SINGER-SONGWRITERS

POP MUSIC'S PERFORMER-COMPOSERS, FROM A TO ZEVON

DAVE DiMARTINO

BILLBOARD BOOKS
An imprint of Watson-Guptill Publications/New York

Copyright © 1994 by Dave DiMartino

Edited by Tad Lathrop
Senior Editor: Paul Lukas
Book and Cover Design: Bob Fillie, Graphiti Graphics
Cover Illustration: Mel Odom
Production Manager: Hector Campbell

First published in 1994 by Billboard books, an imprint of Watson-Guptill
Publications, a division of BPI Communications, 1515 Broadway,
New York, NY 10036

Library of Congress Cataloging-in-Publication Data
DiMartino, Dave.
    Singer-songwriters : pop music's performer-composers, from A to Zevon/
Dave DiMartino.
        p.   cm. — (Billboard hitmakers series)
    Includes index.
    ISBN 0-8230-7629-6
    1. Rock musicians—Bio-bibliography. Composers—Bio
-bibliography. I. Title. II. Series.
ML105.D6 1994
782.42164'092'2—dc20
    [B]   93-44845
                                             CIP
                                             MN

Manufactured in the United States of America

First Printing, 1994

1 2 3 4 5 6 7 8 9 / 99 98 97 96 95 94

This book is dedicated to the first and best singer-songwriter in my life:
Anthony F. DiMartino (1913–1993)

CONTENTS

ABOUT "BILLBOARD HITMAKERS"

Billboard is the home of the pop charts. For a century, those charts have chronicled the hit songs and albums that have come to represent the pinnacle of commercial achievement in the music industry.

But the charts are not the whole story. Of key importance both in and outside the industry are the artists — the rock and roll bands, soul singers, country musicians, and pop icons who produce the vast body of work from which chart successes emerge.

Billboard Hitmakers is about those artists.

The Hitmakers series presents a broad overview of popular music, with separate volumes devoted to such subject areas as Pioneers of Rock and Roll, Singer-Songwriters, Rhythm and Blues, and Country and Western. Each Hitmakers volume is designed to be enjoyed as a separate reference work dedicated to a distinct segment of the pop spectrum, but the books also complement and reinforce each other. Just as the music scene is constantly changing and growing, the Hitmakers series will expand as new volumes covering new subject areas are published. Taken together, the Billboard Hitmakers series adds up to a growing library of information on pop music's prime movers — with a unique Billboard slant.

Each book explores its topic in depth and detail via individual artist profiles arranged alphabetically, with the artists selected for inclusion on the basis of their commercial and/or aesthetic impact on the music scene — including, of course, their history of Billboard chart activity.

The artist profiles themselves provide more than just raw chart data, however. Along with biographical facts and career highlights, each profile gives a sense of the artist's impact, offers insights about the music, and places the subject in the grand musical scheme of things. Artists are viewed not as isolated entities but as contributors to an ever-changing soundscape, drawing music from the past, adding to it in the present, and passing it on to musicians of the future. The volumes in the Billboard Hitmakers series chronicle this ongoing evolution, providing a history of popular music as seen from the perspective of the artists who created it.

In addition, each Hitmakers profile lists the artist's significant songs and albums. Titles are chosen first from the top of the Billboard charts and are listed chronologically, along with the name of the record's label, its year of release, and its peak chart position. In cases where a profiled artist has no top 40 hits, the titles listed are those generally regarded as the artist's best or most significant recordings.

With rock and roll now moving toward the half-century mark and the originators of blues, gospel, country, and jazz slipping into history, popular music is steadily maturing. Its present-day boundaries encompass an intricate latticework of known genres, nascent movements, as-yet-unlabeled trends, and one-person sonic revolutions. Our intent with the Billboard Hitmakers series is to identify the major players within these diverse yet interrelated musical worlds and present their fascinating stories. And if the books also translate into print some of the musical pleasure these hitmakers have given us over the years, so much the better.

PREFACE

Singer-Songwriters is about those artists who do it all—the artists who write the music that they themselves perform.

That said, some explanation is due regarding the criteria used in deciding who would—and who would not—be among the profiled performers in this volume. This book is *not* a series of biographical entries about the 208 highest-charting singer-songwriters in pop music history. It could have been—were simple chart placement the only criterion—but it isn't. While the *Billboard* charts have certainly played a role in the career of each artist to be found here, and while the charts, by definition, are numbers and rankings, other factors that are not so readily quantifiable have also been taken into account. Among them are talent, influence, quality, consistency, career duration, overall uniqueness, and, finally, the ability to write a catchy tune once in a while. All of which is to say: there is a consistency at work within this book, and that consistency isn't solely chart-related.

Given that this book was to focus on singer-songwriters, we first had to arrive at a definition of "singer-songwriter" and then work our way down. Question: What is a singer-songwriter? Answer: Someone who sings and writes songs. Implication: This book could be five feet thick and cover perhaps 20,000 artists. This clearly would not do. So we attempted to set some guidelines, most of which were aimed at pruning down a potentially massive list to a workable number of artists.

The guidelines:

● *The profiled performers must be "pop" artists.* Or, looked at from another angle, if the performer had spent a significant portion of his career and/or chart life in more specialized genres—such as R&B or country—he would not be included. The major reason for this seeming slight, apart from the aforementioned need to pare down a huge list, was to avoid the logistical headaches presented by crossover country artists such as Lyle Lovett, Rodney Crowell, and Rosanne Cash—or pop/R&B giants such as Prince, Smokey Robinson, and Marvin Gaye, all of whom have enjoyed significant (and often more) success on the R&B charts.

● *They must have recorded as solo artists.* In other words, you'll find singer-songwriters like the Who's Pete Townshend in this book, but not the Kinks' Ray Davies. Townshend has been regularly making solo albums since the 1970s; Davies' only "solo" album, 1985's soundtrack *Return to Waterloo,* was a career aberration, essentially a Kinks album without lead guitarist Dave Davies. The sole exceptions to be found here are Jimi Hendrix and Steve Miller, both of whom recorded albums with shifting casts of backing musicians and essentially were the only constants of their respective "groups."

● *They should be regarded not only as solo artists but specifically as singer-songwriters.* This is a sometimes sticky but necessary perceptual distinction that effectively meant that we would avoid such artists as Billy Idol, Lita Ford, Pat Travers, and Sammy Hagar. The key questions: Would anyone normally refer to the performer as a singer-songwriter? Has his material often been covered by other artists? If no in both cases, out they went.

● *They must write most of the material they sing.* Again, a debatable point, but some artists who might initially seem to fit the singer-songwriter classification—such as Joan Baez, Taj Mahal, or even Rick "Garden Party" Nelson—have in fact achieved more fame interpreting other writers' material. Seeming exception to the rule Bonnie Raitt, on the other hand, has penned several key original songs during the course of her career—including the title tracks to her albums *Give It Up* and *Nick of Time*—that we felt merited her inclusion herein.

● *They must have had some measurable degree of commercial success...* In a world where Phil Collins can legitimately be called a singer-songwriter and thus be included here, it may seem odd that other artists who more readily fit the traditional singer-songwriter mold aren't. Still, some likely candidates who have never had a charting album include Wendy Waldman, Paul Siebel, Ellen Shipley, Buzzy Linhart, David Blue, Tim Rose, Judee Sill, Tom Rapp, Michael Hurley, and Paul Brady, among many others.

●*...or, if not, a significant influence in the sphere of songwriting.* Which, for example, explains the presence of Fred Neil.

If this book were simply a recapitulation of *Billboard* chart action, you would very likely be reading about singer-songwriter Bertie Higgins—whose 1982 album *Just Another Day in Paradise* bore the top 10 hit "Key Largo" and peaked at number 38—rather than Fred Neil, who never released an album that charted in his life. As it was, the 200-odd artists discussed in the pages that follow were selected from a master list that originally included 558 names; in the course of writing the book, about 10 other artists that had escaped our attention were then added.

An explanatory note about the *Top Albums* and *Top Songs* lists that follow each artist entry: this is the one aspect of the book in which chart placement plays the major role. Albums and songs were selected in accordance with their chart ranking rather than their overall importance to the artist's career. A maximum total of 10 albums and/or songs are listed for each performer, with their year of release and top 40 chart ranking included. In those instances when an artist has fewer that 10 top 40 albums and songs, other representative works, whether albums or songs, are also listed without ranking. The downside of this system, unfortunately, is that occasionally an artist's most vital work is not found in the listing; ideally, it is given appropriate weight in the accompanying text.

On a personal level, had the criteria for inclusion been slightly different—if, say, this book were a purely critical work devoted to discussion of the arbitrarily selected "best singer-songwriters" in pop—you might be reading about several other artists who aren't mentioned in this volume at all. Ultimately, though, I can't quarrel with the criteria used, and in a very real sense am thankful for them. We have attempted to be as consistent as possible, to offer the reader a mixture of fact and critical evaluation, and to occasionally provide some insight into the careers of some of pop music's finest entertainers. Hopefully, if you care about it, it's here.

DAVE DiMARTINO
Los Angeles
December 1993

ACKNOWLEDGMENTS

Uncredited quotes found in this book were either supplied by the record company or drawn from my own past interviews; I've spoken to about a fourth of the artists.

Sincere thanks to the many people who supplied help, information, and/or camaraderie during the course of the writing of this book. Among the most helpful: my friend Geoff Mayfield at *Billboard;* his assistant Brett Atwood; pals Craig Rosen and Chris Morris, also at *Billboard;* and Bill Holdship at *BAM.* Thanks also to Carole Willcocks and Cable Neuhaus at *Entertainment Weekly* for the use of their computer.

Additionally, I'm much obliged to Simone Seydoux, Kevin Kennedy, Seth Brandler, Joel Amsterdam, Marilyn Arthur, Barbara Shelley, Michelle Krupkin, Angee Jenkins, Carrie Svingen, Beth Catrell, Heather Davis, and Karen Johnson at their respective record companies, as well as John Chelew, Dan Bourgoise, the fine folks at Shanachie and Chesky Records, and the very nice woman from Tony Joe White's office.

Many thanks also to Tad Lathrop for his editing, feedback, guidance, and patience.

Undying thanks also to the used record stores of Los Angeles that as of this writing are selling mint copies of ancient LPs for as little as 29 cents.

And of course the most special thanks to Janet, Michael, and Gregory.

BRYAN ADAMS

Bryan Adams

had signed Adams; ironically, considering Adams' rock roots, his label debut was a dance single called "Let Me Take You Dancing" that reportedly featured a speeded-up recording of Adams' voice and "made me sound like a chipmunk," he complained later. The song was a fluke for the artist and wasn't included on his self-titled debut album, which was co-produced by Adams and Vallance and released in 1980.

Adams' first major hit came in 1983, with his own version of a track he had written three years earlier. "Straight from the Heart" had, in fact, appeared in very similar form on singer Ian Lloyd's 1980 album *3WC* (as had, for that matter, the Adams-Vallance song "Lonely Nights"). From Adams' third album, the pivotal *Cuts Like a Knife*, "Straight" soared to the top 10 and led the way for two more hits, "Cuts Like a Knife" and "This Time." In what must have been harrowing for Adams—but inarguably productive—the singer spent 283 full days on the road in 1983, promoting the album and, clearly, himself as a performing property. The payoff? His quintuple-platinum follow-up, 1984's *Reckless,* which held the Number One slot for two weeks and yielded a staggering six top 20 singles—including Adams' first-ever Number One single, "Heaven," also found on the soundtrack to 20th Century Fox's 1983 film *A Night in Heaven.* Further notice that Adams had internationally arrived came via his July 1985 Live Aid performance, viewed by millions. Following one of the more memorable moments of that show—Adams'

One of the busiest singer-songwriters in the music industry, Kingston, Ontario–born Bryan Adams (b. Nov. 5, 1959) has enjoyed major success on three levels: as a songwriter who's written hits for other artists, as a recording artist whose own work has met huge international acclaim, and as a captivating live performer, whose memorable appearances at Live Aid and on Amnesty International's Conspiracy of Hope tour helped cement his status as an international superstar.

Adams' songs, in fact, helped pave the way for his own record deal. While performing with a local Vancouver group as a teen, Adams met drummer Jim Vallance in 1977 and immediately began a songwriting partnership that still functions today. The pair's work—typically an appealing blend of hard-edged rock and sweet, hook-heavy pop—was soon being covered by such artists as Bachman-Turner Overdrive, Ian Lloyd, and Prism. By 1979, A&M Canada

TOP ALBUMS

CUTS LIKE A KNIFE (A&M, '83, 8)
RECKLESS (A&M, '84, 1)
INTO THE FIRE (A&M, '87, 7)
WAKING UP THE NEIGHBOURS (A&M, '91, 6)

TOP SONGS

RUN TO YOU (A&M, '84, 6)
HEAVEN (A&M, '85, 1)
SUMMER OF '69 (A&M, '85, 5)
HEAT OF THE NIGHT (A&M, '87, 6)
(EVERYTHING I DO) I DO IT FOR YOU (A&M, '91, 1)
CAN'T STOP THIS THING WE STARTED (A&M, '92, 2)

Additional Top 40 Songs: 11

energetic duet with Tina Turner on "It's Only Love"—the *Reckless* single of that song was later nudged up the charts to number 15. Also keeping Adams in the international spotlight was his work on 1985's Ethopian famine relief single "Tears Are Not Enough," by Canadian superstar group Northern Lights.

While Adams' 1987 album *Into the Fire* couldn't accurately be called a failure—it did surpass platinum; it did contain three singles that hit the top 40—it wasn't the sales monster many in the industry had expected. Regardless, Adams continued to maintain a high profile during the late 1980s via his spot on the Amnesty International tour as well as appearances at the Prince's Trust Charity, the 1988 London Freedomfest honoring Nelson Mandela, and Roger Waters' 1990 production of *The Wall* in Berlin.

Anyone predicting a downward slide for Adams' career got a powerful wake-up call in 1991. From the hit film *Robin Hood: Prince of Thieves* came the record of Adams' career: "(Everything I Do) I Do It for You," a chart-topper for seven weeks and the biggest-selling single in the history of A&M Records. It helped boost Adams' long-awaited album *Waking Up the Neighbours* past the triple-platinum mark and pushed him back into the superstar sales range once more. And with that album, keen-eyed observers noticed a change: Adams' new producer, Robert John "Mutt" Lange, was now also his new songwriting partner, co-credited on each song, including four also co-credited to longtime Adams crony Jim Vallance. Why the change? At one point early in his career, Bryan Adams had said, "If you ask me what I do for a living, I'd have to say that I'm a songwriter first." When it comes to success—be it artistic or commercial—Adams still clearly believes it all starts with the song.

PETER ALLEN

Artists are often asked if their material is autobiographical, but with Peter Allen (b. Peter Woolnough, Feb. 10, 1944, Tenterfield, Australia) the question seemed unnecessary. Beginning with its title track, Allen's 1972 album *Tenterfield Saddler,* a quietly touching, understated recording, bore lyrics that essentially laid out Allen's life for all to see. He was the grandson of an Australian saddler, the son of a man who took his own life, and the

---

TOP ALBUMS

I COULD HAVE BEEN A SAILOR (A&M, '79)
BI-COASTAL (A&M, '80)
NOT THE BOY NEXT DOOR (A&M, '83)

---

former husband of, in his words, "a girl with an interesting face"—otherwise known to the world as Liza Minnelli.

Allen, who would soon develop into a flamboyant, world-class live attraction, got his start via someone who'd been exactly that for years: his future mother-in-law, Judy Garland. While in Hong Kong in 1964, she'd seen the hotel lounge act of Allen and Chris Bell, two unrelated Australians performing under the stage name Chris and Peter Allen. Garland loved them, hired them as her opening act, and for a brief while was their manager. The duo was warmly received in the States, where they signed to Mercury Records and reportedly so enthralled Johnny Carson after their "Tonight Show" debut that he signed them for 20 more appearances. After a lengthy engagement—Minnelli had only been 18 when they'd met—the two finally married in 1967, only to separate three years later. On the same day they split, Allen also dissolved his longstanding partnership with Bell and went solo.

In June 1970, Allen opened for comedian David Steinberg at New York's Bitter End. Meanwhile, he'd signed a publishing deal with Valando Music, which had resulted in his writing material for teenidol Bobby Sherman. When executives from Sherman's label, Metromedia Records, caught Allen's live show, he struck a deal that would result in two albums, 1971's *Peter Allen* and the next year's *Saddler*. Though both received rapturous reviews, they sold minimally, and by 1974, Allen had moved over to A&M. Allen's star would rise further that year, thanks largely to "I Honestly Love You," a song he had co-written with Jeff Barry that became a Number One hit for Olivia Newton-John and was awarded the 1974 Grammy for Record of the Year. It was a significant moment in Allen's career: while his own records would sell respectably enough—his highest-charting effort, 1980's *Bi-Coastal*, peaked at number 123—they never quite matched the success other performers had singing his material. "Don't Cry Out Loud," for instance, was a top 10 hit for Melissa Manchester; "I'd Rather Leave When I'm in Love" a hit for Rita Coolidge; and "I Go to Rio" an American hit for Pablo Cruise (though a huge international hit for Allen himself). And the Academy Award–winning song for which he is most famous—"Arthur's Theme (Best That You Can Do)," co-written with Burt Bacharach, Carole Bayer Sager, and Christopher Cross—was, of course, a massive Number One hit for Cross.

In many ways, Allen's celebrity stemmed mostly from his writing and brilliant cabaret-style performances, which became increasingly outrageous as his career progressed, perhaps peaking with his nine-night 1982 stint at Radio City Music Hall with the Rockettes. Following his deal with A&M, Peter Allen made additional records for Arista and RCA, none of which charted. Sadly, he died of AIDS on June 15, 1992.

TORI AMOS

Tori Amos

In January 1992, music journalists around the nation were sent a letter from Douglas P. Morris, president, co-chairman, and co-CEO of Atlantic Records. The letter, printed on fancily embossed personal stationery, was accompanied by a promotional audiocassette. "For those of us who spend most of our waking moments in this frenetic business of music," wrote Morris, "there are very special moments that remind us why we wanted to do this in the first place. For me, the rarest and most special of these moments is when I hear for the first time an artist whose music embodies passion, integrity, and vision." All of which was well and good—as was the accompanying cassette, *Little Earthquakes* by Tori Amos (b. circa 1964, North Carolina). The only problem: Morris had heard Amos for "the first time" nearly five years earlier.

In short, Atlantic was putting a new face on an old artist. In 1988, the company had issued a peculiar hard rock album by a "band" called Y Kant Tori Read; oddly, the album cover depicted only a sultry redhead holding a sword in a typical hard-rock, dangerous babe stance. In fact, Y Kant Tori Read was Tori Amos, and the so-called band essentially a studio concoction. As the cover picture indirectly promised, the album was a predictable batch of Pat Benatar–inspired hard rock; though the singer's voice was much better than average, the lyrics were another story. "Caught my boyfriend/Lookin' at

another/Slender pair of thighs," sang the fetching Tori, whose last name mysteriously was mentioned nowhere in the album credits. But Tori not only couldn't read, she couldn't sell—and the album sank without a trace.

One can't blame Atlantic's Morris for wanting to bury Tori's earlier loser: who'd give a fair shot to a former flop? But more importantly, who could fault him for his enthusiasm over *Little Earthquakes*? In addition to a last name, Tori had a new sound miles removed from her rock-by-numbers debut. Like a peculiar cross of Kate Bush and Laura Nyro, Tori Amos now stood revealed as a superb singer, writer, and pianist—and a talent of jarringly deep proportions. Among the album's highlights was "Me and a Gun," a creepy, first-person account of a rape sung a cappella, and "Silent All These Years," in which the former hard rocker sang, "So you found a girl who thinks really deep thoughts/What's so amazing about really deep thoughts/Boy you best pray that I bleed real soon/How's that thought for you?"

The daughter of a Methodist minister, Amos

turned out to have a strange background indeed: She had spent six years enrolled as a piano student at Baltimore's Peabody Conservatory beginning at the age of five, and by 13 was playing bars and piano lounges with her chaperoning minister father in tow. Encouraged to write by producer Narada Michael Walden, she eventually moved to Los Angeles and made *Y Kant Tori Read*. Following that album's fatal plummet, the singer temporarily moved to England in the early 1990s, where her solo performances drew conspicuous raves. When Amos released *Little Earthquakes* in England in 1991, she was instantly hailed as the Next Big Thing.

For the album's American release in 1992, Atlantic sent out a thick folder of English press raves to accompany it. Predictably, American journalists followed suit and were similarly enraptured, comparing her to Nyro, Bush, and even Patti Smith. How did Amos feel about it? "You know when you feel like sometimes the fairy godmother has put her little dink on your hat, and you just feel like something magical is kind of happening at this moment, and you allow yourself to go with that?" she asked at the time. "I think what people are just comparing is that dink on your head. I think those other women were dinked, too."

While *Little Earthquakes* was hardly an out-of-the-box smash, strong video play and press coverage gave it a long chart life, and the album was soon certified gold. Atlantic quickly followed up the set with a CD-5 that looked to prove the singer's eclectic nature; aside from two originals, it included covers of the Rolling Stones' "Angie," Led Zeppelin's "Thank You," and a much-aired version of Nirvana's smash, "Smells Like Teen Spirit." Any way you looked at it, it smelled like success for Tori Amos—and, one has to hand it to him, yet another winning promotional strategy for Atlantic's Doug Morris.

TOP ALBUMS

Y KANT TORI READ (Atlantic, '88)
LITTLE EARTHQUAKES (Atlantic, '92)

TOP SONGS

CRUCIFY (Atlantic, '92)
SILENT ALL THESE YEARS (Atlantic, '92)
ME AND A GUN (Atlantic, '92)

ERIC ANDERSEN

If it is brought up at all in the 1990s, Eric Andersen's name is never alone. It can be found, typically, midway down a list that also includes Phil Ochs, Tom Paxton, Patrick Sky, Mark Spoelstra, Carolyn Hester, Ian and Sylvia, and Dave Van Ronk. The list will be in a reference text, or a scholarly article, or a nostalgia piece, and the undertone will always somehow convey the impression that "here is the second string" or "and then there were the also-rans." The subject will be the Greenwich Village folk scene of the late 1950s through mid-'60s—and that list will be, as always, extremely convenient and grossly unfair.

In many ways, Eric Andersen (b. Feb. 14, 1943, Pittsburgh, Pennsylvania) seemed the prime candidate to burst from that aforementioned pack when his debut album, *Today Is the Highway,* was released by Vanguard Records in 1965. A young, strikingly handsome singer who'd arrived in Greenwich Village by way of Cambridge, Massachusetts, Andersen was an unabashedly romantic songwriter whose material showed unusual depth and sensitivity. That didn't go unnoticed by better-known contemporaries such as Judy Collins, who covered his song "Thirsty Boots"; or the Blues Project, whose version of "Violets of Dawn" became the first Andersen song heard by the general pop audience; or even Johnny Cash, who recorded his "Close the Door Lightly."

Still, Andersen's critical and commercial fortunes were two different matters. In a highly unusual move, the singer followed up his 1966 acoustic album, *'Bout Changes and Things,* with an "electric" version of the same album the next year and accurately dubbed it *'Bout Changes and Things Take 2.* And anyone comparing that gesture with Bob Dylan's historic "going electric" phase needed only wait for Andersen's 1968 country set, *A Country Dream,* to note it featured the same players Dylan had used on his deliberately sparse *John Wesley Harding* almost a year earlier.

When Andersen departed Vanguard for Warner Bros., his sound became slightly more commercial. 1969's *Avalanche* contained a blatant attempt at a rock song with "Louise," which featured some Claptonesque (circa Cream) guitar riffing and unusually poppish backing vocals, and "Think About It," which was bolstered by an unexpected and prominent horn section. Though follow-up *Eric Andersen* was sedate in comparison, the near-rave-up "She Touched Me" again seemed a transparent bid for the rock market. But the rock market wasn't listening.

It would be Andersen's Columbia debut, *Blue River,* that finally brought him the larger audience he deserved. Generally regarded as the singer's crowning achievement, the album featured two of his best songs in years, "Is It Really Love at All" and the title track, which notably featured friend and backing vocalist Joni Mitchell. The singer's first album to chart—it peaked at number 169—it looked likely to set the stage for Andersen's greater widespread acceptance. But it was not to be. Unbelievably, the final tapes for *Blue River*'s planned follow-up were literally lost by Columbia, and would not be recovered for years. "I was shocked," Andersen later told writer Anthony DeCurtis. "It was really strange. It was surreal. It was like Kafka." The singer then followed departing Columbia president Clive Davis to his new Arista label and rerecorded six of the lost tracks for *Be True to You,* which peaked at number 113 in 1975.

After one more Arista album, Andersen moved to Europe in 1980, eventually settling in Norway. He recorded two albums (*Midnight Son* and *Tight in the Night*) and scored a film (*Istanbul*) there during the 1980s, and many assumed he'd be staying for good. But in 1989, when folk-inspired artists such as Tracy Chapman and Suzanne Vega were making their respective commercial inroads, the singer returned with the surprisingly strong *Ghosts upon the Road,* released here by the so-called "boomer" label, Cypress Records. Its unquestionable highlight, at least for longtime Andersen fans, was the fascinating 10-minute title track, a spoken autobiographical piece in which Andersen recounted his life since being "stranded up in Cambridge" in 1964. And a final career irony came in 1991, when Columbia Records found the master tapes to his great lost album of 1973 and reissued it as *Stages: The Lost Album.* It was as good as it was supposed to be—and

more importantly for Andersen, its three final songs, brand new 1990 recordings that had been additionally tagged on, were as splendid as the other tracks he'd been mourning for the previous 17 years. Lightly or otherwise, the door has yet to close on Eric Andersen.

PAUL ANKA

One of the select few teen idols of the 1950s to maintain a healthy career following the British Invasion of the early 1960s, Paul Anka (b. July 30, 1941, Ottawa, Ontario, Canada) is in some ways more famous for what he did after his initial burst of top 40 fame (which lasted from 1957 to 1963) than for the hits themselves. Among his major claims to fame: he bought the rights to a French melody, slapped new lyrics on it, and wrote "My Way," the song that has become Frank Sinatra's trademark (and as a result become an object of parody when sung by the late punk-rocker Sid Vicious of the Sex Pistols); he wrote "Johnny's Theme," better known as "The Tonight Show Theme" when that NBC property was hosted by Johnny Carson, one of the most performed (and thus royalty-generating) themes in all of popular culture; he also wrote Tom Jones' biggest hit, "She's a Lady," Number One for two weeks in 1971.

Still, Anka's own recording career has been no less phenomenal. What initially set him apart from his teen-idol peers is clearly what's sustained his career since then: unlike most of them, he wrote his own songs, and did so from the very beginning. His first single, "Blau Wildebeeste Fontaine" backed with "I Confess," was released by the Modern Records imprint RPM when Anka—who'd spent the summer away from Ottawa working as a concessions seller in L.A.—was only 15. Within a year, he visited New York and struck up a deal via ABC-Paramount producer Don Costa; the resulting single "Diana," written by Anka about a 20-year-old babysitter his family had hired, rapidly reached Number One in 1957 and went on to sell a staggering 9 million copies worldwide.

"Diana" would be only the first of 24 top 40 hits Anka would have between 1957 and 1963. In the summer of 1959, he began a memorable hot streak that began with "Lonely Boy"—a Number One hit for four weeks—and included four more top 10 hits:

"Put Your Head on My Shoulder," "It's Time to Cry," "Puppy Love" (a top five hit again in 1972 for Donny Osmond), and "My Home Town."

Anka's teen-idol status was further cemented when he appeared in two late-'50s films: 1958's *Let's Rock,* starring Julius LaRosa and Phyllis Newman and featuring Anka singing "I'll Be Waiting for You," and *Girls' Town,* a 1959 teen flick starring Mamie Van Doren and Mel Tormé that included Anka singing "Lonely Boy." In 1962, a 28-minute film short about Anka bearing the *Lonely Boy* name won international accolades as one of the first examples of cinema verité; the film was acknowledged as an influence on the Beatles' *A Hard Day's Night* and the prescient 1967 British fantasy film about rock stars, *Privilege.*

In 1960, 19-year-old Anka became the youngest performer ever to headline at the prestigious Copacabana nightclub. Indeed, the singer spent most of the 1960s establishing himself as a Las Vegas–style performer—a role that would serve him well, as stars of his era seemed increasingly overshadowed by the growing surge of young '60s rock and roll groups.

In 1974, Anka returned amid much controversy with his Number One hit "Havin' My Baby," a duet with singer Odia Coates. The controversy came, of course, via the use of "my" in the title, which greatly enraged feminists of the era. Anka reportedly began singing the words "havin' our baby" to make amends.

TOP ALBUMS

PAUL ANKA SINGS HIS BIG 15 (ABC-Paramount, '60, 4)
ANKA AT THE COPA (ABC-Paramount, '60, 23)
ANKA (United Artists, '74, 9)
TIMES OF YOUR LIFE (United Artists, '75, 7)

Additional Top 40 Albums: 1

TOP SONGS

DIANA (ABC-Paramount, '57, 1)
LONELY BOY (ABC-Paramount, '59, 1)
PUT YOUR HEAD ON MY SHOULDER
    (ABC-Paramount, '59, 2)
IT'S TIME TO CRY (ABC-Paramount, '59, 4)
PUPPY LOVE (ABC-Paramount, '60, 2)
(YOU'RE) HAVING MY BABY (United Artists, '74, 1)

Additional Top 40 Songs: 26

Six more top 40 hits for Anka would follow until 1978's "This Is Love"; his final chart hit, "Hold Me 'Til the Morning Comes," was released by Columbia in 1983.

Anka has played a part in the careers of others, including Annette Funicello, who supposedly inspired a love-struck Anka to write "Puppy Love," and for whom Anka penned the jazz tune "It's Really Love" (which, without lyrics, ultimately became "The Tonight Show Theme"). Additionally, Anka played a role in the discovery of Chicago-based folksinger John Prine.

An extremely astute businessman, Anka wisely bought the rights to his own hits (most recently reissued in the U.S. on Rhino); he's also believed to have amassed a fortune via art collecting and real estate. Ironically, his business acumen led him to conspicuously denounce the selling of used compact discs in 1993—which led many writers to smarmily wonder in print just exactly how many CDs Paul Anka could sell in 1993 in the first place. Anka, probably on his way to the bank, ignored their jibes.

JOAN ARMATRADING

It's ironic that the career of one of pop music's most successful singer-songwriters is often discussed in terms of seeming failures rather than profound accomplishments, but so it goes for Joan Armatrading. Rather than looking at her extraordinary accomplishments—which include crafting 15 very substantial albums for A&M Records in the course of 20 years—pundits typically focus on the bad stuff: how she's never had the huge hit single she's needed to break through, how latecomer Tracy Chapman stole her thunder (and, some maintain, vocal style), how her records sometimes seemed to reflect the taste of her (many) producers rather than her own. What gets overlooked—as often happens in an industry dominated by the quick-fix hit single—is Armatrading's near-astounding consistency through the years: she's simply never made a bad record.

Born December 9, 1950, on the Caribbean island of St. Kitt's, the third of six children, the singer-guitarist moved with her family to Birmingham, England, in 1958 and eventually reached London in the early 1970s. Perhaps predictably, her first album,

1973's *Whatever's for Us,* led some in the industry to compare her to Elton John: it was produced by Gus Dudgeon (Elton's own producer) and featured a vocalist who collaborated with a behind-the-scenes lyricist (Pam Nestor, who vanished by 1976's *Joan Armatrading*). At the time, the fact that Armatrading is black actually proved a curious marketing wrinkle for a business deeply entrenched in formatting and market segmentation: her pop-folkish blend clearly wasn't so-called "soul music," but labels cavalierly being bandied about by critics—such as "the black Joni Mitchell"—and comparisons to artists like Nina Simone seemed off-base and suspect.

It didn't matter, though, to those who heard Armatrading's work for what it was: a thoughtful, varied repertoire of songs dealing with subjects other writers avoided, often told from a unique vantage point. "More Than One Kind of Love," from 1990's *Hearts and Flowers,* for example, features a female protagonist advising a girlfriend not to ignore old friends during a current heated affair. "Just remember that passion fades," sings Armatrading. "Good friendships seldom die." Likewise, her 1983 track "(I Love It When You) Call Me Names" relays the charming tale of a large woman and a short man: "And he loves it/When she beats his brains out," she elaborates. Not exactly moon, spoon, or June material—and that, said fans, was the entire point.

Though a longstanding favorite in the curiously arbitrary "women's music" genre—singers Kris Williamson and Holly Near, the entire Olivia Records roster, and others—Armatrading can't be denied her much broader popular following, which again marks her as unique. Not incidentally, her seeming shift from sensitive folkie to pop artist in the early 1980s corresponds with her commercial peak: with rock producers like Richard Gottehrer, Steve Lillywhite, and Val Garay at the production helm,

Joan Armatrading

she reached the upper reaches of the Top Pop Albums chart twice (1980's *Me Myself I* peaked at number 28, 1983's *The Key* at number 32). In a further show of artistic growth, the singer successfully began producing herself in 1985; she hasn't let up since. With a loyal core audience that's followed her now for two decades—and has kept her recording and concert career well in the green—Armatrading may indeed be one of the most stable forces in the singer-songwriting business.

TOP ALBUMS

JOAN ARMATRADING (A&M, '76)
SHOW SOME EMOTION (A&M, '77)
ME MYSELF I (A&M, '80, 28)
THE KEY (A&M, '83, 32)

TOP SONGS

LOVE AND AFFECTION (A&M, '76)
DROP THE PILOT (A&M, '83

DAVID BAERWALD

An extremely underrated Los Angeles–based songwriter, David Baerwald (b. July 11, 1960, Oxford, Ohio) has chronicled '90s American life more profoundly than most of his contemporaries; the result, particularly evident on his 1993 album *Triage,* has been a repertoire of vivid,

David Baerwald

sometimes painful songs that personalize characters and situations other writers have generally preferred to ignore. Just as the best rap music has typically presented viewpoints and scenarios in almost journalistic fashion—documenting both an attitude for the converted and an inaccessible lifestyle for unknowing, middle-class suburbia—Baerwald, too, reports on what he sees. And perhaps because he lives in L.A., where gang warfare, drug commerce, and drive-by shootings are normal facts of life, what he sees is a society collapsing into itself in fear, hatred, and helplessness.

An extremely literate writer who has drawn inspiration from such writers as Paul Bowles, Raymond Carver, Tennessee Williams, and Raymond Chandler, Baerwald first gained national attention as one-half of David + David, an L.A. duo with partner David Ricketts; generally, Baerwald sang and provided lyrics to music mostly supplied by multi-instrumentalist Ricketts. The pair's A&M album *Boomtown* was a critical sensation upon its arrival in 1986, largely for its unique portrayal of Los Angeles as a land of shattered dreams. "Welcome to the boom-

town," sang Baerwald on the album's opening track. "Pick a habit/We got plenty to go around/And all that money/Makes such a succulent sound." The song's mixture of lyrical resignation and its near-hypnotic drone instantly drew in listeners and made the song a top 40 hit, pushing *Boomtown* to number 39 on the album charts.

When Ricketts became involved in the production of friend Toni Childs' 1988 album *Union*, Baerwald eventually went his own way. After an initial album project with producer Steve Berlin fell by the wayside ("It was just too crazy, it was too unmusical, and it was too personal," the singer later said), Baerwald returned in 1990 with *Bedtime Stories*, an even more mature and focused statement about urban alienation and loneliness. Produced mostly by Larry Klein, who collaborated with Baerwald on six songs, the album contains one of the singer's most memorable works, "Young Anymore," a vignette wherein a father secretly watches his ex-wife wait in her car outside their daughter's ballet class. "And I am her daddy," he sings, "and I'm a coldhearted man." Baerwald's skill as a storyteller, in telling a large

TOP ALBUMS

BEDTIME STORIES (A&M, '90)
TRIAGE (A&M, '93)

tale with very few words, is exceptional. One of *Bedtime Stories'* biggest fans, in fact, was fellow storyteller Bruce Springsteen, who told many journalists at the time that the album was one of his favorites.

Baerwald's next album, 1993's stunning *Triage,* was in many ways an overload, sonically, lyrically, and even visually: its gruesome cover, which depicted two bloodied hands extended before an American flag, may be one reason the record never even entered the charts. Loosely based around the political ramifications of the album title—"triage" is an emergency medical term roughly meaning "save the wounded who can be be saved, and abandon the rest"—the disc was a further refinement of the subject matter Baerwald had already explored, and a very powerful one. Using vocal samples of Jim Jones, George Bush, and congressional testimony that "Jonestown was a CIA mind-control experiment," *Triage* was an elaborate aural montage of moral decay, Baerwald's ambitious statement that the American government had wholly gone awry. Most memorable was the album's sinister opening cut, "A Secret Silken World," the lyrics of which perfectly set *Triage*'s tone: "Don't you love to hurt the weak/ When they refuse to fight/When there's no need to be judgmental/No need to be polite/All you need to know is that/Might equals right/On a lazy kind of night." In case the album didn't make its point succinctly enough—and it certainly did—Baerwald dedicated it to Dean Acheson, Paul Nitze, John J. McCloy, John Foster Dulles, Allen Dulles, Henry Kissinger, James Baker III, and George Bush, "in the sincere hope that there is a God and that He is vengeful beyond all comprehension."

In late 1993, with *Triage* behind him, Baerwald had resumed work with his former partner David Ricketts and was preparing a second David + David album for 1994 release.

RUSS BALLARD

A 30-year veteran of pop music, Russ Ballard (b. Oct. 31, 1947, Waltham Cross, England) is one very unusual case: he seems to have done everything right. From his earliest days backing pre-Beatle sensation Adam Faith in England, to being a key member of hitmaking group Argent in the 1970s, to his own successful solo career, to producing hit albums, to having his songs turned into

hits worldwide—given the time frame, there should be a misstep somewhere in there. But there isn't. To paraphrase one of his better-known songs, he can do magic.

Coolly wearing his habitual sunglasses even from the very beginning, Ballard first gained international notice in 1963 as guitarist with Adam Faith's backing band the Roulettes. Though Faith's fame dwindled as new-lads-on-the-block the Beatles began their historic climb, Ballard's was on the upswing, initially with the Roulettes sans Faith, then in 1967 as a member of Unit Four Plus Two (his memorable guitar work had been heard two years earlier sessioning on their sole U.S. hit "Concrete and Clay"), and then, most notably, with Argent from 1969 to 1974.

Joining forces with former Zombies keyboardist-songwriter Rod Argent, bassist Jim Rodford, and his longtime friend drummer Robert Henrit (with whom he'd played in both the Roulettes and Unit Four Plus Two), Ballard was an integral part of Argent for six albums. His song "Liar," from the group's 1970 debut album, was instantly covered by Three Dog Night (who in retrospect showed remarkable taste in songwriters) and became a top 10 hit; more significantly, Argent's own version of "Hold Your Head Up," penned by Ballard for 1972's *All Together Now,* zoomed all the way to the number five slot. And though Ballard's "God Gave Rock 'n' Roll to You" from the next year's *In Deep* didn't have as strong a chart showing, it was an FM staple throughout the decade. When he opted to leave the group after four and a half years, it seemed inevitable: Ballard's forte was obviously the hookish pop single, while Rod Argent (who kept the group operating for two more years) seemed to be veering toward Emerson, Lake and Palmer–style progressive-rock theatrics, disappointing those fans who so loved his Zombies background.

Ballard then let fly a steady stream of solo albums

from 1974 to 1985. His best, 1978's *At the Third Stroke,* produced by Keith Olsen and featuring most of Toto, remains one of the decade's most severely underrated pop works. That none of his seven albums made as much of a dent on the charts as Argent's might have stung somewhat, but whatever pain Ballard felt was likely mitigated by his other endeavors: he produced successful albums by such artists as Roger Daltry and Leo Sayer (1975's *Ride a Rock Horse* and *Another Year,* respectively) and saw his songs become international hits for Olivia Newton-John, former Zombies vocalist Colin Blunstone, the Bay City Rollers, and many more.

As Ballard's recording career began to wind down—his last album remains 1985's *The Fire Still Burns*—his songs have remained bountiful for many other artists, including Abba's Frida ("I Know There's Something Going On"), Santana ("Winning" and "Nowhere to Run"), and, of course, America ("You Can Do Magic"). Nearly 30 years after backing Adam Faith, he's been reaching a whole new generation, too: courtesy of a 1991 collaborative "updating" by aging rockers Kiss, American youth heard a raucous "God Gave Rock 'n' Roll to You II" as they sat in theatres and witnessed *Bill & Ted's Bogus Journey.* Lucky them—sort of.

CHUCK BERRY
....

If an entire genre of music can be credited to one man, that genre would be rock and roll, and the man would be Chuck Berry (b. Charles Edward Anderson Berry, Oct. 18, 1926, San Jose, California). A brilliant guitarist, songwriter, and lyricist, Berry is responsible for literally dozens of classic songs, including "Roll Over Beethoven," "Sweet Little Sixteen," "Rock & Roll Music," and the immortal "Johnny B. Goode." His work shaped the sound of the biggest groups of the 1960s—including the Beatles, the Rolling Stones, and the Beach Boys, all of whom covered his songs—and remains the largest body of rock standards in existence.

Berry grew up singing in church choirs in St. Louis and started playing the guitar as a teenager. Following an early stretch of imprisonment in 1944–47 for armed robbery, he became a beautician by day and a blues guitarist by night, via his St. Louis–based Chuck Berry Combo. In 1955, he sought professional advice from blues legend Muddy Waters; Waters

introduced him to Chess Records owner Leonard Chess, who heard a song called "Ida Red" on Berry's demo tape and suggested it be renamed "Maybellene." It was, Chess signed Berry and released it, and the song became Berry's first top 10 hit.

Berry's string of Chess hits was remarkable, spanning three decades (he left Chess for Mercury in 1966, but returned by 1970) and including 27 charting singles, seven of which reached the top 10. Yet his charting history is filled with ironies: Berry's biggest single ever was the 1972 double-entendre novelty track "My Ding-A-Ling," by no means representative of his work; additionally, his only top 10 album was the same year's gold *The London Chuck Berry Sessions,* a fairly disposable set that was one in a series of Chess packages featuring prominent blues artists (Waters, Howlin' Wolf, and Bo Diddley among them) in the U.K.

A well-known personality since the early days of rock, Berry appeared in such early rock-based films as *Rock, Rock, Rock* (1956), *Mister Rock and Roll* (1957), *Go, Johnny, Go* (1959), the classic documentary *Jazz on a Summer's Day* (1960), and the legendary pop extravaganza *The TAMI Show* (1965). Much of his fame has also come via extra-musical means: throughout his career, his various run-ins with the law have received enormous publicity. The most famous took place in 1959, when Berry was sentenced to two years in federal prison for violation of the Mann Act; 20 years later, he spent 100 days behind bars for tax evasion. Other incidents have followed.

TOP ALBUMS
....
CHUCK BERRY ON STAGE (Chess, '63, 29)
CHUCK BERRY'S GREATEST HITS (Chess, '64, 34)
CHUCK BERRY'S GOLDEN DECADE (Chess, '67)
THE LONDON CHUCK BERRY SESSIONS (Chess, '72, 8)

TOP SONGS
....
MAYBELLENE (Chess, '55, 5)
SCHOOL DAY (Chess, '57, 3)
ROCK & ROLL MUSIC (Chess, '57, 8)
SWEET LITTLE SIXTEEN (Chess, '58, 2)
JOHNNY B. GOODE (Chess, '58, 8)
MY DING-A-LING (Chess, '72, 1)

Additional Top 40 Songs: 8

Berry's colorful life has been well documented, both in his own words—*Chuck Berry: The Autobiography* was published in 1987—and in such appreciative works as Taylor Hackford's 1987 film *Chuck Berry: Hail! Hail! Rock 'n' Roll.* The latter, a concert documentary honoring the artist's 60th birthday, featured Keith Richards as music director and included Eric Clapton, Etta James, and Linda Ronstadt among its guest stars honoring Berry. In 1988, MCA Records issued a superb Berry box set which contained 71 tracks and included virtually all of Berry's essential works. It is perhaps the most remarkable document of all—a portrait of a sound that shaped a culture, and of the man who shaped that sound—and may be all one ever needs to know about rock and roll.

MICHAEL BOLTON

Michael Bolton

One of the most popular male vocalists of the late 1980s and early '90s, Michael Bolton (b. Michael Bolotin, Feb. 26, 1954, New Haven, Connecticut) has consistently found himself in the center of two distinct camps: those who think he's the greatest, most soulful singer-songwriter of our time, and those who think he's a minor pop songwriter with a penchant for bellowing songs in an annoying, terminally overwrought manner. While critics may rank high on Bolton's hate list—"I was under the delusion that people who are hired to critique music are qualified," he said self-defensively in 1992—he himself ranks even higher among his enormously large and loving fan base.

The lanky singer, whose recording career began as far back as 1975, when he still went by his Bolotin surname, has led a true journeyman's life in the music business. Stylistically, in the course of nearly 20 years he has shifted from (1) a Joe Cocker–influenced rock singer to (2) a hard-rock, even heavy-metal belter to (3) an AOR balladeer to (4) a blue-eyed soul singer to, finally, (5) an adult-contemporary standard bearer. Even more interestingly, Bolton, who is a prolific songwriter, has continued to write the bulk of his material whatever its orientation; that versatility has in many respects been overlooked by critics who only see the singer as a big-voiced, schlocky cynic purposefully filling a hole in the "imitation soul" marketplace.

Bolton began singing in Connecticut bar bands in

the early 1970s, and he signed with RCA Records in 1975 on the basis of demo tapes he'd recorded at the studios of singer Leon Russell's Shelter Records. His two albums for the label, *Michael Bolotin* (1975) and *Every Day of My Life* (1976), were capable if unexceptional recordings that showcased Bolton's Cocker-inspired vocals more than adequately and contained several respectable original compositions, most of them ballads. Neither set caused much of a stir commercially, however, and before long Bolotin returned as the central figure in hard-rock quartet Blackjack. With them, he again recorded two albums—the first of which, *Blackjack*, contained a minor 1979 radio hit in "Love Me Tonight," which reached number 62 on the singles chart. With the exception of a cover version of "My World Is Empty Without You," both *Blackjack* (1979) and *Worlds Apart* (1980) contained a wealth of original material penned by Bolotin and guitarist Bruce Kulick. Appropriately—given the state of the hit parade of the era—Blackjack's material sounded much less inspired by the works of Joe Cocker than by AOR hitmakers Journey.

Following Blackjack's demise, Bolotin de-ethnicized his last name and signed as a solo artist to Columbia. Again, with his 1983 label debut, *Michael Bolton,* the singer's music seemed directly aimed at the heart of AOR radio; luckily for him, the format picked up his track "Fool's Game" and gave it heavy airplay, establishing him for the first time as a solo artist. While his debut sold respectably and peaked at number 89 on the charts, whatever momentum he'd begun to acquire was instantly snuffed with the 1985 release *Everybody's Crazy,* an even harder-rocking effort that radio somehow snubbed altogether; the set failed to even enter the charts.

Perhaps revealingly, most of the album-rock material Bolton had been recording till then had been the result of songwriting collaboration—usually with either Mark Mangold or Mark Radice, both keyboardists who had also appeared on his records. But neither was present on *The Hunger,* the album that signaled a sea change in Bolton's overall musical approach and provided the first inkling of what was to come. From the album's cover shot, in which the formerly leather-clad rocker now stared out looking moody and pensive, it became obvious something was up—and indeed, with both "That's What Love Is All About," penned by Bolton and Eric Kaz, and "Walk Away," by the singer and Dianne Warren, the change became apparent. Both tracks utilized the same adult-contemporary style Bolton soon took on full-time. "That's What Love Is All About" became the singer's first top 20 hit, and his cover of Otis Redding's '60s smash "(Sittin' On) The Dock of the Bay" did even better.

Bolton's career fell immaculately together soon thereafter. Already an accomplished songwriter who'd penned a top 20 hit for Gloria Branigan (1983's "How Am I Supposed to Live Without You," later a Grammy-winning Number One hit for Bolton himself), he did the same for both Cher ("I Found Someone," a top 10 single in 1988) and Barbra Streisand (who covered his "We're Not Making Love Anymore" on her platinum 1989 greatest hits set). He continued to work with a steady stream of top writers—such as Warren, Andy Goldmark, Desmond Child, Barry Mann and Cynthia Weil, and even Bob Dylan (1991's "Steel Bars")—and between 1987 and 1992 scored 11 top 40 hits.

At the height of his success, Bolton was repeatedly attacked by critics on two separate fronts: for his original material—which some contend is too formulaic and pat—and for his successful "whitewashed" covers of R&B material such as Redding's "(Sittin' On) The Dock of the Bay" and Percy Sledge's "When a Man Loves a Woman." In response, he has often spoken harshly of such critics during concert performances. "Yeah, I vent a little onstage," he acknowledged in 1992. "At the same time, I also let the audience know that what matters to me is what matters to them. That the bottom line is, the only critics that really matter are the ones who lay their money down to buy your albums and come and see you in concert. Those people work for a living, and that's what they decide to do with their money and time. Those people are coming and supporting you."

Bolton's abilities as an interpretive singer were further displayed in late 1992 with his Number One album *Timeless (The Classics),* which featured covers of such pop chestnuts as "You Send Me," "Since I Fell for You," "Drift Away," "To Love Somebody," and even "White Christmas." Perhaps because the singer was distressed about the criticism he'd received for his rerecorded R&B hits, he noted on the album liner that a portion of the albums proceeds would go to a special foundation "which has been created to enable young people of color to pursue their dreams in the creative arts."

TOP ALBUMS

THE HUNGER (Columbia, '87)
SOUL PROVIDER (Columbia, '89, 3)
TIME, LOVE & TENDERNESS (Columbia, '91, 1)
TIMELESS (THE CLASSICS) (Columbia, '92, 1)

TOP SONGS

HOW AM I SUPPOSED TO LIVE WITHOUT YOU
  (Columbia, '89, 1)
HOW CAN WE BE LOVERS (Columbia, '90, 3)
WHEN I'M BACK ON MY FEET AGAIN (Columbia, '90, 7)
LOVE IS A WONDERFUL THING (Columbia, '91, 4)
TIME, LOVE & TENDERNESS (Columbia, '91, 7)
WHEN A MAN LOVES A WOMAN (Columbia, '91, 1)

Additional Top 40 Songs: 5

KARLA BONOFF

Karla Bonoff (b. Dec. 27, 1952, Los Angeles) epitomizes the archetypal singer-songwriter that sprang up in the 1970s, long after James Taylor and Carole King had left their respective marks with *Sweet Baby James* and *Tapestry.* First, her initial claim to fame came via her songs, rather than her singing: Linda Ronstadt sang three Bonoff tunes on her 1976 platinum album *Hasten Down the Wind.* Those songs—"Someone to Lay Down Beside Me," "If He's Ever Near," and "Lose Again"—also appeared on Bonoff's own debut album, released by Columbia in the fall of 1977. Secondly, that same album was produced by former Stone Poney and later Ronstadt band member Kenny Edwards and featured the L.A. session-musician "mafia" that dominated most recordings of the genre and era: multi-instrumentalist Andrew Gold, guitarist Waddy Wachtel, bassist Leland Sklar, drummer Russ Kunkel, pianist Jai Winding, and a crew of backing vocalists that included Eagle Glenn Frey, John David Souther, Wendy Waldman, and even Ronstadt herself. Thirdly, Bonoff had connections: before Ronstadt had heard a single song she'd written, Bonoff and her group Bryndle (also featuring Waldman, Gold, and Edwards) had already made an album for A&M Records that had never been released. Finally, after the singer-songwriter era passed its '70s peak, Bonoff was one of the first artists to be "resurrected" via Gold Castle Records, the late-'80s baby-boomer label that also signed Peter, Paul and Mary, Joan Baez, Eric Andersen, and Judy Collins, among others.

If the 1970s saw a surplus of singer-songwriters, as many contend, Bonoff could count herself lucky. Her three Columbia albums all sold well, with 1979's *Restless Nights* peaking at number 31 and 1982's *Wild Heart of the Young* bearing her sole top 20 hit single, "Personally." Ironically, the track was the only song on the album Bonoff hadn't penned; it was a remake of Jackie Moore's 1978 Columbia debut single and the work of R&B writer Paul Kelly. And as fate would have it, her most-heard vocal performance of all time—"Somebody's Eyes" from 1984's platinum *Footloose* soundtrack—came cour-

Karla Bonoff

tesy the pens of songwriters Tom Snow and Dean Pitchford.

Continual comparisons to Ronstadt throughout her career were perhaps inevitable, given Bonoff's path to stardom and the musicians and friends both artists shared; but even then, sometimes she helped things along. When *New World,* Bonoff's first album in six years, hit the stores in 1988, a key contributor was producer Mark Goldenberg, a former member of L.A.'s conspicuously "new wave" group the Cretones, who in 1980 had been brought in to provide Ronstadt's *Mad Love* album some punkish kick. Though *New World* was by no means a sales smash, it clearly indicated that Bonoff's songwriting talents hadn't diminished in the slightest. All of which was further confirmed two years later, when New World's "All My Life" won a BMI Pop Award, after Ronstadt—of course—and Aaron Neville scored a hit duet with it.

TOP ALBUMS

KARLA BONOFF (Columbia, '77)
RESTLESS NIGHTS (Columbia, '79, *31*)
WILD HEART OF THE YOUNG (Columbia, '82)

TOP SONGS

SOMEONE TO LAY DOWN BESIDE ME (Columbia, '77)
LOVE AGAIN (Columbia, '77)
PLEASE BE THE ONE (Columbia, '82)

DAVID BOWIE

One of only a handful of rock artists who have maintained steady recording careers from the 1960s through the '90s, David Bowie (b. David Robert Jones, Jan. 8, 1947, Brixton, South London) became a vastly influential rock figure in the 1970s, known equally for the cutting-edge quality of his music—which stylistically was usually well ahead of its time—and his brilliant incorporation of theatrical elements into live performance. Dubbed early on as "the chameleon of rock," Bowie spent his '70s heyday changing his look, sound, and style with the release of nearly every album. During the course of the 1970s alone, the singer took on the role of futuristic rock star (1972's *The Rise and Fall of Ziggy Stardust and the Spiders from Mars*), slick white-soul singer (1975's *Young Americans*), Euro-rock instrumentalist (1977's *Low*), and even punkish world-music avatar (1979's *Lodger*). If there was a dilemma in any of this—and at the time there didn't appear to be—it may have been that Bowie's constant shifts precluded the establishment of a central artistic focus: in short, the music often seemed to take a back seat to the new look or style.

Though Bowie's arrival on the scene for most fans came via 1972's *Ziggy Stardust,* those captivated by the album soon discovered that much had preceded it. Uncovering the singer's past work seemed much like peeling the layers of an onion: prior to Ziggy came the warm and friendly *Hunky Dory* (1971); before that were the obscure Mercury albums *Man of Words, Man of Music* (1969) and *The Man Who Sold the World* (1970), then already out of print; before even that was the extremely obscure debut album, *David Bowie,* released on Deram Records in April 1967. As the singer's popularity climbed, additional reissue packages emerged that included singles Bowie had recorded as far back as 1964 under such names as Davy Jones and the Kingbees, the Mannish Boys, the Lower Third, and David Bowie (he had changed his name due to the rising Monkees star) and the Buzz. What made all this extremely relevant was that by 1972, when Bowie appeared to be making his American debut with *Ziggy Stardust,* he was already a well-seasoned performer, fully aware of the ins and outs of the

David Bowie

music business and by no means naïve. Unlike most new artists of the '70s, who often took two or three records to fine-tune one particularly well-received aspect of their style or repertoire, Bowie had "arrived" complete and fully formed.

Still, the singer's stylistic shifts were more noteworthy for their disparity than for any sort of innovation; Bowie was often forthright about the artists who directly influenced his sound. In rough order, they included British singer Anthony Newley, Bob Dylan and Lou Reed (both of whom were acknowledged on the liner to 1971's *Hunky Dory*), Iggy Pop (whose name inspired Bowie's "Ziggy" persona and with whom he would often collaborate), Bruce Springsteen, the entire Philadelphia soul sound (Bowie dubbed 1975's R&B-filled *Young Americans* his "plastic soul" phase), Eno, Tangerine Dream and Kraftwerk, and even Talking Heads. Further, his '60s British pop influences were made abundantly clear by his trendsetting 1973 "tribute" album *Pin Ups,* which featured covers of past songs by the Pretty Things, Them, Yardbirds, Pink Floyd, the Who, Australia's Easybeats, and the Kinks, among others.

Bowie's international fame sprang not only from his music but from his work in films. One of the few pop stars to have made a believable transition from music to the screen, the singer won praise for his work in *The Man Who Fell to Earth* (1976), *Just a Gigolo* (1978), *The Hunger* (1983), *Merry Christmas, Mr. Lawrence* (1983), and *Absolute Beginners* and *Labyrinth* (both 1986). Additionally, he starred in the Broadway play *The Elephant Man* in 1980 and the BBC-TV adaptation of Bertolt Brecht's "Baal" in 1982.

Despite Bowie's seeming ubiquitousness, his music was not played much on the radio during the height of his '70s fame. Discounting the 1973 hit "Space Oddity"—which had originally been recorded in 1969 and was thus pre-Ziggy—Bowie had only three top 40 hits during the decade, with his biggest single the Number One "Fame," featuring prominent backing vocals by John Lennon. Perhaps oddly,

---

TOP ALBUMS

DIAMOND DOGS (RCA, '74, *5*)
YOUNG AMERICANS (RCA, '75, *9*)
STATION TO STATION (RCA, '76, *3*)
CHANGESONEBOWIE (RCA, '76, *10*)
LOW (RCA, '77, *11*)
LET'S DANCE (EMI America, '83, *4*)
TONIGHT (EMI America, '84, *11*)

Additional Top 40 Albums: 9

TOP SONGS

FAME (RCA, '75, *1*)
LET'S DANCE (EMI America, '83, *1*)
BLUE JEAN (EMI America, '84, *8*)

Additional Top 40 Songs: 10

Bowie's ascendancy to the top 40 with 1983's "Let's Dance" almost precisely coincided with his gradual falling out of favor with the countless critics who had spent the prior decade praising his every move. While that single's source, the album *Let's Dance,* was initially viewed as yet another "phase" in his chameleon-like career—it combined the R&B sound of co-producer Nile Rodgers with the bluesy guitar of Stevie Ray Vaughan—the same general style remained throughout 1984's much weaker follow-up album, *Tonight.* And where Bowie had once seemed a songwriter with an unlimited supply of catchy new tunes, both albums were distressingly filled with older material, such as remakes of Bowie and Iggy Pop's "China Girl" and "Tonight" as well as covers of songs by Brian Wilson, Leiber and Stoller, and others. The low point came in 1985, when Bowie and Mick Jagger recorded a pointless duet version of "Dancing in the Street," which nonetheless became a top 10 hit.

Unfortunately for Bowie, despite the noticeable improvement in the quality of his material that began with 1987's *Never Let Me Down* (which wrongly received the bad reviews its two predecessors deserved), his singing career has been in a downward spiral ever since. He formed the quartet Tin Machine in 1989, and the band context sparked him to write some of his finest material since 1980's *Scary Monsters.* But the group's three albums were among the least commercially successful records he made, with 1991's *Tin Machine II* peaking at number 126 and 1992's live set *Oy Vey, Baby* incredibly failing to enter the charts at all. Perhaps even more mortifying, when the singer resumed recording under his own name with 1993's *Black Tie White Noise*—again one of his best efforts in years—his new label, Savage Records, went under short weeks after issuing the album, and the set went into commercial limbo.

Whether Bowie will be able to recover his niche in the marketplace remained a major question in late 1993; but as his distinguished track record suggests, platinum sales may be only one more style change ahead of him.

EDIE BRICKELL

Anyone catching 1989's top 10 hit "What I Am" for the first time would be forgiven for thinking (1) It's one of Rickie Lee Jones' best singles, and (2) What the heck do those words mean? It's a natural reaction to the work of Edie Brickell (b. Oak Cliff, Texas), who at the time told the press that, in fact, she'd never heard Rickie Lee Jones until she finished making her album. "So I listened to her records," Brickell told *Rolling Stone* in late 1988, "and I went, 'Wow, I see what they mean.' " Had those words come from an obvious business sophisticate such as Madonna, they'd perhaps be suspect, but originating from the refreshingly naive, charming Brickell, their genuineness was plausible.

Edie Brickell

Those lyrics, apparently inspired by equal measures of Zen, *Sesame Street,* and Popeye (sample lyric: "I'm not aware of too many things/I know what I know if you know what I mean"), seemed street-smart in a strangely disarming way. Combined with the appealing lilt in her Jonesish voice along with the maximum, well-timed exposure she received on "Saturday Night Live" and MTV, the videogenic Brickell won hearts nearly overnight. Over a million hearts, actually, as the source of her hit, *Shooting Rubber Bands at the Stars,* quickly shot to the top five and went platinum—allowing fans to discover such additional intriguing lyrics as "there's nothing I hate more than nothing" and many more. For that matter, they'd discover Brickell had concluded the album with an uncredited track called "I Do," which, she acknowledged in a Geffen Records promotional booklet, was "a song for my cat."

Yet anyone who'd frequented the vibrantly artsy Deep Ellum section of Dallas in the mid-'80s might've been wondering what happened. The Edie Brickell they knew—the one whose father was a professional bowler and whose mother was actually given the name Larry—was only part of a local band called the New Bohemians. Having attracted a large following, the group had already appeared on a 1987 Island Records compilation (called *The Sound of Deep Ellum*) billed by their proper name.

What did happen? Business as usual: in the course of mak-

ing their Geffen debut album, the decision had been made to credit it to Edie Brickell and the New Bohemians. The rationale? The band had been disturbed by their lack of control in the making of the record—producer Pat Moran had used additional players as he saw fit—and Geffen, seeking to protect their investment if something should go wrong, decided to establish Brickell as an artist in her own right. Her contributions to the album were by no means minimal: she'd penned all the lyrics, co-written the music for five tracks, and produced three entirely on her own. Ultimately, though, Geffen's decision caused considerable tension in the band and resulted in several significant personnel shifts.

When *Ghost of a Dog* emerged in 1990, also credited to Edie Brickell and the New Bohemians, it seemed as if a conscious effort had been made to make much of it seem more

---

TOP ALBUMS

SHOOTING RUBBERBANDS AT THE STARS
(Geffen, '88, 4)
GHOST OF A DOG (Geffen, '90, 32)

TOP SONG

WHAT I AM (Geffen, '89, 7)

---

of a band effort—but it was too late. Songs such as the opener, "Mama Help Me," which featured Brickell singing against a loud guitar and rhythm section, simply didn't fit in with the sound the public had come to accept as Brickell's. The album had no hit singles, and it peaked at a disappointing number 32. Still, Brickell had written five of the album's tracks this time out—the better ones, actually (including one with the unique opening line, "Sittin' on the front porch/In Oak Cliff/With my bra")—and seemed poised to take the next step and simply become a solo artist.

Two final facts: In a 1988 interview, Brickell had told the *New York Times* that she admired the lyrics of Paul Simon and Elvis Costello. In 1992, she married Simon and eventually bore their child. One supposes the child will follow Dad's example and read the *Times* regularly, too.

JACKSON BROWNE

Yes I wish I was as mellow/As for instance Jackson Browne," went the lyric to "H-A-T-R-E-D" from Tonio K.'s 1978 album *Life in the Foodchain*, "But 'Fountain of Sorrow' my ass/I hope you wind up in the ground." Lauded by some critics as the finest rock lyricist to emerge during the 1970s, Jackson Browne (b. Oct. 9, 1948, Heidelberg, Germany) so embodied the cliché of the "sensitive singer-songwriter" by 1978 that he made a perfect target for politically minded types who felt his characteristically introverted tunes too often bordered on solipsism at a time when the world, they contended, was going to hell. Ironically, Browne would soon become so politically outspoken himself—on the topics of nuclear energy, Latin American politics, and Amnesty International—that some fans were soon clamoring for the singer to leave his politics at the recording studio door and, as Tonio K. would say, get mellow again.

Though Browne's so-called emergence indeed took place in

the 1970s, via his 1972 Asylum debut album, *Jackson Browne* (a.k.a. *Saturate Before Using*), the singer's songs had been making the rounds for at least the preceding half-decade. Browne, whose family had moved from Germany to California in the early 1950s, was a precocious singer-songwriter who began performing in the early '60s. Together with Orange County friends Steve Noonan and Greg Copeland, he linked with Elektra Records' publishing arm Nina Music following his 1966 high school graduation; by 1967, he saw his earliest tunes appearing on Nico's *Chelsea Girl* ("These Days," "Somewhere There's a Feather," and "The Fairest of the Seasons," co-written with Copeland) and the debut album of Long Beach friends the Nitty Gritty Dirt Band ("Melissa" and "Holding"), with whom he had briefly played. By the next year, his work was on Tom Rush's *The Circle Game* ("Shadow Dream Song") and Noonan's own Elektra debut ("She's a Flying Thing," "Tumble Down," "The Painter," "Shadow Dream Song," and "Trusting Is a Harder Thing," co-written with Noonan). Browne himself is rumored to have recorded an Elektra album of his own in 1968 that never surfaced.

Contextually, however, Jackson Browne could not have picked a finer time to first display his wares than 1972, less than a year after singer-songwriters James Taylor and Carole King had had Number One albums with *Mud Slide Slim and the Blue Horizon* and *Tapestry* respectively. Browne's official debut was marvelous, a mature statement that may remain his finest work. A mostly acoustic set highlighted by such memorable tracks as "Song for Adam," "Something Fine," and "Under the Falling Sky," the album quickly found an audience thanks to its inclusion of the top 10 single "Doctor My Eyes." Significantly, the album helped launch not only Browne but also David Geffen's new Asylum label, which would swiftly become a bustling center of West Coast recording activity during the '70s.

Browne's earliest albums sold increasingly well, and his affiliation with Asylum up-and-comers the Eagles (he co-wrote their first hit, "Take It

TOP ALBUMS

JACKSON BROWNE (Asylum, '72)
LATE FOR THE SKY (Asylum, '74, *14*)
THE PRETENDER (Asylum, '76, *5*)
RUNNING ON EMPTY (Asylum, '78, *3*)
HOLD OUT (Asylum, '80, *1*)
LAWYERS IN LOVE (Asylum, '83, *8*)
LIVES IN THE BALANCE (Asylum, '86, *23*)

TOP SONGS

DOCTOR MY EYES (Asylum, '72, *8*)
RUNNING ON EMPTY (Asylum, '78, *11*)
SOMEBODY'S BABY (Asylum, '82, *7*)

Additional Top 40 Songs: 9

Jackson Browne

the singer himself became deeply engrossed in political and foreign policy issues. His concern was reflected in 1983's *Lawyers in Love,* but after a 1984 trip to Nicaragua it surfaced profoundly in his follow-up *Lives in the Balance.* "What's good about a world in which/War rages at a fever pitch," he sang on "Soldier of Plenty," "And people die for little things/A little corn, a little beans."

Browne participated in Amnesty International's 1986 Conspiracy of Hope tour, and within two years he had aligned himself with the Christic Institute, a nonprofit law and public policy organization for which he did a benefit tour. But while Browne's political muscle was growing, his chart fortunes seemed to be fading: 1989's *World in Motion* was the first album of his career that failed to be certified either gold or platinum or even have a charting single.

Following a four-year break from recording, the singer returned in late 1993 with the impressive *I'm Alive,* a return to form for him in many ways. Most obvious was the overall lack of political content of its songs; if anything, the themes explored on tracks such as "My Problem Is You," "Two of Me, Two of You," and "All Good Things" recalled Browne's memorable '70s work on *Late for the Sky* and *The Pretender.* Some saw the album as deeply autobiographical for the singer: his longtime relationship with actress Daryl Hannah had come to a well-publicized and stormy end, and at the time of the album's release, she was rumored soon to be marrying John F. Kennedy, Jr. "My songs are the residue of my life," Browne had told record executive Joe Smith in his 1988 book *Off the Record.* "When everything else is done, the songs are what's left. Generally, it tends to be sort of looking in the rearview mirror. The songs are about a time that is past—or a resolve about the present that in some ways relates to the past."

JACK BRUCE

Easy," with Glen Frey) by no means harmed him. His best songs of the time typically focused on relationships; more often than not, he was at his best when those relationships seemed to be souring or climaxing in some way, as on the title track to 1974's superb *Late for the Sky* (home of Tonio K. favorite "Fountain of Sorrow"). Though 1976 should have been a banner year for the singer—his album *The Pretender* was his first to make the top 10—it was marred by the tragedy of his wife Phyllis's suicide in March. Browne carried on, and the next year daringly released a live album of all-new material, *Running on Empty,* which ascended to number three on the charts and brought him two hits: the title track, and a cover of Maurice Williams and the Zodiacs' 1960 hit "Stay."

Browne became increasingly involved with the anti-nuclear movement in the late 1970s; he was a co-founder and board member of MUSE (Musicians United for Safe Energy) and played a major role in 1979's historic "No Nukes" concerts at Madison Square Garden. While his music gained more acceptance than ever—1980's *Hold Out* debuted at Number One and his 1982 single "Somebody's Baby" (from *Fast Times at Ridgemont High*) went top 10—

O ften credited as being one of the founding fathers of heavy metal due to his pivotal role in the legendary '60s band Cream, bassist Jack Bruce (b. John Simon Asher Bruce, May 14, 1943, Lanarkshire, Scotland) may be one of the most innovative musicians ever to play rock and roll of any style. While his onetime partner Eric Clapton has gone on to world superstardom, album for album, song for song, and note for note, Bruce remains the more impressive musician. He's certainly the more adventurous.

After briefly studying cello at the Royal Scottish Academy of Music in his late teens, Bruce moved to London in the early 1960s and got in on the ground floor of that city's fabled blues explosion, playing and recording with Alexis Korner, Graham Bond, John Mayall, and even popsters Manfred Mann for an eight-month spell. (He's on their 1966 top 30 hit "Pretty Flamingo.") At that point, Bruce joined forces with two musicians he'd already worked with, Eric Clapton from Mayall's band and Ginger Baker from Bond's; formed the original power trio, Cream; then went on to sell 35 million records.

From the opening note of "I Feel Free"—the first song from the first Cream album, 1966's *Fresh Cream*—listeners heard the work of a song partnership now closing in on its third decade. Jack Bruce's lyricist of choice was Pete Brown, a British "jazz poet" whose very first song lyric was penned for "Wrapping Paper," Cream's initial single. Brown was himself a recording artist, the lead singer of groups such as the Battered Ornaments and Piblokto!, whose scattered few albums are now highly sought by collectors. Working together, Bruce and Brown forged one of the more memorable (and colorful) collaborative relationships in pop history. The pair wrote both of Cream's top 10 hits, "Sunshine of Your Love" (with Clapton also sharing a credit) and "White Room." But more importantly in those self-consciously "underground" days, with Bruce's powerful vocals and Brown's sometimes surrealistic imagery they shaped Cream's overall character completely. Which is one reason why Bruce's ensuing solo albums always felt more like Cream albums than did Clapton's.

Bruce's musical sophistication allowed him to regularly write songs using odd time signatures and arrangements; his first solo album, 1969's *Songs for a Tailor*, was a brilliant tour de force in that regard. Without the constraints that the Cream power trio phenomenon presented, Bruce was free to bring in brass, cellos, organ, and piano wherever he saw fit. And that's what he did.

If anything especially marks Bruce as unique, it's his unfailing ability to excel in genres that have little

TOP ALBUMS

SONGS FOR A TAILOR (Atco, '69)
HARMONY ROW (Atco, '71)
OUT OF THE STORM (RSO, '74)
HOW'S TRICKS (RSO, '77)
I'VE ALWAYS WANTED TO DO THIS (Epic, '80)

in common. From studying classical cello and pioneering hard rock, he then played some of the most adventurous jazz of his time, performing on Carla Bley's mammoth 1972 set *Escalator Over the Hill* and becoming a member of the original, epochal Tony Williams Lifetime. For that matter, Bruce's second solo album—issued in 1971, when Cream nostalgia was just beginning to kick in—was a straight-out instrumental jazz set he'd recorded three years earlier with guitarist John McLaughlin. Indeed, most of Bruce's post-Cream career has been something of a puzzling zigzag, from subtle solo albums like 1971's understated *Harmony Row* to his raucous, heavy-metal fling with West, Bruce and Laing, which lasted for 16 months and resulted in three pounding albums.

Despite Bruce's failure to find as dependable a steady gig as Cream provided, he's managed to work regularly with superb musicians and turn out top-notch albums. Though the musical cast of characters has changed considerably in 20 years (from Mick Taylor and Carla Bley to David Sancious and Billy Cobham to a 1993 Rock and Roll Hall of Fame "reunion" with Cream), Bruce's compositions, still mostly penned with Brown, haven't lost one iota of their original magic. Which may be why pop stars like Belinda Carlisle (in 1987) and David Bowie (in 1993) separately chose to resurrect "I Feel Free" nearly a quarter of a century after Bruce and Brown wrote it. It's difficult to imagine that a member of the most popular rock trio of all time might be undervalued, but with Jack Bruce, that's exactly the case.

LINDSEY BUCKINGHAM

When he joined Fleetwood Mac with partner Stevie Nicks in 1975, the common consensus was that Lindsey Buckingham (b. Oct. 3, 1947, Palo Alto, California) was extending a grand musical tradition that had begun in the 1960s. This was true on an obvious level—that of helping to keep alive a long-lived English blues band—but also on another, more subtle one. As an enormously talented singer, songwriter, guitarist, arranger, and producer, Buckingham brought the sound of California music both to Fleetwood Mac and to pop radio. His use of harmonies, the seductive twang of his guitar during ballads, his often minor-key, hazy melodies—they all suggested a lonely beach sunset, all recalled the sound popularized by Brian Wilson's Beach Boys in their mid-'60s prime. Indeed, as a member of Fleetwood Mac, Buckingham performed a version of Wilson's early-'60s song "The Farmer's Daughter" in concert; it can be found on 1980's *Fleetwood Mac Live,* along with a

TOP ALBUMS

LAW AND ORDER (Asylum, '81, 32)
GO INSANE (Elektra, '84)
OUT OF THE CRADLE (Reprise, '92)

TOP SONGS

TROUBLE (Asylum, '81, 9)
GO INSANE (Elektra, '84, 23)
SOUL DRIFTER (Reprise, '92)
SURRENDER THE RAIN (Reprise, '92)

thank you note to Wilson ("You're the greatest," wrote Buckingham) for providing the song. Four years later, the guitarist ended his brilliant solo album *Go Insane* with the moving "D. W. Suite," an extended composition commemorating Beach Boy drummer Dennis Wilson, who had drowned in December 1983.

"I've been a fan of the Beach Boys since the seventh grade," Buckingham said at the time, "but they began to affect me about the time that Brian started to emerge and I began to appreciate what a great melodicist he has always been. And if you want to talk about experimental, and beautiful experimental things—Brian's music during the *Smile* period, no one has ever done things like that, before or since."

Buckingham's own knowledge of musical experimentalism began early in his life in Palo Alto, when an inheritance from a deceased aunt allowed him to purchased $12,000 worth of recording equipment. He used it to record much of the material he would perform live with his Bay Area band Fritz; also featuring his future girlfriend Stevie Nicks, the band lasted for roughly three years before the pair would split off and eventually sign to Polydor in 1973 as Buckingham Nicks. Now a rarity, their sole album impressed the members of Fleetwood Mac enough to ask the duo to join their group—and the rest, of course, is history.

In one way, Buckingham's contributions to the newly reconstituted Fleetwood Mac exceeded those of any other band member, including partner Nicks. While the number of hits he wrote were exceeded by both Nicks and Fleetwood mainstay Christine McVie—a total of three top 10 Mac hits were penned by Buckingham, including "Go Your Own Way," "Tusk," and "Big Love"—his guitar and production contributions overwhelmingly shaped the sound of Fleetwood Mac during their hitmaking prime. "If I had to choose my main contributing factor to the band," he told *Billboard*'s Timothy White in 1987, "it wouldn't be as a guitarist, a writer, or a singer. It would be as someone who knows how to take raw material from Christine and Stevie and forge that into something. That's a nice gift to have and be able to help people with."

Lindsey Buckingham

Buckingham's sculpting of the Fleetwood Mac sound was perhaps most prominent on his final album with the band, 1987's extraordinary, double platinum *Tango in the Night*. The guitarist not only gave the group four of the best songs he was preparing for an upcoming solo album (an added fifth, "You and I Part I," served as a single B side) but also endowed the songs of McVie and Nicks with such utterly gorgeous arrangements that the album truly stands as Fleetwood Mac's finest. One suspects it was no accident that 1990's *Behind the Mask*—the first post-Buckingham Mac album—was the group's lowest-charting effort since 1974's *Heroes Are Hard to Find*.

While still a band member, Buckingham recorded two solo albums that seemed to purposefully avoid Mac-like songs and pursue the same studio experimentalism he'd admired in Brian Wilson. *Law and Order* (1981) and *Go Insane* (1984) both made the top 40 and bore hits: 1981's "Trouble" reached the top 10, and title track "Go Insane" peaked at number 23. But it was with 1992's *Out of the Cradle* that Lindsey Buckingham—for the first time a bona fide solo artist—created his masterpiece. Without external distractions, and without the need to balance Nicks' and McVie's standard slow-moving ballads with his own upbeat rockers, the guitarist fashioned a marvelously cohesive work, highlighted by two beautiful ballads—"Soul Drifter" and "Surrender the Rain"—that evoked the very best California rock of two decades earlier, yet sounded as up-to-date as any of Fleetwood Mac's finest work.

Because Buckingham enjoys a share in the royalties of *Rumours*, the second-largest selling American album in pop history, it's likely he doesn't need to make another record in his life to earn a living. That he still does speaks less about his ego—or his need for commercial recognition—than of his simple love for the sound of music, which continues to shine through on everything he records.

TIM BUCKLEY

Underappreciated to this day, nearly two decades after his death, Tim Buckley (b. Feb. 14, 1947, Washington, D.C.) remains for the many who have not heard him just one in the blur of Tims and Toms—Paxton, Hardin, Rose, Rush, Rapp—who surfaced in the mid-'60s, guitars in hand

and meaningful songs at the ready. But while each Tim and Tom was distinctly different from one another, Tim Buckley was distinctly different from literally everybody. His status as a musical innovator ranks as high as Bob Dylan, the Beatles, and the Rolling Stones (from the commercial realm) and Captain Beefheart, Can, and the Velvet Underground (from the rock underground). Like all of those artists in their prime, he pursued his muse with little regard for the prospect of eventual commercial reward; the results, in his case, were nine albums produced in a seven-year span (1967–74) that, for the most part, sound like they might have been recorded yesterday, so pure is the artistic drive behind them. His fascinating career trajectory—from teen folksinger to pop singer-songwriter to jazz-rock experimentalist to contemporary classicist to slyly sexual, madcap rock star—is so overwhelming in its breadth, would be so impossible to even attempt to duplicate, that it will likely remain one of pop music's eternal, untouchable mysteries.

Buckley's recording career got its start in 1966 with the help of Frank Zappa's manager Herb Cohen, who took Buckley on as a client after seeing him perform in Los Angeles and then got him a deal with Elektra. *Tim Buckley* was a rich collection of 12 original songs, seven of which the 19-year-old had penned with lyricist Larry Beckett, with whom he'd continue to work through the remainder of his career. Buckley's high-pitched voice suggested a cross between angel and choirboy; the lyrics he sang, whether his or Beckett's, were unabashedly romantic and evocative.

With 1967's *Goodbye and Hello*, Buckley's career took off notably; though it spent only five weeks on the album charts and peaked at number 171, it made a lasting impression and is probably the singer's most-heard work. While his debut album featured full-band accompaniment, there was a certain sparseness to the sound no longer in evidence on this intricately arranged follow-up; a full section of strings and horns accompanied Buckley on the ambitious, nearly nine-minute title track. Beckett, who this time wrote half of the album's lyrics, sometimes went overboard in his ambition—and never so much as on that same title track, which had Buckley singing such wordy passages as "In that hollowest house of the opulent blind," and "Godless and sexless directionless loons/Their sham sandcastles dissolve in the tide."

That wordiness was nowhere to be found on

Buckley's captivating *Happy Sad,* his highest-charting album (it reached number 81) and perhaps his best. Buckley's voice seemed to have dropped an octave, and the last album's intricate arrangements had been replaced by a warm, jazzy groove. Jazz fans instantly recognized the debt its opening track, "Strange Feelin'," owed to Miles Davis's *Kind of Blue* classic "All Blues"—and just as Davis was a pioneer in his use of openness and space, Buckley sounded relaxed and intimate on much of *Happy Sad.* Though Beckett wrote no lyrics this time out, Buckley, especially on the movingly introspective "Dream Letter," was providing his own lyrical peaks.

Happy Sad was Tim Buckley's pivotal album; it marked a clean delineation between his early folk- and pop-based style and his embrace of jazz and avant-garde classical forms on his three next albums, *Blue Afternoon* (1969), *Lorca* (1970), and the sonically staggering *Starsailor* (1971). The latter two undoubtedly lost Buckley whatever degree of loyalty he maintained from *Goodbye and Hello* fans, as the singer—inspired by the jazz saxophonist John Coltrane and classical avant-garde composer Iannis Xenakis, among others—explored his astounding five-octave vocal range with no holds barred; several tracks on *Starsailor* featured a chorus of over-dubbed, howling Buckleys that sounded nearly insectlike.

Buckley's final career phase came via the relatively commercial-sounding *Greetings from L.A.,* a rocking tour de force in which Buckley played the role of erotic bad boy, singing about machine guns, women, bars, and, on the unique "Get on Top," licking his lover's stretch marks. It was a bruising reentry into mainstream rock, but it—like its two even more commercial follow-ups *Sefronia* (1973) and *Look at the Fool* (1974)—was largely ignored by both rock radio and consumers.

Buckley spent much of his later period on the road giving devastatingly electric live performances; his sudden death by drug overdose on June 29, 1975, surprised and saddened many who felt the artist had a long and still very promising future ahead of him.

Though Buckley's records were rarely played on

TOP ALBUMS

TIM BUCKLEY (Elektra, '66)
GOODBYE AND HELLO (Elektra, '67)
HAPPY SAD (Elektra, '69)
BLUE AFTERNOON (Straight, '69)
LORCA (Elektra, '70)
STARSAILOR (Straight, '71)
GREETINGS FROM L.A. (Straight, '72)

TOP SONGS

MORNING GLORY (Elektra, '67)
HAPPY TIME (Straight, '69)
SONG TO THE SIREN (Straight, '71)

radio and fell out of print for a disturbingly long stretch (though all were reissued on CD in the early 1990s), his songs have become familiar to two generations of pop fans. *Goodbye and Hello*'s "Morning Glory" was prominently covered by Linda Ronstadt and Blood, Sweat and Tears in the 1960s; British alternative group This Mortal Coil redid that song, *Blue Afternoon*'s "I Must Have Been Blind," and *Starsailor*'s "Song to the Siren" in the late 1980s and early '90s. Avant-garde guitarist Eugene Chadbourne and Camper Van Beethoven also produced one-half an album of Buckley covers on 1988's *The Eddie Chatterbox Double Trio Love Album.*

In 1990, Enigma/Retro Records unexpectedly released *Dream Letter/Live in London 1968,* a double-CD concert recording featuring Buckley in his prime—right after he'd released *Happy Sad*—that sounded so contemporary it might have been recorded only the week before. We can only wish it had.

JIMMY BUFFETT

I f someone who saw Jimmy Buffett during the early days of his career—say, 1972, when he was the opening act at a Miami coffeehouse/club called the Flick—was plucked from the past and deposited in the midst of a modern-day Buffett concert, that person's jaw would drop lower than Key West. Just as the Grateful Dead have their core following of Deadheads, Buffett's own loyal troops, called "Parrot Heads" due to their tropical taste in hats, are among the most colorful in pop history. Jimmy Buffett: not just a singer, but a cultural icon.

How did it happen? Buffett (b. Dec. 25, 1946, Pascagoula, Mississippi) had humble but well-educated beginnings, graduating from the University of Southern Mississippi with a degree in history and journalism (he was a one-time *Billboard* correspondent) and a hankering to establish himself as a country singer. He moved to Nashville by the end of the 1960s and recorded two albums for Barnaby, but neither sold, and his careeer floundered. Next stop:

Miami, where an expected job didn't materialize, after which a near-broke Buffett took buddy Jerry Jeff Walker's advice and moved south to Key West.

Thereafter, Buffett's career swiftly kicked into gear. The cover of 1973's *A White Sport Coat and a Pink Crustacean*, his first album under a new deal with Dunhill (which would ultimately be absorbed by MCA), instantly established Buffett's redoubtable persona: a droopy-eyed, too-pleasant-to-be-smarmy Buffett was beaming barefoot atop a crate of Florida lobsters. With liner notes by local literary fixture Tom McGuane and the now-classic "Why Don't We Get Drunk" ("and screw" mysteriously missing from the official title) credited to one "Marvin Gardens," Buffett had produced a warm album of colorful story-songs that showed equal traces of humor, sentiment, and a keen grasp of Americana. With 1974's "Come Monday," Buffett produced his first hit single; his next, 1977's "Margaritaville," took him to the top 10 and gave him his first platinum album, *Changes in Attitudes, Changes in Latitudes.*

In one sense, Buffett enjoyed his peak record-selling years between 1977 and 1979: he had three additional top 40 hits (*Changes'* title track, "Cheeseburger in Paradise," and "Fins") as well as one platinum (*Son of a Son of a Sailor*) and two gold (*You Had to Be There* and *Volcano*) albums in that time span. Though he'd again nab platinum honors with 1985's *Songs You Know by Heart* compilation, by then he'd become much more than a mere record seller. For his growing legion of fans, Buffett was an annual summer concert tradition in the same sense that the Beach Boys were; his records may not have been going quadruple platinum, but attendance at his concerts was booming, and he quickly became a regular top-grossing artist. At the same time, Buffett's creative juices were flowing in several other directions as well: he was an entrepreneur (he'd opened two retail operations, the Margaritaville Store & Cafe, first in Key West, then New Orleans); a crusader (he's been instrumental in Florida conservationists' efforts to save the manatee); a sailor (he'd bought a boat with his first big royalty check); a pilot (he flies his own single-engine amphibian plane); a record company head (he launched Margaritaville Records in 1992); and an author of both bestsellers (*Where Is Joe Merchant?* and *Tales from Margaritaville*) and children's books (*The Jolly Mon* and *Trouble Dolls*, co-written with his young daughter).

Not that Buffett's records don't continue to sell. *Boats, Beaches, Bars & Ballads*, a four-CD, career

Jimmy Buffett

TOP ALBUMS

A1A (Dunhill, '75, 25)
CHANGES IN LATITUDES, CHANGES IN ATTITUDES (ABC, '77, 12)
SON OF A SON OF A SAILOR (ABC, '78, 10)
VOLCANO (MCA, '79, 14)
COCONUT TELEGRAPH (MCA, '81, 30)

Additional Top 40 Albums: 1

TOP SONGS

COME MONDAY (Dunhill, '74, 30)
MARGARITAVILLE (ABC, '77, 8)
CHANGES IN LATITUDES, CHANGES IN ATTITUDES (ABC, '77, 37)
CHEESEBURGER IN PARADISE (ABC, '78, 32)
FINS (MCA, '79, 35)

retrospective boxed set issued in 1992, went on to become MCA's biggest-selling boxed set ever. And the Parrot Heads are increasing in number: Buffett made headlines as one of the largest concert draws of the summer of 1993. "What gets so surreal to me is that I figured this was going to peak some time ago," he told a reporter. "I thought everybody would start going to somebody else's shows. But it hasn't happened."

T-BONE BURNETT

Nearly six-and-a-half feet tall, T-Bone Burnett (b. Joseph Henry Burnett, 1948, St. Louis, Missouri) stands out in any crowd in which he might be found. As it happens, that crowd has included some of the finest singers, songerwriters, and performers of the past two decades. Since the Fort Worth–bred guitarist gained international notice in 1975 as part of Bob Dylan's Rolling Thunder Revue, he has steadily built a reputation as a highly skilled producer (for Elvis Costello, Los Lobos, and Peter Case, among others) and an extremely literate, fascinating singer-songwriter. Most unusually, he is a devout Christian moralist (credited by many, in fact, for helping along Dylan's "born again" post–Rolling Thunder phase) who has no compunction about coloring his songs with metaphors and analogies that at times seem clearly biblical—yet never to the point where they overwhelm listener or song.

Burnett began his career in the mid-'60s as an engineer and producer at Fort Worth's Sound City studio. Even then, his songs were getting exposure: the 1968 Uni Records album he produced for obscure Texan group Whistler, Chaucer, Detroit, and Greenhill, for example, bore four early Burnett tracks of surprising high quality, which sounded stylistically similar to Buffalo Springfield. His own debut album, *The B-52 Band & the Fabulous Skylarks,* was issued by Uni in 1972 and featured Burnett with drummer Matt Betton and bassist David Jackson, both later members of his post–Rolling Thunder group, the Alpha Band.

It was with the latter band that Burnett's music received its first serious exposure. Formed in New Mexico in 1976 by Rolling Thunder players Burnett, David Mansfield, and Steven Soles, the short-lived group recorded three superb albums for Arista Records in only 18 months. Though many writers were involved, it was mostly Burnett's music that dominated the discs; 1978's *The Statue Makers of Hollywood* now seems a Burnett album all but in name, its second side opening with his "Perverse Generation" and closing with Hank Williams's "Thank God."

Burnett's series of solo albums followed, led by 1980's impressive *Truth Decay,* which on critical levels finally established him as a major artist. Quirky, funny at times, and noticeably judgmental, it helped lay the groundwork for Burnett's future lyrical explorations of America's institutional underbelly. That came through strongest on the brief, musically understated "Madison Avenue," on which Burnett sang, "Will you tell me this riddle/Who is the father of lies?/Who is the master of half-truth?/What is Madison Avenue?" He would continue in this vein throughout the 1980s, most successfully on 1983's *Proof Through the Night,* which tackled icons as disparate as Walt Disney (whom he compared to Hugh Hefner) and Marilyn Monroe, and on one track, "The Sixties," an entire decade.

Burnett's albums have featured a wide assortment of prominent guest stars, including Pete Townshend, U2's Bono, and Richard Thompson. In the mid-'80s he began an association with Elvis Costello that would result in a joint single—"The People's Limousine," issued in 1985 under the pseudonym the Coward Brothers—and a producer credit on Costello's lauded 1986 album, *King of America.* In 1988, he signed to Columbia Records and released the ambitious *The Talking Animals,* followed by 1992's intriguing *The Criminal Under My Own Hat.*

Though sometimes accused by critics of preachiness and of taking himself too seriously, Burnett remains a major talent who—perhaps because of his religious background—simply can't help telling two

---

TOP ALBUMS

TRUTH DECAY (Takoma, '80)
PROOF THROUGH THE NIGHT (Warner Bros., '83)
THE TALKING ANIMALS (Columbia, '88)
THE CRIMINAL UNDER MY OWN HAT (Columbia, '92)

TOP SONGS

QUICKSAND (Takoma, '80)
THE MURDER WEAPON (Warner Bros., '83)

stories at once. He did, after all, sing these words on his 1992 song "Kill Switch": "There are those who play for money babe/There are those who play for fame/There are still those who only play/For the love of the game."

KATE BUSH

Kate Bush

A towering talent in a tiny package, the diminutive Kate Bush (b. July 30, 1958, Bexley, Kent, England) is an international superstar whose grand artistic ambitions are more than met by her musical capabilities. One of very few performers who have not compromised their art for the sake of commercial convenience, Bush is a respected singer, songwriter, keyboardist, dance, mime, video director, and, most notably, conceptualist. While the United States has been slow in warming up to her in comparison to other markets—where for the past 15 years she has regularly had Number One hits—her

album sales have consistently increased, and she is no stranger to the upper reaches of the charts.

Bush's celebrated 1978 debut single, "Wuthering Heights," was a sensation in her homeland; it soared to Number One, became that year's best-selling single, and noticeably bumped up sales of Emily Bronte's like-named novel. Interest in Bush was heavy not only for the uniqueness of her sound—her high-pitched, piercing voice was like nothing ever heard before—but her curious past. Discovered two years earlier by Pink Floyd guitarist David Gilmour, who had funded her initial three-track demo tape, Bush had been signed by EMI when just 16, then allowed two years to prepare for her debut album. In the interim, she began performing locally in the three-piece KT Bush band and studied dancing and mime, both of which would figure prominently in her later concerts.

One very simple reason America was slow to appreciate Bush's music was its literal inaccessibility to U.S. audiences. Following her 1978 debut *The Kick Inside*—which made the British top 10 but failed to chart stateside—her next two albums, *Lionheart* (also 1978) and *Never for Ever* (1980), were not released in the U.S. until 1984. For the American audience, *Kick Inside*'s "follow-up" was 1982's *The Dreaming*, an extremely sophisticated, self-produced effort that was a significant step up from its comparatively primitive 1978 predecessor. Staying on the charts for nearly three months and peaking at number 157, the album was proof enough for EMI that Bush was a viable U.S. commodity; within a few months they issued *Kate Bush,* a mini-LP of five songs recorded between 1979 and 1982.

Bush's best-selling album both internationally and in the States was 1985's *The Hounds of Love,* an ambitious project that made a particularly strong impression via its accompanying videos. The singer's first U.S. top 40 hit, "Running Up That Hill," was apparently all she'd needed to nudge her album sales; as a result of that exposure, *Hounds* itself entered the top 30. The next year's compilation *The Whole Story* helped consolidate her success by offering new fans a glimpse of her distinguished back catalog.

Bush's music was becoming more sophisticated with every album, largely due to her spirit of adventurousness and precocious skill on the famous Fairlight synthesizer, one of the earliest sampling devices. By 1989, Bush had built a first-rate studio in her Kent, England, home; in it, she recorded most of 1989's *The Sensual World,* a complex but, in its

TOP ALBUMS

THE KICK INSIDE (Harvest, '78)
THE DREAMING (EMI America, '82)
HOUNDS OF LOVE (EMI America, '85, *30*)
THE WHOLE STORY (EMI America, '86)
THE SENSUAL WORLD (Columbia, '89)

TOP SONGS

WUTHERING HEIGHTS (Harvest, '78)
MAN WITH THE CHILD IN HIS EYES (Harvest, '78)
RUNNING UP THAT HILL (EMI America, '85, *30*)

way, sensuous recording featuring musical guests Gilmour, Bulgaria's Trio Bulgarka, and uillean pipe player Davey Spillane. The album's title track—which began with Bush singing, "Mmm, yes/Then I'd taken the kiss of seedcake back from his mouth/ Going deep South, go down, mmh, yes"—was inspired by no less than James Joyce's *Ulysses.*

In late 1993, Bush's ambition again seemed at an all-time high: she released *The Red Shoes,* her first album in nearly four years, and wrote, directed, and starred in the one-hour film *The Line, the Cross, the Curve.* The movie, which also starred Miranda Richardson and famed British mime Lindsay Kemp, drew on several songs from *The Red Shoes,* including "Moments of Pleasure" and "Eat the Music." That the latter song became the number one most added record at alternative radio stations in its first week of release only underscores how Kate Bush—who has recording now for well over 15 years—makes music that may be uncategorizable, but always sounds new.

J.J. CALE

I f it's every songwriter's dream to write that one classic song—the one that will get them in history books and make them a bundle at the same time—then John J. Cale (b. Dec. 5, 1938) may be one of the reasons why. The reclusive guitarist/singer/songwriter probably didn't expect much when "After Midnight" was released on a small independent label in 1965, but when guitarist Eric Clapton covered it on his first solo album and scored an international hit with it, Cale's future started looking brighter. And when Clapton resurrected the song for a Michelob beer commercial nearly 20 years later, it looked brighter still. Toss in both Clapton's 1980 hit version of Cale's "Cocaine" and Lynyrd Skynyrd's 1974 recording of "Call Me the Breeze," and in Cale's own words, circa 1990, "Those three songs there pay my rent. And I wrote them 25 years ago."

Cale's influence is by no means confined to the pervasiveness of his songs; both Clapton and, more notably, Dire Straits have borrowed from Cale's trademark performing style: a laid-back, bluesy guitar shuffle over which a barely audible, introverted lyric regularly insinuates itself. Like the most subtle of blues players, Cale can tell a completely different story with only the slightest variation of lyric or strummed guitar chord. "By the time I started making songwriting type of deals, I was about 32–33 years old," Cale recalled. "I'd already figured out by then that there was plenty of people out there doing hard rock. I thought I'd try a different approach to see if I could slide into a slot nobody had covered. So I kind of underplayed everything. And, uh, that worked."

Cale started playing guitar in the late '40s; among his earliest influences on the instrument were Les Paul, Chet Atkins, Billy Butler, and Scotty Moore. A late-'50s stint with his own band, Johnny Cale and the Valentines, brought him to Nashville, where he eventually got road gigs with such country artists as Red Sovine and Little Jimmy Dickens. In 1964, Cale moved to Los Angeles with Tulsa friends Leon Russell and Carl Radle and spent time working with Delany & Bonnie Bramlett (as did, much later, Clapton), and as an audio engineer. In 1968, one of the more interesting period pieces in Cale's discography emerged on Viva Records: As a member of the Leather Coated Minds, Cale offered a goofily psychedelic album called *A Trip Down Sunset Strip* that's now a prized collectible.

To most fans, though, Cale's recording career started in earnest with *Naturally,* his 1971 debut on Leon Russell's Shelter label, which bore his sole hit single—"Crazy Mama," which reached number 22 in '72—and a newly recorded "After Midnight." With its striking cover painting of a well-dressed raccoon reclining next to a sleeping hound dog, *Naturally* was a polished, mature work that sounds surprisingly contemporary even two decades later. That Cale's own picture was an afterthought, barely evident anywhere on the package, helped create a mystique about him that's ultimately worked to his benefit: Portrayed in the press as an eccentric recluse who rarely gives interviews—who'd just prefer to sit on the front porch and strum—Cale's been able to escape the pop rat race and let his music do the talking.

Spending most of the '70s in Nashville, Cale recorded a series of superb albums for Shelter featuring top session players and a core musical crew consisting of Tim Drummond, Karl Himmel, Bill Boatman, Christine Lakeland, and Jimmy Karstein. Though warmly received by critics, none of the albums contained a follow-up hit to "Crazy Mama," something Cale says he became increasingly conscious of when he started recording for PolyGram in 1982. "I'd got to where I was making records and I'd turn 'em in to the record company, and they'd go 'We don't like these, there's no hits on 'em,' " he later recalled. "A big corporation has to have hits more than a little corporation, because their overhead's so high. And I understand that." Because he felt uncomfortable in the situation, Cale and his longtime publisher/producer Audie Ashworth asked PolyGram to let him out of his contract after 1983's #8. The label did so, releasing a final Cale compilation album, *Special Edition*, in 1984.

Cale spent the next five years in "semi-retirement," performing six weeks out of the year mainly because he enjoyed playing. Then Andrew Lauder—head of England's independent Silvertone label and a longtime Cale fan—offered him a deal he found appealing. The result was 1990's *Travel-Log*, a collection of demo tapes Cale had made since departing from PolyGram. "It doesn't sound like a polished record, but I still have the feel in there," Cale said at the time. "And if you re-record it, sometimes you lose the feel." A second Silvertone set, *Number 10,*

emerged without fanfare in 1992, and it, like all its predecessors, hadn't lost "the feel" in the slightest. Cale continues to tour regularly—usually just for an annual six-week stretch. "You got to remember," he said, grinning, "there's another 10-and-a-half months I don't do nothing. But I'm a songwriter, and I get ideas, get to hear new bands, and get to meet new people. It's what I got in the music business for."

JOHN CALE

One of the most versatile musicians in popular music, John Cale (b. Mar. 9, 1942, Garnant, South Wales) is most widely known for his role in the vastly influential '60s rock group the Velvet Underground. But the breadth of his musical accomplishments both before and after that short-lived group in many ways makes his two-album involvement with them seem only a minor part of a larger, much more fascinating story. Cale's two-pronged talents, musical and lyrical, have resulted in his recording—and producing—some of the finest, most groundbreaking albums in all of pop.

John Cale

TOP ALBUMS

NATURALLY (Shelter, '71)
REALLY (Shelter, '72)
TROUBADOUR (Shelter, '76)
GRASSHOPPER (Mercury, '82)
TRAVEL-LOG (Silvertone, '90)

TOP SONGS

CRAZY MAMA (Shelter, '71, 18)
AFTER MIDNIGHT (Shelter, '71)
COCAINE (Shelter, '71)

A onetime child prodigy who studied musicology at Goldsmith's College at London University, Cale was awarded a Leonard Bernstein scholarship in 1963 to study composition with avant-garde Greek composer Iannis Xenakis at the Berkshire Music Center at Tanglewood in Lenox, Massachusetts. He soon moved to New York and began working with the godfather of classical minimalism, La Monte Young, in an experimental unit dubbed the Dream Syndicate; though they rigorously recorded, none of their performances have yet seen commercial release. Cale soon met songwriter Lou Reed at a party, and the pair, who found they had similar musical goals, eventually formed the legendary Velvet Underground.

Very much a part of the New York underground scene, the band recorded their first album, 1967's *The Velvet Underground and Nico,* under the auspices of nominal producer and friend Andy Warhol. Featuring startlingly streetwise lyrics by Reed, often counterpointed by loud, deliberately grating music above which Cale's electrified viola soared, the album was a trailblazing classic now regarded as one of rock's finest. The second, *White Light/White Heat,* was even more of the same; poorly recorded, its (occasionally) unintended distortion only made it that much more an intense listening experience. Cale, whose contributions on viola and organ were particularly memorable, left the group soon afterward. In 1981, he characterized his experience in the band as being "Lou, it was all Lou—I was a sideman, Lou was the frontman. We just went onstage and made a lot of noise." Indeed, Cale's songwriting credits with the Velvets were meager: he'd co-written 1967's "The Black Angel's Death Song" with Reed and was jointly credited with other band members for the music on four additional tracks.

Instead, Cale's work with original Velvet Underground chanteuse Nico remains among the best early showcases of his formidable talent. Her 1967 album *Chelsea Girl*—which featured former band members Cale, Reed, and Sterling Morrison backing her on several tracks—included Cale's writing credit on

three tracks. More impressive was his work on Nico's 1969 masterpiece, *The Marble Index,* for which Cale provided absolutely remarkable arrangements and played nearly all of the instruments. He took on a similar role in her follow-ups *Desertshore* (1970) and *The End* (1975), but neither could match *The Marble Index* in ferocious intensity.

An inkling of Cale's own approach to songwriting came via his steady stream of eclectic solo albums, which began with 1970's *Vintage Violence.* An appealing and commercial album of pop songs, the album's only indication that its maker had come from the Velvet Underground was Cale's occasionally ominous-sounding lyrics. On the other hand, follow-up *Church of Anthrax,* a full collaboration with minimalist composer Terry Riley, was the closest Cale has yet come to performing the pre-Velvets music he'd played with La Monte Young. Aside from Cale's short pop song "The Soul of Patrick Lee," mysteriously sung by one Adam Miller and contextually out of place, the remainder of the album was a fascinating collection of overdubbed instrumentals highly reminiscent of Riley's own influential 1969 album *A Rainbow in Curved Air.*

In 1971, Cale moved to Los Angeles and signed to Warner Bros. as, unusually, an artist, producer, and A&R man. His 1972 label debut, *The Academy in Peril,* again sounded nothing like his earlier work; billed by Warners as their first "classical" release, the album included several orchestral works performed by the Royal Philharmonic, some improvised piano pieces, a few instrumental oddities, and one song with lyrics, "King Harry," which Cale whispered rather than sang. In contrast, his 1973 follow-up, *Paris 1919,* was a lush collection of pop songs similar in orientation to *Vintage Violence;* featuring both Lowell George and Richie Hayward of Little Feat, the album is thought by many to be Cale's finest work.

Since his days with the Velvet Underground, Cale had largely made music not capable of being performed onstage; that changed in 1974, when the singer moved to London and signed with Island

TOP ALBUMS

VINTAGE VIOLENCE (Columbia, '70)
THE ACADEMY IN PERIL (Reprise, '72)
PARIS 1919 (Reprise, '73)
FEAR (Island, '74)
SLOW DAZZLE (Island, '75)
MUSIC FOR A NEW SOCIETY (Ze/Passport, '82)
WORDS FOR THE DYING (Opal/Warner Bros., '89)
SONGS FOR DRELLA (Sire, '90)

TOP SONGS

ANDALUCIA (Reprise, '73)
BUFFALO BALLET (Island, '74)

Records. Falling in with many of England's rock avant-garde elite, Cale recorded three albums between 1974 and 1975—*Fear, Slow Dazzle,* and *Helen of Troy*—backed by such luminaries as Brian Eno, Phil Manzanera, Chris Spedding, Ollie Halsall, and Robert Wyatt. He soon developed into a fascinating and eccentric live performer.

As punk rock's influence became increasingly strong, John Cale's stature grew along with it. Aside from his innovative work with the Velvets, the Welshman had also played a role in the early careers of most of the genre's forefathers; remarkably, he had produced the debut albums of the Stooges, the Modern Lovers, and Patti Smith. Cale continued to make inroads as a live performer between 1975 and '77, particularly in fledgling punk clubs, and issued two well-received independent records (1977's *Animal Justice* EP and 1979's *Sabotage*) before signing a one-off deal with A&M Records in the early 1980s. The resulting album, *Honi Soit,* reached number 154 and was the first charting album of Cale's solo career.

Cale then spent much of the '80s on the road, perhaps making up for lost time. "One of the things I learned when I was at Warner Bros.," Cale said upon *Honi Soit*'s release, "was of the folly of making albums in a vacuum, and not going out and supporting them." Unfortunately, with the exception of his marvelous 1982 album *Music for a New Society*—a thoughtful, atmospheric set that included two collaborations with playwright Sam Shepard—the road seemed to take its toll on Cale's work. Albums such as *Caribbean Sunset* (1984) and *Artificial Intelligence* (1985) were filled with borderline collaborative material, typically penned by Cale, his guitarist, and writer Ratso Sloman, and were the least distinguished of his career.

After four years of relative silence, Cale returned to former glories with *Words for the Dying.* An ambitious orchestrated work produced by friend Brian Eno, it featured Cale's lengthy "Falklands Suite," a 30-minute composition in which Cale recited four poems by Dylan Thomas backed by a full Russian orchestra and Welsh choir. He further rebounded in 1990 with *Wrong Way Up,* a poppish collaboration with Eno, and *Songs for Drella,* which marked his long-awaited reunion with former partner Lou Reed and commemorated recently deceased luminary and friend Andy Warhol.

Over the years, much of Cale's more interesting work has turned up in places other than his albums.

His film soundtrack work includes the scores to Roger Corman's 1973 film *Caged Heat,* both Jonathan Demme's 1982 short *Who Am I This Time?* and his 1986 film *Something Wild* (with Laurie Anderson), and parts of Alex Cox's 1986 infamous punk biofilm *Sid and Nancy.* His fine soundtrack to *Paris S'Eveille* was issued on a small Belgian label in 1991.

Upon turning 50, Cale showed no signs of slowing at all—though he was looking backward, somewhat. His 1992 release *Fragments of a Rainy Season* was a superb career retrospective, featuring the singer alone at the piano performing works from solo albums as far back as 1970's *Vintage Violence.* Additionally, one of the musical highlights of the decade was his participation in 1993's Velvet Underground reunion. The original quartet's historic European tour was ably documented by the double-CD release *Live MCMXCII,* and further confirmed that John Cale's place among the highest ranks of pop royalty is, to say the least, well deserved.

CAPTAIN BEEFHEART

Given the constraints of normal rock and roll, those select few artists who deliberately push at its boundaries either achieve massive commercial success or are quickly and summarily dropped from the major labels who'd thought they'd signed the Next Big Thing but apparently hadn't. The exception to the rule? The man who in 1969 recorded *Trout Mask Replica*—the staggering album that featured a singer wearing a trout mask on its cover and the most deliriously innovative rock music in history within its sleeves. A truly indescribable blend of avant-garde rhythms and arrangements and unforgettably imaginative lyrics, *Trout Mask* was the best in a series of legendary albums made by one of rock's most towering, creative pioneers: Don Van Vliet, a.k.a. Captain Beefheart.

Beefheart (b. Don Vliet, Jan. 15, 1941, Glendale, California) was a child prodigy with an early devotion to art: he sculpted in clay and, by one account, once "punched a single hole in every rose in the hedge of a Beverly Hills garden." He grew up near Los Angeles in the desert town of Lancaster, where before dropping out of high school he befriended fellow student Frank Zappa, the musical figure to whom he'd be linked for the remainder of his career.

Captain Beefheart

Station and 1982's *Ice Cream for Crow*). If that lengthy chain of comings and goings betrays a lack of proper business direction, the music was by no means directionless. With the exception of the pair of Mercury albums—glossily produced by Andy DiMartino and featuring familiar Magic Band members only on the first—every record bearing the Beefheart name has grown in stature since its release.

For all the critical hoopla, however, only three of Beefheart's albums ever entered the album charts, and all three (*The Spotlight Kid, Clear Spot,* and *Unconditionally Guaranteed*) caught him during his most accessible, relatively "straight"-rocking phase. Ironically, his worst album, *Bluejeans & Moonbeams,* which was specifically intended to be a commercial breakthrough, never charted at all. Beefheart was most widely heard, perhaps inevitably, on the album on which he shared a billing with old friend Zappa, 1975's *Bongo Fury.*

Following 1982's *Ice Cream for Crow,* Captain Beefheart retired from the music business to devote his attention to painting and the visual arts. In the decade that has followed, his artistic works have gained international attention and sold for considerable sums. While his fans continue to clamor for his return to the music business—and his influence in that sphere grows with each passing year—it now seems highly unlikely he'll ever make music again. In a rare interview in late 1993, he explained that at that point in his life, he simply derived more pleasure from painting than he did from making music. Why? "It's all just from the paintbrush to the canvas," he said. "And the paint doesn't say anything, it just allows me to make mistakes." A master in whatever domain he chooses to express himself, Don Van Vliet makes the sort of mistakes of which other artists only wish they were capable.

In 1963 or '64, they recorded a few tracks together as the Soots in Zappa's nearby Cucamonga studio; at least one track from that period, "Metal Man Has Won His Wings," has surfaced on a bootleg (albeit bearing the not-quite-right title *Metal Man Has Hornet's Wings*). Selecting his stage name from a film idea of his and Zappa's called *Captain Beefheart and the Grunt People,* Vliet would later add the "Van" and form the spectacular blues band that was the first to bear the Captain Beefheart and His Magic Band name.

The cast of musicians would change, and so would the major labels on which Beefheart would sporadically appear: A&M (two early singles later collected on a 1984 EP), Buddah (1967's *Safe as Milk* and *Mirror Man,* recorded the same year but released in 1971), Blue Thumb (1968's *Strictly Personal*), Warner Bros./Reprise (*Trout Mask* through *Clear Spot,* 1969–72), Mercury (*Unconditionally Guaranteed* and *Bluejeans & Moonbeams,* 1974), Warners again (*Shiny Beast [Bat Chain Puller],* 1978), and, finally, Virgin (1980's *Doc at the Radar*

TOP ALBUMS

SAFE AS MILK (Buddah, '67)
STRICTLY PERSONAL (Blue Thumb, '68)
TROUT MASK REPLICA (Straight/Warner Bros., '69)
LICK MY DECALS OFF, BABY (Straight/Reprise, '70)
THE SPOTLIGHT KID (Reprise, '72)
CLEAR SPOT (Reprise, '72)
SHINY BEAST (BAT CHAIN PULLER) (Warner Bros., '78)
DOC AT THE RADAR STATION (Virgin, '80)
ICE CREAM FOR CROW (Virgin, 1982)

ERIC CARMEN

An immensely talented tunesmith, Eric Howard Carmen (b. Aug. 11, 1949, Cleveland, Ohio) has spent much of his career being compared to other artists who have "been there" first. Case in point, of course, came with his well-known 1970s pop group the Raspberries, who burst onto the scene in 1972 with a debut album bearing a raspberry-scented sticker and cover art displaying what looked like a typical rock band from a decade earlier. Decked out in matching black suits and shirts, the four Raspberries—who'd formed from the ashes of Cleveland bands the Choir and Cyrus Erie—not only looked but played the part of retro-rockers by providing well-crafted, punchy, and brief rock tunes at a time when groups like the Allman Brothers were devoting two entire LP sides to just one "song."

The obvious comparison for many writers was with the Beatles—and Carmen, who wrote the band's best tunes (and all but one of their singles) and whose taste for sweet-sounding, pleasant melodies seemed noticeably McCartneyesque to most critics, didn't seem to mind at all. But in spite of a string of outstanding singles between 1972 and '74—including "Go All the Way" (a top five hit), "I Wanna Be with You," and "Let's Pretend"— the group's fortunes seemed to be on a terminal decline, both internally and externally. Other band members were upset that Carmen's songs were the ones chosen to be singles; the group's "poppy" image disturbed lead guitarist Wally Bryson, who was itching to rock a little more; and the public itself seemed to be losing interest in the group. Band personnel shifted in time for the final Raspberries album —1974's superb *Starting Over*—but by then it was too late. The group's final hit, the Carmen-penned "Overnight Sensa-

tion (Hit Record)," was a sensual delight recalling the Beach Boys, Phil Spector, and other '60s sensations; but good as it was, it signalled the end of the band.

When Carmen made it known that he was looking for a solo deal, Arista Records president Clive Davis flew to Cleveland, heard a few of the singer's new tunes, then signed him soon after. Davis—who has spent much of his career trumpeting the importance of the song above all—made an astute call. Most of what he heard became part of Carmen's self-titled debut album, released in 1976 and full of hits, including the top 10 gold single "All by Myself," "Never Gonna Fall in Love Again," and "Sunrise." With it, two new developments had surfaced: First, Carmen's early classical training was making itself heard via conspicuous quoting of Rachmaninoff (in "All by Myself" and "Never Gonna Fall in Love Again") and Chopin ("Last Night"). Secondly, at Arista—home of Barry Manilow and Melissa Manchester, among others—Carmen's taste for the sweet sound could go absolutely unrestrained. And with the notable exception of the hard-rocking, autobiographical "No Hard Feelings" (with revealing lyrics about his Raspberries experience), much of the album featured orchestral backing, which to some critics meant Carmen was on his way to becoming Manilow-ized.

Though Eric Carmen went gold, the singer's next three Arista albums couldn't match that success. Despite two top 30 singles with 1977's "She Did It" and 1978's "Change of Heart," the singer was eventually dropped after 1980's *Tonight You're Mine*. His career temporarily derailed, Carmen then stayed out of the spotlight for the most part, resurfacing again in 1983 as co-writer (with Dean Pitchford) of "Almost Paradise," a hit for Ann Wilson and Mike Reno from the film *Footloose*. A brief deal with Geffen followed, resulting in a 1984 album and hit, "I

Eric Carmen

TOP ALBUMS

Eric Carmen (Arista, '75, *21*)
Boats Against the Current (Arista, '77)

TOP SONGS

All by Myself (Arista, '76, *2*)
Never Gonna Fall in Love Again (Arista, '76, *11*)
Sunrise (Arista, '76, *34*)
She Did It (Arista, '77, *23*)
Change of Hearxt (Arista, '78, *19*)
I Wanna Hear It from Your Lips (Geffen, '85, *35*)
Hungry Eyes (RCA, '87, *4*)
Make Me Lose Control (Arista, '88, *3*)

PETER CASE

Peter Case (b. c. 1952, Hamburg, New York) has been described by more than one clever rock and roll scribe as "Bob Dylan in reverse"—mainly because at a crucial point in his career, he "went acoustic." After a captivating late-'70s-to-early-'80s stint in the formidable Los Angeles power-pop quartet the Plimsouls, the singer-songwriter departed, feeling dissatisfied and, he said at the time, detached from his pop audience. Given that both the Plimsouls and Case's earlier band, San Francisco's Nerves, were critically lauded purveyors of pop of the highest order, no one quite expected what they heard on the 1986 solo debut *Peter Case*: mature and accomplished folk-inspired songcraft, expertly produced by Texas cult hero J. Henry "T-Bone" Burnett. With a stunning cast of supporting musicians—including solo artists John Hiatt, Roger McGuinn, Van Dyke Parks, as well as Burnett, Jim Keltner, Jerry Scheff, and Fred Tackett—Case presented a splendidly timeless-sounding, adult masterwork. And perhaps in reaction to the mechanics of the pop music business, or merely because with just one guitar and his voice he could do it, Case took to promoting the album in a strange manner: wandering the country singing in front of nightclubs and

Wanna Hear It from Your Lips." Then came the career uptick, via the phenomenal success of the *Dirty Dancing* soundtrack, which bore his top five hit "Hungry Eyes." Oddly, Carmen signed to Arista again—and scored his second-biggest single ever, 1988's "Make Me Lose Control." Though his career has been comparatively laid-back since then, one never knows what's to come. And that schmaltzy image? Forget it. With '70s nostalgia rearing its head more strongly than ever, some sources say an eventual Raspberries reunion—however brief—may be likely.

Peter Case

record stores, his guitar case open just like any street player's.

While critics clearly accepted Case's change of direction and enthused about it (*Rolling Stone* called it a "masterpiece"; the *New York Times* named it best record of the year), the singer's second album, *The Man with the Blue Post Modern Fragmented Neo-Traditionalist Guitar,* sent his critical standing through the roof. Produced by J. Steven Soles (like Burnett, a previous member of the Alpha Band and Bob Dylan's 1976 Rolling Thunder Revue), Larry Hirsch, and Case himself, the album contained 10 haunting tracks about love, relationships, self-doubt, fear, and the darker side of life. Case sang snippets like "there's a hole in your soul where the wind blows through" and the "worst disease is to be unwanted"—and the title of the album's most musically upbeat track, actually issued as a single, was "Put Down the Gun." With a superb crew of back-up musicians including Ry Cooder, David Lindley, and Los Lobos' David Hidalgo, *Blue...Guitar* appeared on most critics' top 10 lists at 1989's end.

The deeply personal subject matter of Case's material suggested a life filled with turmoil, and, indeed, fans made whispered references to his past "self-destructive habits." He became a born-again Christian in the mid-1980s. Following the collapse of his longstanding relationship with fellow singer-songwriter Victoria Williams, he married fiction writer Dianne Sherry. Sherry, in fact, co-wrote a song on Case's 1992 album *Six-Pack of Love.* And his wife wasn't his only collaborator, either: only two of *Six-Pack*'s 13 tracks were written by Case alone, the rest penned with such distinguished writers as Tonio K., John Prine, Tom Russell, and Bob Neuwirth. Ironically, Case's latest work is no longer stripped-down or folkish. Much of *Six-Pack of Love* sounds, strangely enough, almost Plimsoulish. In

fact, given that band's distinguished reputation and Case's way with a melodic hook, amply displayed since his earliest days, one or two future hit singles don't seem out of the question.

PETER CETERA

A major hazard of being in any well-known rock and roll group is evident in how easily the group's identity supercedes that of any individual band member. Most fans of '60s and '70s rock remember the Grass Roots and Three Dog Night, for example, but who can name any members of those bands? So it was in 1986, when "newcomer" Peter Cetera (b. Sept. 13, 1944, Chicago) scored a Number One record with "Glory of Love," the theme from *The Karate Kid Part II.* While it was his first appearance ever in the top 10 as a solo artist, it was actually his 16th time there since 1970, when as the singing bassist of Chicago he watched "Make Me Smile" hit number nine.

One of the more interesting aspects of Cetera's old band (from which he departed in 1985) was how no one member consistently dominated the writing of material; keyboardist Robert Lamm wrote the most, with horn players James Pankow and Lee Loughane, guitarist Terry Kath, and Cetera himself chipping in regularly. Likewise, three singers sang in Chicago's earliest days, and compared to Lamm's midrange singing and Kath's gruff, bass vocals, Cetera's characteristically high vocals became probably the most instantly identifiable. Thus, by the time Cetera made his top 10 "debut" in 1986, his was one of the most recognizable voices in pop music.

The material that landed the solo Cetera on the charts wasn't especially different from that which he'd provided Chicago, either: typically smooth, laid-back pop verging on MOR. And lots of it. Of the 10 top 20 hits Chicago had between 1976's Number One record "If You Leave Me Now" through 1985's "Along Comes a Woman," Cetera had in fact written eight. Cetera's post-Chicago track record continued that streak, first with "Glory," then another Number One: "The Next Time I Fall," sung with Christian crossover star Amy Grant. After 1988's *One More Story,* an album pairing Cetera with Madonna producer Patrick Leonard that produced the number four hit "One Good Woman," Cetera scored with yet another duet—this time with

---

TOP ALBUMS

PETER CASE (Geffen, '86)
THE MAN WITH THE BLUE POST MODERN FRAGMENT-
    ED NEO-TRADITIONALIST GUITAR (Geffen, '89)
SIX-PACK OF LOVE (Geffen, '92)

TOP SONGS

PUT DOWN THE GUN (Geffen, '89)
HIDDEN LOVE (Geffen, '89)

Cher, on "After All" from the film *Chances Are*.

Pivotal in all this has been well-known producer-keyboardist David Foster—who played a key role in Chicago's early '80s sound (coming aboard circa *Chicago 16* in 1982) and who co-wrote most of the group's hits of that era with Cetera, as well as "Glory of Love" and 1991's Desert Storm "tribute" single, "Voices That Care." Foster is one of several collaborators Cetera has tended to use on a project-by-project basis since going solo. Others include Leonard, guitarist Bruce Gaitsch (with whom he co-produced Agnetha Faltskog's *I Stand Alone* in 1988), and Andy Hill (who co-produced his 1992 album *World Falling Down*).

Cetera has proven to be a popular singer-songwriter, and certainly one with staying power. And he's sharp, too: though with *World Falling Down* he was admittedly doing more singing than writing—he only co-wrote four of 10 tracks—he at least seemed to be making an effort to break out of the schmaltz-duet persona he'd been heading in that might've proven an artistic dead end. In short, he may not have a hardcore contingent of fans beating down his door, but—like him or not—Peter Cetera won't be going away anytime soon.

HARRY CHAPIN

Even in his prime, Harry Chapin (b. Dec. 7, 1942, New York) was never accorded the critical respect many of his singer-songwriter contemporaries regularly received. It might simply have been a matter of appearing too "commercial" for tastemakers of the time; Chapin's 1972 debut album,

Heads & Tales, did, after all, shoot up the charts rapidly as the result of his top 30 hit "Taxi." More likely, though, it was the singer's songwriting style—perfectly illustrated by "Taxi," a tale of a cabdriver picking up a long-gone former girlfriend in his cab one rainy night—that crimped his critical currency. Whereas most of the best singer-songwriters wrote songs that were deliberately open to individual interpretation on several levels, Chapin specialized in the "story-song," little mini–movie musical epics about specific people and specific situations. Typically, each song also had a specific moral: the late-night loser deejay of Chapin's 1974 hit "W-O-L-D," who phones the wife he callously deserted eight years earlier trying to make amends—but is rebuffed—might have had a happier life were he a better person. The downside of the style, unfortunately, was that Chapin often seemed to veer toward preachiness without offering any new insights; once you'd heard the song, in short, you'd heard it, and that was that. Still, the approach won Chapin many fans—and that it continued to have some validity was proven in 1992 when, ironically, considering their genre, alternative band Ugly Kid Joe covered Chapin's sole Number One hit, "Cat's in the Cradle," and made it a smash of their own.

Chapin's family was bustling with musicians: his father was a jazz drummer who'd played with Woody Herman and Tommy Dorsey; his brother Tom was a singer-songwriter in his own right; other brother Stephen, a band member, produced Harry's albums, providing keyboards and musical arrangements. A onetime member of the Brooklyn Heights High School boys' choir (as was classmate and friend Robert Lamm of Chicago), Chapin managed an actual Oscar nomination in 1969 for a film documentary about boxing, *Legendary Champions*, that he produced with Jim Jacobs before signing with Elektra.

Though all of Chapin's 11 albums charted, only one—1974's *Verities & Balderdash*—was a major hit and reached the top five. Nonetheless, he was highly visible figure during the 1970s largely for his near-fanatical charity work for the cause of world hunger. It's estimated that Chapin—who averaged over 200 concerts a year, half of which were benefits—raised a total of over $5 million for starving children. Chapin's artistic endeavors also included a 1975 off-Broadway show called *The Night That Made America Famous* and another in Los Angeles, *Chapin '77*.

Chapin's career was unexpectedly cut short on July 16, 1981, when the singer suffered a heart attack

TOP ALBUMS

HEADS & TALES (Elektra, '72)
SHORT STORIES (Elektra, '73)
VERITIES & BALDERDASH (Elektra, '74, 4)
PORTRAIT GALLERY (Elektra, '75)

TOP SONGS

TAXI (Elektra, '72, 24)
W-O-L-D (Elektra, '74, 36)
CAT'S IN THE CRADLE (Elektra, '74, 1)
SEQUEL (Boardwalk, '80, 23)

on the Long Island Expressway—on the way to yet another benefit—and died. Chapin was posthumously awarded the 115th Congressional Gold Medal Award in recognition of his work for the world hunger cause, and on December 7, 1987, he was the subject of a benefit 45th birthday party at Carnegie. Among those who performed Chapin songs that night were Bruce Springsteen, Judy Collins, Oscar Brand and Pete Seeger, Graham Nash, Richie Havens, the Smothers Brothers, Pat Benatar, and Peter, Paul and Mary. In 1990, Relativity Records released highlights of that night's performance as a benefit album titled *Harry Chapin Tribute*.

TRACY CHAPMAN

What may be the most interesting aspect of Tracy Chapman's virtual explosion upon the music scene in 1988 is, in retrospect, the contrast between her low-key, understated music and the bombast of other stars of the era. In a year when the best-selling music was provided by such loud and formulaic rock-by-numbers bands as Def Leppard, Bon Jovi, and Poison and such overly slick studio creations as Tiffany and Expose, virtually anything with a grain of integrity would stand out. The raw introspection coloring most of the music Chapman (b. 1964, Cleveland, Ohio) played on her eponymous debut album not only sounded good, it reminded listeners that pop music could be subtle and still touch the heart—and signaled to the industry that artist signings based on the greatest common denominator principle weren't necessarily the inevitabilities they seemed.

In short, Tracy Chapman's debut proved that even in the jaded 1980s a folksinger could have a Number One record if it was good enough. Thanks to Chapman's instantly gripping top 10 hit "Fast Car"—an introspective track so unusual most listeners can still recall when they first heard it—the previously little-known singer became an instant international celebrity. It was quite a change for the singer, who'd been raised in Cleveland and had earlier spent her time playing Boston coffeehouses—and the streets of Harvard Square—while attending Tufts University.

What made Chapman so instantly captivating? First, her voice, which was quietly authoratative and powerful; secondly, her lyrics—most of them dealing with struggles of either a personal or political nature; thirdly, the non-flashy, simple musical arrangements surrounding Chapman's voice; and finally, realistically, her absolutely genuine and welcome non–"rock star" appearance. In 1988, a young black woman singing about inevitable political struggle ("Talkin' Bout a Revolution"), spousal abuse ("Behind the Wall"), and assaults on small black girls ("Across the Lines") was simply not everyday MTV fare. And Chapman's saving grace, above all, was her utter listenability; this was not clichéd protest-singer ravings, this was music that had a message and that was also extremely listenable. Chapman so unsettled a nation of cocky, pigeonholing rock critics that the majority of them—after uniformly comparing her to Joan Armatrading (she was black, she sang, etc.)—fell head-over-heels in love.

It was predictable. Chapman was nominated for six 1988 Grammys and won three: Best New Artist; Best Pop Vocal Performance, Female; and Best Folk Recording for "Fast Car." Her album went triple platinum, ultimately selling 9.5 million copies worldwide. She performed with Peter Gabriel, Sting,

TOP ALBUMS

TRACY CHAPMAN (Elektra, '88, 1)
CROSSROADS (Elektra, '89, 9)
MATTERS OF THE HEART (ELEKTRA, '92)

TOP SONGS

FAST CAR (Elektra, '88, 6)
TALKIN' BOUT A REVOLUTION (Elektra, 88)
BABY CAN I HOLD YOU (Elektra, '88)

George Michael, and Whitney Houston, and was a conspicuous presence on the Amnesty International Human Rights tour and Britain's Nelson Mandela Freedomfest.

But did all this mean a lifetime of celebrity for Chapman? No way. Though her 1989 follow-up album, *Crossroads,* hit the top 10 and went platinum, it simply didn't measure up, artistically or commercially. Many critics held that the singer was repeating herself—and in fact, there was a sameness to much of the material. A close look at the copyright dates of songs from both albums provided a clue: her debut featured proven jewels she'd composed as far back as 1982 (when, for example, "Revolution" was copyrighted) through the making of that album. But everything on *Crossroads* was brand new—and that might have made all the difference in the world. As the famous cliché has it: an artist has all the time in the world to write songs for his or her first album, and six months to a year for the second. And with 1992's *Matters of the Heart*—a brutal disappointment, not even cracking the top 40—Chapman sadly seemed less and less a long-term artist and more and more a disappointingly repetitive flash in the pan.

ERIC CLAPTON

T he most popular blues guitarist that ever deigned to play rock and roll, Eric Clapton (b. Mar. 30, 1945, Ripley, England) (1) was part of the Yardbirds and Cream, two of the most popular rock groups of the 1960s, (2) made rock history with Derek and the Dominoes' classic album *Layla* in the '70s, (3) was the subject of one of pop music's most popular boxed-set retrospectives (the four-CD *Crossroads*) in the '80s, and (4) met the the greatest commercial success of his life with his live *Unplugged* set of the '90s. The only rock star to be nicknamed "God" against his will—as British graffiti of the mid-'60s had it—Clapton has had more ups and downs in his lengthy career than most of his contemporaries, but in the literal sense remains very much a survivor.

Clapton's early history involved a thorough appreciation of the blues, which he'd played in early '60s R&B band the Roosters and, between 1963 and 1965, with the Yardbirds. But by the time most Americans had the first inkling the latter band even

existed—via their initial summer 1965 hit "For Your Love"—Clapton had already departed, frustrated by the group's increasingly poppish direction. He embraced the blues wholeheartedly on 1966's *Bluesbreakers—John Mayall with Eric Clapton,* the album that remains the most distinguished in prolific U.K. bluesman John Mayall's bulging catalog, but soon felt dissatisfaction in that context as well.

The guitarist's U.S. introduction essentially came when he joined bassist Jack Bruce and drummer Ginger Baker to form Cream, perhaps the first rock "supergroup" of the era, whose influence on hard rock from 1967 onward cannot be overstated. Renowned mostly for Clapton's stunning guitar work, which was amply displayed during extended solos in live performance, the band's relatively commercial albums were instant hits, with *Disraeli Gears, Wheels of Fire,* and *Goodbye* all rapidly reaching the top five upon their 1967–69 releases. Though bassist Jack Bruce wrote the lion's share of Cream's material, Clapton held a co-writing credit on two of their best-known songs, including the classic top five hit "Sunshine of Your Love" and the later "Badge," co-written with Beatle George Harrison. Additionally, Clapton sang the band's arrangement of Robert Johnson's "Crossroads," a top 30 single in 1969 that has since become even more of a classic rock radio standard than "Sunshine of Your Love."

Following the group's late-'60s demise, Clapton and Baker joined forces with Traffic's Steve Winwood and bassist Rik Grech for the the ill-fated Blind Faith, who lasted long enough to produce one album and briefly tour America in 1969 before disbanding. Though viewed in retrospect as an experiment that failed, the group produced one of Clapton's best early songs in "Presence of the Lord"; in fact, detached from the heavily felt hype of its time, the album sounds remarkably good 25 years later.

A growing friendship with American act Delaney and Bonnie, who had opened for Blind Faith on some American tour dates, led Clapton to invite the duo to England to perform; they did, he joined them on guitar, and the results can be heard on 1970's *On Tour with Delaney & Bonnie & Friends with Eric Clapton.* Clapton, who had lingering doubts about his singing ability, has credited Delaney Bramlett for giving him the emotional nudge he needed to become a front man for his own band. Bramlett further proved his point by producing Clapton's 1970 solo debut, *Eric Clapton,* which boasted eight songs written or co-written by the guitarist and reached the top 15, thanks in part to the top 20 hit "After Midnight" (penned by J. J. Cale) and the radio hit "Let It Rain."

Encouraged, Clapton then formed Derek and the Dominoes, whose inspired album *Layla* featured guest guitarist Duane Allman and showcased both players at their absolute best; regarded by many as one of the best rock albums of the era, the double LP reached the top 20 in 1970 and was reissued in a three-CD "deluxe anniversary edition" by Polygram in 1990. With co-writing credits on "I Looked Away," "Bell Bottom Blues," and the legendary title track, Clapton more than proved his worth on *Layla* as a songwriter; he was no longer regarded by the public as merely Cream's ex-guitarist.

Eric Clapton

TOP ALBUMS

ERIC CLAPTON (Atco, '70, *13*)
461 OCEAN BOULEVARD (RSO, '74, *1*)
SLOWHAND (RSO, '77, *2*)
BACKLESS (RSO, '78, *8*)
JUST ONE NIGHT (RSO, '80, *2*)
ANOTHER TICKET (RSO, '81, *7*)
UNPLUGGED (Duck, '92, *1*)

Additional Top 40 Albums: 12

TOP SONGS

I SHOT THE SHERIFF (RSO, '74, *1*)
LAY DOWN SALLY (RSO, '78, *3*)
TEARS IN HEAVEN (Reprise, '92, *2*)

Additional Top 40 Songs: 12

While Clapton enjoyed great success in the 1970s, problems with heroin and, later, alcohol significantly disrupted his career. Off the scene between 1971 and '73 (except for an uninspired Pete Townshend–organized "comeback" concert, released in 1973 as *Eric Clapton's Rainbow Concert*), the guitarist returned in triumph with 1974's *461 Ocean Boulevard,* which became the first Number One album of his career largely due to its cover of the Wailers' classic "I Shot the Sheriff." Clapton was shifting his musical emphasis more and more into songs rather than the lengthy improvisations that had once been his trademark with Cream. It was a move that had been long in coming; in 1974, he told *Rolling Stone* that he had been impressed some years earlier upon hearing the Band's classic *Music from Big Pink* album. "I thought, well this is what I want to play," he recalled, "not extended solos and maestro bullshit but just good funky songs."

Clapton's songwriting continued to improve, and throughout the remainder of the 1970s he enjoyed a nonstop run of successful albums—four of which made the top 10 between 1977 and '81—and self-penned hit singles, including "Hello Old Friend," "Lay Down Sally" (co-written with Marcy Levy), "Wonderful Tonight," and "I Can't Stand It." In 1983, Clapton moved over to Warner Bros., and with *Money and Cigarettes* began recording on his own Duck Records label. The resulting albums continued to be substantial efforts, often featuring the guitarist with top-notch musical partners including Ry Cooder, Albert Lee, and Phil Collins. Clapton began writing with a host of new collaborators, among them keyboardist Greg Phillinganes, the Band's Robbie Robertson, Collins, Steven Bishop, Foreigner's Mick Jones, and blues guitarist Robert Cray.

By the early 1990s, Clapton had further extended his compositional chops by scoring several film soundtracks, including all three of the *Lethal Weapon* films, Mickey Rourke's *Homeboy,* and *Rush,* which featured Clapton's Grammy-winning single "Tears in Heaven." The moving lyrics of the latter song, co-written with Will Jennings, connected heavily with the public after Clapton's four-year-old son Conor was tragically killed in a 53-story fall in early 1991.

In many ways, Eric Clapton spent much of 1993 looking backward. In January, he reunited and performed with Jack Bruce and Ginger Baker when Cream was inducted into the Rock 'n' Roll Hall of Fame. And throughout the year, his Grammy-winning MTV *Unplugged* set—featuring the guitarist performing acoustic versions of many of his classics—continued to be a true sales phenomenon. By late 1993, the album had sold over 7 million copies in the U.S. alone, and an equal number internationally. A new generation had taken Clapton's newly recorded "Layla" to the top of the charts—and the only Cream they knew went in their decaf capuccinos.

GENE CLARK

A founding member of '60s legends the Byrds — one of the finest rock and roll groups in pop history—Gene Clark (b. Harold Eugene Clark, Nov. 17, 1941, Tipton, Missouri) was a superb singer-songwriter who found himself struggling in the shadow of his enormously popular and influential former band. A prolific songwriter during the Byrds' earliest days, he departed from the group after the release of only their second Columbia album, 1965's *Turn! Turn! Turn!*, and began a solo career that—with scattered Byrds-related interruptions—continued until his unexpected death in 1991.

Clark, a member of the New Christy Minstrels between 1962 and 1964, was inspired by the Beatles to forge his own career in rock and roll. Upon seeing singer Jim McGuinn performing Beatles material at L.A.'s Troubadour club in 1964, he suggested the pair form a band; they did, and soon added David Crosby and named themselves the Jet Set. The group recorded several demos (later reissued as *Preflyte* in 1969) and recorded one single for Elektra (released under the name the Beefeaters) before adding members Chris Hillman and Michael Clark and taking on their Byrds moniker. They signed to Columbia in November 1964.

Though the general public became familiar with the Byrds in 1965 via singles not written by the group—"Mr. Tambourine Man" and "All I Really Wanna Do" were penned by Bob Dylan, and "Turn! Turn! Turn! (To Everything There Is a Season)" was a remake of Pete Seeger's lyrical adaptation from the Book of Ecclesiastes—Gene Clark was in fact the group's dominant songwriter. Among his best songs with the band were "I'll Feel a Whole Lot Better," "Here Without You," "I Knew I'd Want You," "Set You Free This Time," "The World Turns All Around Her," and "If You're Gone," as well as his collaboration with McGuinn, "You Won't Have to Cry." Another of the pair's collaborations, "You Showed Me"—heard on *Preflyte* —became a top 10 hit for the Turtles in 1969.

Whatever Clark's reason for departing from the band—initially it was blamed on his "fear of flying," though many have said it was due to struggles with McGuinn—he never again met the same level of professional success. His final hit with the group was 1966's classic "Eight Miles High," co-written with Crosby and McGuinn. Though he would briefly rejoin them again in 1967 (for only three weeks), his major focus from that point onward was his hit-and-miss solo career. His first album, *Gene Clark with the Gosdin Brothers*, emerged in the stores the same week in 1967 as did the Byrds' *Younger than Yesterday;* the latter album largely overshadowed Clark's own effort, which failed even to register on the album charts. A superior effort that served as a preview for the L.A.-based country-rock scene soon to come, the album was later remixed and reissued by Columbia in 1972 as *Early L.A. Sessions*.

Clark next joined forces with Doug Dillard, of Elektra's pioneering bluegrass band the Dillards, and recorded two highly regarded albums for A&M —*The Fantastic Expedition of Dillard and Clark* (1968) and *Through the Morning, Through the Night* (1969)—before resuming his solo recording career with 1972's excellent *Gene Clark*. A much-heralded Byrds reunion project resulted in a disappointing 1973 Asylum album, which seemed very much a patchy grafting of solo efforts by individual band members. Clark remained with Asylum and issued *No Other* in 1974; one of his best works, and

TOP ALBUMS

GENE CLARK WITH THE GOSDIN BROTHERS (Columbia, '67)
GENE CLARK (A&M, '72)
NO OTHER (Asylum, '74)
TWO SIDES TO EVERY STORY (RSO, '77)

TOP SONGS

TRIED SO HARD (Columbia, '67)
WHITE LIGHT (A&M, '72)
NO OTHER (Asylum, '74)

the one he would later recall as his personal favorite, the album was the only charting album of his solo career. It peaked at number 144. *Two Sides to Every Story*—a similar-sounding follow-up issued by RSO Records in 1977—had no such luck, and quickly fell out of print.

Clark again tried a reunion in 1979 with former Byrds bandmates via *McGuinn, Clark & Hillman,* and this time scored a top 40 hit with McGuinn's "Don't You Write Her Off," which pushed the re-formed trio's debut album into the top 40. Clark, however, became seriously involved with drugs during this period, and was only a featured player on McGuinn and Hillman's 1980 follow-up, *City.* He was nowhere to be found on *McGuinn-Hillman,* also issued that year.

Clark spent much of the 1980s in minor league oblivion, performing older hits in a so-called "tribute to the Byrds" that aroused the ire of other former band members. He released *Firebyrd* on Takoma in 1984; a fair album, it included redone versions of "Mr. Tambourine Man" and "Feel a Whole Lot Better" and several songs co-written by Clark and drummer Andy Kandanes. Three years later, he returned in a duo format with former Textones singer Carla Olson with *So Rebellious a Lover,* which seemed a marked improvement from its predecessor.

By 1991, Clark was again reuniting with his band-mates of 25 years earlier. The occasion was the Byrds' admission into the Rock 'n' Roll Hall of Fame, and Clark was hoping personal disagreements between band members could finally be put behind them. "There are resentments that go back," he said at the time. "By now I think they're kind of silly. I think that they should just be forgotten, and that we should move on and just be friends. Especially now." The group's reunited performance was one of the major highlights of that year's induction ceremony, and the last opportunity anyone would have to see the original Byrds ever again. Gene Clark died of natural causes on May 24, only short months afterward.

BRUCE COCKBURN

Though long acclaimed as a major artist in his native Canada, where he has been awarded 10 prestigious Juno Awards, Bruce Cockburn (b. May 27, 1945, Ottawa, Ontario) remains relatively underappreciated in other parts of the world—

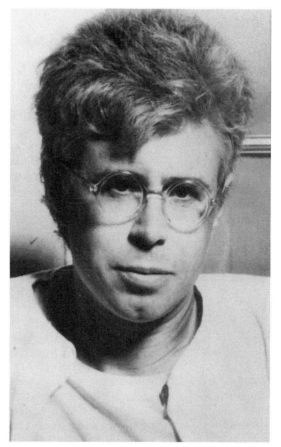

Bruce Cockburn

despite releasing 22 very substantial albums in the course of a near quarter-century. During that time, Cockburn has evolved from an inspiring folk guitarist with a decidedly intimate acoustic style, to a born-again Christian, to a strident political activist. Since the early 1980s, the singer has devoted much of his time to such causes as preservation of the environment and Native American rights; additionally, following an eye-opening journey to Nicaragua he undertook in 1983, he has written songs about Central American political repression.

Much of the above would have been difficult to believe on the basis of 1971's *Bruce Cockburn,* the singer's low-key, tasteful Epic debut album, which placed him squarely in the melodic-folkie genre then being compellingly explored by John Martyn and Nick Drake. Though the album has its fair share of hippie-dippie lyrics, several tracks, including "Going to the Country" and "Thirteenth Mountain," showed Cockburn was an intriguing writer with an eye for detail and a special skill for evoking meditative moods. His obvious skill as an acoustic guitarist helped; the singer had come from a background of rock, ragtime, and country blues and had studied composition at Berklee College of Music in Boston. While Cockburn's debut had considerable impact in Canada, the album went mostly unnoticed in the States. Such would also be the case for 1972's *Sunwheel Dance,* the singer's third album, but second to be released in the U.S. While Cockburn churned out new albums regularly at home, Epic—which had struck a deal with the guitarist's Canadian label, True North—released *Sunwheel Dance* only before giving up on Cockburn altogether. As a result, this country missed out on four of the singer's better albums—*High Winds White Sky* (1971), *Night Vision* (1973), *Salt, Sun and Time* (1974), and *Joy Will Find a Way* (1975)—and missed watching his noticeably linear stylistic evolution.

Consequently, when True North pacted with Island Records in 1976 and issued Cockburn's *In the Falling Dark,* the artistic leap he'd seemed to make was remarkable. Earlier sparse instrumentation had been replaced by flutes, trumpets, and fluegelhorns, and the former folkie sounded like a mature and adventurous pop writer, fusing folk, rock, and jazz forms into a delightful new whole. His former inner-directed lyrics were now encompassing environmental causes, as on his stirring "Silver Wheels": "Black earth energy receptor fields/Undulate under a grey cloud shield/We outrun a river colour brick red

---

TOP ALBUMS

Bruce Cockburn (Epic, '71)
In the Falling Dark (True North/Island, '76)
Dancing in the Dragon's Jaws (Millennium, '79)
Humans (Millennium, '80)
Inner City Front (Millennium, '81)
Stealing Fire (Gold Mountain, '84)
Waiting for a Miracle (Gold Mountain, '87)
Christmas (Columbia, '93)

TOP SONGS

Silver Wheels (Island, '76)
Wondering Where the Lions Are
  (Millenium, '80, *21*)

---

mud/That cleaves apart hills soil rich as blood." In one sense moving toward pop, former folkie Cockburn was now writing material that was intelligent, meaningful, and increasingly radio-ready.

The singer's American breakthrough came in 1980, thanks largely to the top 40 success of the single "Wondering Where the Lions Are" from 1979's *Dancing in the Dragon's Jaws*—which soon crept into the top 50 itself. It was enough to similarly push that year's follow-up, *Humans,* into the top 100, but lacking a single, that album quickly dropped off the charts.

Though Cockburn's melodies and musical arrangements were becoming increasingly catchy in the early 1980s, his tendency toward wordy, poetic lyrics occasionally rendered the point moot. Consider this passage from *Inner City Front*'s otherwise spritely "You Pay Your Money and You Take Your Chance": "Confused and solo in the spawning ground I watch the confusion of friends all numb with love/Moving like stray dogs to the anthem of night-long conversations, of pulsing rhythms and random voltage voices/In spite of themselves, graceful as these raindrops creeping spermlike across the car window." Interestingly, the problem soon vanished after Cockburn took his 1983 trip to Latin America; the resulting songs seemed more a product of the heart and gut than attempted poetry, as Cockburn's well-known "If I Had a Rocket Launcher" perfectly illustrates: "Here comes the helicopter—second time today/Everybody scatters and hopes it goes away/How many kids they've murdered only god can say/If I had a rocket launcher...I'd make somebody pay."

Cockburn spent most of the 1980s deeply involved in political issues. "Becoming a Christian was a factor and having a child was a factor," he told the *Atlanta Journal.* "But the single biggest crystalizing factor was travel—getting into situations where people don't have the luxury of sitting back and wondering if they should be involved in politics because someone who *is* involved may come along with a machete and remove a body part."

Continuing to record regularly, the singer signed with Columbia in 1991 and has since released *Nothing But a Burning Light,* superbly produced by T-Bone Burnett, and 1993's gorgeous *Christmas.* The latter—an unexpectedly pleasurable seasonal album that sounded wonderful all year long—displayed the typical thought and craft that has highlighted all of Cockburn's best work.

Leonard Cohen

LEONARD COHEN
. . . .

A published novelist and poet whose late-'60s entrance into popular music came via one of that decade's most profoundly affecting albums, Leonard Cohen (b. Leonard Norman Cohen, Sept. 21, 1934, Montreal) remains a wholly unique figure in the music industry. His talent as a songwriter was unassailable from the start: Judy Collins had already recorded his classic songs "Suzanne" and "Dress Rehearsal Rag" on her *In My Life* album months before his debut LP was released in late 1967, and by the time of her 1968 follow-up, *Wildflowers*—the same album that introduced Joni Mitchell's songwriting to the world—Collins was covering Cohen's "Sisters of Mercy" and "Hey, That's No Way to Say Goodbye." Cohen's first album, *The Songs of Leonard Cohen*, was in some respects not as "easy" a listen as Collins's work, generally because his voice seemed, at least to some, a droning monotone. But acquired taste or not, Cohen's singing was the perfect vehicle for his intricate and intimate songcraft; the stark, meticulous arrangements of producer John Simon let the singer's reedy voice take the center stage, and its impact,

combined with Cohen's subtle, compelling lyrics, was hypnotically beautiful—and sometimes wrenching. The album was only the first of several that rank among pop music's all-time classics.

Cohen, who at the age of 17 had formed a Montreal country and western band called the Buckskin Boys, studied English literature at both McGill and, later, Columbia universities. As early as 1956, while still an undergraduate, a collection of his poetry was published as *Let Us Compare Mythologies;* before Cohen's first record emerged a decade later, he had published three additional collections (*The Spice-Box of Earth, Flowers for Hitler,* and *Parasites of Heaven*) and two novels, *The Favourite Game* and *Beautiful Losers.* Cohen's adeptness at language made him a natural lyricist, particularly skilled at conveying subtle emotional nuances that were simply beyond the reach of other songwriting contemporaries. Signed to Columbia by legendary A&R executive John Hammond, Cohen has remained with the label (with two peculiar U.S. exceptions) for over a quarter-century.

Over the course of those years, Cohen's songs have touched on many subjects, but the dominant recurring themes have typically centered on sex, religion, and human relationships; the varied cast of characters in his songs has included the son of biblical figure Abraham ("Story of Isaac"), a hunchback ("Avalanche"), a near-suicidal figure plagued with self-doubt ("Dress Rehearsal Rag"), a man listening to his lover having sex in an adjoining hotel room ("The Walls of This Hotel"), and Joan of Arc. Cohen's sometimes searing portrayals of lonely and desperate figures have often branded him as "depressing" by casual listeners; in fact, much of his work is wry and extremely humorous, and that balancing aspect of his repertoire is a vital part of his art.

Cohen's critical reputation was largely made on the basis of his first three Columbia albums, *Songs of Leonard Cohen, Songs from a Room* (1969), and *Songs of Love and Hate* (1971); indeed, the majority of his most-covered songs can be found on them, and with the addition of 1973's *Live Songs,* they constitute the only charting albums of his career. But Cohen's work thereafter may be even more fascinating, in part because of the shifting musical contexts provided for his lyrics. *New Skin for the Old Ceremony*—a 1973 album for which Columbia supplied a "clean" cover due to its original depiction of angels making love, taken from an alchemical text dating back to 1550—was brilliantly arranged by producer John Lissauer, and for the first time offered Cohen in as close to a rock context as he'd come. But the real surprise would be 1977's *Death of a Ladies' Man,* an unexpected collaboration between Cohen and eccentric producer Phil Spector. While Cohen sang some of his most thought-provoking and sexually charged lyrics to date, Spector—who shared co-writing credit on all the tracks—supplied over-the-top music

backing that stunned and alienated many of Cohen's former fans, including critics. "In retrospect, I think the songs that Phil and I wrote together are really good," Cohen recalled in 1988. "I would really like to hear that record done by somebody like Bill Medley, Tina Turner, or Jennifer [Warnes], even—somebody who could really belt the stuff out. Or let me practice for six or seven months. All those were scratch vocals, that's what I really had against it. I never really had a chance to perfect the thing." Nonetheless, the album remains the most interesting item in Cohen's entire catalog, and whether a failed experiment or a monument of excess, it has been severely underrated since its release.

Cohen's *Ladies' Man* had been issued in the U.S. on Warner Bros. due to its Spector affiliation; following 1979's comparatively restrained *Recent Songs* on Columbia, the singer in effect found his label dropping him in the U.S. His 1984 album, *Various Positions,* emerged instead on the small, independently distributed Passport label. While Cohen's status overseas was nearly at superstar levels, his American profile had never been lower. That would soon change, however; in 1987, longtime friend and former Cohen backing vocalist Jennifer Warnes released *Famous Blue Raincoat,* a superb collection of Cohen songs that reached number 72 on the charts. "Jennifer helped me enormously in the country," Cohen said later. "I think in the high smoky rooms of power where these things are determined, maybe my career and name underwent some kind of revision."

Since then, Cohen has indeed been the subject of a massive media resurgence. His 1988 *I'm Your Man,* this time back on Columbia, was the subject of uniform acclaim from critics either old enough to have bought his earliest albums or young enough to hear most of alternative music's biggest stars claim Cohen as a major musical influence. 1991's *I'm Your Fan* bore out the latter point: a Leonard Cohen tribute album featuring such artists as R.E.M., the Pixies, the House of Love, John Cale, and Nick Cave and the Bad Seeds, the likeable set introduced an entire new audience to some of the best pop songwriting of the past 20 years. By 1992, Cohen's elevated status as alternative demigod helped push reviews of his *The Future* into the forefront of the major media. Now likely to be the first songwriter of the rock era to be performing in concert at the age of 60—which he'll reach in 1994—Leonard Cohen is, proudly, old enough not to know better.

TOP ALBUMS

SONGS OF LEONARD COHEN (Columbia, '67)
SONGS FROM A ROOM (Columbia, '69)
SONGS OF LOVE AND HATE (Columbia, '71)
NEW SKIN FOR THE OLD CEREMONY (Columbia, '73)
DEATH OF A LADIES' MAN (Warner Bros., '77)
RECENT SONGS (Columbia, '79)
I'M YOUR MAN (Columbia, '88)
THE FUTURE (Columbia, '92)

TOP SONGS

SUZANNE (Columbia, '67)
BIRD ON A WIRE (Columbia, '69)

MARC COHN

The surprisingly mature 1991 debut album of singer-songwriter Marc Cohn (b. Cleveland) at first couldn't help but seem anachronistic: in an age dominated by loud rap, slickly over-produced song belters like Whitney Houston and Mariah Carey, and the throbbing blare of hard-rock bands like Guns N' Roses and Metallica, Cohn's subtle and emotive songs stood so completely unadorned, so willing to be judged solely on their merits as songs, they might've been recorded 20 years earlier. Cohn played piano and sang with a sincerity that, for many, was instantly captivating. His debut single, "Walking in Memphis"—which found an audience in a wide variety of radio formats and reached number 13—kept his album high on the charts for over a year, during which time he was awarded a Grammy for being 1991's Best New Artist.

A self-taught pianist, the singer honed his style playing solo in Los Angeles clubs following his graduation from UCLA. He then moved to New York, where he put together the Supreme Court, a 14-piece band that featured five horn players and drew a substantial local following; fans included Carly Simon and even Caroline Kennedy, at whose wedding the band performed. Cohn, however, eventually left the group and spent 18 months recording song demos, a half-dozen of which helped clinch his deal with Atlantic.

The singer's stated early influences of Van Morrison, Jackson Browne, and the Band can be heard reverberating through much of his work; like those artists, there is not much "showy" material in his repertoire, nor does he seek to convey a specific attitude. For that reason, his second album, 1993's *The Rainy Season,* seemed more a further refinement of his first than a bold new step forward—despite the presence of featured guests Bonnie Raitt, David Crosby and Graham Nash, Los Lobos's David Hidalgo, Jim Keltner, and Benmont Tench. The major difference to be found was in the subject matter of Cohn's songs: he had become a father since his first album, and several tracks—particularly "Baby King"—reflected it. Additionally, with only one album behind him—albeit one that won him a Grammy—with "Paper Walls" he was already writing about the travails of the road.

Though *The Rainy Season* was a comparative sales disappointment—it lacked a strong hit single and peaked at number 63, lasting only 15 weeks on the charts—its strength as an album was undeniable. Like his singer-songwriter predecessors of two decades ago, Marc Cohn seems very much a long-term artist to whom hit singles appear to be more a means than an end.

TOP ALBUMS

MARC COHN (Atlantic, '91, *38*)
THE RAINY SEASON (Atlantic, '93)

TOP SONGS

WALKING IN MEMPHIS (Atlantic, '91, *13*)
TRUE COMPANION (Atlantic, '91)
SILVER THUNDERBIRD (Atlantic, '91)
WALK THROUGH THE WORLD (Atlantic, '93)
THE THINGS WE'VE HANDED DOWN (Atlantic, '93)

PHIL COLLINS

If anyone can be said to have become a pop superstar by default, Genesis's Phil Collins (b. Jan. 30, 1951, London) is the man. A drummer drafted to replace his group's departing lead singer—when the world assumed that departure really meant the band's demise—Collins took that group to new heights of commercial success, established his own booming solo career as a singer-songwriter, played with and produced albums by many of the world's best musicians, collaborated with world-class songwriters, and became a movie star. And what has endeared Collins to so many in the industry, above and beyond this, is that his reputation as one of the most decent people in the business has never changed despite the acclaim.

While some highfalutin critics may pooh-pooh Collins's commercial accomplishments of the 1980s (merely 13 top 20 singles, including seven at Number One), it's a good bet they respect what he did before: His earliest album, *Ark 2,* recorded in 1969 with his group Flaming Youth, now commands top dollar among record collectors. In 1970, after answering an ad in England's *Melody Maker,* Collins joined Genesis as drummer and backup vocalist. By 1975, lead vocalist Peter Gabriel departed, and Collins was

TOP ALBUMS

FACE VALUE (Atlantic, '81, 7)
HELLO, I MUST BE GOING! (Atlantic, '82, 8)
NO JACKET REQUIRED (Atlantic, '85, 1)
. . . BUT SERIOUSLY (Atlantic, '89, 1)

Additional Top 40 Albums: 1

TOP SONGS

AGAINST ALL ODDS (TAKE A LOOK AT ME NOW)
   (Atlantic, '84, 1)
ONE MORE NIGHT (Atlantic, '85, 1)
SUSSUDIO (Atlantic, '85, 1)
DON'T LOSE MY NUMBER (Atlantic, '85, 4)
TWO HEARTS (Atlantic, '88, 1)
ANOTHER DAY IN PARADISE (Atlantic, '89, 1)

Additional Top 40 Hits: 12

drafted to front the band. That might be enough for some, but not Collins: on the side, he founded highly respected jazz-fusion band Brand X, with whom he recorded seven albums, and he played on hugely influential albums by such rock pioneers as Brian Eno, John Cale, Robert Fripp, and, ironically, Peter Gabriel, as well as by other acclaimed performers.

In one sense, though, this all became overshadowed in 1981 with *Face Value,* Collins's first solo album, which hit the top 10, went double platinum, and changed the industry's perception of the man forever. The main attention-getter was his haunting international hit "In the Air Tonight," which, with its oddly droning intro, tension-filled vocals, and liberating percussion bursts, was simply unforgettable after one hearing. (Three years later, the song would dominate a memorable episode of "Miami Vice"; the next year, Collins himself made an appearance on the show.)

Though till then Collins had solely written only a smattering of post-Gabriel Genesis material (including their biggest U.S. hit at that point, "Misunderstanding," which reached number 14), the bulk of *Face Value*'s compositions showed surprising maturity. Collins was clearly not "just" a drummer by a mile: he played keyboards on each track with notable expertise, his sometimes deeply personal lyrics were more profound than one might reasonably expect from a comparative rookie, and his melodies lingered. Proof officially came when his

memorable *No Jacket Required* won 1985's Album of the Year award at the Grammys.

Whereas Genesis had in the past been criticized for the excessive instrumental rambling style so characteristic of '70s progressive rock, Collins and his own albums were generally seen as offering substance, not just fancy trimmings. Occasionally there have been seeming missteps: though they were both top 10 hits, his remakes of the Supremes' "You Can't Hurry Love" (1982) and the Mindbenders' "Groovy Kind of Love" (1988) seemed creative copouts to many—proof, some said, that the hyperactive Collins was spreading himself too thin. But even with his own material he couldn't win: after releasing 1989's *...But Seriously,* which contains the Number One hit "Another Day in Paradise," a moving track about homelessness, many critics guffawed, asking, sometimes impolitely, what a millionaire like him could possibly know about homelessness.

Overall, though, it seemed Collins was everywhere at once in the 1980s, producing albums (by John Martyn, Abba's Frida, Philip Bailey, Eric Clapton, and Steven Bishop); playing drums and touring with Robert Plant; starring as a small-time thief in the 1988 film *Buster;* appearing at the Prince's Trust 10th Anniversary Party; and, characteristically Collins-like, performing on the same day at both the London and Philadelphia sites of 1985's momentous Live Aid concerts. In the 1990s, the Collins phenomenon doesn't appear to be coming to an end, either. With the success of Genesis now paralleling his own, Collins continues to play awesome double-duty: his 1990 solo tour, his third, saw him give 127 shows across the world; in 1992, he was central in Genesis's enormously successful international tour, which resulted in two separate live albums and, of course, continued massive exposure. No one knows how Phil Collins does it, but—uniformly—they're always glad he does.

ELVIS COSTELLO

Dubbed "the most talented pop tunesmith of his generation" by the *New York Times* in 1982, Elvis Costello (b. Declan Patrick McManus, August 25, 1955, Paddington, London) was by far the best songwriter to emerge from Britain's explosive punk and new wave scene in the late 1970s. A lyricist of the highest order, Costello initially looked deliberately nerdy, wore Buddy Holly–style horn-rimmed glasses, and wrote scathing songs that seemed to focus mainly on themes of anger, revenge, and personal betrayal. While such topics went hand in hand with the era's thriving punk scene, Costello's songs carried an intellectual and emotional weight that nearly obliterated all his competition. Though early songs like "Less than Zero" and "Oliver's Army" dwelt on decidedly political topics such as British fascism, his first American single "Alison"—covered to his professed displeasure by the increasingly MOR-ish Linda Ronstadt in 1978—was an early indication that his real lyrical strength lay in songs of more personal focus. "Sometimes I wish that I could stop you from talking," he sang, "When I hear the silly things that you say/I think somebody better put out the Big Light/'Cause I can't stand to see you this way."

Like all major artists, Costello quickly evolved on both lyrical and musical levels: he assembled his much-admired backing group the Attractions by the time of his second album, 1978's *This Year's Model,* and the quartet rapidly became one of the most searing live units of the period, providing a near-physical punch to Costello's sometimes brutal lyrics. He gained tremendous exposure that year when he appeared as a surprise musical guest (after the scheduled Sex Pistols pulled out) on NBC's "Saturday Night Live"; his unrehearsed performance of "Radio Radio"—a scathing assault on the medium in which he prophetically sang "I wanna bite the hand that feeds me"—was galvanizing, and won him many new fans.

Still, while Costello was bemoaning the state of radio programming, he wasn't especially an underdog: of the 10 albums he released between 1977 and 1984, only one—1981's atypical country session, *Almost Blue*—failed to enter the top 40. All the more remarkable was the fact that his fans were willing to follow him through the myriad of stylistic changes he'd undergo in that time span. Very much a fan of American music, he explored not only country via *Almost Blue* but also soul and R&B on the jam-packed, 20-song *Get Happy!!,* which included his cover of Sam and Dave's "I Can't Stand Up for Falling Down." Additionally, his choice of cover versions, which would often surface live or on numerous single B sides and EPs, included songs by Burt Bacharach and Hal David ("I Just Don't Know What to Do with Myself"), Doc Pomus and Mort Shuman ("Little Sister"), Smokey Robinson ("Don't Look

Back" and "One More Heartache"), Bob Dylan ("Knockin' on Heaven's Door"), the Amazing Rhythm Aces ("Third Rate Romance [Low Rent Rendezvous]"), and even Rodgers and Hart ("My Funny Valentine").

Costello's affinity for the finest of American songwriters was noticed by critics, some of whom began tagging him as "the Cole Porter of the 1980s." Flattered, Costello told journalist Robert Palmer in 1982, "That kind of songwriting—Porter, Kern,

Elvis Costello

Rodgers & Hart—is something I'm very fond of and aspire to. When people ask me to name a great song, I mention something like 'Love for Sale' or 'Someone to Watch Over Me.' In the last 20 years or so, very few people have been up to that standard of lyric writing." If Costello has any lyrical weaknesses of his own, they stem from his being too clever —making a lyrical pun because he can't resist it, not because it entirely fits, as in his otherwise superb "Man Out of Time": "But for his private wife and kids/Somehow life becomes a rumor/Days of Dutch courage, just three French letters and a German sense of humor/He's got a mind like a sewer and a heart like a fridge/He stands to be insulted and he pays for the privilege."

By no means did Costello abandon the political issues of his day in the 1980s. In response to his country's struggle in the Falklands Islands, he penned the gorgeous ballad "Shipbuilding" with Clive Langer in 1983 and gave it to singer Robert Wyatt, whose ethereal version remains one of the period's finest singles. That same year, he recorded the biting "Pills and Soap" to coincide with England's springtime general election, released it under the name the Imposter, and—to hammer home his anti-Thatcherite message—deleted the single on election day. The next year, he produced the Special AKA's "Free Nelson Mandela," which bitterly commemorated and highlighted the 20th anniversary of the South African liberationist's political imprisonment.

The quality of several of Costello's albums fluctuated between 1983's *Punch the Clock* and 1986's *Blood and Chocolate,* the last of which signaled his parting company with the Attractions. None matched the quality of what may be Costello's masterwork, 1982's *Imperial Bedroom;* that ambitious album, Costello's most probing look at troubled relationships, was exceptional for both its superb production and spotless thematic unity—the latter of which the prolific singer, for all his scattered output, has yet to duplicate.

Onetime new wave outcast Costello found him-

TOP ALBUMS

MY AIM IS TRUE (Columbia, '77, *32*)
THIS YEAR'S MODEL (Columbia, '78, *30*)
ARMED FORCES (Columbia, '79, *10*)
GET HAPPY!! (Columbia, '80, *11*)
TRUST (Columbia, '81, *28*)
IMPERIAL BEDROOM (Columbia, '82, *30*)
PUNCH THE CLOCK (Columbia, '83, *24*)
SPIKE (Warner Bros., '89, *32*)

Additional Top 40 Albums: 3

TOP SONGS

EVERYDAY I WRITE THE BOOK (Columbia, '83, *36*)
VERONICA (Warner Bros., '89, *19*)

self very much a central figure in the music industry by the late 1980s, when he began collaborating with ex-Beatle Paul McCartney. The fruits of their labors could be found on his 1989 album *Spike* ("Pads, Paws and Claws" and "Veronica") and 1991's *Mighty Like a Rose* ("So Like Candy" and "Playboy to a Man"), as well as on McCartney's 1989 set *Flowers in the Dirt* ("My Brave Face," "You Want Her Too," "Don't Be Careless Love," "That Day Is Done") and 1993's *Off the Ground* ("Mistress and Maid" and "The Lovers That Never Were"). It was a productive team-up; Costello scored his highest-charting hit ever with the McCartneyesque "Veronica," and the ex-Beatle's "My Brave Face," sounding much like Costello, peaked at number 25 and remains McCartney's last top 40 hit.

In 1993, Costello's increasing interest in other musical idioms, particularly classical music, led to his unusual collaboration with the Brodsky Quartet, *The Juliet Letters.* A true merging of genres, with both singer and quartet members contributing words and music, the album was described by the singer as "no more my stab at 'classical music' than it is the Brodsky Quartet's first rock 'n' roll album. It does, however, employ the music which we believe touches whichever part of the being that you care to mention."

Costello's repertoire of over 250 songs has been covered by a widely divergent range of artists, including Chet Baker, Johnny Cash, Roger McGuinn, Roy Orbison, George Jones, and Charles Brown. His seeming ability to write on demand was most recently illustrated on the curious debut solo album of Transvision Vamp singer Wendy James, *Now Ain't the Time for Your Tears,* which featured 10 new Costello songs that he reportedly had written or co-written in a few days' time. Hampered only by her unexceptional voice, the album was a surprisingly solid collection of "tossed-off" songs—and further evidence that Elvis Costello, one of pop music's greatest talents, may simply have more talent than he knows what to do with.

MARSHALL CRENSHAW

That Detroit-born singer-songwriter Marshall Crenshaw (b. 1954) once had a role as John Lennon in a road company version of *Beatlemania* made for good press, true. From a career standpoint, though, it might have been wiser to have kept that bit of trivia to himself: if there was one phrase listeners really didn't need to be reminded of, it was "not the real thing but an incredible simulation." Why? Because Crenshaw's best moments—be they songs or vocal performances—seemed borrowed from another singer, another song, and, unfailingly, another era.

Crenshaw's rise to prominence in the early 1980s came via the "new wave" credibility of writer-producer Alan Betrock and his tiny, independent Shake Records label, which issued his first single "Something's Gonna Happen" shortly before Warner Bros. jumped in with a long-term album deal. Crenshaw's 1982 Warner debut, one of the most critically lauded albums of the decade, is as concise a career statement as one could want—but, sad to say, about as good as the singer ever got. Ask any fan what their favorite Crenshaw song is, and it'll surely be found here, "There She Goes Again," "Someday, Someway," "She Can't Dance," and "Cynical Girl" being the likeliest candidates.

Stylistically, Crenshaw borrowed chord progressions and lyrical themes from the late '50s to early '60s era; one song might contain a snatch of Buddy Holly here, of Ricky Nelson there, or even of Bobby Fuller. But where a superior songwriter working in the same mode—Crenshaw's "power pop" contemporaries such as Alex Chilton or Dwight Twilley, for instance—would be able to take those scattered influences and weld them together into one believable, singular whole, Crenshaw never seemed much

more than a songwriter who simply was up on good music by other people.

The singer-guitarist's first top 40 hit—"Someday Someway" reached number 36 in 1982—was also his last. As his career rolled on, the critical buzz began to subside; disappointing second album sales had many pointing the finger at producers and such (wrongly—*Field Day* sounds superb) and ignoring the main problem: where were all the hooks? By the time of his last Warner Bros. album, 1989's *Good Evening*, the songwriter was covering tunes by John Hiatt, Richard Thompson, Bobby Fuller, even Diane Warren (whom one might think would be anathema to one of Crenshaw's rocking persuasion), and had only penned two tracks on his own.

All the while, Crenshaw kept plugging away in the shadow of others. How odd was it, after all, that a musician who spent a portion of his paid career imitating John Lennon would portray Buddy Holly in Taylor Hackford's 1987 Richie Valens film *La Bamba*? (This after appearing in the Holly-inspired *Peggy Sue Got Married*, no less.) In concert, Crenshaw even covered Elvis Presley's bogus Broadway send-up Conrad Birdie, via *Bye-Bye Birdie*'s "You've Gotta Be Sincere." Clever? Sure. But the unfortunate conclusion—which Crenshaw must suspect by now—is that, as Dobie Gray sang in 1965's "The In Crowd," the original is still the greatest.

JIM CROCE

As an increasing number of early '70s singer-songwriters began to share their most intimate feelings on records sometimes dripping with sensitivity, Jim Croce's upbeat and down-to-earth demeanor seemed like a breath of fresh air—even despite his characteristic cigar. Croce (b. Jan. 10, 1943, Philadelphia, Pennsylvania) enjoyed just a brief interlude of international fame before his unexpected death in a 1973 plane crash, but he left behind a sturdy catalog of classics certain to be listened to—and covered—for years.

Croce learned to play guitar comparatively late, at the age of 16, but by the time he was a freshman at Villanova University, he was a professional entertainer. His influences were typically folkie: a sprinkling of Kerouac and the beat poets, Oscar Brand, Woody Guthrie, Ramblin' Jack Elliot, Bob Dylan, Leadbelly. Serving as a judge at a Philadelphia hoo-

---

TOP ALBUMS

MARSHALL CRENSHAW (Warner Bros., '82)
FIELD DAY (Warner Bros., '83)

TOP SONGS

SOMEDAY, SOMEWAY (Warner Bros., '82, 36)

TOP ALBUMS

YOU DON'T MESS AROUND WITH JIM (ABC, '72, *1*)
LIFE AND TIMES (ABC, '73, 7)
I GOT A NAME (ABC, '73, 2)
PHOTOGRAPHS & MEMORIES/HIS GREATEST HITS
(ABC, '74, 2)

TOP SONGS:

YOU DON'T MESS AROUND WITH JIM (ABC, '72, *8*)
BAD, BAD LEROY BROWN (ABC, '73, *1*)
I GOT A NAME (ABC, '73, *10*)
TIME IN A BOTTLE (ABC, '73, *1*)
I'LL HAVE TO SAY I LOVE YOU IN A SONG (ABC, '74, *9*)

Additional Top 40 Songs: 3

tenanny contest, he met his future wife, Ingrid, with whom he'd form a folk duo and, by 1963, start performing at various clubs in Greenwich Village. The couple married in 1966 and lived in Philadelphia; while Ingrid attended Moore College of Art, Croce, through various solo gigs, further honed his folksy live performance style. Then a call from college friend Tommy West—whose production company Cashman, Pistilli and West had just inked a deal with Capitol Records—summoned the pair to New York, where they recorded *Ingrid and Jim Croce,* released by Capitol in 1969. Not quite their big break, the album made little impression, and the Croces, dejected and not enamored of life in the Bronx, moved to rural Lyndell, Pennsylvania. There they were joined by another artist from West's production company, guitarist Maury Muehleisen, who'd recorded his own bomb for Capitol. With wife Ingrid now pregnant, Croce and his new partner began serious woodshedding. The results were the songs that would soon make Jim Croce a star.

After sending a tape of the new demos to West, then at ABC Records, Croce soon scored a new record deal. In May of 1972, his *You Don't Mess Around with Jim* hit the stores; by the end of the year, the title track had gone top 10 and "Operator (That's Not the Way It Feels)" top 20. Croce's appealingly romantic style, subtle and never condescending, had managed to tap into the general pop audience to an extent matched by few of his singer-songwriter contemporaries. For the next nine months he prospered, attaining his first Number One

single, "Bad, Bad Leroy Brown" (later often performed by Frank Sinatra), in July 1973, taken from his top 10 album *Life and Times.*

On September 20, 1973, at the peak of his career, both Croce and his guitarist partner Muehleisen were killed when their small plane crashed on take-off at Natchitoches, Louisiana. Perhaps predictably, his sales then soared: First "I Got a Name" from the film *The Last American Hero* hit the top 10; by the year's end, Croce's classic "Time in a Bottle" became the second Number One single of his abbreviated career. His posthumous album *I Got a Name* swiftly went to number two upon its December release, and in January, *You Don't Mess Around with Jim* held the Number One slot for five weeks, almost three years after its release.

The premature death of any artist leaves open the question of how their career might have further developed, but critics generally agree that Croce's best work was probably ahead of him. For once, though, a taste of what might have been did come: in 1993, A. J. Croce—the son of Jim and Ingrid—released his debut album on the Private Music label. Like the father of its maker, it was highly praised.

DAVID CROSBY

A colorful figure who by the 1990s had achieved nearly matching levels of fame and notoriety, David Crosby (b. Aug. 14, 1941, Los Angeles) was a key member of two enormously popular and influential '60s rock groups, the Byrds and Crosby, Stills and Nash. Certainly very much a songwriter, Crosby's other major asset was his tremendous ability as a harmonizing vocalist; it's no coincidence both his former groups are renowned for their unique vocal abilities, which had influenced an entire school of rock by the early 1970s. But several personal problems came to a head for Crosby in the early '80s, and by 1986, troubles with drugs landed him in jail for several months. Finally cleaning up by the later part of the decade, the singer went on to record with both of his reunited former groups and on his own; remarkably, and happily for him, his voice seemed in better shape than it had ever been.

The son of well-known cinematographer Floyd Crosby, the singer grew up in southern California and began performing as a folk singer in Santa Barbara in 1958. By the age of 19, he'd taken his act farther south to Los Angeles, playing "God Bless the

Child," "Willie Gene," and assorted blues songs at venues such as the Unicorn Club. After an extended bout of traveling to such locales as Greenwich Village, Miami, and San Francisco—where he struck up protracted friendships with future '60s Jefferson Airplane and Quicksilver Messenger Service members Paul Kantner, Dino Valenti, and David Freiberg— Crosby had a brief stint with a folk group called Les Baxter's Balladeers, then united with Jim McGuinn and Gene Clark in 1964 to form the Jet Set. Following a one-off single on Elektra as the Beefeaters, the Jet Set added bassist Chris Hillman and drummer Michael Clarke, and the Byrds were born.

Crosby spent three exciting, sometimes tension-filled years with the Byrds and before departing in October 1967 had contributed to five albums bearing their name, from *Mr. Tambourine Man* through *The Notorious Byrd Brothers*. His role as a songwriter increased considerably upon the 1966 departure of Gene Clark; of the music on those five albums, Crosby had penned three songs on his own (including "What's Happening?!?!," "Everybody's Been Burned," and "Mind Gardens") and 10 with other band members (highlighted by "Eight Miles High," "I See You," "Why," "Renaissance Fair," and "Draft Morning"). Also of note was the group's Crosby-written "Lady Friend" single, as well as his controversial "Triad," which—after later covers by the Jefferson Airplane and Crosby, Stills, Nash and Young—finally saw release under the Byrds name in a 1989 anthology. "When we finally parted company," Crosby reminisced in 1990, "and actually, they

David Crosby

tossed me out—I thought they were terrible villains. But the truth is they're wonderful guys, and they're amongst my closest friends now." Crosby, who considers himself only a "minor writer" in the group, said he looks back at his work as a harmony singer as his major contribution to the band.

Since then, Crosby's historic role with partners Stephen Stills, Graham Nash, and, occasionally, Neil Young has been documented in books, films (their second-ever performance can be seen in the *Woodstock* film), and several video documentaries. A phenomenally successful act, it would be no exaggeration to say they were probably America's most popular rock group between 1969 and 1971. The group's initial three albums each went top 10—with 1970's *Déjà Vu* a Number One hit, selling platinum seven times over, and the double LP *4 Way Street* similarly Number One and quadruple platinum.

As all three albums were hanging steadily on the charts by April 1971, they had been joined a month earlier by David Crosby's first solo album, the delightful *If I Could Only Remember My Name*. Still very much an underrated effort—though it went gold and reached number 12 on the charts—the album featured musical backing by members of the

TOP ALBUMS

IF I COULD ONLY REMEMBER MY NAME
  (Atlantic, '71, *12*)
GRAHAM NASH/DAVID CROSBY (with Graham Nash,
  Atlantic, '72, *4*)
WIND ON THE WATER (with Graham Nash,
  ABC, '75, *6*)
WHISTLING DOWN THE WIRE (with Graham Nash,
  ABC, '76, *26*)
OH YES I CAN (A&M, '89)
THOUSAND ROADS (Atlantic, '93)

TOP SONGS

LAUGHING (Atlantic, '71)
TRACTION IN THE RAIN (Atlantic, '71)

Grateful Dead, Jefferson Airplane, Santana, Quicksilver, and Joni Mitchell. While the album had its share of memorable songs—including "Laughing," "Traction in the Rain," and the surrealistic "Cowboy Movie"—more interesting was Crosby's willingness to include several near-instrumental tracks featuring only his wordless vocals, most of which were absolutely gorgeous.

As Crosby, Stills and Nash became a huge multiplatinum machine, its members broke off into occasional subgroups, returning less and less frequently to make "reunion" albums such as 1977's *CSN* and 1982's *Daylight Again.* Crosby repeatedly paired with Graham Nash, and between 1972 and '77, they released four albums, three of which went gold and two of which made the top 10. The duo typically shared the songwriting, and Crosby's contributions came steadily—again, occasionally relying on beautiful wordless harmony on tracks such as "Dancer" and "Critical Mass."

Crosby's run-ins with the law in the mid-1980s greatly disrupted his personal and professional life. "I saw very little of anybody," he recalled in 1990. "I was mostly hiding in the bathroom with a base pipe. It's only since I've gotten straight that I could really be friends with anybody. Or that anybody would want to be friends with me." When he resurfaced drug-free on 1988's *American Dream* by the reunited Crosby, Stills, Nash and Young, one of his most telling compositions was the deeply felt "Compass," on which he sang, "I have wasted ten years in a blind-fold/Ten-fold more than I've invested now in sight/I have traveled beveled mirrors in a fly-crawl/Losing the reflection of a fight."

Crosby resumed his own solo recording career with 1989's *Oh Yes I Can* on A&M, a strong effort that showed him brimming with an energy he hadn't displayed in years, which he ascribed to "the benefits of sobriety." Crosby went full-bore back into music, singing with the reunited Byrds, Bonnie Raitt, Bob Dylan, Phil Collins, and many others. In 1993, he released his third solo album, *Thousand Roads,* which featured only a smattering of Crosby originals—including collaborations with Joni Mitchell and Phil Collins—and seven songs by other writers. Since the mid-1980s, the singer has also displayed an interest in acting; to date, he has appeared in the films *Backdraft, Thunderheart,* and *Hook* and on the TV shows "Roseanne," "Flying Blind," and "The Simpsons." Ever ambitious, David Crosby continues to make up for lost time.

CHRISTOPHER CROSS

When film directors of the future want to evoke the America of the early 1980s, it's a sure bet Christopher Cross (b. May 3, 1951) will show up somewhere on the soundtrack. Born Christopher Geppert in San Antonio, Texas, Cross absolutely dominated the airwaves then with his eminently listenable 1979 debut album—perhaps to the point where it ultimately hurt him. Like so many others to whom too much fame comes too soon, Cross has spent the rest of his career trying to live up to his own past, and, sad to say, he hasn't been so successful.

Christopher Cross was by any standard an anonymous-looking debut album: one side of the cover depicted a flamingo standing in water, the other just the water, and not a single picture of the artist was to be found anywhere. Smooth almost to the point of scientific precision, the record featured Cross's own quartet (including keyboardist Rob Meuer, bassist Andy Salmon, and drummer Tommy Taylor), the cream of L.A. session musicians, and top-notch backing vocalists like Michael McDonald, Don Henley, J. D. Souther, Nicolette Larson, and Valerie Carter. The tunes were uniformly catchy, surprisingly poppish, and oftentimes (particularly on the hit-bound "Never Be the Same") reminiscent of the work of Todd Rundgren or Carole King.

Within a year the album was a chart fixture, spawning a run of top 20 hits including "Ride Like the Wind," "Sailing," "Never Be the Same," and

TOP ALBUMS

CHRISTOPHER CROSS (Warner Bros., '80, 6)
ANOTHER PAGE (Warner Bros., '83, 11)

TOP SONGS

RIDE LIKE THE WIND (Warner Bros., '80, 2)
SAILING (Warner Bros., '80, 1)
NEVER BE THE SAME (Warner Bros., '80, 15)
ARTHUR'S THEME (BEST THAT YOU CAN DO) (Warner Bros., '81, 1)
ALL RIGHT (Warner Bros., '83, 12)
THINK OF LAURA (Warner Bros., '83, 9)

Additional Top 40 Songs: 2

Christopher Cross

itself—entered the top 40 at all. Why? No one knew for sure, though some critics were contending that Cross was already old news and, they added uncharitably, physically not exactly MTV material, either.

With his third album a sales disappointment, Cross started seeming sadly on the defensive. "Once people develop a perception of who you are," he noted in a company press release, "you get scared to break out of the mold they've made for you." Despite collaborating with old friend and former bandmate Rob Meurer for five tracks on his next album, 1988's *Back of My Mind,* it never entered the charts at all, and 1980's newest star exited the decade an apparent conspicuous overachiever. Cross hasn't released an album since.

CHRIS DeBURGH

Chris DeBurgh's past reads as if it belongs to one of the romantic characters that populate his songs. The son of a British diplomat, Christopher John Davidson was born in Argentina on October 15, 1948, and grew up in exotic locations like Malta, Nigeria, and Zaire. Upon finally settling in Ireland, his parents promptly purchased a 12th-century Norman castle, which they then converted to a hotel. Eventually learning to play guitar, DeBurgh, ever well rounded, put it aside long enough to study French and English at Dublin's Trinity College. By 1972, he had signed a publishing deal that ultimately led to a contract with A&M Records—the label for whom he continues to record two decades later.

DeBurgh's audience is fittingly international in scope, and was from day one. His first single, "Flying," from 1975's *Far Beyond These Castle Walls,* actually broke in Brazil (where it stayed at Number One for 17 weeks); next, his 1977 album *Spanish Train and Other Stories* promptly hit in Canada, where it went platinum.

Artistically, DeBurgh seemed very much to fit the dictionary definition of "troubadour"—or, as A&M referred to him on the back of his third album, "the British equivalent of the French 'chanteur.' " Not so much a folksinger as a balladeer, DeBurgh hasn't much changed his writing style over the years, just his musical context. His American breakthrough came via his 1983 hit "Don't Pay the Ferryman," which, thanks to the skilled production of Rupert

"Say You'll Be Mine" and selling more than four million copies worldwide. It also won Cross five Grammys, including Album of the Year, Record of the Year ("Sailing"), Song of the Year ("Sailing"), and, predictably, Best New Artist honors. Then, after most of pre-MTV America got their first look at him during the Grammy show, came his biggest record yet. From the hit movie *Arthur*, "Arthur's Theme (Best That You Can Do)" bore a lengthy composer's credit that included Burt Bacharach, Cross, Carole Bayer Sager, and Peter Allen. It stayed in the Number One slot for three weeks, went gold (no small achievement at the time for a single)...and Cross never did as well again.

With second album *Another Page* shooting three more singles up the top 40 charts in 1983 ("All Right," "No Time for Talk," and "Think of Laura"), Cross, now minus his old bandmates, seemed to be holding on respectably, but holding on nonetheless. Not so with 1985's *Every Turn of the World.* Not one of its singles—not even the album

TOP ALBUMS

THE GETAWAY (A&M, '83)
MAN ON THE LINE (A&M, '84)
INTO THE LIGHT (A&M, '86, 25)

TOP SONGS

DON'T PAY THE FERRYMAN (A&M, '83, 34)
THE LADY IN RED (A&M, '87, 3)

Hine, was the most upbeat, poppish thing he'd ever done. In fact, the two albums Hine produced—1982's *The Getaway* and 1984's *Man on the Line*—had DeBurgh sounding markedly like British rock group the Fixx, another of Hine's artists; for older fans, it must have seemed a considerable genre leap.

But the biggest leap of all came with "The Lady in Red," DeBurgh's massive international smash of 1987, which reached number three on the U.S. charts, was an acknowledged favorite of the Duchess of York, and won the heart of nearly every female listener who'd heard it. The simple song of love may be as timeless a composition as DeBurgh has written—and when he told interviewers the song had actually been inspired by his wife, he established his fan base for life.

Further solidifying his image as a romantic family man were "For Rosanna" and "Just a Word Away," songs he'd written especially for his newly born daughter Rosanna, and, later, son Hubie. Indeed, though he remains a top concert attraction around the world, it's likely those children—and the tremendous success of "The Lady in Red"—may be why Chris DeBurgh doesn't make records much anymore.

SANDY DENNY

One of the finest singer-songwriters ever to emerge from Great Britain, Sandy Denny (b. Jan. 6, 1941, London) has grown in critical stature since her career was tragically cut short in 1978. Renowned mainly as a central figure in England's long-lived folk aggregation Fairport Convention, Denny also became known to many for peripheral reasons: her composition "Who Knows Where the Time Goes"—only the second song she'd ever written—was the title track of Judy Collins's

bestselling album of 1968; additionally, longtime fans Led Zeppelin invited Denny to sing on "The Battle of Evermore" from their 1971 set *Led Zeppelin IV*.

A former nursing student, Denny began her musical career in various English pubs and clubs in the mid-1960s. While performing at the Troubadour club in Earls' Court in 1967, Denny was spotted by Dave Cousins, leader of British folk act the Strawbs, who asked her to join his group. She did; they then recorded an album together in Copenhagen titled *All Our Own Work,* which featured "Who Knows Where the Time Goes." While Cousins was out seeking a British distributor for the set, Denny accepted an offer to replace departing singer Judy Dyble in Fairport Convention and became a member in May 1968.

From the start, Denny proved a brilliant addition to the group. Her song "Fotheringay," which opened *What We Did on Our Holidays* (released in America as *Fairport Convention* on A&M), was a warm, elegantly reserved acoustic track that instantly set the tone for Fairport's coming stylistic shift. Fairport's first album with Dyble (which saw delayed U.S. release in 1970 on Cotillion Records) had displayed a British band clearly taken with American musical forms, covering songs by Joni Mitchell, Bob Dylan, and Emitt Rhodes; with Denny's addition, the group still sounded faintly American ("Mr. Lacey" might've come from the first Jefferson Airplane album; "Book Song" sounded much like the early Byrds) and still covered Dylan and Mitchell, but they were heading toward a unique synthesis contemporizing traditional British folk. When vocalist Iain Matthews left to go solo, the roles of both Denny and Fairport guitarist Richard Thompson increased markedly; both pushed quickly toward the new style.

Denny stayed with Fairport for two more albums, leaving on the heels of what has been uniformly acclaimed the pivotal album of British folk-rock, *Liege and Lief.* The group's all-time international bestseller (though it failed to chart in America), it memorably combined original material like "Come All Ye" by Denny and bassist Ashley Hutchings with English traditional songs such as "Tam Lin," and essentially laid out the course that Fairport Convention would follow without Denny for many years to come. In 1970, both Hutchings and Denny left the group. Hutchings went on to form the successful, similarly folk-oriented Steeleye Span, and Denny, with her eventual husband Trevor Lucas, an Australian, formed Fotheringay.

Though that group recorded but one album, it was dominated by a wealth of superb Denny originals such as "Nothing More" and "The Sea"; it became obvious that with Fairport's heading toward traditional territories, Denny's songs might not have been entirely appropriate in the context of that band.

After an aborted attempt at a second Fotheringay album, the group broke up. Denny began recording a series of solo albums, the best of which was 1972's *Sandy*. As in the early Fairport Days, Denny occasionally interpreted other artists' songs—Bob Dylan being a particular favorite—but her originals were consistently unique and appealing. Musicians came from the same revolving case of British folk players, including members of Fairport Convention.

Ironically, Trevor Lucas became a Fairport Convention member himself in 1974. Denny, who'd apparently left the group amicably, returned as well, touring the States with Fairport in 1974 and contributing to its 1975 album *Rising for the Moon*. Both she and Lucas left Fairport in 1976; in 1977, she bore a baby daughter, Georgia. The next year, after falling down a flight of stairs, Denny died of a brain hemorrhage on April 21st.

A top-notch four-LP set of Denny's work was released by Hannibal Records in 1985; commendably comprehensive, the collection shows Denny's singing and songwriting to have timeless appeal. She remains greatly missed.

JOHN DENVER

It's difficult to believe that the bland-voiced, achingly sincere character gazing out at us from the cover of 1970's *Whose Garden Was This* was one of that decade's biggest recording stars. Still, shirtless and wearing a medallion bearing the inscription "War is not healthy for children and other living things," John Denver (b. John Henry Deutschendorf, Dec. 31, 1954, Roswell, New Mexico) would soon become a recording phenomenon so deeply a part of '70s culture that he would star in

films with George Burns, record an album with the Muppets, star in his own Emmy-winning television special, and even be officially declared the poet laureate of Colorado. Offending nobody except for most rock critics, Denver's general shtick—that cities and war were bad, nature and peace good—was perfectly encapsulated in his debut hit, "Take Me Home, Country Roads," in which the singer relayed his first of several requests to escape troublesome urban torment and enjoy the wild country, whether it be West Virginia or his wonderful, sunshine-filled, adopted state of Colorado. As he would soon sing in his Number One hit "Sunshine on My Shoulders"—a lyric that delighted an audience increasingly disturbed by the drug problems of a younger generation—"Sunshine almost always makes me high."

Born to an Air Force family—his father had broken a world speed record in a B-58 Hustler bomber in 1961—young John Deutschendorf spent much of his youth on the move and eventually attended Texas Tech, where he majored in architecture. Leaving school in 1964, he moved to Los Angeles and, as John Denver, soon replaced the departing Chad Mitchell in the Chad Mitchell Trio, staying with them for four years. His recordings with that group would later be partially collected and reissued by Mercury Records in 1974 as *Beginnings with the Mitchell Trio*. Then playing briefly in an act with former Kingston Trio member John Stewart, Denver penned his song "Leaving on a Jet Plane," which was covered by Peter, Paul and Mary in 1967 and became a Number One hit for them two years later.

Denver's solo career began in 1969 with *Rhymes and Reasons,* the first of roughly 25 albums he made in affiliation with RCA Records. The disc contained his own version of "Jet Plane" and—perhaps to further establish his politically hip folk-singer credentials—"The Ballad of Richard Nixon" and "The Ballad of Spiro Agnew," among other tracks. Denver's earliest material was largely serviceable, country-tinged, ecologically based folk music; he covered a significant number of other artists' songs on such 1970–71 albums as *Whose Garden Was This, Take Me to Tomorrow,* and *Poems, Prayers & Promises,* including those of Tom Paxton, Jacques Brel, Lennon and McCartney, James Taylor, and the Band's Robbie Robertson. But the hits that made him an eventual superstar were uniformly penned by Denver, or co-written with friends Bill Danoff and Taffy Nivert (of Fat City, later the Starland Vocal Band) or his band members Mike Taylor and Dick Kniss.

Denver's peak as a record seller came between 1971 and '75, when he scored 10 hits that reached the top 15, seven of which made the top five, six of which went gold, four of which were Number One singles. All of them—from "Rocky Mountain High" and "Sunshine on My Shoulders" to "Back Home Again" and "Thank God I'm a Country Boy"— helped shape his near-perfect just-folks persona, which made his transition from pop star to media personage a relatively effortless procedure. Perhaps the most telling proof of his popularity was his 1973 *Greatest Hits* set, which sold over 10 million copies and stayed on the album charts for an astounding 175 weeks.

But by no means was he merely a singles artist: Between 1971 and '76, the singer released seven albums that reached the top five. He also briefly helmed his own RCA-distributed label, Windsong, for which Bill and Taffy Danoff, under the Starland Vocal Band moniker, recorded their 1976 Number One hit "Afternoon Delight."

While Denver continued to score hits well into the next decade—his last encounter with the top 40 was 1982's "Shanghai Breezes"—he became a larger-than-life presence on many levels, whether on television for his own specials and with the Muppets, on the screen with George Burns in *Oh, God!*, or even being named the Entertainer of the Year by the Country Music Association—no mean feat for a pop star. His last charting album for RCA came in 1985

with *Dreamland Express,* which peaked at 90; in 1990, he briefly reappeared on the small, independently-distributed Windstar label, but his album *The Flower That Shattered the Stone* spent only a measly six weeks on the chart and peaked at number 185.

It's probable that Denver's musical ties to the 1970s are simply too strong for him to escape at this point; additionally, the level of success he enjoyed then has, in retrospect, hindered rather than helped boost his reputation in critical circles. The unpleasant flip side of fame, at least for John Denver, is that in the mid-1990s, he is remembered much more for the degree of his fame than for the quality of his songwriting.

JACKIE DeSHANNON

Despite her long and distinguished career as a singer-songwriter—and as a pioneering female during a time when the songwriting business was almost exclusively the domain of men—Jackie DeShannon remains one of the most underrated performers in pop history. An extremely prolific tunesmith with over 600 tunes to her credit, DeShannon (b. Sharon Myers, Aug. 21, 1944, Hazel, Kentucky) has had a hand in writing or performing some of the most memorable songs of the rock era— most notably '60s classics "What the World Needs Now Is Love" and "Put a Little Love in Your Heart" and 1981's international smash "Bette Davis Eyes."

DeShannon's lengthy singing career has provided her with memorable encounters with nearly all of pop's royalty: As a teenager, she reportedly was encouraged to move to California by rocker Eddie Cochran; by the same account, she was slated to appear at the same show to which Buddy Holly, the Big Bopper, and Ritchie Valens were flying when their plane crashed en route. In 1964, she played 26 American dates with the Beatles; the next year, she was in England writing songs with Jimmy Page for Marianne Faithfull. She played an important role in in the careers of two of folk-rock's most illustrious practitioners: the Searchers had hits covering her two 1963 singles "Needles and Pins" (written by DeShannon's producer Jack Nitzsche and Sonny Bono) and "When You Walk in the Room" (penned by DeShannon), and the Byrds covered "Don't Doubt Yourself, Babe" on their famous *Mr. Tambourine Man* Columbia debut album. Her breadth,

TOP ALBUMS

ROCKY MOUNTAIN HIGH (RCA, '72, *4*)
BACK HOME AGAIN (RCA, '74, *1*)
AN EVENING WITH JOHN DENVER (RCA, '75, *2*)
WINDSONG (RCA, '75, *1*)

Additional Top 40 Albums: 11

TOP SONGS:

TAKE ME HOME, COUNTRY ROADS (RCA, '71, *2*)
SUNSHINE ON MY SHOULDERS (RCA, '74, *1*)
ANNIE'S SONG (RCA, '74, *1*)
BACK HOME AGAIN (RCA, '74, *5*)
THANK GOD I'M A COUNTRY BOY (RCA, '75, *1*)
I'M SORRY (RCA, '75, *1*)

Additional Top 40 Songs: 9

in retrospect, appears amazing: As early as 1961, she'd written the top 10 hit "Dum Dum" for Brenda Lee and composed the theme music for the film *Splendor in the Grass.* She appeared in the films *Surf Party, Hide and Seek,* and *C'mon, Let's Live a Little.* And as a staff writer for Metric Music she collaborated with—and covered songs by—a teenaged Randy Newman.

Yet even with all these credits, DeShannon's own recording career never really took off to the degree it might have. Part of it may have been the slapdash nature of her early albums (on Liberty and its subsidiary Imperial), which often lacked cohesion and generally failed to properly establish her as songwriter. Her shoddily packaged 1965 set *This Is Jackie DeShannon,* for instance, cheesily bore the prominent titles of five songs on its cover—but aside from hits "What the World Needs Now Is Love" and "A Lifetime of Loneliness" (both written and produced by Burt Bacharach and Hal David), who'd be interested in her versions of "Summertime," "I'm Gonna Be Strong," and "Don't Let the Sun Catch You Crying"? Likewise, other Imperial albums such as *New Image* and *For You* featured superb writer DeShannon singing standards such as "Night and Day" and "I'll Be Seeing You" with orchestral backing. They weren't bad albums—DeShannon was too good a singer for that—but during some of rock's most explosive years, she was driving noticeably in the middle of the road.

DeShannon's only album to enter the top 100 turned out to be 1969's *Put a Little Love in Your Heart,* pushed there largely by its top five title track. By then, though, she'd assumed more control over her work and had writing credits (shared with Jimmy Holiday and Randy Myers) on 10 of the album's 12 tracks. By 1971 she was jumping labels, from Capitol to Atlantic, then to Columbia, and finally, by

1977, to tiny Amherst, where she recorded her last album, *You're the Only Dancer.* Her best album was 1972's *Jackie,* produced for Atlantic by Jerry Wexler, Tom Dowd, and Arif Mardin and recorded mainly in Memphis. On it, DeShannon sings wonderfully, her original tune "Vanilla 'Olay" ranks with her best, and her choice of covered songwriters—including John Prine, Neil Young, Steve Goodman, and Van Morrison (with whom she'd both sing and later write the 1978 song "Santa Fe")—thoroughly inspired. Her sole Columbia album, 1975's *New Arrangement,* featured the original version of the DeShannon–Donna Weiss song "Bette Davis Eyes," which Kim Carnes would redo to enormous success in 1981. Still active as a writer, if not a singer, DeShannon—who married songwriter–film scorer Randy Edelman—has without exaggeration accomplished more than most pop artists can ever hope to.

NEIL DIAMOND

It's entirely possible a generation of young music lovers spun *Up on the Roof: Songs from the Brill Building,* the 1993 collection of pop classics sung by Neil Diamond (b. Noah Kaminsky, Jan. 24, 1941, Brooklyn, New York), looked heavenward, and assumed the aging MOR star was going through his "rock and roll phase." But that delightful collection, informatively annotated by Diamond himself, again reminded a slightly older generation just how deeply involved Diamond had been in rock and roll since its formative years.

Inspired to write his first song after seeing Pete Seeger perform at his summer camp, a teenaged Diamond formed an early singing duo with friend Jack Packer; together, they released two Everly Brothers–styled singles under the name Neil and Jack on New York's tiny Duel label in 1960–61.

While attending New York University on a fencing scholarship, intending to study medicine, the singer continued to pursue a career in music on the side. He landed a $50-a-week job with Sunbeam Music six months before finishing school, and, slowly but steadily, that music career soon came. A 1963 deal with Columbia Records resulted in a one-off single ("Clown Town") that failed to chart; soon after, Diamond met songwriting team Jeff Barry and Ellie Greenwich, who would help get him signed to

<hr>

TOP ALBUMS

Put a Little Love in Your Heart (Imperial, '69)
Jackie (Atlantic, '72)

TOP SONGS

What the World Needs Now Is Love
  (Imperial, '65, 7)
Put a Little Love in Your Heart (Imperial, '69, 4)
Love Will Find a Way (Imperial, '69,

Leiber and Stoller's Red Bird label. When that ultimately proved unproductive, Barry and Greenwich asked Diamond to join them in forming their own publishing company, Tallyrand Music. By 1965, Diamond's songs began getting covered by such artists as Jay and the Americans ("Sunday and Me"), Jimmy Clanton, Bobby Vinton, and Cliff Richard—which was cause enough for Bang Records head Bert Berns to offer a recording deal to Diamond himself.

At Bang, Diamond recorded a memorable string of nine top 40 hits, including "Cherry, Cherry," "Solitary Man," "You Got to Me," and "I Thank the Lord for the Night Time." His status as a hit songwriter soared in 1966, when the Monkees took his "I'm a Believer" to the top of the charts, where it stayed for seven weeks; two singles later, they'd do the same with his "A Little Bit Me, a Little Bit You," a Number One hit for two weeks. British group Deep Purple also scored with a Diamond song via their 1968 version of his "Kentucky Woman."

When Bang president Berns expressed reluctance to release Diamond's "Shilo" as a single, the disappointed singer soon struck a new deal with Uni Records, for whom he'd record 11 hits, including four of his biggest—"Sweet Caroline," "Holly Holy," "Cracklin' Rosie," and "Song Sung Blue"—all of which went gold. Anxious to market Diamond as an album artist rather than simple top 40 hitmaker, Uni watched with pleasure as Diamond, beginning with 1969's *Touching You Touching Me*, scored an unbroken string of eight gold albums for the label.

Diamond made the transition from simple pop star to major live performer while at Uni; his final album for the label, 1972's *Hot August Night*, was recorded at Hollywood's 5,000-seat Greek Theatre, shortly before he would give an unprecedented 20 performances at Broadway's Winter Garden Theater. Following those appearances, Diamond took a four-year sabbatical from the concert circuit.

In 1973, the singer struck a reported $5 million deal with Columbia Records, for whom he has continued to record ever since. His debut for the label, the soundtrack to *Jonathan Livingston Seagull,* remains his second all-time bestseller; it began a streak of platinum or gold releases that, with one exception (1991's *Lovescape*) has yet to be broken. Diamond's popularity continued to rise through the 1970s, and his music—once the very essence of simple, catchy pop—took a notable turn toward MOR.

Neil Diamond

While he still wrote nearly all of his songs, he began using a steady stream of collaborators, including Alan Lindgren, Richard Bennett, Alan and Marilyn Bergman, Tom Hensley, Gilbert Becaud, and Burt Bacharach and Carole Bayer Sager. "You Don't Bring Me Flowers," his 1978 duet with Barbra Streisand, became his first Number One single since 1972's "Song Sung Blue"; it was also his last.

Since 1980, when Diamond starred with Sir Laurence Olivier in the film remake *The Jazz Singer,* he has become one of America's most popular general entertainers. (Though his soundtrack to the film went quintuple platinum and produced three top 10 singles, in retrospect it seems a feat he isn't likely to duplicate.) A phenomenally successful live draw, Diamond also became one of the first '60s-era pop stars to demonstrate that concertgoers and record buyers were not necessarily the same audiences. Indeed, his last single to enter the top 40—the top five "Heartlight"—came over a decade ago.

Still, hitless or not, Diamond's massive fan base has so far ensured that almost all of his releases will at least go gold. He has sold over 92 million albums during his career, and his continued value as a recording artist was amply demonstrated in 1993, when he and Sony concluded an impressive new recording deal. His chosen stage name remarkably appropriate, Neil Diamond remains one of the most widely recognized entertainers in the world.

TOP ALBUMS

MOODS (Uni, '72, 5)
JONATHAN LIVINGSTON SEAGULL (Columbia, '73, 2)
SERENADE (Columbia, '74, 3)
BEAUTIFUL NOISE (Columbia, '76, 4)
THE JAZZ SINGER (Capitol, '80, 3)

Additional Top 40 Albums: 17

TOP SONGS

SWEET CAROLINE (GOOD TIMES NEVER SEEMED
   SO GOOD) (Uni, '69, 4)
CRACKLIN' ROSIE (Uni, '70, 1)
SONG SUNG BLUE (Uni, '72, 1)
YOU DON'T BRING ME FLOWERS (with Barbra
   Streisand, Columbia, '78, 1)
LOVE ON THE ROCKS (Capitol, '80, 2)

Additional Top 40 Songs: 32

DR. JOHN

One of popular music's most respected musicians, Dr. John (b. Malcolm John "Mac" Rebennack, Nov. 21, 1941, New Orleans, Louisiana) received his official launch as a pop star in 1968 with *Gris-Gris,* released under his unique stage name of Dr. John Creaux, a.k.a. "the Night Tripper." The album was a strange mix of voodoo, blues, jazz, rock, and mysticism, and considering that very peculiar era—when artists such as British singer Arthur Brown would perform onstage wearing a flaming hat—it seemed both appropriate and deliciously psychedelic. Musicologists of the period, however, might have looked at the lineup of professional musicians appearing on *Gris-Gris* and felt a warm rush of familiarity. The central player of the album was singer, writer, pianist, and guitarist Mac Rebennack, and he—along with many of the album's musicians—was a New Orleans stalwart with a distinguished musical pedigree.

In fact, Rebennack had been playing on classic New Orleans R&B, country, and rock and roll records since the mid-1950s, doing session work at Cosimo Matassa's studios and elsewhere for such labels as Ace (where he also served as an A&R rep), Ric and Ronn, Specialty, and Ebb. He had worked with such noted musicians as Professor Longhair, Leonard James and the Nighttrainers, Paul Gayten, Frankie Ford, Lee Allen, Red Tyler, and Joe Tex, and he had released his own recordings on the Rex and Ace labels. A member of producer-arranger Harold Battiste's AFO (All for One) cooperative, he left New Orleans for Los Angeles in 1962 with plans to record with Sam Cooke. When that fell through, he began a lucrative career as an L.A. session musician, backing Sonny and Cher and many others; additionally, he played with several New Orleans friends in loose aggregations the Zu Zu Band (with Jessie Hill) and Morgus and the Three Ghouls. Those friends and more can be found accompanying Dr. John on *Gris-Gris,* which was reportedly recorded on session time originally bought for Sonny and Cher.

The music of *Gris-Gris* caught ears far and wide. "I Walk on Gilded Splinters," the album's closing track, was later covered by Humble Pie and Johnny Jenkins, among others; "Jump Sturdy" was likewise redone by Manfred Mann's Earth Band. In retrospect, Dr. John's much more substantial follow-up, *Babylon,* remains his most underrated work by far.

A mixture of psychedelia and unique jazz arrangements provided by Harold Battiste, the album features some of Dr. John's best songs, particularly "Glowin'" and the distinctly odd "Twilight Zone." Sample lyrics from the latter: "Martians kidnap the First Family/They're gonna demand New York City for ransom money/We're gonna outsmart 'em, leave a note for 'em to read/The best they can get is Milwaukee/In the Twilight Zone." Very much ahead of its time, both lyrically and musically, the album is an unsung classic of the 1960s.

With Dr. John himself providing the arrangements on 1970's *Remedies* and 1971's *The Sun, Moon & Herbs,* both albums are still deliberately spacey but (with the exception of *Remedies*' side-long "Angola Anthem") relatively traditional-sounding compared to their predecessors. *The Sun, Moon & Herbs,* his first charting album (it peaked at number 184), boasted a stellar guest list that included Mick Jagger and Eric Clapton; oddly, their contributions seemed muted and largely inaudible. Most importantly, the two albums were the the the last to be issued bearing the "Night Tripper" tag; they closed the book on Dr. John's psychedelic phase.

Beginning with *Gumbo,* Mac Rebennack embraced his past as a New Orleans R&B artist—and his music was never the same again. Vastly praised by critics, *Gumbo* featured Dr. John playing the music he loved best, covering songs popularized by Huey "Piano" Smith, Professor Longhair, Ray Charles, and Earl King, as well as a version of his own 1960 recording (as

TOP ALBUMS

Gris-Gris (Atco, '68)
Babylon (Atco, '69)
Gumbo (Atco, '72)
In the Right Place (Atco, '73, 24)
Desitively Bonnaroo (Atco, '74)

TOP SONGS

I Walk on Gilded Splinters (Atco, '68)
Babylon (Atco, '69)
Iko Iko (Atco, '71)
Right Place Wrong Time (Atco, '73, 9)
Such a Night (Atco, '73)

Drits and Dravy, with Ronnie Barron) "Somebody Changed the Lock." *In the Right Place,* Dr. John's all-time bestseller, followed in 1973; produced by Allen Toussaint and featuring backup band the Meters, the album included both the top 10 title track and "Such a Night," the top 50 hit that would be his last. Both songs were penned by Rebennack and stand as his best-known work.

Following *Triumvirate,* an unsatisfying 1973 collaboration with guitarists Mike Bloomfield and John Hammond, Jr., Dr. John returned with *Desitively Bonaroo,* which peaked at number 105 and became his last charting album for 15 years. He recorded several albums (many instrumental) for various labels in the interim, the most interesting perhaps 1978's *City Lights on Horizon,* on which he cowrote three tunes with Doc Pomus. In 1989, his traditional set *In a Sentimental Mood* won a Grammy for its duet version of "Makin' Whoopee" featuring Rickie Lee Jones.

Though it's possible Mac Rebennack may look back on his years as "the Night Tripper" as a brief aberration in a career otherwise devoted to R&B, blues, and jazz, his brilliant musicianship and inspired, voodoo-flavored lunacy make those albums some of the most enjoyable relics of the era. No matter what his approach, or his genre of choice, the Doctor, in short, has always been in.

THOMAS DOLBY

 One of the most underrated singer-songwriters currently working in the pop field, Thomas Morgan Dolby Robertson (b. Oct. 14, 1958) may be a little *too* good—or so it may seem to those who picked up his 1982 debut album *The Golden Age of Wireless* and immediately fell in love. In the years since, Dolby has released only three similarly poppish albums, and his rock star days seem increasingly behind him. What happened? Ironically, *he* did. Between becoming a funk artist, scoring films, playing keyboards on superstar recording sessions, and producing other artists' records—including one of the best of the 1980s, *Two Wheels Good* by U.K. group Prefab Sprout—his own records, few as they have been, have almost seemed afterthoughts.

But of course, they weren't. Dolby's background was quirky: Born in Cairo to British parents, son of

an archeologist, he'd attended various boarding schools and taught himself piano and guitar. He'd tried playing jazz piano at bars, investigated the electronic music German groups like Kraftwerk and Roxy Music's Eno were pioneering, and even built and operated sound systems for several London punk groups. In short, he played—and liked—a little of everything. It showed. His career took off via a playing gig with English group Bruce Wooley and the Camera Club; soon after, his tune "New Toy" became a hit for Lene Lovich in 1980, and his solo career began in earnest.

Dolby's remarkable ear for keyboard-driven, gloriously melodic pop songs was amply evident on the original version of *Wireless* that Capitol released in 1982. But with the surprise international success of 1983's top five hit "She Blinded Me with Science," things changed. Stylistically not much more than a danceable funk hit—and absolutely skeletal compared to his earlier work—"Science" was quickly grafted onto both a makeshift mini-LP (*Blinded by Science*) and, with two other new songs and other subtle changes, the earlier *Wireless.* Though Dolby had already gone on record claiming such diverse influences as Soft Machine, Joni Mitchell, and Chick Corea, those who knew him only from the funk-filled "Science" couldn't be blamed for assuming he'd been joking.

Dolby's 1984 sequel, *The Flat Earth,* inevitably contained a funky follow-up in "Hyperactive," but more interesting were two slow-moving, nearly cinematic tracks: a gorgeous version of Dan Hicks and the Hot Licks' "I Scare Myself" and "Screen Kiss," which manages to combine two of Dolby's themes,

TOP ALBUMS

BLINDED BY SCIENCE (Capitol, '83, *20*)
THE GOLDEN AGE OF WIRELESS (Capitol, '83, *13*)
THE FLAT EARTH (Capitol, '84, *35*)
ALIENS ATE MY BUICK (EMI-Manhattan, '88)
ASTRONAUTS & HERETICS (Giant, '93)

TOP SONGS

EUROPA AND THE PIRATE TWINS (Capitol, '83)
SHE BLINDED ME WITH SCIENCE (Capitol, '83, *5*)
SCREEN KISS (Capitol, '84)
I LOVE YOU GOODBYE (Giant, '93)
I LIVE IN A SUITCASE (Giant, '93)

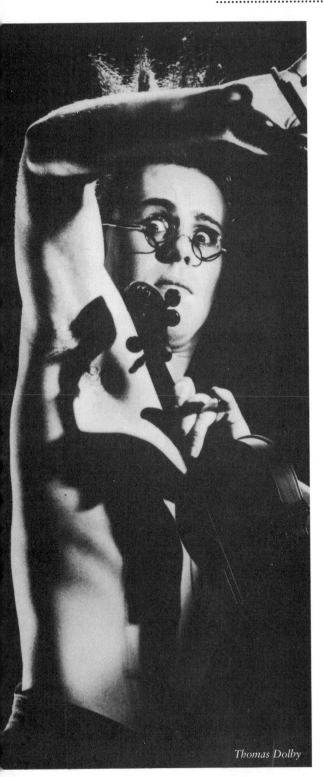

Thomas Dolby

emotional discontent and glitzy Los Angeles, in a surprisingly effective, moving way.

At this point, Dolby continued what he'd already been doing: collaborating with strangely varied artists. He'd already played on sessions by Foreigner, Joan Armatrading, Adele Bertei, and Malcolm McLaren; via the magic of trans-Atlantic collaboration, he'd also written and produced a hit record by New York rappers Whodini. He went on to work with funk king George Clinton; produce Joni Mitchell (her 1985 *Dog Eat Dog* album), Prefab Sprout, and world music singer Ofra Haza; score the film *Fever Pitch* and Ken Russell's surreal *Gothic;* and provide a full side of music for the little-heard *Howard the Duck* soundtrack.

Thereafter, Dolby moved from England to L.A., took out an advertisment in local weekly newspaper the *Recycler* for "some new talent" to join his band, and within a year, with his newly dubbed band the Lost Toy People, released *Aliens Ate My Buick.* On its cover he can be seen hugging his wife, American actress Kathleen Beller from the TV show *Dynasty.*

Comparative quiet followed for five years, though fans were eventually rewarded in 1993 with Dolby's best album since his first, *Astronauts & Heretics.* Despite being conspicuously jam-packed with a circus of big-name guest stars—Jerry Garcia, Edward Van Halen, Beausoleil, and Ofra Haza being only a few—the album sounds like a complete work, not the patchwork it might've been, and therein lies its beauty. Boasting two of Dolby's best songs ever— "I Love You Goodbye" and "I Live in a Suitcase"— and a sequel to *Wireless*'s opener "Europa & the Pirate Twins," the album is a major work by someone who, one suspects, might be just as happy doing something else entirely.

DONOVAN

As the years move onward, perceptions about artists and their worth—culturally, materially, or otherwise—shift unpredictably. Take, for instance, Scottish singer-songwriter Donovan (b. Donovan Phillip Leitch, May 10, 1946, Glasgow, Scotland), who during his mid-'60s prime was deemed the hippest of the hip by tastemakers worldwide. By the time the 1970s slid in, he was viewed as an aging, out-of-it hippie troubadour; by the 1980s, a virtual nonentity more famous for the actor children he spawned rather than his music; and, by the 1990s…well, he was hip again.

Aside from being a great listen, Epic Records' 1992 *Troubadour: The Definitive Collection* confirms what may be obvious: the songs haven't changed, *we* have. More importantly, it reveals that unlike many of his contemporaries, Donovan removed from his cultural context still holds up remarkably well. And if the best gauge of a performer's success is the degree to which he or she has permeated the culture, consider this: Donovan's music named a soda pop (Mello Yello), promoted an entire line of cosmetics (via his 1967 "Wear Your Love Like Heaven"), and enjoyed the distinct honor of having a 1968 hit ("Hurdy Gurdy Man") covered 22 years later by no less a name than the Butthole Surfers.

Though critics tend to dismiss Donovan's early material as blatantly Dylan-derived (a view partially encouraged by D. A. Pennebaker's historic Dylan documentary *Don't Look Back*), it's a short-sighted view. Similarities: he was a "protest singer," he wore the characteristic accessories (denim cap, acoustic guitar, harmonica in holder), he sang songs like "Universal Soldier." Differences: he was launched via a TV show (England's "Ready Steady Go"), he didn't write "Universal Soldier" (Buffy Sainte-Marie did), and he had an uncanny ear for catchy pop tunes. Viewed in retrospect, he was very much his own man.

From 1966 to 1969, the streak of pop hits Donovan enjoyed was—in terms of how much each differed from the last—rivaled only by the Beatles themselves. Beginning with his Number One hit "Sunshine Superman," the singer shifted personas and musical style each time out. From "Mellow Yellow" to "Epistle to Dippy" to "Hurdy Gurdy Man" to "Atlantis," the singer also had an amazing talent for weaving meaning into what on paper might have looked like complete nonsense (e.g., his 1969 hit "Goo Goo Barabajagal"). The key—and one reason his material holds up so well decades later—is that his "nonsense" never becomes dated; his "electrical banana" lyric sounds as peculiar now as it did then. Further, his records themselves were brilliant: British producer Mickey Most did his best work with Donovan, even managing to seamlessly incorporate distinctive guest artists like Jeff Beck and Jimmy Page (whom he also produced) into some of Donovan's flakiest songs.

But when Donovan was cold, he was very cold. His last top 40 single ("Barabajagal") came in 1969; his final album to reach the top 40 was 1973's *Cosmic Wheels*. Thereafter, his name was used by comedians as verbal shorthand to evoke the silliness of the 1960s (and perhaps some previous fans were a little sheepish about how much they'd liked the man who once wrote a song called "I Love My Shirt").

After a series of poorly received albums—including a Nashville set (1974's *7-Tease*) that became a touring theatre piece—the singer effectively retired from the road. Donovan's last "new" American album, 1991's *The Classics Live,* celebrated his 25th anniversary in the business with newly performed versions of his better-known songs. Now a grandfather—and no doubt an "electrical" one—Donovan lives in Ireland with his wife, whom he met and fell in love with in 1965.

TOP ALBUMS

Sunshine Superman (Epic, '66, *11*)
Mellow Yellow (Epic, '67, *14*)
A Gift from a Flower to a Garden (Epic, '68, *19*)
Donovan in Concert (Epic, '69, *18*)
Open Road (Epic, '70, *16*)

Additional Top 40 Albums: 5

TOP SONGS

Sunshine Superman (Epic, '66, *1*)
Mellow Yellow (Epic, '66, *2*)
There Is a Mountain (Epic, '67, *11*)
Hurdy Gurdy Man (Epic, '68, *5*)
Atlantis (Epic, '69, *7*)

Additional Top 40 Songs: 7

NICK DRAKE

Just as our memories of such film stars as James Dean and Marilyn Monroe limit us to experiencing them in past tense—through their films, through the photographs taken of them at their physical zenith, and before age, slowing careers, or personal hardships diluted their peak intensity—four records are all we can know about Nick Drake (b. June 19, 1948, Burma). The British folksinger, who died in 1974, has become the object of cult worship since his death; his albums have been boxed, his songs individually analyzed, and his life story told and retold to the point of attaining near-mythhood. He has been the subject of a tribute album (*Brittle Days,* on England's Imaginary Records, 1992), and even his practice tapes have been studied, analyzed, and covered by a guitarist who admired Drake's instrumental ability (*Nine of Swords* by Scott Appel, on Kicking Mule, 1988). He is a performer who sold very few albums during his lifetime, whose work never appeared on any album sales chart, but whose influence grows yearly—and isn't likely to decrease in the future.

Born in Burma, the son of prosperous parents, Drake grew up in Tamworth-in-Arden, a small village near Coventry, England. By one account, he listened to performers like Van Morrison, Tim Buckley, and Randy Newman while attending college in Cambridge, where he began performing during his first year. Fairport Convention member Ashley Hutchings saw Drake and recommended him to producer Joe Boyd, an American who headed up a British recording company called Witchseason Productions— home to John Martyn, the Incredible String Band, and Fairport's Richard Thompson, among others. Boyd called and asked Drake for a tape, and the ultimate result was the album *Five Leaves Left,* issued in 1968, when he was 20.

The music of *Five Leaves Left* was—and is— utterly spellbinding: Drake's soft, bassy voice, typically accompanied by his acoustic guitar and occasional orchestration, sang songs that were gentle, dreamy, and often melancholy; his lyrics, tied to no specific time or lyrical theme, might have been written a century ago yet still instantly pulled the listener in. By the next year's equally impressive *Bryter Layter,* Drake's spirits in some ways seemed to be picking up; the memorable "Poor Boy" featured a backing female chorus and jazz piano by noted South African player Chris McGregor, and "Hazey Jane I" was as close as Drake would ever come to a love song. Still retaining its melancholic tinge, Drake's music was alluringly rich and captivating.

Personally troubled and prone to serious depression, Drake sought psychiatric help following the

TOP ALBUMS

FIVE LEAVES LEFT (Island, '68)
BRYTER LAYTER (Island, '69)
PINK MOON (Island, '72)

TOP SONGS

THREE HOURS (Island, '68)
RIVER MAN (Island, '68)
POOR BOY (Island, '69)
ONE OF THESE THINGS FIRST
    (Island, '69)
AT THE CHIME OF A CITY CLOCK
    (Island, '69)
HAZEY JANE I (Island, '69)
THINGS BEHIND THE SUN
    (Island, '72)

making of *Bryter Layter* and was prescribed antidepressants. He reportedly recorded his third album, 1972's *Pink Moon,* in only two days; the lushness of his prior albums was replaced by the stark sound of only the singer's voice, guitar, and occasional piano. The lyrics were equally spare, and sometimes harrowing. The brief "Know" featured only one short verse ("Know that I love you/Know I don't care/Know that I see you/Know I'm not there"); more oblique, but no less revealing, was the snippet from "Things Behind the Sun" in which Drake sang, "And the movement in your brain/Sends you out into the rain."

After committing himself to a psychiatric hospital for five weeks, Drake returned to the recording studio one final time to record four songs, none of which would be issued until after his death. To some, the songs' lyrics seem more a cry for help than anything else he'd yet recorded; most chilling was the simple imagery of "Black Eyed Dog," in which Drake seemed to moan, helpless and dispirited, "I'm growing old and I wanna go home/I'm growing old and I don't wanna know." According to writer Arthur Lubow, Drake told studio engineer John Wood at the time, "I can't think of words. I feel no emotion about anything. I don't want to laugh or cry. I'm numb—dead inside."

Drake died at his parents' house on November 25, 1974, of an overdose of the antidepressant Tryptizol; the coroner's office declared the death a suicide, though no note was left.

The four songs that Drake had recorded in 1974 emerged on *Fruit Tree,* a boxed set of Drake's complete works released in 1979. The same set was reissued and expanded in 1986, when Hannibal took those four tracks and added 10 other previously unreleased ones to make the posthumous *Time of No Reply,* included in the new box with the singer's three original albums. Predictably, a new generation of critics and consumers was enchanted by the singer's work. A tragic hero maybe, but a brilliant singer and songwriter most assuredly, Nick Drake will not be forgotten.

Bob Dylan

BOB DYLAN
••••••••••••••••••

The most profoundly influential singer-song-writer of the rock era, Bob Dylan (b. Robert Allen Zimmerman, May 24, 1941, Duluth, Minnesota) has released over 40 albums since his 1962 debut and remains today as vital an artist, and as imposing a figure, as he was in his '60s heyday. The changes he wrought in all of pop music have been the subject of countless essays, articles, books, films, and documentaries, as have the changes he himself has undergone, musical or otherwise. There are literally no artists in popular music who have not been affected by Dylan on one level or another: He was a major catalyst in the careers of the Beatles and Rolling Stones in the 1960s; his song "All Along the Watchtower" was the sole hit single by the Jimi Hendrix Experience; he was the figure to whom such distinguished singer-songwriters as Bruce Springsteen, John Prine, and Loudon Wainwright III were

compared upon their debuts; he was the subject of a song by David Bowie and the central inspiration of "new wave" up-and-comer Elvis Costello in the 1970s; his "Mr. Tambourine Man" sparked the Byrds' success and thus spawned the entire genre of folk-rock (and later, R.E.M.); and his many songs have been covered by literally hundreds of artists of nearly every musical genre. Dylan's memorable 30th Anniversary Concert, held at Madison Square Garden on October 16, 1992, gave just an inkling of the number of superstar artists who consider themselves indebted to the singer-songwriter: among those performing were Neil Young, George Harrison, Eric Clapton, Lou Reed, Johnny and June Carter Cash, Roger McGuinn, Tom Petty and the Heartbreakers, Willie Nelson, Stevie Wonder, John Mellencamp, the Band, the O'Jays, Chrissie Hynde, Sinead O'Connor, Kris Kristofferson, and even Eddie Vedder of Pearl Jam.

Dylan has said that he listened most to rock and roll artists such as Little Richard, Carl Perkins, and

Jerry Lee Lewis before hearing Leadbelly and turning toward folk music, then burgeoning in the late 1950s. He read and was moved by Woody Guthrie's *Bound for Glory* and began performing in coffeehouses near the University of Minnesota, where he enrolled briefly in 1959. By 1961, he had moved to New York, where he visited the hospitalized Guthrie in New Jersey and began performing in such Greenwich Village folk clubs as Gerde's Folk City. Finding early session work as a harmonica player, Dylan met legendary Columbia Records producer and talent scout John Hammond at a Carolyn Hester recording session; Hammond invited Dylan to make a demo tape. A rave review by *New York Times* critic Robert Shelton of a Dylan Gerde's appearance further drew attention to the singer, and by October, Hammond had signed Dylan to Columbia.

Dylan's earliest records were very much folk music in the tradition of Guthrie and Pete Seeger. Though his 1962 *Bob Dylan* bore only two original tunes ("Talkin' New York" and "Song to Woody," both talking blues), by the next year's *The Freewheelin' Bob Dylan*, the singer had produced enough original material to base an entire career upon. Among the best-known songs were "Blowin' in the Wind" and "Don't Think Twice, It's Alright" (both top 10 hits for Peter, Paul and Mary in 1963), "Masters of War," and the uniquely wordy "A Hard Rain's A-Gonna Fall." Written during the 1962 Cuban missile crisis, the latter track was "a desperate kind of song," Dylan said at the time. "Every line

in it is actually the start of a whole song. But when I wrote it, I thought I wouldn't have enough time alive to write all those songs so I put all I could into this one."

Though Dylan would not "go electric" until 1965, his earlier albums still found a wide audience: *Freewheelin'* reached number 22 on the charts, and 1964's *The Times They Are A-Changin'* peaked at number 20. And while 1965's *Another Side of Bob Dylan* only reached number 43, the songs it contained were among Dylan's best known due to cover versions by other artists: "My Back Pages" and "All I Really Want to Do" were both top 40 hits by the Byrds, the latter also a top 15 hit by Cher, and "It Ain't Me Babe" was a top 10 hit for the Turtles.

If any year was Bob Dylan's, it was 1965: he added an electric backing band on half of *Bringing It All Back Home,* was booed at the Newport Folk Festival for the same offense, and in June released what would be the most galvanizing single of his career—and perhaps of all time—"Like a Rolling Stone." An immediate hit that held the number two slot for two weeks (the Beatles' "Help" was Number One), it would inspire a generation and become as close to a theme song as the budding countercultural movement of the 1960s would ever have. The two albums that followed, *Highway 61 Revisited* and *Blonde on Blonde,* are considered the singer's all-time classics, and indeed, Dylan's impact was felt everywhere: in the songs of contemporaries the Beatles and Rolling Stones, in the surge of former folksingers who were picking up electric guitars, and in the entranced media, that typically saw Dylan as a mysterious, charismatic figure who might provide a clue into the workings of what seemed an increasingly disenfranchised youth culture.

In July 1966, a serious motorcycle accident kept Dylan in seclusion for many months, during which time he would eventually record material with a backing group soon to be known as the Band. Though that material was widely heard on many late-'60s bootlegs, its first legitimate release came in 1975, when Columbia issued it as *The Basement Tapes.* Had it been issued when it was recorded, it might've explained the jarring transition between *Blonde on Blonde* and 1968's *John Wesley Harding,* a stripped-down, starkly acoustic album of songs filled with noticeably religious imagery. While in retrospect it seems a logical move—particularly in light of the verbal-imagery overload of *Blonde on Blonde*'s final track, "Sad Eyed Lady of the Low-

---

TOP ALBUMS

HIGHWAY 61 REVISITED (Columbia, '65, *3*)
JOHN WESLEY HARDING (Columbia, '68, *2*)
NASHVILLE SKYLINE (Columbia, '69, *3*)
PLANET WAVES (with the Band, Asylum, '74, *1*)
BEFORE THE FLOOD (Columbia, '74, *3*)
BLOOD ON THE TRACKS (Columbia, '75, *1*)
DESIRE (Columbia, '76, *1*)
SLOW TRAIN COMING (Columbia, '79, *3*)

Additional Top 40 Albums: 23

TOP SONGS

LIKE A ROLLING STONE (Columbia, '65, *2*)
RAINY DAY WOMEN #12 & 35 (Columbia, '66, *2*)

Additional Top 40 Songs: 10

lands," which might have signaled an approaching stylistic blind alley—it surprised many fans at the time. In truth, it was just another instance of onetime folkie Bob Dylan reinventing himself. Upon the release of his wholly countrified *Nashville Skyline*, which featured the singer's voice sounding a near-octave lower than normal on such uncomplicated songs as "Country Pie," some wayward fans were suggesting Dylan's motorcycle accident was more serious than had been let on.

Dylan had many more surprises up his sleeve, and for the first time in his career he was beginning to lose faithful critics. His 1970 double LP *Self-Portrait*—on which rock's songwriting legend covered both Paul Simon and Gordon Lightfoot—confused many and was widely panned; when he seemed to return to form short months later with *New Morning*, initially giddy critics were soon moping about a perceived lack of depth in Dylan's new material. In the meantime, Dylan took on an acting role in Sam Peckinpah's *Pat Garrett and Billy the Kid* and recorded its soundtrack, which included "Knockin' on Heaven's Door," a song that has since grown to become a classic in Dylan's canon.

Though Dylan's two ensuing ventures with the Band—1974's *Planet Waves* and the live *Before the Flood*—won a fair amount of praise (and sales: *Planet Waves* was the singer's first Number One album), it was his magnificent *Blood on the Tracks* that stands as his crowning achievement of the 1970s. Seemingly a mixture of autobiography and romantic nostalgia, the album's "Tangled Up in Blue," "Simple Twist of Fate," and "Lily, Rosemary and the Jack of Hearts" were richly rewarding tracks, certainly the equal of much of his past work, and in many ways more lyrically mature. The set was the second Number One album in Dylan's career, and would only be bested commercially by its follow-up, *Desire*, which was Number One for five weeks and greatly pushed by the singer's much-publicized Rolling Thunder Revue tour of 1975–76.

Increasingly, Dylan's recordings began to be marked by cycles of seeming dead ends and critical rebirths. When the singer surprised many by announcing he was a born-again Christian in 1979, it was accompanied by the marvelously peculiar *Slow Train Coming*, which featured religious-themed tracks such as "Gotta Serve Somebody," "Man Gave Names to All the Animals," and "When He Returns"; the oddest facet of Dylan's conversion, as displayed in *Slow Train*'s songs, was his apparent belief in a merciless and venegeful God. Follow-up albums *Saved* (1980) and *Shot of Love* (1981) lacked the superb songs of *Slow Train*, but by 1983's *Infidels*, Dylan was writing some of his sharpest songs in ages. Their political orientation bothered some critics who considered Dylan's religious conversion to have gone hand in hand with a new political conservatism; indeed, with their references to Israel and greedy labor union leaders, many songs such as "Neighborhood Bully" and "Union Sundown" were scathingly attacked by former staunch fans.

Since then, there have been many Bob Dylans on display for both critics and fans to choose from:

The Dylan of the Past, whose glorious works have been resurrected twice now in much-lauded CD boxed-set format: *Biograph* (1985) and *The Bootleg Series—Volumes 1–3 (Rare and Unreleased) 1961–1991* (1991)

The Dylan of the Never-Ending Tour, who has continued to document his nonstop live performance activities with *Real Live* (1985) and *Dylan and the Dead* (1989)

The Dylan of Traveling Wilburys Fame, who recorded two hit albums between 1988 and 1990 with George Harrison, Roy Orbison, Jeff Lynne, and Tom Petty

The Dylan of Today, who continues to roll out new albums with a celebrity-studded cast of musicians and producers, including *Knocked Out Loaded* (with Tom Petty and the Heartbreakers, 1986), *Down in the Groove* (with Eric Clapton, Mark Knopfler, Ron Wood, and members of the Grateful Dead, Clash, and Sex Pistols, 1988), *Oh Mercy* (produced by Daniel Lanois, 1989), and *Under the Red Sky* (with David Crosby, George Harrison, Bruce Hornsby, Elton John, Jimmy and Stevie Ray Vaughan, and Slash of Guns N' Roses, 1990)

The Dylan as He'd Like to Be Remembered, in which the former fledgling folksinger who started out with a guitar, harmonica, and other people's songs does it all over again with *Good as I Been to You* (1992) and *World Gone Wrong* (1993)

Less than a year after his massive 30th Anniversary Concert gathered together some of the finest musicians in the world to pay him tribute, Bob Dylan was gearing up for the road yet again, this time touring with old friend Carlos Santana. "It's all about a livelihood," he told an Associated Press writer at the time. "It's all about going out and playing. That's what every musician who has crossed my path strives for."

JONATHAN EDWARDS

When discussion turns to the so-called singer-songwriter era of the early 1970s, James Taylor and Carole King are—logically, in light of their respective sales—the names brought up most often. But it wouldn't be a full-fledged era unless there was a complete cast of first-string, second-string, and bargain-basement players involved. Place Jonathan Edwards (b. July 28, 1946, Minnesota) at the top of that second string. He had one hit record, and in over 20 years and more than a half-dozen albums, he never managed a respectable follow-up to match that success.

Like most early '70s singer-songwriters, Edwards got his start in rock and roll. His first major label appearance was with Boston-based band Sugar Creek, a quartet whose 1968 Metromedia album *Please Tell a Friend* was a pleasant collection of country-tinged rock songs. Eventually tiring of the quartet, Edwards picked up an acoustic guitar and went solo, played most of New England, and got signed to the fledgling Capricorn label, home of the Allman Brothers and other southern-fried sounds. By 1971, his eponymous solo album had emerged, bearing his big hit, "Sunshine," a gold top five single, and a collection of similar-sounding (but not as catchy) tracks. Edwards had written or co-written all but two (which were the work of his former Sugar Creek bandmate Malcolm McKinney), and each bore his trademark sound: a shuffling rhythm guitar, a hint of country twanging, and Edwards' distinctive tenor, sounding not quite like James Taylor, but almost. With its memorable passage "He can't even run his own life/I'll be damned if he'll run mine," the lyrics of "Sunshine" fit the Vietnam War time frame perfectly; this writer recalls seeing a nameless hard rock trio energetically playing the song, shamelessly bor-

Jonathan Edwards

rowing from the style of Robin Trower, and it seemed an even more effective version than Edwards' original.

When Capricorn's distribution deal then shifted from Atlantic Records to Warner Bros., Edwards opted to stay with Atlantic, via Atco. "That was a mistake," he later recalled, "because I was the only thing like me at the label." Sure enough, Edwards' next three albums—1972's *Honky-Tonk Stardust Cowboy,* 1973's *Have a Good Time for Me,* and 1974's live set *Lucky Day*—were consecutively dead on arrival, and the singer wanted out. He moved to Nova Scotia.

Edwards returned to the States a few years later with his two best albums, *Rockin' Chair* and *Sailboat,* issued by Reprise in 1976 and 1977 respectively. What made them Edwards' best, however,

---

TOP ALBUMS

JONATHAN EDWARDS (Capricorn, '71)
HONKY-TONK STARDUST COWBOY (Atco, '72)

TOP SONG

SUNSHINE (Capricorn, '71, *4)*

---

had less to do with his songs than Brian Ahern's production, along with the stellar group of musicians (James Burton, Albert Lee, and Glen D. Hardin among them) rounded up for the sessions. Edwards' originals actually seemed to be drying up: half or more of each album featured material by other writers, including Jesse Winchester, Rodney Crowell, Hoyt Axton, and the Louvin Brothers. When both discs proved commercial flops, Edwards left Reprise and thereafter kept his career in low gear. He made an album that was never released, then collaborated with the Seldom Scene for a bluegrass set released in 1984.

Upon later taking the lead role in the road-show version of the musical *Pumpboys and Dinettes,* Edwards met up with old friend Wendy Waldman in Nashville. Together, they produced Edwards' most recent album, *The Natural Thing,* issued quietly by Curb/MCA in 1989. Edwards' only original tune was co-written with Gary Nicholson and titled—ironically—"It's Easy to Write a Love Song." Were that true—and were it easy to write a good love song—then we'd probably have heard much more from Jonathan Edwards.

MELISSA ETHERIDGE

For much of pop history, the image of a woman walking onstage carrying a 12-string guitar has traditionally suggested that a set of sensitive ballads would soon be sweetly unleashed upon a fawning, equally sensitive audience. But when Melissa Etheridge (b. circa 1960, Leavenworth, Kansas) was herself unleashed via her Island Records debut of 1988, that stereotype was swiftly shattered. Etheridge found enormous success belting out her material in a passionate, near-religious fervor as captivating as it was unique. And her fervor was contagious: one after another, her albums have lodged themselves in the upper reaches of the charts and gone gold.

Etheridge's climb to success began in Kansas, where she started writing songs on the guitar at the age of 10 and was playing in local bands by her teens. At 18, she enrolled at the Berklee College of Music in Boston and regularly played local coffeehouses, honing her style until, like so many, she headed to L.A. to seek her musical fortune. But what came next didn't really follow the standard procedure: playing at various clubs in the area—some of them extremely off the beaten path—she was spotted at a Long Beach bar by no less than Island Records founder Chris Blackwell, who was so taken with her he signed her instantly.

Etheridge contributed four songs to the DEG film *Weeds* before settling down to record her debut set. Halfway through the making of the album, it was decided overproduction was burying the natural live intensity Etheridge projected; the solution, unusually, was to go back and rerecord everything live in the studio as a three-piece band (with select overdubs added later). The strategy worked, and Etheridge was at once perceived as something unique and genuine by her audience. Bolstered by uniformly rave reviews greeting her numerous live performances, *Melissa Etheridge,* her 1988 debut, stayed on the charts for 65 weeks and climbed to number 22.

When Etheridge's follow-up arrived in late 1989, some trendwatchers pointed to the success of Bonnie Raitt's *Nick of Time* and wondered aloud if a resurgence of "female rockers" was taking place. To some extent it was: *Brave and Crazy* quickly duplicated its predecessor's success, peaking again at number 22 and staying on the chart for more than a year. Additionally, Etheridge copped three Grammy nominations for the set and won Canada's prestigious Juno Award as Best International Entertainer of the Year.

"Ain't It Heavy," from Etheridge's third album, *Never Enough,* brought the singer her first Grammy (in the Best Female Rock Performance category) and further helped expand her fan base, still growing through her extensive live performances. Etheridge became a regular for many political causes, including the 1992 presidential campaign, and in 1993 was one of many performers at the Clinton inauguration ceremonies. Perhaps more notably, she was extensively involved with various women's causes and benefits and created something of a stir by publicly acknowledging she was a lesbian. Thought to be further acknowledgment was the title of

TOP ALBUMS

MELISSA ETHERIDGE (Island, '88, 22)
BRAVE AND CRAZY (Island, '89, 22)
NEVER ENOUGH (Island, '92, 21)
YES I AM (Island, '93, 16)

TOP SONGS

SIMILAR FEATURES (Island, '88)
NO SOUVENIRS (Island, '89)

her 1993 album *Yes I Am.* The robust set contained several songs with themes seemingly aimed at women, however ambiguously, including "I Will Never Be the Same" (from the film *Welcome Home Roxy Carmichael*), "Silent Legacy," and "All American Girl."

By now it's clear Etheridge has successfully established herself as an overall performing artist, rather than as a singer of hit singles. In fact, she has yet to actually have one; her only charting singles, "Similar Features" and "No Souvenirs," barely squeaked into the bottom reaches of the Hot 100. Still, that hasn't been a factor in the sales of her albums, which boom along regardless. One strong hit single, say many in the industry, and her career is likely to skyrocket.

DONALD FAGEN

As one half of the creative core of Steely Dan, Donald Fagen (b. Jan. 10, 1948, Passaic, New Jersey) established a reputation in the 1970s as a musical perfectionist that, if anything, has only increased with time. Known for wanting endless retake-upon-retake during his former band's recording sessions, Fagen took over 10 years to follow up his 1982 debut solo album *The Nightfly* with 1993's *Kamakiriad.* And while it's doubtful he took a decade to actually record that sturdy follow-up, one suspects it wouldn't be beyond him.

Fagen met his longtime musical partner Walter Becker while attending Bard College in the mid-1960s; the pair instantly bonded, played together in several college bands, and decided to seek their fortune as singer-songwriters. Among their earliest gigs was a late-'60s stint performing with Jay and the Americans (for whose 1970 album *Capture the Moment* the pair wrote string and horn arrangements). During the same period, many of the demos they recorded between 1968 and 1970 were used as the basis for an unproduced, *Hair*-influenced play by writer Richard Lifschutz called *Ego—The Making of a Musical.* The same demos, which included such songs as "The

Android Warehouse," "Brain Tap Shuffle," and "Yellow Peril," began surfacing on albums in the early 1980s under such titles as *Becker & Fagen: The Early Years, Sun Mountain,* and *Berry Town,* undoubtedly much to the pair's chagrin. Similarly, an early soundtrack they recorded to Peter Locke's obscure film *You Gotta Walk It Like You Talk It (Or You'll Lose That Beat),* originally issued on Spark Records in 1971, was rereleased by Visa Records in 1978 when the Original Soundtrack—as Becker, Fagen, and guitarist Denny Dias were then called—became better known as Steely Dan.

An early '70s meeting with future ABC-Dunhill producer Gary Katz—then at Avco-Embassy Records working with singer Eric Mercury—eventually landed both Becker and Fagen jobs in Los Angeles as staff writers for ABC-Dunhill. Having already placed their "I Mean to Shine" on Barbra Streisand's 1971 album *Barbra Joan Streisand,* the move seemed entirely plausible, but the duo's songs appeared on scattered, relatively obscure albums by John Kay ("Giles of the River"), Thomas Jefferson Kaye ("American Lovers" and "Jones"), Navasota ("Canyon Ladies"), and Christopher Kearney ("Runnin' Child"), and little came of them. Eventually, at the prodding of Gary Katz, a band was formed around the pair in 1972. Taking their name from William Burroughs' novel *Naked Lunch,* the group became Steely Dan, and their music, very swiftly, became famous.

By 1981, every one of Steely Dan's eight albums had entered the top 40 and gone gold or platinum, pushed by a string of 10 top 40 hits that began with "Do It Again" and ended with "Time Out of Mind." In the interim, the group had changed markedly. Beginning as a six-piece on 1972's *Can't Buy a Thrill,* they gradually lost members—each of whom was replaced on records by a number of highly skilled session players—until by 1975's *Katy Lied,* live concerts were a memory and "Steely Dan" became Becker, Fagen, and the finest studio sessions players money could buy. And their reputation as studio perfectionists was becoming legend. "They are the most demanding group of people in the industry that I've

TOP ALBUMS

THE NIGHTFLY (Warner Bros., '82, *11*)
LIVE AT THE BEACON (with the New York Rock and Soul Revue, Giant, '91)
KAMAKIRIAD (Reprise, '93, *10*)

TOP SONGS

I.G.Y. (WHAT A BEAUTIFUL WORLD) (Warner Bros., '82, *26*)
NEW FRONTIER (Warner Bros., '82)
TOMORROW'S GIRLS (Reprise, '93)
SNOWBOUND (Reprise, '93)

worked for," guitarist Larry Carlton told the *New York Times* in 1977. "Nothing goes with a flutter in it. If three of the guys are cutting the part great and one part doesn't feel right, they'll call in a whole new band and redo the whole thing."

"Donald's and Walter's music was evolving," producer Gary Katz recalled in 1984. "And it was opening into more sophisticated [territory] and sort of an expansion of their own style. And they wanted the freedom to be able to utilize as many-styled players as fit the different tunes that were starting to be written." Because band members like guitarist Jeff Baxter and backing singer Michael McDonald had other opportunities elsewhere, "it just naturally happened," said Katz. "There was no big blow-up or argument."

Becker and Fagen finally parted ways in 1981. "I had been thinking of doing an album that would basically be autobiographical for a long time," Fagen told writer Bruce Pilato in 1983. "But I didn't know how I was going to go about doing it. At the same time, Walter and I decided we needed a break from each other. After being together for 14 years, we decided we wanted to do something different, so I guess the circumstances were right." Received with open arms by Steely Dan fans, *The Nightfly* quickly went gold and reached number 11 on the charts; its first single, "I.G.Y. (What a Beautiful World)," likewise was a top 30 hit. Aside from its version of Leiber and Stoller's "Ruby Baby"—the first cover version Fagen had ever sung—the album was as autobiographical as the singer had intended: "The songs on this album," Fagen noted on the liner, "represent certain fantasies that might have been entertained by a young man growing up in the remote suburbs of a northeastern city during the late '50s and early '60s, i.e., one of my general height, weight and build." Despite the absence of Becker, many fans noted that *The Nightfly* sounded very much like a brand new Steely Dan album.

Fagen laid low—extremely low—for most of the 1980s, emerging only toward the end of the decade as catalyst of the New York Rock and Soul Revue. The informal group, which mostly played '50s and '60s rock and soul covers, provided the context for Fagen's first live performances since Steely Dan's final live concert in 1974. An album documenting the show—featuring guest stars Michael McDonald, Phoebe Snow, Boz Scaggs, and Charles Brown, among others—was released by Giant Records in 1991.

1993 was a banner year for Steely Dan fans on two levels: Fagen finally released *The Nightfly*'s follow-up *Kamakiriad*—which entered the charts at number 10 and quickly went gold—and had reunited with Becker, who was the album's producer. Another Fagen album with a theme, *Kamakiriad* was set sometime in the future and featured such songs as "Trans-Island Skyway" and "Tomorrow's Girls," all of which again sounded like prime Steely Dan. But the biggest surprise of all was the summer's accompanying Steely Dan tour—one of the year's hottest concert tickets, and one of the most critically lauded reunion tours in rock history. Though it had been a decade since the singer's last record, and nearly two since Steely Dan had last played live, the reception was ample proof that music fans could not be more eager to hear Donald Fagen—as the song goes—do it again.

MARIANNE FAITHFULL

Few artists have led as interesting or eventful a life as Marianne Faithfull (b. Dec. 29, 1946, London); in some ways, perhaps, few would want to. But in her transition from the angelic-voiced teenager who sang "As Tears Go By"—the 1965 hit penned for her by the Rolling Stones—to the startlingly sophisticated, raspy-throated chanteuse she has since become lies one of the most fascinating and life-affirming stories in popular music.

Discovered at a London party in 1964 by Rolling Stones manager Andrew Loog Oldham, Faithfull was a 17-year-old convent school student and the daughter of a London University professor and an Austrian baroness. Oldham introduced her to Stones Mick Jagger and Keith Richard, who then wrote "Tears" for her; the song became an international hit, reaching the top 30 in 1965, and established her singing career. Faithfull's beauty in some ways handicapped her, however; many viewed her at the time as a gorgeous hanger-on whose success was handed to her courtesy of Mick Jagger, who soon became her boyfriend. Still, she produced three very credible albums for London Records between 1965 and 1966, the first of which (*Marianne Faithfull*) nearly entered the top 10, and proved an able interpreter of non-Stones material via three additional top 40 hits

("Come and Stay with Me," "This Little Bird," and "Summer Nights") in 1965.

Faithfull stopped making records after 1966's *Faithfull Forever,* though one final British single emerged in 1968: "Something Better," which bore on its B side the Jagger-Richards-Faithfull composition "Sister Morphine." Instead, she made movies…and headlines. Her film roles began with 1968's *I'll Never Forget What's 'is Name* and *Girl on a Motorcycle* (released in America as *Naked Under Leather*); she also appeared in London stage productions of *Hamlet* and *Early Morning.* But much of that activity was overshadowed by the publicity she received after moving in with Jagger in 1967: she was involved in that year's much-publicized Stones drug bust; she accompanied Jagger to India to visit Maharishi Mahesh Yogi; she was busted once more; she became addicted to heroin; and, eventually, she attempted suicide while in Australia with Jagger (then starring in the film *Ned Kelly*), after which she and the Stone split up.

At seeming rock bottom, Faithfull gradually rebuilt her career. In 1974 she appeared as part of David Bowie's televised *1980 Floor Show,* later shown in the States as a special segment of NBC's "Midnight Special"; the next year, she signed a new recording deal with the British NEMS label, and by 1977 released *Dreaming My Dreams,* her first album in 10 years. That effort served as the groundwork for a 1979 deal with Island Records, for whom the singer continues to record today.

Marianne Faithfull truly began anew with 1979's *Broken English.* A stunning, powerful work bearing extremely vivid lyrics—Island in fact slapped a warning sticker on it—the album presented the now-husky-voiced Faithfull singing about politics and sexuality in a manner considerably more sophisticated than her approach of a decade earlier. Highlights included the title track—inspired by the Berlin Wall—and the graphically sexual "Why'd Ya Do It," which provoked much critical comment. Faithfull, whose songwriting in the past had been minimal, was now much more involved in the creation of her work, particularly her lyrics, and continued to be on the albums that followed, including *Dangerous*

TOP ALBUMS
....
BROKEN ENGLISH (Island, 1979)
DANGEROUS ACQUAINTANCES (Island, '81)
A CHILD'S ADVENTURE (Island, '83)
BLAZING AWAY (Island, '90)

TOP SONGS
....
AS TEARS GO BY (London, '64, 22)
COME AND STAY WITH ME (London, '65, 26)
THIS LITTLE BIRD (London, '65, 32)
SUMMER NIGHTS (London, '65, 24)
WHY'D YA DO IT? (Island, 1979)

Acquaintances (1981) and *A Child's Adventure* (1983).

A meeting with producer Hal Willner resulted in Faithfull singing "Ballad of a Soldier's Wife" on his 1985 Kurt Weill tribute album, *Lost in the Stars.* Following her appearance on the soundtrack to 1986's *Trouble in Mind,* Willner then produced Faithfull's superb *Strange Weather,* a collection of standards including "Boulevard of Broken Dreams," "Penthouse Serenade," "Yesterdays," and Faithfull's own past hit "As Tears Go By." The 1987 album sparked Faithfull's first live performances in years, which drew raves and several comparisons to Lotte Lenya and Marlene Dietrich. Appropriately, Faithfull's follow-up was the live *Blazing Away,* which boasted versions of the many important songs in her life—from "Tears" and "Sister Morphine" to "Broken English" and "Why'd Ya Do It"—and established her as a world-class performer. Faithfull then briefly taught lyric-writing seminars at a Colorado arts college; she has since moved to Ireland with her husband, American playwright Giorgio Dellaterza. Still an enigmatic figure, Marianne Faithfull now has a past of which she can be very proud indeed.

DAN FOGELBERG

While his career has never been especially flashy, nor his name the first to arise when anyone cites the most influential singer-songwriters, Dan Fogelberg (b. Aug. 13, 1951, Peoria, Illinois) has quietly produced one of the more substantial bodies of work of any practicing singer-songwriter. Not to mention bestselling: between 1975 and 1984, eight consecutive Fogelberg albums went platinum or gold.

Since his 1972 debut album, *Home Free,* Fogelberg has managed to carve himself a stylistic niche somewhere between the Crosby, Stills and Nash school of folk-rock harmony, the Harry Chapin–Billy Joel school of blustery lyric realism, and the Tim Hardin school of overwhelming romantic sensitivity. Which may make him nothing more than the sum of someone else's parts, true—but still, it's been a unique enough combination to keep an audience fascinated for over two decades.

A former student of art at the University of Illinois, where he'd been playing local coffeehouses, Fogelberg quit school in 1971 to move to Los Angeles. He then signed a deal with Columbia that put him in a Nashville studio with country producer Norbert Putnam. *Home Free,* the result, was Fogelberg's first and last album for Columbia. Eighteen months later—after working with artists like Randy Newman, Roger McGuinn, Eric Anderson, Joe Walsh, and Jackson Browne—he had a new album out on Epic, 1974's *Souvenirs,* and a serious career on his hands. "Part of the Plan," Fogelberg's memorable first hit, featured a catchy hook, guitar playing by producer Joe Walsh, and backing vocals by Graham Nash; the combination was enough to send *Souvenirs* into the top 30—where every album he'd put out for the next 10 years would also land.

Fogelberg's next hit, "The Power of Gold," was the product of an interesting collaboration between the singer and flute player Tim Weisberg—"an experiment that worked," as he'd later call 1978's *Twin Sons of Different Mothers.* The mostly instrumental album featured "Gold" and an extraordinary version of the Hollies' "Tell Me to My Face" (a top 40 hit for singer Keith in 1967) that revealed an aspect of Fogelberg's rock roots that hasn't been on display since.

Dan Fogelberg

TOP ALBUMS

NETHER LANDS (Full Moon, '77, *13*)
TWIN SONS OF DIFFERENT MOTHERS
  (with Tim Weisberg, Full Moon, '78, *8*)
PHOENIX (Full Moon, '79, *3*)
THE INNOCENT AGE (Full Moon, '81, *6*)
WINDOWS AND WALLS (Full Moon, '84, *15*)

Additional Top 40 Albums: 4

TOP SONGS

LONGER (Full Moon, '80, *2*)
SAME OLD LANG SYNE (Full Moon, '80, *9*)
HARD TO SAY (Full Moon, '81, *7*)
LEADER OF THE BAND (Full Moon, '81, *9*)
THE LANGUAGE OF LOVE (Full Moon, '84, *13*)

Additional Top 40 Songs: 6

From the early 1980s onward, Fogelberg began a stretch of hits that has, for better or worse, defined his sound for most people: slow, introspective lyrics laden—some have said overly laden—with sensitivity. Three top 10 hits in a row are what did it: "Same Old Lang Syne," an autobiographical account of the singer meeting an old girlfriend; "Hard to Say," about a lost love; and "Leader of the Band," an ode the singer wrote about his former bandleader father. All three tracks came from Fogelberg's ambitious double album of 1981, *The Innocent Age.* Supposedly inspired by the singer's turning 30, the album reportedly remains Fogelberg's favorite. In retrospect, it could have served as the central inspiration for the 1980s television hit "thirtysomething."

Since then, Fogelberg has purposely shifted his musical approach several times, from bluegrass and country explorations on 1985's *High Country Snows* to noticeably rocking on 1987's *Exiles.* The latter album was every bit as lyrically revealing as was *The Innocent Age;* Fogelberg said at the time its subject matter was "the anatomy of the breakup of a marriage," and the singer was indeed going through a divorce at the time. Regardless, the album was the first he'd made that didn't crack the top 40 since *Home Free,* and he hasn't been back there since. Still, no one—least of all Fogelberg—can deny that selling over 15 million albums in the course of 20 years remains one very impressive run.

JOHN FOGERTY

As leader of the most popular rock singles band of the late 1960s, John Fogerty (b. May 28, 1945, Berkeley, California) took Creedence Clearwater Revival to the top 10 nine times between 1969 and 1971, on each occasion providing a song that has worked its way into American culture like no other artist since Elvis Presley. While his legendary group was sometimes scoffed at for their hit singles—mostly by hipsters who then deemed the very idea unfashionable—20 years later, "Proud Mary" and "Bad Moon Rising" are remembered with deep affection while most 20-minute-long, acid-rock "jams" of the era have been long forgotten. Though many predicted a long and prosperous career of hitmaking for Fogerty upon Creedence's split in 1972, his withdrawal from the scene has so far resulted in a meager four albums in over 20 years—and proven to be one of pop's larger mysteries and disappointments.

The roots of Creedence went back as far as 1959, when Fogerty, his older brother Tom, and high school classmates Doug Clifford and Stu Cook first recorded together in Oakland as the Blue Velvets. The young quartet released three singles on the small Orchestra label starting in 1961, and by 1963 had pacted with San Francisco's Fantasy Records; recording under the name the Golliwogs (the label's Beatle-conscious idea), the band released a total of seven singles, all of which would be collected and reissued in 1975, three years after CCR disbanded. In 1967, Fantasy changed hands and new owner Saul Zaentz insisted the Golliwogs change their name; thus, in November of that year, the single "Porterville" became the first release by the newly dubbed Creedence Clearwater Revival.

If one term can be said to encompass all that CCR

played, it would be "swamp rock." Though situated far from Louisiana, Fogerty and company concocted a mixture of bluesy R&B and potent, swirling guitar textures that combined with their "Revival" tag and evoked images of the hot, steamy Deep South. Not that the band didn't help foster the image: After breaking through with a memorable reworking of "Suzie Q." by Louisiana-born Dale Hawkins, Creedence scored a top 10 hit with their second album, *Bayou Country.* The latter, which featured "Proud Mary" and the hypnotic "Born on the Bayou," became the first of five top 10 albums CCR would produce in, incredibly, less than two years. Driven by a nonstop string of top 10 hit singles—including "Bad Moon Rising," "Green River," "Down on the Corner," "Travelin' Band," "Up Around the Bend," "Lookin' Out My Back Door," "Have You Ever Seen the Rain," and "Sweet Hitch-Hiker"—Creedence ruled the charts like no other American band.

John Fogerty's first post-Creedence solo album was a surprise in more ways than one. Though he had played all the instruments, 1973's *The Blue Ridge Rangers* seemed the work of a brand new band—and on it, Fogerty's name was nowhere to be found. Loaded with country covers such as Hank Williams' "Jambalaya," which became Fogerty's first post-Creedence top 20 hit, the album seemed a purposeful stepping back from the limelight for the songwriter. His official "return" came two years later, with a self-titled debut on Asylum Records. Though the record scored a hit with "Rockin' All Over the World" (later covered in concert by Bruce

---

TOP ALBUMS

THE BLUE RIDGE RANGERS (Fantasy, '73)
JOHN FOGERTY (Asylum, '75)
CENTERFIELD (Warner Bros., '85, *1*)
EYE OF THE ZOMBIE (Warner Bros., '86, *26*)

TOP SONGS

JAMBALAYA (as Blue Ridge Rangers, Fantasy, '73, *16*)
HEARTS OF STONE (as Blue Ridge Rangers, Fantasy, '73, *37*)
ROCKIN' ALL OVER THE WORLD (Asylum, '75, *27*)
THE OLD MAN DOWN THE ROAD (Warner Bros., '85, *10*)
ROCK AND ROLL GIRLS (Warner Bros., '85, *20*)

Springsteen) and included his popular "Almost Saturday Night," it was viewed by many as a disappointment; it peaked at number 78 and fell off the charts in only seven weeks. Fogerty's next record would come a full 10 years later.

"You have to understand my state of mind back then," he explained in 1985. "I recorded an album back in 1975 because I felt I owed it to the public. When it was done it just didn't ring my bell. I don't know what was wrong, but there was something missing, and that was confirmed by the people I trusted in the business. So (Elektra Chairman) Joe Smith told me to take my time, that I didn't have to make a record. When that happened it sort of freed me to be John Fogerty again, instead of a musician who has to do his job despite the fact that his heart isn't in it."

Fogerty spent much of the time in the interim struggling over control of his music with Fantasy Records head Zaentz—and dealing with his own creative problems. As he told his former boss Smith in the exec's 1988 book *Off the Record:* "I was slowly drying up. I kept trying, and it kept coming out lousy. Suddenly, I began to feel like I could no more

make a hit record than the guy out in the street running a jackhammer. It went away, I knew it was gone, and I also knew I would get it back if I worked hard at it."

Even when Fogerty staged his long-awaited return with 1985's Number One *Centerfield,* there were problems. Its final track "Zanz Can't Danz" so aroused the wrath of Fantasy's Zaentz, the song's poorly disguised subject—of whom Fogerty sang "Zanz can't dance/But he'll steal your money/Watch him or he'll rob you blind"— legal pressure forced Fogerty to change the song to "Vanz Kant Danz" on second pressings of the album. Additionally, Zaentz filed a lawsuit against Fogerty claiming his 1985 top 10 hit "Old Man Down the Road" had "plagiarized" the earlier Creedence music to which Fantasy owned the rights. Fogerty eventually prevailed.

After the double platinum success of *Centerfield,* it looked likely that the singer was back on track, and indeed *Eye of the Zombie* followed by the next year. But the album received strangely muted reviews, and its sole charting single, the title track, peaked at number 81. Whatever the reason, the album was again perceived as a disappointment; it peaked at number 26, and then slowly slid off the charts, barely going gold. It remains the last John Fogerty album to date.

Fogerty's bitterness about his past with Creedence surfaced unpleasantly in 1993, when the band was inducted into the Rock 'n' Roll Hall of Fame. At the same gathering where Cream had reunited and performed for the first time in years, Fogerty stood onstage with former bandmates Clifford and Cook to receive the band's award—but later refused to allow the pair to perform onstage with him, reportedly for their dealings with Fantasy's Zaentz. On a night intended to honor Creedence Clearwater Revival's massive contribution to rock and roll, the bad moon had risen for John Fogerty once again.

through two years of junior college. He then went solo, and, after losing his hometown job as a truck driver, moved to New York City in 1976. Staying at a local YMCA, Forbert scouted out the music scene and soon found gigs aplenty, the mythical punk club CBGB becoming a regular venue for him. A recording deal with the CBS-distributed Nemperor label followed, then *Alive on Arrival*—and there was Forbert, 23, maybe even encouraging those Dylan comparisons a little bit with songs like "Steve Forbert's Midsummer Night's Toast," which didn't sound a lick like "Bob Dylan's 115th Dream," honest.

Forbert's debut drew uniformly good reviews; his artfully plainspoken songs, delivered with an addictively intimate rasp quite like Rod Stewart's, hit

STEVE FORBERT

Steve Forbert

Steve Forbert (b. 1955) may have been the last singer-songwriter, guitarist, and harmonica player to be seriously pegged by some poor fool (a journalist? a person at his label?) as "the new Dylan" before that career-killing appellation was wisely retired forever. But given the earnest look in Forbert's eyes on the cover of his 1978 debut *Alive on Arrival,* his standard folkie uniform (a tattered denim jacket and harmonica dutifully in holder, strummed Gibson in hand), and his just-from-the-sticks life story, of which much was made, you can't blame anyone for making the easy comparison.

Part of a large family, Forbert grew up in Meridian, Mississippi, and played in rock bands with school friends

TOP ALBUMS

ALIVE ON ARRIVAL (Nemperor, '79)
JACKRABBIT SLIM (Nemperor, '79, *20*)
LITTLE STEVIE ORBIT (Nemperor, '80)
STREETS OF THIS TOWN (Geffen, '88)

TOP SONGS

YOU CANNOT WIN IF YOU DO NOT
 PLAY (Nemperor, '79)
ROMEO'S TUNE (Nemperor, '80, *11*)
GET WELL SOON (Nemperor, '80)

home for aging folkies and young punksters (the CBGB affiliation helped) alike. Instrumentally, *Arrival* was comparatively unadorned—a standard guitar–keyboard–rhythm section combo accompanied him—letting Forbert's wry lyrics stand front and center. When distinguished producer John Simon was brought in for 1979's *Jackrabbit Slim,* instrumentation was beefed up (there were horns and accordians) and so were Forbert's sales: thanks to "Romeo's Tune," a track he dedicated to the late Supreme Florence Ballard, he scored a number 11 hit single, and *Jackrabbit* zoomed to number 20 on the Top Pop Albums chart.

Forbert once called his music "folk, country, rockabilly, soul, pop, gospel, rock 'n' roll, blues music"—which was cute, but wrong. In reality, he started out a folkish stripped-down rocker and simply got less folkish and more rocking as his career progressed. To this day, his 1980 set *Little Stevie Orbit* may be the best representation of everything he does well: tracks like "Get Well Soon" combined *Blonde on Blonde*–style lyrics with the sound of Bruce Springsteen's E Street Band; other highlights like "Cellophane City" and the intimate "A Visitor" still sound fresh and revealing a decade later.

When *Orbit* and 1982's *Steve Forbert* failed to duplicate *Jackrabbit Slim*'s success, no one expected Forbert's career to seriously decline—but that's exactly what happened. The singer asked to be released from his Nemperor deal and sign directly with Columbia; an album he made with Pat Benatar's guitarist husband Neil Girardo never materialized (though a track from it surfaced on a compilation Epic slipped out in 1993); and Forbert rode out most of the decade without any product whatsoever. He moved to Nashville in 1985 and signed a deal with management firm Praxis International, which handled Jason and the Scorchers and the Georgia Satellites, among others. Label or no, he gigged all over.

Eventually, Forbert's recording career was resuscitated by two very different people: E Street Band bassist Garry Tallent, who produced several sessions for Forbert after seeing him play with the Crickets at New York's Lone Star Cafe; and Geffen Records' Tom Zutaut, the same A&R executive who signed Motley Crue and Guns N' Roses to their respective labels. Tallent produced Forbert's first Geffen album, 1988's *Streets of This Town;* Pete Anderson, producer of Michelle Shocked and Dwight Yoakum, oversaw

1991's *The American in Me.* Sure enough, Forbert's newer work still shows the maturity and lyrical vision that made him a standout 15 years earlier…but some things do change with time. Now he's making lyrical references to Guns N' Roses. Moral: never underestimate the influence of a powerful A&R man, especially when he's yours.

PETER FRAMPTON

Peter Frampton (b. Apr. 22, 1950, Kent, England) has seen the up and down sides of success more often than most performers. A singer-songwriter who also happens to be an exceptionally skilled lead guitarist, Frampton achieved the success of a lifetime with his 1976 live album *Frampton Comes Alive!;* then through a series of tactical marketing blunders—not to mention so-so albums—he watched it all go down the drain.

Frampton's entry into the rock marketplace came early via British pop group the Herd, with whom he played guitar, sang, and toured the U.K. and Europe between 1966 and 1967. Declared "the Face of '68" by respected U.K. journalist Penny Valentine, pop idol Frampton purposely went the non-teenybopper route when that band split, forming Humble Pie with Steve Marriott (the former Small Faces singer whose career ironically paralleled Frampton's). That band played an interesting blend of sophisticated hard rock and acoustic pop that simply couldn't last: where Marriott favored the harder, boogie-oriented material, Frampton—certainly capable of letting stun-guitar riffs fly when he chose to—was in contrast an acoustic balladeer, generally favoring subtle, jazzy chord changes (jazz legend Django Reinhardt was a favorite of his). In one sense, Frampton departed from Humble Pie at exactly the wrong moment, one month before 1971's breakthrough live album (featuring Frampton) *Performance—Rockin' the Fillmore* took the band to the next level of international success. But in another sense, it was precisely the right time to leave, if he didn't want to be bogged down in boogie. And he didn't.

Most of the songs on Frampton's 1972 solo debut, *Wind of Change,* had in fact been demoed and rejected by his bandmates when the guitarist was still in Humble Pie. It was their loss. The album catches Frampton at his creative peak, and features several of his best songs, including "The Lodger,"

"All I Want to Be (Is By Your Side)," "Fig Tree Bay," and the title track—which, with odd lyrics like "God knows I weren't meant to do no cooking," clearly indicated where Frampton's weak spot might be.

Wind of Change had featured friends and session musicians like Ringo Starr and Billy Preston; for the next album, Frampton wanted to put together an actual band. He did, calling it Camel (temporarily), and together, for countless months, they slogged it out across America. Releasing one solid album after another—*Frampton's Camel, Somethin's Happening,* and *Frampton*—between 1973 and 1975, Frampton gradually cultivated an enthusiastic, snowballing concert audience.

One reason *Frampton Comes Alive!* was *Billboard*'s Number One album of 1976 was simply because of what it delivered: two LPs' worth of solid, catchy material—material that most of mid-America had never heard—performed live by a notably charismatic and, er, cute performer.

Did "cute" hurt? Maybe not when Frampton was playing "Walk on Gilded Splinters" with Humble Pie, but absolutely in 1977, when *Alive!*'s follow-up *I'm In You* arrived, featuring Frampton languidly posing in true teen idol fashion on its cover. Both that and its gooey hit title track completely turned off Frampton's hard-rock constituency. So did his appearance in the widely panned *Sgt. Pepper* film. He himself has acknowledged this period as the low point of his career. (Being parodied by Frank Zappa —"I Have Been in You" opened Zappa's *Sheik Yer-*

Peter Frampton

TOP ALBUMS

WIND OF CHANGE (A&M, '72)
FRAMPTON (A&M, '75, 32)
FRAMPTON COMES ALIVE! (A&M, '76, 1)
I'M IN YOU (A&M, '77, 2)
WHERE I SHOULD BE (A&M, '79, 19)

TOP SONGS

SHOW ME THE WAY (A&M, '76, 6)
BABY, I LOVE YOUR WAY (A&M, '76, 12)
DO YOU FEEL LIKE WE DO (A&M, '76, 10)
I'M IN YOU (A&M, '77, 2)
I CAN'T STAND IT NO MORE (A&M, '79, 14)

Additional Top 40 Songs: 1

bouti album—might have stung, too.) The result, unfortunately, was a steady stream of sales disappointments for Frampton, from 1979's *Where I Should Be* (which contained his final top 20 hit, "I Can't Stand It No More") through 1981's *Breaking All the Rules* to the next year's *The Art of Control*—his last for longtime label A&M, who'd been with him since Humble Pie. The final indignity, Frampton later told a writer, was that "Certain people had suggested that I write an album 'that doesn't sound like a Peter Frampton album.' That was awful, what do you do then?"

Frampton did many things: he took four years off and played with David Bowie and Chris Spedding; he recorded two albums for Atlantic; and, finally, he recorded again with Steve Marriott immediately prior to the latter's accidental death in 1991. Only two of the resulting tracks have surfaced so far, on an A&M Frampton compilation called *Shine On*, and they show Frampton and Marriott to be able, compatible, and obviously willing collaborators. Unfortunately again for Peter Frampton—and for his fans—wondering what might have been is a very big part of the job.

MICHAEL FRANKS

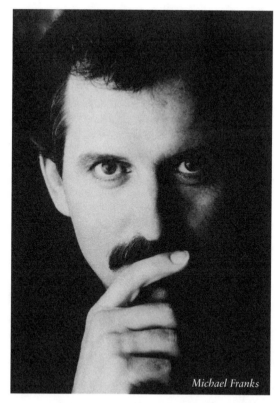

Michael Franks

It's one thing to create your own artistic niche; it's another to do that and then fill it, with consistent creativity, for over 20 years. That's precisely what Michael Franks (b. Sept. 18, 1944, La Jolla, California) has achieved since 1973, when his Brut Records debut displayed a singer-songwriter with a gift for wry, sexy lyrics and an inimitable voice perfectly suited to sing them. One album later, Franks' memorable *The Art of Tea* hooked a much broader audience—and began a long-term relationship with Warner Bros. Records that has lasted well into two decades. Even though Franks isn't likely to duplicate the pop chart achievements of current top Warner acts Prince and Madonna, it is likely the label is still immensely grateful for his consistency—both artistically and commercially.

For want of a better term, Franks has produced a substantial body of "jazzy pop" tunes—or, more precisely, has presented his clever pop songs in a jazzy musical context. The key to his consistent sound may lie in that context, which most often has been provided by top-line sessionmen on both coasts, e.g., the Crusaders, David Sanborn, the Brecker Brothers, Eric Gale, Hiram Bullock, Steve Khan, and the Yellowjackets (whose 1992 live set *Live Wires* features Franks as a guest).

What makes the music stand out from normal well-played session fodder, though, is Franks himself. His shaky,

often double-tracked vocals borrow stylistically from jazz and "cool" Brazilian bossa nova vocal styles (original "Girl from Ipanema" chanteuse Astrud Gilberto in fact guested on his 1983 album *Passion Fruit*) and are often sung slightly sharp; his appealingly hip lyrics presume listeners are jazz fans, too. (His 1977 song "The Lady Wants to Know" contains this characteristic snippet: "Daddy's just like Coltrane/Baby's just like Miles/The lady's just like heaven when she smiles.")

Franks, who attended UCLA, the University of Montreal, and the University of California at Berkeley, got his break in 1972 via bluesmen Sonny Terry and Brownie McGhee. The legendary duo recorded three of his tunes ("You Bring Out the Boogie in Me," "White Boy Lost in the Blues," and "Jesus Gonna Make It Alright") on their A&M album *Sonny & Brownie,* which also featured Franks himself on guitar and banjo; then,

---

TOP ALBUMS

THE ART OF TEA (Reprise, '76)
SLEEPING GYPSY (Warner Bros., '77)
BURCHFIELD NINES (Warner Bros., '78)
TIGER IN THE RAIN (Warner Bros., '79)
OBJECTS OF DESIRE (Warner Bros., '82)

TOP SONGS

POPSICLE TOES (Reprise, '76)
LADY WANTS TO KNOW (Reprise, '77)

while recording a film soundtrack for new Buddah Records subsidiary Brut, the pair recommended the fledgling label sign Franks. It did, and though the resulting album died on the racks, interest in the singer was substantial enough for it to be reissued by CBS offshoot John Hammond Records 10 years later. And—you want long-term appeal?—10 years after *that*, Franks was turning in *Dragonfly Summer*, his 11th album for Warner Bros.

In retrospect, Franks seems something of a visionary: he discovered and played to the yuppie audience before it was even known to exist; like Steely Dan's best work (and Steely founder Walter Becker has indeed produced Franks), his supremely polished albums don't seem dated in the slightest (although "Burchfield Nines" does name-drop Mr. T); and, finally, his seamless merger of jazz and pop was precisely the music that defined the early-'90s "Wave" radio format, sometimes called "new adult contemporary." He'll likely be making records for that audience until he drops.

It may be difficult for blues fans to fathom, but, yes, thanks to Sonny Terry and Brownie McGee, the man who gave us "In Search of the Perfect Shampoo" is absolutely thriving.

GLENN FREY

A founding member of the vastly successful Eagles, one of America's premier rock and roll bands, Glenn Frey (b. Nov. 6, 1948, Detroit, Michigan) has had a co-writing credit on some of the best-known songs of the rock era, among them all five of the Eagles' Number One hits, including "Best of My Love," "One of These Nights," "New Kid in Town," "Hotel California," and "Heartache Tonight." Together with Don Henley, his co-writing partner (among others) on all but one of the band's top 40 songs, Frey stayed with the superstar group for its entire 1971–82 run, then went solo and established a healthy career that brought him to the top five twice. But while his former partner Henley's own solo work has proven fruitful and established him as a near superstar, Frey's career took a mysterious nosedive in the early 1990s from which it has yet to recover.

A former Motor City rock and roller who long ago shared the stage with Bob Seger, Frey came to the Eagles with respectable credentials. He'd been a

member of Longbranch Pennywhistle (whose sole 1970 Amos Records album remains an eminent collectible) with J. D. Souther, himself a later solo artist and co-writer of three Eagles hits with Frey and Henley. Additionally, Frey and other future Eagles had backed Linda Ronstadt on her 1970 *Silk Purse* album as well as in concert, and would later appear on her 1972 *Linda Ronstadt* album. But it was with the Eagles that Frey established himself as a major player. Beginning with their first hit, 1971's "Take It Easy," co-written by Frey and Jackson Browne, the group built upon past attempts to merge country and rock by the Byrds, Poco, and Flying Burrito Brothers and smoothed down the rough edges into palatable and appealing pop that instantly found its audience.

Unlike other groups of that era such as Buffalo Springfield, Poco, or even Crosby, Stills and Nash, the Eagles seemed very much a democratic unit. Where the other bands had a clear division of duties—typically, one band member would write a song and then sing it—the Eagles generally worked as a team. Though the group's debut included two songs penned solely by Frey—"Chug All Night" and "Most of Us Are Sad"—albums thereafter generally featured Frey and Henley working on songs together, often with additional input from Souther, Browne, other band members, and even Bob Seger. Furthermore, vocals on Henley-Frey compositions were split: on 1975's *One of These Nights,* for instance, Henley sang the hit title track while Frey sang "Lyin' Eyes."

If a distinction could be made—and it became

TOP ALBUMS

No Fun Aloud (Asylum, '82, *32*)
The Allnighter (MCA, '84, *22*)
Soul Searchin' (MCA, '88, *36*)
Strange Weather (MCA, '92)

TOP SONGS

The One You Love (Asylum, '82, *15*)
Sexy Girl (MCA, '84, *20*)
The Heat Is On (MCA, '85, *2*)
Smuggler's Blues (MCA, '85, *12*)
You Belong to the City (MCA, '85, *2*)
True Love (MCA, '88, *13*)

Additional Top 40 Songs: 1

more noticeable as the group neared its end—Frey, from the land of Motown, generally gave more of an R&B feel to much of his material. Indeed, after the Eagles' breakup, when Frey was freed from the considerable constraint of a group containing four other writers (Henley, Joe Walsh, Timothy B. Schmit, Don Felder), he quickly slipped a cover of Johnny Taylor's 1974 Stax hit "I've Been Born Again" onto *No Fun Aloud,* his solo debut of 1982.

In fact, Frey's own career started off healthily: his first album bore two top 40 hits in "The One You Love" and "I Found Somebody." Those songs and three others were the product of a writing collaboration between the singer and writer Jack Tempchin, a onetime member of the Funky Kings and an Arista solo artist who'd previously penned the Eagles hits "Peaceful Easy Feeling" and "Already Gone"; Tempchin has remained Frey's primary songwriting partner now for over a decade.

A year after the 1984 release of Frey's second solo album, *The Allnighter,* which boasted one top 20 hit in "Sexy Girl," his career suddenly took off dramatically. The reason? "The Heat Is On," a number two hit from *Beverly Hills Cop,* and "You Belong to the City" and "Smuggler's Blues," which peaked at numbers two and 12 respectively, both from the "Miami Vice" soundtrack.

If there was to be any downside to Frey's enormous success, it was simply this: his biggest solo hits have thus far come from soundtrack albums and not his own. After his previous hit streak, the singer must have been extremely disappointed in 1988 when *Soul Searchin',* his first solo album in four years, brought him only one hit (the top 20 "True Love") and became his first effort in 17 years that failed even to go gold. But that was only a prelude to the heartbreak to come in 1992: *Strange Weather,* Frey's finest solo album ever—easily as good as any of his Eagles work—failed to enter the album chart at all. And the same thing happened with his 1993 live set, on which he reprised six Eagles songs.

It therefore came as no great surprise when Frey hit on another means to express himself artistically. The singer had already appeared as a guest on "Miami Vice," in the 1986 film *Let's Get Harry,* and in seven episodes of the TV series "Wiseguy." In late 1993, he was cast as the detective lead in the CBS television series "South of Sunset." The show was canceled after only one episode aired—for drawing the lowest premiere ratings on record on any of the Big Three networks.

RICHIE FURAY

A peculiar case of an artist being in the right place at the right time and still not quite getting it right, Richie Furay (b. May 9, 1944, Yellow Springs, Ohio) has a musical pedigree ranking up there with the best. A founding member of the Buffalo Springfield, and of Poco, and of the Souther-Hillman-Furay Band, Furay spent much of the 1960s and '70s watching his former bandmates garner all the rewards of fame—economic and otherwise—while he worked away industriously to little avail. And when the time finally came, years later, for his band Poco to trendily reunite and record a surprisingly successful gold comeback album, Furay wasn't chomping at the bit for any long-owed financial reward: he was a born-again, practicing Christian minister with much more on his mind than any old rock and roll band—even his own.

Furay grew up in Ohio and dropped out of college to pursue a career in music; upon moving to New York in the early 1960s, he and future Buffalo Springfield partner Stephen Stills made their recording debut as members of folk group the Au Go-Go Singers. Their sole album, *They Call Us Au Go-Go Singers,* was issued by Roulette in late 1964. Within two years, both Furay and Stills had separately moved to Los Angeles and, with the vital additions of Neil Young, Bruce Palmer, and Dewey Martin, formed the Springfield in 1966.

A rhythm guitarist with an exceptionally sweet singing voice, Furay ultimately found himself the group's third wheel as a songwriter. With Stills and Young both contributing one brilliant song after another, Furay was mostly consigned to singing. (He proved a marvelous interpreter of Young's material in particular.) In the course of two years and three albums with the group, Furay penned only seven Springfield tunes, the best being "A Child's Claim to Fame," "Sad Memory," and the superb "Kind Woman." The latter track, which closed out their final album, *Last Time Around,* featured Furay with newly recruited bassist (and album producer) Jim Messina and steel-guitarist Rusty Young. It served as a stripped-down introduction to Furay's next group, Poco, which included those three players plus bassist (and future Eagle) Randy Meisner and drummer George Grantham.

Poco's contribution as one of the very first bands to play country rock (most tend to credit Gram Parsons' International Submarine Band as the genre's originator) has historically been overshadowed by the achievements of his two former bandmates in Crosby, Stills, Nash and Young. Ironically, while CSN&Y judiciciously juggled writing credits, Furay, for the first time, had comparative free rein in Poco; his compositions dominated that group's repertoire. The only fly in the ointment was radio's reaction to Poco's music: "We were too rock for country stations and we were too country for rock stations," Jim Messina recalled in 1989. As it was, despite Furay's steady stream of excellent songs such as "Pickin' Up the Pieces" and "Anyway Bye Bye," Poco went mostly unheard on the radio. While America was engrossed in Crosby, Stills and Nash's "Suite: Judy Blue Eyes," "Marrakesh Express," and "Woodstock," Poco—whose only top 20 hits would come after Furay had departed—built its audience through live performance only.

After six albums with the group, Furay split, encouraged by David Geffen to become part of fledgling "supergroup" the Souther-Hillman-Furay Band. The group seemed artifical and forced—particularly compared to the Springfield and Poco—but their two albums hit the top 40 in 1974 and '75, and Furay's "Fallin' in Love" cracked the top 30 and helped the debut go gold.

1976's *I've Got a Reason* was a significant departure for Furay on two fronts: it was his first real solo album (though it was initially credited to the Richie Furay Band), and, as he noted when it was reissued by the contemporary Christian Myrrh label in 1982, it was "the beginning of Jesus working in and changing my life that I might see Him at the center." Furay's material had become distinctly religious and revealingly autobiographical—noticeably so on songs like "Still Rolling Stones," in which he sang, "Well God only knows I'm polite/But I can't sing this song/And halfway belong and feel right." *Reason* was Furay's last charting solo album, though two

additional efforts would follow on Asylum. His last solo set, 1982's *Season of Change* on Myrrh, included scriptural references penned by Furay annotating each number.

Furay's songwriting participation on Poco's 1989 *Legacy* reunion album was limited to two tracks. On one, he only contributed half the lyrics and none of the music. The other, "If It Wasn't for You," distinctly sounded as if it were addressed to God. "[Furay] has another profession now," Messina said at the time.

PETER GABRIEL

One of very few performers to emerge from a full-blown '70s art rock group and become a critical favorite, Peter Gabriel (b. Feb. 13, 1950, England) is a remarkably creative singer and songwriter whose dedication to music of all forms—particularly world music—ranks among the very highest. From 1966 through 1974, Gabriel was the lead singer of Genesis, and with his animated, theatrical style established himself as the most charismatic front man of the progressive rock era. Upon his departure from the group following 1974's *The Lamb Lies Down on Broadway,* many expected his solo career to simply echo his earlier work; instead, Gabriel shifted into an experimental pop mode and aligned himself with several of the U.K.'s most admired members of the rock avant-garde. Displaying marked artistic growth with each successive release, the singer was wise enough to take advantage of the growing importance of rock video and—even wiser—to never forget that all great pop songs need distinct melodic hooks. With his artistic ambitions running closely parallel to his considerable songwriting talents, Peter Gabriel has recorded some of the most distinctive and revelatory pop music of the last 20 years.

Gabriel's 1977 solo debut, *Peter Gabriel,* was the first of three consecutive albums by the singer to bear that name; the fourth was titled *Security* by Geffen Records upon its 1982 U.S. release, but internationally it stands as his fourth eponymous set. "I thought it would be like a magazine cover," he explained later, "something like *Time* or *Newsweek.* You have the same format and the same logo, only a different picture. Sort of like, 'Well, who's on the cover this year?...The only difference is I'm on the cover every

TOP ALBUMS

I've Got a Reason (Asylum, '76)
Dance a Little (Asylum, '78)
I Still Have Dreams (Asylum, '81)

TOP SONG

I Still Have Dreams (Asylum, '79, 39)

Peter Gabriel

African activist Steven Biko, which has since been covered by Simple Minds and Robert Wyatt and become one of the singer's signature tunes. Gabriel's ascension to the mainstream continued with 1982's *Security*, which boasted his first-ever top 30 hit, "Shock the Monkey," a compelling song that became an MTV standard due to its remarkable video, one of the genre's finest. By the next year, *Plays Live*—a double-LP concert set recorded on the singer's 1982 North American tour—served as a fine retrospective of Gabriel's career to that point, and allowed him to move on to other, more esoteric concerns.

With the 1984 soundtrack to Alan Parker's film *Birdy*, the singer made a bold artistic move that essentially signaled a new phase of his career. Bearing a notation on its back cover reading, "WARNING: This record contains re-cycled material and no lyrics," the album was a fascinating combination of older material that Gabriel had pilfered from his back catalog, remixed without the vocals, and combined with a few new instrumental tracks. It was one of the first indications that the singer was shifting his critical attention to sound, rather than simple songs. *So*, officially the first Peter Gabriel album bearing a title, remains the singer's all-time best-seller, a triple platinum collection highlighted by the singer's Number One hit "Sledgehammer," the top 10 "Big Time," and "In Your Eyes." His most fully realized work, *So* blended the danceable pop of his hits with soft, melodic material such as "Mercy Street," dedicated to poet Anne Sexton, and "Don't Give Up," which prominently featured singer Kate Bush. It sold over five million copies worldwide—and became Gabriel's last pop album for over six years.

year." Where Genesis's lyrics had often focused on mythological and fantasy-based concepts, Gabriel's own seemed much more reality-oriented, often shaded with a subtle but noticeble apocalyptic tinge. "Home Sweet Home" from his second album, for example, was based on a newspaper account of a young British mother who leapt to her death from her high-rise apartment, holding her baby in her arms.

It may forever be to Atlantic Records' regret that the company refused to issue Gabriel's third album in 1980; though they had deemed it too non-commercial, Mercury Records didn't—and when that company finally released it, the album was the singer's first to crack the top 40. Fueled by the radio hit "Games Without Frontiers," a top five hit in Britain, the record also featured "Biko," Gabriel's homage to murdered South

In the period that followed, the singer put his rock star career on the back burner and became involved in an extraordinary number of activities centering on music and political issues, including Amnesty International (he was part of its 1988 Human Rights Now! tour), and further work with WOMAD (World of Music Arts and Dance), which he co-founded in 1980 and with whom he established his Real World Records world music label in 1989. And though he stopped

TOP ALBUMS

PETER GABRIEL (Atco, '77, *38*)
PETER GABRIEL (Atlantic, '78)
PETER GABRIEL (Mercury, '80, *22*)
PETER GABRIEL (Security)
   (Geffen, '82, *28*)
SO (Geffen, '86, *2*)
US (Geffen, '92, *2*)

TOP SONGS

SHOCK THE MONKEY (Geffen, '82, *29*)
SLEDGEHAMMER (Geffen, '86, *1*)
IN YOUR EYES (Geffen, '86, *26*)
BIG TIME (Geffen, '87, *8*)

making pop records, *Passion,* his beautiful, sonically adventurous 1989 soundtrack to Martin Scorsese's film *The Last Temptation of Christ,* won a well-deserved Grammy in 1989.

In 1992, Gabriel made his long-awaited return with *Us,* and found himself in such demand that the album debuted on the charts at number two. While tracks such as "Digging in the Dirt" were being played hourly on MTV, he lined up the first American WOMAD concert tour; headliners on the 10-city tour were typically eclectic, including Crowded House, P. M. Dawn, Ziggy Marley, Sheila Chandra, the Drummers of Burundi, and Russian folk artists the Terem Quartet. Also performing, of course, was Gabriel himself, who had brought Sinead O' Connor along on the tour to provide accompanying vocals (she contributed to *Us*'s "Blood of Eden") and sing her own material. "There is more 'world music,' as it is known, here than in other countries," Gabriel told the *Los Angeles Times* at the time, "yet it's more segregated than in any other country I can think of. There is a state here which [Ugandan musician] Geoffrey Oryema calls musical apartheid." Still looking to break down barriers wherever he may find them, Peter Gabriel is that rare artist to whom commercial success simply matters less than personal satisfaction. We should be grateful.

JERRY GARCIA

So well known they named an ice cream flavor after him, Jerry Garcia (b. Jerome John Garcia, Aug. 1, 1942, San Francisco), has spent over 30 years playing music of every genre—from jug band, country, bluegrass, and folk to blues, R&B, jazz, and rock and roll. He remains the central figure in pop music's phenomenal Grateful Dead, a long-lived aggregation that began in 1965 and within three decades became one of the highest-grossing concert attractions in the industry. His music has taken him to the most historic events in rock history, including the Monterey, Woodstock, and Watkins Glen festivals, 1969's infamous Altamont concert, and 1982's massive US Festival. With the Dead, he performed for three nights in front of the Sphinx and the Great Pyramid of Cairo; he has also appeared in the similarly immortal setting of Las Vegas. He is the paternal figure to one of the largest, strangest, and most socially acceptable cults of all time—the Dead-

heads—and he has twice been near death but came back playing stronger and more passionately than ever. Finally, he is a superb musician and excellent singer-songwriter whose work continues to be appreciated by several generations of rock fans—most recently demonstrated in 1993 by alternative rock band Cracker's cover of Garcia's "Loser" on *Kerosene Hat,* a college-radio favorite.

Within the context of the Dead—which with members Bob Weir, Phil Lesh, and Garcia has three consistently sturdy songwriters—Garcia's songs have generally been most prominent. Just one of many aspects of the Dead's unique approach has been their longtime association with lyricist Robert Hunter; since the group's 1969 album *Aoxomoxoa,* Hunter has co-written songs with nearly every member of the band. Another is the remarkable degree of respect the band accords the many songs that make up its repertoire, particularly in comparison to performers of similar vintage. Typical Dead sets of the 1990s feature material that extends back as far as the '60s, and often obscure material at that—and since the band has had only one hit single (1987's "Touch of Grey," by Garcia and Hunter) in their nearly 30-year career, what's being "promoted" is not new product, but a song the band and its audience both clearly love. Among the older Garcia-Hunter tunes that continue to regularly surface in the '90s are "Ripple," "Dark Star," "Candyman," "Uncle John's Band," "Deal," "China Cat Sunflower," "Sugaree," and many, many more.

The democracy and artistic freedom the Dead have long enjoyed have allowed its individual members to prolifically record their own solo projects. Garcia became the first to do so with 1971's

TOP ALBUMS

GARCIA (Warner Bros., '72, 35)
GARCIA (Round, '74)
REFLECTIONS (Round, '76)
CATS UNDER THE STARS (Arista, '78)
RUN FOR THE ROSES (Arista, '82)
JERRY GARCIA/DAVID GRISMAN (Acoustic Disc, '91)
JERRY GARCIA BAND (Arista, '91)

TOP SONGS

SUGAREE (Warner Bros., '72)
DEAL (Warner Bros., '72)

Hooteroll?, an instrumental set on which he was second-billed to organist Howard Wales. *Garcia*, his first real solo album, came the next year; featuring the guitarist playing all the instruments but drums, the set boasts many of his and Hunter's finest songs, including "Deal," "Sugaree," "Loser," and "The Wheel," all still part of the Dead's repertoire 20 years later. Solo projects also gave Garcia the space to cover songs that might not always be appropriate for Dead albums; on *Live at Keystone,* a 1973 set recorded with jazz organist Merle Saunders, for instance, the guitarist covered Bob Dylan's "Positively Fourth Street," Jimmy Cliff's "The Harder They Come," and Rodgers and Hart's "My Funny Valentine."

Through the course of many solo albums to come—*Garcia* (1974), *Reflections* (1975), *Cats Under the Stars* (1978), and *Run for the Roses* (1982)—Garcia continued to record original material, most of which would later pop up at Dead shows: "Might as Well," "They Love Each Other," "Gomorrah," "Mission in the Rain," and "Comes a Time" are some of the best known to Dead fans. Since he was still writing for the Dead regularly, the albums served a secondary function of indicating what music and which artists the guitarist particularly valued; by the time of 1991's live *Jerry Garcia Band,* he was singing songs by such diverse writers as Dylan, Smokey Robinson, Bruce Cockburn, Allen Toussaint, Lennon and McCartney, Robbie Robertson, Peter Tosh, and Los Lobos.

Jerry Garcia

What may be most remarkable about the Grateful Dead is the manner in which they've continually built their audience without seeming to lose any longtime fans. It's a testament to the phenomenon of their staying power that their 23rd charting album, *In the Dark,* became their first to actually enter the top 10. As is evident at any of their shows, when Garcia sings the lyrics to "Touch of Grey," lines like "I will get by/I will survive" take on an emotionally powerful, almost palpable resonance. After taking the longest, strangest trip in all of pop, Jerry Garcia always proves the point simply by singing it.

DAVID GATES

Though some "serious" music fans might look down their noses at the soft rock sound of the early-1970s group Bread, 20 years has been ample time for many to reconsider: few bands could match Bread's knack for crafting so many near-perfect singles so consistently. While hipsters of the time were busy knocking the quartet's steady stream of hits and listening to the "underground" sounds of early FM heroes like Leon Russell and J. J. Cale, few suspected group leader David Gates (b. Dec. 11, 1940) was in fact an old Tulsa, Oklahoma, buddy of Russell's and Cale's and that he, like them, had played with some of the very best musicians in the business.

Gates, who had played in a high school band with Russell, moved to Los Angeles after graduation to work as a session musician. Among those he worked with were Elvis Presley (on a film soundtrack), country star Merle Haggard, and a quartet called the Pleasure Fair—whose 1967 Uni debut album he produced and arranged. Together with that group's singer-guitarist Robb Royer and singer James Griffin (who had co-written the Oscar-winning, eventual Carpenters hit "For All We Know" from the 1969 film *Lovers and Other Strangers*), Gates formed Bread.

Starting out as just a trio (and eventually settling for a permanent drummer, Mike Botts), the group split song-

writing duties from the start. Typically, Gates penned soft, romantic ballads, while Griffin and Royer—who most often worked in tandem—wrote less consistent, often upbeat pop. Each would typically write half of each album. One suspects that Griffin and Royer remain chagrined that during the course of the group's career—from 1969 to 1973, with a brief 1976 reunion—virtually every one of Bread's 12 hit singles had been penned by Gates. Beginning with 1970's "Make It with You," Bread's first and only Number One record, the group managed a top 40 single every three months up through 1973's "Aubrey"—hitting the top 10 with "It Don't Matter to Me," "If," "Baby I'm-a Want You," and "Everything I Own."

Stylistically, many of Gates's songs and records were similar: slow, delicately strummed rhythm guitar; double-tracked vocals; romantic, almost overly-sentimental lyrics typically written in the second person; and, in all, about the best slow-dance music of the era. Remarkably, Bread seemed to have a musical monopoly of sorts, too: for a band so distinctly popular, they had remarkably few imitators.

By 1971's *Manna,* guitarist Royer had left the group and been replaced by well-known studio pianist Larry Knechtel; by 1973, Bread was, as they say, toast, and Gates and Griffin went solo. Griffin's Polydor album of the same year stiffed unmercifully, but the title track of Gates's second solo set, 1975's *Never Let Her Go,* at least netted him a top 30 single. Bread's brief 1976 reunion—apparently inspired by floundering solo careers—resulted in a final top 30 album, *Lost Without Your Love,* and its top 10 title track, Bread's final hit.

Back on his own again, Gates managed two more hits in 1978—the top 20 film theme "Goodbye Girl" and top 30 hit "Took the Last Train"—before vanishing from the charts entirely. Two low-key albums followed, *Falling in Love Again* and 1981's *Take Me Now,* his sole album for Arista Records.

Gates hasn't made records since. He should. Play any of the early Bread records for someone who missed them the first time around and watch their faces light up, guaranteed. If any 1970s artist deserves serious critical reappraisal, David Gates may be the man.

TOP ALBUMS

First (Elektra, '73)
Never Let Her Go (Elektra, '75)
Goodbye Girl (Elektra, '78)

TOP SONGS

Never Let Her Go (Elektra, '75, 29)
Goodbye Girl (Elektra, '78, 15)
Took the Last Train (Elektra, '78, 30)

LOWELL GEORGE

As leader of Little Feat, one of the most highly respected American rock bands of the 1970s, the late Lowell George (b. Apr. 13, 1945, Los Angeles) crafted eight much-admired albums, in their own way as distinctly American-sounding as the Band's. Merging rock, funky rhythms, R&B, and a divinely wicked sense of humor—evident from the surrealistic Neon Park artwork that graced most of their albums' covers—George provided the heated emotional counterpoint to the slick, equally well-played music of Steely Dan, the only other '70s band to similarly inspire rabid devotion in both fans and musicians of the era.

George's career, unfortunately, was never greeted with the sort of commercial success that might have assured a steady flow of inspired work. That may be an understatement, considering that the debut album of his first group, the Factory—formed in Los Angeles in 1965—was essentially recorded for Uni Records in the late 1960s but finally released in 1993, 14 years after his death. In fact, the guitarist's participation in the bustling L.A. music scene of the '60s was almost consistently ignored or covered after the fact: Uni had released only one Factory single; George participated only as sideman on the Fraternity of Man's 1969 album *Get It On!*; his brief membership in the Mothers of Invention was documented only by scattered album tracks and a missing mugshot on the cover of their 1969 album *Uncle Meat*; and two of his best early songs, "Truck Stop Girl" (co-written with Feat's Bill Payne) and "Willin' "—both found on Little Feat's poor-selling 1970 debut—were initially heard by the mass public when covered by the Byrds and Sea Train in 1970–71.

In many ways, the first two albums by Little Feat—the original quartet that George had put together following his departure from Zappa's Mothers—are the best examples of the guitarist's work to be had. Loaded with many of his finest songs, including "Willin'," "Easy to Slip," and "Sailin' Shoes," the records display a group both musically at the top of their form—George's slide guitar playing was consistently enthralling—and lyrically sharp enough to outclass nearly all of their contemporaries. Consider George's mutated take on the blues on *Sailin' Shoes'* "A Apolitical Blues": "Well my telephone was ringing and they told me it was Chairman Mao/Well my telephone was ringing

and they told me it was Chairman Mao/You got to tell him anything 'cause I just don't want to talk to him now."

But dismal sales of the band's second album, *Sailin' Shoes,* caused the quartet to temporarily split; when they returned in 1973 with *Dixie Chicken,* they'd lost a bassist to Captain Beefheart and gained three new players—bassist Kenny Gradney and conga player Sam Clayton, both from New Orleans, and additional guitarist Paul Barrere. While the six-piece format gave the band room to expand musically—and in fact started them on their way to playing the heated, funky rock they became most famous for—it also gave George enough room to slacken off in both his songwriting contributions and overall participation in the group. Though he still dominated *Dixie Chicken*—which stands as the Mark II band's finest overall work—by 1975's *The Last Record Album,* Barrere and Payne had taken over the majority of the songwriting duties, with George nabbing credits for only two-and-half songs.

Seemingly always on the verge of breaking up—which they did often, but only temporarily—the band broke through commercially with 1974's *Feats Don't Fail Me Now,* which reached number 36 on the charts and went gold. As they toured nonstop and became an extremely successful live outfit (many fans claim the group's bootlegged concerts outshine their records), they released five albums between 1975 and 1981 that likewise made the top 40, with 1978's live *Waiting for Columbus* cracking the top 20 and going platinum.

As George's input lessened, Little Feat gradually evolved into a slick, jazzy outfit far removed from the earthiness displayed on their first two albums. Having already produced albums by singer Tret Fure

TOP ALBUMS

THANKS I'LL EAT IT HERE (Warner Bros., '79)

TOP SONGS

WILLIN' (with Little Feat, Warner Bros., '70)

TRUCK STOP GIRL (with Little Feat, Warner Bros., '70)

EASY TO SLIP (with Little Feat, Warner Bros., '72)

SAILIN' SHOES (with Little Feat, Warner Bros., '72)

TEENAGE NERVOUS BREAKDOWN (with Little Feat, Warner Bros., '72)

and the group Howdy Moon (whose singer Valerie Carter later made a solo album featuring George prominently), the guitarist went off to produce the Grateful Dead's *Shakedown Street* in 1978. After repeatedly threatening to make his own solo album, he finally followed through in 1979 with *Thanks I'll Eat It Here*. But longtime George fans were disappointed to find it featured little of his guitar playing—he had intended the set to showcase his bluesy voice—and only four of his songs, one of which ("Two Trains") originated on *Dixie Chicken*. While on the road promoting the album, George died of drug-related heart failure on June 29, 1979 in Arlington, Virginia.

Little Feat soon disbanded, but by 1988, they successfully re-formed with both seasoned guitarist Fred Tackett (a longtime band friend who'd appeared on earlier albums) and former Pure Prairie League vocalist Craig Fuller taking George's place. The band had been so heavily missed in the interim, their reunion album shot into the top 40 and eventually went gold. It had the sound, it had the shake, and it had the funk—but it didn't have Lowell George, said critics, so it wasn't Little Feat.

DEBBIE GIBSON

Anyone in their mid-20s attempting to break into the music business must look at Debbie Gibson (b. Aug. 31, 1970, Long Island, New York) and shudder. While jazz and classical music have had their share of musical prodigies, the youngest pop performers, with very few exceptions, have historically been figureheads, singing or performing within a context provided to them by someone older and much less photogenic—or newsworthy. But when her 1988 single "Foolish Beat" reached Number One in 1988, young Debbie Gibson, barely 17, became the youngest artist in history to have written, produced, and performed a chart-topping single. And anyone thinking of those special two words "novelty

act" should consider that the album bearing that single was certified triple platinum and yielded three other self-penned top five singles.

One also suspects that a certain world-famous singer-songwriter who is married to supermodel Christie Brinkley must have felt a mixture of gratitude and a sense of his own mortality when Debbie Gibson proudly announced, "When I was eight, I got my first pop album, Billy Joel's *52nd Street*. About a year later, I saw him in concert at Nassau Coliseum, and ever since that day, I knew exactly what I wanted to do." If Billy Joel got his first pop album when he was eight, it very likely could have been Bing Crosby's *Merry Christmas*.

Whether Gibson was pushed into her music career by her parents or simply pulled them along with her remains an interesting question. She reportedly spent her childhood attending a plethora of various lessons, auditions, and performances; according to a record company bio, her parents even gave her a drum machine and synthesizer upon her confirmation, after which the family set up a "recording studio" in the Gibson basement. Regardless, Gibson proved a very capable tunesmith, and through sending various demo tapes around to major record companies, she eventually landed a contract with Atlantic Records at 16.

Within a year, Gibson's debut album, *Out of the Blue*, sat comfortably in the top 10; before departing, it generated five hits, four of them in the top five.

What was the appeal? Her music was pleasant and catchy, and while not exactly lyrically profound, such songs as "Only in My Dreams" and "Staying Together" offered lyrics to which a young teen audience could relate. Furthermore, Gibson was a natural candidate for wide MTV exposure; given that, and a nation full of bored adolescents with remote controls in their hands, her success seemed a natural.

Ironically, another teenaged singer released her first album the same month Gibson debuted. Her name was Tiffany, and her self-titled debut album actually outdid Gibson's, selling quadruple platinum and holding the Number One slot

---

TOP ALBUMS

OUT OF THE BLUE (Atlantic, '87, 7)
ELECTRIC YOUTH (Atlantic, '89, 1)
ANYTHING IS POSSIBLE (Atlantic, '90)
BODY MIND SOUL (Atlantic, '93)

TOP SONGS

ONLY IN MY DREAMS (Atlantic, '87, 4)
SHAKE YOUR LOVE (Atlantic, '87, 4)
OUT OF THE BLUE (Atlantic, '88, 3)
FOOLISH BEAT (Atlantic, '88, 1)
LOST IN YOUR EYES (Atlantic, '89, 1)
ELECTRIC YOUTH (Atlantic, '89, 11)

Additional Top 40 Songs: 3

Debbie Gibson

Gibson made headlines in early 1992 for her Broadway debut as Eponine in *Les Miserables,* a well-received stint that lasted a full three months. That she was looking to broaden her image became even more obvious when her fourth album, *Body Mind Soul,* arrived in early 1993. Her song "Shock Your Mama" might have done exactly that to many mothers, so brazen was its sexy promotional video. Collaborating with the powerhouse R&B team Carl Sturken and Evan Rogers on five tracks, Gibson fashioned a dance-heavy album that obviously looked to recast the former sweet teenager into some sort of PG-rated Madonna. Whether it worked or not is debatable; the album became another sales disappointment.

ANDREW GOLD

A primary architect of the '70s Los Angeles singer-songwriter sound, due mostly to his work as guitarist and arranger with Linda Ronstadt on her 1974 platinum breakthrough *Heart Like a Wheel,* Andrew Gold (b. Aug. 2, 1951, Burbank, California) seemed destined for greater things than he's so far achieved. Gold is a capable multi-instrumentalist, and, unlike so many other West Coast sessioneers with splendid musical chops, has a smart ear for simple pop hooks. Though it may be overly picky to find fault with a career that includes one top 10 hit (1977's "Lonely Boy") and another top 30 hit that will be heard for all eternity as the theme song from "Golden Girls" (1978's "Thank You for Being a Friend"), Gold once seemed a likely candidate to take '60s pop, merge it with '70s studio professionalism, and emerge a vital pop figure. On the evidence of what he's produced so far, that hasn't been the case and probably won't be.

Gold may have been genetically predisposed for his line of work: his father is film composer Ernest Gold (*Exodus, On the Beach, It's a Mad, Mad, Mad, Mad World*), and his mother is singer Marnie Nixon, whose voice was dubbed in for the non-singing stars of such films as *The King and I* (Deborah Kerr), *West Side Story* (Natalie Wood), and *My Fair Lady* (Audrey Hepburn).

In the late 1960s, Gold formed the group Bryndle with Wendy Waldman, former Stone Poney Kenny Edwards, and Karla Bonoff; they recorded one A&M album that was never released. Gold and

for two weeks. But where Gibson was intimately involved with all aspects of her music, Tiffany was much more a novelty figure, owing much of her success to top 10 cover versions of '60s hits like "I Think We're Alone Now" and (the gender-changed) "I Saw Him Standing There." Tiffany barely lasted one more album; Gibson is still going relatively strong.

Gibson's second album, *Electric Youth,* shot to Number One and held that slot for five weeks, eventually going double platinum; on it were the gold Number One single "Lost in Your Eyes" and the title track, which peaked at number 11 but went gold as well. Her third album, *Anything Is Possible,* was in comparison a significant disappointment: it only reached number 41, though still going gold, and generated only one top 40 single via its title track, which stalled at number 26. And for the first time, Gibson was collaborating with another writer—though in this case, few could quibble with her choice of Lamont Dozier, who co-wrote four of the album's tracks.

Edwards then formed the Rangers, whose demo tape impressed Ronstadt enough to ask the pair to join her working band. Gold became an integral part of the Ronstadt group during what can fairly be called her golden era, appearing on her platinum trilogy *Heart Like a Wheel, Prisoner in Disguise,* and *Hasten Down the Wind* between 1974 and '76. In 1975, he inked his own deal with Ronstadt's label, Asylum Records, and released his first and best album, *Andrew Gold.* Like select few other multi-instrumentalists who know their way around the studio—Todd Rundgren comes immediately to mind—Gold played nearly all the instruments on his record; luckily, he was proficient enough to escape the common trap of making it sound cold and mechanical. The singer wrote all his material, and much of it sounded like superior British pop: texturally, the superb closing track "I'm Coming Home" might've been the work of either the Searchers or the Hollies from a decade earlier.

Gold's next two albums, *What's Wrong with This Picture* and *All This and Heaven Too,* respectively yielded his two hits "Lonely Boy" and "Thank You for Being a Friend." Rather than play most of the instruments as he'd done on his debut, Gold increasingly used L.A. session musicians, and it showed: both albums sounded less quirky and original than the first and more like typical L.A. studio rock. Though both albums made the top 100, his final Asylum effort, 1980's uninspired *Whirlwind,* bore no hit singles and failed to chart at all.

Gold's studio skills made him a natural as a producer, and between 1980 and 1982 the singer found himself behind the boards for former partner Karla Bonoff, Rita Coolidge, Nicolette Larson, Moon Martin, and 10cc. For the latter, on 1982's *Ten Out of 10,* Gold produced three tracks he'd co-written with 10cc's Graham Gouldman and Eric Stewart. It was a collaboration that clicked, and the result was

Andrew Gold

a new band by Gold and Gouldman called Wax. For Gold—an artist whose best work emulated great British pop of the 1960s—working with the man who'd penned hits for the Yardbirds, the Hollies, and Herman's Hermits seemed wonderfully appropriate. It was fruitful, too: the pair released two solid albums between 1986 and 1988 and had a top 50 hit with "Right Between the Eyes."

TOP ALBUMS

ANDREW GOLD (Asylum, '76)
WHAT'S WRONG WITH THIS PICTURE? (Asylum, '77)
ALL THIS AND HEAVEN TOO (Asylum, '78)

TOP SONGS

LONELY BOY (Asylum, '77, 7)
THANK YOU FOR BEING A FRIEND (Asylum, '78, 25)

STEVE GOODMAN

Best known for his song "The City of New Orleans," a top 20 hit for Arlo Guthrie in 1972, Steve Goodman (b. July 25, 1948, Chicago) left an admirable recorded legacy behind after his death of leukemia in 1984. A former University of Illinois student who left school in 1969 to pursue a career in music, the spunky singer-songwriter first made his name performing in Chicago-area folk clubs, while occasionally writing local advertising jingles on the side. In the summer of 1971, a series of fortuitous circumstances—instigated by the odd musical pair of Kris Kristofferson and Paul Anka—brought both Goodman and his singer-songwriter pal John Prine to New York, where each would score their first record deals.

Prine, who swiftly signed a deal with Atlantic, became the focus of massive critical attention for his 1971 debut; though Goodman, who had inked with Buddah, wasn't quite as fortunate, his 1971 debut, *Steve Goodman,* still drew plenty of raves, not only for its songs—which included the original "City of New Orleans" track—but for the outstanding playing of the Nashville musicians on the sessions, produced by Norbert Putnam and Kristofferson. Goodman's 1972 follow-up, *Somebody Else's Troubles,* was produced by the equally distinguished Arif Mardin; among its guest musicians was one "Robert 'Milkwood' Thomas—better known as Bob Dylan—as well as Maria Muldaur and David Bromberg.

After finding little commercial success at Buddah, Goodman moved to Asylum in 1975, for whom he produced five albums through 1980. His most successful, *Jessie's Jig and Other Favorites,* peaked at number 144 on the album charts. An often funny writer whose best songs were typically warm and sentimental, Goodman had a special lyrical knack for touching the heart while never quite indulging in overt corniness. An excellent example was "My Old Man," from 1977's *Say It in Private:* "I miss my old man tonight/And I can almost see his face/He was always trying to watch his weight/And his heart only made it to fifty-eight/For the first time since he died/Late last night I cried/I wondered when I was gonna do that/For my old man." Goodman often wrote songs with others; among his regular collabo-

rators were Steve Burgh, Jim Rothermel, Rick Chudacoff, Mike Smith, and Bill LaBounty, as well as Prine (1977's "The Twentieth Century Is Almost Over") and Jimmy Buffett (1974's "Door Number 3").

Goodman departed Asylum after 1980's *Hot Spot,* and next appeared on his own Red Pajamas label with *Artistic Hair, Affordable Art,* and *Santa Ana Winds.* A much-loved performer, he was deeply missed when he finally succumbed to leukemia on September 20, 1984. "We lived with it for so long," singer Prine later told *Rolling Stone*'s David Fricke. "He'd had leukemia since 1968. It was something he always talked about, a dark-humor thing. We'd go to airports, and he'd look up at the word 'terminal,' shake his head, and go, 'Why do they have to have that sign up there?' It was like that for years."

Following Goodman's death, a live tribute concert was held in Chicago, featuring Prine, Arlo Guthrie, Richie Havens, John Hartford, David Bromberg, and the Nitty Gritty Dirt Band, among others. A live recording documenting the event won the Best Contemporary Folk Recording Grammy in 1986.

ARLO GUTHRIE

Having the most famous figure in folk music for a father might seem intimidating, but the music made by Arlo Guthrie (b. July 10, 1947, Coney Island, New York) has, from the very start, been filled with a joyful self-confidence as appealing as the man who made it. Just as Woody Guthrie influenced an entire generation of folksingers, whether Ramblin' Jack Elliot or Bob Dylan, his eldest son, Arlo, made music that spoke to another generation—spoke so eloquently, in fact, that they made a movie about it. The music was Guthrie's 18-and-a-half-minute epic of 1967, "Alice's Restaurant," the generation was of the Woodstock era, and the 1970 movie, directed by Arthur Penn and starring Guthrie himself, remains a refreshing look back at an era when much more than beer was being drafted.

Though Arlo Guthrie never saw his father perform (he was hospitalized with Huntington's chorea in 1954, when Arlo was only seven, and died 13 years later), he received his first guitar from the elder folksinger as a present on his sixth birthday. At 13 he gave his first public performance, singing some of his father's songs onstage at a Greenwich Village

TOP ALBUMS

STEVE GOODMAN (Buddah, '71)
SOMEBODY ELSE'S TROUBLES (Buddah, '73)
JESSIE'S JIG AND OTHER FAVORITES (Asylum, '75)
WORDS WE CAN DANCE TO (Asylum, '76)
SAY IT IN PRIVATE (Asylum, '78)

TOP SONGS

THE CITY OF NEW ORLEANS (Buddah, '71)
BANANA REPUBLICS (Asylum, '76)

Arlo Guthrie

1972 and 1974; *Hobo's Lullaby* (which included his top 20 hit version of Steve Goodman's "City of New Orleans"), *The Last of the Brooklyn Cowboys,* and *Arlo Guthrie* all featured a mixture of non-original material (such as his father's classic "Deportees") as well as Guthrie's own folk-based songs. One of the best, "Presidential Rag," was a scathing post-Watergate indictment of Richard Nixon, in which Guthrie sang, "You're the one we voted for/And you must take the blame/For handing out authority/To men who are insane." Other later material was even further removed from the comparatively upbeat fare of *Alice's Restaurant,* dealing with such topics as Arab-Israeli relations, the slain Chilean poet Victor Jara, and by 1979's *Outlasting the Blues,* the singer's conversion to Catholicism.

In 1986, Guthrie started Rising Son Records and acquired his Warner Bros. back catalog, most of which he has since reissued. The singer released *Son of the Wind,* a collection of cowboy tunes such as "Buffalo Gals," "Shenandoah," and "Red River Valley," in 1992; additionally, he recorded the Grammy-nominated children's album *Woody's 20 Grow Big Song* with his brother Joady and sister Nora. After buying the original "Alice church" in Great Barrington, Massachusetts, the same year, Guthrie moved his Rising Son offices there and founded the Guthrie Foundation, a not-for-profit organization devoted to helping abused children, the elderly, and people afflicted with AIDS and other terminal illnesses. Both in his art and way of life, Guthrie has stayed true to the principles he has long espoused, and seems a son of which any father would be more than proud.

folk club. After graduating high school, he spent the summer in Europe playing in clubs and on street corners; he returned to the States and attended college in Montana for only six weeks before dropping out at 18 to pursue music professionally.

In 1967, Guthrie sang his famous "Alice's Restaurant" at the Newport Folk Festival; it made such an impression during his afternoon set that he was called back to reprise it at the close of the festival. The ultimate result was a record deal with Warner Bros. and his 1967 debut album *Alice's Restaurant*—which cost only $3,500 to record but stayed on the charts for 99 weeks and went platinum. Guthrie's unique story-song became legendary and nearly ubiquitous, and was further boosted by Arlo's memorable appearance at the 1969 Woodstock Festival (the film of which captured his performance of "Coming into Los Angeles") and by the next year's Penn film.

Most of Guthrie's records for Warner Bros.—he made 12 over a period of 15 years—are surprisingly sturdy, well-made works sounding little like his most famous song. Three of the best were expertly produced by John Pilla and Lenny Waronker between

TOP ALBUMS

ALICE'S RESTAURANT (Reprise, '67, *17*)
RUNNING DOWN THE ROAD (Reprise, '69)
WASHINGTON COUNTY (Reprise, '70, *33*)
HOBO'S LULLABY (Reprise, '72, *38*)
LAST OF THE BROOKLYN COWBOYS (Reprise, '73)
ARLO GUTHRIE (Reprise, '74)
AMIGO (Reprise, '76)

TOP SONGS

ALICE'S RESTAURANT (Reprise, '67)
COMING INTO LOS ANGELES (Reprise, '69)
CITY OF NEW ORLEANS (Reprise, '72, *18*)

JOHN HALL

At least one critic pegged John Hall's best-known band, Orleans, as the East Coast version of Steely Dan—and in some respects, that wasn't far from the truth. Both bands got their start at ABC Records in 1972, and both featured musicianship that was consistently impeccable. Hall, in particular, was an outstanding guitarist who had recorded with some of the most demanding players and producers in the business, including Taj Mahal, John Simon, Bonnie Raitt, Al Kooper, and Seals and Crofts, all in their late-'60s and early-'70s prime. But unlike Steely Dan, session players didn't crowd out Orleans' regular band members during recording dates; playing next to Hall, Wells Kelly and Lance and Larry Hoppen could and certainly did hold their own—which explains why Orleans was an acclaimed live band during the course of its career (especially with the 1976 addition of drummer Rick Marotta) and Steely Dan was not.

But by no means did Hall's entire career revolve around Orleans. Before that group formed in New York in 1972, he'd already recorded an album with a quartet called Kangaroo (on MGM Records, 1968), released his first solo album (*Action,* on Columbia, 1970), written the music for a Broadway play (*Morning, Noon and Night*), written and arranged "Half Moon" on Janis Joplin's classic album *Pearl,* and produced the debut album by Tom Pacheco and Sharon Alexander.

By the time Orleans released its debut album, Hall had acquired a steadfast songwriting partner: his wife, Johanna. Together they wrote all but two tracks on the first album, and would continue to dominate Orleans' material until Hall departed to go solo in 1977. They were responsible for the group's two top 10 hits, "Dance with Me" (from 1975's *Let There Be Music*) and "Still the One" (from 1976's *Waking and Dreaming*). The latter track remains Hall's most famous song, due, oddly enough, to ABC-TV's constantly using it at the time to promote their upcoming television season.

TOP ALBUMS

JOHN HALL (Asylum, '78)
POWER (ARC/Columbia, '79)
ALL OF THE ABOVE (EMI America, '81)
SEARCHPARTY (EMI America, '83)

TOP SONGS

POWER (ARC/Columbia, '79)
CRAZY (KEEP ON FALLING)
    (EMI America, '81)
LOVE ME AGAIN (EMI America, '83)

Hall's visibility was definitely on the upswing once he left Orleans—though much of that was for extramusical reasons. Along with Jackson Browne, Graham Nash, and Bonnie Raitt, Hall was a major organizer of Musicians United for Safe Energy (MUSE), the aggressively anti-nuclear-power organization that sponsored five highly publicized benefit concerts at Madison Square Garden in 1979 (documented on the triple *No Nukes* album and its accompanying film). Hall's song "Power"—performed by the Doobie Brothers, Hall, and James Taylor—played a conspicuous role through the proceedings and served as the title track to Hall's solo album of the same year.

Without Orleans, however, Hall found his own solo work was selling meagerly at best. Though he shifted labels repeatedly, from Asylum to ARC/Columbia to EMI-America in just six years, nothing clicked. To add to the irony, Orleans, who had continued on in his absence, managed a top 20 hit without him in 1979 with "Love Takes Time." As might've been predicted, Hall and his former partners eventually reunited and attempted to recapture their formula for past success: *Grown Up Children,* released by MCA in 1986, featured Hall and the Hoppen Brothers and—as also might've been predicted—came and went quickly. It was another verse of the same old song: they may have still been the ones, but anyone who still cared had apparently long gone.

TIM HARDIN

One of the most gifted singer-songwriters of the rock era, Tim Hardin (b. Dec. 23, 1941, Eugene, Oregon) wrote extraordinarily sensitive and deeply personal songs—and lived a tragic life needlessly cut short by a drug overdose. He left behind a catalog of songs that were hits for other performers, including "If I Were a Carpenter" and "Reason to Believe," and also, more importantly, some of the most emotionally compelling albums in all of pop.

The product of a musical family—his mother was a violinist with the Portland Symphony Orchestra, his father a onetime jazz bassist—Hardin was older than many of his '60s contemporaries, and spent the late '50s in the Marines, stationed in Indochina. Upon getting discharged, he moved to the East Coast and began performing in various folk clubs in Cambridge, Massachusetts. He quickly developed a following, and by 1966 appeared at the influential Newport Folk Festival. Soon he was signed to Verve Records, where he recorded his best-known songs, including "Carpenter," "Reason to Believe," "Misty Roses," "Lady Came from Baltimore," and many more.

Hardin's songs seemed unabashedly romantic, a tinge autobiographical, and—significantly—perfectly suited for interpretation by other singers. Bobby Darin's version of "Carpenter" was a top 10 single in 1966; four years later, Johnny Cash and June Carter released a hit duet version of the same song. Likewise, Rod Stewart's huge-selling *Every Picture Tells a Story* album contains an especially emotive cover of Hardin's "Reason to Believe." Other artists to cover Hardin's songs included Frank Sinatra, the Youngbloods, Joan Baez, Bob Seger, the Nice, Scott Walker, Leon Russell, Nico, Ian Matthews, and the Dream Academy, among many others.

As popular as Hardin's many songs were, other people's versions are what most people heard, not Hardin's own definitive renderings, sung in his inimitably airy, jazz-blues style. Though he did play Carnegie Hall, minimal airplay and album sales had him spending much of the late 1960s playing coffee-houses and college concerts. Eventually he moved to upstate New York (his appearance at the Woodstock Festival ended up being cut from the famous concert film, though it resurfaced in a "lost performances" home video two decades later) and recorded three very different albums for Columbia. The first, 1969's *Suite for Susan Moore and Damion—We Are—One, One, All in One,* was a beautiful cycle of love songs Hardin had written for his wife and young son; the second, 1971's *Bird on a Wire,* was a harrowing, sometimes despondent mix of covers and originals apparently documenting his disintegrating relationship with his wife; the third, 1973's *Painted Head,* featured no new material, just Hardin singing the likes of "Nobody Knows You When You're Down and Out" and "Lonesome Valley" in a strangely upbeat musical context.

Hardin's longtime abuse of alchohol and drugs had in part led to his early-'70s move to London, where he sought treatment via England's liberal methadone program. There he recorded both *Painted Head* and the more respectable *Nine* (which at least bore six new Hardin tunes)—but the days of "Misty Roses" and "Reason to Believe" were clearly long behind him. He had already lost the rights to his own song catalog and was struggling simply to make ends meet. Hardin returned to America in the late 1970s and died of a heroin overdose in his rented Hollywood apartment on December 29, 1980. Two final albums were released posthumously: *The Homecoming Concert,* recorded live in Hardin's hometown of Eugene in January 1980, and *Unforgiven,* his final unfinished recordings, compiled by executive producer Don Rubin, who'd worked with Hardin from the beginning. Hardin's distinctly unglamorous death put an end to what had become a tragic life; fortunately, his beautiful songs will be with us forever.

TOP ALBUMS

TIM HARDIN 1 (Verve/Forecast, '66)

TIM HARDIN 2 (Verve/Forecast, '67)

TIM HARDIN 3/LIVE IN CONCERT
(Verve/Forecast, '68)

SUITE FOR SUSAN MOORE AND DAMION—WE ARE—
ONE, ONE, ALL IN ONE (Columbia, '69)

BIRD ON A WIRE (Columbia, '71)

TOP SONGS

MISTY ROSES (Verve/Forecast, '66)

REASON TO BELIEVE (Verve/Forecast, '66)

IF I WERE A CARPENTER (Verve/Forecast, '67)

LADY CAME FROM BALTIMORE (Verve/Forecast, '67)

LENNY'S TUNE (Verve/Forecast, '68)

GEORGE HARRISON

Given his membership in the most famous rock and roll band of all time, there's no point in attaching the word "obscurity" to any of the doings of former Beatle George Harrison (b. Feb. 24, 1943, Liverpool, England). While it's true that the Fab Four may be most famous for the songs written and sung by John Lennon and Paul McCartney, Harrison's contributions both as a guitarist and song-

George Harrison

writer were integral parts of the band from its celebrated beginning—and a Beatles without George
Harrison would have been unthinkable in every way.
Proof? In the late 1980s, when performing rights
group BMI handed out "Million-Airs" awards to
songwriters whose specific works had received radio
airplay exceeding 50,000 hours, only three Beatles
songs could be found at or above the four-million
mark—signifying more than 22 years of continuous
airplay. What were they? All-time winner "Yesterday" and "Michelle," both by Lennon and McCartney, and "Something" by George Harrison—which,
significantly, was a newer song by four years.

Onetime "quiet Beatle" Harrison made his songwriting debut in 1963 with "Don't Bother Me," first

available in the U.S. on 1964's *Meet the Beatles.* "It
took me a while to pluck up the courage," Harrison
told *Billboard*'s Timothy White in 1992, "because
we'd already had a bunch of hits—'Love Me Do,'
'Please Please Me,' 'From Me to You'—with Lennon
and McCartney songs. They were getting what
seemed like quite expert at it. I just had to try and
write something that was acceptable that I wouldn't
get laughed out of the room with." In fact, most of
Harrison's songs were anything but laughable; solidly constructed, often in minor keys not favored by
Lennon and McCartney, they provided a valuable
musical contrast that served to round out albums
already brimming with brilliance. All told, the Beatles recorded 21 Harrison songs between 1963 and

1970. Many are among the band's best known, including "If I Needed Someone," "Taxman," "While My Guitar Gently Weeps," "Here Comes the Sun," and, of course, "Something."

Harrison's pioneering incorporation of Indian music into the Beatles' Western pop is well documented; the most exotic songs in the Beatles' canon were typically Harrison's, including his "Within You Without You" from *Sgt. Pepper's Lonely Hearts Club Band* and the B side "The Inner Light." Still another musical area where Harrison excelled—one that has gone relatively uncredited—was his knack for crafting superlative nuggets of '60s psychedelia; both "It's All Too Much" from *Yellow Submarine* and "Blue Jay Way" from *Magical Mystery Tour* are among the finest examples of the genre, their use of droning sounds—perhaps inspired by his love of Indian music—still sounding very much ahead of its time.

The ever-esoteric Harrison was also the first Beatle to release a solo album. 1969's *Wonderwall Music* was a well-crafted soundtrack of largely Indian-inspired instumental music; its swift follow-up, *Electronic Sound,* was, as its name suggested, an uncommercial bit of early sonic exploration on the Moog synthesizer. What may be forgotten in the haze of time, however, is that of all the Beatles

TOP ALBUMS

ALL THINGS MUST PASS (Apple, '70, *1*)
THE CONCERT FOR BANGLA DESH (with Bob Dylan,
　Ringo Starr, Leon Russell, Eric Clapton, etc.,
　Apple, '72, *2*)
LIVING IN THE MATERIAL WORLD (Apple, '73, *1*)
DARK HORSE (Apple, '74, *4*)
EXTRA TEXTURE (READ ALL ABOUT IT)
　(Apple, '75, *8*)
CLOUD NINE (Dark Horse, '87, *8*)

Additional Top 40 Albums: 4

TOP SONGS

MY SWEET LORD (Apple, '70, *1*)
ISN'T IT A PITY (Apple, '70, *1*)
GIVE ME LOVE (GIVE ME PEACE ON EARTH)
　(Apple, '73, *1*)
GOT MY MIND SET ON YOU (Dark Horse, '87, *1*)

Additional Top 40 Songs: 10

post–Fab Four solo albums, it was Harrison's three-LP *All Things Must Pass* that was by far the most successful. Holding the Number One slot for a full seven weeks, the double platinum seller was co-produced by Phil Spector and included three top 10 hits, including the dual-sided Number One "My Sweet Lord" b/w "Isn't It a Pity" and "What Is Life." (A major controversy eventually ensued over "My Sweet Lord" when parties representing the author of the Chiffons' 1963 hit "He's So Fine" sued Harrison for allegedly appropriating the tune; settled in 1976, the lawsuit reportedly cost Harrison close to a million dollars.)

Harrison's involvement in the 1971 Concert for Bangla Desh—captured on vinyl and film—was another conspicuous success; the record won 1972's Album of the Year Grammy, was number two for six weeks, and was highlighted by guest appearances by Bob Dylan, Ringo Starr, and Eric Clapton, among others. By 1973, when Harrison returned with *Living in the Material World,* it looked like he could do no wrong. Number One for five weeks, the album had a substantial hit—the Number One "Give Me Love (Give Me Peace on Earth)"—and with such enjoyably wry songs as "Sue Me, Sue You Blues," Harrison proved a witty chronicler, well deserving of extended solo success. But 1974's *Dark Horse* did not bode well for him: while the album slid into the top five and went gold, its title track peaked at number 15 and, for Harrison, seemed mildly undistinguished; worse, the follow-up single "Ding Dong, Ding Dong" only peaked at number 36 and became the worst-performing single of his career. Worse yet, all this took place despite Harrison's being the subject of enormous publicity for his first American solo tour—during which he had been continually plagued by vocal hoarseness.

Because it was only the mid-'70s, when the Beatles were still a fresh memory for many, Harrison's next few albums generally performed well, but not exceptionally so. Between 1975 and 1979 he released four singles that entered the top 40, but even the highest-charting one—1979's number 16 hit "Blow Away"—was minor, and stylistically seemed more a look backward than forward. With 1981's *Somewhere in England,* Harrison released his first album not to be gold certified since the Beatles split—this despite the presence of the aggressively nostalgic number two hit "All Those Years Ago." Even worse, 1982's *Gone Troppo* weakly peaked at number 108 and was off the charts in less than two months. Perhaps wisely, Harrison then stopped recording for a period, focusing his attention on film productions such as *The Life of Brian* and those of his own HandMade company, which included *Time Bandits, The Missionary, Shanghai Surprise, Mona Lisa,* and *Withnail and I,* among others.

The ex-Beatle made a powerful return to form with 1987's *Cloud Nine,* which with the assistance of producer Jeff Lynne (of ELO and the Move) was his first album that sounded almost deliberately Beatle-ish, yet not negatively so. Featuring "Got My Mind Set on You," a non-original tune that became his first Number One hit in 14 years, and the humorous "When We Was Fab," the album reached number eight, went platinum, and quickly reestablished his major artist stature. Two platinum sets recorded with supergroup the Travelling Wilburys—featuring Harrison, Dylan, Roy Orbison, Tom Petty, and Lynne—further consolidated his "comeback" in 1988 and 1990. Still, the mild reception given his 1992 two-CD *Live in Japan*—a concert retrospective that included material as ancient as "Taxman" and featured guest guitarist Eric Clapton—might have given him pause: it peaked at number 126 and charted for all of two weeks.

A clear sentimental favorite among fans, Harrison is a pop figure very few people actively dislike. His accomplishments are among the most major in all of rock and roll, and his distinguished track record—both with the Beatles and early in his solo career—shows him capable of carrying his own weight and more. But apart from all that, and apart from the media fixation that has followed the Beatles from their earliest days in Liverpool, George Harrison in the 1990s is just like any other artist: he eats, he sleeps, he breathes—and he needs a hit record now and then, too.

JIMI HENDRIX

Justifiably renowned as the finest rock and roll guitarist of all time, Jimi Hendrix (b. James Marshall Hendrix, Nov. 27, 1942, Seattle, Washington) is often overlooked for his unique talents as a songwriter. Well before there was an MTV to supply lazy listeners visual accompaniment to the music they enjoyed, Hendrix was writing songs packed with enough lyrical imagery to put any contemporary "Buzz Bin" clip to shame. As just a cursory glance at some of his better-known song titles reveals, the man who wrote "Purple Haze," "Fire," and "Castles Made of Sand" wrote songs that, like his guitar playing, painted singular visual pictures that once heard were rarely forgotten.

Perhaps the single most-documented rock performer of the 1960s, Hendrix has been the subject of an extraordinary number of books, films, magazine retrospectives, and, no doubt, unproduced film scripts. Most surprising of all, in light of this, is the fact that the guitarist's fame has come essentially as the result of only the four albums he produced in his lifetime, and a fifth which he'd nearly finished before his September 1970 death. Since 1967's *Are You Experienced?,* however, there have been an astounding total of 25 charting Jimi Hendrix albums, and well over a hundred bootleg recordings that made the rounds during the same period.

Hendrix's well-trod story began in the early 1960s, when the guitarist began a post-army career backing the likes of Little Richard, the Isley Brothers, and Sam Cooke. By 1966, he'd made his way to Greenwich Village and formed Jimmy James and the Blue Flames; Chas Chandler, former member of British pop group the Animals, saw the guitarist perform at a club there and invited him to London. By October, with Chandler acting as his manager, the former Jimmy James joined forces with bassist Noel Redding and drummer Mitch Mitchell, and the Jimi Hendrix Experience was born.

An immediate sensation after his spectacular performance at 1967's Monterey Pop Festival—captured for all the world to see on director D. A. Pennabaker's historic film *Monterey Pop*—Hendrix won further national attention with songs such as "Purple Haze" and "Foxy Lady," both of which boasted some of the most unusual-sounding guitar playing the world had ever heard. Hendrix was a true master not only of the fretboard but also of the electronic effects that were becoming very much a part of rock's overall sound. With the accompaniment of howling feedback, sqealing sustained tones, and electronic growls that moved from speaker to speaker, the guitarist's music was more than psychedelic: it was otherworldly.

Hendrix took hold of the late 1960s and refused to let it go. By October 1968, all three of the Experience's albums were in the charts at once: *Are You Experienced?,* the milestone debut, had peaked at number five; *Axis: Bold as Love* had nudged higher to number three; and the double-LP set *Electric*

Ladyland reached Number One and stayed there for two weeks. The last of the three had been helped by Hendrix's unforgettable top 20 cover of Bob Dylan's "All Along the Watchtower"; the only hit single in Hendrix's career, its effect was so overwhelming that Dylan himself would use Hendrix's arrangement thereafter.

"I felt like 'Watchtower' was something I'd written but could never get together," Hendrix said at the time. "I often feel that way about Dylan. I could never write the kinds of words he does, but he's helped me out in trying to write, 'cause I've got a thousand songs that will never be finished; I just lay around and write about two or three words. Now I have a little more confidence in trying to finish one."

Hendrix's songwriting influences included much more than Dylan; he was a longtime science fiction fan, and it showed in his work. "Purple Haze" was reportedly inspired by a short story by science fiction writer Philip José Farmer. Hendrix's explanation of the song said much about his overall lyrical approach: "It's about going through this land," he said, " 'cause that's what I like to do, write a lot of mythical scenes, like the history of the wars on Neptune. Like how they got the Greek gods and all that mythology—well you can have your own mythology scene, or write fiction, complete fiction." Several of Hendrix's better-known songs —such as "Third Stone from the Sun," "Up from the Skies," "And the Gods Made Love," and "1983...(A Merman I Should Turn to Be)"—fit that pattern precisely.

TOP ALBUMS

ARE YOU EXPERIENCED? (Reprise, '67, *5*)
AXIS: BOLD AS LOVE (Reprise, '68, *3*)
ELECTRIC LADYLAND (Reprise, '68, *1*)
BAND OF GYPSYS (Capitol, '70, *5*)
CRY OF LOVE (Reprise, '71, *3*)
CRASH LANDING (Reprise, '75, *5*)

Additional Top 40 Albums: 4

TOP SONGS

PURPLE HAZE (Reprise, '67)
ALL ALONG THE WATCHTOWER (Reprise, '68, *20*)
LITTLE WING (Reprise, '68)
ANGEL (Reprise, '71)

Additionally, the guitarist often used earth-air-water-fire imagery in his writing: consider only the titles of "The Wind Cries Mary," "Castle Made of Sand," "One Rainy Wish," "Burning of the Midnight Lamp," "Rainy Day, Dream Away," "House Burning Down," and, of course, "Fire" itself. All from the man who set his guitar afire on the Monterey Festival stage.

Hendrix's live work often included many cover songs, by well-known artists such as Dylan, the Troggs (both "Like a Rolling Stone" and "Wild Thing" were performed at Monterey), the Beatles ("Day Tripper" and "Sgt. Pepper's Lonely Heart's Club Band"), Cream ("Sunshine of Your Love"), Chuck Berry ("Johnny B. Goode"), Carl Perkins ("Blue Suede Shoes"), and others.

Though Hendrix's own songs were the subject of thousands of bar- and high-school-band cover versions in their time, comparatively few—considering his stature and influence—have been redone professionally by other artists. One suspects that's largely due to the overwhelming personal stamp he placed on all his work; covering a one-of-a-kind artist is a losing proposition for any performer. Still, there have been several well-known recordings of Hendrix songs, including Stevie Ray Vaughan's "Voodoo Chile (Slight Return)," Rickie Lee Jones's "Up from the Skies," and Rod Stewart's top 40 hit "Angel." Hendrix was the subject of two tribute albums in the early 1990s. *If 6 Was 9: A Tribute to Jimi Hendrix,* on the obscure Imaginary Records label, featured a crew of alternative bands such as Thin White Rope, the Shamen, the Mock Turtles, and Thee Hypnotics. 1993's *Stone Free: A Tribute to Jimi Hendrix* was a powerhouse effort on Warner Brothers featuring Eric Clapton, the Cure, Pat Metheny, the Spin Doctors, the Pretenders, P. M. Dawn, and Paul Rodgers (who recorded his own Hendrix tribute set the same year), among others.

That Hendrix's influence will last well through the millenium was evidenced in late 1993, when MCA Records reissued *Are You Experienced?, Axis: Bold as Love,* and *Electric Ladyland* in deluxe packaging. The release coincided with, in the words of the label, a "state-of-the-art audio/video exhibition featuring cutting-edge digital and computer technology designed to catapult Hendrix into the 21st century." While the exhibit's choice of a title—"Jimi Hendrix: On the Road 1994"—may sound somewhat tasteless, it's a good bet the concept would have suited Hendrix's taste for mythological scenes to a T.

DON HENLEY

A major American superstar who successfully made the transition from '60s rocker to '70s country rocker to '80s solo artist, Don Henley (b. July 22, 1947, Gilmer, Texas) is best known for his role as co-founder of the Eagles. During the span of their 10-year career, the band met enormous international success and sold over 80 million albums worldwide; at the time of their 1981 breakup, they had four Number One albums, five Number One singles, and four Grammys to their credit.

Though Henley was the band's drummer, he co-wrote all 10 of the group's top 10 hits and sang lead on many of them. Both he and band co-founder Glenn Frey each went on to significant solo success, but significantly, as Frey's career began cooling down in the late 1980s, Henley's was getting hotter by the minute.

Henley got his start playing in a late '60s Texas band named Shiloh, who moved to L.A. and recorded an eponymous debut album for Amos Records in 1970. Oddly enough, another Amos act named Longbranch Pennywhistle made its bow the same year; featured in that group's ranks was one Glenn Frey, who would soon invite Henley to join him in Linda Ronstadt's backup band. He did, and by 1971 the pair had hooked up with guitarist Bernie Leadon and bassist Randy Meisner to form the Eagles.

With a 1972 debut album boasting two top 20 singles—"Take It Easy," co-written by Frey and Jackson Browne, and "Witchy Woman," penned by Henley and Leadon—the Eagles soared from the start. Though Frey and Henley had written no songs together on their first album, on the 1973 follow-up, *Desperado,* they launched a fruitful songwriting partnership that lasted for the duration of the group's tenure.

When Glenn Frey announced his plans to make a solo record in 1980, his decision would ultimately result in the breakup of the Eagles. But the band that three years earlier had scored a top 20 hit with "Life in the Fast Lane" had apparently also been singing from experience: Henley, in a legal scrape that generated much bad press that year, was given two years probation for drug possession and fined for "contributing to the delinquency" of a teenaged girl. The roasting the singer received at the time, ironically,

Don Henley

gave him sufficient fuel to start his own solo career with his first hit single, the top five "Dirty Laundry." An embittered protest against the scandal-hungry press, Henley's memorable song was driven by a pounding beat, over which he sang, "We got dirty little fingers in everybody's pie/We love to cut you down to size/We love dirty laundry/We can do 'The Innuendo'/We can dance and sing/When it's all said and done we haven't told you a thing/We all know that Crap is King/Give us dirty laundry!" The song helped push Henley's 1982 debut album, *I Can't Stand Still,* to number 24; Frey's debut, *No Fun Aloud,* which had been released three months earlier and boasted two top 40 hits, had only managed to reach number 32.

Interestingly, the solo careers of Henley and Frey share another parallel: each writer, either due to habit or limitations, is heavily dependent on using songwriting collaborators. When together in the Eagles, neither Henley nor Frey had ever written a song solely on his own; the vast majority of their songs were written together, often with other writers. Alone, Frey has penned exactly two songs on his own—1982's "All Those Lies" and 1992's instrumental "Agua Tranquillo"—and Henley, none. While Frey has typically used Jack Tempchin, Henley generally works with guitarist- producer Danny "Kootch" Kortchmar.

With 1984's double platinum *Building the Perfect Beast,* Henley's solo career markedly heated up. "The Boys of Summer," the album's opening track, was a brilliant single which, with its memorable

lyrics about a Cadillac bearing a "Deadhead" sticker and the refrain "Don't look back, you can never look back," conveyed a new maturity that has suited Henley well—and helped take him into the 1990s perceived as a relevant artist. Three additional top 40 hits, including the top 10 "All She Wants to Do Is Dance," kept the album high in the charts for well over a year.

Henley's third solo album, 1989's *The End of the Innocence,* reached number eight, went triple platinum, and, perhaps most amazingly, enjoyed a marathon stay on the charts of 148 weeks. Considering that the singer had previously been singing "don't look back," there was some irony in the fact that the album's first single—the top 10 title track, written by Henley and Bruce Hornsby—began by asking, "Remember when the days were long/And rolled beneath a deep blue sky/Didn't have a care in the world/With mommy and daddy standin' by?" But rather than a simple nostalgia piece, the song railed against "this tired old man that we elected king" and lawyers.

Henley's growing political activism and concern with environmental issues became increasingly evident on *Innocence*—and in his personal life. In 1990, the singer spearheaded a major campaign to preserve the Walden Woods, the forest area surrounding Henry David Thoreau's celebrated retreat at Walden Pond. By 1993, the cause was furthered by the all-star benefit tribute album *Common Thread: The Songs of the Eagles,* featuring well-known country singers Clint Black, Vince Gill, Alan Jackson, Trisha Yearwood, and others performing the songs Henley and his former band had made famous two decades earlier.

The future of Henley's recording career was the object of much industry speculation in mid-1993, after the singer declared he would no longer record for Geffen Records due to severe disagreements about his treatment there and the overall validity of his contract. Geffen then sued the singer for breach of contract, and the singer fired back another lawsuit, claiming the label had conspired against him by asking other labels not to consider signing him. A final irony: four years earlier, referring to *The End of the Innocence,* Henley told the *New York Times*'s Stephen Holden, "I mention lawyers several times on the album. That's because of the pervasive sense of every man for himself and every woman for herself. These days you see more men and women suing each other. It's a very insidious thing."

TOP ALBUMS

I CAN'T STAND STILL (Asylum, '82, *24*)
BUILDING THE PERFECT BEAST (Geffen, '84, *13*)
THE END OF THE INNOCENCE (Geffen, '89, *8*)

TOP SONGS

DIRTY LAUNDRY (Asylum, '82, *3*)
THE BOYS OF SUMMER (Geffen, '84, *5*)
ALL SHE WANTS TO DO IS DANCE (Geffen, '85, *9*)
SUNSET GRILL (Geffen, '85, *22*)
THE END OF THE INNOCENCE (Geffen, '89, *8*)
THE LAST WORTHLESS EVENING (Geffen, '89, *21*)
THE HEART OF THE MATTER (Geffen, '90, *21*)

Additional Top 40 Songs: 2

JOHN HIATT

Though Indianapolis-born John Hiatt (b. Aug. 20, 1952) has never attained superstar status, the prolific singer-songwriter has enjoyed a career remarkable in its consistency and duration. Equally respected by critics and fellow musicians, Hiatt has had a hand in the music business since the early '70s, when he left Indiana for a planned songwriting career in Nashville and fell into the habit of regularly making records. His first appearance came as a member of Uni Records recording group White Duck, a Wisconsin band that drafted Hiatt as rhythm guitarist and secondary songwriter for its second album, 1972's *In Season.* By that time he'd struck a songwriting deal with Tree Publishing—pulling down a grand total of $25 weekly, he'd later mirthfully recall—and was making inroads on securing his own record deal.

Hiatt's solo career began in earnest when the manager of singer Tracy Nelson introduced him to executives at Epic Records, who signed him to a singles deal that resulted in two albums, 1974's *Hanging Around the Observatory* and 1975's *Overcoats,* both recorded in Nashville. Neither album was successful, and Hiatt was dropped—from Epic and, eventually, Tree (where his salary had risen to $250 weekly and actually become his sole income). Moving back to Indianapolis, then to San Francisco, Hiatt next spent two-and-a-half years performing on the road.

Hiatt's reentry into the recording scene came via a new publishing deal split between Bug Music and a company funded by guitarist Leo Kottke; the resulting 1979 album *Slug Line,* issued on MCA Records, bore an arty cover designed by John Van Hammersveld and seemed to position Hiatt directly in the middle of the era's "new wave" explosion. Though it was by no means a big seller, the biting wit displayed on such tracks as "The Negroes Were Dancing" helped establish Hiatt as a hipster among critics who'd otherwise ignored his past work. A second MCA album, 1980's *Two Bit Monsters,* was similarly admired but commercially ignored.

TOP ALBUMS

HANGIN' AROUND THE OBSERVATORY
(Epic, '74)
SLUG LINE (MCA, '79)
RIDING WITH THE KING (Geffen, '83)
BRING THE FAMILY (A&M, '87)
STOLEN MOMENTS (A&M, '90)

TOP SONGS

SHE LOVES THE JERK (Geffen, '83)
THING CALLED LOVE (A&M, '87)
HAVE A LITTLE FAITH IN ME
(A&M, '87)

Internationally, Hiatt's critical stature was significantly boosted at this time through a series of collaborations with guitarist Ry Cooder—including appearances on Cooder's *Borderline* (1980) and *The Slide Area* (1982) albums, and the soundtrack from the 1981 film *The Border.* Additionally, Cooder had invited Hiatt to join his band—playing guitar and singing—for a well-received 1980 European tour.

In the meantime, Hiatt had left MCA for yet another new label, Geffen Records, for whom he recorded three diverse-sounding albums, *All of a Sudden* (1982), *Riding With the King* (1983), and *Warming Up to the Ice Age* (1985). Despite the varied musical approach of each—producers Tony Visconti, San Francisco's the Durocs, England's Nick Lowe, and Nashville's Norbert Putnam couldn't be more stylistically dissimilar—they were uniformly rejected by the public, and Hiatt soon found himself without a record contract again.

"It was a point in my life where I had to take a good look, you know?" Hiatt recalled a few years later. "I had to consider that maybe I wouldn't make another record. And I *did* consider that." From this seeming low point came what would be the pivotal album in his career: *Bring the Family,* his triumphant A&M Records debut of 1987. Garnering Hiatt the best reviews of his career, the album was recorded in just four days by an exceptional quartet consisting of Hiatt, guitarist Cooder, British producer/bassist Lowe, and highly respected drummer Jim Keltner. The set's comparative lack of polish helped provide a sense of immediacy that, combined with Hiatt's lyrics—which seemed much more personal than usual this time out—displayed him at an all-time peak and kick-started his career once more.

Further A&M albums followed, including 1988's *Slow Turning* and 1990's *Stolen Moments.* Ironically, Hiatt's former labels became interested in him again: Epic and MCA reissued some of his earlier, long-deleted titles on CD, and in 1989, Geffen released *Y'All Caught* (subtitled *The Ones That Got Away, 1979–1985*), a near-comprehensive compilation that also included MCA material. Longtime fan

Bonnie Raitt also covered two Hiatt songs on her multi-platinum Capitol "comeback" albums, which enhanced his public profile considerably. Finally, fans of Hiatt's *Bring the Family* were thrilled in 1992 when that album's players—Hiatt, Cooder, Lowe, and Keltner—reunited to form Little Village, an informal quartet whose upbeat, eponymous Reprise album seemed a sheer labor of love.

DAN HICKS

Though he may be a peripheral figure in the overall pop pantheon, Dan Hicks (b. Dec. 9, 1941, Little Rock, Arkansas) wrote and performed some of the more interesting music of the early 1970s. Once describing the sound of his inimitable combo, the Hot Licks, as "a cross between the Andrews Sisters and the Jim Kweskin Jug Band," Hicks showed young and impressionable members of that era's burgeoning counterculture that "old-fashioned" music—for that's indeed what he played—easily held as much validity as half-hour, poorly played, acid-rock-inspired drum solos. His saving grace, even for those who didn't appreciate his group's brilliant musicianship, was his wicked sense of humor.

Hicks, who played both guitar and drums, was a founding member of San Francisco's legendary '60s band the Charlatans, whose 1969 album came at the end of their career, after Hicks had already departed. Even before he had left, though, he'd already formed the Hot Licks. Notable for their instrumental lineup—Hicks on guitar, two female vocalists, a bassist, no drummer, and a violinist—the group changed personnel slightly and then signed a deal in 1969 with Epic Records. From its very cover, which featured a deliberately ancient-looking photo of Hicks duded up in cowboy regalia and leaning on an acoustic guitar, *Original Recordings* seemed to be promising something different. And different it certainly was.

Officially billed as Dan Hicks and his Hot Licks (the female vocalists would later be known as Lickettes), the sextet opened its debut album with three of Hicks' finest songs: "Canned Music," "How Can I Miss You When You Won't Go Away?," and the eerily seductive "I Scare Myself" (which was cannily covered 15 years later by Thomas Dolby). Jaws must have dropped in communes from Maine to Min-

neapolis when unprepared fans of the era's "San Francisco sound" heard Hicks' music, which clearly drew inspiration from the legendary early-1930s jazz of guitarist Django Reinhardt and violinist Stephane Grappelli and threw in female harmonies like those heard on Army PX jukeboxes during World War II. As pianist Ben Sidran noted on the liner to 1972's *Striking It Rich* as he compared Hicks to underground cartoonist Robert Crumb: "They use the mood of the past to rewire your brain for the future."

Hot Licks personnel shifted through the course of their four albums, though both Hicks and superb violinist "Symphony" Sid Page were constants. As a lyricist, Hicks loved to devise various characters and scenarios that made his better songs especially memorable; among those songs were "Shorty Takes a Dive," "O'Reilly at the Bar," "Shorty Falls in Love," and "Moody Richard (The Innocent Bystander)."

The group's three Blue Thumb albums all made the album chart, with 1973's *Last Train to Hicksville* reaching a high of number 67. Additionally, Maria Muldaur covered Hicks' "Walkin' One and Only" on her top five 1973 set *Maria Muldaur*. The group broke up in 1974, but several members accompanied Hicks on his 1978 Reprise solo album, *It Happened One Bite*.

The "nostalgic" sound provided by the Hot Licks predated similar approaches later taken by the Pointer Sisters, Manhattan Transfer, and even Bette Midler. What made Hicks' music so much better, though, was that simply recreating an era was never his intention; providing a memorable context for those still-marvelous songs was.

Though he still performs occasionally, Dan Hicks hasn't made an album since 1978.

TOP ALBUMS

ORIGINAL RECORDINGS (Epic, '69)
WHERE'S THE MONEY? (Blue Thumb, '71)
STRIKING IT RICH! (Blue Thumb, '72)
LAST TRAIN TO HICKSVILLE (Blue Thumb, '73)

TOP SONGS

I SCARE MYSELF (Epic, '69)
HOW CAN I MISS YOU WHEN YOU WON'T GO AWAY? (Epic, '69)
CANNED MUSIC (Epic, '69)
WALKIN' ONE AND ONLY (Blue Thumb, '72)

PETER HIMMELMAN

One of the most notable benefits of the late-'70s and early-'80s punk–new wave music scene was the new method of exposure provided by its so-called DIY ethic—Do It Yourself. New, young bands could play live, low-budget gigs, record for small independent labels or even their own, and, with luck, build viable careers at a minimum of expense. So it was that Peter Himmelman established himself as the major creative force behind Minneapolis new wave group Sussman Lawrence. Between 1980 and '84, the band released two albums (*Hail to the Modern Hero* and *Pop City*), continuously played small bars throughout the Midwest, and gained a small but loyal audience and press following. Upon moving to New York in late 1984, the group played a steady stream of East Coast club dates, consolidated that following even more, and within two years released *This Father's Day* on their own Orange Records label.

In the interim, however, the group had dropped the Sussman Lawrence moniker and instead become Peter Himmelman and his band. Hardly a power play, the move simply recognized the obvious: Himmelman, who played guitar and sang, had written all the group's material from the start—Sussman Lawrence was actually a onetime Himmelman pseudonym. And the change was artistically appropriate as well: in the six years between Sussman Lawrence's debut and *This Father's Day,* Himmelman progressed from a too-obvious Elvis Costello sound-alike to a much more mature, individualistic songwriter. That was quickly recognized both by MTV, who gave regular rotation in 1986 to the singer's cheaply produced video of "Eleventh Confession," and Island Records, who picked up and

Peter Himmelman

TOP ALBUMS

THIS FATHER'S DAY (Orange, '86)
GEMETRIA (Island, '87)
SYNESTHESIA (Island, '89)
FROM STRENGTH TO STRENGTH (Epic, '91)

TOP SONGS

THIS FATHER'S DAY (Orange, '86)
ELEVENTH CONFESSION (Orange, '86)

rereleased *This Father's Day* the same year.

Himmelman's evolution from new wave copycat to warm, humanistic songwriter was evident as early as *This Father's Day*—which bore a title track the singer had specially written and recorded in 1983 as a present for his dying father. The albums that followed—*Gemetria* (1987), *Synesthesia* (1989), and *From Strength to Strength* (1991), his first for Epic—showed the singer was learning to drop the inessentials (he had a tendency to be wordy) and concentrate on simple, more direct songs and sentiments. At the same time, Himmelman was acquiring a reputation as a vastly enjoyable live performer, who—perhaps taking a cue from late comedian Andy Kaufman—would often ask his club audiences to accompany him outside for further performances.

Like his father-in-law, Bob Dylan, Himmelman has very often worn his religious beliefs on his sleeve. An orthodox Jew, the singer crafted a memorable biographical account of an encounter with a white supremacist cab driver on his 1992 album *Flown This Acid World*. The song, "Untitled," concludes with the singer seeking consolation and advice from a former concentration camp victim "with death camp numbers on his arm." An unusual subject for any songwriter to pursue, the song is always emotionally received when performed in concert—and typifies the uniqueness of the singer's relationship with his loyal audience. Still nowhere near his peak, Peter Himmelman apparently wants to take his audience with him in more ways than one.

ROBYN HITCHCOCK

Robyn Hitchcock

Considering the vivid, surrealistic imagery that runs through the songs of Robyn Hitchcock (b. Mar. 3, 1952, London), there's no reason to assume that any of his material is particularly autobiographical. Still, it's tempting now to look back at the opening track of his first solo album, 1981's *Black Snake Diamond Role,* and wonder who "The Man Who Invented Himself" could be if not the singer himself. The founder of British cult band the Soft Boys, whose few albums sold minimally during the band's 1976–80 duration, Hitchcock has seen both his legacy and that of his former band grow by leaps and bounds during the 1980s and well into the '90s. Though the majority of his best material was never even released in the U.S.

until Rykodisc reissued it in 1992–93, by 1989 A&M Records was proudly stickering copies of Hitchcock's *Queen Elvis* with the enthusiastic accolade "#1 Post-Modern Artist."

A very clever tunesmith with an extremely vivid imagination, Robyn Hitchcock won his large '80s alternative following by, ironically, emulating the sounds of two decades earlier. Above all, one can't fault him for his taste. Vocally, he resembles no one so much as legendary Pink Floyd founder Syd Barrett; with the Soft Boys, in fact, he covered Barrett's little-known "Vegetable Man" and "Gigolo Aunt" as well as Floyd's "Astronomy Domine." He has also covered the Byrds, raved endlessly about the Beatles, and, as recently as 1993, released a song called "The Wreck of the Arthur Lee"—referring, of course, to the central figure in the mythic '60s rock band Love. Much of his music delights in references and puns that undoubtedly go over the heads of most of his younger audience; it's a sure bet, for example, that some listeners still have no idea that part of his "He's a Reptile" is sung precisely to the tune of the Crystals' Phil Spector–produced 1962 hit "He's a Rebel."

But Hitchcock is more than a walking jukebox (though in defense of his covers, most of his older fans are usually thrilled that a performer they admire grew up listening to the same obscure records that they did). Hitchcock may not be entirely original, but he's got a great ear for melody and is an absolutely superb lyricist…most of the time. From 1981 to 1985, his peak period as a solo artist, he produced his four best albums—*Black Snake Diamond Role, Groovy Decay, I Often Dream of Trains,* and *Fegmania!*—all of which were highlighted by his careful balance of humor ("Sometimes I Wish I Were a Pretty Girl"), surrealism ("The Man with the Lightbulb Head"), and sometimes surprising emotional depth ("52 Stations"). But on his albums of the later 1980s, Hitchcock went much heavier on the surrealism, a tad more on the humor, and almost completely neglected songs of any emotional depth whatsoever. Perhaps because he spent much of that period touring America (which remains his largest market by far), alternately being asked if he "took drugs" by naive young journalists and being expected to "act weird" while onstage, he instinctively shifted his writing style to fill that perceived need. Whatever the reason, his work suffered.

As the 1990s unwind, however, Hitchcock seems to be getting back to that special balance that made his records of the early '80s so delightful. Things are looking up: his 1993 album *Respect* was his best in nearly a decade, he remains a remarkably prolific writer, and his own songs are now being covered by others—even by R.E.M., who in 1992 recorded Hitchcock's "Arms of Love" for European release. As any Robyn Hitchcock fan will tell you—and as he himself surely knows by now—who covers whom sometimes makes all the difference in the world.

TOP ALBUMS

Fegmania! (Slash, '85)
Element of Light (Relativity, '86)
Globe of Frogs (A&M, '88)
Queen Elvis (A&M, '88)
Respect (A&M, '93)

TOP SONGS

52 Stations (Albion, '82)
The Man with the Lightbulb Head (Slash, '85)
Arms of Love (A&M, '93)

BUDDY HOLLY

Perhaps the only rock and roll performer of the 1950s to rival Elvis Presley in terms of influence and sheer rocking ability, Buddy Holly (b. Charles Hardin Holley, Sept. 7, 1936, Lubbock, Texas) had something even the King himself lacked: an impressive repertoire of self-penned classics. A mere glance at the familiar songs Holly made famous—from "That'll Be the Day" and "Peggy Sue" to "It's So Easy" and "Not Fade Away"—illustrates how deeply Holly's influence touched rock from its very beginning.

The pervasiveness of Buddy Holly's music and image can be felt in nearly every generation of performers that arose since his tragic death in 1959: from the Beatles and Rolling Stones, who recorded his "Words of Love" and "Not Fade Away" at the beginning of their careers in the 1960s; to Linda Ronstadt, who brought Holly's music to a new generation with her hit versions of "It's So Easy" and "That'll Be the Day" in the 1970s; to distinguished film director Francis Ford Coppola, who made a film based on Holly's song "Peggy Sue Got Married" in 1986. The singer's familiar horn-rimmed glasses made a deep enough visual image that when bespectacled performers such as Elvis Costello and Marshall Crenshaw made their respective public debuts two decades later, Holly's name somehow found its way into the lead paragraph of nearly every review. The meek-looking Texan has been immortalized in both a film (1978's *The Buddy Holly Story*) and stage musical (1989's London-based *Buddy: The Buddy Holly Story*). And finally, perhaps the most convincing proof of the singer's ultimate worth: his entire song catalog was purchased in 1975 by astute musicologist Paul McCartney.

Holly began his career playing country music in the early 1950s; by 1956, he had signed a contract with Decca and cut several singles in Nashville, none of which were successful. He returned to Texas, continued performing, and was reportedly inspired to play rock and roll after opening for a young Elvis Presley in Lubbock. (Ironically, Presley himself was quoted saying some years later, "Looking back over the last 20 years, I guess the guy I've admired most in rock 'n' roll is Buddy Holly.") Holly soon found a friend and more in producer Norman Petty, who owned the studio in nearby Clovis, New Mexico, where the singer soon recorded the demo of "That'll

Buddy Holly

non–pop star looks endeared him to many younger fans perhaps seeking nonthreatening role models. Further hits followed at two-month intervals, among them "Peggy Sue," "Oh, Boy!," "Maybe Baby," and "Rave On." Holly split with both the Crickets and manager Petty by the fall of 1958 and relocated to New York, where he very quickly married; his band continued without him for several years.

Needing money, Holly picked up a new band and continued touring through early 1959. While on the road as part of the Winter Dance Party touring caravan, he, the Big Bopper, and Richie Valens were killed on February 3, 1959, when their chartered plane crashed near Mason City, Iowa. A month later, Coral released his final top 20 hit, a version of Paul Anka's (ironically titled, considering the circumstances) "It Doesn't Matter Anymore." Though his voice was stilled at only 22, Holly's records kept coming: several recordings he'd made earlier, whether unreleased or demos, surfaced for many years afterward, most of them bearing overdubbed vocal or orchestral backing.

Holly's classic recordings have continue to be reissued over the years and remain true gems in the MCA Records catalog. He is unlikely to ever be forgotten. His tragic plane crash is referred to as "the day the music died" in Don McLean's classic 1971 smash "American Pie," and newer rock heroes such as Bruce Springsteen have unfailingly lauded the man at every opportunity. "I play Buddy Holly every night before I go on," Springsteen once said. "It keeps me honest!"

Be the Day" that landed him a contract from the Coral/Brunswick label in 1957. Holly's arrangement with the label was in some ways peculiar: while his records on the Coral label were solely credited to him, those released bearing the Brunswick imprint were attributed to the Crickets, his famous backing band. Holly's recording arrangement with Petty afforded him countless hours of studio time in which to experiment; among his stylistic innovations was his practice of often double-tracking his own voice, common years later, but then very new.

Holly's Brunswick debut single, "That'll Be the Day," was an immediate smash that hit Number One on *Billboard*'s Best Seller chart; the result would be a nonstop schedule of touring—in the U.S., U.K., and Australia—intermittently mixed with recording. Holly was a sensation: his quirky vocal style seemed very much the voice of exuberant youth, and his

---

TOP ALBUMS

THE BUDDY HOLLY STORY (Coral, '59, *11*)
REMINISCING (Coral, '63, *40*)

TOP SONGS

THAT'LL BE THE DAY (with the Crickets, Brunswick, '57, *1*)
PEGGY SUE (Coral, '57, *3*)
OH, BOY! (with the Crickets, Brunswick, '57, *10*)
MAYBE BABY (with the Crickets, Brunswick, '58, *17*)
RAVE ON (Coral, '58, *37*)
THINK IT OVER (with the Crickets, Brunswick,'58, *27*)
EARLY IN THE MORNING (Coral, '58, *32*)
IT DOESN'T MATTER ANYMORE (Coral, '59, *13*

BRUCE HORNSBY

One of the more interesting singer-songwriters to emerge in the 1980s—and certainly one of the most difficult to assign to a specialized genre—is Williamsburg, Virginia–born pianist Bruce Hornsby. Recipient of the 1986 Best New Artist Grammy award, Hornsby (b. Nov. 23, 1954) shot to instant prominence in 1986 with his hugely appealing Number One single "The Way It Is." Part of its appeal was how completely unique its piano-heavy arrangement sounded during a music year dominated by Whitney Houston, Madonna, and Janet Jackson; another part was, of course, the unremitting catchiness of its hooky chorus.

But there was more: Hornsby seemed to arrive already fully formed musically, in the same manner that one of his major influences, the Band, had two decades earlier. And while his piano solos (his, not a paid sessioneer's) were adventurously jazzy—his touch not unlike jazz star Keith Jarrett's, in fact—his song lyrics held the same timeless air of Americana as those of the Band's Robbie Robertson. Hornsby seemed a genuine artist, not a pop star, who coincidentally, almost accidentally, was finding favor with the public. All of which became obvious when it was later revealed that Hornsby, a former music student at the University of Miami and Berklee College of Music, had been microseconds away from signing a deal with new age–instrumental label Windham Hill before RCA nabbed him.

Though Hornsby's first three albums were consistently credited to Bruce Hornsby and the Range,

Bruce Hornsby

his band—which included David Mansfield (later replaced by Peter Harris), George Marinelli, Joe Puerta, and John Molo—was not involved in any songwriting; Hornsby's sole collaborator, at least on his own albums, consistently has remained his attorney brother, John. They work very well together; where his brother's lyrics are more image-laden, almost consciously literate, Hornsby himself tends to write more simple, emotional lines. Though his label once referred to him in jest as "a young William Faulkner with a backbeat," the description isn't far from the truth.

Hornsby made quite a splash, initially. Aside from nabbing the aforementioned Grammy, his debut album sent three singles into the top 20 ("The Way It Is," "Mandolin Rain," and "Every Little Kiss"); furthermore, longtime friend Huey Lewis, who'd produced three of the album's tracks, recorded his own version of Hornsby's "Jacob's Ladder" and sent it to Number One in early 1987. By 1988, Hornsby was off and running: while second album *Scenes from the Southside* hit the top five with hits "The Valley Road" and "Look Out Any Window," Hornsby himself was out collaborating with just about everybody in the business, including Don Henley (with whom he co-wrote Henley's top 10 hit "The End of

TOP ALBUMS

THE WAY IT IS (RCA, '86, *3*)
SCENES FROM THE SOUTHSIDE (RCA, '88, *5*)
A NIGHT ON THE TOWN (RCA, '90, *20*)
HARBOR LIGHTS (RCA, '93)

TOP SONGS

THE WAY IT IS (RCA, '86, *1*)
MANDOLIN RAIN (RCA, '87, *4*)
EVERY LITTLE KISS (RCA, '87, *14*)
THE VALLEY ROAD (RCA, '88, *5*)
LOOK OUT ANY WINDOW (RCA, '88, *35*)
ACROSS THE RIVER (RCA, '90, *18*

the Innocence"), the Nitty Gritty Dirt Band (with whom he won the 1989 Grammy for Best Bluegrass Recording from their *Will the Circle Be Unbroken Vol. 2*), Leon Russell (whose *Anything Can Happen* comeback set he produced), and many more.

Hornsby's final album with the Range, 1990's *A Night on the Town*, was considered a sales disappointment; only one single hit the top 20 ("Across the River"), while the album itself couldn't quite crack the top 40. Where was Hornsby? Out being guest keyboardist with the Grateful Dead (for over 100 shows), contributing to over 40 albums by other artists, touring himself, and—fair enough—having twins. Was he spreading himself too thin? Very possibly. By 1993, his album *Harbor Lights*—his first without the Range—quickly sank off the charts, hitless, despite a stellar musical cast that included Jerry Garcia, Pat Metheny, Bonnie Raitt, Phil Collins, and Branford Marsalis—all, by now, Hornsby's pals.

To be fair, no one can deny Hornsby's talents, which he's already ably demonstrated, nor the degree to which he's respected by his peers. But whether he's got another "The Way It Is" in him—and whether an audience will still be around that wants to hear it—may be the two biggest questions he now faces.

IAN HUNTER
. . . .

The lead singer of England's lovable, hard-rocking Mott the Hoople, Ian Hunter (b. Ian Patterson, June 3, 1946, Shrewsbury, England) was very much a central figure in rock and roll during the 1970s. As leader of a band that seemed to get nearly everything wrong but do it wonderfully, Hunter stayed with Mott from its 1968 inception through 1974, in the process recording eight very colorful albums that are among the most spirited (and sometimes extraordinary) in British pop. He successfully established a solo career in 1975 that continued through the mid-'80s, then returned in 1989 with *Y U I Orta*, his last album and final collaboration with longtime partner Mick Ronson, who died of cancer four years later.

The perpetually sunglassed Hunter was a flamboyant character from the very beginning. Initially a struggling songwriter who'd placed a few songs with '60s British artists like Freddie and the Dreamers and Dave Berry, the singer won his spot in Mott the

Hoople at the suggestion of legendary English producer Guy Stevens, who was bowled over by Hunter's rendition of "Like a Rolling Stone" during an audition. The choice of song was telling: the earliest Mott albums sounded much like *Highway 61 Revisited*–era Dylan being backed by an amphetamine-driven Procol Harum. The group's 1969 debut, *Mott the Hoople*, is an amazing take on all that was right with rock and roll at the time, mixing covers of the Kinks, the Sir Douglas Quintet, and Sonny Bono with Hunter's Dylanesque original "Backsliding Fearlessly" and Mott guitarist Mick Ralphs's "Rock 'n' Roll Queen"—a bruising, straightforward number that rocked like the Rolling Stones and Jerry Lee Lewis. While the band's British contemporaries were readying art rock "masterpieces" like *Tarkus, Fragile,* and *To Our Children's Children's Children,* Mott was rocking in very grand tradition.

The three albums that followed were equally as interesting and even more eclectic. By 1971's *Wildlife*, Hunter was mixing crazed covers of Little Richard's "Keep A'Knockin" and Melanie's "Lay Down" with self-penned songs of much greater depth and originality, particularly the wistful "Angel of Eighth Avenue" and "Waterlow" (which he has called the best song he's ever written). Following 1971's fascinating *Brain Capers*—which with the raving "Death May Be Your Santa Claus" and "The Moon Upstairs" remains one of rock's most joyously excessive classics—the band, weary of minimal sales and unrewarding gigs, prepared to disband.

In 1972, David Bowie effectively rescued Mott

TOP ALBUMS
. . . .

IAN HUNTER (Columbia, '75)
ALL-AMERICAN ALIEN BOY (Columbia, '76)
YOU'RE NEVER ALONE WITH A SCHIZOPHRENIC
    (Chrysalis, '79, 35)
IAN HUNTER LIVE/WELCOME TO THE CLUB
    (Chrysalis, '80)
SHORT BACK N' SIDES (Chrysalis, '81)
ALL OF THE GOOD ONES ARE TAKEN (Columbia, '83)
Y U I ORTA (with Mick Ronson, Mercury, '89)

TOP SONGS
. . . .

ONCE BITTEN TWICE SHY (Columbia, '75)
SHIPS (Chrysalis, '79)
CLEVELAND ROCKS (Chrysalis, '79)

the Hoople, not only by providing them their first top 40 hit with "All the Young Dudes," but by producing the hit album of the same name. The affiliation with Bowie—then at the height of his Ziggy Stardust fame—combined with the group's astute cover of the Velvet Underground's "Sweet Jane" and made Mott the darlings of the growing glitter rock scene. The albums that followed, 1973's *Mott* and 1974's *The Hoople,* were top 40 hits—and the increasingly popular band became the first rock group to play Broadway in a week-long engagement at the Uris Theater in May 1974. Hunter became the central focus of the band and edged out founding guitarist Ralphs, who exited to form Bad Company and was replaced by Spooky Tooth's Luther Grosvenor and, briefly, Mick Ronson. Meanwhile, the songs Hunter was writing—such as "Ballad of Mott the Hoople," "Marionette," and "Saturday Gigs"—were becoming increasingly self-referential and sentimental. It became evident the band would soon run out of steam, and by 1974, Hunter, with final Mott guitarist Ronson in tow, left the band to go solo.

While his career alone may not have been as colorful as Mott's, Hunter essentially carried on in his former band's tradition. "Once Bitten Twice Shy," the opening track from 1975's solo debut, *Ian Hunter,* sounded like prime *Dudes*-era Mott; it wasn't a hit at the time, but L.A. hard-rock band Great White took the song to the top five in 1989. In fact, Hunter would have no more hit singles in his career

after Mott, though his career as an album artist prospered. Despite the weak showing of follow-up *All-American Alien Boy* (which adventurously featured jazz stars Jaco Pastorius and David Sanborn), 1979's *You're Never Alone with a Schizophrenic* was often heard on album rock stations and climbed to number 35 on the charts. The album spawned one of the most unlikely cover versions imaginable when "Ships"—a beautiful song Hunter had written about his father, stylistically in Mott's *Wildlife* mode— became a top 10 hit for Barry Manilow in 1979.

Hunter's currency among the rising new generation of pop stars was exceptionally high due to his Mott roots: He was asked to produce Generation X's *Valley of the Dolls* in 1979, and the Clash's Mick Jones, who had long sung Mott's praises, co-produced Hunter's *Short Back and Sides* in 1981. But while Hunter's musical progeny flourished, after 1983's *All of the Good Ones Are Taken,* the singer seemed to vanish. Except for scattered contributions to film soundtracks such as *Teachers, Fright Night, The Wraith,* and *Light of Day,* the singer laid low for nearly eight years, finally returning in 1989 with *Y U I Orta*—which peaked at number 157 and was his most recent album to date. Still affectionately remembered by many loyal fans, Ian Hunter remains a sorely missed perpetrator of much divinely inspired rock and roll.

Ian Hunter

JANIS IAN

Janis Ian

Just about everything strange that can happen to a singer-songwriter has happened to Janis Ian (b. Janis Eddy Fink, May 7, 1951) during the lengthy course of her career—and the marvel is she's still out there singing and songwriting. Ian was catapulted to national prominence in 1967, when no less a public figure than conductor Leonard Bernstein pronounced her "a marvelous creature" on national television as she performed her controversial hit "Society's Child (Baby I've Been Thinking)." All of 15 years old, Ian suddenly found herself singing on "The Tonight Show" and elsewhere —and, chillingly, often being harrassed with disturbing cries of "nigger lover," since the song's subject matter of interracial romance upset many at the time. By 1968, the apparent child prodigy was performing at the Newport Folk Festival, hanging out with Jimi Hendrix, and being sent home from parties by a concerned Janis Joplin

when drugs were in use. A year later, after releasing four albums (*Janis Ian, For All the Seasons of Your Mind, The Secret Life of J. Eddy Fink,* and *Who Really Cares*) and facing both declining sales and accusations of selling out from the folk community that had earlier championed her, 10th-grade dropout Ian retired from the business.

Eventually she'd return—first with the 1970 Capitol album *Present Company* and live performances, then, after Roberta Flack took Ian's song "Jesse" to the top 30, with a reborn career on Columbia. Her 1974 label debut, *Stars,* was a surprisingly sophisticated, musically complex effort that—coming on the heels of the early-'70s singer-songwriter era—struck both the industry's and the public's fancy. And with 1975's *Between the Lines,* Janis Ian made the album of her career. At its center was her unforgettable top five ballad "At Seventeen," a sensitive account of the awkwardness of adolescence that, with its jarring lines about "ugly girls like me," was obviously deeply felt by the singer. Ian had honed a style that was lyrically moving and confessional; that combined folk, pop, and jazz forms intriguingly; and—most rewardingly for any singer-songwriter—that had touched her audience. "At Seventeen" won Ian her first Grammy (for Best Pop Vocal Performance, Female), while *Between the Lines* won honors for Best Engineered Recording (Non-Classical). She continued in the same manner for the next seven years and produced a series of consistently interesting albums, but none had a track as gripping as "At Seventeen," and only 1976's *Aftertones* reached the top 20.

Having been on the celebrity treadmill already with "Society's Child," Ian plugged away dutifully, but the insistent grind of the business eventually wearied her. ("Eleven solid years of make a record for three months, tour for eight months, write for two months, start all over again," she later complained.) In 1982, Ian walked away from her Columbia contract, eventually studying theater with Stella Adler, and then, unfortunately, suffering several hellish years: bad financial advice she'd received resulted in her being nearly wiped out by the I.R.S. for back taxes; a burst intestine nearly killed her; she divorced an abusive hus-

TOP ALBUMS

JANIS IAN (Verve/Forecast, '67, *29*)
BETWEEN THE LINES (Columbia, '75, *1*)
AFTERTONES (Columbia, '76, *12*)
MIRACLE ROW (Columbia, '77)

TOP SONGS

SOCIETY'S CHILD (BABY, I'VE BEEN THINKING) (Verve/Forecast, '67, *14*)
AT SEVENTEEN (Columbia, '75, *3*)

band; and, finally, she discovered that most major record labels weren't especially interested in signing a two-time "has-been" star who was nearing 40.

Deciding to concentrate on songwriting, Ian then teamed with Nashville writer Kye Fleming and saw her songs covered by Amy Grant, Uta Lemper, Dianne Schuur, and Maura O'Connell, among others. The singer took permanent residence in Music City in 1989, finding the city's treatment of music writers infinitely preferable to what she'd experienced in the past on both coasts. After contributing a track ("Days Like These") to the 1992 film *Fall from Grace*, Ian released her first album in 12 years in 1993, the superb and fully realized *Breaking Silence*. Though most of the publicity she received at the time focused on her "coming out" and making public she was a lesbian, some astute critics ironically noted that Ian's album sounded every bit as contemporary as the latest works by Suzanne Vega and other conspicuously younger artists on larger labels. But as Ian learned three decades earlier, that's show biz.

CHRIS ISAAK

Chris Isaak

It's ironic that MTV, which prides itself on replacing the old and tired with the new and exciting, played a major role in establishing Chris Isaak (b. June 26, 1956) as a star in the early 1990s. While the video of his 1990 single "Wicked Game" followed all of the network's unspoken rules—it was shot by trendy "name" director Herb Ritts, it featured the handsome singer erotically embracing "name" model Helena Christensen on a beach—the song itself could have been written and sung 30 years earlier. Chris Isaak's circle of business acquaintances may include hot '90s icons like David Lynch, Jonathan Demme, Keanu Reeves, and Bridget Fonda, and his face may appear on the cover of such up-to-the-minute fashion magazines as *Elle*, but his music comes from the same territories Roy Orbison, Elvis Presley, and Ricky Nelson explored long ago.

Isaak, who grew up in Stockton, California, claims a childhood of listening to country and western music, crooners like Dean Martin and Bing Crosby, and, in his words,

TOP ALBUMS

SILVERTONE (Warner Bros., '85)
CHRIS ISAAK (Warner Bros., '87)
HEART SHAPED WORLD
  (Reprise, '89, 7)
SAN FRANCISCO DAYS
  (Reprise, '93, 35)

TOP SONGS

WICKED GAME (Reprise, '91, 6)

the "obscure genius" of Louis Prima. He attended college in Japan, where he pursued amateur boxing (as evidenced by the shape of his nose) and initially heard Presley's famous Sun Records recordings, which, he says, inspired him to begin his singing career. He eventually returned to San Francisco, where he performed as a soloist and then assembled a backing trio dubbed Silvertone. An extended stay at a local club brought him to the attention of producer Erik Jacobsen, who had previously worked with the Lovin' Spoonful, Tim Hardin, and Sopwith Camel, among others, and he helped Isaak sign his deal with Warner Bros.

Isaak garnered much early press attention with 1985's *Silvertone*, though most of it focused on what he seemed to represent—an attractive musical throwback who looked like Elvis Presley and sounded like Roy Orbison—rather than the quality of his songs, which despite their retro-rockabilly feel were substantial. Both his debut and 1987's *Chris Isaak* sold poorly domestically (only the second charted, peaking at number 194 in two weeks), but the latter's "Blue Hotel" was a major hit in France; the group subsequently spent much time working the European market to great success.

A cameo appearance in Jonathan Demme's 1988 film *Married to the Mob* triggered an entirely new career for Isaak; further film work would include another cameo in Demme's *Silence of the Lambs,* a role in David Lynch's *Twin Peaks—Fire Walk with Me,* and by 1993, a starring role in Bernardo Bertolucci's *Little Buddha.* Rather than interfering with his music, Isaak's film activities have actually helped him. An Atlanta disc jockey who'd heard "Wicked Game" in Lynch's 1990 film *Wild at Heart* single-handedly resuscitated the song and helped make it a top 10 single 18 months after its release on Isaak's 1989 set, *Heart Shaped World*—a record both Isaak and Warner Bros. had thought long dead. As a result, the album finally entered the top 10 and went platinum in 1991.

After renegotiating his contract, Isaak returned in 1993 with *San Francisco Days,* a respectable effort that broke no new ground but was still typically enjoyable. The album went gold and peaked at number 35, and singing actor Isaak was off for a summer tour with Tina Turner. Though it seemed a strange double billing, it indicated the dilemma an artist like Isaak faces in the genre-conscious mid-'90s: he may have the look and the feel of a young alternative artist, but he has the sound middle-aged Americans heard on their car radios 30 years ago. The major downside? Eventually, of course, they got tired of it.

JOE JACKSON

The only thing "new" about Joe Jackson, one of the select few "new wave" artists to stick around after the ensuing marketing shtick died down, was, and is, the height of his ambition. Though his 1979 debut, *Look Sharp,* seemed the essence of punk confrontation at the time of its release—with Jackson glaring and pointing angrily from the album's back cover and its tunes about the sleazy press in "Sunday Papers"—in retrospect, it

now seems a viable music business entrée from a young upstart sharp enough to know all the right marketing moves. A lanky, piano-playing singer with a noticeably receding hairline, Jackson (b. Aug. 11, 1954, Burton-on-Trent, England) then seemed like a watered-down version of Elvis Costello, singing snappy, sarcastic tunes about "Happy Loving Couples," "Fools in Love," and "Pretty Girls." The difference, evident even then, was the feeling that deep down inside, Jackson was probably a decent, nice, well-adjusted fellow just looking to make a living.

His saving grace? A great ear for pop hooks, evident with his first hit "Is She Really Going Out with Him?," a track about as far removed from punk rock as were the Eagles. But all the trappings were there—even the clothes—and Jackson's first two "new wave" albums charted much higher than Costello's had two years earlier: *Look Sharp!* went top 20 and eventually gold, and quick follow-up *I'm the Man* swiftly reached number 22.

After one more similar-sounding album, 1980's *Beat Crazy,* Jackson disbanded his favored quartet and gave the first indication that he—a former student of London's Royal Academy of Music, member of a jazz trio, and pianist at a Playboy club—wasn't just any pop star. In essence, beginning with 1981's *Joe Jackson's Jumpin' Jive,* a one-off "affectionate tribute" to 1940s swing music, Jackson became purposely unpredictable, swinging from genre to genre and back again. Luckily for him, the very next genre he tackled was sophisticated, piano-driven Latin pop inspired by "the streets of New York," where he'd

TOP ALBUMS

LOOK SHARP! (A&M, '79, *20*)
I'M THE MAN (A&M, '79, *22*)
NIGHT AND DAY (A&M, '82, *4*)
BODY AND SOUL (A&M, '84, *20*)
BIG WORLD (A&M, '86, *34*)
LAUGHTER & LUST (Virgin, '91)

TOP SONGS

IS SHE REALLY GOING OUT WITH HIM? (A&M, '79, *21*)
STEPPIN' OUT (A&M, '82, *6*)
BREAKING US IN TWO (A&M, '83, *18*)
YOU CAN'T GET WHAT YOU WANT (TILL YOU KNOW WHAT YOU WANT) (A&M, '84, *15*)

Joe Jackson

just moved. *Night and Day*—named not just for the Cole Porter tune but also to delineate album sides—begat Jackson's biggest hit to date, the top 10 single "Steppin' Out," and brought Jackson his first and only top five album.

From that career high point, Jackson's path began to strangely waver. His first film soundtrack—for James Bridges' film *Mike's Murder*—was issued in 1983, oddly months before the film's actual release; when it finally hit theatres, Jackson's music was nowhere to be found. His next "real" album, 1984's *Body and Soul*—featuring Jackson clutching a cigarette and a tenor sax, a stunning tribute to a classic, identical Sonny Rollins Blue Note album cover of the 1950s—offered Jackson's last top 20 hit, "You Can't Get What You Want (Till You Know What You Want)." Cover art and all, it was readily becoming apparent that Jackson was treating each new album as a special project—which may have made him unpredictable, as he likely wanted to be, but also was confusing his audience. So it was that he recorded his "special, three-sided, direct-to-two-track digital" album *Big World,* followed by his curious (but quite

impressive) instrumental album, 1987's *Will Power*—which peaked at number 131 on the charts and remains his poorest-selling non-soundtrack effort ever. (His next album, the score from *Tucker: The Man and His Dream,* didn't chart at all.)

Following a double live set that served as a welcome career recap, Jackson recorded what he would later refer to as his best album, 1989's *Blaze of Glory.* His first set of new songs in three years, it was indeed superb—and, better yet, noticeably nonconceptual. When it peaked disappointingly at number 61, Jackson, miffed at what he felt was underpromotion from his longtime label A&M, departed for Virgin Records. While his first album for Virgin, 1991's *Laughter & Lust,* did even worse, it still showed Jackson capable of writing great pop songs when he wanted to, particularly the little-heard "The Other Me" and "When You're Not Around."

Ultimately, Jackson's incredible creative drive may in some ways be his greatest handicap. In the early days of MTV, he spoke out forcefully against rock videos; yet in steadfastly refusing to do some when he might have, he may have sabotaged his own career momentum. Furthermore, increasingly noticeable on some of his more recent songs—such as "Hit Single" and "The Old Songs" from *Laughter & Lust*—is an unpleasant lyrical bitterness that, one suspects, stems from his own personal experience in the music business. If he's not careful, he'll turn into a punk rocker before he knows it.

MICK JAGGER

As one-half of the composing team that has guided the Rolling Stones from their obscure 1962 beginnings to the present, singer Mick Jagger (b. Michael Philip Jagger, July 26, 1943, Dartford, England) shares with guitarist Keith Richards songwriting credits for 36 of the band's 41 top 40 hits—and for all eight of their Number One songs, starting with 1965's all-time classic, "(I Can't Get No) Satisfaction." Discerning precisely who contributed what, and where, seemed more difficult before both Jagger and Richards began recording their own albums in the mid-1980s. By 1993, with each artist three albums deep into his respective solo career, it appears that the work was split exactly where one might think: Jagger, the witty and verbal Stone, wrote the lyrics; Richards, the chugging muse with the rock and roll heart, wrote the riffs.

Unfortunately for Richards — and for the future of his solo career—his guitar-playing and songwriting style are much more easily replaceable commodities than are Jagger's vocals and lyrics. While Richards continues to struggle as a barely passable lead vocalist, Mick Jagger can—and does—hire any player he wants. And if a "Stones-style" guitar part is called for, chances are any studio pro will be able to deliver it in an instant. Sad to say, Richards' playing since the early '70s days of "Brown Sugar" has settled into a recognizable groove that may indeed be his stylistic hallmark, but it has also dragged down much of the Stones' post-'60s music for its lack of innovation.

The flip side, of course, is that without Richards as his co-writer, one might expect Jagger to soar in

entirely new musical directions. But he hasn't. Beginning with 1985's *She's the Boss,* Jagger has brought in distinguished producers such as Nile Rodgers and Bill Laswell and equally distinguished guitarists like Jeff Beck—and recorded three successive albums of music that sounds very much like the Stones, only weaker. While *She's the Boss* went platinum and offered a top 15 single with "Just Another Night," it peaked at number 13, the first time a new, non-compilation album featuring Jagger failed to make the top 10 since 1964 (and the release of *England's Newest Hitmakers/The Rolling Stones,* the group's debut album, which managed to climb two notches higher than Jagger's debut nonetheless).

Primitive Cool, Jagger's 1987 follow-up, was even more of a disappointment. With the novelty of what a Mick Jagger solo album might sound like no longer an issue, it failed even to crack the top 40, and its one meager hit, the Stonesish "Let's Work," peaked at number 39. Ironically, the album's title track boasted some of Jagger's best lyrics in ages; rather than the typical one-syllable patter that characterized much of the Stones' later work—and of which "Let's Work" was a prime example—"Primitive Cool" showed the sort of thoughtful lyrical approach Jagger hadn't used since the late 1960s.

Despite using the very credible contemporary producer Rick Rubin on 1993's *Wandering Spirit,* Jagger had only middling luck with it. Though it was loaded with Stonesy material bearing the sort of song titles the band had made famous— "Don't Tear Me Up," "Put Me in the Trash," "Wired All Night"—it failed to connect critically and entered the chart at number 11, proceeding downward thereafter. And oddly, the most promising song on the album, "Angel in My Heart," gave rise to new questions about the division of songwriting duties in the Stones. A gentle acoustic track sung rather than shouted by Jagger, it sounded much like the melodic material the Stones were regularly performing circa their 1967 *Flowers* album—which in many ways was their best. The question: how much of that era's material *did* Jagger write? And why did he stop?

In late 1993, Mick Jagger and Keith Richards

TOP ALBUMS

SHE'S THE BOSS (Columbia, '85, 13)
PRIMITIVE COOL (Columbia, '87)
WANDERING SPIRIT (Atlantic, '93, 11)

TOP SONGS

JUST ANOTHER NIGHT
  (Columbia, '85, 12)
LUCKY IN LOVE (Columbia, '85, 38)
DANCING IN THE STREET (with David
  Bowie, EMI America, '85, 7)
LET'S WORK (Columbia, '87, 39)

were reported to be holding auditions for a new bass player to replace 57-year-old Bill Wyman, whose departure had marked a historic turn for the group. Unsurprisingly, in light of their non-stellar solo careers, the pair was again planning to record a new Rolling Stones album and follow it up with a tour. Though it may be too early to know what the band's new material will sound like, here's a safe guess: Stonesy. Very Stonesy.

GARLAND JEFFREYS

To some it might seem odd that critic Robert Christgau once, in his wiseguy way, called Garland Jeffreys "a living breathing advertisment for the mongrelization of the races." But odd it wasn't, by any stretch. Jeffreys (b. 1944, Brooklyn, New York), an outstanding singer and writer, has spent most of his recording career composing songs dealing explicitly with his peculiar heritage—a mix of black, white, Puerto Rican, and possibly Native American—and how that ethnic blend has affected even the most minute aspects of his life. He's worn his hair in dreadlocks, he's written songs about being called "Buckwheat" by a white man at a Mets game, and he's seen the other side as well. "I don't go through a lot of stuff that real dark people go through," he once told writer Toby Goldstein. "I can, as they [say], I can pass. People never know what I am, which is a real asset in terms of survival in this world."

An art major at Syracuse University, where he struck up a longtime friendship with fellow student Lou Reed, Jeffreys graduated in 1965 and spent some time studying art in Florence, Italy, before returning to New York. Once there, he began playing in various Manhattan clubs and eventually formed the group Grinder's Switch. Billed as Penguin, the group backed Jeffreys' friend (and, like Reed, former Velvet Underground member) John Cale on his 1969 debut album *Vintage Violence*, a brilliant set that climaxed with Jeffreys' own composition, "Fair-

weather Friend." The band got its own deal with Vanguard, and in 1970 it released one album credited to "Grinder's Switch featuring Garland Jeffreys" that sold poorly.

A solo deal with Atlantic resulted in an eponymous 1973 album that was artfully produced and included one track recorded in Jamaica—an early indication of the reggae leanings later to color Jeffreys' most popular work. Oddly, while the album did little business, a non-album track next released by Atlantic called "Wild in the Streets" garnered scattered airplay and provided the singer a significant critical buzz. After a mismatched deal with newly founded Arista resulted in just one single—1975's "The Disco Kid Part 1"—Jeffreys found a new home at A&M, not only for himself but for "Wild in the Streets." *Ghost Writer,* his 1977 label debut, became his first charting album (it hit number 140) and was a critical sensation. Top-notch production by David Spinozza and Jeffreys himself and the performer's best batch of songs to date made *Ghost Writer* almost maddeningly addictive ear candy. Jeffreys' unique combination of politically hot topics (his song "Why-O" was about mandatory busing and "I May Not Be Your Kind" about interracial romance; the album itself was dedicated to "the abused and battered children of the world") and the album's clever blend of R&B and reggae feels was in many ways stunning.

Jeffreys' next two albums continued in a similar direction, but neither was ultimately as gripping. He left A&M after 1979's *American Boy and Girl* and headed to Epic. While there, he seemed on the verge of breaking through several times, mostly due to what appeared to be a marketing effort to present him as some sort of Springsteenian rock figure. *Escape Artist,* his 1981 commercial peak, helped in that regard: it featured E Street Band members Roy Bittan and Danny Federici, as well as Graham Parker's rhythm section, the Rumour. True, the singer hadn't given up on his multicultural approach: also on hand were important reggae figures like Linton Kwesi Johnson and Big Youth. But while the album

TOP ALBUMS

GHOST WRITER (A&M, '77)
ONE-EYED JACK (A&M, '78)
AMERICAN BOY & GIRL
  (A&M, '79)
ESCAPE ARTIST (Epic, '81)
ROCK 'N' ROLL ADULT (Epic, '81)
GUTS FOR LOVE (Epic, '83)
DON'T CALL ME BUCKWHEAT
  (RCA, '91)

TOP SONGS

SHE DIDN'T LIE (Atlantic, '73)
WILD IN THE STREETS (Atlantic, '74)
I MAY NOT BE YOUR KIND
  (A&M, '77)

prominently featured Jeffreys singing the praises of rock and roll on tracks like "R.O.C.K.," it buried his most topical song—"Miami Beach," about that town's Liberty City riots—by sticking it on an accompanying "bonus" four-song EP. Two more albums for Epic were to come, then the singer laid low for nearly eight years.

Jeffreys' 1991 comeback effort, *Don't Call Me Buckwheat,* was an unexpected pleasure containing some of the most pointed songs he'd ever written. Dealing almost exclusively with the subject of race and racism, the album in some therapeutic way seemed to be directed as much at Jeffreys himself (on such autobiographical songs as "I Was Afraid of Malcolm" and the title track) as any kind of general audience. It was a mature statement by an artist by no means past his peak, and it was welcome indeed.

BILLY JOEL

A prolific recording superstar whose 1977 smash *The Stranger* became the biggest-selling album by a solo artist in Columbia Records history, Billy Joel (b. William Martin Joel, May 9, 1949, Hicksville, New York) long ago won the war—now he's just wrapping up the battles. At one point the object of derision by critics who felt his work hacklike and lacking in rock and roll "spirit," Joel received unstinting praise from all quarters for his 1993 album *River of Dreams.* And while that might have mattered to the singer, chances are the fact that it was the fastest-selling album in his career —and spent the first three weeks of its chart life sitting comfortably at Number One—meant a bit more.

A journeyman rocker who has led one of the most tumultuous lives in the recording business, Billy Joel first recorded as Billy Joe Joel as a member of late-'60s rock group the Hassles, a Long Island combo that claimed the Vagrants, Young Rascals, and Vanilla Fudge as contemporaries. After releasing five singles and two albums between 1967 and 1969, all of which flopped, Joel formed the "power duo" Attila with his former drummer; their sole album, released on Epic in 1970, similarly stiffed.

Billy Joel's solo career officially commenced in 1971, when a deal he struck with industry figure Artie Ripp resulted in the making of *Cold Spring Harbour,* issued on Ripp's Paramount-distributed Family label. Any way you look at it, though, it was

a bad deal for Joel: The album was slightly sped up in the mastering, which made his voice sound like, in his words, "a chipmunk." Additionally, he had signed a heavy-duty contract with Ripp that gave away most of his publishing royalties and ultimately proved to have disastrous consequences. Chagrined, Joel headed to Los Angeles and began playing cocktail piano as "Bill Martin" (a situation that would result in his writing his first hit, 1974's "Piano Man"). When Columbia Records heard that a taped performance of Joel singing his song "Captain Jack" was getting repeat radio airplay on Philadelphia station WMMR, they tracked the singer down and eventually signed him—after concluding a hefty settlement with Family's Ripp, who reportedly was allotted 25 percent of Joel's future sales royalties.

Success came quickly. The autobiographical title track of 1973's *Piano Man,* the singer's first effort for Columbia, reached number 25 on the Hot 100 and soon propelled the album to gold certification; "The Entertainer," from Joel's follow-up, *Streetlife Serenade,* also proved a top 40 hit. But it was with 1977's *The Stranger* that Billy Joel delivered his sales monster. Spending an astounding 137 weeks on the charts, the seven-times-platinum set produced the gold single "Just the Way You Are" and further hits "Movin' Out (Anthony's Song)," "Only the Good Die Young," and "She's Always a Woman." In short, it was the album that has come to define Billy Joel for most people. A sometimes upbeat, sometimes blatantly romantic pop record, it elevated the

TOP ALBUMS

THE STRANGER (Columbia, '77, 2)
52ND STREET (Columbia, '78, 1)
GLASS HOUSES (Columbia, '80, 1)
STORM FRONT (Columbia, '89, 1)
RIVER OF DREAMS (Columbia, '93, 1)

Additional Top 40 Albums: 8

TOP SONGS

JUST THE WAY YOU ARE (Columbia, '77, 3)
MY LIFE (Columbia, '78, 3)
IT'S STILL ROCK 'N' ROLL TO ME (Columbia, '80, 1)
TELL HER ABOUT IT (Columbia, '83, 1)
WE DIDN'T START THE FIRE (Columbia, '89, 1)

Additional Top 40 Songs: 27

Billy Joel

singer to the position of a top-notch pop craftsman, a songsmith with a great ear for hooks in the tradition of Elton John.

Joel's story thereafter is essentially one of nonstop success and broken sales records. His equally strong follow-up, *52nd Street,* stayed at Number One for eight weeks, showing *The Stranger* was by no means a career fluke; its three hits included the gold top five "My Life" as well as "Big Shot" and "Honesty." Joel recorded an astounding string of 20 top 40 hits during the course of the 1980s, nine of which reached the top 10. Most interesting was the variety in the sound of all his singles; as a writer, he deliberately worked in many genres, from the simple pop style of his earlier "Honesty" to rock ("It's Still Rock 'n' Roll to Me") and even early-'60s pop ("Uptown Girl" and "Tell Her About It"). Joel was one of the first major singer-songwriters to take advantage of the burgeoning rock video format, and he did so with consistent creativity; several of MTV's most-played videos of the 1980s were his.

Billy Joel has had his share of personal happiness and grief during the course of his career. On a personal level, his marriage to supermodel Christie Brinkley looks to be one of the happiest unions within the industry; Brinkley, who appeared in the singer's "Uptown Girl" video, painted the cover of his 1993 *River of Dreams* set. The couple's daughter, Alexa Ray, also had an impact on the album: Joel wrote "Lullabye (Goodnight, My Angel)" for her. On the downside, however, have been the series of business dealings that have devastated Joel financially through the years. In 1989, he fired and filed suit against Frank Weber, his business manager and former brother-in-law, after an independent audit allegedly revealed the theft of millions of dollars. In 1993, he additionally sued the extremely powerful music business attorney Allen Grubman and his New York firm for fraud and breach of contract; the suit, which contained several conflict-of-interest claims that heated the music industry, was eventually settled later in the year.

Otherwise, with the instant success of *River of Dreams*, things could not be looking brighter for Billy Joel. The man who in 1979 was named Columbia Records' biggest-selling solo artist of the 20th century has approached middle age with dignity and considerable grace. What's next? In late 1993, he told *Newday*'s Ira Robbins it may be the Great White Way. "I had been approached by other people about doing a Broadway musical," he told Robbins, "but when Pete Townshend told me that, it was the first time I really seriously have considered that I am going to do that. I intend to do it." On the basis of past performance, few others could be as capable.

DAVID JOHANSEN

A major figure in rock and roll due mainly to his central role in '70s glam/punk precursors the New York Dolls, David Johansen (b. Jan. 9, 1950, Staten Island, New York) is an interesting and much underrated songwriter, whose grasp of the essential elements of rock—sex, romance, and, often, non-stop partying—is second to very few others. Ironically, that last element of dusk-till-dawn partying may be what he has come to be most associated with, via his grinning and buffoonish alter ego Buster Poindexter—whose visibility and record sales in the late 1980s actually exceeded his earlier work both with the Dolls and on his own.

Johansen formed the Dolls with guitarist partner Johnny Thunders in 1971. Soon, the five-piece rock group was the center of massive international attention, receiving unanimous press raves for their pioneering blend of trash, glamour, and classic rock and roll. As the group's colorful lead vocalist, Johansen proved both a charismatic and creative figure: of the 21 songs the Dolls recorded on their two albums, the singer had a writing or co-writing credit on 15. Following the group's 1975 demise, Johansen took two years to put together a new band, the David Johansen Group, who recorded his solo debut, *David Johansen*, in 1978.

At least initially, the differences between the Dolls' and Johansen's material were slight; if anything, the singer's post-Dolls outfit comprised much better musicians—but since part of the Dolls' appeal was their endearingly sloppy amateurishness, that was almost incidental. Without exception, the best material to be found on Johansen's first two albums—including 1979's *In Style*—was co-written by the singer and his former partner Syl Sylvain, second guitarist in the Dolls. The most memorable tracks, "Funky but Chic," "Cool Metro," "Frenchette," and "Flamingo Woman," all took the Dolls' earlier trash aesthetic and carried it through to an interesting, noticeably more sophisticated level. The songs were mostly romantically based and about women, unobtainable or otherwise, to which Johansen's characteristically yowling vocals added surprising warmth and sincerity.

From *In Style* onward, Johansen's work hovered in the bottom reaches of the album charts; though his straightforward, Rolling Stones–inspired rock style was often replaced with attempts at Motownish soul ("Melody" being a nearly perfect Four Tops tribute), R&B, and even reggae, no commercial breakthroughs were to come. After 1981's semi-successful *Here Comes the Night*, which featured Johansen co-writing with late-model Beach Boy Blondie Chaplin, the singer scored his biggest solo hit via *Live It Up*, an excellent live album that led off with an Animals medley ("We Gotta Get Out of This Place"/"Don't Bring Me Down"/"It's My Life") that met some radio success. Still, it charted at a mere number 148.

After 1984's piecemeal *Sweet Revenge*—a poorly distributed effort featuring the singer collaborating with producer-songwriter-manager Joe Delia—Johansen began to cultivate his sporadic Buster Poindexter persona into a full-blown career commitment. He made several appearances on "Saturday Night Live" prior to releasing his official Buster debut album, *Buster Poindexter*, in 1988; the album, which featured a cover picture of the tuxedo-clad singer slyly sipping a martini, included standards, big band rhythm and blues, and the soca-inspired top 50 hit "Hot Hot Hot." Johansen was soon seen everywhere, not only singing but

TOP ALBUMS

DAVID JOHANSEN (Blue Sky, '78)
IN STYLE (Blue Sky, '79)
HERE COMES THE NIGHT (Blue Sky, '81)
LIVE IT UP (Blue Sky, '82)
BUSTER POINDEXTER (RCA, '88)

TOP SONGS

FUNKY BUT CHIC (Blue Sky, '78)
FRENCHETTE (Blue Sky, '78)
MELODY (Blue Sky, '79)
HOT HOT HOT (RCA, '88)

David Johansen

ELTON JOHN

On the basis of the charts alone the most popular artist of the 1970s, Elton John (b. Reginald Kenneth Dwight, Mar. 25, 1947, Pinner, Middlesex, England) is a master showman whose electrifying performances and nonstop stream of hit records have made him an international superstar of the highest caliber. But the charts also tell another, even more impressive story: Beginning with his first American hit, "Your Song," in 1970, the singer-pianist has so far amassed an astounding total of over 50 top 40 hits in his still-fruitful career. In 1993, he surpassed Elvis Presley for the most consecutive years of top 40 hits on *Billboard*'s Hot 100 and became the only artist in pop history to have reached the top 30 for 24 uninterrupted years. With his status as a hot artist still very much intact, John looks likely to break many more records—in both senses of the word—before he finally hangs up his (formerly platform) rock and roll shoes and heads off to the Great Player Piano in the sky.

Young Reggie Dwight began playing piano at an early age and studied at the Royal Academy of Music before before making his move into rock and roll in the mid-1960s. He began playing with an R&B group called Bluesology in 1964, backing American R&B artists such as Major Lance, Patti LaBelle and the Blue Belles, and Billy Stewart prior to working full-time behind lanky U.K. singer Long John Baldry. In June 1967, he answered a Liberty Records talent-seeking advertisement he'd seen in England's *New Musical Express;* the roundabout result was a songwriting partnership at music publisher Dick James Music with lyricist Bernie Taupin—who'd responded to the same ad—that would last into the 1990s. Initially assigned to write songs for the likes of Tom Jones and Engelbert Humperdinck—which they attempted to do, but were unsuccessful—the pair were told by a company executive to stop trying to write "hits" and simply write music they themselves liked. "We basically went home and started writing what we felt like writing," Taupin later told writer Michael Amicone, "and those songs became the nucleus of our first album, *Empty Sky.*"

In the U.S., 1969's *Empty Sky* would not see release until 1975, short months after *Elton John's Greatest Hits* had concluded its 10-week run as America's Number One album. Instead, the U.S.

acting: he played a record promoter in "Miami Vice" and later appeared in such films as *Married to the Mob, Let It Ride, Tales from the Darkside: The Movie,* and *Freejack.*

1989's *Buster Goes Berserk,* included his version of "Hit the Road, Jack" from the film *The Dream Team,* but was otherwise unexceptional; it failed to chart. Containing only two meager originals, the album seemed to signal that David Johansen the songwriter was now long gone. In his place was a cartoonish character that would probably go down a storm in Las Vegas—which may, in the long run, be where he'll end up. Always a savvy player and performer, David Johansen can be counted on to take his trash aesthetic where it's needed most.

debut of Elton John—a moniker Dwight had constructed by combining the names of Long John Baldry and Bluesology saxophonist Elton Dean—would be 1970's *Elton John*. To help launch the album, the singer had flown to Los Angeles to give a now-legendary show at the Troubadour. "People just went crazy," John later recalled to British deejay Andy Peebles, "and a guy called Robert Hilburn from the *Los Angeles Times* gave me the rave review of all time, and it spread across America and I became an overnight sensation." Bolstered by the top 10 success of "Your Song," the album indeed soared to the top five and spent a year on the charts; by the end of 1971, no fewer than four other Elton John albums had been released—*Tumbleweed Connection*, *Friends* (a film soundtrack recorded in 1970), *11-17-70* (a live New York City concert that had been broadcast on WPLJ-FM), and *Madman*

Elton John

Across the Water. All entered the top 40; all but the concert set were certified gold.

John and Taupin were a brilliant team; the pianist was a captivating singer with a powerful voice, able to wring nuances out of even the vaguest of Taupin's image-laden lyrics. John excelled as a balladeer, particularly when emoting on such surrealistic songs as "Levon"—which, some suggested, with its odd story line about a man who "wears his war wound like a crown" and "calls his child Jesus," needed whatever help could be brought to it. From 1972's top 10 hit "Rocket Man" through 1976's "Sorry Seems to Be the Hardest Word," the singer produced a nonstop series of 16 top 20 singles, 12 of which had entered the top five. John's commercial enormity was unprecedented; in the same period, three of his albums (*Captain Fantastic and the Brown Dirt Cowboy*, *Elton John's Greatest Hits*, and *Rock of the Westies*) entered the album charts at Number One, giving him a grand total of seven Number One albums in only a three-year span.

If lyricist Taupin needed any reassurance about the value of his contributions to John's songs, it came immediately after 1976's *Blue Moves*, the last album on which he'd work full-time with the singer until 1983's *Too Low for Zero*, and also the last top 10 Elton John album for 16 years. Beginning with 1978's *A Single Man*, the singer began collaborating with other lyricists including Gary Osborne, Tom Robinson, Judie Tzuke, and Tim Rice. Coinciding with that period was a noticeable drop in the popularity of his singles; where the singer had previously typically charted in the single-digit range, beginning with 1978's "Ego," which peaked at number 34, double digits were more often the rule rather than the exception.

The singer spent much of the late 1970s and mid-'80s appearing in a variety of new contexts. He released the three-song EP *The Thom Bell Sessions*, produced and arranged by Philly soul specialist Thom Bell, in 1979; its "Mama Can't Buy You Love" was one of John's few top 10 hits of the period. Scant months later he appeared on the extremely curious "disco album" *Victim of Love*, which featured a cover of "Johnny B. Goode" and a plethora of non-originals by producer Pete Bellotte; the album sold poorly and is generally considered a failed experiment. Additionally, he was heard on

Dionne and Friends' 1985 Number One hit "That's What Friends Are For" with Dionne Warwick, Gladys Knight, and Stevie Wonder, and sang on Jennifer Rush's top 40 hit "Flames of Paradise" in 1987.

By the mid-1980s, Elton John began hitting the top 10 again with singles such as 1986's "Nikita," "I Don't Wanna Go On with You Like That," and a remake of "Candle in the Wind." He returned to MCA Records, after being at Geffen for seven comparatively disappointing years. Critics, who in recent years had often tended to dismiss him as a talented but ultimately lightweight sales phenomenon, began looking fondly at him, perhaps realizing his artistic consistency was much more of a phenomenon than the number of units he shipped. Beginning with 1987's *Live in Australia,* his MCA albums took on a renewed sales vigor, and by 1989's *Sleeping with the Past,* he scored his first all-new platinum album in 11 years. And with 1992's *The One,* again platinum, John had his first top 10 album since 1976's *Blue Moves.* Perhaps helping spur that success along was 1991's *Two Rooms,* a special tribute album to the songs of John and Taupin that featured top-line guest stars Eric Clapton, Kate Bush, Phil Collins, Rod Stewart, Tina Turner, and Sting, among others.

In late November 1993, industry expectations were high for *Duets,* featuring the singer's 1991 hit remake of "Don't Let the Sun Go Down on Me" with George Michael, and 10 other new duets sung

---

TOP ALBUMS

HONKY CHATEAU (Uni, '72, *1*)
DON'T SHOOT ME, I'M ONLY THE PIANO PLAYER (MCA, '73, *1*)
GOODBYE YELLOW BRICK ROAD (MCA, '73, *1*)
CARIBOU (MCA, '74, *1*)
CAPTAIN FANTASTIC AND THE BROWN DIRT COWBOY (MCA, '75, *1*)
ROCK OF THE WESTIES (MCA, '75, *1*)

Additional Top 40 Albums: 21

TOP SONGS

CROCODILE ROCK (MCA, '72, *1*)
BENNIE AND THE JETS (MCA, '74, *1*)
PHILADELPHIA FREEDOM (MCA, '75, *1*)
ISLAND GIRL (MCA, '75, *1*)

Additional Top 40 Songs: 47

---

with such artists as k.d. lang, Little Richard, Leonard Cohen, Don Henley, Bonnie Raitt, Tammy Wynette, P. M. Dawn, and old friend Kiki Dee. An exciting, generous artist whose fan base seems on the increase even in the 1990s, Elton John is one of pop music's true giants.

RICKIE LEE JONES

An extremely talented singer-songwriter whose career has occasionally stumbled, Rickie Lee Jones (b. Nov. 8, 1954, Chicago) has a superb ear for melody and writes surprisingly subtle, personal lyrics. Had her impressive 1979 platinum debut, *Rickie Lee Jones*—which won her that year's Best New Artist Grammy—arrived 10 years earlier, the singer would have likely been considered in the same league as Laura Nyro (whom she sounds very much like) and Joni Mitchell. As it was, with her conspicuous beret, her hipster mannerisms, and her repertoire of songs with titles like "Coolsville," Jones was looked upon with suspicion in some quarters as a poseur who deliberately affected her beatnik pose for marketing purposes. That she was the former girlfriend of Tom Waits—and had already appeared on the cover of his 1978 album *Blue Valentine*—only added fuel to her apparent "wannabe" fire. But by her second album, *Pirates,* by far her best work, Jones quickly doused that fire, cut out the finger-popping stylisms, and proved herself an atmospheric songwriter capable of extraordinary depth.

Ironically, as details of her earlier life surfaced, it became apparent that her onetime street-urchin image wasn't far removed from the truth; she'd been a teenage runaway expelled from high school for insubordination, and the child of two orphaned parents whose father—an actor-musician who'd taught Jones to play and sing—had eventually deserted the family. A onetime former waitress at an Italian restaurant in Los Angeles, the singer received her first national exposure when Little Feat founder Lowell George performed her song "Easy Money" on his 1979 solo album *Thanks, I'll Eat It Here;* shortly afterward, she struck her own deal with George's label, Warner Bros.

Though Jones's career took off instantly thanks to the top five success of the upbeat, rollicking single "Chuck E.'s in Love," written about L.A. musical

Rickie Lee Jones

fixture Chuck E. Weiss, the song has proved to be an oddity in her career. Even as early as 1981's gold *Pirates*, Jones began moving into more atmospheric, meditative realms. For that album alone she deserves the comparisons to Laura Nyro she's received; a gorgeous, sometimes orchestrated work populated with characters named Woody, Dutch, Zero, Louie, and Eddie, the album seemed the logical successor—call it the West Coast version—of Nyro's classic *New York Tendaberry.*

Rather than continue in that impressive direction, Jones resurfaced two years later with *Girl at Her Volcano,* an odd package not only for its 10-inch vinyl EP format but also for its paucity of new self-penned material: included were covers of Billy Strayhorn's "Lush Life," the Left Banke's "Walk Away Renée," Rodgers and Hart's "My Funny Valentine," and the Drifters hit "Under the Boardwalk." After moving to Paris in 1984, Jones—who didn't speak French—penned several songs for *The Magazine,* an

excellent return to creative form that served as her last album for five years. In the interim, she traveled to Tahiti and met her eventual husband Pascal Nabet-Meyer, with whom she had a daughter in 1988.

Jones's 1989 *Flying Cowboys* displayed how much in her life had changed in the previous five years; four of its tracks were collaborations she'd written with her husband, and one—"The Horses"—was written for her infant daughter, Charlotte. And while names such as "Rodeo Girl" and "Jupiter Ray" still cropped up in her lyrics, it became obvious Jones's songs were becoming increasingly autobiographical. Boasting a superb production supplied by Steely Dan's Walter Becker, *Cowboys* was not as instantly accessible as Jones's past work but remains a self-assured effort that sounds better with each playing.

With five top 40 albums behind her, Jones blundered mightily with 1991's *Pop Pop,* an unnecessary all-acoustic album comprising mostly standards (jazz, show tunes, and pop) on which her singing sounded horribly nasal and conspicuously inappropriate. The album was ill-received by both critics and the public; it stayed on the charts for an embarrassing five weeks and peaked at number 139. In 1993, Jones's *Traffic from Paradise* was a welcome return to form; though the singer's marriage was coming to an unpleasant end, she was writing better lyrics than ever, some unavoidably autobiographical. In short, she seemed more in control of her graceful art than ever before. A major artist whose work is occasionally overlooked due to an image she discarded more than a decade ago, Rickie Lee Jones sings from the heart—and about the heart—with uncompromising consistency.

TOP ALBUMS

RICKIE LEE JONES (Warner Bros., '79, 3)
PIRATES (Warner Bros., '81, 5)
GIRL AT HER VOLCANO (Warner Bros., '83, 39)
THE MAGAZINE (Warner Bros., '84)
FLYING COWBOYS (Geffen, '89, 39)
TRAFFIC FROM PARADISE (Geffen, '93)

TOP SONGS

CHUCK E.'S IN LOVE (Warner Bros., '79, 4)
YOUNG BLOOD (Warner Bros., '79, 40)

PAUL KELLY

Little known in this country despite the major-label release of three of his albums, Australian singer-songwriter Paul Kelly (b. circa 1955, Adelaide, South Australia) may be one of the finest rock tunesmiths to emerge in the 1980s. An extraordinary lyricist with a knack for telling touching personal stories in three-minute vignettes, the prolific Kelly has yet to repeat himself lyrically or musically; his marvelous command of pop song structure has provided him with a seemingly endless supply of catchy hooks and riffs. His failure to break through commercially in this country seems much more a statement about the promotional failings of major record labels than of his own bursting talents.

Kelly's star began to rise in Melbourne, Australia, in the late 1970s, first with the High Rise Bombers, then with his own band, the Dots. Signed to Mushroom Records, the band released two albums stylistically in the Elvis Costello–Graham Parker vein, *Talk* (1981) and *Manila* (1982). When the group split in 1984, Kelly moved to Sydney and recorded his first solo album, *Post* (1985), backed by the musicians who would later make up his band the Messengers, originally named the Coloured Girls.

In 1987, Kelly's first American record, *Gossip,* was issued by A&M; bearing 17 tracks, a distillation of the original 24-song Australian double LP, it was about as rich a debut album as any artist could hope for. Because the singer had already spent close to a decade honing his songwriting talents, *Gossip* was a strikingly mature set—in a sense, the equivalent of Dylan or Costello "debuting" with their own *Blonde on Blonde* or *Imperial Bedroom* albums. Difficult to digest in one sitting, *Gossip* was a virtual treasure trove of songs, stories, and characters that revealed new aspects with every listening.

Unlike its predecessor, *Under the Sun* (1988) went down easy; Kelly's 14 songs had the same fresh feel of the early work of England's Mott the Hoople, and his lyrics were even more masterfully concise. The singer's greatest skill lay in his ability to summarize complex relationships in lyrical shorthand and fragmented scenarios, whether it was former lovers seeing each other at the airport ("Same Old Walk") or a jittery estranged husband seeking to make his failed marriage work ("To Her Door"), Kelly conveyed volumes with his well-chosen lyrical snippets.

As a writer, Kelly's all-time peak may have come with 1989's *So Much Water, So Close to Home.* Featuring two of his finest songs—"I Had Forgotten You," about an older man remembering an ancient unfinished love affair, and "Careless," about a self-destructive lost soul—the album also showed Kelly was delving deeper into the actual craft of songwriting. "Everything's Turning to White," based on the Raymond Carver short story from which Kelly's album took its title, is actually sung from a woman's perspective—as are several other tracks on the album. At the time, Kelly said his initial motivation stemmed from being asked to write songs for various Australian female singers. "In literature it's quite normal for male writers to write stories from the point of view of a woman," he said, "or for women writers to write from a point of view of a man. It happens a lot in folk music as well. The song is the thing, not the singer. The singer can take on the character of the songs. I've always written a lot of my songs in character, so writing in the character of a woman is an extension of that."

Despite typically over-the-top press raves for Kelly's works, none of them charted at all, and he was quietly dropped from the A&M roster. In 1991, the independent Dr. Dream label picked up his superb *Comedy* album—which intriguingly featured a version of John Cale's little-covered "Buffalo Ballet"—but lacking A&M's distribution clout, the album had minimum visibility and sold poorly. It's inconceivable that an artist of Paul Kelly's proven talent is without a major American label in the 1990s, but sadly, in an increasingly hits-conscious music industry, he's not the only one.

TOP ALBUMS

GOSSIP (A&M, '87)
UNDER THE SUN (A&M, '88)
SO MUCH WATER SO CLOSE TO HOME (A&M, '89)
COMEDY (Dr. Dream, '91)

TOP SONGS

SAME OLD WALK (A&M, '88)
I HAD FORGOTTEN YOU (A&M, '89)
CARELESS (A&M, '89

GREG KIHN

I f context is everything, the arrival of Greg Kihn (b. 1952, Baltimore, Maryland) held promise: it placed him squarely in the center of Matthew King Kaufman's much-liked, loopy independent label Beserkley Records. Founded in the mid-1970s, the San Francisco–based Beserkley boasted a roster that would impress many during the early days of the punk and new wave explosion—due in large part to the presence of the one-of-a-kind Jonathan Richman, whose earlier band the Modern Lovers would enjoy international acclaim among punk fans well after their 1972 breakup. Also prominent on the roster were San Francisco's Earthquake (previously on A&M) and the Rubinoos, who both embraced the upbeat, melodic sounds of '60s pop in the face of the rising tide of so-called "progressive" music played by '70s groups like Yes and Emerson, Lake and Palmer. Kihn, an acquaintance of Kaufman's from Baltimore, rounded out the roster. He seemed cast from the late-'60s and early-'70s singer-songwriter mold, with a taste for early-'60s rock and roll that would grow as his career developed.

The Beserkley lineup made its initial splash in 1975 with the superb compilation *Beserkley Chartbusters Vol. 1*, signaling to most critics that something special was brewing in the West. Kihn's contribution included backing vocals on the album's most prominent track—Richman's "Roadrunner," a later punk standard—and two of his own tracks, "All the Right Reasons" and "Mood Mood Number." His own album, *Greg Kihn*, followed in the next year and was a pleasantly substantial surprise. Kihn had a clear ear for pop hooks, most notably heard on "Any Other Woman," which at times sounded much like the distinctly unfashionable '60s band the Grass Roots; at the same time, he could write warm and sentimental acoustic rock, typified by the lovely "Kid from Louieville," which harked back to early tracks by the Lovin' Spoonful. Kihn additionally showed his taste with a cover of Jerry Butler's 1960 hit, "He Will Break Your Heart."

TOP ALBUMS

ROCKIHNROLL (Beserkley, '81, *32*)
KIHNTINUED (Beserkley, '82, *33*)
KIHNSPIRACY (Beserkley, '83, *15*)
CITIZEN KIHN (EMI America, '85)

TOP SONGS

KID FROM LOUIEVILLE (Beserkley, '76)
THE BREAKUP SONG (THEY DON'T WRITE 'EM) (Beserkley, '81, *15*)
JEOPARDY (Beserkley, '83, *2*)
LUCKY (EMI America, '85, *30*)

By far Beserkley's best-selling artist, Kihn found an audience early in his career. His second album, *Next of Kihn,* which further showed his rock roots via a cover of Buddy Holly's "Love's Made a Fool of You," received much FM radio exposure thanks to his smart cover of Bruce Springsteen's early track "For You"—significantly, an arrangement Springsteen himself would use in later performances. Kihn's music would continue on in this direction—mostly original tunes, with occasional covers—all the while becoming increasingly rock-oriented. He covered Springsteen again on 1979's *With the Naked Eye*—this time an inspired cover of "Rendezvous," a track Springsteen often sang in concert but hadn't recorded at the time (it would later appear on bootlegs jointly sung by Springsteen and Kihn)—and also showed his hip '70s roots via a cover of Richman's "Roadrunner."

Kihn became a popular live attraction and a prolific record maker. He jumped smack into the mainstream with his 1981 album *Rockihnroll*, which hit number 32 on the charts thanks to his first top 20 single, "The Breakup Song (They Don't Write 'Em)"; still, even then, his affection for early '60s pop was vividly displayed with a cover of Tommy Roe's 1962 hit "Sheila." Follow-up *Kihntinued* peaked only one notch lower on the album chart than its predecessor, garnering airplay with two charting singles, particularly "Happy Man." His all-time bestseller, *Kihnspiracy*, arrived in 1983, bringing with it Kihn's hit single "Jeopardy," which held the number two slot for two weeks. The song received massive exposure on MTV, which at the time was just beginning to build its power base among the nation's pop music consumers, and became so prominent that no less than "Weird" Al Yankovic parodied it in 1984 via his "I Lost on Jeopardy," also an early MTV favorite.

After a long run at Beserkley, Kihn moved to the EMI America label in 1985. There, he'd produce both his final charting album, *Citizen Kihn* (which peaked at number 51), and his last top 40 hit, "Lucky." An additional album came the next year, but *Love and Rock and Roll* curiously failed to make any impression on the chart whatsoever—even though it had stayed close to his proven formula mix of originals and well-known covers (in this case, "Little Red Book," popularized by Love, and "Another Girl, Another Planet" by U.K. punk icons the Only Ones).

Despite an excellent overall track record, Kihn and company then dropped out of the scene, returning only for the somewhat unnecessary (and disappointing) live album *Unkihntrollable*, issued by Rhino in 1989. While his recording absence since then is a minor mystery, his 12-album catalog remains an impressive career run for any artist. Kihn will be remembered as an artist who made his mark purely by doing what he liked—and doing it remarkably consistently.

CAROLE KING

O ne of the most vital figures in pop music throughout both the 1960s and 1970s, Carole King (b. Carole Klein, Feb. 9, 1942, Brooklyn, New York) is renowned both for her songwriting skill—displayed via the countless hits she penned for dozens of performers in the '60s—and her own best-selling recordings of the '70s. If she had done nothing in her career but record 1971's *Tapestry*, she would still be a major presence: the album, which sold over 15 million copies, was Number One for 15 weeks, stayed on the charts for an astounding 302 weeks, and was the third-biggest seller of the 1970s (topped only by Fleetwood Mac's *Rumours* and the *Saturday Night Fever* soundtrack). Additionally, King and friend James Taylor are generally credited with ushering in the early '70s era of the singer-songwriter; Taylor's first Number One hit, in fact, was his version of King's "You've Got a Friend" from his 1971 album *Mud Slide Slim and the Blue Horizon,* on which King herself played piano. Throughout most of the 1970s, King enjoyed massive popularity with her series of Ode albums that continued in the same warm vein as *Tapestry,* but by the late '70s

her popularity started to fade somewhat. Spending much of the '80s away from the recording scene, she returned in 1989 with the warmly received *City Streets,* her vast writing talent still amply in evidence.

King spent her early years in Brooklyn very much immersed in music. She formed a quartet called the Co-Sines, and in 1958 met lyricist Gerry Goffin while a student at Queens College. The pair, who married, began working together on early singles such as 1969's "Baby Sittin' " on ABC-Paramount and 1960's "Oh! Neil," her "answer" song to Neil Sedaka's 1959 hit "Oh! Carol." By 1960, King and Goffin were major players in the so-called "Brill Building" era of pop, working at Don Kirshner and Al Nevins's Aldon Music next to the likes of Sedaka and Barry Mann and Cynthia Weil.

While King still made occasional records—and had her own first hit in 1962 with "It Might as Well Rain Until September"—the songs for which she and Goffin remain best known were hits for other artists. Following their first Number One hit, 1961's "Will You Love Me Tomorrow" by the Shirelles, she wrote what amounts to one of the most remarkable lists of hits in pop history, including "The Loco-Motion," "Take Good Care of My Baby," "One Fine Day," "Go Away Little Girl," "Up on the Roof," "I Can't Stay Mad at You," "I'm into Something Good," "Pleasant Valley Sunday," "Just Once in My Life," "Hey, Girl," "Chains," and "Sharing You," among many, many others.

In 1968, King and Goffin divorced, and the singer formed a short-lived band called the City with her eventual second husband Charles Larkey and guitarist Danny Kootch (formerly of James Taylor's Flying Machine). The group's one album, 1969's oft-bootlegged *Now That Everything's Been Said,* was a commercial failure but included an early version of the Taylor hit-to-come, "You've Got a Friend." The same players and a few others (Taylor, the group Jo Mama) backed the singer on her 1970 solo debut, *Writer;* mixed by her ex-husband Goffin, the album featured King singing her own versions of past hits "Up on the Roof" and

TOP ALBUMS

Tapestry (Ode, '71, *1*)
Music (Ode, '71, *1*)
Rhymes & Reasons (Ode, '72, *2*)
Wrap Around Joy (Ode, '74, *1*)
Thoroughbred (Ode, '76, *3*)

Additional Top 40 Albums: 3

TOP SONGS

It's Too Late (Ode, '71, *1*)
I Feel the Earth Move
  (Ode, '71, *1*)
Sweet Seasons (Ode, '72, *9*)
Jazzman (Ode, '74, *2*)
Nightingale (Ode, '75, *9*)

Additional Top 40 Songs: 8

"Goin' Back" and laid the groundwork for the next year's *Tapestry.*

King's colossal hit album bore her double-sided smash single "It's Too Late"—a collaboration with lyricist Toni Stern, one of many post-Goffin writers she'd work with—as well as "I Feel the Earth Move" and "So Far Away." Also on the album were her own versions of past Goffin-King songs "Will You Love Me Tomorrow" and "(You Make Me Feel Like) A Natural Woman" (co-written with Jerry Wexler); King would often return to the Goffin-King well, performing "Some Kind of Wonderful" on *Tapestry*'s follow-up and later devoting an entire album (1980's *Pearls*) to their collaborations. Though King continued to pen songs occasionally with her ex-husband, others she regularly wrote with through the 1970s included Stern, David Palmer, and her third husband, the late Rick Evers.

Through her 1978 collection *Her Greatest Hits,* King's records regularly went gold and typically placed in the top 10 or top 20. Most of them seemed further refinements of her earlier work, though such albums as 1973's *Fantasy* surprisingly enjoyed a significant R&B audience. Between 1971's "It's Too Late" and 1977's "Hard Rock Cafe," she scored 11 top 40 hits, including her second-biggest single, 1974's "Jazzman." Beginning with 1978's *Welcome Home,* on the Capitol-distributed Avatar label, however, her star seemed on the wane; her albums no longer went gold, and only one—her 1980 Goffin-King retrospective set *Pearls*—even made the top 100. With 1983's *Speeding Time,* she stopped charting at all.

King spent most of the mid-1980s living in Idaho, devoting much of her time to wilderness issues in the northern Rockies. She resumed recording in 1989 with *City Streets,* which featured guests Eric Clapton, Branford Marsalis, and Max Weinberg as well as significant help from her keyboardist son-in-law, Robbie Kondor. In 1992, she enjoyed adult-contemporary radio success with her song "Now and Forever" from the film *A League of Their Own,* and in 1993 returned with *Colour of Your Dreams.*

Carole King remains one of the most talented artists in pop music. "I'm so tired of reading articles and reviews that talk as if people of my generation have to prove they've still got it," she told the *Los Angeles Times*'s Richard Cromelin in 1993. "That's not the perpective I see. I see us as survivors. We have survived, we have transcended generations. We're not poor things desperately holding on."

AL KOOPER

The resume of Al Kooper (b. Feb. 5, 1944, Brooklyn, New York) weighed in so heavily he gave it the name *Backstage Passes* and sold it as his autobiography in 1977. A scenemaker beyond belief, Kooper played with the Royal Teens ("Short Shorts") in the late 1950s, was central to both the Blues Project and Blood, Sweat and Tears in the 1960s, and discovered and produced Lynyrd Skynyrd in the 1970s. He has played keyboards and guitar with most of the major stars in '60s pop, typically when those artists were in their prime: search album credits and you'll find him on Jimi Hendrix's *Electric Ladyland,* the Rolling Stones' *Let It Bleed,* the Who's *The Who Sell Out,* and perhaps most notably, Bob Dylan's "Like a Rolling Stone" and *Blonde on Blonde.* For better or for worse, he was also responsible for creating a legitimate market for rock "jam sessions" via his gold *Super Session* album of 1968, which featured him improvising in the studio alongsideguitarists Mike Bloomfield and Steve Stills.

Kooper's entrée into the music business came through songwriting and session work at the start of the 1960s. During an extended period of hustling, Kooper worked as a writer for both Sea Lark and We Three music publishers and eventually struck gold in 1965. Two of his songs (co-written with Bob Brass and Irwin Levine) became hits, including "This Diamond Ring," Number One for Gary Lewis and the Playboys in 1965, and Gene Pitney's "I Must Be Seeing Things," which climbed to Number 31. More importantly, that was the year Columbia Records producer Tom Wilson invited Kooper to watch Bob Dylan recording in the studio—and set into motion a chain of events that led to Kooper's playing organ on "Like a Rolling Stone" and performing with Dylan during his historic "electric" Newport Folk Festival appearance that summer. Kooper's involvement then led to a nonstop series of "electric folk" sessions for such theretofore-acoustic artists as Tom Rush, Phil Ochs, Judy Collins, Peter Paul and Mary, and others.

By 1966, Kooper had appeared as a solo artist on Elektra Records' landmark *What's Shakin'* compilation (alongside the Lovin' Spoonful, Eric Clapton and the Powerhouse, the Paul Butterfield Blues Band, and Tom Rush) and became a full-time member of the Blues Project. The semi-legendary New York band was among the first to combine blues with rock and roll, and Kooper—who played keyboards and sang—wrote many of the group's best original numbers, including "No Time Like the Right Time" (their only charting single) and their live solo showcase, "Flute Thing." Each of the three Blues Project albums featuring Kooper entered the top 100, with 1966's *Projections,* their biggest seller, peaking at number 52.

Kooper then left and formed Blood, Sweat and Tears, whose one album featuring him as leader— 1968's brilliant *Child Is Father to the Man*—stands as one of the greatest pop albums of the era. Featuring superb interpretations of songs by Randy Newman, Nilsson, Gerry Goffin and Carole King, and Tim Buckley, as well as many of Kooper's best originals—including "I Can't Quit Her," "I Love You More Than You'll Ever Know," and "House in the Country"—the album was an exciting merging of pop, rock, and big-band brass that bowled over many critics. Though the group went on to greater success on both the albums and singles charts after Kooper departed and was replaced by Canadian vocalist David Clayton-Thomas, their debut remains their finest hour.

Between 1968 and 1970, Al Kooper's career was a jumble of recording sessions, producing stints, and prolific solo work. He accepted a job as a staff producer at Columbia and produced albums by Appaloosa, Don Ellis, and Sweet Linda Devine; he guested on sessions with Dylan, Hendrix, the Stones, the Who, the Paupers, and Jim and Jean; he record-

Al Kooper

ed *Super Session* with Bloomfield and Stills, then carried the format further with Moby Grape's *Grape Jam* (1968), *The Live Adventures of Mike Bloomfield and Al Kooper* (1969), and young guitarist Shuggie Otis's *Kooper Session* (1970). Additionally, he continued the approach he'd used with Blood, Sweat and Tears on his own solo albums—five of which were released within a three-year span. The best, 1969's *You Never Know Who Your Friends Are,* showed Kooper to be a superior tunesmith adept at most styles; aided by arranger and conductor Charlie Calello, the singer produced a handful of adventurous tracks ("Anna Lee," "Never Gonna Let You Down," and "The Great American Marriage/ Nothing") that equal or surpass his Blood, Sweat and Tears work.

In retrospect, Kooper's solo albums illustrate his knack for recognizing other songwriters' talent: the few cover versions to be had were typically early works of artists destined for greater fame, including Nilsson, Steve Winwood, James Taylor, Elton John and Bernie Taupin, and John Prine. Spotting worthy artists was a talent Kooper also put to good use as head of the MCA-distributed, Atlanta-based Sounds of the South label in the early and mid-1970s, where

TOP ALBUMS

SUPER SESSION (with Michael Bloomfield and Stephen Stills, Columbia, '68, *12*)

I STAND ALONE (Columbia, '69)

YOU NEVER KNOW WHO YOUR FRIENDS ARE (Columbia, '69)

EASY DOES IT (Columbia, '70)

NEW YORK CITY (YOU'RE A WOMAN) (Columbia, '71)

A POSSIBLE PROJECTION OF THE FUTURE/CHILDHOOD'S END (Columbia, '72)

ACT LIKE NOTHING'S WRONG (United Artists, '77)

TOP SONGS

ANNA LEE (WHAT CAN I DO FOR YOU) (Columbia, '69)

(PLEASE NOT) ONE MORE TIME (United Artists, '77)

he produced Lynyrd Skynyrd's first three albums for the label, as well as debuts by Southern Rock bands Mose Jones and Elijah.

Kooper spent much of the 1970s producing other artists (the Tubes, Nils Lofgren, Eddie and the Hot Rods) rather than making his own records. He produced and played on a live Blues Project reunion album in 1973; released *Act Like Nothing's Wrong* on United Artists in 1976; played a dominant role in rock-disco band 4 on the Floor, whose obscure album was issued by Casablanca in 1979; then returned to Columbia in 1982 for the bizarre *Championship Wrestling,* a failed concept album that featured several guest vocalists. Having already scored the United Artists film *The Landlord* in 1970, Kooper resumed that line of work in the '80s, first with the television series "Crime Story," then with a portion of John Waters' film epic, *Cry Baby.*

Kooper's 35-year involvement in pop music would likely make perfect fodder for an autobiographical film or miniseries. While that seems unlikely, the singer's own account of his past can be found in *Backstage Passes: Rock 'n' Roll Life in the Sixties* (with Ben Edmonds, Stein & Day, 1977), still one of the best behind-the-scenes accounts of the music industry to be had.

LENNY KRAVITZ

Blessed—or cursed—by his relative youth, Lenny Kravitz (b. circa 1965, Brooklyn, New York) has built a growing audience in the 1990s by playing music that draws conspicuous inspiration from such '60s figures as Jimi Hendrix, the Beatles, Curtis Mayfield, and Sly and the Family Stone. What seems to gall his many critics most? That he actually dresses the part. With his bellbottom pants, his boots, and his necklaces and medallions, he could be an extra from the cast of *Hair,* were it not for the telling modern touches of dreadlocks and a nose ring.

Kravitz's affection for the 1960s runs much deeper than mere matters of his appearance, or even his songwriting; deeply involved in the production of his own albums, he is, for instance, militantly in favor of analog recording methods that use tubes rather than transistors. Referring to his unique studio approach, Kravitz noted with some pride in 1992, "Now when people try for that sound, they feel that all you have

to do is turn the reverb off. They don't understand the whole process—going from the microphone to the amplifiers to compressors into EQ units that have tubes and back to the tape machine. It's a lost art." The art that Kravitz has not only found but displayed with love throughout his three albums has won him a large international audience and, with 1992's *Are You Gonna Go My Way?,* taken him to platinum sales levels.

The Brooklyn-born son of "Jeffersons" actress Roxsie Roker and NCB-TV producer Sy Kravitz, Kravitz grew up on New York's Upper East Side, immersed in the music of Bobby Short, Count Basie, and Ella Fitzgerald. At one point in his childhood, he's said, he sat on Duke Ellington's lap as the master jazz composer played the piano. After his mother moved to Los Angeles for her "Jeffersons" role, Kravitz spent three years with the California Boys Chorale, with whom he participated in conductor Zubin Mehta's recording of Mahler's Third Symphony. Attending Beverly Hills High School, where he would meet future Guns N' Roses guitarist Slash—who would later guest on Kravitz's albums—the singer led what was by no means a "normal" childhood. Or adulthood: even before signing his deal, Kravitz was nationally known due to his marriage with actress Lisa Bonet of "The Cosby Show." Though they have since divorced, Kravitz dedicated his 1991 breakthrough album, *Mama Said,* to the actress.

Kravitz met his longtime musical partner, Henry Hirsch, in the early 1980s; Hirsch, who ran a New Jersey recording studio, shared Kravitz's interest in pre-digital technology. Kravitz's talents as musician and producer have been heavily in demand since 1989's *Let Love Rule.* His productions have includ-

---

TOP ALBUMS

LET LOVE RULE (Virgin, '89)
MAMA SAID (Virgin, '91, *39*)
ARE YOU GONNA GO MY WAY (Virgin, '93, *12*)

TOP SONGS

LET LOVE RULE (Virgin, '89)
IT AIN'T OVER 'TIL IT'S OVER (Virgin, '91, *2*)
STAND BY MY WOMAN (Virgin, '91)
ARE YOU GONNA GO MY WAY (Virgin, '93)
SWEET THING (Virgin, '93)

ed part of the *Superfly II* soundtrack, Madonna's "Justify My Love" (for which he has partial composing credit), and an album with French singer Vanessa Paradis. In 1993, he duetted with Mick Jagger on the Rolling Stones singer's 1993 version of Bill Withers' "Use Me" and co-wrote a track on Aerosmith's platinum-plus *Get a Grip* album.

As derivative as his own music may sometimes be, Lenny Kravitz is a unique figure, and his albums are aural treats. Though his critics may scoff at his seeming deliberately retro look, it has very much worked to his benefit in the modern MTV era. "If you really listen to my records," Kravitz told writer Steve Hochman in late 1993, "there's elements of folk, elements of gospel...lots of R&B, lots of soul, jazz, classical with my arrangements, reggae. I'm really covering a lot of ground. But because of the clothes and things, it all gets clumped up." Is Lenny Kravitz bothered by critics? "They dogged Bob Marley, they dogged John Lennon, they dogged everybody," said the singer. "Who cares?"

ARTHUR LEE

Consider two mid-'60s groups. Each is from Los Angeles, each is signed to Elektra Records, and each releases a series of albums that stand as some of the finest rock and roll of the era. But in the early '70s, one of the groups' lead singers dies—and the then-defunct band's popularity grows to unbelievably massive proportions. By the early '90s, the group is immortalized when a prestigious film director devotes an entire movie to them.

Now consider that the two groups' names are the Doors and Love, and consider that in 1993, while the legend of late Doors vocalist Jim Morrison continued to grow two decades after his death, Love's singer Arthur Lee—in his 19th year without a major American record deal—was actually opening for a Doors cover band at a small Los Angeles club. One suspects he would have rather been hit by a bus.

Just one in a series of major ironies for Arthur Lee (b. 1944, Memphis, Tennessee) is the fact that his pioneering work with Love is now as revered internationally—at least on some critical levels—as the music of Jim Morrison's Doors. The first rock group to be signed by Elektra, Love was an unusual group by many standards, not least because both Lee, the band's lead singer and main songwriter, and John

Echols, the band's guitarist, were black men who played rock and roll. Very much an underground group (they rarely performed outside Los Angeles), Love first made their name on the basis of two superb 1966 singles: a remake of Manfred Mann's "My Little Red Book" (penned by Burt Bacharach and Hal David) from *What's New Pussycat?* and Lee's own "Seven and Seven Is," a top 40 hit. But much more influential were Love's albums, the first three of which displayed remarkable diversity and artistic growth.

The 1966 debut album, *Love,* was a much better than average collection of melodic, Byrds- and Beatles-inspired pop, most of it written by Lee himself. By 1967's *Da Capo,* Love's original quintet had added two members, and the group's sound had grown much more sophisticated (including flute, saxophone, and harpsichord)—as had Lee's compositions. Tracks like "Stephanie Knows Who" and "The Castle" were enormously inventive and dynamic, filled with complex chords and atmospheric shadings that sound contemporary even today. Additionally, the group had experimented even further by filling the second side of their LP with a 19-minute single track called "Revelation."

Still, all this served only as a prelude to 1967's *Forever Changes,* Love's all-time classic and an album many hold to be pop's finest. A mixture of hard rock and soft symphonic pop, it featured gorgeous string arrangements, trumpets, and pleasingly surreal lyrics by Lee. Released months after the so-called Summer of Love, the album's back cover bore

---

TOP ALBUMS

FOREVER CHANGES (with Love, Elektra, '67)
VINDICATOR (A&M, '72)

TOP SONGS

SEVEN AND SEVEN IS (with Love, Elektra, '66, *33*)
STEPHANIE KNOWS WHO (with Love, Elektra, '67)
SHE COMES IN COLORS (with Love, Elektra, '67)
A HOUSE IS NOT A MOTEL (with Love, Elektra, '67)
MAYBE THE PEOPLE WOULD BE THE TIMES OR BETWEEN CLARK AND HILLDALE (with Love, Elektra, '67)
YOU SET THE SCENE (with Love, Elektra, '67)
AUGUST (with Love, Elektra, '69)
GOOD TIMES (with Love, Elektra, '69)

a picture of Lee holding a broken jug of obviously dead flowers; inside, he was singing lines like "They're locking him up today/They're throwing away the key/I wonder who it'll be tomorrow/You or me?" A timeless album better heard than described, it will keep Arthur Lee's name in circulation well into the next century. "Those were my last words to the world," Lee recalled in 1981, "and I've been here ever since. Just like a guy saying goodbye, and you look out your front door and he's still there. I know I was real young, but I just thought that would be the year for me to exit."

Arthur Lee disbanded that version of Love and continued with several newer editions of the group, none ever as graceful or good as the first. 1969's hard-rocking *Four Sail* remains the last fully excellent album he was involved with; though nearly all of the Love albums to come between it and 1974's final *Reel-to-Real* boast many high points—including an appearance by Jimi Hendrix on 1970's *False Start*—Lee's seeming genius was slowly winding down. He recorded one respectable solo album in 1972's *Vindicator* (credited to Arthur Lee and Band-Aid) and one fairly shoddy one (including covers of the Bobbettes' 1957 hit "Mr. Lee" and Jimmy Cliff's "Many Rivers to Cross") released on the fledgling Rhino label in 1981, and he hasn't made an American album since.

Though there have been several attempted Love reunions—including a 1978 concert issued by Rhino in 1982—it seems increasingly unlikely the group's magic could ever be duplicated again. Arthur Lee has continued to perform in the Los Angeles area through the 1990s, and sometimes—not often, but sometimes—he still seems capable of making his audience believe it's 1967 all over again.

JOHN LENNON

As one-half of the most famous pop songwriting team of all time, John Lennon (b. Oct. 9, 1940, Liverpool, England) will go down in history not only for noting with irony that his band the Beatles was "more popular than Jesus," but for having more than one member of the clergy sadly, if quietly, agree with him. Lennon's songwriting relationship with Paul McCartney may be the most thoroughly examined, well-documented collaboration in musical history. In the course of their momentous

career—beginning with the October 5, 1962, U.K. release of debut single "Love Me Do" through the year of McCartney's April 10, 1970, announcement that the group had dissolved—the Beatles released 46 top 40 singles and 26 charting albums, many of which were reissues of earlier material or contained only interview snippets. Because of the massive press attention the Beatles received through the course of their career, and because the eyes of the world were focused on John Lennon's every move until his death in 1980, his music away from the group has taken on that much more importance in retrospect.

The John Lennon who co-wrote "She Loves You" and "Love Me Do" with Paul McCartney was a young and ambitious singer-songwriter who merely wanted to become part of "the Goffin and King of England"; the John Lennon who would pose nude on the cover of *Two Virgins* with his bride-to-be, Yoko Ono, was instead one of the world's most famous individuals. His very existence was a statement, his every recording was examined thoroughly, held up against his past work as a Beatle, and dissected: What was its motivation? Is this the music he wanted to do, but the other Beatles wouldn't let him? Did he hate his past work? Did he think listeners wanted to hear him and Yoko Ono grunting, groaning, laughing, and screaming? More to the point, did he think fans wanted to pay money for the privilege of hearing it?

In fact, most of those question died down following the release of 1970's *John Lennon/Plastic Ono Band*, which in many ways marked Lennon's resumption of his Beatles-styled songwriting ways. But the four albums that preceded it, all released within a year, were a far cry from the polished work of *Abbey Road* or even *Let It Be*: Between February and December of 1969, Lennon and Ono released *Unfinished Music No. 1: Two Virgins, Unfinished Music No. 2: Life with the Lions,* and *Wedding Album*—three albums of "experimental music," avant-garde ramblings that tried the patience of most Beatle fans. And when Lennon "returned" to rock in January 1970 with *The Plastic Ono Band—Live Peace in Toronto 1969*, one-half of a potentially great live album, featuring Eric Clapton on lead guitar and versions of "Dizzy Miss Lizzy," "Yer Blues," "Blue Suede Shoes," and "Cold Turkey," was marred by the unsettling, screeching yawps of Ono.

Still, when Lennon released the comparatively accessible *John Lennon/Plastic Ono Band*, he came back with a stark rawness he'd never displayed while in the Beatles. His greatest solo work, the album was an intense but rewarding listening experience that contained many of his best-known songs—including "Mother," "Working Class Hero," and "God," the latter two of which include some of his most oft-quoted lyrical passages. The brutal, inward-looking nature of such tunes as the album closer "My Mummy's Dead"—on which Lennon sang "My Mummy's dead/It's hard to explain/So much pain/I could never show it/My Mummy's dead"—offered a revealingly close (some said too close) look at Lennon's inner turmoil; the album is still cited by many as one of rock's finest.

Lennon's best-known solo work, *Imagine,* followed in 1971; perhaps surprisingly, the title track, now very much a pop standard, peaked at only number three on the pop charts. Still in the introverted mode, Lennon turned his gaze outward long enough to craft what may be one of the meanest songs in pop, directed at former partner McCartney. "How Do You Sleep" took the famous bassist to task for, among other things, his composing skills: "A pretty face may last a year or two," sang Lennon, "But pretty soon they'll see what you can do/The sound you make is muzak to my ears/You must have learned something in all those years." But balancing out that vitriol, and the seeming self-effacement of "Crippled Inside," were such beautiful tracks as "Oh My Love," a simple and elegant love song for which even the era's Yoko haters could be grateful.

Yoko's presence was felt on Lennon's most disposable effort, 1972's *Some Time in New York City,* which was jointly credited to John & Yoko/Plastic Ono Band and came wrapped in a mock *New York Times* cover. The album, which peaked at number 48 and was Lennon's lowest-charting release since his 1969 "experimental" phase, was a mostly strident diatribe that was, appropriately, very newspaperish in tone. Though it contains the infamous Lennon/Ono composition "Woman Is the Nigger of the World"—which was actually released as a single, and peaked at number 57—the album's songs about Angela Davis, the prison riots at Attica, and the imprisoned John Sinclair now inevitably seem dated and slight.

When Lennon returned to his more normal pop mode with 1973's *Mind Games,* it seemed a strangely empty gesture. Though he had a hit with the title track—a minor one, it peaked at number 18—many of the songs had little focus and even less melody; for the first time it became acutely evident Lennon

John Lennon

would have derived great benefit from a helping of McCartney's skill at making so-called "muzak." The album's ascent to the top 10 now seems much more a function of Lennon's ex-Beatle status than its inherent worth; with the exception of its title track, *Mind Games* may be the least-heard in Lennon's entire pop canon.

Even more disturbingly, while the singer's 1974 set *Walls and Bridges* seemed something of a return to form—it did, after all, reach Number One—its popularity generally stemmed from two singles, one of which ("Whatever Gets You Through the Night") featured conspicuous backing vocals from the 1970s' hottest superstar, Elton John, and the other of which ("#9 Dream") was a self-consciously Beatle-esque track that almost seemed an artistic retreat of sorts. Where was the intensity of *Plastic Ono Band* or *Imagine?* Following the even further artistic retreat of 1975's *Rock 'n' Roll,* Lennon's interesting but minor retreading of rock classics such as "Be-Bop-A-Lula," "Stand by Me," and "Peggy Sue," and the greatest-hits compilation *Shaved Fish,* the singer dropped out of the business for five years to raise his young son Sean.

Lennon returned with what would win a Grammy as 1981's Album of the Year, *Double Fantasy,* his long-awaited comeback and one very much worth waiting for. Divided into two parts—one-half Lennon songs, one-half Ono songs—the album was an inspired work that was rapturously received by fans. Featuring three top 10 hits—including the Number One hit "(Just Like) Starting Over," "Woman," and "Watching the Wheels," the album was in some ways as introverted as ever; this time, however, Lennon seemed a much happier man, filled with love for Ono and, as documented wonderfully on "Beautiful Boy," his young son Sean. But as "(Just Like) Starting Over" made its way to the top of the charts, Lennon's triumphant return ended horrendously on December 8, 1980, when he was shot in front of the Dakota apartment building on New York's Upper West Side; he died en route to Roosevelt Hospital.

Lennon's tragic death was eventually followed by the inevitable release of several albums of unfinished songs, outtakes, and live performances on such albums as 1984's *Milk and Honey* and 1986's *Live in New York City* and *Menlove Ave.;* his last charting album was the soundtrack to Andrew Solt's 1988 film *Imagine: John Lennon.* Though the albums may continue to come—there are many unre-

leased Beatles tracks in EMI's vaults, most of which are expected to surface eventually—there will never, obviously, be any new music from John Lennon ever again. The finality of his death remains a gruesome reminder for an entire generation that the brightest lights in pop music and elsewhere can be unexpectedly extinguished at any time.

GORDON LIGHTFOOT

A highly respected and prolific folk troubadour, Gordon Lightfoot (b. Nov. 17, 1938, Orillia, Ontario, Canada) rose to prominence in the mid-1960s via his superb songs, several of which were first recorded by Peter, Paul and Mary, Ian and Sylvia, and country singer Marty Robbins. Introduced to New York–based managers Albert Grossman and John Court by friends Ian and Sylvia—who'd heard the Canadian singer performing in Toronto in 1964 and covered his "Early Mornin' Rain" and "For Lovin' Me" in 1965—Lightfoot signed with them, made his solo recording debut in 1966, and began a healthy career that has continued, with few interruptions, for more than 25 years.

Unlike many of his contemporaries who earned volumes of critical plaudits but failed to reach a mass audience, Lightfoot has enjoyed the best of both worlds during his long career. After a series of five widely praised albums for United Artists—highlighted by his superb 1966 debut, *Lightfoot!,* which featured his classics "The Way I Feel," "For Lovin' Me," "I'm Not Sayin'," and "Early Morning Rain—the singer signed to Reprise in 1970 and immediately struck gold. Or, more accurately, after eight months or so: Lightfoot's Reprise debut was initially titled *Sit Down Young Stranger* when released in June 1970, but after a Seattle radio station began regularly playing "If You Could Read My Mind," the album track gradually snowballed into a top five hit by early 1971, and Reprise then rereleased the album as *If You Could Read My Mind.* With that title, the album soon climbed to number 12 on the charts and established the Canadian singer as a worthy pop presence.

Fitting comfortably into an era when singer-songwriters were prospering, Lightfoot rarely varied from his warm, acoustic-flavored style. His follow-up albums sold well, and by 1974 he reached his

TOP ALBUMS

JOHN LENNON/PLASTIC ONO BAND (Apple, '70, 6)
IMAGINE (Apple, '71, *1*)
MIND GAMES (Apple, '73, 9)
WALLS AND BRIDGES (Apple, '74, *1*)
DOUBLE FANTASY (with Yoko Ono, Geffen, '80, *1*)

Additional Top 40 Albums: 6

TOP SONGS

INSTANT KARMA (We All Shine On) (Apple, '70, *3*)
IMAGINE (Apple, '71, *3*)
WHATEVER GETS YOU THROUGH THE NIGHT (Apple, '74, *1*)
(JUST LIKE) STARTING OVER (Geffen, '80, *1*)
WOMAN (Geffen, '81, *2*)

Additional Top 40 Songs: 8

TOP ALBUMS

SIT DOWN YOUNG STRANGER (Reprise, '70, *12*)
SUNDOWN (Reprise, '74, *1*)
COLD ON THE SHOULDER (Reprise, '75, *10*)
SUMMERTIME DREAM (Reprise, '76, *12*)
ENDLESS WIRE (Warner, '78, *22*)

Additional Top 40 Albums: 2

TOP SONGS

IF YOU COULD READ MY MIND
   (Reprise, '71, *5*)
SUNDOWN (Reprise, '74, *1*)
CAREFREE HIGHWAY (Reprise, '74, *10*)
RAINY DAY PEOPLE (Reprise, '75, *26*)
THE WRECK OF THE EDMUND FITZGERALD
   (Reprise, '76, *2*)

Additional Top 40 Songs: 1

commercial peak: both *Sundown* and its title-track single claimed the Number One spot on their respective charts, and Lightfoot claimed his first platinum album. After follow-up hits "Carefree Highway" and "Rainy Day People," the singer then wrote a song that may have been the decade's best example of the living folk music tradition: "The Wreck of the Edmund Fitzgerald," Lightfoot's eerie ballad based on the real-life 1975 sinking of a ship in Lake Superior. The song became a massive hit and stayed at number two for two weeks.

Lightfoot remained a consistent seller throughout the remainder of the 1970s, reaching the platinum mark twice again, with *Gord's Gold*—a 1975 two-LP hits collection, the first disc of which featured the singer redoing his earlier United Artists material—and 1976's *Summertime Dream*. He reached the top 40 one more time with "Circle Is Small (I Can See It in Your Eyes)," from 1978's gold *Endless Wire*, but by the start of the 1980s saw his album sales slackening. Following 1986's *East of Midnight*, which peaked at number 165 and stayed on the charts for a mere six weeks, Lightfoot announced that he had nothing more to say as a songwriter, and planned to stop recording. To add insult to injury, *Gord's Gold II*, a second hits collection released in 1988, then failed to chart at all.

By 1989, Lightfoot felt his enthusiasm for songwriting surging again. "I got married and got my household and life reorganized," he later explained to *Billboard*'s Larry LeBlanc. "Then I got a new method of working. I started getting up in the middle of the night and working through sunrise." Following a lengthy period of preparation, Lightfoot reemerged in 1993 with *Waiting for You,* a finely polished set bearing many songs comparable to those of his early '70s peak along with a cover of Bob Dylan's "Ring Them Bells." He then undertook his most extensive American tour in many years.

Through the lengthy course of his career, Lightfoot has seen—quite amazingly—over 130 of his songs being covered by an impressive array of artists, including Bob Dylan, Barbra Streisand, Elvis Presley, Johnny Cash, and Judy Collins, among countless others. He remains one of very few '60s folk performers who continue to thrive in the mid-'90s.

NILS LOFGREN

An extremely talented guitarist and still promising songwriter, Nils Lofgren (b. 1952, Chicago) has a long and impressive resume. The diminutive rocker, who spent his teenage years performing around Washington, D.C., has worked with three of rock and roll's all-time greats, Neil Young, Bruce Springsteen, and Lou Reed; played on the enormously influential first album by Young's backing group Crazy Horse; and also managed a spotlight position on ex-Beatle Ringo Starr's acclaimed tour of the early 1990s. But Lofgren is much, much more than a guitarist-for-hire. Beginning with the 1971 debut album of his first group, Grin, he has displayed occasional flashes of singing and songwriting brilliance that, without exaggeration, have equalled the work of his more famous collaborators.

A 1970 encounter with Neil Young led to Lofgren's providing piano and backing vocals on Young's top 10 album *After the Gold Rush* as well as a spot on Crazy Horse's 1971 debut, for which he provided two songs, including the memorable "Beggar's Day" (later covered by hard rockers Nazareth on their platinum 1975 set *Hair of the Dog*). All of which served as a prelude to Lofgren's center-stage bid with his own trio, Grin, who signed a deal with CBS subsidiary Spindizzy as a result of his spreading fame. Together with local friends Bob Berberich (drums) and Bob Gordon (bass), Lofgren recorded one of rock's finest debut albums.

Though it only spent three weeks on the charts and peaked at number 192, *Grin* was an utter tour de force for Lofgren. His songwriting skills were clearly major—he'd penned everything—and the songs he crafted were an unusual blend of toughness and tenderness, an appealing aspect of his work that has stayed with him since. While guitars crackled wildly on rocking tracks like "See What Love Can Do" (courtesy of guests Young and Crazy Horse), Lofgren displayed a mile-wide romantic streak on softer ballads such as "Take You to the Movies Tonight." That he was conscious of the schism became evident on 1972's *1+1*, probably his finest work. The album was segmented into a "Rockin' Side," featuring his single "White Lies," and a "Dreamy Side," highlighted by the wistful "Lost a Number" and the overpoweringly sentimental finale, "Soft Fun." Still, the album sold only slightly better than the first; its follow-up, the slightly inferior *All Out*, did worse.

In 1973, Lofgren took time out to accept an invitation to join mentor Young for his "Tonight's the Night" tour; the ultimate result, a 1975 album centering on the death of mutual friend Danny Whitten, Crazy Horse guitarist and central songwriter, is a harrowing album and one of Young's truly classic works. Following the tour, Lofgren reformed Grin (which, since *All Out,* also included his brother Tom as rhythm guitarist) for one disappointing A&M album that signalled that group's demise.

In 1975, Lofgren rebounded in total triumph with his first and finest solo album, *Nils Lofgren*. A near-perfect display of every aspect of his talent, it featured hard-rocking classics like "Back It Up" (later the name of a promotional-only bootleg issued by A&M) and "Keith Don't Go" (directed at Rolling Stones guitarist Keith Richards, of whom Lofgren was a major fan) mixed with wonderfully melodic tracks such as "The Sun Hasn't Set on This Boy Yet" and "Two by Two." Best of all was the absolutely enchanting reading of Goffin-King's "Goin' Back" that rivalled the Byrds' classic '60s version from their *Notorious Byrd Brothers* album.

From that point onward, Lofgren spent much of the 1970s on the road establishing himself as a gui-

tar-hero type, successfully charting with such albums as *Cry Tough* (1976) and *I Came to Dance* and the double live set *Night After Night* (both 1977). Unfortunately, Lofgren's songwriting began to slip somewhat at the same time, perhaps the result of spending so much time on the road. The situation was partially rectified on 1979's *Nils*, on which Lofgren co-wrote three songs with Lou Reed (three others appeared on Reed's 1979 album *The Bells*) and more with guitarist Dick Wagner, among others. That pattern continued to some extent on Lofgren's next record, 1981's *Night Fades Away,* on which he collaborated with producer Jeff Baxter. But while that album just cracked the midpoint of the album chart, his next, 1983's *Wonderland,* failed to chart at all—and Lofgren's solo career looked shaky.

Having played with Young once more on his 1982 *Trans* tour, Lofgren clearly had no problem playing second banana to anyone. Thus, Bruce Springsteen's 1984 request that he replace departed guitarist "Miami" Steve Van Zandt for his 1984–85 tour came at precisely the right time. He did so—garnering more visibility than he ever had in his life—then came back refreshed for the very substantial *Flip,* issued by Columbia in 1985. He soon joined Springsteen again for his late '80s *Tunnel of Love* tour and was also highly visible as part of Ringo Starr's 1990 All-Starr Band.

In 1991, Lofgren surfaced again on the indie Rykodisc label, for whom he'd record *Silver Lining* (which featured a guest spot by Springsteen) and the next year's *Crooked Line* (on which Young guests), both of which received enthusiastic reviews. Also in 1992, he again backed Neil Young—this time on Young's "Unplugged" MTV special, later released in both album and video formats. As a final irony, in the fall of 1993, only weeks after his former Springsteen bandmate Max Weinberg was named music director of NBC's "Late Night with Conan O'Brien," Lofgren was named music director of ABC-TV's (short-lived) primetime comedy program, "The Paula Poundstone Show." It may be tempting to note that you can't keep a good man down—but as his resume indicates, Lofgren hasn't been down yet.

TOP ALBUMS

NILS LOFGREN (A&M, '75)
CRY TOUGH (A&M, '76, 32)
I CAME TO DANCE (A&M, '77, 36)
NIGHT AFTER NIGHT (A&M, '77)

TOP SONGS

BACK IT UP (A&M, '75)
I DON'T WANT TO KNOW (A&M, '75)
KEITH DON'T GO (ODE TO THE GLIMMER TWIN) (A&M, '75)
TWO BY TWO (A&M, '75)
SHINE SILENTLY (A&M, '79)

KENNY LOGGINS

While never viewed as an especially cutting-edge performer, Kenny Loggins (b. Jan. 7, 1947, Everett, Washington) has managed to stay in business, integrity and sales intact, longer than almost all of his contemporaries. From country-rocking folkie to slick pop star to ubiquitous soundtrack presence, Loggins has, in the course of two decades, shifted his approach to music making skillfully and without much noticeable compromise. Maybe he has gone the soundtrack route once too often—but consistent top 10 singles are, after all, awfully difficult to argue with.

Like many of his contemporaries, Loggins started out in comparative obscurity; he recorded with two little-known late-'60s rock bands (Gator Creek and Second Helping) before signing a publishing deal with ABC/Wingate. As a result of that deal, the Nitty Gritty Dirt Band recorded four of his songs and scored a small hit in 1971 with "House at Pooh Corner." Columbia Records then stepped in and offered Loggins a recording contract. His first album's slated producer, former Buffalo Springfield and Poco member Jim Messina, became so involved with the recording it was credited to "Kenny Loggins with Jim Messina" and thus began one of the more lucrative musical partnerships of the 1970s. Together through 1976, Loggins and Messina recorded two platinum and five gold albums and scored a top five single in 1972 with the jointly penned "Your Mama

Kenny Loggins

Don't Dance" (which again hit the top of the charts 17 years later when covered by hard-rock group Poison).

"It was one of the highlights of my life," Jim Messina said years later of his time with Loggins. "I considered my relationship with Kenny in the beginning very special, and a creative relationship. I learned a lot from him as a singer, and he helped me indirectly as a writer—in the sense that he was a very quality writer. There was a creative competitiveness there, a healthy competitiveness, that I think brought both of us up to a real special place."

Significantly, though, when Loggins and Messina split, it was Loggins's career that took off, while Messina's floundered by comparison. Loggins's first three solo albums each went platinum—*Celebrate Me Home, Nightwatch,* and *Keep the Fire,* all released between 1977 and 1979—and, maybe more importantly, Loggins was striking up musical relationships with some of the dominant musical forces of the era. To wit: Fleetwood Mac's Stevie Nicks, who sang on the top 10 single "Whenever I Call You 'Friend,' " and the Doobie Brothers' Michael McDonald, with whom Loggins had written "What a Fool Believes" (a Number One Doobies hit in

TOP ALBUMS

CELEBRATE ME HOME (Columbia, '77, 27)
NIGHTWATCH (Columbia, '78, 7)
KEEP THE FIRE (Columbia, '79, 16)
KENNY LOGGINS ALIVE (Columbia, '80, 11)
HIGH ADVENTURE (Columbia, '82, 13)

TOP SONGS

WHENEVER I CALL YOU "FRIEND" (Columbia, '78, 5)
I'M ALRIGHT (Columbia, '80, 7)
FOOTLOOSE (Columbia, '84, 1)
DANGER ZONE (Columbia, '86, 2)
NOBODY'S FOOL (Columbia, '88, 8)

Additional Top 40 Songs: 9

1979) and "This Is It," a top 20 hit for Loggins, among many other tracks.

The next phase in Loggins's career is in some ways the most controversial: a series of hit singles from film soundtracks that, despite their success, may have altered the industry's perception of the singer. The onetime album-rock staple was hitting top 40 radio regularly with hits from *Caddyshack* ("I'm Alright"), *Footloose* (the title track, written by Loggins and Dean Pitchford, topped the Hot 100 for three weeks and went platinum), *Top Gun* ("Danger Zone"), *Over the Top* ("Meet Me Halfway"), and even *Caddyshack II* (the top 10 hit "Nobody's Fool"). What was the downside? First, Loggins had nothing to do with the writing of either "Danger Zone" or "Meet Me Halfway"—Giorgio Moroder and Tom Whitlock did—and secondly, few of those hits were to be found anywhere on his own albums, which had stopped their regular ascension to the top 40 with 1985's *Vox Humana.*

By the time Columbia issued *Outside from the Redwoods,* Loggins's live career retrospective of 1993, a notation in the CD booklet mentioned only five albums that were "also available from Kenny Loggins." Curiously not listed were 1980's *Kenny Loggins Alive,* 1982's *High Adventure,* and, most surprisingly, *Back to Avalon,* a comparatively recent 1988 effort. Did this mean Loggins's audience was vanishing? Not likely—his 1991 album *Leap of Faith* had gone gold, after all, and included well-known adult contemporary hits like "I Would Do Anything" and "If You Believe." More likely, Loggins's "adult contemporary" audience was simply growing up and away—and wisely, like other singer-songwriters of his vintage, Loggins was preparing for it. By 1994, the co-writer of "Your Mama Don't Dance" was scheduled to produce his first album of children's songs.

JACKIE LOMAX

One of the first artists introduced to the world on the Beatles' new, prestigious Apple Records label, Jackie Lomax (b. May 10, 1944, Liverpool, England) was a lanky, good-looking singer-songwriter who took an appealingly soulful approach to singing but never commercially clicked. A longtime performer whose onetime group the Undertakers played in Hamburg in the early

---

1960s, as did the Beatles, Lomax had signed a management deal with Beatle manager Brian Epstein and released one single under the name the Lomax Alliance. Though little came of it, the singer convinced Beatle George Harrison he had the goods; the result was a series of recordings leading to 1968's "Sour Milk Sea," Lomax's first Apple single, which was penned by Harrison and featured a band that included Eric Clapton, Harrison, Paul McCartney, Ringo Starr, and pianist Nicky Hopkins. Lomax's first album, *Is This What You Want?,* followed in May 1969, containing "Sea" and 11 other self-penned tracks, the majority of which were excellent. The album sold respectably, staying on the charts for nine weeks and peaking at number 145, but after one more single ("How the Web Was Woven") Lomax was no longer on the label.

Briefly thereafter the singer worked with two groups that never properly gelled: Balls, featuring ex-Moody Blues and future Wings guitarist Denny Laine and Move bassist Trevor Burton; and Heavy Jelly, in which Lomax was accompanied by members of the Aynsley Dunbar Retaliation. Though neither group released an album at the time, in 1984 the U.K.'s Psycho label released *Take Me Down to the Water,* a collection of Heavy Jelly recordings circa 1970, which featured eight songs written and sung by Lomax.

The singer then moved to Woodstock, New York, in 1970 and signed to Warner Bros.—the same label that would likewise scoop up his former Apple labelmate James Taylor. His two albums for the label, *Home Is in My Head* (1971) and *Three* (1972), were surprisingly good; Lomax was an especially emotive singer, and his songwriting on these discs was mature and varied. Highlights included his tender "You Within Me" from *Home* and *Three*'s upbeat opener "No Reason," the latter aided greatly by John Simon's sympathetic production. Both albums proved virtual nonentities on the charts, and in 1974 the singer returned to England, where he fronted Badger—the group formed by keyboardist Tony Kaye upon leaving Yes—for their curious 1974 album *White Lady*. Produced by Allen Toussaint, the record comprised 10 Lomax tunes and more accurately should have been issued under the singer's name. Better for him that it wasn't: underdeveloped and weak-sounding, the album was not exactly a career high point for Lomax.

The singer got one more shot the next year, when he returned to Los Angeles and signed to Capitol. But his two records for the label, *Livin' for Lovin'* and 1976's *Did You Ever Have That Feeling?*, were disappointments; his songs often veered toward the ordinary, and the production buried his vocals too deeply in the mix. Dropped by the label soon after, Lomax has been without a label since. He has continued performing in Los Angeles through the 1990s, occasionally with such fellow expatriates as Terry Reid, Mick Taylor, and Brian Auger. Still an engaging vocalist and performer, Lomax turned 50 in 1994; a further stint on a major label seems unlikely.

NICK LOWE

Nick Lowe

One of the founding members of Brinsley Schwarz, England's most famous "pub rock" group of the late 1960s and early '70s, Nick Lowe (b. Mar. 25, 1949, Woodbridge, Suffolk, England) played a vital role in the early days of England's colorful punk scene. A distinguished songwriter in his own right, Lowe became best known as a producer of some of the era's most prominent acts, including the Damned (whose 1977 debut album *Damned Damned Damned* is generally credited as the first U.K. punk album), Dr. Feelgood, and singers Graham Parker, Elvis Costello, and Wreckless Eric. Lowe seemed very much a jack-of-all-trades and stylistic chameleon; his early solo singles parodied the Bay City Rollers and the disco phenomenon and would later explore diverse styles such as pop, hard rock, rockabilly, and even electro-pop. A long-term relationship with Welsh guitarist Dave Edmunds, formerly of rock group Love Sculpture, resulted in many collaborative albums released under both of their names—though together with two other play-

ers they were members of the well-traveled touring band Rockpile. The latter group disbanded in 1981, shortly after the release of the sole album bearing the group's moniker, and Lowe has continued releasing albums under his own name ever since.

Heavily associated with Stiff Records, Britain's ground-breaking independent label of the mid-1970s, Lowe released the company's first single ("So It Goes" b/w "Heart of the City") in 1976, and essentially became its house producer. By 1977, he had become bassist with Rockpile—which, at the time, was simply the backing group of Dave Edmunds, who was touring to promote his Swan Song Records debut album, *Get It*. That album featured two tunes by Lowe ("I Knew the Bride" and "What Did I Do Last Night?") and another pair by both Lowe and Edmunds ("Here Comes the Weekend" and "Little Darlin' ") and marked the start of the pair's long, sometimes rocky relationship.

While Edmunds was himself very much a studio genius type—enormously skilled at replicating the production and overall sound of '50s and '60s rock—Lowe was well known for his "bash it out" studio philosophy, often contending that the best pop music was spontaneous, not polished until all the rough edges were removed. Regardless, the pair were a highly respected and complementary duo; Edmunds typically played upbeat rootsy rock, and Lowe more often opted for witty and melodic pop. Given the context of the times—the rawness of primitive punk versus the tired slickness of album-rock fodder such as Journey, Styx, and Kansas—both Lowe's and Edmunds' approaches were welcome, very refreshing changes of pace.

After Lowe scored a top 15 American hit with 1979's "Cruel to Be Kind," expectations were high at Columbia Records when the first official Rockpile album, *Seconds of Pleasure,* was released in 1980. "Even when we were making Dave Edmunds records," Lowe insisted at the time, "we all had the same sort of shout—the same sort of voice—as we did when we were making Nick Lowe records." Added partner Edmunds: "The only thing that's changed now is that if we were doing a Nick Lowe album, Nick's say would be final, because it was his album, and it was the same for me if I was doing an album. Now with a Rockpile album, it turns out that whoever is singing the songs gets the last say, 'cause it was his idea to sing the thing in the first place." While *Seconds of Pleasure* was indeed a commercial success—it reached number 27 on the charts—it was regarded by critics as a disappointment precisely for the reason Edmunds said: it sounded like the work of two different artists, not one distinct group.

Lowe's commercial fortunes as a solo artist declined gradually in the 1980s. His albums lost the eclectic and poppish sound that had made both his pre-Rockpile efforts, *Pure Pop for Now People* and *Labour of Lust,* so distinctive; later lesser works such as *The Abominable Showman, Nick Lowe and His Cowboy Outfit,* and *The Rose of England* bore no distinctive hits to maintain his diminishing audience and give his career the boost it sorely needed. By 1988, his album *Pinker and Prouder than Previous* failed to chart at all; he left Columbia soon afterward.

Lowe's abilities as a musician were very much on display as part of John Hiatt's band on his critically hailed 1987 album *Bring the Family;* the experience gave him much food for thought regarding the direction his own career was taking. "I got the feeling that as a songwriter, I had a role to play," Lowe recalled in 1990, "and not just as some aging lounge lizard. I persist in hoping that writing good songs will lead to commercial success. I want to be successful, but I've learned that if I water it down here and break off a bit there to try and get it to fit, it just doesn't wash."

Though Lowe signed a new deal with Reprise and released his best record in years with 1990's *Party of One,* the album spent only three weeks on the charts and peaked at number 182. He returned in 1992 with the same band that had backed Hiatt—which included guitarist Ry Cooder, drummer Jim Keltner, and Hiatt himself—but the resulting album, released under the group name Little Village, was regarded by many as an unfocused disappointment. The problem—as it was with Rockpile—was simple: great band, no bandleader. But if getting there is half the fun, Nick Lowe was clearly having the time of his life in the early '90s.

TOP ALBUMS

PURE POP FOR NOW PEOPLE (Columbia, '78)
LABOUR OF LUST (Columbia, '79, *31*)
SECONDS OF PLEASURE (with Rockpile, Columbia, '80, 27)
NICK THE KNIFE (Columbia, '82)
THE ABOMINABLE SHOWMAN (Columbia, '83)
PARTY OF ONE (Reprise, '90)

TOP SONGS

I LOVE THE SOUND OF BREAKING GLASS (Columbia, '78)
CRUEL TO BE KIND (Columbia, '79, *12*)
I KNEW THE BRIDE (WHEN SHE USED TO ROCK 'N' ROLL) (Columbia, '85)

BARRY MANILOW

One of the most recognizable figures in popular music, Barry Manilow (b. Barry Alan Pincus, June 17, 1946, Brooklyn, New York) dominated the charts during the latter half of the 1970s. His music, pleasant and overwhelmingly sentimental, touched the hearts of an extremely large and loyal, mostly female audience, who found it easy to relate romantic hits like "Looks Like We Made It" and "Can't Smile Without You" to their personal lives. Though much of his music is remembered as schmaltzy and corny and has often been the subject

Barry Manilow

of pointed satire, Manilow's enormous impact on pop culture—he has sold over 50 million records worldwide—should not be underestimated.

A onetime student at Juilliard, Manilow worked as a mail clerk at CBS, where at the age of 18, he was asked by a director to arrange music for a stage adaptation of *The Drunkard;* instead, he composed an entire new score, and the musical had an eight-year off-Broadway run. In 1967, he became music director of WCBS-TV's "Callback!" musical variety series, and he began writing and singing radio and television commercials for Dr. Pepper, Pepsi, State Farm Insurance, McDonald's, and more. In 1971, he co-wrote "Could It Be Magic" with longtime collaborator Adrienne Anderson; produced by Tony Orlando, it was his first single, released on Bell Records in 1971 and credited to "Featherbed featuring Barry Manilow." The next year, he met Bette Midler while serving as house pianist at New York's Continental Baths, and soon became her musical

director, arranger, and pianist. One of his most notable early credits came via his co-producing and arranging her Grammy-winning debut, *The Divine Miss M,* and its follow-up, *Bette Midler.*

Manilow's own recording career soon blossomed at Bell—or, more accurately, Arista, as the label was called after Clive Davis took it over in 1974. Davis retained very few of Bell's artists upon his arrival; Manilow, one of the lucky few who made the cut, soon saw both of his poor-selling Bell albums (1973's *Barry Manilow I* and 1974's *Barry Manilow II*) reissued and remarketed by Arista. Beginning with his Number One single "Mandy"—a remake of a charting 1971 single by Scott English—Manilow enjoyed an amazing run of 25 consecutive top 40 hits by 1983, 11 of which made the top 10. In 1978, five of his albums—all either gold or platinum—were on the chart simultaneously, a feat previously accomplished only by Frank Sinatra and Johnny Mathis—elite company indeed.

There's substantial irony in the fact that his Number One hit "I Write the Songs"—perhaps the biggest single in Manilow's career—was penned not by him but by Beach Boy Bruce Johnston. In fact, of Manilow's 25 top 40 hits, he wrote only eight: "It's a Miracle," "Could It Be Magic," "This One's for You," "Even Now," "Copacabana (At the Copa)," "Daybreak," "I Made It Through the Rain," and "Some Kind of Friend." As a rule, Manilow's music was accompanied by lyrics supplied by others—typically Anderson, Marty Panzer, or Bruce Sussman and Jack Feldman, though other collaborators included Johnny Mercer, Enoch Anderson, and Lisa Sennett. As Manilow's career unfolded into the 1980s and early '90s, he wrote even less frequently, occasionally using writers such as Tom Kelly for musical support as well.

Beginning with 1984's *Swing Street*—a surprising jazzy departure for Manilow that featured guests Sarah Vaughn, Gerry Mulligan, Mel Tormé, and Shelly Manne—the singer began to focus on concept works rather than hit singles, which is reflected in his absence from the top 40 charts since then. Among his projects was *Swing Street,* the soundtrack to a 1987 CBS-TV special, a live-on-Broadway album, a gold-certified Christmas album, and 1991's *Showstoppers,* a collection of Broadway show tunes. Now perceived as much more an overall live entertainer than simple record maker, Barry Manilow has moved on—and, fortunately for him, his loyal audience has conspicuously followed, ever faithful.

John Martyn

TOP ALBUMS

BARRY MANILOW II (Arista, '74, 9)
TRYIN' TO GET THE FEELING (Arista, '75, 5)
THIS ONE'S FOR YOU (Arista, '76, 6)
BARRY MANILOW/LIVE (Arista, '77, 1)
EVEN NOW (Arista, '78, 3)

Additional Top 40 Albums: 9

TOP SONGS

MANDY (Arista, '74, 1)
COULD IT BE MAGIC (Arista, '75, 6)
I WRITE THE SONGS (Arista, '75, 1)
LOOKS LIKE WE MADE IT (Arista, '77, 1)
CAN'T SMILE WITHOUT YOU (Arista, '78, 3)

Additional Top 40 Songs: 20

JOHN MARTYN

Attempt to categorize John Martyn (b. June 28, 1948) at your own risk. The Glasgow-born singer-songwriter-guitarist, who has been making brilliant records since 1968, really does play a little bit of everything: folk, blues, jazz, rock, reggae, even space music. His numerous albums—there have been over 20, and more keep coming year after year—have featured a steady stream of superstar sidemen, including Eric Clapton, Phil Collins, Steve Winwood, and Pink Floyd's David Gilmour, all of whom are clearly sitting in for love, not money. Though when an artist the caliber of Clapton sees fit to record a Martyn tune—in this case, "May You Never" for his platinum *Slowhand* album back in 1977—love and money may go hand-in-hand.

Martyn's very early signing to England's fledgling Island Records label resulted in 1968's quaintly folkish U.K. debut, *London Conversation.* Initially, Martyn seemed an enchanting vocalist with a guitar style owing much to English folkie heroes like Davy Graham, John Renbourn, and Bert Jansch—though that didn't stop him from covering Bob Dylan's "Don't Think Twice It's Alright." In short order, though, Martyn's eclecticism kicked in. His next album, *The Tumbler,* had a few jazzy touches, courtesy of respected Brit flautist Harold McNair; the next featured a new partner and wife, singer Beverley, and was recorded in Woodstock, New York. *Stormbringer,* issued by Warner Bros. in 1970, was Martyn's first American release and was officially credited to John and Beverley Martyn. The earlier sparse folkie sound was becoming fuller by the minute: *Stormbringer* paired the Martyns with American rock players like Levon Helm, Harvey Brooks, and Billy Mundi; follow-up *The Road to Ruin,* issued the same year, threw in three horns and the prominent playing of acoustic bassist Danny Thompson, whose relationship with Martyn would prove pivotal.

Already Martyn seemed a folkie turned folk rocker; when wife Beverley dropped out of the professional scene, even newer directions were beckoning. Within two years, Martyn had redefined his musical and songwriting approach and made a pair of albums that still rank as his best: 1971's *Bless the Weather* and 1973's *Solid Air.* Though he still was writing what could fairly be called pop music—pop group America, after all, covered *Weather*'s "Head and Heart" on its gold 1972 set, *Homecoming*—bassist Thompson had brought in a jazzy element that made all the difference. Martyn's vocals, earlier full of earnestness and plainly sung, became purposefully slurred, almost indistinct; his guitar took on a more prominent atmospheric role; his songs, still gently personal pieces about people and relationships, didn't sound at all out of place when set alongside a wild cover of bluesman Skip James's "I'd Rather Be the Devil."

TOP ALBUMS

BLESS THE WEATHER (Island, '71)
SOLID AIR (Island, '73)
INSIDE OUT (Island, '73)
SUNDAY'S CHILD (Island, '74)
GRACE AND DANGER (Antilles, '80)
PIECE BY PIECE (Island, '86)
NO LITTLE BOY (Mesa, '93)

TOP SONGS

SOLID AIR (Island, '73)
MAN AT THE STATION (Island, '73)
MAY YOU NEVER (Island, '73)

Throughout the 1970s, Martyn continued exploring the outer perimeters of sound: In 1975, he issued a privately pressed concert album, *Live at Leeds,* that featured an 18-minute-and-57-second guitar and Echoplex instrumental track. In 1976, he visited Jamaica to check out the burgeoning dub scene there and work with well-known reggae producer Lee Perry. When his marriage to wife Beverley fell apart in the late 1970s, the resulting album, *Grace and Danger,* a deeply personal and sometimes harrowing listen, was reportedly delayed release by label executives who found it too depressing.

In 1981, Martyn had a new album, *Glorious Fool;* a new producer and drummer, Phil Collins; and, on one track at least, a new guitarist, Eric Clapton. That album, and the next few that followed, seemed a stepping back from the emotionalism that made *Grace and Danger* so memorable. And ironically, despite the presence of heavy-hitters like Collins and Clapton on those earlier works, it was 1986's guest star–free *Piece by Piece* album that was his comparative breakthrough: thanks to the growth of "Wave"-format radio stations, Martyn's softer stuff—particularly "Lonely Love"—was a favorite of many stations leaning toward "adult contemporary" music.

Entering the 1990s without an American label, Martyn seemed to be settling into a future of independent-only releases. Both 1990's *The Apprentice* and 1991's *Cooltide,* issued on the U.K.'s Permanent Records label, were certainly the equal of anything Martyn had done during the 1980s—but in the age of MTV, what label really cared? The answer, oddly enough, was Mesa Records, a label that had demonstrated a knack for the so-called new adult contemporary music that by now (and by default) provided a convenient category for Martyn's music.

In 1993, Mesa issued Martyn's *No Little Boy,* featuring guests Phil Collins, David Gilmour, Levon Helm, and jazzers Peter Erskine and Andy Sheppard. The tunes were redone versions of Martyn's all-time classics, nearly half from *Bless the Weather* and *Solid Air.* And one thing's for sure: if nobody heard them the first time, it hasn't been John Martyn's fault.

RICHARD MARX

No one can deny Richard Marx his rightful due: from out of nowhere, the Chicago-bred singer-songwriter emerged in 1987 with a triple platinum top 10 album, a nonstop series of hits, and a knack for crafting songs that album-rock radio embraced wholeheartedly—and instantly. Marx's uncanny success in that medium was such that his record company took to emphasizing it above all else, sometimes to ridiculous extremes. Richard Marx, recounted one Capitol Records press release, was "the first new artist ever played on 117 radio stations nationwide during his initial week on the charts." What, quipped skeptical journalists, does this mean other new artists get played on 200?

In fact, despite his success, Marx found himself getting the short end of the stick from the press more often than not—both for his music, which many critics pegged as being too formulaic and bland, and for his hair, which was, well, big a lot of the time. While Marx could take care of his hair with a quick trip to the barber, his music was another story: to many ears, it seemed like a further refinement of the California rock sound produced by the likes of the Eagles and other Asylum Records rockers of the mid-1970s. Which is why album-rock radio loved it, of course: it went down easy and felt good on the way.

Marx came from a distinguished musical family in the Windy City. His father was a former jazz pianist who later made his name in the jingle busi-

Richard Marx

TOP ALBUMS

RICHARD MARX (EMI-Manhattan, '87, 8)
REPEAT OFFENDER (EMI, '89, 1)
RUSH STREET (Capitol, '91, 35)

TOP SONGS

DON'T MEAN NOTHING (Manhattan, '87, 3)
SHOULD'VE KNOWN BETTER (Manhattan, '87, 3)
ENDLESS SUMMER NIGHTS (EMI-Manhattan, '88, 2)
HOLD ON TO THE NIGHTS (EMI-Manhattan, '88, 1)
SATISFIED (EMI, '89, 1)
RIGHT HERE WAITING (EMI, '89, 1)
ANGELIA (EMI, '89, 4)

Additional Top 40 Songs: 5

ness; his mother sang on television commercials—as did Marx himself at the early age of five. But by the time he was 17, he was writing his own material. Marx's break into the business came via Lionel Richie, who by chance had heard one of the singer's tapes and invited him to sing background vocals on his albums; a further link with producer David Foster saw him co-writing two Kenny Rogers hits ("What About Me" and "Crazy") in 1985, and later tracks by Chicago, Philip Bailey, and Durell Coleman.

Marx struck his own deal with Manhattan Records in early 1986, and the rest is chart history. His first album sent four singles into the top three ("Don't Mean Nothing," "Should've Known Better," "Endless Summer Nights," and the Number One hit "Hold On to the Nights"); his second, 1989's *Repeat Offender,* brought him three top three hits (dual Number One smashes "Satisfied" and

"Right Here Waiting" along with "Angelia") and additional top 20 hits "Too Late to Say Goodbye" and "Children of the Night." Combined, both albums sold more than 10 million copies worldwide.

Though Marx writes most of his music and lyrics, he occasionally teams with an interesting collaborator: Fee Waybill, former lead singer of the Tubes, a band so colorful and visual they seem almost Marx's diametric opposite. Marx have an image problem? You bet. In 1991, when politics within the EMI group of labels dictated that Marx's third album would be released on Capitol (*Repeat Offender* had been on EMI), his new label went to unprecedented lengths to pump up Marx's public persona. Renting a huge MGM Grand charter jet, Capitol sent Marx, his band, and a crew of noisy media people to five cities in one day; in each, Marx would give a brief concert to promote his new album, *Rush Street*. By the end of a very long day, Marx had played Baltimore, New York, Cleveland, Chicago, and Los Angeles—and journalists, unfortunately, were still talking about his hair. Hits, Richard Marx has got; it's respect he needs.

DAVE MASON

Anyone who assumes that writing one successful pop song will automatically lead to a life of fame and fortune ought to take a look at Dave Mason (b. May 10, 1945, Worcester, England), who wrote the oft-covered tune "Feelin' Alright" in 1968 as a member of Traffic, began a bang-up solo career, then slowly watched his fortunes slip away. Nineteen years later, hoping to kickstart his career with a new album for a new label, the guitar-playing singer-songwriter glumly explained his misfortune. "I've gone through two bankruptcies and basically ended up with not a lot to show for anything," he said. "Most of my songs have been either lost through bankruptcies, publishers, or things from the past."

Certainly no one expected anything but terrific singing, writing, and guitar playing from Mason when, in 1968, he departed Traffic—a group he founded a year earlier with drummer Jim Capaldi, flautist Chris Wood, and multi-instrumentalist whizkid Steve Winwood. He'd already penned the group's second British hit, "Hole in My Shoe," and with "Feelin' Alright" and "You Can All Join In"

contributed two of the strongest tunes on Traffic's highly regarded second album, his last with the group. But even early on, Mason's post-Traffic career seemed spontaneous to the point of liability: just when he needed to establish himself as a vital creative entity on his own, one planned group fell apart (Mason, Wood, Capaldi and Frog), and another high-profile 1969 gig—with Delaney and Bonnie and Friends—kept him in the background as just a guitarist (though trading riffs with another "Friend," Eric Clapton, was doubtless a joy).

His first solo album, 1970's *Alone Together,* featured Mason front and center—and remains one of the finest album of the 1970s. With a backing group of superb musicians (including Leon Russell, Jim Keltner, and Delaney and Bonnie themselves), Mason played and delivered his classic: taut, tension-filled tunes such as "Look at You Look at Me," bolstered by his still-underrated, legato lead guitar style; "Sad and Deep as You," a tender track that wouldn't have been out of place on a Traffic album; and the upbeat and rocking "Only You Know and I Know," rerecorded and made a top 20 hit by Delaney and Bonnie a year later.

Though *Alone Together* wasn't Mason's only gold album, it was his highest charting and, significantly, by far his most artistically successful. Next for the artist came a series of puzzling career maneuvers that quickly halted whatever momentum he'd just achieved: a live album by a temporarily reunited Traffic (*Welcome to the Canteen*), a bizarre joint album with Mama Cass Elliot (1971), a half-studio/half-live *Headkeeper* (the live side featured no new material), and yet another live set, *Dave Mason Is Alive* (1973). Mason, who felt the problems to be related to his label Blue Thumb, moved to Columbia and got his career back on track with 1973's *It's Like You Never Left,* with guests George Harrison (billed "Son of Harry"), Graham Nash, and Stevie Wonder conspicuous contributors. As his career moved back into gear and Mason assembled a fairly steady band, including guitarist Jim Krueger and organist Mike Finnegan, his former label helpfully issued two greatest hits sets (1974's *Best of Dave Mason* and 1975's *Dave Mason at His Best*)—poor form, considering the only studio albums he'd made for Blue Thumb were *Alone Together* and half-each of the Mama Cass and *Headkeeper* sets.

Two things happened to Mason at Columbia: he had hits and he lost focus. Though three of his albums (1974's *Dave Mason*, 1975's *Split Coconut,* and 1977's *Let It Flow*) reached the *Billboard* Top Pop Albums chart's top 40 (*Mason* and *Flow* going gold), each had progressively fewer songs penned by the singer. Mason took to covering Bob Dylan's "All Along the Watchtower," Sam Cooke's "Bring It On Home to Me," and Buddy Holly's "Crying, Waiting, Hoping," eventually scoring his final top 40 hit in 1978 with Goffin-King's "Will You Still Love Me Tomorrow." Mason's final album for Columbia, issued two years later, when the punk and new wave bands were making commercial inroads on the charts, was self-consciously titled *Old Crest on a New Wave.*

Mason then left Columbia, feeling what he called a lack of "personal commitment" from the company. "It took me a year to get off the label," he later recalled. "Then my mother died of cancer. After that happened, I really didn't care if I made another record. I was very soured on the business." After a serious depression, Mason resurfaced in 1987 with two albums, only one of which—*Two Hearts,* on MCA/Voyager—he fully authorized. (The other, *Some Assembly Required,* was of indeterminate vintage and slipshod, featuring four solo tracks by guitarist Jim Krueger.)

Whatever the ups and downs of his career, Mason clearly has a hard time losing old friends: his former bandmate Steve Winwood prominently played and sang on *Two Hearts,* and—speaking of old English ties—in 1993, Mason signed on to join Fleetwood Mac. Hard to believe? As the saying goes, they'll get to everyone, eventually.

TOP ALBUMS

ALONE TOGETHER (Blue Thumb, '70, 22)
DAVE MASON & CASS ELLIOT (with Cass Elliot, Blue Thumb, '71)
DAVE MASON (Columbia, '74, 25)
SPLIT COCONUT (Columbia, '75, 27)
LET IT FLOW (Columbia, '77, 37)

TOP SONGS

ONLY YOU KNOW AND I KNOW (Blue Thumb, '70)
BABY...PLEASE (Columbia, '73)
WE JUST DISAGREE (Columbia, '77, 12)
LET IT GO, LET IT FLOW (Columbia, '77)
WILL YOU STILL LOVE ME TOMORROW (Columbia, '78, 39)

IAIN MATTHEWS

While Iain Matthews (b. June 1946, Lincolnshire, England) hasn't ever officially been a music critic, he'd likely be one of the best there ever was, if having good taste in little-known songs was that occupation's sole requirement. With over 32 albums to his credit, either in solo or group context, Matthews, an exquisite singer, has consistently rescued some of the least heard but best songs in pop from undeserved obscurity.

Born Iain McDonald, Matthews began using his middle name in the late 1960s to avoid confusion with the early King Crimson member with the same name (he returned to the original Gaelic spelling of "Ian" much later, in 1990). It's doubtful anyone would confuse the amphetamine-driven roar of King Crimson's showstopping "21st Century Schizoid Man" with Matthews' first major band (he'd earlier recorded with obscure British pop group Pyramid), legendary English folk-rockers Fairport Convention, which also boasted Sandy Denny and Richard Thompson as members. Matthews stayed with the group long enough to contribute to their first three albums, which were much more rock-oriented compared to the group's later traditional folk approach, giving Fairport their peculiar (and short-lived) status as "England's Jefferson Airplane."

Matthews' early association with American music was significant: his initial exposure here came via his 1971 hit recording of Joni Mitchell's "Woodstock," which reached number 23 on the Hot 100 despite already being taken there (and higher, to number 11) a year earlier by supergroup Crosby, Stills, Nash and Young. The hit was credited to Matthews' Southern Comfort, the countryesque folk group the singer formed following his first solo album, 1969's *Southern Comfort.* Two other albums with the Southern Comfort banner followed, each bearing a mixture of original tunes by Matthews and other band members and a revealing batch of covers, including songs penned by Neil Young, James Taylor, Jesse Winchester, and Al Anderson of the Wildweeds and NRBQ.

Matthews has continued this pattern for most of his solo career, mixing his own compositions with a smattering of others that truly had to have been sought out to have ever been heard in the first place. Examples: "Right Before My Eyes," from Matthews' 1971 album *Tigers Will Survive,* originated from

Moby Grape's dismally selling *Truly Fine Citizen* album; "Shake It," Matthews' 1978 hit (his biggest ever: it reached number 13), was one of two songs he'd covered by Terence Boylan, who'd recorded two undeservedly obscure albums for Asylum during the same era. A partial list of songwriters that self-confessed record junkie Matthews has covered during his career, in fact, is quite an eye-opener. To those already mentioned, add Richard Farina, Eric Andersen, Pete Carr, Paul Siebel, Jerry Yester and Judy Henske, Jackson Browne, Steve Young, Randy Newman, Michael Nesmith, Don Gibson, Tom Waits, Danny Whitten, Gene Clark, Donald Fagen and Walter Becker, Mickey Newbury, Tim Hardin, Jimmy Webb, Merle Haggard, Jesse Colin Young, Van Morrison, Tim Moore, Daryl Hall, Terry Reid, John Martyn, Marc Jordan, Stevie Nicks, the Left Banke's Michael Brown and Steve Martin—even Peter Gabriel. All of which would be a moot point if the tunes Matthews himself has written weren't up to snuff. They are. And what's especially interesting is that unlike many singer-songwriters whose skills sometimes seem to plateau after an initial flash of brilliance, Matthews seems a better writer the longer he's at it.

His taste in music hasn't gone unnoticed at record company levels, either: after his 1983 album *Shook* did not see an American release, the disillusioned Matthews—who had moved to Seattle and was playing with low-profile group Hi-Fi—actually worked A&R for Island Music (where he helped in the career of Bourgeois-Tagg) and Windham Hill Records. His return to recording, 1988's *Walking a Changing Line,* showed just how much good songs continued

to mean to him: it was devoted entirely to the compositions of Jules Shear. Though a risky move for any singer-songwriter, it didn't signify a dry spell for Matthews: within four years, his triumphant *Skeleton Keys* marked the first time he'd written every song on an album.

PAUL McCARTNEY

Just as Beatle fans professed amusement at the mythical young record buyer of the 1970s who'd note in amazement, "Hey, did you know Paul McCartney was in another band before Wings?," Wings fans can now be amused by a new, even younger generation of CD buyers unaware that solo artist McCartney was once even in a band. An exaggeration, of course, but still a possibility for the man whom in 1979 the *Guinness Book of Records* honored as the most successful popular music composer ever. Since that singular distinction, McCartney (b. James Paul McCartney, June 18, 1942, Liverpool, England) has released 14 more albums, four of which were certified platinum, and 12 top 40 singles, including the Number One hits "Coming Up," "Ebony and Ivory," and "Say Say Say." The legendary Liverpudlian's career has continued at a more productive pace than ever into the 1990s: between the release of 1989's gold *Flowers in the Dirt*—which was highlighted by the singer's songwriting collaborations with Elvis Costello—through 1993's *Paul Is Live,* McCartney issued a total of seven albums, or roughly half the number of albums he recorded while a member of the Beatles.

Indeed, there's a good chance that the still-active McCartney will soon match the astounding number of top 40 hits he and John Lennon penned for the Beatles—a total of 40—since the group's famous split of 1970. Though that doesn't take into account the many hits he and Lennon wrote for the likes of Peter and Gordon, Billy J. Kramer, and other '60s British Invasion stars—another facet of his extraordinary success—it's a fact that may surprise diehard Beatle fans who assume McCartney's track record with the Beatles remains unapproachable.

In some ways, despite his monumental achievements, McCartney has fought an uphill battle since leaving the Beatles. Much of it has stemmed from the longheld critical perception that the Lennon and McCartney songwriting team offered listeners

---

TOP ALBUMS

TIGERS WILL SURVIVE (Vertigo, '72)
VALLEY HI (Elektra, '73)
SOME DAYS YOU EAT THE BEAR...(Elektra, '74)
GO FOR BROKE (Columbia, '76)
STEALIN' HOME (Mushroom, '78)
WALKING A CHANGING LINE (Windham Hill, '88)
PURE AND CROOKED (Gold Castle, '90)
SKELETON KEYS (Mesa, '92)

TOP SONGS

KEEP ON SAILING (Vertigo, '72)
SHAKE IT (Mushroom, '78, *13*)

a perfect balance of harshness and sweetness—that Lennon was the diehard rock and roller of the pair, while McCartney was the softer, sweeter crooner. Early on, critics point out, McCartney preferred to cover the likes of "A Taste of Honey" and "Till There Was You" while Lennon opted for Chuck Berry tunes like "Roll Over, Beethoven" and "Rock 'n' Roll Music." After the pair split, the dichotomy became a matter of public record: Lennon aimed his biting 1971 song "How Do You Sleep" directly at McCartney, declaring "the sound you make is muzak to my ears"; five years later, McCartney's "Silly Love Songs" indirectly responded with "You'd think that people would have had enough of silly love songs/But I look around me and I see it isn't so." The bottom line, at least on the commercial level, is that by the time Lennon began his five-year leave from the music business in 1975, he had only nine top 40 hits to his credit, compared to McCartney's 16.

Perhaps ironically, while a significant amount of Lennon's post-Beatles work has dated poorly—particularly 1972's *Some Time in New York City*—McCartney's early unpolished solo work such as 1970's *McCartney* and 1971's *RAM* still sounds

Paul McCartney

remarkably fresh and current. Where Lennon at times seemed to strive to make massive statements, whether personal or political, McCartney's deliberately informal, lighthearted approach to music making, perfectly illustrated by his new group Wings' 1971 near-primitive debut *Wildlife,* had an even more alluring, timeless charm. Though Wings quickly grew into an extremely polished, sometimes slick aggregation by the time of their second album, *Red Rose Speedway,* which bore the Number One hit "My Love," they displayed an overall playfulness, and a sense of not taking themselves too seriously, that was all the more endearing.

Furthermore, while critics continued to maintain that McCartney gravitated toward the schmaltzy—and admittedly, ballads like "My Love" didn't help—the former Beatle recorded a signicant number of outright rockers, whether on his albums or as single B sides; among the best were the top 10 hits "Hi, Hi, Hi," "Helen Wheels," "Jet," and "Band on the Run." The latter was the title track of McCartney's best and most successful album ever, a 1973 set that drove home to many the fact that the former Beatle was making a full-fledged career on his own, and clearly no longer in need of his former bandmates to churn out hits regularly.

Before Wings officially disbanded in 1981, McCartney scored 24 top 40 hits with them, 14 of which made the top 10, six of which went to Number One. With the exception of the 1978 platinum compilation *Wings Greatest,* all of the band's nine albums reached the top 10; additionally, each of the five consecutive albums between *Red Rose Speedway* and 1976's *Wings over America* went to Number One. After being part of the highest-charting group of the 1960s, by the end of the '70s, McCartney was second only to Elton John as the highest-charting artist of that decade as well.

Starting the 1980s with *McCartney II,* his first true solo album since 1970's *McCartney,* the ex-Beatle began a noticeable commercial slide that, considering his status during the previous two decades, was probably inevitable. He recorded only one Number One album—1982's *Tug of War*—and had his biggest hits via duets with Stevie Wonder (1982's seven-week Number One smash "Ebony and Ivory") and Michael Jackson (1982's number two single "The Girl Is Mine" and 1983's six-week Number One "Say, Say, Say"). The latter singles were particularly significant: Jackson, who was experiencing the greatest fame of his life with *Thriller,* was beginning

TOP ALBUMS

MCCARTNEY (Apple, '70, 1)
BAND ON THE RUN (with Wings, Apple, '73, 1)
VENUS AND MARS (with Wings, Capitol, '75, 1)
WINGS AT THE SPEED OF SOUND (with Wings, Capitol, '76, 1)
TUG OF WAR (Columbia, '82, 1)

Additional Top 40 Albums: 15

TOP SONGS

MY LOVE (with Wings, Apple, '73, 1)
SILLY LOVE SONGS (with Wings, Capitol, '76, 1)
COMING UP (with Wings, Columbia, '80, 1)
EBONY AND IVORY (with Stevie Wonder, Columbia, '82, 1)
SAY SAY SAY (with Michael Jackson, Columbia, '83, 1)

Additional Top 40 Songs: 30

to enjoy the same sort of superstar status McCartney himself had known for the previous 20 years; it's more likely the two duets' extended success came through his participation in the tracks rather than McCartney's.

The former Beatle finished out the 1980s in a somewhat low-key fashion. He had two more top 10 hits with 1984's "No More Lonely Nights," from his lukewarmly received film *Give My Regards to Broad Street,* and 1985's "Spies Like Us," from the film of the same name. For the first time in his career, he released albums that failed even to go gold (1986's *Press to Play* and 1987's hits compilation *All the Best!*).

McCartney's critical standing got a shot in the arm with 1989's *Flowers in the Dirt.* The accompanying Get Back world tour, the singer's first in 13 years, was a huge, high-grossing success, featuring as its high point McCartney unexpectedly performing such Beatles songs as "Sgt. Pepper's Lonely Hearts Club Band," "The Fool on the Hill," and "Hey Jude." *Tripping the Live Fantastic* was the live double CD that documented the tour; a month after its release, Capitol Records released an abbreviated "highlights" version that featured 13 of McCartney's Beatle covers (as well as four of his solo songs) on a single disc. Revealingly, perhaps, only the second set was certified platinum.

In a very active 1991, McCartney released one of the first MTV-related *Unplugged* albums; *Unplugged (The Official Bootleg)* featured the debut recording of "I Lost My Little Girl," the first song he'd ever written, and was surprisingly strong despite its informal origin. Five months later brought the worldwide issue of *CHOBA B CCCP—The Russian Album,* a collection of non-Beatle oldies he'd recorded in 1988 exclusively for distribution in the Soviet Union. The same week, he released *Liverpool Oratorio,* his first full-length work of classical music, which he'd composed with conductor Carl David and recorded at the Liverpool Cathedral with the Royal Philharmonic Orchestra and Choir. Not much of a pop smash, nor passionately embraced by music critics, the album nonetheless soared to the top of the classical charts.

McCartney continued in the productive mode with 1993's *Off the Ground,* which contained two more collaborations with Elvis Costello and the single "Hope of Deliverance," which disappointingly peaked at number 83. Having thoroughly enjoyed his 1989–90 touring experience, the singer embarked on yet another trek. The New World Tour, the biggest in McCartney's career, reached five continents and featured performances of long-unheard Beatle hits such as "All My Loving," "Here There and Everywhere," and "I Wanna Be Your Man." In late 1993, he again released a live album: its cover was a parody of that of the Beatles' *Abbey Road,* depicting McCartney walking a dog while crossing the street in front of the famed London studio, its title, *Paul Is Live,* a play on the "Paul is dead" rumors rampant at the time of *Abbey Road*'s release.

Clearly at peace with himself and his illustrious past, Paul McCartney has, in the course of his lifetime, sold over one billion albums worldwide. He will very likely sell many more.

DELBERT McCLINTON

Pity the poor record store clerk who opens a box of new CDs by Delbert McClinton (b. Nov. 4, 1940, Lubbock, Texas) and then has to put them out on the sales racks. Is he country? Blues? R&B? Rock and roll? The clerk won't want to hear it, but the answer is: all of the above. An immensely talented singer, writer, and harmonica player, McClinton boasts one of the most diverse musical resumes going. In the late 1950s, he was a member of the Straitjackets—the house band for an all-black blues club near Fort Worth—and backed up blues greats Howlin' Wolf, Jimmy Reed, and Sonny Boy Williamson, among others. In 1960, he covered Williamson's "Wake Up Baby" on the small Le Cam label and became the first white artist heard on Fort Worth blues station KNOK. He played on Bruce Channel's 1962 hit "Hey Baby," and while touring in England shortly thereafter taught Beatle John Lennon some of his harmonica licks—which Lennon then proudly displayed on his group's early hit "Love Me Do." His local Texas group the Ron-Dels had a 1965 chart hit with "If You Really Want Me To, I'll Go" on Smash Records, which, though it only reached number 97, was later covered by both Waylon Jennings and Doug Sahm.

McClinton's first album appearance came in 1972, when he and Texas friend Glen Clark formed the duo Delbert and Glen in Los Angeles. After signing with Atlantic offshoot Clean Records, the pair produced two excellent albums that often seamlessly merged the R&B and country genres. The first, co-produced by Daniel Moore and T-Bone Burnett, included " 'B' Movie Box Car Blues," a song Dan Aykroyd and John Belushi would record on their 1980 double platinum *Blues Brothers* LP, and "I Received a Letter," also later covered by Jennings. The second, 1973's *Subject to Change,* featured McClinton's "California Livin'," in which the transplanted Texan declared, "I've made up my mind what I'm gonna do/I'm going back to Texas in a day or two." He soon did exactly that.

The most interesting phase of McClinton's career followed. Back again in Fort Worth, he signed with ABC Records and produced three memorable (and now quite rare) albums that simply defied any attempt at genre classification. *Victim of Life's Cir-*

cumstances (1975) was mostly—but not totally—a country album, loaded with superb McClinton originals such as "Object of My Affection," "Honky Tonkin' (I Guess I Done Me Some)," and "Two Bottles of Wine," a Number One country hit for Emmylou Harris in 1978. The object of many rave reviews and indeed his best album, *Victim* quickly sank without a trace. 1976's *Genuine Cowhide* was more obviously a rocking R&B effort, as was 1977's *Love Rustler;* between the two of them, though, they contained only three McClinton songs. McClinton's cover of James and Bobby Purify's "Let Love Come Between Us" was delightful, as was his remake of Tony Joe White's "Hold On to Your Hiney," but the lack of new material was troublesome.

Still signed to ABC when that label folded, McClinton moved over to Capricorn for two albums. He charted with 1979's *Keeper of the Flame,* which reached number 146, but even there, the only two songs penned by McClinton were his well-known "Two More Bottles of Wine" and "I Received a Letter." After Capricorn went under, the singer moved to Capitol Records' Muscle Shoals-based MSS imprint. Though he had written no new material for it whatsoever, 1980's *The Jealous Kind* was the biggest album of his career. Clearly pushing the album to its number 34 slot was McClinton's sole top 10 hit, "Giving It Up for Your Love," written by Jerry Williams.

Unlike its predecessor, the singer's next set, *Playin' from the Heart,* contained some new McClinton songs, though only two; otherwise heard, curiously, were songs by rock performers Frankie Miller and Andy Fraser, among others. After his record label dissolved—the third time it happened in his career—McClinton spent a lengthy period out on the road, sorting out various drug and alcohol problems. "Every record company I've been with since 1971 has folded while I was on the label," he later told writer Thomas Goldsmith, "And it's pretty frustrating."

McClinton reemerged in 1989 with *Live from Austin,* a set originally recorded for the "Austin City Limits" television show then picked up by the Chicago-based Alligator label. After nearly nine years, McClinton was in excellent voice; more interestingly, much of his older material, once so difficult to classify, now seemed absolutely contemporary. The singer signed to Curb Records the same year and released *I'm with You,* half of which was filled with new McClinton songs, and 1992's *Never Been*

TOP ALBUMS

VICTIM OF LIFE'S CIRCUMSTANCES (ABC, '75)
KEEPER OF THE FLAME (Capricorn, '79)
THE JEALOUS KIND (Capitol, '80, 34)
NEVER BEEN ROCKED ENOUGH (Curb, '92)

TOP SONGS

OBJECT OF MY AFFECTION (ABC, '75)
TWO MORE BOTTLES OF WINE (ABC, '75)
GIVING IT UP FOR YOUR LOVE (Capitol, '80, 8)

Rocked Enough, which featured a duet with Bonnie Raitt and several tracks produced by studio hotshot Don Was. Very well received—McClinton's reputation had grown considerably in his absence—the album sold well and peaked at number 118. McClinton's most recent records have more of a rocking edge than many of his earlier ones, but his hard-edged but soulful singing thankfully remains unclassifiable. As always, he remains one of a kind.

COUNTRY JOE McDONALD

One of the more fascinating musical figures of the 1960s, Country Joe McDonald (b. Jan. 1, 1942, El Monte, California) will be remembered by the masses for what was at best an insignificant moment in his very colorful career: onstage at the Woodstock Festival with his hip, left-ist Berkeley band the Fish, he caused the nearly half-million members of the audience to simultaneously shout an infamous four-letter word while leading his famous "Fish Cheer." Joe McDonald was funny, but he was no clown, and it's to his credit that he—unlike nearly all of his contemporaries—spent the quarter-century that followed staying true to the political and philosophical principles he and his generation so conspicuously preached between songs.

An ex-Navy man, McDonald attended college in Los Angeles and moved to Berkeley in the early 1960s, where he performed at various folk clubs and eventually published *Rag Baby,* a local low-budget political magazine. When that magazine issued a special "audio" edition in October 1965—in the form of a four-song EP—it introduced the world to McDonald's newly formed band, Country Joe and the Fish. They began by making fun of President Lyndon Baines Johnson via McDonald's song "Superbird" and spent the rest of their six-year career mixing passionate politics with humor in an often unforgettable manner. What remains their most memorable number, the "I-Feel-Like-I'm-Fixin'-to-Die Rag," best displayed their aggressively anti-war approach: to a ragtime beat, the group exhorted its listeners to "Be the first ones on your block/To have your boy come home in a box." Though humor was a vital part of the band's character, it didn't dominate all their political material;

McDonald's "An Untitled Protest" from the group's 1968 *Together* album was a haunting, somewhat creepy view of the Vietnam War seen through the eyes of a Vietnamese villager.

Musically, Country Joe and the Fish had much to offer as well. Though they are sometimes viewed in retrospect as more of a "political" band than their San Franciscan contemporaries the Grateful Dead, Jefferson Airplane, Quicksilver Messenger Service, and Big Brother and the Holding Company, their earliest records contain some of the best representations of psychedelic music available. Likewise, their performance of "Section 43" at the 1967 Monterey Pop Festival, captured in filmmaker D. A. Pennebaker's *Monterey Pop,* was one of that film's surrealistic highlights. The group was amply appreciated in terms of record sales and saw five of its six LPs reach the top 100 of the charts before they disbanded in 1970.

Joe McDonald's solo career revealed much more about his musical roots than did his work with the Fish. His pioneering 1969 album *Thinking of Woody*—a 10-song collection of Woody Guthrie songs that began with "Pastures of Plenty" and

Country Joe McDonald

ended with "This Land Is Your Land"—introduced the writer's classic material to a generation more familiar with the works of his son Arlo. Similarly, the same year's *Tonight I'm Singing Just for You*, recorded at Bradley's Barn in Nashville, featured McDonald singing his favorite country songs at a time when rock hipsters thought the genre the province of illiterate rednecks.

McDonald released a steady stream of nearly 20 records on Vanguard, Fantasy, and his own Rag Baby labels throughout the 1970s and '80s, and while none were big sellers—the exception perhaps 1975's *Paradise with an Ocean View*, which reached number 124—each was interesting in its own way. With the Vietnam War long over, political activist McDonald found plenty of other just causes to sing about; environmentalism and the anti-nuclear movement were central topics, as were women's rights. McDonald should be highly lauded by feminists for his militancy on the issue, as well as his actions: his 1973 All-Star Band, heard on his *Paris Sessions* album, was a quintet featuring three women; among the material they performed then was McDonald's own "Sexist Pig."

Nearly 20 years later, referring to his song "Clara Barton," the singer wrote on the liner notes to his 1991 album *Superstitious Blues*, "I despair over the lack of real women as role models, it's my cause of the moment. Rock and roll and blues have a way of playing on the cliché of the evil woman who'll break your heart. I was thinking about my three daughters and I wanted some heroes for them to think about."

TOP ALBUMS

HOLD ON IT'S COMING (Vanguard, '70)
INCREDIBLE LIVE! (Vanguard, '72)
PARIS SESSIONS (Vanguard, '73)
COUNTRY JOE (Vanguard, '74)
PARADISE WITH AN OCEAN VIEW (Fantasy, '75)
PEACE ON EARTH (Rag Baby, '84)
SUPERSTITIOUS BLUES (Rag Baby, '91)

TOP SONGS

Country Joe and the Fish:
SUPERBIRD (Rag Baby, '65)
NOT SO SWEET MARTHA LORRAINE (Vanguard, '67)
THE FISH CHEER & I-FEEL-LIKE-I'M-FIXIN'-TO-DIE
 RAG (Vanguard, '67)

Now closing in on his 30th aniversary in the music business, Country Joe McDonald seems less and less a political prankster and more and more like a '60s version of his hero, Woody Guthrie.

MICHAEL McDONALD

Easily one of the most recognizable vocalists in pop music, Michael McDonald (b. Dec. 2, 1952, St. Louis, Missouri) has had much to sing about in his life: membership in two hugely successful rock bands at the height of their respective careers, five prestigious Grammy Awards, and singing and co-writing credits on some of the most successful records in pop. Most importantly, his singing and writing style conveys a quality of warmth and urbanity that is uniquely his.

Getting his start in St. Louis nightclubs in the late 1960s, McDonald soon moved to Los Angeles, where in 1972 he cut a series of singles for Bell Records with producer Rick Jarrard. Though no album was issued then, 10 years later those tracks and four previously unreleased ones (including a cover of the Allman Brothers' "Midnight Rider") were issued by Arista Records as *That Was Then/The Early Recordings of Michael McDonald*. By 1973, at the recommendation of drummer Jeff Porcaro, McDonald had been hired to join Steely Dan's touring band, playing keyboards and providing backing vocals. It was a relationship that would prove rewarding: McDonald would thereafter contribute to every Steely Dan album from 1975's *Katy Lied* through 1980's *Gaucho*. (He would much later join Fagen as part of the New York Rock and Soul Revue, whose live album was released in 1991.) Additionally, the friendship he'd strike up with Dan guitarist Jeff "Skunk" Baxter, who soon departed for the Doobie Brothers, resulted in Baxter's bringing him to that band in 1975 as a substitute for founding member Tom Johnston.

McDonald's effect upon the Doobies was drastic: the former good-time, rocking party band was transformed into a slick, soulful unit, and the material that McDonald wrote and sang provided the group with hit after hit. Among them: "Takin' It to the Streets," "It Keeps You Runnin'," "Minute by Minute," "Real Love," and the gold, Number One, multiple-Grammy-winning single "What a Fool Believes," co-written by McDonald and Kenny Loggins. For seven years, McDonald was an ever-present fixture on the radio, guesting and singing harmony with Christopher Cross (on the huge hit "Ride Like the Wind"), Kenny Loggins ("This Is It"), Nicolette Larson (1980's duet "Let Me Go, Love"), and countless others.

McDonald revved up his solo career while the Doobies were gearing to split; his first solo album, *If That's What It Takes,* emerged in 1982, the same year the Doobies disbanded. As expected, it was a hit; landing in the top 10, the album went gold and gave the singer his first and only solo top five hit, "I Keep Forgettin' (Every Time You're Near)." Following the Doobies' farewell tour, McDonald produced the Capitol debut album of singer Amy Holland, contributing several new songs he co-wrote with such writers as David Pack, Ed Sanford, Robert Akers Terry, and Holland herself. (Further collaborations with Holland—whom he'd soon marry—included his two children.) In 1984, his familiar voice graced "Yah Mo B There," a duet with singer James Ingram that netted both a Grammy.

Though the title track of McDonald's first official post-Doobies set, *No Lookin' Back,* reached the top 40, it later became a matter of discomfort for the singer that his hits were coming from sources other than his own albums and own pen. "On My Own"—his powerful duet with singer Patti LaBelle that was Number One for three weeks in 1986—was drawn from LaBelle's *Winner in You* MCA album (and was written by Burt Bacharach and Carole Bayer Sager); "Sweet Freedom," which hit the top 10

Michael McDonald

short months later, was from the soundtrack to *Running Scared* (and penned by Rod Temperton). And though his 1990 album *Take It to Heart* featured a bushel of collaborators (Peter Leinheiser, Paul Carrack, Diane Warren, George Hawkins, and more) and two songs McDonald played no part in writing, it still fared poorly, not even entering the top 100. To add insult to injury, its one chart single, the title track, peaked disappointingly at number 96. But *Blink of an Eye,* the singer's 1993 follow-up, offered an encouraging sign: of nine new McDonald originals, five had no collaborators, and each was superb. In all, while the gruff familiarity of Michael McDonald's voice may in some ways be a handicap—he's just too '70s, some hapless program director may object—his talent continues to shine through regardless.

TOP ALBUMS

IF THAT'S WHAT IT TAKES (Warner Bros., '82, 6)
NO LOOKIN' BACK (Warner Bros., '85)
TAKE IT TO HEART (Warner Bros., '90)
BLINK OF AN EYE (Warner Bros., '93)

TOP SONGS

I KEEP FORGETTIN' (EVERY TIME YOU'RE NEAR)
(Warner Bros., '82, 4)
YAH MO B THERE (with James Ingram,
   Qwest, '84, 19)
NO LOOKIN' BACK (Warner Bros., '85, 34)
ON MY OWN (with Patti LaBelle, MCA, '86, 1)
SWEET FREEDOM (MCA, '86, 7)

ROGER McGUINN

Leader of one of the 1960s' most acclaimed American rock groups—and one of the few to meet the challenge of the British Invasion groups head on—guitarist Roger McGuinn (b. James Joseph McGuinn, July 13, 1942, Chicago) was the heart, soul, and most especially the sound of the legendary Byrds. A former folkie whose transition to rock and roll came via an electrified version of Bob Dylan's "Mr. Tambourine Man" and instantly catapulted him to stardom, McGuinn founded the Byrds in 1964 and was the group's only original member at the time of their 1973 demise. Enormously innovative, the band has been credited with originating folk-rock, "raga-rock," and country rock during their nine-year career. Along with New York's Velvet Underground, the Byrds remain perhaps the most influential American rock group of the 1960s; echoes of their sound can be heard today in the mainstream rock of Tom Petty and the Heart-breakers, in the alternative rock of R.E.M. and the Church, and even the hardcore rock of Hüsker Dü, who recorded a memorable cover of the Byrds' "Eight Miles High" in 1984. McGuinn launched a post-Byrds solo career with 1973's *Roger McGuinn* and has since spent the past two decades performing and sporadically recording, both on his own and occasionally with former Byrds members. Encouragingly, McGuinn's most recent album, 1991's *Back from Rio*, was the highest-charting solo work of his lengthy career.

Prior to his days with the Byrds, McGuinn was a respected folk artist in Chicago; he moved to New York's Greenwich Village and soon was backing the Limeliters, the Chad Mitchell Trio, and Bobby Darin. One of his earliest major credits included being music director and second guitarist for Judy Collins's 1964 album *Judy Collins #3*; interestingly, the album featured three tracks (Woody Guthrie's "Deportee" and Pete Seeger's adaptations of "The Bells of Rhymney" and "Turn! Turn! Turn!/To Everything There Is a Season") McGuinn would later perform with the Byrds. The same year, he

formed the Jet Set with L.A. musicians Gene Clark, David Crosby, Chris Hillman, and Michael Clarke; following some recording sessions and a lone Elektra single as the Beefeaters, the group was signed to Columbia as the Byrds.

In retrospect a near-phenomenal batch of fine songwriters, the Byrds ironically wrote fewer than half of their seven top 40 hits. Dylan supplied three ("Mr. Tambourine Man," "All I Really Want to Do," and "My Back Pages"), while Seeger essentially provided their biggest hit—a Number One record for three weeks—with 1965's "Turn! Turn! Turn!" McGuinn had a composing credit on the three remaining tracks, however: "Eight Miles High" (co-written with Crosby and Clark), "So You Want to Be a Rock 'n' Roll Star" (penned with Hillman), and his own "Mr. Spaceman." By the time of 1968's *Sweetheart of the Rodeo*, the initial quintet had dwindled down to only McGuinn and Hillman; briefly stepping in as a replacement was still another major singer-songwriter, Gram Parsons, whose contributions to the album helped establish it as the definitive country-rock classic. When Hillman finally departed in October 1968 to join Parsons' pioneering Flying Burrito Brothers, McGuinn was the only original Byrd remaining.

While most critical appraisals of the Byrds contend that the Byrds effectively ended at that point—and continued for another five years in name only—McGuinn in fact continued to write some of the best material of his career. Highlights were "Candy" (co-written with new bassist John York) from *Dr. Byrds & Mr. Hyde*, "Ballad of Easy Rider" (reportedly an uncredited collaboration with Bob Dylan) from *Ballad of Easy Rider*, and a wealth of songs McGuinn composed with new lyricist partner Jacques Levy, including "Chestnut Mare," "Lover of the Bayou," "Just a Season," and "Kathleen's Song," among others.

McGuinn finally disbanded the the group following 1972's *Farther Along*. "I really thought it was more or less like keeping a brand name together for the sake of having a brand name," McGuinn recalled in 1988. "And it wasn't musically as good as it had been, or creatively. And it was a little frustrating."

TOP ALBUMS

ROGER McGUINN (Columbia, '73)
PEACE ON YOU (Columbia, '74)
CARDIFF ROSE (Columbia, '76)
BACK FROM RIO (Arista, '91)

TOP SONGS

I'M SO RESTLESS (Columbia, '73)
MY NEW WOMAN (Columbia, '73)
WITHOUT YOU (Columbia, '74)
TOGETHER (Columbia, '74)
TAKE ME AWAY (Columbia, '75)
KING OF THE HILL (Arista, '91)

After a much-maligned "Original Byrds" reunion album in 1973, McGuinn let fly with his first solo album and received the best reviews he'd seen in years. *Roger McGuinn* was an impressive debut; featured guests included the original Byrds on one track, Bob Dylan playing harmonica on another, and Beach Boy Bruce Johnston vocalizing on the Beach Boys–inspired "Draggin'." Still, McGuinn's past as a Byrd followed him with each album to come: the cover of 1974's *Peace on You* depicted a bald eagle clutching McGuinn's trademark Rickenbacker 12-string guitar and included "Same Old Sound," a tune on which he bemoaned his fate as the expected provider of the instantly recognizable "Byrdsy" guitar sound ("And everywhere I'm bound/I got to play that same old sound").

McGuinn's solo albums were noticeably inconsistent; 1975's *Roger McGuinn & Band,* which featured few originals, was particularly uninspired. "I was kind of out of it," the singer noted in 1988. "I was doing a lot of drugs and alcohol, and I was not really paying attention to what I was doing. I was being lazy mentally and creatively. What you see there are some flashes of creativity, but moments of real apathy. It shows up in the work." Certainly one of the singer's most creative flashes was 1976's *Cardiff Rose;* recorded after McGuinn toured as part of Dylan's 1975–76 Rolling Thunder Revue, the album was superbly produced by guitarist Mick Ronson and featured a brace of excellent McGuinn/Levy collaborations and previously unreleased tracks both by Dylan ("Up to Me") and Joni Mitchell ("Dreamland"). After 1977's *Thunderbyrd,* which included McGuinn's extremely appropriate cover of Tom Petty's "American Girl"—a tune that in its original form had sounded like a McGuinn song in the first place—the singer finally left Columbia after 23 years with the label.

In 1979, McGuinn reunited with former Byrds Hillman and Gene Clark and scored his biggest post-Byrds hit to date with "Don't You Write Her Off." Much in the style of the ill-advised Byrds reunion album of 1973, the three collaborative albums that resulted sounded less like a group than a series of solo tracks by each individual artist. "Once I got into the studio," McGuinn later recalled, "the Albert brothers, who were producing, decided they didn't want it to sound at all like the Byrds—which meant I couldn't play guitar or sing very much. So I was kind of sidelined for it; it was frustrating." After the 1980 release of *McGuinn-Hillman,* the singer left

Capitol and spent most of the 1980s without a record deal and on the road.

In the 1990s, McGuinn returned to the forefront of the pop scene with both the highly regarded *Back to Rio*—which boasted an all-star lineup including Tom Petty, Elvis Costello, and Crosby and Hillman, among others—and a lavishly praised four-CD Byrds box set, which included four new recordings by McGuinn, Crosby, and Hillman. Additionally, in 1991, all five of the original Byrds performed together when inducted into the Rock and Roll Hall of Fame. The seeming blitz of Byrds-related publicity launched a noticeable reappraisal of McGuinn's work, both with the Byrds and on his own. "I look at it sort of philosophically," McGuinn said at the time. "Like, 'to everything there is a season.' It's just time for things like that to happen."

DON McLEAN

Any performer fortunate enough to be involved in a true phenomenon had better be prepared to deal with it, one way or another, for the rest of his or her life. Don McLean (b. Oct. 2, 1945, New Rochelle, New York) must thank his lucky stars that his phenomenon, 1971's massive hit single "American Pie," came late enough in his career as a singer-songwriter to be dealt with for what it was—an extramusical, sociological event—rather than as the albatross it might have become for any less experienced artist. Career surges come and career surges go, but McLean has never lost what it takes to win over any audience—regardless of its size or his fluctuating status as a record seller.

A well-respected writer and player who'd given countless performances in folk clubs and coffeehouses for nearly a decade before "Pie," McLean had struck up an early friendship with many well-known folk figures, including Pete Seeger, who provided him significant extended exposure as part of the performing troupe on the fabled Clearwater sloop in 1969. McLean then signed with the small Mediarts label and recorded *Tapestry,* which went mostly unheard until its 1973 reissue by United Artists (who had purchased Mediarts two years earlier). The reason for its rerelease? Inevitably, "American Pie."

Issued in late 1971, McLean's allegorical story of rock and roll has been analyzed to near death, though McLean himself has consistently (and wisely)

refused to be drawn into protracted explanations regarding its meaning. Its extended stay at the top of the charts—it was Number One for four weeks, while the *American Pie* album held the top slot for seven in 1972—might've guaranteed a raft of imitations, perhaps by a dazzled McLean himself, but it was not to be. His next single, the lovely "Vincent" (a tribute to artist Vincent Van Gogh), was a moving, intimate track that sounded nothing like "American Pie" but hit the top 20 regardless. A huge international hit, the song in some ways shaped McLean's future—and later musical approach— much more so than did "Pie."

By 1973, McLean was gaining fame via truly unique sources: Perry Como had recorded his *Tapestry* track "And I Love You So" and scored a top 30 hit with it; and Roberta Flack's smash Number One hit "Killing Me Softly with His Song," it became known, was directly inspired by a live McLean performance. Following the relative success of "Dreidel," a single pulled from *American Pie*'s follow-up, *Don McLean,* the singer spent the remainder of the 1970s hitless. While his international fame grew, particularly as a concert attraction in the U.K., McLean, partially stymied by a perceived need to follow up "American Pie," at one point refused to play the track in concert—though he later relented.

One early indication that McLean knew there was more to his life than one extraordinary hit single was his rootsy *Playin' Favorites* album of 1973, which featured the singer's versions of classics by Buddy Holly, Dale Evans's "Happy Trails," and other more traditional folkie fare. In fact, when McLean's star surged once more in the early 1980s, it was again with cover versions—of Roy Orbison's

"Crying," which hit the top five, followed by the Skyliners' "Since I Don't Have You," which peaked at number 23. He followed both with a top 40 remake of *Tapestry*'s "Castles in the Air."

For the Memories, two separate volumes of standards McLean issued during the late 1980s, were charming recordings that might have suggested to some that McLean's own creative well was tapped out. Yet in 1991, the singer produced a respectable collection of originals called *Headroom* that easily measured up to past work. There might not have been a new "American Pie" in there, true—but Don McLean, from every indication, doesn't plan to stop killing them softly anytime soon.

MELANIE

With her shaky, quivering voice, her hippy-dippy flower-power image, and her decision to professionally use only her first name, Melanie (b. Melanie Safka, Feb. 3, 1947, Queens, New York) in retrospect seems more tied to her time than virtually any other singer-songwriter. And why not? She not only played at Woodstock, she got a top 10 hit and gold album out of it. When it rained during her set at the 1969 festival, a stage announcer suggested the audience light candles to ward off the storm; they did, she sat onstage watching the mass of lit candles, and, inspired, she soon wrote "Lay Down (Candles in the Rain)." Recorded with the Edwin Hawkins Singers, the 1970 single was loaded with melodrama and sold by the boatload, as did the album bearing the same name. It was a convincing enough piece of pop music for English rockers Mott the Hoople to cover—which they did, royally, sending its melodrama quotient through the roof on their 1971 *Wildlife* album.

Initially signed to Columbia Records, who released her single "Beautiful People" in 1967, Melanie recorded her first album for Neil Bogart's upstart Buddah label in late 1968. That album (*Born to Be,* later cleverly reissued as *My First Album*) sold meagerly, as did its successor, *Melanie,* which boasted a rerecorded version of "Beautiful People" to little commercial avail, as the album peaked at number 196.

But by the next year, Woodstock was history, and Melanie was among the first to bear its fruit, via "Lay Down." *Candles in the Rain* is the most representative of Melanie's albums, and probably her best.

TOP ALBUMS

AMERICAN PIE (United Artists, '71, *1*)
DON MCLEAN (United Artists, '72, *23*)
CHAIN LIGHTNING (Millennium, '81, *28*)

TOP SONGS

AMERICAN PIE (United Artists, '71, *1*)
VINCENT (United Artists, '72, *12*)
CASTLES IN THE AIR (United Artists, '72, *12*)
DREIDEL (United Artists, '73, *21*)
CRYING (Millennium, '81, *5*)
SINCE I DON'T HAVE YOU (Millennium, '81, *23*)

It contains three of her better songs—the title track, "What Have They Done to My Song Ma" (a top 20 hit later that year by the New Seekers), and "Leftover Wine"—as well as cover versions of James Taylor's "Carolina in My Mind" and the Rolling Stones' "Ruby Tuesday." Cover versions were no small part of her repertoire; she tended to favor Bob Dylan and the Rolling Stones, though commendably she often chose their more obscure works (Dylan's "Sign on the Window," the Stones' "Jigsaw Puzzle"). Surprisingly, her interpretations usually worked, largely due to her bizarre, wavering vocal style, which effectively "Melanized" each song enough to make it sound like one of her own.

Yet Melanie's fate was sealed in 1971, when her biggest hit, the playfully sung "Brand New Key," topped the charts for three weeks and instantly branded the former sensitive singer-songwriter as teenybopper radio fodder to the hipper masses. And it didn't help that her next hit, "The Nickel Song," was similarly gimmicky. Despite some very convincing adult-themed material on later albums such as 1972's *Stoneground Words*, Melanie was thereafter taken less and less seriously by tastemakers of the era.

In 1971, she and her longtime husband and producer Peter Schekeryk formed their own label, Neighborhood Records. Melanie would ultimately record six albums for the label, each of which sold less than its predecessor. Beginning with 1978's *Phonogenic* on Midsong International, she started label hopping, first to Atlantic (*Photograph*), then

Tomato (*Ballroom Streets*), and finally, in 1982, to small, independently distributed Blanche (*Arabesque*). Little has been heard from her since, though many were surprised when the singer received a 1989 Emmy Award for penning the lyrics to "The First Time I Loved Forever" from the network television show "Beauty and the Beast."

Though it would be inaccurate to say Melanie has been widely missed by her fans, she has certainly been remembered. In penning the bio to his 1992 album *History*, singer-songwriter Loudon Wainwright III wryly noted that he had once been touted as "the New Bob Dylan," "the Woody Allen of folk," "the Charlie Chaplin of rock," and "the male Melanie."

JOHN MELLENCAMP

Few artists have had to face the uphill climb that greeted John Mellencamp (b. Oct. 7, 1951, Seymour, Indiana) after recording his ill-advised 1976 debut album, *Chestnut Street Incident*. First, there was the horrible name problem: Johnny Cougar. Then there was the "MainMan" logo on the back—the trademark of the company helmed by former David Bowie manager and strategist Tony DeFries. Then there was the pretty-boy, almost androgynous picture on the album jacket, looking as if it had been taken by a camera with a vaseline-covered lens. Finally, there was the music—or what could be found of it, once you'd gotten through the pointless versions of songs previously sung by the Doors, Roy Orbison, Elvis Presley, and the Lovin' Spoonful. But 16 years later, when many of the world's most prestigious recording artists gathered together at Madison Square Garden to pay tribute at Bob Dylan's 30th Anniversary Concert, who not only opened the show but opened it with a cover of "Like a Rolling Stone"? Mrs. Cougar's little boy Johnny.

The transition of Johnny Cougar to today's entirely respectable John Mellencamp is an exemplary illustration of (1) how much an artist will compromise himself to break into the music business, (2) how much manipulation of image a manager or record label will engage in to break an artist, (3) how all the manipulation in the world can't help a flawed record, and, finally, (4) how long it can take to repair a reputation once it has become nearly irreparably damaged by all of the above.

TOP ALBUMS

CANDLES IN THE RAIN (Buddah, '70, *17*)
LEFTOVER WINE (Buddah, '70, *33*)
GATHER ME (Buddah, '71, *15*)

TOP SONGS

BEAUTIFUL PEOPLE (Buddah, '69)
LAY DOWN (CANDLES IN THE RAIN) (with the Edwin Hawkins Singers, Buddah, '70, *6*)
PEACE WILL COME (ACCORDING TO PLAN) (Buddah, '70, *32*)
BRAND NEW KEY (Neighborhood, '71, *1*)
RING THE LIVING BELL (Neighborhood, '72, *31*)
THE NICKEL SONG (Buddah, '72, *35*)
BITTER BAD (Neighborhood, '73, *36*)

From the very small southern Indiana town of Seymour, a 23-year-old John Mellencamp grabbed his demo tape in 1974 and went to New York in search of a record deal. He eventually visited the offices of MainMan's DeFries, and before long he struck a deal that would ultimately result in *Chestnut Street Incident,* his embarrassing "Cougar" moniker, and a manager who wanted to push him to stardom the only way he knew how. "He tried to do the same exact thing with me that he did with Bowie," Mellencamp said in 1983, "but guess what? It was cool the first time around, but not the second—hey, we've seen this act before, Jack!"

After the album flopped and MCA opted not to release the intended follow-up, *The Kid Inside* (though it would finally be released in the U.K. in 1982), Mellencamp signed a new deal with England's Riva label. Though the resulting album, 1978's *A Biography,* never saw American release, two of its tracks could be found on 1979's domestic *John Cougar*—and one of them, "I Need a Lover," finally helped the singer crack the American marketplace. Already a hit in Australia, the song was covered by Pat Benatar on her platinum debut and became a top 30 hit for Mellencamp himself in 1979.

With the *Chestnut Street* album a virtual sales nonentity, *John Cougar* was largely perceived by the public as the debut of a new artist. And far from the Bowie-esque figure DeFries might have planned, the singer struck many as a straight rock and roller from the heartland, much in the tradition of a Bob Seger or a Bruce Springsteen. Within a year, follow-up album *Nothin' Matters and What If It Did* was in the top 40, and two of its hits— "This Time" and "Ain't Even Done with the Night"—were suitable proof the singer wasn't a one-shot hitmaker. And when 1982's *American Fool* shot to Number One and stayed there for nine weeks—as two of its singles, "Hurt So Good" and "Jack and Diane," simultaneously sat comfortably in the top five—proof of anything was hardly an issue. John Cougar had produced 1982's biggest-selling album.

Rather than sitting still and

John Mellancamp

basking in success, Mellencamp got busy. He produced Mitch Ryder's 1983 "comeback" LP *Never Kick a Sleeping Dog,* he recorded his own album *Uh-Huh* (this time credited to John Cougar Mellencamp) in an Indiana farmhouse converted into a recording studio—and he began to stretch artistically. With 1985's triple platinum *Scarecrow,* his lyrics took on such serious topics as the plight of the American farmer; the same year, he performed at Farm Aid I, later returning to both Farm Aid II in 1986 and Farm Aid III in 1987. Additionally, Mellencamp's straightforward rock sound was evolving: with 1987's *The Lonesome Jubilee,* he added new band members and began featuring violins, accordions, pedal steel guitars, and dulcimers prominently. Still another sign of the singer's desire to expand his horizons, the album was his most artistically mature statement to date. And the audience wasn't

TOP ALBUMS

AMERICAN FOOL (Riva, '82, *1*)
UH-HUH (Riva, '83, *9*)
SCARECROW (Riva, '85, *2*)
THE LONESOME JUBILEE
  (Mercury, '87, *6*)
BIG DADDY (Mercury, '89, *7*)
HUMAN WHEELS (Mercury, '93, *7*)

Additional Top 40 Albums: 1

TOP SONGS

HURTS SO GOOD (Riva, '82, *2*)
JACK & DIANE (Riva, '82, *1*)
LONELY OL' NIGHT (Riva, '85, *6*)
R.O.C.K. IN THE U.S.A. (Riva, '86, *2*)

Additional Top 40 Songs: 14

being left behind, either: *Jubilee* bore three hit singles, with both "Paper in Fire" and "Cherry Bomb" cracking the top 10.

Mellencamp's growth since has been amply displayed on such albums as *Big Daddy, Whenever We Wanted,* and 1993's *Human Wheels.* The latter, a top 10 album, may be the singer's finest ever; it's certainly the most forward-looking, perhaps due to the touch of co-producer Malcolm Burn, whose past work with associate Daniel Lanois cast a distinctive sheen on much of the 1990s' finest pop and alternative rock music. You'd never have suspected it from 1976's *Chestnut Street Incident,* but at the rate John Mellencamp undergoes stylistic shifts with each new album, he could prove to be the next David Bowie. Think he'd enjoy the comparison?

GEORGE MICHAEL

One of the major international pop stars of the 1980s, George Michael (b. Yorgos Kyriatou Panayiotou, June 25, 1963, Finchley, North London) ascended the pop ladder with the significant help of rock video, which—as its influence quickly spread throughout the world—consistently glued his pretty, deliberately stubble-faced mug to nearly every television screen in the Free World. Helping considerably, of course, was the singer's noticeable growth as both singer and songwriter since his earliest days in the pop duo Wham!—which began as a nondescript pop-dance group and quickly metamorphosed into a huge international hit machine.

Michael's entry into the music business came in the late 1970s, when he and friend Andrew Ridgely, under the spell of such dance artists as Chic and Sylvester, began writing songs together. Soon fascinated by the music of the U.K.'s ska revival, the pair formed their own ska group, the Executives; by 1982, the duo had signed a deal with the CBS-distributed Innervision label as Wham! and released their first single, "Young Guns (Go for It)," which swiftly became a club hit. A string of similarly successful singles, including "Wham Rap (Enjoy What You Do)," "Bad Boys," and "Club Tropicana," all shot to the U.K. top 10, and before long Wham! were teen-idol contemporaries of New Romantic sensations Duran Duran.

Enough of a buzz was felt in American clubs to send the duo's 1983 debut album, *Fantastic,* into the top 100, despite the comparative mainstream failure of their earlier singles. All that changed, however, with 1984's "Wake Me Up Before You Go-Go," Wham!'s international hit, which climbed to the top of the Hot 100 and stayed there for three weeks. An immediate MTV smash, the track merely opened the floodgates for hits to come. Next up was "Careless Whisper"—credited solely to singer Michael in the U.K., but to "Wham! featuring George Michael" in the States. In both countries, the lush, romantic track established Michael as a swoonworthy crooner of the first degree; like its predecessor, it held the Number One slot for another three weeks. Two more hits ("Everything She Wants" at Number One and "Freedom" at number three) helped propel *Make It Big* to the top of the album charts and send it into quintuple platinum territory.

Wham! became superstars of the highest order: singer Michael duetted with Elton John at Live Aid, the pair became the first Western pop group to perform in China, and the antics of Andrew Ridgely, who drove racing cars for sport and often crashed them, made newpapers worldwide. Many wondered why Ridgely remained around: since Michael wrote and sang virtually all the pair's hits (except the rhythm-heavy "Wham Rap" single), his pretty partner seemed largely expendable. Indeed, after the release of three more top 10 singles—"I'm Your Man" and "The Edge of Heaven," both credited to Wham!, and "A Different Corner," released only under Michael's name—the singer pulled the plug in 1986, and Wham! was no more. A final album hodgepodge of new and old singles, *Music from the Edge of Heaven,* commemorated the duo's demise and made the top 10 that summer.

George Michael's 1987 return to the spotlight remains his most impressive achievement to date: *Faith* was a royal tour de force for the singer, loaded with, unbelievably, a total of six top five hits, four of which ("Faith," "Father Figure," "One More Try," and "Monkey") went to Number One. Establishing him as an extremely credible writer and singer, the album was Number One for 12 weeks and won the 1988 Grammy for Album of the Year.

Michael's ascension into the highest ranks of superstardom then led him to make a bold decision: he made himself scarce. Specifically, after recording his 1990 follow-up, *Listen Without Prejudice,* he opted to refuse all interview requests and—much more courageously—not appear in any rock videos promoting the album. The result? *Listen* peaked at number two, and bore only two top 10 hits: "Praying for Time" and "Freedom." Compared to *Faith,* which had sold over 15 million copies worldwide, it was a major commercial disappointment and sold barely a third of that figure.

Though Michael would later score hits in 1993 with Elton John ("Don't Let the Sun Go Down on Me") and Queen ("Killer/Papa Was a Rollin' Stone"), his own recording career suddenly ground to a halt. Claiming his contract with Sony Music was grossly unfair, the singer filed suit against his label in British High Court in 1993. Among his complaints was that the company's U.S. division was "not prepared" to support the singer's change of career direction, as evidenced by their handling of *Listen Without Prejudice.* According to Michael's attorney, the singer's decision to not appear in his own music videos was a major factor in the suit: "Following the success of [*Faith*], Michael felt that he needed a change of direction—he wanted to concentrate on his music and play down the image of being a sex symbol...He was entitled by his contract to make these decisions, but at the same time he realized he needed the cooperation of the record company, and was anxious that it should support him...However, he felt that his record company in the United States was not prepared to do this."

At the heart of it, claimed Michael, was that the Columbia Records he had initially signed to was not the same company once it had been acquired by Sony in 1987. "With CBS, I felt that I was believed in as a long-term artist," Michael said, "whereas Sony appears to see artists as little more than software." While the eyes of the international music industry watched warily, George Michael's future recording career remained on hold in late 1993.

STEVE MILLER

Among pop music's most interesting and prolific artists, Steve Miller (b. Oct. 5, 1943, Milwaukee, Wisconsin) has been making records of nearly every genre since 1968. A well-traveled blues guitarist who arrived in San Francisco in 1966, just one year prior to that city's fabled Summer of Love, Miller signed a lucrative deal with Capitol Records that resulted in some of the most substantial, texturally interesting music of the era. In the course of 20 years at Capitol, Miller and a varying cast of musicians—always billed as the Steve Miller Band—would produce music that was alternately psychedelic, bluesy, R&B-inspired, country-tinged, gorgeously poppy, discofied, highly synthetic, and straight-out jazzy. Even more remarkable than that variety was his ability to perform skillfully in those modes without submerging the core of his sound or his own personality. In short, Steve Miller's 17 albums sound nothing alike—but always very much like the work of Steve Miller.

The son of a music-loving physician, Miller had a childhood that any musician would envy: world-class instrumentalists such as Les Paul, Red Norvo, Tal Farlow, and Charlie Mingus would often drop by to visit his father while performing in the Milwaukee area. "[They'd] just come and eat and hang out on a Sunday afternoon," Miller has said. "I saw the respect my dad had for them, and it seemed like musicians were just the neatest people of all." By the time he was 12, his family had moved to Dallas and Miller had formed his first blues band, the Marksmen Combo, soon to include later Miller Band stalwart Boz Scaggs. The pair continued to be bandmates while attending college at the University of Wisconsin, where Miller led local blues-rock combo the Ardells in the early 1960s. Following a brief period as a student at the University of Copenhagen, Miller returned to the States and moved to Chicago, where he spent nearly three years playing blues guitar and jamming with some of the Windy

---

TOP ALBUMS

MAKE IT BIG (with Wham!, Columbia, '84, *1*)
MUSIC FROM THE EDGE OF HEAVEN (with Wham!, Columbia, '86, *6*)
FAITH (Columbia, '87, *1*)
LISTEN WITHOUT PREJUDICE (Columbia, '90, *2*)

TOP SONGS

CARELESS WHISPER (with Wham!, Columbia '84, *1*)
FAITH (Columbia, '87, *1*)
FATHER FIGURE (Columbia, '88, *1*)
ONE MORE TRY (Columbia, '88, *1*)
MONKEY (Columbia, '88, *1*)
PRAYING FOR TIME (Columbia, '90, *1*)

Additional Top 40 Songs: 14

City's superlative blues talent. He briefly formed a group with keyboardist Barry Goldberg, later of the Electric Flag.

Upon Miller's 1966 arrival in San Francisco, he put together the Steve Miller Blues Band, whose earliest work can be heard backing Chuck Berry on his 1967 *Live at the Fillmore* album; additionally, the band supplied three songs to the soundtrack of the 1967 film *Revolution*. By the time the Steve Miller Band flew to England to record their memorable 1968 debut, *Children of the Future*, the group consisted of Miller, Scaggs, drummer Tim Davis, bassist Lonnie Turner, and organist Jim Peterman. That version of the band lasted long enough to record both *Children* and its remarkable follow-up, *Sailor*; Scaggs then left to begin his solo career and Peterman also departed. True '60s classics, both albums, viewed in retrospect, functioned as samplers of the directions Miller would be following as his career unfolded. They contained blues covers ("Key to the Highway"); ethereal, pre–new age instrumentals ("Song for Our Ancestors"); simple pop ("You've Got the Power"); psychedelic rock ("The Beauty of Time Is That It's Snowing"); and raving rock and roll ("Living in the U.S.A.").

Though it's difficult to call the eclectic mix above a "formula," it's accurate to say Miller proceeded in that direction for many albums to come. As band members began departing circa 1969's *Brave New World,* Miller used supplementary musicians such as Ben Sidran and pianist Nicky Hopkins to flesh out his sound. By 1971's *Rock Love,* Miller was the only remaining member of the original Steve Miller Band. The latter album was his first since *Children of the Future* not to enter the top 40; though he'd yet to score a hit single, regular FM radio play of such songs as "Living in the U.S.A." had previously made Miller a very respectable album seller and significant concert attraction.

But something clicked in Miller's career with 1973's *The Joker.* The good-timey, deliberately simple aspect of his music—present as far back as *Sailor*

and *Brave New World*'s "Space Cowboy"—kicked in massively via *The Joker*'s title track, which soared to become Miller's first Number One single ever and pushed the album to number two. The records that followed were even more successful: 1976's *Fly Like an Eagle* went quadruple platinum and offered three major hits, including the Number One "Rock'n Me" and the familiar, gold-certified title track. His triple platinum *Book of Dreams* was also hit-filled, but with one significant difference: of its three hits—"Jet Airliner," "Jungle Love," and "Swingtown"—only the last was a Miller original, for which he shared a writing credit with Chris McCarty.

The man who had penned 1976's "Take the Money and Run" then did exactly that. In 1978, he moved to Oregon and built a 24-track recording studio; he emerged with the music he'd recorded there in 1971. The results? *Circle of Love* went gold, thanks to top 40 hit "Heart Like a Wheel," and 1982's platinum *Abracadabra* included the third Number One in Miller's career with its bouncy title track. Nearly 15 years after the mature artistic statement of *Children of the Future,* Miller was making hits out of lyrics such as "Abra-abra-cadabra/ I want to reach out and grab ya."

But Miller's career then took a tumble. 1983's follow-up to the number three *Abracadabra* was a live album that only reached number 125 on the charts, and its studio successor, *Italian X-Rays*—actually one of Miller's better efforts in years—peaked at number 101 and fell off the charts in less than three months. "I was having a hard time with my record company," Miller recalled in 1993. "They weren't very interested in what I was doing, didn't have much of a plan for it. On the [studio] follow-up to *Abracadabra* we ran into the independent promotion thing, and I refused to pay independent promotion. I didn't know what it was, I didn't care about it, and I sold 26,000 albums."

Sensing his longtime relationship with Capitol was near its end, Miller made two unusually genre-specific albums—1986's bluesy *Living in the 20th Century* and 1988's jazz-filled *Born to Be Blue*—and

---

TOP ALBUMS

BRAVE NEW WORLD (Capitol, '69, 22)
THE JOKER (Capitol, '73, 2)
FLY LIKE AN EAGLE (Capitol, '76, 3)
BOOK OF DREAMS (Capitol, '77, 2)
ABRACADABRA (Capitol, '82, 3)

Additional Top 40 Albums: 5

TOP SONGS

THE JOKER (Capitol, '73, *1*)
ROCK'N ME (Capitol, '76, *1*)
FLY LIKE AN EAGLE (Capitol, '77, 2)
JET AIRLINER (Capitol, '77, 8)
ABRACADABRA (Capitol, '82, *1*)

Additional Top 40 Songs: 4

---

left the label in 1988. He spent the next several years out on the road, where he developed an enormous live following that the media eventually compared to the Grateful Dead's Deadheads. As his 1978 *Greatest Hits 1974–1978* set became one of the strongest catalog sellers in the industry, rap artists were vigorously sampling his music, and hot '90s rock band the Spin Doctors were uniformly described by critics as sounding "Steve Miller-like."

Miller returned in 1993 with *Wide River,* the first album of his career on a label other than Capitol. After thinking long and hard about his experience in the record industry, Steve Miller finally decided to sign with Polydor. "The deal I made with my record company was that I wanted the highest royalties they'd ever paid any living human being in the world, I wanted complete artistic control, and I didn't want a penny up front," Miller remarked at the time. "I'm lucky now, I don't need the money up front—but a lot of bands do, to get started. And that's when they have to give everything up."

JONI MITCHELL

A singer-songwriter of the highest order, Joni Mitchell (b. Roberta Joan Anderson, Nov. 7, 1943, Fort McLeod, Alberta, Canada) has, on purely musical terms, shown more growth as an artist than nearly any other pop performer during her 25-year career. In that period, she has evolved from a sweet-voiced confessional folksinger best known for writing songs popularized by Judy Collins ("Both Sides Now," "Michael from the Mountains") and Crosby, Stills, Nash and Young ("Woodstock") to a top 10 hitmaker in her own right via 1974's "Help Me" to, finally, a musical explorer whose works have incorporated jazz, world music, and slick electronic pop. Since her 1968 debut, *Joni Mitchell* (often referred to as *Song to a Seagull*), the Canadian-born singer has released 16 albums, all of which have charted and half of which have been certified either gold or platinum. Unlike nearly every one of her '60s contemporaries—except, perhaps, Neil Young—the sound of each of Mitchell's new releases, even this far into her career, cannot easily be predicted; if not her style, then certainly her musical context conspicuously changes with each outing. She is, as a result, one of the most respected artists in all of pop music.

Joni Mitchell

A talented visual artist whose paintings have graced several of her album covers, Mitchell studied art in Calgary before moving to Toronto, where she performed in area folk clubs and married her first husband, singer Chuck Mitchell. The couple moved to Detroit in 1965 and split the next year; thereafter, she moved to New York and was signed to Reprise Records in 1967. Several of her songs had already been or were being recorded by others at the time, including "The Circle Game," the title track of Tom Rush's acclaimed 1968 album; the aforementioned Judy Collins tracks, both on her 1968 set *Wildflowers;* and "I Don't Know Where I Stand" and "Chelsea Morning," from U.K. group Fairport Convention's 1967 debut.

Mitchell's 1969 album, *Clouds,* and 1970's *Ladies of the Canyon* were largely acoustic affairs very much in keeping with the era's folk styles. Still, her 1970 track "Big Yellow Taxi" showed enough pop verve to chart as a single: though it only reached number 67 that year, when redone four years later with the live backing of Tom Scott and the L.A. Express, it reached the top 25. Mitchell, however, was very much an album artist, and both *Ladies of the Canyon* and its follow-up, *Blue,* entered the top 30 and went platinum. The latter record, a deeply personal accounting of many of Mitchell's celebrated romances, is ranked by many as one of the finest works of the 1970s.

Moving to David Geffen's Asylum Records in 1972 with *For the Roses,* Mitchell began making a musical transition into pop that was first evidenced with the top 30 success of "You Turn Me On, I'm a Radio" then driven home with the enormous impact of 1974's *Court and Spark.* Backed by a superb group of studio musicians, including Tom Scott and members of the Crusaders, Mitchell was playing an intriguing blend of jazz, folk, and pop. Boasting both her first cover—"Twisted," popularized by jazz singing trio Lambert, Hendricks and Ross—and first top 10 hit in "Help Me," the album stayed at the number two spot for a full month and represents the singer's finest commercial hour. The follow-up double-live set *Miles of Aisles,* on which the singer was backed by saxophonist Scott's group the L.A. Express, was a welcome restating of much of the singer's best-known work, in one sense making much of it accessible to non-folk-inclined ears.

Accessibility was the major issue with 1975's bold *The Hissing of Summer Lawns,* an adventurous sonic experiment that featured Mitchell backed, at

least on one track, by the warrior drums of Burundi and that, to her credit, showed her to be more interested in art than album sales. Though it reached number four on the charts, it met a mixed reception; oddly, one of its most vocal fans in the years to come would be Prince. Mitchell was entering an interesting exploratory phase of her career that would bring together the most eclectic groupings of musicians imaginable. *Hejira* and *Don Juan's Reckless Daughter* were fascinating jazzy excursions prominently featuring the late bassist Jaco Pastorius as well as jazz saxophonist Wayne Shorter, Neil Young, Eagle Glenn Frey, J. D. Souther, and orchestrator Michael Gibbs. The latter album—the cover of which showed the composer of "Chelsea Morning" dressed as a black man—attracted the attention of legendary jazz bassist-composer Charles Mingus; in the final months before his 1979 death, he and Mitchell collaborated on an album that would be titled *Mingus.* A controversial work that seemed to please neither jazz fans nor longtime Mitchell followers, it was her first album since 1969's *Clouds* to fail to be certified gold. She came back with yet another double live album via 1980's *Shadows and Light;* featuring many of her latter-day songs, the set was boosted by an incredible backing band of jazz stars, including guitarist Pat Metheny, saxophonist Michael Brecker, keyboardist Lyle Mays, and bassist Pastorius, as well as backing vocalists the Persuasions.

In 1982, Mitchell moved to a new label—Geffen Records—and married producer-bassist Larry Klein. In some ways a return to "pop," albeit pop of

TOP ALBUMS

BLUE (Reprise, '71, *15*)
FOR THE ROSES (Asylum, '72, *11*)
COURT AND SPARK (Asylum, '74, *2*)
MILES OF AISLES (Asylum, '74, *2*)
THE HISSING OF SUMMER LAWNS (Asylum, '75, *4*)
HEJIRA (Asylum, '76, *13*)

Additional Top 40 Albums: 6

TOP SONGS

YOU TURN ME ON, I'M A RADIO (Asylum, '72, *25*)
HELP ME (Asylum, '74, *7*)
FREE MAN IN PARIS (Asylum, '74, *22*)
BIG YELLOW TAXI (live, Asylum, '75, *24*

remarkable sophistication, *Wild Things Run Fast* included a much-played version of the Leiber and Stoller–penned Elvis Presley hit, "(You're So Square) Baby, I Don't Care" and was generally admired by critics. With the 1980s, however, Mitchell's commercial popularity was gradually sliding; though that album reached number 25, none of the three she has made since have even entered the top 40. 1985's *Dog Eat Dog* was nonetheless marvelous, featuring several tracks co-produced by English popster Thomas Dolby, a typical odd mix of performers (James Taylor, Wayne Shorter, Michael McDonald, and shakahachi player Kazu Matsui), and a cameo "evangelist speech" by actor Rod Steiger. Mitchell's material—about the Ethiopian famine, about rampant consumerism, about the "three great stimulants" (artifice, brutality, and innocence), and about her own smoking habit—was a far cry from her earlier confessional love songs, but its intelligence and her craft were no less remarkable.

Mitchell's most recent albums—1988's *Chalk Marks in a Rainstorm* and 1991's *Night Ride Home*—were co-produced by Mitchell and her husband Klein, and again showed her to be an artist who has never rested on her laurels. The intricacies of her latest work make it seem unlikely she'll have another hit single anytime soon; indeed, if there's one negative aspect to the singer's post–*Court and Spark* work, its the simple fact that it has become increasingly difficult to find a simple hummable melody within it. Regardless, her audience has yet to leave her, and probably won't: most fans of Mitchell's early work have grown up as much as she has and are more than satisfied with the lyrical themes she now explores so intelligently. Mitchell's mark on America was felt at the most profound level with the 1992 election of President Bill Clinton: it was the first time in history a member of the First Family was named after a pop song. One can only wonder whether Chelsea Clinton knows that the writer of "Chelsea Morning" grew up in Saskatoon, Saskatchewan.

ESSRA MOHAWK

The most interesting lives in pop music are rarely those of the superstars, whose typical rags-to-riches stories eventually become a blur of self-congratulation; instead, it's the artists who almost made it—who through a series of circumstances beyond their control had a taste of fame, some small level of tantalizing success, and watched as it all slipped further and further away. Consider the case of Essra Mohawk (b. Sandy Hurvitz, Long Island, New York), who in 30 years has released only six albums—none of which entered the album charts, though most of which were of extremely high quality. Though that part of her story isn't altogether unique—many artists, in fact, only wish they were allowed the opportunity to make six albums—her talent as a vocalist and songwriter certainly is.

Breaking into the business early, the singer released the 1965 Liberty single "The Boy with the Way" under the name Jamie Carter when she was only 16. It flopped, but started her career rolling. At 17, she was offered songwriting deals by both Koppelman and Rubin and United Artists, neither of which she accepted. A meeting with producer Shadow Morton eventually resulted in two of her early tunes being recorded, one by girl group the Shangri-Las, the other by the Vanilla Fudge. (The latter tune, "The Spell That Comes After" from 1968's *Renaissance,* was credited to Mohawk's non-songwriting boyfriend of the time, artist Cal Schenkel, due to business conflicts.) After a 1967 encounter with Frank Zappa, who with his Mothers of Invention was playing an extended run at New York's Garrick Theater, Mohawk opened for and performed with the band and eventually recorded her first album. Released on Verve Records and bearing Zappa's Bizarre imprint, the 1968 album was called *Sandy's Album Is Here at Last* and credited to Sandy Hurvitz. Despite its bare-boned, somewhat drab production, Mohawk seemed a promising new talent stylistically not too far removed from Laura Nyro.

When next heard from, the former Sandy Hurvitz had moved to Los Angeles, met and married her producer Barry Friedman—then going by the pseudonym Frazier Mohawk—and officially become Essra Mohawk. Her 1970 Reprise album *Primordial Lovers* was a stunning step forward; one of the unsung masterpieces of the era, it was an atmospheric delight easily on par with the best work of contemporaries like Nyro or Joni Mitchell. Not only was Mohawk a superb writer, she was a breathtaking, adventurous vocalist, simultaneously sexy and soulful. But serious personal problems soon disrupted both Mohawk's marriage and her recording career; she moved back to the East Coast and resurfaced four years later on Elektra/Asylum Records.

Essra Mohawk

TOP ALBUMS

SANDY'S ALBUM IS HERE AT LAST (Verve, '68)
PRIMORDIAL LOVERS (Reprise, '70)
ESSRA MOHAWK (Asylum, '74)
PEOPLE WILL TALK (Private Stock, '76)
E-TURN (Eclipse, '85)

TOP SONGS

I HAVE BEEN HERE BEFORE (Reprise, '80)
I'LL GIVE IT TO YOU ANYWAY (Reprise, '80)
NEW SKINS FOR OLD (Asylum, '84)
PEOPLE WILL TALK (Private Stock, '76)

Despite the high quality of 1974's *Essra Mohawk* and its 1976 follow-up, *People Will Talk,* all was not going well with the career of Essra Mohawk. She had initially recorded *Essra Mohawk* for Paramount Records, and when that label was purchased by ABC in 1974, her manager Johannan Vigoda took the master and sold it to Elektra/Asylum. "Paramount was into me," the singer recalled years later, "they were involved, they had done everything. Elektra got a finished package and could care less. So they put it out—they just threw it out there—and then they were into the next one. But the next one had a really low budget, and it went over budget and sat for eight months—until Johannan got Private Stock Records to put it out. And they did the same thing. So I just said, 'Stop. No more. I will not do this three times in a row.' "

Since then, Mohawk's visibilty as a recording artist has severely declined. She released a now very rare album on Matthew Katz's San Francisco Sound label in the early 1980s; following her move to Philadelphia, her final album, *E-Turn,* surfaced on the independent Eclipse label in 1985. Though she has persistently sought another major label deal, none have been forthcoming. Fortunately for her, she's had much better luck with her songwriting; Cyndi Lauper scored a top three hit with Mohawk's "Change of Heart" in 1986, and the title track of Lisa Fischer's top 100 album *So Intense* was co-written by Mohawk. Additionally, her songs have been covered by Lorrie Morgan, who scored a 1992 country hit with "So Intense," and Lowen and Navarro (1993's "I've Had It All").

A practicing Buddhist since 1979, the singer continues to have a positive outlook about both her career—despite its occasional bumpiness—and her life. "In Buddhism, it's cause and effect," she says. "If you don't like the effect you're receiving, then you take responsibility. You make the cause, you get the effect. So anything that happened to me in the past—or will happen now or later—I can't really blame on anyone else."

EDDIE MONEY

With roughly 25 charting singles to his credit—slightly half of which entered the top 40—Eddie Money (b. Edward Mahoney, Mar. 2, 1949, Brooklyn, New York) proved to be one of pop's most consistent hitmakers of the late 1970s and '80s, if not one of the most exciting. The son of a New York policeman and a onetime attendee of the New York Police Academy, Money gave up his planned police career to pursue rock and roll in the mid-1970s. His break came after he moved to Berkeley, inked a management deal with West Coast powerhouse Bill Graham, and signed with Columbia Records. *Eddie Money,* his late-1977 debut album, featured two extremely radio-friendly singles in "Baby Hold On" and "Two Tickets to Paradise," both of which hit the top 30 and established Money as a tough-but-friendly singer with a nearly perfect album-rock voice much like Bad Company's popular singer, Paul Rodgers.

Working in tandem with guitarist Jimmy Lyon, with whom he'd often write songs, Money connected with his audience more often that not throughout the 1980s. All but one of the seven albums he released between 1977 and 1988 reached the top 50, bearing a total of eight top 30 singles between them. Additionally, many of his non-single tracks received significant radio airplay. Money's music typically rocked, but in a smoothed-down—some critics would say bland—manner, which perhaps helped make him a special favorite of increasingly demographic-conscious rock radio programmers. That especially seemed the case with his biggest hit, 1986's "Take Me Home Tonight," which featured original Ronette Ronnie Spector singing the lead line from her 1963 smash "Be My Baby"—a song likely to bring tears to the eyes of any aging, sentimental program director at the time.

As Money's career progressed, his involvement in his own songwriting lessened noticeably; though he'd generally be a collaborator, his name often appeared alongside two, three, or even four others in song credits by the early 1990s. Money seemed to be a victim of his own earlier radio success in 1992, when *Right Here,* his first new album since 1988's *Nothing to Lose,* peaked at an unprecedentedly low chart position of number 160. Some at the time ascribed its comparative failure not to its quality—it was a very solid record—but to an overall shift in the rock audience, which was now buying the work of alternative acts such as R.E.M. and Nirvana in record numbers. To that exceedingly MTV-con-

TOP ALBUMS

EDDIE MONEY (Columbia, '78, 37)
LIFE FOR THE TAKING (Columbia, '79, 17)
PLAYING FOR KEEPS (Columbia, '80, 35)
NO CONTROL (Columbia, '82, 20)
CAN'T HOLD BACK (Columbia, '86, 20)

TOP SONGS

BABY HOLD ON (Columbia, '78, 11)
TAKE ME HOME TONIGHT (Columbia, '86, 4)
I WANNA GO BACK (Columbia, '87, 14)
WALK ON WATER (Columbia, '88, 9)
PEACE IN OUR TIME (Columbia, '89, 11)

Additional Top 40 Songs: 4

scious crowd, Money was clearly last decade's news.

In a move that acknowledged MTV's exploding influence, Money released *Unplug It In* in late 1992, a live seven-track EP featuring acoustic versions of past songs such as "Two Tickets to Paradise" and other of Money's "favorites." The irony, of course, was that the release had no actual affiliation with MTV's enormously influential "Unplugged" series— and that aging rocker Money himself seemed an unlikely candidate to ever be booked on the show. With album-rock radio's ratings continuing to plummet, "Baby Hold On" may indeed have taken on whole new meaning for Eddie Money in the '90s.

VAN MORRISON

One of the most talented figures in all of rock and roll, Van Morrison (b. George Ivan Morrison, Aug. 31, 1945, Belfast, Ireland) is an extraordinary performer whose artistic consistency during his 30-year career is virtually unmatched by any other pop artist. He is a spectacularly emotive vocalist whose influence has been felt since his early days as leader of the Irish rock group Them and whose records—especially his 1968 masterpiece *Astral Weeks*—are commonly regarded by critics as among the finest of the rock era. From the 1960s through the '90s, many of the most revered artists in pop—including Bruce Springsteen, Rod Stewart, Bob Seger, and Patti Smith—have drawn inspiration from Morrison's rich recorded legacy. That the inimitable Irish singer has retained his commercial appeal into the 1990s was amply evident in late 1993, as his platinum 1990 Mercury Records compilation *The Best of Van Morrison* approached its 190th week on the album chart, where it has steadily dwelled in the mid-100 range for over two years. Though he hasn't had an American hit single since 1971's "Wild Night," it would not be inaccurate to say Van Morrison's career is nonetheless booming more than 20 years later.

Like other rockers of his generation, Morrison cut his teeth performing rock and R&B in clubs near American army bases in Germany during the early 1960s. Following a stint playing saxophone with the Monarchs, Morrison returned to Belfast and formed Them in 1964. While together for only two years, the band scored several hits, including "Here Comes the Night," a top 25 single given to the band by

writer-producer Bert Berns, and the Morrison-penned "Mystic Eyes," which cracked the top 40 in December 1966. Oddly, though Morrison's "Gloria" is one of the best-known songs in all of rock and roll, Them's original version of the track spent only one week at the bottom of the Hot 100 in May 1965; instead, Chicago rockers the Shadows of Knight had a top 10 hit with it a year later.

Morrison's recognition as a solo artist came after Them disbanded in 1966 and producer Berns sent the singer a one-way plane ticket to New York to do some recording. Out of those sessions came Morrison's first solo hit—1967's top 10 single "Brown Eyed Girl"—and an accompanying album of alleged "demos" on Berns's Bang Records label called *Blowin' Your Mind.* A disgruntled Morrison still maintains that the record should not have been released; regardless, it is a superb set that features some of his most fascinating work, including the tracks "T. B. Sheets," written about a friend with tuberculosis; the bluesy "He Ain't Give You None"; and initial versions of two songs that would later pop up on *Astral Weeks,* "Madame George" and "Cypress Avenue."

Already suspicious of the workings of the music business due to his experience with Them, Morrison would see those "demos" be issued twice more by Bang Records (first in 1970 as *The Best of Van Morrison,* then in 1974 as *T. B. Sheets*) and again by Sony Music as *Bang Masters* in 1991. Though producer Berns is long since dead, Morrison still holds a grudge, as his 1993 track "Big Time Operators" attested: "Well they told me to come on over/I made my way to New York/And they tried to have me deported/Stop me from getting work/Blacklisted me all over/They were vicious and they were mean/They were big time operators/Baby, on the music business scene."

Morrison signed to Warner Brothers and in 1968 released *Astral Weeks,* an album that failed to chart at the time of its release but is now ranked alongside the Beach Boys' *Pet Sounds,* Bob Dylan's *Blonde on Blonde,* and the Beatles' *Sgt. Pepper's Lonely Hearts Club Band* as one of the finest rock and roll albums of all time. An introspective, romantic merging of folk, jazz, and rock, the album contains autobiographical lyrics by Morrison that are at once private and universally applicable; open to interpretation by any listener, *Astral Weeks* works both as pleasant music and on the deepest personal level. By 1970, Morrison shifted more into the jazz and R&B mode

with *Moondance,* his most popular work, which entered the top 30 and went platinum. Featuring its title-track single, now a true standard, as well as the singer's well-known "Caravan" and "Into the Mystic," the album essentially laid the musical groundwork for most of the work Morrison would produce through the 1970s; particularly in live performance, his show-stopping numbers are most often drawn from this album.

Morrison's next few efforts—including *His Band and Street Choir* (1970), *Tupelo Honey* (1971), *St. Dominic's Preview* (1972), and *Hard Nose the Highway* (1973)—all worked the same musical territory and easily climbed into the top 40, aided by such hits as "Domino," "Blue Money," and "Wild Night." In 1974, Morrison recapped that portion of his career admirably with the much-acclaimed double live set *It's Too Late to Stop Now;* he then went through a series of directional shifts that resulted in some fascinating music. After visiting Belfast for the first time in years, he released 1974's *Veedon Fleece,* his finest work since *Astral Weeks,* an album with which it shared many musical similarities—though such

songs as as "Linden Arden Stole the Highlights" and "You Don't Pull No Punches, But You Don't Push the River" did not lend themselves as easily to listeners' own personal interpretations as did the songs on Morrison's earlier record.

After several false starts and more than one aborted album attempt, Morrison returned three years later with the accurately titled *A Period of Transition,* which leaned heavily on the keyboards and arrangements of Dr. John. A year later, his *Wavelength* met a stronger reception from both radio and retail; older fans were tickled by its inclusion of keyboardist Peter Bardens, a former bandmate of Morrison's in Them. While both albums were satisfactory, neither felt as substantial as Morrison's early '70s work, and some critics felt Morrison was slipping somewhat.

Beginning with 1979's impressive *Into the Music,* however, the singer entered a phase of his career from which he has yet to depart. Incorporating Irish and Celtic music forms and featuring his best band ever—including trumpeter Mark Isham, bassist David Hayes, and drummer Peter Van Hooke—the album seemed to bring together the disparate elements of Morrison's work on *Astral Weeks* and *Moondance*. Upbeat and joyous, yet at the same time serene and wistful, it—and the many albums that followed in the same mode—signaled a new artistic maturity for Morrison. The singer took to regularly invoking the names of poets and mystics on such tracks as *Common One*'s "Rave On, John Donne" and began featuring gorgeous instrumental pieces like *Beautiful Vision*'s "Scandanavia"; he also became associated with various religious philosophies such as Christianity, Scientology, and Theosophy. After a nonstop string of gorgeously meditative albums, the singer further tipped his hand regarding his philosophical orientation with "In the Garden," from his best album of the decade, 1986's *No Guru, No Method, No Teacher:* "No Guru, no method, no teacher/Just you and I and nature/And the Father and the Son and the Holy Ghost/In the garden wet with rain."

Morrison took to performing with other musicians in the late 1980s, such as Ireland's Chieftains, with whom he recorded 1988's *Irish Heartbeat,* and U.K. pop figures such as Cliff Richard (they dueted on *Avalon Sunset*'s "Whenever God Shines His Light") and Georgie Fame. Organist Fame, who scored American '60s hits of his own with "Yeh, Yeh" and "The Ballad of Bonnie and Clyde," has been a regular contributor to Morrison's albums and concerts since 1989's *Avalon Sunset.*

As the 1990s unfolded, a new groundswell of appreciation for Van Morrison's work became apparent. The *Best of Van Morrison* collection—drawing from the singer's work since his Them days, became only his second platinum album since 1970's *Moondance* as it played out its lengthy run on the album charts. Additionally, 1991's two-CD *Hymns to the Silence* went gold; aside from the preceding year's compilation, the singer hadn't had a gold record since 1971's *Tupelo Honey*. Polydor released *The Best of Van Morrison Volume Two* in 1993, then quickly followed it up with the singer's fascinating *Too Long in Exile*. Featuring a guest appearance by longtime Morrison friend and bluesman John Lee Hooker (who duets on an unexpected remake of "Gloria") and covers of songs by Doc Pomus, Sonny Boy Williamson, and Brook Benton—all sitting side-by-side with Morrison's adaptation of a text by W. B. Yeats, no less—the album was a perfect blend of *Blowin' Your Mind* and *Veedon Fleece*. It was a reminder that there is no one else in pop music who hears or plays music like Van Morrison and—as if it was needed—further proof that there will never be.

MORRISSEY

The most compelling British pop star of the 1980s, Morrissey (b. Steven Patrick Morrissey, May 22, 1959, Manchester, England) and his legendary pop group the Smiths were responsible for some of the most thought-provoking and intelligent rock and roll of the post-punk era. Always quotable, always enmeshed in controversies regarding song lyrics or deliberately provocative public statements, Morrissey proved to be the wisest manipulator of the press since David Bowie invented Ziggy Stardust a decade earlier. While the group's superstardom in Britain vastly exceeded their fame in the United States, their initial cult following—which began with their eponymous 1984 debut—steadily grew through their 1987 demise; it has since continued to snowball as Morrissey has pressed ahead with his even more lucrative solo career. Beginning with 1988's *Viva Hate*, which attained a higher chart position than any of the Smiths' work, Morrissey's American popularity has blossomed, even while slightly fading in his homeland; by 1992, the onetime cult figure was releasing top 30 albums and filling venues no less prestigious than the Hollywood Bowl.

TOP ALBUMS

MOONDANCE (Warner Bros., '70, 29)
HIS BAND AND STREET CHOIR
  (Warner Bros., '70, 32)
TUPELO HONEY (Warner Bros., '71, 27)
SAINT DOMINIC'S PREVIEW (Warner Bros., '72, 15)
HARD NOSE THE HIGHWAY (Warner Bros., '73, 27)

Additional Top 40 Albums: 1

TOP SONGS

BROWN EYED GIRL (Bang, '67, 10)
COME RUNNING (Warner Bros., '70, 39)
DOMINO (Warner Bros., '70, 9)
BLUE MONEY (Warner Bros., '71, 23)
WILD NIGHT (Warner Bros., '71, 28)

Morrissey

What made the Smiths very special to so many was, of course, the consistently high quality of the group's songs; with the pairing of singer Morrissey, who provided the lyrics, and guitarist Johnny Marr, who composed the wonderfully varied and multitextured music, the group boasted one of the finest songwriting teams in pop. Yet in a sense that consistency has hampered the artistic development of Morrissey's own career. Whether playing hard-charging rock, Byrdsy folk melodies, or English Music Hall–inspired pop, the Smiths built a repertoire that, however eclectic, seemed all of one piece. But without Marr, Morrissey's lyrics have accompanied music written by a diverse crop of writers including Stephen Street, Kevin Armstrong, Clive Langer, Mark Nevin, and most recently, Alain Whyte—none of whom have yet to display Marr's craft at writing catchy, memorable pop hooks. As a result, Morrissey's output has been noticeably inconsistent in both sound and style.

One place Morrissey has yet to fall short, however, has been in his lyrics; he remains one of best in pop music. Early in the Smiths' career he drew attention for his unusual practice of writing songs that were deliberately sexually ambiguous—that often spoke in the second person, to a "you" that could be either male or female, all open to personal interpretation. "It's an absolutely intentional move," the singer said in 1985. "It has to be that way. Because I think all the great writers that I ever liked were writers who spoke for everybody. I don't like it when there's this separatism, that certain groups can be put into absolutely defined categories, that this group could only possibly appeal to men, or women, or certain sects."

Morrissey's lyrical abilities may rank among the highest, but his way with song titles is absolutely unmatched; his best tell an entire story in only a few words, often humorously, while reinforcing his persona as a determined miserablist. Among the best: "I Want the One I Can't Have," "Last Night I Dreamt That Somebody Loved Me," "Some Girls Are Bigger Than Others," "That Joke Isn't Funny Anymore," "There's a Place in Hell for Me and My Friends," "(I'm) The End of the Family Line," "You're the One for Me, Fatty," and "We Hate It When Our Friends Become Successful." A onetime music journalist prior to the Smiths, Morrissey clearly knows the value of a good headline.

Still, if he were merely clever, but incapable of writing songs that deeply touched their audience,

TOP ALBUMS

VIVA HATE (Sire, '88)
BONA DRAG (Sire, '90)
KILL UNCLE (Sire, '91)
YOUR ARSENAL (Sire, '92, *21*)

TOP SONGS

SUEDEHEAD (Sire, '88)
EVERYDAY IS LIKE SUNDAY (Sire, '88)
NOVEMBER SPAWNED A MONSTER (Sire, '90)
WE HATE IT WHEN OUR FRIENDS BECOME
    SUCCESSFUL (Sire, '92)

Morrissey would not have developed the rabidly loyal fan base he now enjoys. The best of his lyrics paint small, purposely ambiguous pictures that allow the listener to devise his or her own story, to fill in the blanks and draw their own conclusions. One of his finest songs, "This Night Has Opened My Eyes," recorded with the Smiths in 1984, illustrates the point superbly: "In a river the color of lead/Immerse the baby's head/Wrap her up in the News of the World/Dump her on a doorstep, girl/ This night has opened my eyes/And I will never sleep again." The song's chorus contains two final lines, "And I'm not happy/And I'm not sad," that concisely convey a depth of emotion—or, literally, a lack of it—that few other artists could begin to approach, let alone match.

"Sometimes people come up to me and say, well obviously this song is about whatever," Morrissey noted in 1985, "and it's a completely erroneous, unintelligent interpretation that they've put on the song. But that's the risk that has to be taken. For me, it's good enough that people just actually think about the songs, regardless of what conclusion they come to about them. And I know that people do think about the words a great deal, because they tell me so. And ultimately, that's the biggest prize of all."

ELLIOTT MURPHY

Elliott Murphy (b. Mar. 16, 1949) once had a very small role in a Fellini movie, which, considering the sometimes very surreal course his career has taken in two decades, couldn't be more appropriate. He has been on four major labels. His records have featured such sidemen as Billy Joel, Phil Collins, and members of the Talking Heads, Violent Femmes, and Velvet Underground. When American labels stopped caring, European labels kept his career afloat for nearly a decade. And the man who once embodied the heart of New York's early-'70s rock and roll scene now lives in Paris with his wife Francoise and young son Gaspard.

Murphy's debut album, *Aquashow,* drew critical huzzahs galore in 1973, and indeed there was much to write about. The album cover: a handsome, elegantly dressed young blond man, looking directly at the camera, his expression halfway cocky, halfway uncertain; a picture of his father's original Aquashow, a water-ballet restaurant and nightclub

---

TOP ALBUMS

AQUASHOW (Polydor, '73)
LOST GENERATION (RCA, '75)
NIGHT LIGHTS (RCA, '76)
JUST A STORY FROM AMERICA (Columbia, '77)
UNREAL CITY (Razor & Tie, '93)

TOP SONGS

LAST OF THE GREAT ROCK STARS (Polydor, '73)
LIKE A GREAT GATSBY (Polydor, '73)

---

in Flushing Meadows (at the site of the 1939 World's Fair). The music: Dylanesque lyrics, melodies, and instrumentation (organist Frank Owens had played on Dylan's *Highway 61 Revisited*), with a touch of *Loaded*-era Velvet Underground; a batch of memorable songs about rock and roll itself and family relationships, and including the candidly titled, heartfelt "White Middle Class Blues." Having already created a buzz via gigs at New York's Mercer Arts Center and Max's Kansas City, Murphy found himself on posters everywhere in Manhattan, courtesy of Polydor Records, hyping this *Village Voice* quote: "Elliott Murphy is going to be a Monster."

That wasn't to be, but not for lack of trying— both by Murphy and his various record labels. His next two albums emerged on RCA, but despite that label's bang-up job with central '70s figures Lou Reed, David Bowie, and the Kinks, Murphy captivated only critics, not consumers. 1975's *Lost Generation,* recorded in L.A., sported songs about "getting felt up" in Hollywood and Eva Braun, both topics top 40 wasn't aching to jump on. *Night Lights,* produced by former Blues Project and Blood, Sweat and Tears member Steve Katz, featured a fascinatingly diverse lineup of guest musicians (many of whom would go on to much greater things later), a cover depicting Murphy posing in Times Square, and a near-classic opener in "Diamonds by the Yard."

Released by Columbia in 1977, *Just a Story from America* was Murphy's final album for a major label. It, too, featured interesting guest musicians— pre-star Phil Collins on drums and Rolling Stone Mick Taylor on guitar—and it, too, bombed. An ensuing disagreement between Murphy's management and his label resulted in the singer being dropped, and Murphy went his independent way.

Forming his own label in 1980, the singer released *Affairs,* a six-song EP that stirred enough interest overseas to spark Murphy's first European tour ever. Since then, he's been prolifically churning out nearly an album a year, writing articles, novels, and short stories, and slowly coming into vogue domestically again. In 1992, the independent Razor & Tie label issued a comprehensive 1973–77 career retrospective called *Diamonds by the Yard;* a year later, the same company released *Unreal City,* Murphy's first nationally distributed album in over a decade. It was reassuringly superb. He had opened 1973's *Aquashow* with "Last of the Rock Stars"; in 1993, he not only wrote a song called "On Elvis Presley's Birthday," he noted in the CD booklet that it's "the most important song on the album." Who knows? That Elliott Murphy still cares enough to share that with us just may be part of his secret.

GRAHAM NASH

Graham Nash

A singer-songwriter whose achievements have often been camouflaged within the larger contexts of his bands, Graham Nash (b. Feb 2, 1942, Blackpool, England) established himself as a key member of both the Hollies in the 1960s and Crosby, Still, Nash and Young in the 1970s. Nash, a superb vocalist with a trademark knack for high-pitched harmonies, co-wrote five top 40 hits for the Hollies between 1966 and 1968 then went on to write more than half of CSN&Y's hits between 1969 and 1982. While his solo career has met only limited success—his two hits, "Chicago" and "Immigration Man" (recorded with David Crosby), came over 20 years ago at the height of CSN&Y's fame—the degree of fame he reached within both bands is undoubtedly great consolation. Well respected within the industry, and largely perceived as the most "stable" member of CSN&Y, Nash has quietly written a repertoire of songs that for many have come to define quality pop of the 1960s and '70s.

As early as the age of 14, Nash, who lived in Manchester, displayed an interest in performing. With lifelong friend Allan Clarke, he formed a singing partnership that would take the pair through a succession of skiffle-oriented bands with such names as the 2 Teens, the Levins, the Guytones, the Fourtones, and the Deltas. By late 1962, the latter band had evolved into the Hollies; within a few

months the group had signed to EMI's Parlophone label in the U.K., and a deal with America's Liberty Records soon followed. The Hollies' first American single, a remake of Maurice Williams and the Zodiacs' "Stay," emerged on Liberty in January 1964; thereafter further releases were issued domestically on the label's Imperial imprint, and then on Epic.

Nash stayed with the Hollies through December 1968, appearing on seven albums with the group and close to 20 singles—seven of which were top 40 hits, five of which he'd co-written, including "Stop Stop Stop," "On a Carousel," "Pay You Back with Interest," "Carrie-Anne," and "Jennifer Eccles." Frustration with the group's direction, and their discomfort with his increasingly adventurous newer songs, eventually brought him into his fateful partnership with the Buffalo Springfield's Stephen Stills and ex-Byrd David Crosby.

TOP ALBUMS

SONGS FOR BEGINNERS (Atlantic, '71, *15*)
GRAHAM NASH/DAVID CROSBY (with David Crosby, Atlantic, '72, *4*)
WILD TALES (Atlantic, '74, *34*)
WIND ON THE WATER (with David Crosby, ABC, '75, *6*)
WHISTLING DOWN THE WIRE (with David Crosby, ABC, '76, *26*)
EARTH & SKY (Capitol, '80)
INNOCENT EYES (Atlantic, '86)

TOP SONGS

CHICAGO (Atlantic, '71, *35*)
IMMIGRATION MAN (with David Crosby, Atlantic, '72, *36*)

Beginning with the 1969 album *Crosby, Stills & Nash,* the trio instantly established itself as one of pop's most compelling acts. Their first single was Nash's own "Marrakesh Express"—a song he'd written while in the Hollies but that they'd refused to perform—and it shot straight into the top 30. Soon adding on Stills's former Buffalo Springfield partner Neil Young and releasing 1970's *Deja Vu,* the group became enormously successful, and it scored two additional Nash-penned hits that year with "Our House" and "Teach Your Children."

Though the group officially disbanded after the release of 1971's quadruple platinum *4 Way Street* to pursue solo careers, they remained friendly and worked together again often. Nash's 1971 debut, *Songs for Beginners,* quickly went gold and produced his first hit single, "Chicago"—which was written about the trial of the radical Chicago Seven and was about as far removed from the Hollies' "Bus Stop" as Nash could ever hope. While Young and Stills quickly went their separate ways and recorded their own solo albums (though briefly forming the Stills-Young band in 1976), both Nash and David Crosby instead formed their own partnership, recording several albums together through the 1970s, most of which went gold. Both 1972's *Graham Nash/David Crosby* and 1975's *Wind on the Water* reached the top 10, the former spurred to its number four position by the Nash-penned top 40 hit "Immigration Man."

By 1977, Crosby, Stills and Nash had reunited to

record *CSN.* In many ways that reformation signaled the arrangement that the trio and even Neil Young continue to work under even today: though each artist would continue with his own solo career, occasional reunion albums and tours provided the best of both worlds. Ironically, the group had to reform before scoring the biggest single hits of their career—first with 1977's "Just a Song Before I Go," then with 1982's "Wasted on the Way," two Nash compositions that became top 10 singles. (Another temporary reunion with an old group came with 1983's *What Goes Around* by the Hollies; Nash wrote none of the material, and the album peaked at number 90.)

Nash's own solo career has generally been overshadowed by both his work with CSN&Y and David Crosby. Following *Songs for Beginners,* sporadic solo albums such as *Wild Tales* (1974), *Earth and Sky* (1980), and *Innocent Eyes* (1986) scored progressively lower chart rankings, with his 1986 effort peaking at number 136 and staying on the charts for a mere seven weeks. Much of the better material from those albums appeared on the superb *Crosby, Stills & Nash* four-CD boxed set, issued by Atlantic in 1991. Featuring the trio's songs placed side-by-side with samplings of the members' various solo recordings, it was further evidence that Graham Nash's work—alone or with his very famous band—deserved all the acclaim it had received over the years and, considering its very noticeable consistency, perhaps even more.

FRED NEIL

An artist whose musical impact vastly exceeded his own renown, Fred Neil (b. 1937, St. Petersburg, Florida) is remembered today for his wide sphere of influence as part of the Greenwich Village folk scene of the early 1960s and, more importantly, for his wonderful songs. The best known by far, "Everybody's Talkin'," was the theme from *Midnight Cowboy* and a top 10 single for Nilsson in 1969. About a half-dozen others became standards performed by some of the 1960s' most prominent artists. Two of them were "The Other Side of This Life," covered by the Jefferson Airplane and the Youngbloods, and "The Dolphins," likewise redone by Linda Ronstadt, Tim Buckley, It's a Beautiful Day, and the Youngbloods. Other well-covered tracks included "Candy Man" (Roy Orbison), "That's the Bag I'm In" (H.P. Lovecraft), and "Blues on the Ceiling."

Neil, who is said to have played at the Grand Ole Opry in the mid-1950s, recorded a series of excellent records from 1964's *Hootenanny Live* at the Bitter End (FM) through 1971's *The Other Side of This Life* (Capitol). None were big sellers, and in fact the singer never had a charting record of his own during the course of his career. The best album, though it lacks most of his better-known songs, is 1968's *Sessions,* a gorgeous, revealing, "live in the studio" session in which Neil—a superb 12-string guitarist —weaves an almost ethereal spell throughout the seven tracks, three of which run over seven minutes. Fans of Tim Buckley are often astounded upon hearing *Sessions* for the first time, as the younger, very talented singer recorded music similar to it later in the 1960s.

Neil's 1964 album *Bleecker & MacDougal,* reissued in 1970 as *Little Bit of Rain* with the success of "Everybody's Talkin'," featured the singer with well-known accompanists John Sebastian (later of the Lovin' Spoonful) and Felix Pappalardi (later producer and member of Mountain). Recalling those days, Sebastian later told writer Bruce Pollock, "Freddy had a classic case of ambivalence. You see, he hung out with a lot of jazz musicians, to whom making it was synonymous with selling out. I came from the next generation, which didn't know from selling out. We just knew from Is it a hit or is it not a hit?" While with the Lovin' Spoonful, Sebastian once wrote a song called "Coconut Grove"; it was the name not only of Fred Neil's publishing company but of the South Florida community in which Neil chose to live upon retiring from the business in the early 1970s.

TOP ALBUMS

BLEECKER & MACDOUGAL (Elektra, '64)
EVERYBODY'S TALKIN' (Capitol, '66)
SESSIONS (Capitol, '68)
THE OTHER SIDE OF THIS LIFE (Capitol, '71)

TOP SONGS

BLEECKER & MACDOUGAL (Elektra, '64)
OTHER SIDE OF THIS LIFE (Elektra, '64)
EVERYBODY'S TALKIN' (Capitol, '66)

MICHAEL NESMITH

A farsighted businessman whose superb work as a singer-songwriter remains obscured by his membership in '60s pop group the Monkees, Michael Nesmith (b. Robert Michael Nesmith, Dec. 30, 1942, Dallas, Texas) is one of the most fascinating figures in American pop. Following his stint in the famed made-for-TV quartet, whose 58-episode run on NBC-TV between 1966 and 1968 generated huge record sales and made him one of the most recognizable stars in America, Nesmith pursued a low-key but highly praised solo career and went on to become a pioneer in the budding genre of music video. Credited as being the man who "invented MTV," the former Monkee founded his own communications company, Pacific Arts Corporation—which has since become a highly respected home video software distribution company in the 1990s—and later produced several cultish but well-received feature films.

The Texas-born son of the woman who invented Liquid Paper, Nesmith moved to Los Angeles in 1963 to explore a career in music. After cutting a folk single with John London and Bill Sleeper under the name Mike, John and Bill and briefly playing in a local band called the Survivors, he was drafted into the Air Force. Upon his release in 1965, Nesmith cut two unsuccessful singles for Colpix Records as Michael Blessing—"The New Recruit" and Buffy Sainte-Marie's "Until It's Time for You to Go"—and became stage announcer at the weekly hootenannies held at the Troubadour, an extremely influential L.A. venue that served as a hotbed of new local talent. Responding to an ad seeking four young musician types to star in a planned TV series, Nesmith—along with Micky Dolenz, Peter Tork, and Davy Jones—was selected to become a Monkee, and stardom soon ensued.

The degree of success achieved by the Monkees seems nearly unbelievable in retrospect; their debut album, *The Monkees,* was the Number One album of 1966, and its follow-up, *More of the Monkees,* claimed the same honor in 1967—beating out no less a contender than the Beatles' *Sgt. Pepper's Lonely Hearts Club Band.* During the two-year course of their much-watched TV show—which every week provided their music the best promotional push in musical history—the group released five albums, four of which went to Number One, the last of which (1968's *The Birds, the Bees & the Monkees*) peaked at number three. While the group's commercial appeal was undeniable, critics of the era were less inclined to praise the band, distrustful of their "manufactured" teen-idol status. The much-repeated irony, of course, is that most of the Monkees' releases were excellent pop records that showcased songs by many of the finest songwriters of the 1960s—including Gerry Goffin and Carole King, Barry Mann and Cynthia Weil, Tommy Boyce and Bobby Hart, Neil Diamond, Nilsson, John Stewart, and David Gates, among others.

Nesmith's own songwriting prowess had been demonstrated via his song "Different Drum," a 1967 single by Linda Ronstadt's band the Stone Poneys that hit the top 15; additionally, Ronstadt covered Nesmith's "Some of Shelly's Blues." But within the context of the Monkees, comparatively few of Nesmith's songs were recorded, typically only one or two per album. As it was, of the group's 12 top 40 hits, 10 were penned by outside writers, and only "The Girl I Knew Somewhere" and "Tapioca Tundra"—the lowest charting ones—were written by Nesmith. Though he had already released an obscure instrumental solo album called *Mike Nesmith Presents/The Wichita Train Whistle Sings* in 1968, by mid-1970 Nesmith had left the Monkees to pursue a solo career full-time and formed the First National Band.

Unusually for the time, Nesmith's new band featured a pedal-steel guitarist—Orville J. "Red" Rhodes—and had a decidedly countryish sound. "Hank Williams, Jerry Lee Lewis and Jimmie Rodgers are to me something of a musical triumvirate," Nesmith explained on the back of his new band's 1970 debut album, *Magnetic South*. "Somehow I always get back to them." Boasting a healthy supply of new songs by Nesmith, the album included the top 30 hit, "Joanne," and was soon followed by two new records bearing similar cover treatments, *Loose Salute* and 1971's *Nevada Fighter*. When that group disbanded, Nesmith returned with the Second National Band, whose excellent *Tantamount to Treason, Vol. 1* was mistitled, for there would be no follow-up.

Despite the great start "Joanne" had provided, Nesmith's album sales were beginning to falter; *Loose Salute*, which had peaked at number 159 and slid off the chart in four weeks, would be his last charting album for nine years. In the interim, Nesmith took his new non-celebrity status in appar-

ent stride by titling his best album yet *And the Hits Just Keep On Comin'* in 1972. He followed it up with another superb effort, *Pretty Much Your Standard Ranch Stash*, and upon its commercial failure left to form the Pacific Arts Corporation.

The first product from Nesmith's new multimedia company came in 1975 with his ambitious "book with a soundtrack," *The Prison*. Buyers were instructed to listen to the album and read the book at exactly the same time; the effect, declared Nesmith, was a "soundtrack to a movie that plays out in your mind's eye." The singer released two more albums on his new label—1976's *From a Radio Engine to a Photon Wing* and 1979's *Infinite Rider on the Big Dogma*, the latter of which reached number 151 on the charts—but otherwise devoted most of his time to his growing interest in combining music with video to produce, in his words, "video records." He'd already made an early rock video with 1976's single "Rio" and by 1979 had created "Popclips," a half-hour music video show that he sold to Warner-Amex, who aired it on their new Nickelodeon cable network and eventually used its concept to create MTV.

"They asked me if I wanted to [run] it," Nesmith recalled in 1993, "and I said, 'No, I want to make these things, I don't want to run a network.' Then suddenly there was a management team in place who came from radio, and they said, 'This is not really

TOP ALBUMS

MAGNETIC SOUTH (with the First National Band, RCA, '70)
TANTAMOUNT TO TREASON (with the Second National Band, RCA, '72)
AND THE HITS JUST KEEP ON COMING (RCA, '72)
PRETTY MUCH YOUR STANDARD RANCH STASH (RCA, '73)
FROM A RADIO ENGINE TO A PHOTON WING (Pacific Arts, '77)
TROPICAL CAMPFIRE'S (Pacific Arts Audio, '93)

TOP SONGS

JOANNE (with the First National Band, RCA, '70, 21)
LISTEN TO THE BAND (RCA, '70)
PROPINQUITY (I'VE JUST BEGUN TO CARE) (RCA, '71)
DIFFERENT DRUM (RCA, '72)

about video records—there's no such thing as video records. This is really a commercial for an audio record, and that's what we should do. We should just focus ourselves on the *Billboard* charts, and we'll force people to make videos for their records.' I always thought the video was the record," Nesmith continued, "and that MTV—instead of being a 24-hour-a-day commercial channel—was a sampling window, that you would then go out and buy these things. Well, it turns out they were more right than I was at the end of the day—but when I look at it, I still think I'm looking at commercials for records."

Nesmith won the first video Grammy Award in 1982 for his video record *Elephant Parts* and spent much of the rest of the 1980s working on film productions such as *Timerider, Repo Man, Square Dance,* and *Tapeheads.* In 1989, he put together a compilation of unreleased songs and material from his later albums for Rhino Records called *The Newer Stuff;* in 1991, a companion volume of material from his early '70s records appeared, appropriately titled *The Older Stuff.*

In mid-1993, Nesmith released his first collection of entirely new material in 14 years, *Tropical Campfire's,* on his newly created Pacific Arts Audio label. Featuring his stalwart pedal-steel player Red Rhodes, the set was a charming collection of country-tinged pop that showed the ex-Monkee still in his songwriting prime. That he is wealthy enough to make records only when he wants to—and only when he feels he has something to say—made the album that much more delightful.

RANDY NEWMAN

A brilliant songwriter and satirist whose humor often cuts too close to the bone for many, Randy Newman (b. Nov. 28, 1943, Los Angeles) has the sort of impeccable credentials money can't buy: he is the nephew of famous film composers Alfred, Lionel, and Emil Newman, who collectively scored literally hundreds of films since the 1930s. While Newman has to some degree followed in his uncles' footsteps—composing the scores for *Cold Turkey, Ragtime, The Natural, Parenthood, Avalon,* and *Awakenings*—he remains best known for his infrequent, uniformly superb pop albums, which he began making for Warner Bros. in 1968.

Newman's pop songs are unusual in several respects, not least because they typically seem to endorse outrageous and offensive viewpoints—viewpoints that are consistently those of the songs' central characters, rather than Newman himself. Among the protagonists in Newman's repertoire have been southern rednecks, a slave recruiter in Africa, a white resident of Capetown, South Africa, and God Himself. "I like the idea of the untrustworthy narrator," Newman told writer David Seay in 1988. "The people in my songs are generally exaggerations; what they say and what they think is colored by who they are. When a song works, the audience understands the character's point of view. And they don't mistake it for mine."

Newman began writing professionally at an early age and by 17 became a staff writer working for publishing companies such as Metric Music and January Music. He had early success with "Just One Smile" (a chart hit for Gene Pitney in 1965, later covered by Blood, Sweat and Tears and Dusty Springfield), "I Don't Want to Hear it Anymore" (recorded by Springfield and the Walker Brothers), "I Think It's Gonna Rain Today" (on Judy Collins's 1966 album *In My Life*), and "Simon Smith and His Dancing Bear" (a 1967 U.K. hit for the Alan Price Set); additionally, he wrote or co-wrote three songs on the 1964 *Breakin' It Up on the Beatles Tour!* album by fellow Metric Music staffer Jackie DeShannon.

A longtime friend of future Warner Bros. Records president Lenny Waronker, Newman was signed by that label's Reprise division and made his debut via 1968's elaborate *Randy Newman,* an impressive orchestrated effort fully arranged by Newman himself. Its 1970 follow-up, *12 Songs,* was a collection of brilliant demos originally recorded before its predecessor; included was Newman's version of "Mama Told Me Not to Come," a Number One hit that year for Three Dog Night. Newman's next album, *Randy Newman/Live,* initially wasn't even intended for commercial release: Reprise had recorded a September 1970 solo performance at New York's Bitter End and pressed up promotional copies for radio and the press; the strong response compelled the label to issue it by the next year. It was Newman's first charting album.

Newman had put in an appearance singing "Gone Dead Train" on Jack Nitzsche's 1970 *Performance* soundtrack, but his next real studio outing was 1972's *Sail Away,* the album many feel to be his

Randy Newman

best work. Newman's caustic wit was in evidence from the opening title track, in which a slave recruiter in Africa was selling the merits of his country: "In America you'll have food to eat/Won't have to run through the jungle/And scuff up your feet/You'll just sing about Jesus and drink wine all day/It's great to be an American." The album's equally memorable closer, "God's Song (That's Why I Love Mankind)," featured the Deity Himself intoning, "I burn down your cities— how blind you must be/I take from you your children and you say how blessed you are/You all must be crazy to put your faith in me / That's why I love mankind."

Newman's deliberate outrageousness delighted his fans, but occasionally provoked some controversy: his song "Rednecks" from 1974's *Good Old Boys* used the word "nigger," and his number two hit "Short People," from 1977's *Little Criminals,* angered many of the height-impaired with Newman's declaration that short people "got no reason to live." Perhaps predictably, the publicity only helped

his record sales: *Good Old Boys* was his first top 40 album, and *Little Criminals* entered the top 10 and went gold. Newman later took on targets such as ELO and Kiss on 1979's *Born Again* (he was decked out in the latter band's makeup style, albeit with dollar-sign designs, on its cover), and with such songs as "It's Money That I Love" and his later "It's Money That Matters" began focusing on fatcat moneymen as unlikely sympathetic heroes.

Newman's public profile isn't the highest, though occasionally his songs catch the masses' fancy; 1983's "I Love L.A." garnered much exposure, for example, though not a single. The writer's growing involvement in film scoring in the late 1980s made his pop albums that much more infrequent; his most recent, *Land of Dreams,* notable for being his first deliberately "autobiographical" project, came five years after its predecessor. In late 1993, the singer had completed songs for an upcoming Disney film called *The Toy Story* and was working on a musical adaptation of Goethe's *Faust.* Scheduled for

TOP ALBUMS
••••••••••••••••••••••

RANDY NEWMAN (Reprise, '68)
12 SONGS (Reprise, '70)
SAIL AWAY (Reprise, '72)
GOOD OLD BOYS (Reprise, '74, 36)
LITTLE CRIMINALS
    (Warner Bros., '77, 9)
BORN AGAIN (Warner Bros., '79)
TROUBLE IN PARADISE
    (Warner Bros., '83)
LAND OF DREAMS (Reprise, '88)

TOP SONGS
••••••••••••••••••••••

SHORT PEOPLE (Warner Bros. '77, 2)
IT'S MONEY THAT MATTERS
    (Reprise, '88)

1994 release, the latter will feature a variety of well-known artists in casted roles, including James Taylor, Don Henley, Linda Ronstadt, Bonnie Raitt, and Elton John. Newman, who cast James Taylor as God, was undoubtedly pleased with his self-appointed role as Satan.

STEVIE NICKS

One of the 1970s' true superstars, Stevie Nicks (b. Stephanie Nicks, May 26, 1948, Phoenix, Arizona) played a major role in resuscitating the career of distinguished English blues band Fleetwood Mac in the mid-'70s before establishing herself as a platinum-selling solo artist while still retaining her membership in the group. Equally known for her sometimes flaky "Welsh witch" stage persona, perhaps inspired by her first top 20 hit with Fleetwood Mac, "Rhiannon," Nicks is an occasionally superb songwriter whose fragile, often sensuous voice remains an essential part of her commercial appeal.

Nicks attended high school in the Los Angeles area and moved to San Francisco in 1966; there she met future boyfriend and bandmate Lindsey Buckingham and joined him for three years in a local psychedelic band named Fritz. The pair relocated to Los Angeles in 1972, further focused on songwriting, and—following a series of demos they recorded at a coffee factory owned by Buckingham's family—signed a deal with Polydor's Anthem Records imprint the next year. Featuring the duo naked on its cover, 1973's *Buckingham Nicks* has since become a valuable collectible; it sold few copies and was quickly deleted. Actually an excellent work, the set offered an early preview of the Fleetwood Mac to come. When producer and engineer Keith Olsen then played tapes of the album to members of the English band as a sample of his studio abilities, they were so impressed they asked Nicks and Buckingham to come aboard and join the band.

The Americanization of Fleetwood Mac was a successful experiment indeed: Since 1975's *Fleetwood Mac,* the group's first album with Nicks and Buckingham, the band has repeatedly scored gold or platinum with every effort, often many times over. While their 1975 effort was a huge success—a Number One album that went quintuple platinum and bore three top 20 hits—it, and nearly everything else in industry history, was overshadowed by their follow-up, *Rumours.* The latter, which held its position at Number One for an amazing 31 weeks, went on to be certified platinum 13 times over and became the second-largest-selling American album of all time, bested only by Michael Jackson's *Thriller.*

Nicks' role in the band was crucial, not least because her consistent supply of hit songs lent the band character and an appealing image—something it hadn't really had since original band founder Peter Green departed in 1970. In one sense, the presence of both Nicks and Buckingham suddenly brought the band an embarrassment of songwriting riches; not only were they prolific writers, so was longtime member Christine McVie. Between the three of them, they wrote 15 top 40 hits between 1975 and 1990—five of which were penned by Nicks, including "Rhiannon," "Dreams," "Sara," "Gypsy," and (partially) "Seven Wonders."

But that success is only part of Nicks' story; beginning with 1981's *Bella Donna,* a Number One album that went quadruple platinum, she became a radio fixture completely apart from Fleetwood Mac. By far the group's most successful solo artist, Nicks had 11 top 40 hits of her own between 1981 and '91, four of which made the top 10. Because her initial hits were duets—with Tom Petty ("Stop Draggin' My Heart Around") and Don Henley ("Leather and Lace") respectively—there was little confusion

TOP ALBUMS

BELLA DONNA (Modern, '81, *1*)
THE WILD HEART (Modern, '83, *5*)
ROCK A LITTLE (Modern, '85, *12*)
THE OTHER SIDE OF THE MIRROR (Modern, '89, *10*)

Additional Top 40 Albums: 1

TOP SONGS

STOP DRAGGIN' MY HEART AROUND (with Tom Petty and the HEARTBREAKERS, MODERN, '81, *3*)
LEATHER AND LACE (with Don Henley, Modern, '81, *6*)
EDGE OF SEVENTEEN (JUST LIKE THE WHITE WINGED DOVE) (Modern, '82, *11*)
STAND BACK (Modern, '83, *5*)
IF ANYONE FALLS (Modern, '83, *14*)
TALK TO ME (Modern, '85, *4*)

Additional Top 40 Songs: 4

among the pop audience that they were hearing new Fleetwood Mac material; since both tracks had made the top 10, she was already well established by the time her first "true" solo single, "Edge of Seventeen," reached its number 11 slot in 1982.

Nicks has used many songwriting collaborators in her solo work, among the most frequent Mike Campbell of Tom Petty's Heartbreakers, friends Sandy Stewart and Rick Nowels, and Rupert Hine, who produced her 1989 album *The Other Side of the Mirror*. Additionally, she has recorded other writers' material; her best-known non-originals include "Stop Draggin' My Heart Around," by Petty and Campbell and "Talk to Me," by Chas Sanford. Her 1991 greatest hits collection, *Time Space—The Best of Stevie Nicks,* was peculiarly marred, however, by her inclusion of two new non-originals by Jon Bon Jovi and Billy Falcon ("Sometimes It's a Bitch") and Bret Michaels (of Poison) and Pat Schunk ("Love's a Hard Game to Play"), writers distinctly beneath her; it seemed a calculated commercial move and was disappointing.

In late 1993, it was announced that the release of Nicks' upcoming album *Street Angel* had been pushed back to early 1994. Produced by Glyn Johns, it was scheduled to feature guests David Crosby, Heartbreakers Campbell and Benmont Tench, Eagles co-founder Bernie Leadon, and Andy Fairweather-Low. According to her label, Nicks "wrote or cowrote" seven of the album's promised 12 tracks.

WILLIE NILE

A performer whose discography may puzzle music historians of the future, Willie Nile (b. Robert Noonan, 1949, Buffalo, New York) is a superior singer-songwriter who delivered two highly praised albums on Arista Records in the early 1980s then seemed to vanish for 10 years. He'd gone nowhere except to court, unfortunately; a legal wrangle kept him preoccupied—and out of the recording studio—for nearly three years, after which his recording career was as kaput as his public profile. It therefore came as some surprise to former fans when the singer suddenly reappeared on Columbia Records in 1991 with *Places I Have Never Been,* an album as engaging as his two of a decade earlier.

Nile, whose grandfather had been a well-known vaudeville pianist, studied philosophy and wrote

---

TOP ALBUMS

WILLIE NILE (Arista, '80)
GOLDEN DOWN (Arista, '81)
PLACES I HAVE NEVER BEEN (Columbia, '91)

TOP SONGS

IT'S ALL OVER (Arista, '80)
POOR BOY (Arista, '81)

---

poetry at the University of Buffalo during the late 1960s. Eventually adding music to the mix, he made his way down to Greenwich Village in the 1970s and began performing in small folk clubs. In 1978, a long-term stint at Kenny's Castaways built up a local audience that swiftly grew after a rave *New York Times* review by respected critic Robert Palmer; his deal with Arista Records followed.

Both 1980's *Willie Nile* and 1981's *Golden Down* came during a strange time in pop music: Critics and record companies were still preoccupied with finding "new" somebodies. A steady parade of talents such as Loudon Wainwright III, John Prine, and Steve Forbert had each already been hyped in some quarters as a "new Dylan"; similarly, a less distinguished batch of artists including D. L. Byron, Billy Falcon, and Arlyn Gale were being positioned as "new Springsteens." For better or worse, Willie Nile seemed to fit somewhere between those designations. Tracks such as "It's All Over" on his debut bore passing resemblance to the Byrds, while *Golden Down*'s opener "Poor Boy" was given a vaguely Springsteenish feel courtesy of producer Jimmy Iovine. Adding to the eclectic mix were Nile's ties to New York's punk-rock scene: earlier, he'd often played at New York's fabled CBGB's club, and his '80s band included members of both Television (bassist Fred Smith) and the Patti Smith Group (drummer Jay Dee Daugherty).

Nile won acceptance both from critics, who listened and found him very much his own man, and from other players—such as Pete Townshend, who liked Nile enough to ask him to open several of the Who's 1980 stadium dates. Both albums held respectable chart positions (peaking at numbers 145 and 158 respectively) in light of bearing no hit singles, and it seemed likely Nile might break wide open with a strong third album. He didn't—mainly because that third album came 10 years later.

During his decade away from record making, Nile continued to write and landed a job at MCA Music, resulting in songs placed with Patty Smyth ("Sue Lee" from her 1987 album *Never Enough*) and the Hooters ("Washington's Day," from 1987's *One Way Home*). In 1987, Nile flew to Oslo to give his first concert performance in five years; while there, he struck up a writing relationship with singer Eric Andersen that produced a newly recorded track on Andersen's 1991 *Stages: The Lost Album,* "Soul of My Song."

While Nile had lost the opportunity to be the "new" anything with 1991's *Places I Have Never Been,* the album was nonetheless widely praised upon its release. With a cast of guest stars including Roger McGuinn, Richard Thompson, Loudon Wainwright III, and members of the Roches and the Hooters, Nile's delayed return still sounded like the work of a fresh, sometimes inspired songwriter of great promise. One can only hope that promise is fulfilled before another decade passes.

HARRY NILSSON

One of the truly enigmatic figures in pop music, Harry Nilsson (b. Harry Edward Nelson III, June 15, 1941, New York) was a brilliant but erratic singer-songwriter who, strangely, has become more famous in retrospect for his extra-musical friendships and partying personality than for his own marvelous songs. Furthering the irony, his two biggest hits, both Grammy winners, were actually penned by other writers: "Everybody's Talkin'," the theme from *Midnight Cowboy,* was the work of Fred Neil, while "Without You," a Number One single for four weeks in 1972, was originally done by Badfinger. And with the exception of a brief one-night appearance during a 1990s Ringo Starr performance, Nilsson has steadfastly refused to perform in public—which, if nothing else, has added much to his mystery.

Moving to Los Angeles with his family as a child, Nilsson worked as a computer specialist for Security First National Bank in Van Nuys during the early 1960s, writing songs on the side. Several of them clicked, impressing no less a figure than Phil Spector: in 1965, the Ronettes recorded Nilsson's song "Paradise" and the Modern Folk Quartet his "This Could Be the Night," with Spector producing both tracks.

RCA signed the singer in 1967, and though his superb debut album, *Pandemonium Shadow Show,* didn't chart, it was a wonderful display of his songwriting ability, containing songs that had been or would soon be recorded by an impressive cast including the Monkees ("Cuddly Toy"), Yardbirds ("Ten Little Indians"), Blood, Sweat and Tears ("Without Her"), and Tom Northcott (who hit the Hot 100 in 1968 with "1941"). His follow-up album, *Aerial Ballet,* which bore liner notes from Beatles publicist Derek Taylor proclaiming Nilsson "the best contemporary soloist in the world," featured "One," a later top five hit for Three Dog Night in 1969.

Nilsson's earliest songs were true pop gems, brimming with melody and appealingly intricate. His musical expertise extended in other directions as well: he wrote the scores for Otto Preminger's 1968 film *Skidoo* and the 1969 TV show "The Courtship of Eddie's Father." At the time, he seemed like something of a renaissance man—which may explain why the Beatles invited him to London to observe the recording of their famous 1968 double set *The Beatles* (a.k.a. the White Album). From that point onward, Nilsson maintained a friendship with Beatle John Lennon that would last the remainder of the late Beatle's life; Lennon, in fact, would later produce and play on Nilsson's 1974 set *Pussy Cats.*

Nilsson's records became increasingly eclectic affairs. He devoted one album to the songs of friend Randy Newman (*Nilsson Sings Newman,* 1970), another to his songs from an animated TV special (*The Point!,* 1970), and still another to orchestrated

---

TOP ALBUMS

PANDEMONIUM SHADOW SHOW (RCA, '67)

THE POINT! (RCA, '71, *25*)

NILSSON SCHMILSSON (RCA, '71, *3*)

SON OF SCHMILSSON (RCA, '72, *12*)

TOP SONGS

EVERYBODY'S TALKIN' (RCA, '69, *6*)

I GUESS THE LORD MUST BE IN NEW YORK CITY (RCA, '69, *34*)

WITHOUT YOU (RCA, '72, *1*)

JUMP INTO THE FIRE (RCA, '72, *27*)

COCONUT (RCA, '72, *8*)

SPACEMAN (RCA, '72, *23*)

Additional Top 40 Songs: 2

versions of early classics such as "Always," "As Time Goes By," and "Makin' Whoopee" (*A Little Touch of Schmilsson in the Night,* 1973). His best seller and only top five album was 1971's *Nilsson Schmilsson,* which contained the hits "Without You," "Coconut," and "Jump into the Fire"; its follow-up, *Son of Schmilsson,* provided "Spaceman."

Nilsson's "Schmilsson" persona—as depicted on the cover of his 1971 set, the singer looking scruffy, barely awake, and unshaven—may unfortunately turn out to be the way the singer is remembered by many. The polished pop he made in the late 1960s became increasingly harder to find after the Schmilsson efforts, replaced by more spontaneous-sounding tracks that simply weren't as appealing or hookfilled. As his partying reputation with the likes of Lennon and the Who's Keith Moon grew, his records became increasingly similar, notable only for mildly humorous or pun-filled songs such as "Jesus Christ You're Tall" and "The Flying Saucer Song." Nilsson needed two things, a shave and more hits, and for the remainder of his career got neither.

After contributing the music to Robert Altman's 1980 film *Popeye,* Nilsson took an extended sabbatical from the business and suffered from several personal problems, including diabetes and, in 1993, a major heart attack. His movie production company, Hawkeye, which he'd started after his semi-retirement, was dogged by several business problems and went under; additionally, the work of a thieving longtime accountant (later sentenced to jail) resulted in his declaring personal bankruptcy. When he died of another heart attack on January 15, 1994, two-time Grammy winner Nilsson was working on his autobiography and seeking a new record deal. Sadly, it was not exactly the way "the best contempory soloist in the world" was expected to be winding down his career.

LAURA NYRO

One of the most fascinating singer-songwriters in pop, and one who has determinedly followed her muse more often that many others would dare, Laura Nyro (b. Laura Nigro, Oct. 18, 1947, Bronx, New York) continues to defy categorization. She is an archetypal pop figure to whom others are often compared, though she herself is rarely compared to anyone.

Nyro's startling originality captivated many from the start, when her 1966 Verve/Forecast album *More than a New Discovery* introduced three songs that would become ubiquitous in other artists' hands: "Stoney End," "And When I Die," and "Wedding Bell Blues," top 10 hits by Barbra Streisand, Blood, Sweat and Tears, and the Fifth Dimension respectively. Still, Nyro was much more than a simple songwriter: her soulful voice could sound happy, angry, and yearning all at once, her unique piano style playfully percussive yet at times even gospel-inspired. A New Yorker who had spent her formative years attending Manhattan's High School of Music and Art, she wrote music that seemed warm, joyful, and sophisticated, very much like the city in which she was raised.

After an unpleasant experience at 1967's famous Monterey Pop Festival—she'd been hooted offstage by the audience, reportedly ill at ease with her gypsy-style clothes and her black backing singers—Nyro spent much of her career in the studio rather than on the stage. With mogul-to-be David Geffen handling

Laura Nyro

TOP ALBUMS

MORE THAN A NEW DISCOVERY (Verve/Forecast, '66)

ELI AND THE THIRTEENTH CONFESSION (Columbia, '68)

NEW YORK TENDABERRY (Columbia, '69, 32)

CHRISTMAS AND THE BEADS OF SWEAT (Columbia, '70)

TOP SONGS

AND WHEN I DIE (Verve/Forecast, '66)

STONEY END (Verve/Forecast, '66)

WEDDING BELL BLUES (Verve/Forecast, '66)

STONED SOUL PICNIC (Columbia, '68)

ELI'S COMING (Columbia, '68)

SAVE THE COUNTRY (Columbia, '69)

her career, she signed to Columbia Records in 1968 and recorded her classic *Eli and the Thirteenth Confession.* Though it merely tweaked the bottom of the charts, peaking at number 181, it bore songs that would bolster her reputation (and pocketbook) considerably: "Stoned Soul Picnic," a top three hit and gold record for the Fifth Dimension; "Sweet Blindness," a top 20 hit, again by the Fifth Dimension; and "Eli's Coming," which Three Dog Night took to the top 10 in 1969.

Nyro's follow-up, *New York Tendaberry,* was a dazzling artistic success and probably her best album ever; it was also her most successful, peaking at number 32. An extremely dynamic album that between near-silent passages and brassy blares may have blown a fair share of speakers, *Tendaberry* was, notably, produced by Nyro herself (with Roy Halee). Given her stylistic evolution, there was one downside to be had: as her music became more intricate, less of it could be covered by hit-seeking artists—though the ever-faithful Fifth Dimension did manage to send "Save the Country" into the top 30 in 1970.

Perhaps ironically, Nyro's sole single to enter the Hot 100 was one she had not written—a version of Goffin-King's "Up on the Roof," which admittedly barely made it, peaking at number 92. Still, the album from which it came, *Christmas and the Beads of Sweat,* had solidly connected with its intended audience and reached number 51 on the album charts. Its 1971 follow-up, *Gonna Take a Miracle,* did even better and peaked at number 46, but for Nyro, that album was a significant change. Backed by LaBelle and produced by R&B powerhouse team Gamble and Huff, *Miracle* was chock-full of cover

versions of the singer's favorite oldies—such as "Jimmy Mack" and "Nowhere to Run"—and contained no new material by Nyro at all.

At this point, essentially, Nyro's career as an innovator ended. She withdrew from the music business for several years, returning sporadically with well-crafted works such as 1976's *Smile* and a long-awaited live album. She was in excellent voice—time could not take that from her—but much of her newer material seemed less distinctive than her earlier work. Further albums such as *Nested* (1978) and *Mother's Spiritual* (1984) continued the pattern, though Nyro's lyrics were now beginning to conspicuously touch on social and political issues such as ecology, animal rights, vegetarianism, and most profoundly, feminism.

Already sporadic, Nyro's recordings became less and less frequent. In 1989, *Laura Nyro Live at the Bottom Line* proved an especially welcome treat; mixing older songs such as "And When I Die" with new material like "Women of the One World" gave the latter needed contextual strength. Additionally, Nyro—who proudly told the press that she had given up smoking—was singing better than ever. Four years later, Laura Nyro returned triumphantly with *Walk the Dog & Light the Light.* Produced by Gary Katz and Nyro herself, it was her strongest work in over a decade. Though her subject matter often provoked comment—"The Descent of Luna Rose," for example, was "dedicated to my period" and borrowed its guitar riff from the Archie Bell and the Drells' hit "Tighten Up"—she sounded confident, upbeat, and, as ever, as supremely soulful as only Laura Nyro can be.

RIC OCASEK

As leader of the Cars, the first new wave band of the late 1970s to attain massive commercial success, Ric Ocasek (b. Richard Otcasek, Mar. 23, 1949, Baltimore, Maryland) had it covered on both fronts. His impeccable ear for simple pop hooks gave his earliest Cars hits "Just What I Needed" and "My Best Friend's Girl" a punch even the most backward-looking album rock or top 40 radio formats could go for; at the same time, his wavering, slightly off-center vocals and well-publicized affection for punk pioneers the Velvet Underground and Suicide gave even his most ordinary pop songs a context that trend-conscious new wave fans could confidently appreciate.

The combination worked well enough between 1978 and 1984 to take four of the band's first five albums into the top 10, and all five well past platinum; when the group finally disbanded in 1988, they had 13 top 40 hits to their credit. But as an adventurous solo artist, Ocasek's chart fame seemed inextricably tied to his visibility within the band. Though the two albums he released while the Cars still functioned (1983's *Beatitude* and 1986's *This Side of Paradise*) sold well and easily sailed into the top 40, his post-Cars product (1991's *Fireball Zone* and 1993's *Quick Change World*) failed even to dent the top 200.

While the Cars had gotten the green light from the starting gate, Baltimore-born Ocasek had been a sales non-starter once before in his career. Together with future Cars bassist Ben Orr—when the pair were known by real names Richard Otcasek and Benjamin Orzechowski—he had been a member of an obscure rock trio named Milkwood, who recorded their sole Paramount album in 1972 in Massachusetts. Now a rarity, the album showed that Ocasek's earliest influences—at least on the basis of the songs he was then writing—may have been less Velvet Underground and more Crosby, Stills and Nash or America. Consider this typical lyric, to the soft, folksy "Dream Trader": "There was a man from Maryland/They said he could not feel/He had a hard time telling what was real."

Once in the Cars, though, Ocasek's solo work seemed a creative outlet that allowed him to stretch from the creative confines in which his band increasingly found itself. *Beatitude,* produced by Ocasek himself, sounds much like a Cars album with a more pronounced Suicide influence; Ocasek had in fact produced an album by the influential synth-punk duo for Ze Records in 1980 and had presented them as special guests when he had hosted NBC's "Midnight Special" a year earlier. *This Side of Paradise* had a more commercial sheen than its predecessor—thanks largely to the production work of Tears for Fears producers Chris Hughes and Ross Cullum—and bore Ocasek's one hit single, the top 15 "Emotion in Motion."

TOP ALBUMS

BEATITUDE (Geffen, '83, 28)
THIS SIDE OF PARADISE (Geffen, '86, 31)
FIREBALL ZONE (Reprise, '91)
QUICK CHANGE WORLD (Reprise, '93)

TOP SONGS

SOMETHING TO GRAB FOR (Geffen, '83)
EMOTION IN MOTION (Geffen, '86, 15)

Many were surprised when the singer's *Fireball Zone* flopped so visibly in 1991; since the Cars had disbanded three years earlier, the album was as close as the industry could ever come to a brand new album from the band. Still, that disappointment was probably nothing compared to what Ocasek faced in 1993. After planning a multimedia event involving "an album, a book of poetry, a collection of photographs, and a performance art piece and rock concert"—all of which would be centered around his already-recorded *Negative Theater* album—Reprise pulled the plug at the last minute and scrapped more than half of it. Advance tapes of the esoteric *Negative Theater* proved the set to be Ocasek's most ambitious project ever; some of it can now be found buried on the second half of *Quick Change World,* which otherwise sounds so much like an early Cars album it borders on self-plagiarism. To add to the irony, Ocasek labeled all the new material the "right side" and whatever remained of *Negative Theater* the "left side." Whether recut at Reprise's request or not, the album's dismal showing in late 1993 could hardly have pleased Ric Ocasek or, more ominously, his label.

PHIL OCHS

Some have contended that '60s folksinger Phil Ochs (b. Dec. 19, 1940, El Paso, Texas) was less an actual protest singer than a writer who pursued the New Journalism via his gift of song. In a way that's very true: just as much of the best New Journalism has dated noticeably after two decades, much of Ochs's best-known material deals in political specifics tied so closely to the 1960s that it now seems—however sincerely delivered—sweetly naive and even quaint. In his liner notes to *There & Now: Live in Vancouver, 1968*—a previously unreleased Ochs performance issued in 1990—British folk troubadour Billy Bragg, like many before him, compared Ochs to Bob Dylan. "[Dylan] produced the most lyrical poetry of his generation, yet after 1964 he never addressed the burning issues of the

TOP ALBUMS

ALL THE NEWS THAT'S FIT TO SING (Elektra, '64)
I AIN'T MARCHIN' ANYMORE (Elektra, '65)
PLEASURES OF THE HARBOR (A&M, '67)
TAPE FROM CALIFORNIA (A&M, '68)
PHIL OCHS' GREATEST HITS (A&M, '70)

TOP SONGS

I AIN'T MARCHIN' ANYMORE (Elektra, '65)
DRAFT DODGER RAG (Elektra, '65)
THERE BUT FOR FORTUNE (Elektra, '66)
OUTSIDE OF A SMALL CIRCLE OF FRIENDS (A&M, '67)
TAPE FROM CALIFORNIA (A&M, '68)

day," Bragg wrote. "The man who wrote 'The Times They Are A-Changing' never wrote a song about the Vietnam War." Phil Ochs, on the other hand, did— but while "Like a Rolling Stone" remains a timeless classic, Ochs's "White Boots Marching in a Yellow Land," 20 years after the fact, simply sounds like a too-strident history lesson. In short, it's entirely possible today's younger music fans may now see the famous cover of Ochs's 1969 album *Rehearsals for Retirement,* which depicts a tombstone reading "Phil Ochs, Died: Chicago, Illinois, 1968," and assume it to be a literal rather than political statement.

Phil Ochs was indeed a mass of contradictions: a former student at a Virginia military school, he was fervently anti-military; a fan of John Wayne and a self-proclaimed patriot, he spent much of his early career feverishly trying to tear down his own government. Ochs, who was a journalism student at Ohio State University, departed Columbus in 1961 and headed for Greenwich Village, where he quickly established himself as a major figure in the burgeoning folk/protest movement. He signed to Elektra Records in 1964 and with *All the News That's Fit to Sing* and its 1965 follow-up, *I Ain't Marchin' Anymore,* became perhaps the leading topical protest singer of his era; indeed, his music was banned by many radio stations at the time. Referring to the latter album's title track—a song that became a true '60s anti-war anthem—Ochs revealed in his liner notes much about what drove him: "This borders between pacifism and treason, combining the best qualities of both. The fact that you won't be hearing this song over the radio is more than enough justification for the writing of it." In 1966, he released *In*

Concert, a highly regarded live album that featured two of his better-known songs in "Love Me, I'm a Liberal" and "There But for Fortune," the latter of which had been a top 50 hit for Joan Baez the previous year.

When Ochs signed to A&M in 1967, his once barely adorned music was often given full accompaniment by studio musicians. This served him well on such tracks as "Outside of a Small Circle of Friends" and "Flower Lady" from *Pleasures of the Harbor;* Ochs was a superb, often underrated melodist. He moved to California in time to record 1968's *Tape from California,* an interesting set that, between his bare-bones version of "Joe Hill" and the marvelously catchy title track, peculiarly positioned him midway between protest singer and pop star. That dichotomy continued with *Rehearsals for Retirement* and even more so on 1970's ironically titled *Phil Ochs' Greatest Hits*—which featured all-new material, a cover shot of Ochs decked out in gold lamé and clutching an electric guitar, and the (Elvis-inspired) legend "50 Phil Ochs fans can't be wrong!" on the album's backside.

Ochs's next record, the controversial, live *Gunfight at Carnegie Hall,* actually did feature him singing Elvis Presley and Buddy Holly tunes, as well as Merle Haggard's infamous "Okie from Muskogee," among other tunes. A strange aural document featuring a very rowdy audience actually booing Ochs, it was released only in Canada in 1971. In retrospect, that album was only the start of the downward spiral that overtook Ochs as the 1970s progressed. While traveling in Africa in 1973, he was attacked and nearly strangled; the assault caused permanent damage to his vocal cords. Extremely depressed thereafter, Phil Ochs released only one more single—1974's "Here's to the State of Richard Nixon" b/w "Power and Glory"—before he hanged himself at his sister's house in Far Rockaway, New York, on April 6, 1976.

SINEAD O'CONNOR

In the bizarre position of being one of the most famous female vocalists of the 1990s for reasons that have little to do with her own music, shaven-headed Sinead O'Connor (b. Dec. 8, 1967, Dublin, Ireland) has made many more enemies than friends in the course of her brief career. Particularly so in

America, where she has caused a nonstop series of well-publicized stirs by (1) refusing to allow "The Star-Spangled Banner" to be played prior to her concert performance; (2) refusing to appear as booked on NBC's "Saturday Night Live" in protest over its scheduled guest host Andrew Dice Clay; (3) refusing to participate in the Grammy Awards ceremony due to her disdain for the industry it represented—despite appearing earlier on the MTV and American Music Awards shows; (4) memorably ripping up a photograph of the Pope when she finally did appear on "Saturday Night Live"; and, finally, (5) being booed off the stage in 1992 as she began to sing at Bob Dylan's 30th Anniversary Concert at Madison Square Garden. To add to the irony, O'Connor—who is without question a skilled singer-songwriter—became famous largely on the basis of her four-week Number One single of 1992, "Nothing Compares 2 U," a song penned not by her but by Prince.

The former lead vocalist of Dublin group Ton Ton Macoute, O'Connor was signed to Ensign Records in the mid-1980s and made an appearance prior to her first album on the soundtrack to *Captive,* a film scored by U2 guitarist the Edge and Michael Berkeley. For most listeners, though, her career began with the 1988 gold album *The Lion and the Cobra,* which established her as an alternative artist with an extremely eclectic sound, sometimes including both hard rock and Irish folk. Her peculiar mix of sensuous vocals and strident yelps—a strange cross

of punk-rock queen Siouxsie Sioux and musical experimentalist Laurie Anderson—added to her inescapable image of a skin-headed waif and made O'Connor the subject of international attention. When the album entered the top 40, it appeared that she was slowly laying the groundwork for what might become a major career.

The follow-up, 1990's *I Do Not Want What I Haven't Got,* came with O'Connor's wildly emotional rendition of "Nothing Compares 2 U," written by Prince and first performed by the Family in 1985. Its accompanying video—which featured an extreme close-up of the face of the singer, crying as she sang—became a huge MTV favorite; it strongly helped the song quickly rise to Number One, where it stayed for four weeks. The album, on the chart for a full year, similarly climbed to Number One and remained there for six weeks.

Even before that staggering success, O'Connor had been deeply affected by her sudden fame, and the mostly autobiographical songs on *I Do Not Want* revealed a woman in turmoil. Songs such as "Feel So Different" and "The Emperor's New Clothes" were sometimes embarrassingly open; the latter's lyrics featured the singer musing, "He thinks I just became famous/And that's what messed me up / But he's wrong / How could I possibly know what I want/When I was only 21?" Making the work no less an emotional roller coaster was the fact that O'Connor had given birth to a son, Jake, fathered by her drummer, John Reynolds, before completing the album.

Following much of the tumult surrounding the "Star-Spangled Banner" and Pope picture brouhahas detailed above, O'Connor returned in 1992 with *Am I Not Your Girl?,* an ill-advised album of cover versions of standards and "favorites" that included Marilyn Monroe's "I Want to Be Loved by You," Billie

Sinead O'Connor

TOP ALBUMS

THE LION AND THE COBRA (Chrysalis, '88, 36)
I DO NOT WANT WHAT I HAVEN'T GOT
(Ensign, '90, 1)
AM I NOT YOUR GIRL? (Ensign, '92, 27)

TOP SONGS

MANDINKA (Chrysalis, '88)
NOTHING COMPARES 2 U (Ensign, '90, 1)
EMPEROR'S NEW CLOTHES (Ensign, '90)

Holiday's "Gloomy Sunday," and *Evita*'s "Don't Cry for Me Argentina." The album peaked quickly at number 29 but stayed on the chart for an extremely brief nine weeks. And while her previous album had been greatly aided by her video version of "Nothing Compares 2 U," one suspects her video to this album's first single, "Success Has Made a Failure of Our Home," didn't help matters; it prominently featured pictures of torture victims supplied courtesy of Amnesty International. Additionally hampering her career: having already claimed to be a victim of child abuse, O'Connor gave interviews at the time mostly devoted to discussions of that topic and her personal politics, rather than her own music. "People are always trying to make me out a bad girl," she told *Billboard*'s Timothy White in 1992, "and I'm trying to say I'm not. I'm a nice girl, and I have a heart."

Sinead O'Connor now has the eyes of the world watching her every move. Whether she will ultimately be judged as an exceptionally talented, outspoken artist or as an exceptionally visible flash in the pan remains to be seen.

DANNY O'KEEFE

Danny O'Keefe's career might seem inconsequential to those who gauge success purely by record sales and chart positions; the singer-songwriter-guitarist's sole brush with the top 10 came once, in 1972, when his "Good Time Charlie's Got the Blues" reached the number nine slot. But consider who recorded their own versions of the song: Elvis Presley, Willie Nelson, Leon Russell, Waylon Jennings, Jerry Lee Lewis, and Charlie Rich.

And consider that two of the hottest artists of the 1970s—Linda Ronstadt and the Eagles—took time out to essentially become O'Keefe's backing band on his 1975 album *So Long Harry Truman*. And, finally, consider that the thematic centerpiece of Jackson Browne's 1978 platinum-selling *Late for the Sky* was O'Keefe's memorable ode to the musician's dreary life, "The Road." With that kind of talent, and those kinds of friends, who could be blamed for thinking O'Keefe just another underachiever? Listen to any of O'Keefe's uniformly fine albums, though, and you'll suspect the only underachievers were at the promotion departments of his various record labels.

One thing's for certain: O'Keefe can't say he never had the chance. His first album, 1966's *Introducing Danny O'Keefe* on Panorama, was actually a collection of demos the Spokane-born singer had made in Seattle that he'd never intended to be released to the general public. "To have sued would have taken a great deal of time and a great deal of money," O'Keefe now wearily remembers. Those

Danny O'Keefe

TOP ALBUMS

O'KEEFE (Signpost, '72)
BREEZY STORIES (Atlantic, '73)
SO LONG HARRY TRUMAN (Atlantic, '75)
AMERICAN ROULETTE (Warner Bros. '77)
GLOBAL BLUES (Warner Bros. '78)

TOP SONGS

GOOD TIME CHARLIE'S GOT THE BLUES
   (Signpost, '72, 9)
THE ROAD (Signpost, '72)
MAGDELENA (Atlantic, '73)
ANGEL SPREAD YOUR WINGS (Atlantic, '72)

early recordings continue to be reissued to this day—most recently as *The Seattle Tapes,* a two-volume set—and, as always, O'Keefe earns not a penny from their sale.

Next, he was a rock and roll singer in a charmingly '60s-ish band called Calliope, whose sole album, *Steamed,* was released by Buddah in 1968. Buried amid the mostly nonadventurous covers ("California Dreaming," "Like a Rolling Stone," "Hound Dog," and "Nadine") were two early O'Keefe originals, "Rainmaker's Daughter" and the quaintly psychedelic album closer, "Atlas" (which O'Keefe would revive 11 years later on his solo album *The Global Blues*). "I was hired to sing by the man that formed that band," he now recalls, "but I was never satisfied with the direction it was pursuing—a poor man's version of the Vanilla Fudge."

When stardom didn't beckon, O'Keefe went solo, signing to Atlantic Records' Cotillion subsidiary and releasing a 1970 self-titled album that went virtually unnoticed. It contained early versions of both "Charlie," which would become a hit two years later when redone for his next album, and "Steel Guitar," which he'd recut with the Eagles and David Lindley on *Harry Truman.* Featuring the hit version of "Charlie" and the original "The Road," 1972's *O'Keefe* was a marked step up both in production (thanks to Arif Mardin) and lyrical sophistication. And with "Louie the Hook vs. the Preacher," O'Keefe's stylistic device of populating his songs with memorable characters became more pronounced: Reverend Stone, Good Time Charlie, Magdelena, Angel, Mad Ruth, and Rainbow Girl were just part of his large, colorful cast.

What should have clinched O'Keefe's place in music history was 1973's *Breezy Stories,* his best album ever, again immaculately produced by Mardin and featuring the cream of New York's sessionmen playing O'Keefe's finest material yet. But what should have happened didn't; the record was a comparative stiff (though Atlantic saw fit to reissue it on compact disc in 1992, with "The Road" and "Charlie" as extra bonus tracks). None of O'Keefe's records ever reached the upper reaches of the Top Pop Albums chart, though most were accorded the respect they deserved by the press. He jumped to Warner Bros. with 1977's *American Roulette,* and finished up his major label run there with the prescient *Global Blues.* O'Keefe then spent time out on the same road he'd always sung about, finally quietly releasing *The Day to Day* on a small Sausalito, California–based label in 1984. Five years later, three new tracks were added, and it was reissued by the independent Chameleon Music Group.

O'Keefe now lives on an island in the Northwest and hasn't made a record since. "There's basically been no [label] interest, as far as I can tell," he says resignedly. These days he spends his time writing and co-writing songs both at home and in Nashville or Los Angeles, where, he adds, he regularly goes "a couple of times a year."

ROY ORBISON

Dubbed "the greatest singer in the world" by Elvis Presley, Roy Orbison (b. Roy Kelton Orbison, Apr. 23, 1936, Vernon, Texas) was inducted into the Rock and Roll Hall of Fame in 1987 by Bruce Springsteen. "In 1975," the Jersey-born singer announced from the podium, "when I went into the studio to make *Born to Run,* I wanted to make a record with words like Bob Dylan that sounded like Phil Spector, but most of all I wanted to sing like Roy Orbison." That was the sort of praise the perpetually sunglassed Orbison received while still alive; the universal accolades following his unexpected death by heart attack in 1988 made the earlier plaudits seem begrudging in comparison. With a career spanning over three decades and including such classic self-penned singles as "Only the Lonely (Know How I Feel)," "Crying," "Running Scared," "It's Over" and "Oh, Pretty Woman," Roy Orbison remains one of pop music's true giants.

Growing up in Wink, in the heart of the Texas oil region, Orbison played and sang in several local bands, including his first, the Wink Westerners, and the better-known Teen Kings. The latter band had recorded a regional single, "Ooby Dooby," that Orbison sent to Sun Records founder Sam Phillips at the urging of Sun artist Johnny Cash; Phillips liked it, Orbison drove to Memphis to recut it, and by June 1956, Sun Records had released its first Roy Orbison single. It was not an altogether happy time for Orbison; now renowned for his strength as a balladeer, his early Sun singles such as "Sweet and Easy to Love," "Chicken Hearted," and "Rock House" were mostly upbeat rockers, and only "Ooby Dooby" had made much of a chart impression. He left the label in 1957 and signed to music publishers Acuff-Rose, convinced his true calling was as a songwriter—and indeed, his song "Claudette" was a top 30 hit for the Everly Brothers in 1958. Following a brief stint at RCA, where he recorded two singles produced by Chet Atkins, the singer soon found his niche at the Washington, D.C.–based Monument Records label.

Orbison began collaborating with fellow Texas songwriter Joe Melson at the time of his Monument deal; beginning with "Uptown," one of the first Nashville sessions to incorporate a string section, the pair began a long, extremely productive writing partnership. Of Orbison's first 15 top 40 hits, six were were penned by the Orbison-Melson team, including "Only the Lonely"—regarded by many as the starting point of the singer's classic ballad sound—and the top 10 hits "Blue Angel," "Running Scared," "Crying," and "Blue Bayou." Additionally, Orbison scored as sole author of his 1963 number seven single "In Dreams" as well as the hits "Leah," "Working for the Man," and "Falling."

A late-1963 falling out between Orbison and Melson—who was attempting to establish himself as a solo artist on Hickory Records at the time—soon split the pair for several years, though by 1967 they would again work together periodically.

TOP ALBUMS

CRYING (Monument, '62, 21)
IN DREAMS (Monument, '63, 35)
MYSTERY GIRL (Virgin, '89, 5)

Additional Top 40 Albums: 2

TOP SONGS

ONLY THE LONELY (KNOW HOW I FEEL) (Monument, '60, 2)
BLUE ANGEL (Monument, '60, 9)
RUNNING SCARED (Monument, '61, 1)
CRYING (Monument, '61, 2)
IN DREAMS (Monument, '63, 7)
OH, PRETTY WOMAN (Monument, '64, 1)
YOU GOT IT (Virgin, '89, 9)

Additional Top 40 Songs: 16

With new songwriting partner Bill Dees, another Texan, Orbison first crafted his extraordinary top 10 hit "It's Over" then produced the biggest-selling single of his life, 1964's "Oh, Pretty Woman." The latter track, estimated to have sold over seven million copies in the year of its release alone, held the Number One slot for three weeks—and showed Orbison capable of holding his own against powerful British Invasion bands such as the Animals and Manfred Mann, who claimed respective Number One hits with "House of the Rising Sun" and "Do Wah Diddy" before and after Orbison's smash.

Whether Orbison truly could hold his own against such powerhouse talents as the Beatles and the Rolling Stones—not to mention the enormous press attention these new bands were getting—became a major issue soon after "Oh, Pretty Woman." Offered an extremely lucrative deal with MGM Records that dangled the potential of Elvis-style movie stardom—and, indeed, he did star in MGM's forgettable 1968 film *The Fastest Guitar Alive*—Orbison signed on and watched his career falter dramatically after only three more middling hits. On a personal level, there was much more disturbing trouble as well: in the midst of a reconciliation with his ex-wife Claudette, she was killed in a motorcycle accident with Orbison in 1966; two years later, two of his sons were tragically killed in a housefire.

Orbison eventually remarried, rebounded, and turned to country music, recording for Mercury and Asylum in the 1970s. His reputation began to soar again via hit covers of his earlier work by Linda Ronstadt (1977's top five "Blue Bayou") and Don McLean (1981's top five "Crying"). He won a Grammy for his 1980 duet with Emmylou Harris—"That Loving You Feeling Again" from the soundtrack to *Roadie*—and saw his 1963 hit "In Dreams" play a central role in director David Lynch's 1986 film *Blue Velvet*. Orbison quickly was moving back into musical prominence: In 1986, he signed to Virgin Records and released *In Dreams: The Greatest Hits*, a rerecorded double set of his best-known songs; in 1987, he was inducted into the Rock and Roll Hall of Fame; the next year, he was a member of the Traveling Wilburys alongside Bob Dylan, George Harrison, Tom Petty, and Jeff Lynne. He recorded a duet version of "Crying" with singer k.d. lang that earned a 1989 Grammy, and was the subject of the superb 1988 Cinemax TV special "Roy Orbison and Friends: A Black and White Night," featuring guest stars Bruce Springsteen, Tom Waits, Elvis Costello, U2's Bono, and T-Bone Burnett, among others.

Following Orbison's death in 1988, his 1989 album *Mystery Girl* shot to the top five, went platinum, and became the biggest-selling album of his career. Included on the set was Orbison's final hit, the top 10 "You Got It," written by the singer with fellow Wilburys Petty and Lynne. Three years later, Virgin released *King of Hearts,* a collection of previously unissued and posthumously completed tracks. While the world and a very impressive cast of musical friends continued to mourn the loss of one of pop music's greatest performers, there was at least some consolation to be had: Roy Orbison departed at a time when his vast talent was conspicuously receiving the recognition it had long been due.

GILBERT O'SULLIVAN

At a time when virtually every pop performer looked as if a stint in the fictional group Spinal Tap was in their near future, clean-cut Gilbert O'Sullivan (b. Raymond O'Sullivan, Dec. 1, 1946, Waterford, Ireland), wearing a letter sweater, his hair barely covering his ears, was one of the more curious fashion aberrations of the early 1970s. Musically, however, he fit right in: his massive hit "Alone Again (Naturally)" topped the charts for a total of six weeks during the summer of 1972, its almost gleefully morose lyric of personal abandonment suitably signalling the start of the Me Decade. O'Sullivan's voice seemed a cross between Paul McCartney's and that of former Herman's Hermit Peter Noone; his songs seemed to borrow from the same English

music hall tradition from which British bands such as the Kinks and Herman's Hermits had lovingly borrowed for years.

Ironically, the man who signed and managed O'Sullivan and helped cultivate his image was producer Gordon Mills, who managed smooth ladies'-man performers Tom Jones and Engelbert Humperdinck—again, pop stars whose images were slightly out of sync with the era's pop-rock norm, but who were no less famous for it.

O'Sullivan—who while in Swindon Art School had shared a band with future Supertramp member Richard Davies—had previously met little success as a singles artist at two other labels. But with Mills's MAM label backing him, his career took off rapidly. Though he was more popular in England, where he scored 15 top 50 hits over a 10-year span, O'Sullivan hit the U.S. quickly in one very hot streak. Within 16 months, he managed three top 10 hits ("Alone Again," "Clair," and "Get Down") and two others in the top 30. But then it was over as quickly as it had started; the singer never had another American hit.

O'Sullivan had more than a fair share of legal troubles, which put a decided crimp in his career. By the late 1970s, a feud with manager Mills over unpaid royalties had escalated into a full-blown, protracted lawsuit. It was resolved by 1985, at which point the singer recovered the rights to all his material and over $3 million in back royalties. Additionally, in the early 1990s, O'Sullivan instigated a lawsuit over the unauthorized use of "Alone Again (Naturally)" on "Alone Again," a track from rapper Biz Markie's 1991 album *I Need a Haircut.* O'Sullivan won, resulting in Warner Bros. taking the unusual step of recalling the album from retailers and reissuing it without the offending track. Markie's 1993 follow-up album was titled, appropriately, *All Samples Cleared!*

Though O'Sullivan still commands a loyal following internationally—especially in Japan—his luster has faded conspicuously in America. As of this writing, the only U.S. title available by the singer—who did, after all, have three charting albums in the 1970s —is a hits compilation issued by Rhino Records in 1991.

TOP ALBUMS

GILBERT O' SULLIVAN—HIMSELF (MAM, '72, 9)
BACK TO FRONT (MAM, '73)
I'M A WRITER, NOT A FIGHTER (MAM, '73)

TOP SONGS

ALONE AGAIN (NATURALLY) (MAM, '72, 1)
CLAIR (MAM, '72, 2)
OUT OF THE QUESTION (MAM, '73, 17)
GET DOWN (MAM, '73, 7)
OOH BABY (MAM, '73, 25)

GRAHAM PARKER

The career of Graham Parker (b. Nov. 18, 1950, East London) has seemed a series of what-ifs and if-onlys for so long that his actual accomplishments as a singer-songwriter are often overlooked. The sometimes brilliant British artist's masterful 1976 debut, *Howlin' Wind,* arrived as a surprisingly mature, fully-formed musical statement that, unusually, instantly established him as a major artist who could fairly withstand comparison to his very obvious influences. That those influences (Bob Dylan, American rhythm and blues, and the unique rhythm and horn sections of Memphis's Stax label) almost exactly coincided with those of Van Morrison was all for the better to many critics, who have deified that Irish singer and historically most enjoyed American music when it is fed back to them in pieces by foreign musicians.

That said, Graham Parker has been unusually proficient working within his chosen musical confines—and remarkably consistent in his songwriting. Parker's adopted persona—the classic Angry Young Man figure—was evident from the start on *Howlin' Wind, Heat Treatment* (1977), and to some extent *Stick to Me* (1978), and it fit snugly with the attitudes of the inferior musicians playing the punk rock that was developing in Britain at the same time. Unlike many of those artists, however, Parker knew precisely what he was railing against: in dull moments, social injustices; but very often, when he was at his peak, personal injustices. Like Dylan, he wrote some songs we could simply admire and others, better ones, that we could deeply relate to. The difference came when the songs were being directly addressed to another party—a friend, a lover, an ex-lover, a hated acquaintance—instead of the world at large.

Of course, Graham Parker is no Bob Dylan; most of his songs are neither social or personal statements. They're just songs, in the same way that Van Morrison's "Domino," "Blue Money," and "Wild Night" were just songs, directed mainly at a paying audi-

Graham Parker

TOP ALBUMS

HOWLIN' WIND (Mercury, '77)
HEAT TREATMENT (Mercury, '77)
SQUEEZING OUT SPARKS
 (Arista, '79, *40*)
THE UP ESCALATOR (Arista, '80, *40*)
THE MONA LISA'S SISTER (RCA, '88)
BURNING QUESTIONS (Capitol, '92)

TOP SONGS

WHITE HONEY (Mercury, '77)
YOU CAN'T BE TOO STRONG
 (Arista, '79)
LIFE GETS BETTER (Arista, '83)
WAKE UP (NEXT TO YOU)
 (Elektra, '85, *39*)

ence. Only with Parker's *Squeezing Out Sparks* (1979), which surprisingly remains the biggest-selling record of his career, did he venture into deeper, more emotionally compelling turf. The much-discussed highlight of that album, "You Can't Be Too Strong," is unusual on several levels: it's about an abortion, it's directed to a woman who has had an abortion, and it studiously avoids taking a position on the matter, focusing instead on the harrowing range of emotions involved. Which is exactly why it's a nearly perfect song.

Parker didn't return to that level of songwriting for several years. Following *Sparks,* he was paired with one "hot" producer after another, apparently in search of that one hit record that would take him to the very top. As it was, he was doing surprisingly well: between 1980's *The Up Escalator* and 1985's *Steady Nerves,* his albums consistently charted in the top 60, with the latter album actually sending one song ("Wake Up [Next to You]") into the bottom of the top 40. Parker's history of jumping from one record label to another has been documented to the point of exhaustion; the very real turning point for him, however, may have been when he signed to Atlantic and found himself at odds with their plan to stick him in the studio with another hotshot producer. He left without releasing an album on the label and went on to issue some of the best music of his career, all relatively unadorned, on RCA, starting with 1987's *The Mona Lisa's Sister.*

What exactly has changed about Parker's music since 1987 is difficult to pinpoint; it may simply be that he's matured as a songwriter, or realized that in an industry dominated by MTV's towering presence, a man in his mid-40s isn't likely to explode into superstardom anytime soon. More likely, he's followed the example of many great artists before him and chosen to ignore incidentals like chart positions, radio play, and fickle fan bases, to more fully focus on his chosen craft. Referring to his 1985 hit "Wake Up (Next To You)" Parker once told writer Jimmy Guterman, "This is everything I wanted to write, nothing about worrying what Graham Parker is supposed to write about. Smokey Robinson could have written this. My aim is to write something like 'Just My Imagination' or 'Being with You.' That's perfect songwriting." That Graham Parker still has a goal, two full decades into his career, best explains why he remains a vital artist.

VAN DYKE PARKS

Van Dyke Parks (b. 1943, Hattiesburg, Mississippi) may be one of the most peculiar musical talents in popular music. Since 1968, he has released only five albums, most the subject of enormous critical praise, only two of which sound at all similar. He has collaborated with many of the most talented musicians in music—most notably Brian Wilson in the mid-'60s, when the famous Beach Boy was at his artistic peak—and played keyboards on some of rock music's most highly regarded albums. In 1971, he produced a Trinidadian steel

TOP ALBUMS
....

SONG CYCLE (Warner Bros., '68)
DISCOVER AMERICA (Warner Bros., '72)
THE CLANG OF THE YANKEE REAPER
   (Warner Bros., '75)
JUMP! (Warner Bros., '84)
TOKYO ROSE (Warner Bros., '89)

TOP SONGS
....

PALM DESERT (Warner Bros., '68)
THE ALL GOLDEN (Warner Bros., '68)

drum album for Warner Bros. Records, where he held a position as audio/visual vice president; the same label remains the only company ever to release one of his albums. He has scored several films, including *Goin' South, Popeye,* and *The Two Jakes.* He is one of very few pop performers ever seriously to be termed a genius by respected writers who disdain that word's casual use. And he has very rarely written songs that are capable of being hummed.

Parks, who was raised in Lake Charles, Louisiana, attended the Columbus Boychoir School in Princeton, New Jersey, in the early 1950s. He was a child actor, appearing in several early New York television productions, and played the role of Andrew Bonino on the 1953 TV series "Bonino." After attending Carnegie Tech, Parks eventually settled in Los Angeles, where he played on several recordings produced by Terry Melcher, who introduced him to Beach Boy Wilson in 1965. Wilson, then recording the Beach Boys' classic 1966 album *Pet Sounds,* chose Parks as his lyrical collaborator for its planned follow-up, *Smile;* when that well-documented project collapsed (for many reasons, including other Beach Boys' reactions to Parks's complex lyrics), their jointly composed songs would be released piecemeal over several albums. Among the best known were "Heroes and Villains" (a 1967 top 20 hit) and "Surf's Up," which finally saw release on the 1971 album of the same name (and which bore lyrics such as "Columnated ruins domino," which particularly aroused the wrath of Beach Boy singer Mike Love).

Parks's own recording career began shortly after he landed a songwriting deal at Warner Bros., where he would produce hits for both Harper's Bizarre and the Mojo Men before recording his own master-work, 1968's *Song Cycle*. A very arty project that involved aural montage, extremely sophisticated, pun-filled lyrics, and odd covers of Randy Newman's "Vine Street" and Donovan's "Colours," the album sold so poorly that Warner Bros. actually advertised the fact in the pop press and offered the album for next to nothing in a bizarre trade-in mail-order offer.

Parks then became a staff producer at Warner Bros., where he headed up label debuts by some of the company's most prestigious artists, including Randy Newman and Ry Cooder. Additionally, he played keyboards on such albums as the Beau Brummels' *Triangle,* Judy Collins's *Who Knows Where the Time Goes,* Tim Buckley's debut, Biff Rose's *Children of Light,* and Phil Ochs's *Tape from California* and *Greatest Hits* (the latter of which he produced in 1970).

In 1971, Parks produced a highly unusual album by the Esso Trinidad Steel Band (though the album listed as producer Warner Bros. head Mo Ostin). That same sound dominated most of Parks's second solo album, 1972's *Discover America.* As peculiar a listening experience as was *Song Cycle*, it featured material by Little Feat, Allen Toussaint, and John Philip Sousa among its deliberately exotic-sounding originals—and, like its predecessor, sold diddly. Parks returned in 1975 with *The Clang of the Yankee Reaper,* a set of eclectic covers he said he'd recorded "with nothing in mind but my love for Caribbean music." Unfortunately for him, record-buying America did not share that same love, and the album quickly stiffed.

When Parks returned nine years later with *Jump!,* it became clear the singer was unlikely ever to record an album lacking some sort of overriding theme. In the case of *Jump!,* that theme was the mythical/historical figure Uncle Remus. Sounding much like a stage musical, the album featured 11 new songs by Parks based on the tales of Brer Rabbit; lyrics were mostly supplied by Martin Kibbee, a friend of Parks who had played both in the Fraternity of Man and in an early group with Little Feat guitarist Lowell George. In 1989, Parks took on still another unusual theme with *Tokyo Rose;* billed as "a musical without a stage," the album examined the relationship between Japan and America. "What came out of this record," Parks said at the time, "which was really a process of discovery, was a concern for the future of my own country. I felt it was time to put a rein on

Van Dyke Parks

the landlords-in-absentia who don't care what happens to the roofs over our heads that they own."

Though Parks's records, like his viewpoints, are never less than fascinating, their ambition has too frequently overwhelmed them. He appears to be considered a treasure by Warner Bros., who have stuck with the artist for over 25 years—and who, in fact, proudly reissued all of his long-deleted albums on compact disc in 1990. The irony—and one Parks has no doubt come to expect—was the brief amount of time they stayed in print before being deleted from the catalog once more.

GRAM PARSONS

Widely credited as the founding father of country rock, the late Gram Parsons (b. Ingram Cecil Conner, Nov. 5, 1946, Winter Haven, Florida) has grown in stature since his 1973 death of an alleged drug overdose at the age of 26. Like other major talents who died in their creative prime and left no glaring evidence of later artistic decline, Parsons produced a small but vital body of work to which countless fans, old and new, continually return—whether seeking inspiration from or taking comfort in the heartfelt richness of his music. From his days with the obscure International Submarine Band, through his brief time with the Byrds and trailblazing work with the Flying Burrito Brothers, to his tragically abbreviated solo career, Gram Parsons made music that mattered then and may matter even more today.

Brought up in an extremely wealthy southern household—his grandfather had made his fortune in citrus groves and cattle—Parsons grew up knowing his trust fund would support him for the remainder of his life. He felt a passion for music while young and played in early bands such as the Legends (with later pop stars Jim "Spiders and Snakes" Stafford and Kent "Lobo" Lavoie) and folk group the Shilos (whose 1963–65 recordings were issued by Sierra Records in 1979). Enrolling briefly in Harvard as a divinity student, Parsons formed the International Submarine Band in 1966, made two unsuccessful singles, and by 1967 moved to Los Angeles, where his group recorded its one and only album.

The extremely rare *Safe at Home,* released on Lee Hazlewood's LHI Records, remains one of the most collectible items in pop. Bearing liner note testimonials from Glen Campbell, Duane Eddy, and Don Everly, the album contains a back-cover blurb by Hazlewood himself that could not have been more accurate. "The first sounds of contemporary Country Music," wrote Hazlewood. "Unique in concept —interesting in performance—the BEGINNING." Featuring four Parsons originals including "Blue Eyes" and "Luxury Liner" along with covers of

songs by Johnny Cash and Merle Haggard, the album was indeed the beginning of an historic merger of country music and post-'50s rock and roll.

When the group unofficially dissolved, Parsons played in a loose-knit group of L.A. musicians that informally dubbed themselves the Flying Burrito Brothers. By February 1968, he was invited to join the Byrds. He left his mark on the group—and on pop in general—with that year's *Sweetheart of the Rodeo* album, which featured two Parsons songs, "One Hundred Years from Now" and his later signature tune (co-written with the Submarine Band's Bob Buccanan), "Hickory Wind." Much more widely heard than *Safe at Home, Sweetheart* is now generally regarded as the album that spawned the

---

TOP ALBUMS

SAFE AT HOME (with the International Submarine Band, LHI, '67)
SWEETHEART OF THE RODEO (with the Byrds, Columbia, '68)
THE GILDED PALACE OF SIN (with the Flying Burrito Brothers, A&M, '69)
GP (Reprise, '73)
GRIEVOUS ANGEL (with Emmylou Harris, Reprise, '74)
GRAM PARSONS AND THE FALLEN ANGELS—LIVE 1973 (Sierra, '82)

TOP SONGS

HOT BURRITO #1 (with the Flying Burrito Brothers, A&M, '69)
HOT BURRITO #2 (with the Flying Burrito Brothers, A&M, '69)
SHE (Reprise, '73)
BRASS BUTTONS (Reprise, '74)

---

genre of country rock. Parsons remained with the Byrds for only a few months—long enough, in fact, for the group to make its historic appearance onstage at Nashville's Grand Ole Opry—before departing in opposition to the group's plan to perform in South Africa. Asked years later about his influence on the group's music, Parsons concisely commented, "I suppose I convinced the Byrds that they should be doing country music instead of trying to write their own Bob Dylan material. I guess Chris [Hillman, founding Byrd member] had been trying to say something like that all along."

Parsons left and formalized the Flying Burrito Brothers, joined only months later by disgruntled Byrd Chris Hillman. Aiming to play what he called "Cosmic American Music," Parsons recorded two albums with the Burritos before embarking on a solo career. The best, 1969's *The Gilded Palace of Sin,* boasted some of Parsons' finest songs, including "Hot Burrito #1" and "Hot Burrito #2" (both co-written with Burrito bassist Chris Ethridge) and "Sin City" (co-written with Hillman); its follow-up, *Burrito Deluxe,* emerged in 1970 shortly after Parsons left the group following a motorcycle accident. Parsons then spent some time in England with the Rolling Stones, whose classic track "Wild Horses" bears a noticeable Parsons influence, and reportedly sings uncredited backing vocals on "Sweet Virginia" from 1972's *Exile on Main Street.*

As influential a figure as Parsons may be, there are only three full solo albums to his credit: 1973's *GP,* which introduced to many the vocals of Emmylou Harris and featured Elvis Presley's backing band; 1974's posthumous *Grievous Angel,* again with Harris, and a new version of "Hickory Wind"; and *Gram Parsons and the Fallen Angels—Live 1973,* a superb live set taken from a radio broadcast and issued by Sierra Records in 1982. Still, between the three albums, there are 11 new Parsons songs to be heard, the best of which include "Brass Buttons," "She" (co-written with the Burritos' Ethridge), "$1000 Wedding," and "A Song for You."

Parsons' unexpected demise in California's Joshua Tree National Monument on September 19, 1973, was marked by much mystery. The cause of his death has variously been attributed to massive drug abuse and heart failure; further, his road manager and a friend stole his coffin on its way to burial in New Orleans and burned it in the desert—later claiming Parsons had, against his family's wishes, wished to be cremated.

In the course of his recording career, Gram Parsons was never involved in any best-selling album: his highest charting appearance came via the Byrds' *Sweetheart of the Rodeo,* which peaked at number 77; his Burritos albums rose no higher than number 164; and of his solo albums, only *Grievous Angel* charted—at number 195, for one week. Nonetheless, his influence has touched a wide variety of pop artists since the 1970s and continues to be felt strongly in the 1990s. In late 1993, Rhino Records issued *Conmemorativo: A Tribute to Gram Parsons,* which featured alternative artists such as the Mekons, Steve Wynn, Uncle Tupelo, and Bob Mould and Vic Chesnutt singing Parsons songs from as far back as 1965. On it, to his eternal credit, Gram Parsons' best songs sound both surprisingly contemporary and as old as the hills—which is, of course, merely another way of saying timeless.

TOM PAXTON

Unlike many of the major singer-songwriters to emerge from the Greenwich Village folk scene of the early 1960s, Tom Paxton (b. Oct. 31, 1937, Chicago) has remained perfectly content with his chosen genre. Some may call him a folksinger who simply never crossed over, but that's inaccurate. His marvelous repertoire of original songs—among them "The Last Thing on My Mind," "Ramblin' Boy," "Whose Garden Was This," and "Wasn't That a Party"—includes pop standards that have been covered by such diverse artists as John Denver, Jimmie Gilmer and the Fireballs, Judy Collins, British pop group the Move, the Irish Rovers, and Peter, Paul and Mary.

For many, though, Paxton, with his everpresent cap and moustache, remains one of the most prominent so-called "protest singers" of the 1960s. His mixture of humor and deep seriousness were amply displayed on the memorable "Talking Vietnam Pot-Luck Blues"; his biting social commentaries "Mr. Blue" (covered in memorably melodramatic style by '60s rockers Clear Light) and the anti-war "Jimmy Newman," though clearly tied to the 1960s, remain vivid listening experiences two decades later. In liner notes he penned for a 1988 compilation, Paxton noted that he'd written the latter track in the late '60s immediately after the Tet Offensive. "We were all beginning to see that this thing would go on forever if people didn't force it to stop," he noted. "I did many songs during and about the war, but I think this one was the best."

TOP ALBUMS

RAMBLIN' BOY (Elektra, '65)
OUTWARD BOUND (Elektra, '66)
THE THINGS I NOTICE NOW (Elektra, '69)
THE COMPLEAT TOM PAXTON (Elektra, '71)
HOW COME THE SUN (Reprise, '71)

TOP SONGS

I CAN'T HELP BUT WONDER WHERE I'M BOUND (Elektra, '65)
THE LAST THING ON MY MIND (Elektra, '65)
GOIN' TO THE ZOO (Elektra, '65)
TALKIN' VIETNAM POT-LUCK BLUES (Elektra, '71)

Tom Paxton

witty titles such as 1986's *One Million Lawyers ...and Other Disasters.* Paxton has a large international following—particularly in Great Britain, where he and his family lived for three years in the early 1970s—and a uniformly loyal one as well. Again unlike many of his early '60s contemporaries, Tom Paxton continues to be treated with the respect someone of his songwriting stature certainly deserves.

TOM PETTY

While the press treated him as a "power pop"–inspired new wave artist at the time of his group's 1976 debut album, Tom Petty (b. Oct. 20, 1953, Gainesville, Florida) and his band the Heartbreakers were playing pure rock and roll in the very finest American tradition. From the opening chords of "Rockin' Around (With You)," Petty and his much-acclaimed band sounded "new wave" only in the sense that they paid no heed to the overblown, pompous rock styles that mid-'70s bands such as Styx, Journey, and Kansas would lucratively explore; instead, they played rock that borrowed from the Beatles, Byrds, and Rolling Stones but still sounded fresh and contemporary. More than a few enthused critics noted that the album's closing track, "American Girl," sounded like some Great Lost Byrds Track; most were thrilled when Petty then received the official seal of approval from the Byrds' own Roger McGuinn, who covered the song on his 1977 *Thunderbyrd* album and subsequently became Petty's good friend. Since then, the Florida-born singer has released a string of gold and platinum records and made many more friends among rock's royalty—including his fellow Traveling Wilburys Bob Dylan, George Harrison, Jeff Lynne, and the late Roy Orbison.

Paxton, who studied drama at the University of Oklahoma, has said his earliest musical influences included Woody Guthrie, Oscar Brand, the Weavers, and Burl Ives. "I remember getting an extended-play record of Burl Ives singing 'The Fox Went Out on a Chilly Night' and 'The Streets of Laredo,' and I just loved it," he told writer Sherwood Ross in 1982. "I still love those songs." Fittingly, just as Ives's music was greatly appreciated by young children, Paxton himself has enjoyed considerable success with that same audience via such tunes as "Goin' to the Zoo" (covered by Peter, Paul and Mary), "Jennifer's Rabbit," and "The Marvellous Toy."

Paxton has been a prolific recording artist, and his work has appeared on many labels. The stretch of records he made for Elektra—from 1965's *Ramblin' Boy* through 1971's *The Compleat Tom Paxton*—remains his most memorable, though his Reprise debut, *How Come the Sun*, was his highest-charting effort, reaching number 120 in late 1971. Since then, Paxton albums have appeared on the Private Stock, Vanguard, Flying Fish, and Mountain Railroad labels, typically bearing characteristically

Petty grew up playing music in the university town of Gainesville, Florida, where he sang alongside future Heartbreakers Mike Campbell and Benmont Tench in a popular local band called Mudcrutch. In search of fame, the band moved to Los Angeles in the early 1970s but soon fell into disarray; when Petty himself got a deal with Leon Russell's Shelter Records label, Campbell, Tench, and L.A. musicians Stan Lynch and Ron Blair joined him in 1975 as the Heartbreakers. Though their 1976 debut album, *Tom Petty & the Heartbreakers,* was well received by the press—who at the time were drooling for something new and exciting in a world of side-long Yes "songs" on albums like *Tales of Topographic Oceans*—it took a full year's time and a flood of U.K. press raves to finally send the album into the charts, where it would climb to number 55 and eventually go gold, helped by the top 40 success of "Breakdown."

Its follow-up, *You're Gonna Get It!*, lacked songs with the distinct impact of "Breakdown" and "American Girl," but the mid-level success of the singles "I Need to Know" and "Listen to Her Heart" and the group's growing appeal sent the album into the top 30. What next followed was one of the many

---

TOP ALBUMS

DAMN THE TORPEDOES (with the Heartbreakers, Backstreet, '79, 2)
HARD PROMISES (with the Heartbreakers, Backstreet, '81, 5)
LONG AFTER DARK (with the Heartbreakers, Backstreet, '82, 9)
SOUTHERN ACCENTS (with the Heartbreakers, MCA, '85, 7)
FULL MOON FEVER (MCA, '89, 3)

Additional Top 40 Albums: 4

TOP SONGS

DON'T DO ME LIKE THAT (with the Heartbreakers, Backstreet, '79, 10)
STOP DRAGGIN' MY HEART AROUND (with Stevie Nicks and the Heartbreakers, Modern, '81, 3)
DON'T COME AROUND HERE NO MORE (with the Heartbreakers, MCA, '85, 13)
I WON'T BACK DOWN (MCA, '89, 12)
FREE FALLIN' (MCA, '89, 7)

Additional Top 40 Songs: 9

Like That" and "Refugee," co-written by Petty and Campbell. It was the right sound at the right time, and the album soared to number two and stayed there for seven weeks. Yet even that success didn't ensure a smooth ride for Petty for long: in 1981, MCA planned to initiate a raise of list price for "superstar product" beginning with the singer's upcoming album; vehemently objecting to their plans, Petty threatened to withhold the album from the label, until MCA relented and issued *Hard Promises* at standard list price. Both it and its 1982 follow-up, *Long After Dark,* again cracked the top 10, between them bearing three top 25 hits: "The Waiting," "You Got Lucky," and "Change of Heart." Additionally, Petty and the Heartbreakers made their first appearance in the top five with Stevie Nicks' 1981 single "Stop Draggin' My Heart Around," a track penned by Petty and Campbell.

The mid-'80s were an eventful period for Tom Petty and the Heartbreakers, filled with both disappointments and glory. Petty broke his hand in a moment of frustration during the recording of 1985's ambitious *Southern Accents,* which featured songwriting collaborations with the Eurythmics' David A. Stewart and a track co-produced by the Band's Robbie Robertson. In 1986, the band undertook a major world tour with no less a figure than Bob Dylan; aside from a flood of good reviews, the experience resulted in "Jammin' Me," the top 20 Petty-Dylan collaboration that opened 1987's *Let Me Up (I've Had Enough)* and undoubtedly paved the way for their partnership in the Traveling Wilburys, whose double-platinum debut album was released in late 1988.

Ironically, the best-selling album in Tom Petty's career to date has been the only one not to fully feature the Heartbreakers. 1989's *Full Moon Fever,* co-produced by Wilbury/ELO member Jeff Lynne, was officially a Tom Petty solo album; most of its songs were Petty-Lynne collaborations, including the three hits "I Won't Back Down," "Runnin' Down a Dream" (co-written with Campbell), and the top 10 "Free Fallin'." Having already helped relaunch the career of Del Shannon in 1982 by producing his Elektra album *Drop Down and Get Me,* Petty,

struggles Petty would face during his career: When MCA Records bought out ABC Records in 1978, the label assumed it had bought the right to all product from ABC subsidiary Shelter as well; Petty maintained that his contract stipulated he didn't have to go along with the deal. A lengthy court battle ensued, after which *Damn the Torpedoes* emerged in 1979 on a new MCA imprint, Backstreet Records, and went on to sell nearly three million copies.

Damn the Torpedoes was the album that shot Petty and the Heartbreakers into pop's forefront. Produced by Petty and Jimmy Iovine, the record boasted a booming, contemporary sound and two of Petty's best singles yet: the top 15 hits "Don't Do Me

Iggy Pop

together with Lynne and the Heartbreakers, then began working with the late singer on a new project; issued posthumously in 1991, Shannon's *Rock On!* was highlighted by the Shannon-Petty-Lynne collaboration "Walk Away."

Jeff Lynne also co-produced Petty and the Heartbreakers' 1991 "reunion" album, *Into the Great Wide Open,* which contained Petty's most recent top 30 hit, again co-written with Lynne, "Learning to Fly." Also present on the album was former Byrds leader Roger McGuinn, for whose 1990 comeback, *Back from Rio,* Petty had penned and sung on the duet "King of the Hill." In a sense the closing of a circle that had started in 1976 with "American Girl," it was yet another signal of Petty's ascendance into the highest rock pantheon. Not that it hadn't already been noted. As the *Los Angeles Times* quite accurately reported in a 1990 concert review: "Tom Petty has arrived at the summit of stardom where, when joined in encore [by] what in rock terms amounts to a visitation from the gods—Bob Dylan and Bruce Springsteen—he didn't seem outranked. This, as far as the crowd was concerned, was a meeting of equals."

IGGY POP

The founding father of punk rock and an acutely intelligent, severely underrated lyricist, Iggy Pop (b. James Newell Osterberg, Apr. 21, 1947, Ann Arbor, Michigan) is one of the most exciting live performers in the history of rock and roll. With his trailblazing band of the late '60s, the Stooges, Pop's single-minded intensity confused many critics of the era who had expected the best new rock and roll to display—and perhaps even further develop—the sophisticated lyrical achievements of a Bob Dylan or the melodic inventiveness of the Beatles. Instead, atop a deliberately repetitive, monochromatic rock drone, Pop began his first album singing, "Well it's 1969, okay/All across the USA/It's another year for me and you/Another year with nothing to do.../Now last year I was 21/I didn't have a lot of fun/And now I'm gonna be 22/I say oh my and boo-hoo." That the album, 1969's *The Stooges,* was produced by John Cale of the Velvet Underground—one of the most fiercely intelligent bands of the 1960s—was in itself an indication that this seemingly amateurish Detroit-based quartet was approaching pop music from an angle that had yet to be explored. However sporadically, and with the occasional interference of some of the most severe roadblocks and personal setbacks imaginable, Iggy Pop has continued to pursue his absolutely unique vision of rock and roll through the 1990s with unshakeable determination.

The son of a schoolteacher father and executive secretary mother, young James Osterberg grew up in an Ypsilanti, Michigan, trailer park and displayed an early interest in music. He formed a high school rock band named the Iguanas—from which "Iggy" was eventually derived—and, he has said, was heavily influenced by the early Rolling Stones. After dropping out of the University of Michigan in 1966, he played in the Prime Movers, a blues band that played bars in the Detroit and Chicago areas; in 1967, he founded the Stooges. "Totally did our own thing, like nobody else," Pop succinctly—and very accurately—summarized in a self-penned record company bio in 1993.

One manner in which Pop did his own thing with the Stooges involved confrontation with the audience. Typically, crowd members would scream names or hurl objects at the singer, while he would often leap into the crowd and grab—or kiss—them, sometimes telling male audience members from the stage that he'd had sex with their girlfriends. Occasionally he would physically cut himself onstage, smearing blood over his body while singing. *Metallic K.O.*, a 1976 bootleg recording (and later semi-legitimate release on Import Records) of what purports to be "the last ever Iggy and the Stooges show" suitably documents the Stooges concert experience; as a sociological document it remains an unforgettable listen.

Though the group disbanded after 1970's *Fun House*, the intervention of fan David Bowie resulted in 1973's final Stooges album, *Raw Power*. An intense record marred by Bowie's strangely muted mix, the album captures what seems like the work of a man truly bent on self-destruction; including tracks such as "Gimme Danger," "Your Pretty Face Is Going to Hell," and the self-explanatory "Death Trip," the album essentially laid the groundwork for

most of the punk rock that would come at the end of the decade. "Went nuts from the life," Pop later wrote, "got screwed in the business, went L.A., went underground, more arrests, hard times."

When Pop reemerged in March 1977 with *The Idiot,* this time fully produced by David Bowie, he sounded less like a man at his wit's end than a sophisticated lyricist with a jarringly dark outlook. Recorded in Berlin and containing many of his best-known (and often-covered) songs, all co-written by Pop and Bowie—including "Sister Midnight," "Nightclubbing, "Funtime," and "China Girl"—the album relaunched the singer as a potential long-term serious artist. It rose to number 72 and remains his highest-charting effort. He followed through with another fine album, the upbeat *Lust for Life,* which featured the former self-immolator grinning happily like a human caricature of *Mad* magazine's Alfred E. Neuman. Contained within were "The Passenger" and "Tonight," the latter again co-written with producer Bowie, who would rerecord the song as the title track of his own 1984 platinum album.

After 1978's *TV Eye Live*, a disappointingly restrained live album that featured Bowie on piano, Pop issued records regularly through the 1980s. Most boasted one or two superb tracks but seemed otherwise diffuse and unfocused; the stability that Bowie had provided was replaced by a constant turnover of new guitarists and/or collaborators, including Scott Thurston, Glen Matlock of the early Sex Pistols (who had covered the Stooges' "No Fun" in 1977), Ivan Kral of the Patti Smith Group, and guitarist Rob duPrey. Pop again collaborated with Bowie in the mid-'80s, the results of which could be seen on Bowie's *Tonight* and Pop's own 1986 album *Blah-Blah-Blah,* which at number 75 was his highest-charting album in nine years. Also on the album, and throughout 1988's *Instinct*, was former Sex Pistols guitarist Steve Jones, who co-wrote several songs with the singer.

Increasingly, Pop was performing and collaborating with younger musicians who had clearly been significantly influenced by his work with the Stooges; unfortunately, the net effect—particularly in live performance—was much like seeing the singer

TOP ALBUMS

THE IDIOT (RCA, '77)
LUST FOR LIFE (RCA, '77)
BLAH-BLAH-BLAH (A&M, '86)
BRICK BY BRICK (Virgin, '90)
AMERICAN CAESAR (Virgin, '93)

TOP SONGS

FUNTIME (RCA, '77)
CHINA GIRL (RCA, '77)
LUST FOR LIFE (RCA, '78)
TONIGHT (RCA, '78)
CANDY (Virgin, '90)

fronting a Stooges cover band. Pop signed to Virgin Records in 1990 and released *Brick by Brick;* produced by Detroit hometown boy Don Was, the album featured the singer's first and only top 30 hit, "Candy," which received heavy MTV play, and included unlikely songwriting collaborations with John Hiatt ("Something Wild") and Slash of Guns N' Roses ("My Baby Wants to Rock 'n' Roll").

In late 1993 Pop released *American Caesar,* his best record in many years, which unfortunately met a dismal commercial reception. Nevertheless, it vividly displayed how the singer's songwriting style now increasingly tends to go in two distinct directions. First, there's the silly, purposely buffoonish Iggy Pop who sings "Boogie Boy": "I like to eat spaghetti with tomato sauce/I like to eat clams with Spanish moss/I like to go down to mash potato town/'Cuz that's where a Boogie Boy can get down." Secondly, and more interestingly, there's the surprisingly candid Iggy Pop of "Jealousy": "She comes from top cheekbones/She never worried hard/You could camp an army/On her family's yard/When I look at blue blood/I want to make it mud/And tear that difference down/Rock 'n' roll is how."

Now in his late 40s and still in superb physical shape—a necessity considering his live performing style—Iggy Pop is one of few performers left in pop music who is clearly much more interested in pursuing his muse for the sake of art rather than simple commerce. "I want to do something that's coming from inside, and see if anybody wants to hear it," he told writer Pamela DesBarres in 1990. "In the end what's real is real. My feelings about things is most music is bad, most films are bad, most TV is bad, most people are bad—but, hopefully, you can find a little good in anything."

ALAN PRICE

The official American debut of Alan Price (b. Apr. 19, 1942, Fairfield, Durham, England) came inconspicuously on March 5, 1964. Looking to get a piece of the same action Capitol Records was enjoying via their new band the Beatles—whose "I Want to Hold Your Hand" was in its sixth week at Number One—MGM Records that day released the first single by their own new British group, the Animals. "Baby Let Me Take You Home" flopped, but three months later, with the

---

TOP ALBUMS

O LUCKY MAN! (Warner Bros., '73)
BETWEEN TODAY AND YESTERDAY (Warner Bros., '73)
ALAN PRICE (Jet, '77)
LUCKY DAY (Jet, '79)

TOP SONGS

O LUCKY MAN! (Warner Bros. '73)
JARROW SONG (Warner Bros. '73)

---

release of second single "House of the Rising Sun," Newcastle quintet the Animals were swiftly on their way to stardom. The first non-Beatles English single to reach Number One—where it stayed for three full weeks—"House" was a mesmerizing, almost menacing-sounding record, a lethal combination of powerful singing and a loud, dominating organ. The vocals were provided by a small man with a big voice named Eric Burdon; the organ came courtesy of one Alan Price.

Initially named the Alan Price Combo when they formed in Newcastle in 1960, the group took on their famous moniker at the suggestion of new arrival Burdon, who joined the group well after they'd established themselves locally. A powerhouse of a blues-rock band, the Animals went on to have 14 American top 40 hits through 1968—though by that time, Alan Price (and everyone but Burdon) had long gone. Price, who played an integral role in shaping the band's earliest hits, had departed in 1965 to form a new band called the Alan Price Set—of which he would, naturally, be lead vocalist. "I was tired and confused," he explained years later to writer Jeff Tamarkin, "and I gave up the struggle between the demands that were made on us and what we were trying to experience. [Management] never took into account what we felt or even what our ideas were. It had a castrating effect."

Between 1966 and '67, Price quickly established himself as a hitmaker in his homeland with three top 10 U.K. singles in little over a year. One of those singles—"Simon Smith and His Amazing Dancing Bear"—had been penned by Randy Newman, the American songwriter to whom, perhaps ironically, Price would find himself being continually compared for much of his later career. Though the Alan Price Set's sole American album, *Price Is Right* (issued by Parrot in 1968), never even charted, and much of his music to come would never see Stateside release, Price's U.S. profile was soon heightened considerably.

In 1973, the onetime Animal appeared onscreen in Lindsay Anderson's much-praised British film *O Lucky Man!*, singing a series of superb songs that also served as its soundtrack. Issued in the U.S. by Warner Bros., the set reached a surprisingly high chart position of number 117. Price's finest album, *Between Today and Yesterday,* emerged on the same label the next year; though it sold poorly, it received rave reviews in important places and in England spawned the top five hit "Jarrow Song."

A brief reunion of the Animals resulted in 1977's surprise set *Before We Were So Rudely Interrupted,* which sold respectably (peaking at number 70) but seemed disappointingly restrained. The same year, Price released his first of three albums on the Jet label (*Alan Price,* 1979's *Lucky Day,* and 1980's *Rising Sun*), all of which were substantial but somewhat slickly produced. And at a time when punk and new wave rock were making substantial inroads into the American heartland, Price, glibly decked out in a tuxedo on his 1977 album cover, looked dishearteningly out of place and very much like last decade's news.

In 1983–84, another much more successful Animals reunion took place, resulting in *Ark* (which peaked at number 66) and a live greatest hits album, both on I.R.S. Records. Ever ambitious, Price continued to extend himself in many other directions as well. During the 1980s he started his own label, Key Records; hosted his own British TV show; wrote and co-starred in a stage musical based on the "Andy Capp" comic strip; and scored such films as 1982's *Britannia Hospital* and the 1987 hit *The Whales of August.* In all, it has been a bright and distinguished legacy, and clearly—whatever his Animal roots—not the work of someone operating on instinct alone.

JOHN PRINE

Perhaps the most significant '70s singer-songwriter to be lauded with the inescapable "new Dylan" tag, John Prine (b. Oct. 10, 1946, Maywood, Illinois) has proven a deeply compelling talent with an uncanny knack for touching on universal truths via songs populated with everyday, small-town characters. His best-known compositions—among them "Angel from Montgomery," about a middle-aged woman facing an empty life, and

TOP ALBUMS

JOHN PRINE (Atlantic, '71)
SWEET REVENGE (Atlantic, '73)
COMMON SENSE (Atlantic, '75)
BRUISED ORANGE (Atlantic, '78)
THE MISSING YEARS (Oh Boy, '91)

TOP SONGS

ANGEL FROM MONTGOMERY (Atlantic, '71)
SAM STONE (Atlantic, '71)
ILLEGAL SMILE (Atlantic, '71)
HELLO IN THERE (Atlantic, '71)
DEAR ABBY (Atlantic, '73)

the resonating "Sam Stone," about a struggling Vietnam veteran—have been covered by a diverse array of artists renowned for their ability to spot winning tunes, including Bonnie Raitt, Bette Midler, Tammy Wynette, and even Manfred Mann's Earth Band.

The third of four children, Prine, a former mailman, was raised in the Chicago suburb of Maywood by Kentucky-bred parents. He spent much time as a child visiting their hometown of Paradise, a coal town later to be the subject of a song on his debut album; the small town reciprocated in 1992 by officially naming one of its streets John Prine Avenue. The singer's big break came at the behest of an unlikely trio of fellow performers: Steve Goodman, the late Chicago-based songwriter who became one of Prine's closest friends; Kris Kristofferson, who Goodman dragged along to see Prine in a small club in 1971 (and who'd pen the liner notes of Prine's debut); and Paul Anka, also present that night, who would fly Goodman and Prine to New York—where each would sign a label deal—and initially manage both artists.

Within 24 hours of arriving in New York, Prine played a conspicuous mini-set during a Bottom Line show by Kristofferson and was offered a $25,000 recording contract by Atlantic Records' Jerry Wexler. He was sent to American Recording Studios in Memphis, where he recorded his self-titled debut album with no less a backing band than Elvis Presley's. It was a critical sensation, launching instant Dylan comparisons and bearing several songs that would swiftly be covered by other artists.

Prine's other albums for Atlantic included *Diamonds in the Rough* (1972), *Sweet Revenge* (1973), and *Common Sense* (1975). Each was similarly appreciated by critics, with *Revenge* earning the highest praise but *Common Sense*—which miffed some fans because of its string-section sweetening provided by producer Steve Cropper—reaching the highest chart level of his career, peaking at number 66. In some ways it was evident then that Prine was at a career plateau; he seemed unlikely to have a hit single of his own, and his albums generally sold at the same levels. He didn't really seem to mind—Prine, typically self-effacing, was clearly in it for the songs, not the glory—but he nonetheless signed a new deal with Asylum Records. Many consider his 1978 label debut, *Bruised Orange,* close to his best work, from the title track that deals with death and emotional isolation to the wry but affecting "Sabu Visits the Twin Cities Alone."

John Prine

Prine released two more albums for Asylum, then, lacking a label deal, moved to Nashville. There he collaborated with other songwriters such as Roger Cook (with whom he'd pen Don Williams's Number One country hit "Love Is on a Roll"), Bobby Braddock (their "Unwed Fathers" was sung by Tammy Wynette), and even pop songwriter John Mellencamp, who would include their joint composition "Jackie O" on his 1983 album *Uh Huh.*

That same year, Prine officially launched his own independent record label, Oh Boy, for which he still records. His series of Oh Boy albums showed the singer still very much at the top of his game: 1986's *German Afternoons* was nominated for a Grammy in the Contemporary Folk category, and 1991's excellent *The Missing Years*—loaded with famous guest stars and superbly produced by Heartbreaker Howie Epstein—not only was nominated but won. In 1993, Rhino Records released an outstanding Prine anthology set that, track for track, showed the singer to be one of the most consistent and enjoyable practitioners of American songwriting.

GERRY RAFFERTY

In the annals of pop, there are a select few instantly recognizable sound bites, and Gerry Rafferty's responsible for one of them. Play someone the six-note saxophone riff that haunts Rafferty's biggest hit record, and chances are they'll know they're hearing "Baker Street." It's that simple.

However big that 1978 hit may have been, it wasn't the first for Gerry Rafferty (b. Apr. 16, 1947, Paisley, Scotland), nor was it his last. He was an experienced singer-songwriter well before Raphael Ravenscroft played that "Baker Street" sax solo—so experienced, in fact, that he'd nearly had his fill of the business.

In the late 1960s, the bespectacled Rafferty first appeared as one half of Scottish folk duo the Humblebums (the other half being comedian-actor Billy Connolly), who released two albums on Liberty before splitting. His first solo album, the superb *Can I Have My Money Back?* (recorded in 1971, released in the U.S. in '73) featured many of the players who would eventually become his next group, Stealer's Wheel, including his pre-Humblebum bandmate Joe Egan. With Rafferty and Egan playing that group's Lennon and McCartney, Stealer's Wheel recorded three impressive albums and netted two hit singles: 1973's memorably Dylanesque "Stuck in the Middle with You," co-written by Rafferty and Egan; and its follow-up, "Star." Rafferty's experience with Stealer's Wheel was, apparently, anything but pleasant. He'd already departed to go solo when "Stuck in the Middle" hit, then had to rejoin. Further problems with management ultimately made the group's 1975 album its last.

Rafferty spent the next few years sorting out legal problems, finally returning in high style with *City to City*—which, with superhit "Baker Street" included, soared to Number One, spawned additional hits "Right Down the Line" and "Home and Dry," and eventually sold more than five million copies worldwide. Key to its success, most agree, was Rafferty's unfailingly melodic ear, a uniformly fine batch of Beatlish pop tunes, and superb radio-ready production by Rafferty and Hugh Murphy.

Rafferty continued in the same direction with 1979's *Night Owl*, which brought him two final brushes with the top 40—"Days Gone Down (Still Got the Light in Your Eyes)" and "Get It Right Next Time"—and still impressive world sales of 2.5 million. When his next two albums, *Snakes and Ladders* (1980) and *Sleepwalking* (1982), didn't take off in the same manner, Rafferty—by no means hurting for money—took time off to travel with his family and build a home studio. In that very studio he would record *North and South,* his most recent album, released quietly in June 1988. Because he rarely tours, and seems to make records only when he wants to, Rafferty remains one of the more reclusive, and interesting, figures in pop music.

TOP ALBUMS

CAN I HAVE MY MONEY BACK? (Blue Thumb, '73)
CITY TO CITY (United Artists, '78, *1*)
NIGHT OWL (United Artists, '79, *29*)
SNAKES AND LADDERS (United Artists, '80)

TOP SONGS

BAKER STREET (United Artists, '78, *2*)
RIGHT DOWN THE LINE (United Artists, '78, *12*)
HOME AND DRY (United Artists, '79, *28*)
DAYS GONE DOWN (STILL GOT THE LIGHT IN YOUR EYES) (United Artists, '79, *17*)
GET IT RIGHT NEXT TIME (United Artists, '79, *21*)

BONNIE RAITT

While never a particularly prolific songwriter herself, Bonnie Raitt (b. Nov. 8, 1949, Burbank, California) has, through the course of a dozen albums, demonstrated an enviable knack for finding precisely the right song and making it seem her own. The list of songwriters Raitt has covered since her 1971 debut album spans an impressive range of musical genres: she has sung the blues of Robert Johnson, Sippie Wallace, and Fred McDowell; the reggae of Toots and the Maytals; the classic songs of New Orleans legend Allen Toussaint; the R&B of Isaac Hayes and David Porter; and the little-known work of semi-obscure songwriters she has continually championed. Even when performing the work of well-known writers like Randy Newman, Jackson Browne, John Hiatt, James Taylor, Joni Mitchell, or John Prine, Raitt's inimitably warm and bluesy style has never allowed those works to overshadow her own musical persona.

Raitt, the daughter of Broadway star John Raitt (*Oklahoma!, Carousel, The Pajama Game*), was raised a Quaker in the unlikely locale of Burbank, California. She began playing guitar as an adolescent, and in 1967 she left to attend Radcliffe, where she'd stay for only two years before dropping out to begin a career in music. The key to her success came via her signing with blues manager Dick Waterman, who often placed her on bills with other clients such as Fred McDowell, Son House, and Sippie Wallace, whom Raitt greatly admired. As a result of that exposure, she signed a deal with Warner Bros. that led to her superb 1971 debut album *Bonnie Raitt*, which featured the gravelly-voiced Raitt accompanied by such Chicago blues stars as Junior Wells and A. C. Reed.

From the start, Raitt would share the spotlight with other songwriters, though her debut did feature two original tunes, "Thank You" and "Finest Lovin' Man." She established herself as a potent performer throughout much of the early 1970s, building a loyal fan base particularly among college students, who were impressed by the breadth of her musical knowledge, her ability as a slide guitarist, and her charming, sometimes salty demeanor. Raitt's second album, *Give It Up*, displayed a considerable broadening of her material, especially with what would become her early signature song, "Love Has No Pride," a distinctly non-bluesy ballad penned by Eric

Bonnie Raitt

TOP ALBUMS

BONNIE RAITT (Warner Bros., '71)

GIVE IT UP (Warner Bros., '72)

SWEET FORGIVENESS (Warner Bros., '77, *25*)

THE GLOW (Warner Bros., '79, *30*)

GREEN LIGHT (Warner Bros., '82, *38*)

NICK OF TIME (Capitol, '89, *1*)

LUCK OF THE DRAW (Capitol, '91, *2*)

TOP SONGS

SOMETHING TO TALK ABOUT (Capitol, '91, *5*)

I CAN'T MAKE YOU LOVE ME (Capitol, '91, *18*)

NOT THE ONLY ONE (Capitol, '91, *34*)

Justin Kaz and Libby Titus. *Give It Up* signalled the singer's first appearance on the album chart, peaking at number 138; every record she's made since has done even better.

Give It Up included three Raitt originals—the best being album opener "Give It Up or Let Me Go"—and gave many the impression she'd devote even more time to songwriting on future albums. It was not to be: the four albums that followed contained no Raitt songs whatsoever. Instead, she seemed to be heading into the same interpretive mold as Linda Ronstadt, who was enjoying enormous popularity at the time.

Though Raitt's song selection continued to impress, each new recording had a different producer (John Hall, Jerry Ragavoy, and Paul A. Rothchild were among those employed), giving each disc a noticeably different spin that somewhat diluted Raitt's consistency. By 1979's *The Glow*, Ronstadt producer Peter Asher himself was called in; ironically, the album would contain Raitt's first new song in seven years, "Standin' By the Same Old Love," which more than held its own against material penned by Browne, Tracy Nelson, and Robert Palmer. *Green Light,* her rocking 1982 effort, further featured two originals Raitt had co-written with her group at the time, the Bump Band.

Raitt's lack of original material never hampered the sales of her albums, however. She'd scored a gold record with 1977's *Sweet Forgiveness,* and indeed all of her work since 1973's *Takin' My Time* has placed comfortably in the Top 100. Her one major sales disappointment, 1986's *Nine Lives,* was in many ways a career aberration for her: two years earlier, she'd turned in an album called *Tongue in Groove* that her label felt was unsatisfactory. Raitt, then in the midst of drug and alchohol problems, was actually dropped from the label for a time before returning with the new, drastically reworked *Nine Lives,* which, with its blend of old and new material, seemed very much a hodgepodge.

Raitt's dramatic career comeback with 1989's triple platinum *Nick of Time* has been well documented. With producer Don Was at the helm, the singer fashioned a superlative album containing choice material by John Hiatt, Jerry Williams, and Bonnie Hayes, along with two excellent new originals, the title track and the autobiographical "The Road's My Middle Name." The larger story, however, wasn't the album, but the reception it and Raitt herself were accorded. A full year after *Nick of Time* made its chart debut, it became Raitt's first Number One album. The surge came largely from the singer's memorable 1990 Grammy sweep, in which, after several past nominations, she received awards for Album of the Year, Best Female Rock Vocal Performance, Best Pop Vocal Performance, and Best Traditional Blues Recording (the result of her appearance on John Lee Hooker's "In the Mood" from his album *The Healer*).

Raitt's popularity continued with 1991's *Luck of the Draw*, the sales of which actually exceeded its remarkable predecessor. Especially interesting was Raitt's apparently growing confidence in her own material: for the first time, she'd made an album with four original songs, one of which ("All at Once") ranks among the finest songs she'd ever sung. More than 20 years after her first album, the future has never looked brighter for Bonnie Raitt. Now one of the most popular female performers in all of pop music, she has to work harder than ever to convince anyone she's got the blues.

KENNY RANKIN

A singer-songwriter whose career extends back to the late 1950s and early '60s, Kenny Rankin (b. circa 1943) recorded his first single, "Saturday After the Game," at the age of 17. Over the years he has been signed to numerous labels—including Columbia, Mercury, Little David, and Cypress, and as of 1991, Chesky—and, while very much a songwriter, has instead grown in stature largely as an interpreter of other writers' material. Enough of a family man to feature an album cover (1969's *Family*) depicting himself holding his two toddler daughters—in the nude, no less—Rankin has collaborated with two separate wives during the course of his writing career. Now viewed as a mostly MOR-styled crooner, Rankin became one of the first critically respected artists of the adult-contemporary genre in the 1970s with songs such as "Peaceful," a latter-day soft-pop standard.

Spending much of the early 1960s immersed in New York's Greenwich Village scene, Rankin showed his roots on his 1967 Mercury album *Mind-Dusters*. Boasting liner notes by Johnny Carson— "Kenny Rankin has all of the qualities to become one of the top musical personalities in the country," wrote the Late Night King—the album featured Rankin's original recording of "Peaceful," as well as material by Fred Neil ("The Dolphin"), Bob Dylan ("Mr. Tambourine Man"), and Gordon Lightfoot ("Song for a Winter's Night"). As would be the case with many Rankin albums to come, the album was produced by Monte Kay and Jack Lewis; in the early 1970s, the pair founded Little David Records, for whom Rankin recorded throughout most of that decade.

As early as 1969's *Family*, Rankin seemed headed in the interpretive direction. While *Mind-Dusters* boasted seven original songs—two co-written by the singer with his lyricist wife Yvonne—its follow-up included only one new song, "Soft Guitar," and a wealth of covers by the likes of Goffin-King, Lightfoot, Stephen Stills, Bert Jansch, and even Otis Redding. When the singer returned in 1972 with *Like a Seed*, the album offered a conspicuous helping of original material; perhaps significantly, the album was Rankin's first charting effort. Containing a new version of "Peaceful"—likely the first version many people had heard—the album established the singer as a velvet-smooth crooner with his own very distinct, almost jazzy sound. Indeed, Rankin has claimed Brazilian composer-guitarist Joao Gilberto as a major influence. "I heard Joao," he once recalled, "and then [producer-arranger] Don Costa gave me my first set of La Bella classical strings and I was in heaven."

Becoming more of a stylist with each successive album, Rankin found a growing audience in the mid-'70s with *Silver Morning, Inside,* and *The Kenny Rankin Album*. Typically, his silky treatments of familiar pop songs such as the Impressions' "People Get Ready," the Beatles' "Blackbird," and the Rascals' "Groovin' " sat side-by-side with standards like "When Sunny Gets Blue" and "Here's That Rainy Day." His

TOP ALBUMS

MIND-DUSTERS (Mercury, '67)
LIKE A SEED (Little David, '72)
SILVER MORNING (Little David, '74)
INSIDE (Little David, '75)
THE KENNY RANKIN ALBUM
(Little David, '77)
HIDING IN MYSELF (Cypress, '88)

TOP SONGS

PEACEFUL (Mercury, '67)
HAVEN'T WE MET (Little David, '74)
IN THE NAME OF LOVE
(Little David, '74)

originals grew fewer and fewer; on 1980's *After the Roses,* he contributed only three, co-composed with either Jack Siegel or Terry Costa. His albums, which had become heavily orchestrated, verged very much on mood music.

Rankin spent a lengthy period without a record deal in the 1980s, but—like many other seasoned performers in his situation—returned in the late '80s on a "boomer" label, Cypress Records. *Hiding in Myself,* released in 1988, featured the singer working with another lyrical collaborator—and another wife—Aime Ulrich Rankin. Though there were still covers to be had via Marvin Gaye ("Trouble Man" and "Let's Get It On") and Jimmy Webb ("She Moves, Eyes Follow"), the album seemed less a mood piece and more the work of a singer who'd spent the past decade immersed in live performance. He returned in 1991 with *Because of You* on the audiophile Chesky Records label and enjoyed significant success, spurred by radio play on both adult-contemporary and so-called "Wave" radio formats. While massive future success looks increasingly unlikely for the aging singer, it's probable Kenny Rankin's loyal fan base—generated by regular soft-rock radio play and a busy touring schedule—won't be deserting him anytime soon.

CHRIS REA

Chris Rea

Count Chris Rea (b. Mar. 4, 1951, Middlesbrough, England) among the few singer-songwriters to be glad we may not precisely remember him. Sort of. Rea's first claim to fame, the 1978 hit single "Fool (If You Think It's Over)" did, after all, help earn his debut album, *Whatever Happened to Benny Santini?,* a Grammy nomination. But that same soft-rock hit, produced by longtime Elton John associate Gus Dudgeon, also helped create a lightweight crooner image that took Rea years to shake. Shake it he finally did, though, and in the process he became an international star of some magnitude. These days, you'll find the supposed "crooner" reeling, rocking, playing a mean slide guitar, and getting compared to Dire Straits regularly.

Rea's first taste of the music business came via a rock and roll band called Beautiful Losers (after the Leonard Cohen novel) which included a pre-Whitesnake David Coverdale among its members. Upon being signed to Magnet Records, Rea—a superb slide guitarist—found himself packaged as a pensive sentimentalist, staring out from his albums wearing a scarf and leather jacket, or moodily strolling down a beach as the waves crashed behind him. At the height of England and America's buzzing punk and new wave scene, tracks like Rea's "Fool"—which he said he'd written for his sister—and "Bows and Bangles" were virtually guitarless.

Rea's first sign of being more than another MOR snoozer came with the opening track of 1980's *Tennis,* his best album yet, and the first he himself produced. With a decidedly non-schlocky, pounding bass behind him, Rea's world-weary voice sang distinctively odd lyrics about a world gone awry ("Freedom is a man with a red grenade/She ran out of gas, got beat and raped/Do you like tennis?"). It would be a lyrical theme he'd continue to explore throughout most of his career, most effectively on 1989's *The Road to Hell.*

Rea's "Fool" audience continued to shrink with *Tennis,* however, and following 1982's *Chris Rea,* it dwindled nearly to nothing. Ironically, the album that would then turn his career around internationally—1983's *Water Sign*—was never released in the U.S. Nor were the next three—*Wired to the Moon, Shamrock Diaries,* or *On the Beach*—despite wide European success. Rea's next appearance in the States came, strangely enough, courtesy of Motown, when the legendary black music label picked up his 1987 *Dancing with Strangers* for American distribution.

Shortly thereafter, Rea signed to Geffen and quite wisely reintroduced himself to America. The vehicle: *New Light Through Old Windows,* a collection of material taken from his last few albums, newly recorded with a notably excellent band featuring pianist Max Middleton and guitarist Robert Ahwai. A tour soon followed, as did the quietly foreboding *The Road to Hell.* Possibly Rea's best work, certainly his most mature, the album showed all the aspects of great rock and roll: superb playing, an intriguing lyrical theme (in the memorable "Texas," a move to the Lone Star State is posited as a be-all, end-all cure to familial woes), and, as always, great singing.

Whether Rea will attain the success here he's achieved internationally is questionable. His 1987 track "Let's Dance"—a huge hit elsewhere—simply didn't crack the U.S. market despite being included on no fewer than three consecutive Rea albums. And when Atco Records released *Auberge* domestically in 1991, they couldn't break him either. Still, considering the sheer accessibility of Rea's music, one suspects the problem ultimately lies with label marketing departments rather than Rea himself. And as the saying goes, we might be fools to think he's over.

LOU REED

With his reputation as a rock lyricist second only to Bob Dylan's by most critical accounts, Lou Reed (b. Lewis Allen Reed, Mar. 2, 1942, Brooklyn, New York) has never enjoyed the level of commercial popularity that placed his contemporaries on the cover of *Time* or *Newsweek.* Nor, for that matter, did his legendary group the Velvet Underground sell many records in their heyday: the band many regard as the second most influential rock and roll group of the 1960s in fact reached their all-time chart peak at number 171, with their debut, *The Velvet Underground & Nico.* Still, despite a career that has conspicuously twisted from one extreme to another—and resulted in the release of an album (1975's *Metal Machine Music*) that many have called the most unlistenable record ever made—Lou Reed has produced many of the most compelling recordings in rock and roll.

A onetime Syracuse University student and former staff writer–performer at Pickwick International, Reed founded the Velvet Underground in 1965 and was the group's principal singer-songwriter until his departure in 1970. His reputation had largely been built upon the foundation of the four albums he made with them, including 1967's *The Velvet Underground & Nico,* 1968's *White Light/White Heat,* 1969's *The Velvet Underground,* and 1970's *Loaded.* Interest in the group has not abated since; in 1974, two separate live albums emerged, *Live at Max's Kansas City* and *1969 Velvet Underground Live;* in 1985, PolyGram issued *VU,* an album of unreleased Velvet Underground recordings, and the next year followed with yet another collection, *Another View.*

Volumes have been written about the unique appeal of the Velvet Underground, and most critics agree the band was groundbreaking on two major levels. Musically, the band's purposeful use of drones, dissonance, repetition, and feedback was far ahead of its time. Much of the credit belongs not only to Reed—an outstanding guitar stylist whose

---

TOP ALBUMS

WHATEVER HAPPENED TO BENNY SANTINI? (United Artists, '78)
TENNIS (Columbia, '80)
THE ROAD TO HELL (Geffen, '89)
AUBERGE (Atco, '91)

TOP SONGS

FOOL IF YOU THINK IT'S OVER (United Artists, '78, *12*)
TENNIS (Columbia, '80)
LET'S DANCE (Motown, '87)
YOU MUST BE EVIL (Geffen, '89)
TEXAS (Geffen, '89)

breathtakingly abrasive work on such *VU* tracks as "I Heard Her Call My Name" continues to influence alternative bands of the 1990s—but also to John Cale, a classically trained multi-instrumentalist who had spent time working with minimalist pioneer La Monte Young. Secondly, the group's lyrics, all penned by Reed, were far more sophisticated than the norm, and drew upon such subject matter as hard drugs, homosexuality, transsexualism, and sadomasochism, topics few pop songwriters dared even approach in their work. More important than the seeming taboo nature of Reed's subject matter was his skill at humanizing the characters in his songs; the most chilling aspect of "Heroin," for example, from the group's debut album, is the not entirely irrational explanation of its use presented by the song's lyric.

Reed's solo career began inauspiciously with a self-titled 1972 solo album that spent only two weeks on the chart. Consisting of several songs he'd written for the Velvet Underground that had gone unreleased up to that point—including "Ocean," "I Can't Stand It," and "Lisa Says"—the album is dryly produced and boasts a curious musical cast, including Yes members Steve Howe and Rick Wakeman and members of Elton John's band. Its follow-up, *Transformer,* found a much wider audience, however, thanks to the rising popularity of its producers—longtime Reed fan David Bowie and Mick Ronson—and the top 20 success of "Walk on the Wild Side," a colorful, unlikely hit about various associates of Andy Warhol, who had produced the Velvet Underground's first album and would be long associated with Reed.

1973's *Berlin,* Reed's finest album of the decade, was a heavily arranged, ultimately depressing concept album about failed relationships that garnered bad reviews upon its release but has since increasingly gained favor. Critics who moaned about Reed's seeming "selling out" of traditional rock and roll values—on *Berlin,* he'd been accompanied by strings and woodwinds—were amply appeased by 1974's *Rock N Roll Animal,* the singer's only gold album, which featured the twin-guitar attack of Steve Hunter and Dick Wagner and received heavy radio play. Reed's sole top 10 album, *Sally Can't Dance,* followed half a year later; its major highlight remains his offhandedly delivered but gripping "Kill Your Sons," a personal account about dysfunctional families and electroshock therapy. A dissatisfied Reed, who nearly disowned the album upon its release and

was surprised at its success, commented at the time, "This is fantastic—the worse I am, the more it sells. If I wasn't on the record at all next time around, it would probably go No. 1." After RCA released *Lou Reed Live,* another concert set culled from the same New York performances that had produced *Rock N Roll Animal,* Reed made history with *Metal Machine Music,* a two-LP set of extremely grating, electronically produced music including feedback, howls, squeals, and hums. More astounding than the music was the fact that RCA actually released the set.

Reed signed with Arista Records in 1976 and produced a brace of inconsistent records, some of which were superb (1978's memorable *Street Hassle*), some disappointingly bland (1976's *Rock and Roll Heart*), and some brutally hilarious (1978's double live *Take No Prisoners*). For the first time in years, Reed began collaborating with other musicians, beginning with 1979's *The Bells.* Still a much-underrated album, the set features songs he co-wrote with various band members, jazz trumpeter Don Cherry, and singer-songwriter Nils Lofgren. In many

Lou Reed

cases, the "co-writing" was less formal than one might expect; Reed said in a 1980 interview that he often enjoyed working in an improvisatory style in the studio. "Go in the studio with zero, write it on the spot, make the lyrics up as the tape's running, and that's it," he explained. "Nobody can change it—they can't ask you to do it again because you don't know what there is already on it. That's it. And then you learn the record afterwards. Bam! That way, no matter what the sound was, my records came out my way. And they sound that way."

Given the overall quality of Reed's work, there are still noticeable peaks and valleys in his recording output. *Berlin* was a peak, as was *Street Hassle* to a lesser extent, and so too was 1982's *The Blue Mask,* a gripping album that marked the singer's return to RCA Records and the beginning of an artistic stability from which he has yet to falter. Boasting a skilled new band including acclaimed guitarist Robert Quine—who had been highly influenced by Reed's own playing approach with the Velvets—the album showcased a singer who had never seemed more balanced or at peace with himself. Still, while Reed was now capable of writing serene, meditative songs such as "My House"—a tribute to poet Delmore Schwartz, whom he'd befriended while a student in Syracuse—his lyrics could also be more graphic than ever before, as on the album's title track: "The pain was lean and it made him scream/ He knew he was alive/He put a pin through the nipples on his chest/He thought he was a saint.../Don't take death away/Cut the finger at the joint/Cut the stallion at his mount/And stuff it in his mouth."

Reed's second stretch with RCA was his most consistent in terms of album sound quality and overall workmanlike songwriting; nonetheless, his most interesting albums were often his most erratic. Thus such efforts as *Legendary Hearts* (1983), *New Sensations* (1984), and *Mistral* (1986) were satisfying, but still somehow seemed lacking. Furthermore, Reed's voice—one of the most imitated speak-song croaks in pop—began shifting toward a near-constant conversational style, and actual singing was becoming less and less frequent.

Reed entered the 1990s on a new label and on the heels of his most successful album in 14 years. 1989's *New York* verged on political commentary and magazine-style journalism and included memorable songs about AIDS, crack, anti-Semitism, violence, and urban disintegration. "Manhattan's sinking like a rock," sang Reed, "Into the filthy Hudson what a shock." About the first true concept album he'd done since *Berlin,* Reed commented at the time, "This is what eight years of Reagan does to you. I knew I wasn't the only one feeling these things. Especially in New York...It's the strongest thing I've ever done."

Much to the excitement of Velvet Underground fans, Reed reunited with John Cale to produce 1990's tribute to their departed friend Andy Warhol, *Songs for Drella.* Death further played a role in Reed's follow-up, *Magic and Loss,* a stark offering Reed undertook after losing two close friends; a sometimes harrowing listen, Reed called it "an adult album, but right now it's something people can relate to." More than ever before, the singer was merging his musical and literary interests. "Party music is great," said Reed. "Dance music is great, but I wish you could approach rock 'n' roll with the same intensity as a great novel."

Those who felt Reed was straying too far from his rock and roll roots were deeply satisfied in 1993, when the original Velvet Underground reformed to play a series of European summer dates. The live album that resulted, *The Velvet Underground Live MCMXCIII,* was a superb recap of much of the band's best material; unlike nearly all of the so-called "reunion" albums to be had in the rock genre, it presented four unique musicians at the height of their powers and transcended the nostalgia factor to a remarkable degree. Roughly akin to hearing Bob Dylan performing the whole of *Blonde on Blonde* in the 1990s, the album was shockingly good, and further testament to the fact that Lou Reed's achievements as singer, songwriter, and musician continue to be unmatched. Oddly, despite nearly 30 years of overwhelming press adoration, Lou Reed's importance as an artist in some ways has yet to be overstated.

TOP ALBUMS

TRANSFORMER (RCA, '72, 29)
BERLIN (RCA, '72)
SALLY CAN'T DANCE
  (RCA, '74, 10)
STREET HASSLE (Arista, '78)
THE BLUE MASK (RCA, '82)
NEW YORK (Sire, '89, 40)

TOP SONGS

WALK ON THE WILD SIDE
  (RCA, '73, 16)
SWEET JANE (RCA, '74)
HEROIN (RCA, '74)
ROCK 'N' ROLL (RCA, '74)

TERRY REID

If raw talent were the only factor in major commercial success, if there were no such thing as luck, record company politics, or being at the right place at the right time, Terry Reid (b. Nov., 1949) might be one of the more famous names in pop music.

He isn't, of course. And consider:

At the height of her '60s fame, Aretha Franklin, returning to the States after a trip to Great Britain, uttered one sentence that must haunt Reid to this day: "There are three things going on in London: the Beatles, the Stones, and Terry Reid."

When classic '60s rock group the Yardbirds were on their last legs, lead guitarist Jimmy Page asked Reid to form a new band with him. Reid, who had his own commitments, politely declined—and ultimately suggested Page try singer Robert Plant and drummer John Bonham instead. He did, and called the legendary result Led Zeppelin.

In over 25 years, singer-songwriter Reid has released a grand total of six albums. On five labels. One of which went under within a few weeks after releasing Reid's album.

Englishman Reid was young when he first gained entry into the music business: his first U.K. single, 1967's "The Hand Don't Fit the Glove," hit the shops when he was all of 15. Playing a mixture of cover tunes and R&B-influenced originals, Reid and his unique guitar-organ-drums trio rapidly became the talk of the U.K. Getting the most attention was Reid's unforgettably powerful, big voice—an instrument certainly the equal of contemporaries who became much more famous, such as Steve Winwood and Rod Stewart.

Hooking up with famous British producer Mickie Most, Reid spent much of his early career in the U.S., in fact releasing his 1968 debut album *Bang, Bang You're Terry Reid* only in the States, not in England. It still stands as a perfect example of Reid's talent: wonderfully melodic original material such as "Erica" and "Without Expression" (which Crosby, Stills, Nash and Young recorded for their platinum *Deja Vu* set but dropped at the last minute); unique covers such as Cher's "Bang, Bang (My Baby Shot Me Down)" and Donovan's "Season of the Witch"; and, finally, Eddie Cochran's "Summertime Blues" merged with his own piece, "Writing on the Wall." The next year's even better *Move Over for...Terry*

Reid contained his oft-covered "Speak Now or Forever Hold Your Peace" (later recorded by Cheap Trick and Christopher Milk) and "Rich Kid Blues" (likewise redone by Tim Davis); but as good as it was, it ended up being his last album for several years after protracted contractual litigation with producer Most.

By the time Reid's next album, *The River*, emerged nearly a full four years later, he'd moved to Los Angeles, and whatever career momentum he'd had was long gone. Though the album boasted a superb band (including guitarist David Lindley) and an especially gorgeous second side of original material, it fizzled instantly, as did the next—1976's *Seed of Memory*, produced by friend and supporter Graham Nash—when Reid's new label, ABC Records, folded shortly after its release.

Sadly for Reid, much hasn't changed since then. The rockish *Rogue Waves*, issued on Capitol in 1978, contained an exuberant mix of originals and well-known oldies—so well known, in fact ("Baby I Love You," "Then I Kissed Her," and others), that were it anyone but Reid singing, further covers would be pointless. After living a comfortable, relatively anonymous life as a session player, recording with Bonnie Raitt, Jackson Browne, and Don Henley, among others, Reid popped up on the soundtrack for 1990's *Days of Thunder* singing "Gimme Some Lovin'," originally made famous by Steve Winwood in the Spencer Davis Group. Reid's last album, 1991's *The Driver*, needlessly included that tune among an otherwise outstanding batch of new material, yet it still passed without much notice.

TOP ALBUMS

BANG BANG YOU'RE TERRY REID (Epic, '68)
TERRY REID (Epic, '69)
RIVER (Atlantic, '73)
SEED OF MEMORY (ABC, '76)
ROGUE WAVES (Capitol, '78)
THE DRIVER (Warner Bros., '91)

TOP SONGS

WITHOUT EXPRESSION (Epic, '68)
RICH KID BLUES (Epic, '69)
SPEAK NOW OR FOREVER HOLD YOUR PEACE
   (Epic, '69)
LAUGH AT LIFE (Warner Bros., '91)

Now performing regularly in L.A. with such old friends as Jackie Lomax, Mick Taylor, and Joe Walsh, Reid hasn't lost one iota of his talent. It's that bad luck he needs to lose.

EMITT RHODES

One of the greatest mysteries in pop music remains how, given two hypothetical artists of equal talent, one can prosper while the other fails dismally. For every rich rock star convinced that "talent will out" is an absolute truism, there's another poor one banging his head against the wall complaining about his incredible bad luck. It's a common scenario, brought up here only to illustrate that album and singles charts can only tell one side of the story. Whether Emitt Rhodes (b. 1949) was ever the sort of artist inclined to head-banging is another mystery. But one thing's for sure: in the six-year span of 1967 to 1973, he made some of the best pop records that nobody ever heard.

Actually, enough people heard Rhodes's first two records to make them Number One in Los Angeles during the very eventful music year of 1967. A 17-year-old from the L.A. suburb of Hawthorne, Rhodes had formed a group in his garage called the Merry-Go-Round. After recording a few demos, the quartet was signed to A&M, who quickly released their first single, "Live," and watched it explode…at least locally. Sounding much like the Beatles—and who better at the time?—the single was melodically sophisticated, filled with gorgeous harmonies, and oozing with promise. Nationally, however, that promise only extended to number 63 on the singles chart. Equally as popular in L.A. was the second single, "You're a Very Lovely Woman," not as immediately catchy as "Live" but even more elegant melodically. It sputtered on the charts for three weeks and peaked at number 94. Two months later, when A&M released the Merry-Go-Round's only album, it too escaped national notice, holding a chart position for a meager two weeks.

Why did the album flop? Surely not for lack of talent. Rhodes, who wrote nearly all of the material, could sing like Paul McCartney or John Lennon at will, and often did—yet he was more than a slavish Beatle imitator. It was recognized early on by England's distinguished Fairport Convention, whose cover of the Merry-Go-Round's "Time Will Show the Wiser" actually opened their 1968 debut album, otherwise filled with original material (by members Richard Thompson and Ian Matthews, no less) and songs by Bob Dylan and Joni Mitchell. It was likewise recognized by the Bangles 16 years later, when they chose to cover Rhodes's "Live" on their debut album. And it was very likely recognized by Rhodes himself—who, when his group collapsed amid much bickering while working on a second album, decided to become his own band.

In 1969, Emitt Rhodes bought himself an Ampex four-track recorder and became one of the very first one-man bands in pop. Already fascinated with recording studio technology, and a capable multi-instrumentalist, Rhodes spent the remainder of his music career making beautiful music with himself. He recorded his first album, sold it to Dunhill Records in 1970 for only $5,000, and, remarkably, watched it soar into the top 30. Its single, "Fresh as a Daisy," received significant airplay and at number 54 became the highest-charting single Rhodes had ever made. Seeing that success, A&M—as record companies typically do—soon issued their own new Emitt Rhodes album, *American Dream*, that comprised unreleased tracks Rhodes and his former band had recorded between 1967 and '68. Oddly enough, it was very good indeed. Building a full-fledged recording studio in his Hawthorne garage, Emitt Rhodes then made two more albums—*Mirror* (1971) and the especially eloquent *Farewell to Paradise* (1973). Neither fared as well as his first, however, and after *Paradise*, for whatever reason, he simply stopped making records.

Why didn't Emitt Rhodes become a household name? Maybe because he might've actually needed a band. Maybe because a one-man studio band couldn't readily go onstage and win new fans. Maybe because the insular environment in which he deliberately placed himself didn't allow the kind of helpful feedback many artists acutely need. Maybe because his record company did a lousy job of promoting his

TOP ALBUMS

EMITT RHODES (Dunhill, '70, 29)
AMERICAN DREAM (A&M, '71)
MIRROR (Dunhill, '71)
FAREWELL TO PARADISE
    (Dunhill, '72)

TOP SONGS

LIVE (A&M, '67)
FRESH AS A DAISY (Dunhill, '70)

records. And, of course, maybe because he just had bad luck. But when anyone hears an Emitt Rhodes record for the first time, count on it: it's a sure bet they won't be able to figure it out, either.

KEITH RICHARDS

One has to give Rolling Stones guitarist Keith Richards (b. Dec. 18, 1943, Dartford, England) his due: he never really *wanted* to be a solo artist. From the start, the much-admired performer, who with Mick Jagger co-wrote nearly all of the Rolling Stones' vast catalog of hits, sat comfortably perched in his slot with the Stones while other band members—including Jagger, Bill Wyman, Brian Jones (indirectly, via 1972's *Brian Jones Presents the Pipes of Pan in Joujouka*), Mick Taylor, Ronnie Wood, and even drummer Charlie Watts—released albums under their own names. "I never saw myself as anything but a Stone," Richards said in 1988. "I felt perfectly content to create music as a Rolling Stone. I had no need to express myself in any other way. Unlike some other original rockers, I didn't have to get out there on my own in order to make my creative juices flow. They always flowed as a Stone."

Still, Richards uttered those words by way of explaining the existence of *Talk Is Cheap*, his first solo album, and the first record ever released under his own name (with the exception of his obscure 1979 single cover version of Chuck Berry's seasonal "Run Rudolph Run"). One couldn't argue with Richards' rationale: Stones albums and tours were coming at best once every three years, his partner Jagger was off recording his own solo albums, and Richards, whose life was devoted to making music, was left holding the bag—however filled with money it might have been. There had already been a precedent set in 1979, when, following the previous year's extended Stones tour, an antsy Richards took Wood, jazz bassist Stanley Clarke, and Meters drummer Ziggy Modeliste on a unique one-off American tour as the New Barbarians. Further, Richards had independently served as music director for Chuck Berry's 60th birthday concert, filmed by director Taylor Hackford as the 1987 documentary *Hail! Hail! Rock 'n' Roll.*

That said, *Talk Is Cheap* was a fairly sturdy set that offered all that was good about the '80s-era Rolling Stones but one fairly important thing: Mick Jagger's vocals. While Richards had sung on such past Stones tracks as "Connection," "You Got the Silver," "Before They Make Me Run," and even 1972's top 30 hit "Happy," his weak, reedy voice often made those cuts serve best as novelty tracks, welcome breaks from Mick Jagger's ever-less-subtle, by-number vocal romps. *Talk Is Cheap* featured 11 tracks penned by Richards and drummer Steve Jordan, and on such tracks as "How I Wish," his opening guitar chording sounded so precisely and distinctly Stones-like that his wheezy vocal rasp was jarring and, unavoidably, a mild anticlimax.

Interestingly, even without Jagger, Richards' songs were thematically similar to those of the Stones during the 1980s—as suggested by the mere titles of such tracks as "Take It So Hard," "Whip It Up," "Big Enough," and "Locked Away." While radio loyally played the album's first single, "Take It So Hard," the track failed to chart; nonetheless, Richards' reputation was enough to take *Talk Is Cheap* into the top 30, where it eventually went gold. That would hardly be the case with the live album that followed, recorded during Richards' tour to promote its predecessor. The informatively titled *Keith Richards & the X-Pensive Winos Live at the Hollywood Palladium December 15, 1988,* sold both separately and as part of a limited edition box set, failed to enter the charts at all.

Lacking the element of surprise, Richards' 1992 album *Main Offender* failed to match *Talk Is Cheap*'s relative success by a significant margin: the album only crawled into the top 100, peaking at number 99 and similarly failing to produce any charting singles. Sounding much like *Talk Is*

TOP ALBUMS

TALK IS CHEAP (Virgin, '88, 24)
KEITH RICHARDS & THE X-PENSIVE WINOS LIVE AT
    THE HOLLYWOOD PALLADIUM DECEMBER 15, 1988
    (Virgin, '91)
MAIN OFFENDER (Virgin, '92)

TOP SONGS

TAKE IT SO HARD (Virgin, '88)
HOW I WISH (Virgin, '88)
WICKED AS IT SEEMS (Virgin, '92)
DEMON (Virgin, '92)

Cheap—and thus much like the Rolling Stones without Jagger—the album featured songs written by Richards with band members Jordan, Waddy Wachtel, bassist Charlie Drayton, and background singer Sarah Dash.

While *Main Offender* offered songs of some substance and was hampered mainly by the lack of a strong lead vocalist, one suspects that if Jagger were actually singing the songs, all would still not necessarily be well. Richards' guitar riffing and songwriting style have not progressed much since the mid-'70s; much of what is on display on his albums sounds "classic" in the sense of the Stones' archetypal style—but noticeably static, even old. In late 1993, while the Stones auditioned bass players to replace the departed Bill Wyman and readied for yet another album and tour—five full years after 1989's *Steel Wheels*—it was interesting to ponder who might be waiting to hear them.

JONATHAN
RICHMAN

Jonathan Richman

Genius or crackpot? That it's hard to tell the difference—and that it probably doesn't even matter—may be one reason Jonathan Richman (b. May, 1951, Boston) has remained both unequalled and unimitated throughout his performing career. No one does it like Richman, whether it be adenoidal singing, songwriting, or making Mister Rogers look like a Mafia kingpin in comparison. Richman's legendary early-1970s Boston band the Modern Lovers can fairly be credited with playing punk rock before the media invented it a half-decade later. He is one of pop's most fascinating figures, essentially because he has kept himself and his music nearly unaffected by outside influences for over two decades.

Jonathan Richman has pursued two styles of music, and those styles could not be more divergent. An early fanatical follower of '60s pioneers the Velvet Underground, Richman put together a group that borrowed the Velvets' drive and emotional intensity and took it, in some ways, even further. The Modern Lovers played powerfully and, with Richman leading them, seemed to spit mightily into the face of convention. At a time when the Allman Brothers were taking duelling twin guitar leads and James Taylor

and Carole King were ruling the airwaves, the Modern Lovers were pounding out songs like "She Cracked," in which Richman, almost chanting, sang: "She'd/Eat garbage/Eat shit/Get stoned/I'd stay/Alone/Eat health food/At home." His all-time classic, "Roadrunner," later covered by the Sex Pistols and Joan Jett among hordes of others, took the Velvets' nightmarish "Sister Ray" chord cycle and sung the praises of driving alone at night listening to AM radio. And before the word took on its current sole connotation of sexual orientation, Richman proudly sang "I'm Straight" to his open-mouthed, mostly hippie audience.

But few heard. There were several attempts made by labels to record the Modern Lovers, including demo sessions paid for by Warner Bros. (with former Velvet then Warner Bros. staff producer John Cale at the helm) and A&M, but by the time the Modern Lovers were finally noticed, they were no more: Jonathan Richman had moved into the second phase of his music making. In 1975, the San Francisco–based Beserkley label provided Richman his first national exposure on *Beserkley Chartbusters Volume 1,* a sampler that featured label acts Earth Quake, the Rubinoos, Greg Kihn, and solo artist

Jonathan Richman—whose four tracks included a cover of the Showmen's 1961 hit "It Will Stand," a new version of "Roadrunner," "Government Center," and "The New Teller." The lyrics of the upbeat latter track gave the best indication of Richman's peculiar new direction: "Well everybody in the bank line knows/That I got a crush on the new teller/It's plain as day, I might as well tell her/She looks my way and she knows quite well, uh."

By the next year there was no doubt about the style change: Beserkley issued both *The Modern Lovers,* a mesmerizing collection of original early-'70s demos by the band, and the newly recorded *Jonathan Richman & The Modern Lovers,* Richman's first "official" album. Featuring an entirely new version of the Modern Lovers, the new package included songs such as "Abominable Snowman in the Market," "Hey There Little Insect," and "Here Come the Martian Martians," and was apparently intended for children of all ages. Richman's earlier focused intensity had been replaced by a noticeably childlike naïveté, and the music, in his words, showed "some of the '50s doowop, the 'outdoor-backyard' flavor" that would be central to his music thereafter.

Fans of the early Modern Lovers sessions initially assumed Richman's stylistic turnabout was some sort of insincere joke—that he wasn't actually serious about such songs as "Ice Cream Man," "I'm a Little Dinosaur," and "Dodge Veg-O-Matic." A half-dozen albums later, they weren't so sure. In the meantime, Richman had scored a European hit in 1978 with his instrumental "Egyptian Reggae," and he eventually became much more popular overseas than in his homeland. Since then, his works have appeared on several domestic labels, including Twin/Tone, Sire, and Rounder.

Richman offered a succinct—and rare—explanation for his mid-'70s directional shift in a bio he penned in the early 1990s titled "Jonathan Richman's First 20 Years in Show Business." In it he noted, "Richman's idea was not to make songs aimed specifically at children, but ones they could enjoy along with the rest of the audience. Sometimes this works and sometimes it doesn't…But the larger part of his songs were still more or less adult subject matter—the songs which had subject matter."

Not a single record Richman has made (his discography now includes over a dozen albums) has ever landed on the American charts, and given the self-imposed restraints of his subject matter along with his preference for minimal production, no future efforts are likely to. Which, no doubt, will be fine by him.

ROBBIE ROBERTSON

Regarded by many as one of the very finest singer-songwriters of the rock and roll era, Robbie Robertson (b. Jamie Robbie Robertson, July 5, 1944, Toronto, Ontario, Canada) at his best has the mystical ability to evoke times, places, and people long gone in his music. As the major songwriter and driving force of the legendary Band, Robertson crafted some of the most distinctly unforgettable pop music in history—most memorably so on 1969's *The Band,* his group's second album, on which with such songs as "The Night They Drove Old Dixie Down," "The Unfaithful Servant," and "King Harvest (Has Surely Come)" he painted a vivid picture of early rural America. "I feel that part of my job is to write American mythology," Robertson said in 1987, upon the release of his first album of new songs in 10 years. "And if there's a connection between what I did in the past and what I do now, it's that I'm continuing to to write this saga of what goes on in the Shadowland out there in the middle of this country someplace."

Though the Canadian-born son of a mother of Mohawk descent, Robertson's familiarity with mid-America was real indeed; in the early 1960s, as part

---

TOP ALBUMS

THE MODERN LOVERS (Beserkley, '76)
JONATHAN RICHMAN & THE MODERN LOVERS (Beserkley, '76)
ROCK 'N' ROLL WITH THE MODERN LOVERS (Beserkley, '77)
BACK IN YOUR LIFE (Beserkley, '79)
JONATHAN SINGS! (Sire, '83)
MODERN LOVERS 88 (Rounder, '87)
I, JONATHAN (Rounder, '92)

TOP SONGS

ROADRUNNER (Beserkley, '76)
SHE CRACKED (Beserkley, '76)
THAT SUMMER FEELING (Sire, '83)

Robbie Robertson

of rocker Ronnie Hawkins's backing group the Hawks, Robertson had repeatedly toured the club circuit of the U.S. and Canada. After splitting from Hawkins in 1963, the Hawks—who included all of the future members of the Band—toured, recorded some singles ("Leave Me Alone" and "The Stones That I Throw") for Atco as the Canadian Squires, and met up with blues singer John Hammond, Jr., who released three albums between 1965 and '68 on which Robertson played guitar.

In 1965, Robertson met Bob Dylan in New York City and his life changed dramatically. He and fellow Hawk Levon Helm backed Dylan on his historic Forest Hills "electric" concert, toured the U.S. with the singer, then recorded with him; Robertson's guitar can be heard on Dylan's classic 1966 set *Blonde on Blonde*. Together, Dylan and the Hawks moved

to Woodstock, New York, where, while the singer recuperated from a serious motorcycle accident, he and the Hawks made the informal series of recordings that would soon be bootlegged as *The Great White Wonder* and eventually see legitimate release in 1975 as *The Basement Tapes*.

By 1968, the Hawks had officially become the Band; their debut album, *Music from Big Pink*, became one of the most widely admired recordings of the decade. Featuring Robertson's well-known songs "The Weight," "Caledonia Mission," and "Chest Fever" (later covered on Three Dog Night's gold 1969 debut), the record also boasted three Dylan-penned tracks, including "Tears of Rage" (co-written with the Band's Richard Manuel), "This Wheel's on Fire (co-written with Band member Rick Danko), and the debut appearance of his monumental "I Shall Be Released." While *Big Pink* also featured excellent songs ("Lonesome Suzie" and "We Can Talk") penned solely by Richard Manuel, with later albums Robertson's compositions would almost completely dominate the Band's output.

Critics and fans alike were drawn by the unusual maturity and character to be found in the Band's work. Their 1969 masterwork, *The Band,* which featured the group's first top 30 hit, "Up on Cripple Creek," entered the top 10 and went platinum; 1970's follow-up, *Stage Fright,* which contained Robertson's well-known "The Shape I'm In," made the top five and was certified gold. The Band were indeed central pop figures throughout most of the early 1970s: Robertson received much acclaim for his production work on Jesse Winchester's brilliant 1970 debut; the group's superb double live LP, *Rock of Ages,* reached number six on the charts, went gold, and bore a top 40 hit cover version of Holland-Dozier-Holland's "Don't Do It"; with the Allman Brothers and the Grateful Dead, the group played before over 650,000 people at 1973's historic Watkins Glen Festival; and again with Dylan, the Band recorded both 1974's *Planet Waves* and its live follow-up, *Before the Flood.*

But with 1975's excellent *Northern Lights— Southern Cross*—the first collection of new Band material in four years—and its disappointing follow-up, *Islands,* much of the group's earlier magic seemed to be dwindling. The group soon undertook a final farewell tour, and on Thanksgiving Night in 1976 gave their final performance. The spectacular San Francisco show, which featured guest appearances by Dylan, Ronnie Hawkins, Van Morrison, Neil Young, Eric Clapton, Muddy Waters, and Neil Diamond (whose two albums *Beautiful Noise* and *Love at the Greek* were produced by Robertson), was filmed by director Martin Scorsese and became *The Last Waltz,* deemed by many critics to be the best rock film ever made.

Robertson spent most of the next few years absorbed in film work. He produced, composed source music for, and starred in 1979's *Carny,* then provided music for Scorsese's 1980 film *Raging Bull* and 1983's *The King of Comedy.* The latter's sound-

track album also featured Robertson's first post-Band recording, "Between Trains." In the mid-'80s, he signed a solo recording deal—which began at EMI-America but ended up at Geffen Records, due to a label move by A&R Executive Gary Gersh, who'd signed him—and worked further with Scorsese on his 1986 film *The Color of Money,* co-writing "It's in the Way That You Use It" with Eric Clapton.

Ironically for a writer of Robertson's stature, when his debut album, *Robbie Robertson,* emerged on Geffen Records in 1987, more than a few people were uncertain of how it would sound; with three superb singers in the Band like Levon Helm, Richard Manuel, and Rick Danko, Robertson very rarely was lead vocalist on his own songs. It was only a brief mystery, however; the album was both a critical and commercial hit, reaching number 38 and soon going gold. The selection of fellow Canadian Danois Lanois as the album's co-producer was a particularly astute move. Renowned for his work with U2 and Peter Gabriel, Lanois provided Robertson his typically atomspheric and airy sonic canvas, and the singer supplied some of his best work in ages. "I didn't want to make a Band album," Robertson said at the time of its release. "I wanted to make an album that reflects the way I feel now. The sounds are 99% organic—the real thing. It's real people playing. Instead of getting things on Synclaviers and synthesizers, I wanted to get them on guitars." With guest appearances by the BoDeans, Gabriel, Lone Justice's Maria McKee, and U2 (who played on two tracks and co-wrote "Sweet Fire of Love"), the album was ample proof Robertson remained one of pop's finest songwriters.

Storyville, the singer's 1991 follow-up, was a comparably sturdy effort, this time co-produced by Robertson, Stephen Hague, and Geffen A&R exec (and current Capitol Records president) Gersh. Featuring several songwriting collaborations by Robertson and guest musicians such as Bruce Hornsby, David Ricketts of A&M act David + David, Ivan Neville, and Martin Page (who had co-written two tracks on the singer's 1987 set), the album purported to tell the story of a boy and girl who meet and fall in love in the fabled Storyville district of New

---

TOP ALBUMS

ROBBIE ROBERTSON (Geffen, '87, *38*)
STORYVILLE (Geffen, '91)

TOP SONGS

FALLEN ANGEL (Geffen, '87)
SWEET FIRE OF LOVE (Geffen, '87)
SOMEWHERE DOWN THE CRAZY RIVER (Geffen, '87)
NIGHT PARADE (Geffen, '91)
SIGN OF THE RAINBOW (Geffen, '91)

Orleans. "Life isn't places and events," Robertson explained at the time. "It's the stuff in between, that mystery of emotion and relationships. The boy and the girl in this story share that mystery with each other."

Though the singer offered those words only to explain *Storyville*, they reveal much about what continues to make Robbie Robertson one of pop's premiere songwriters. Both with and without the Band, his music carries with it an air of timelessness that makes it as meaningful today as it was the day it was written; rather than places or events, it very artfully explores that same "stuff in between."

TODD RUNDGREN

Todd Rungren

A pioneer in combining music with both video and CD-interactive technology, Todd Rundgren (b. June 22, 1948, Upper Darby, Pennsylvania) may be pop's ultimate hyphenate: a singer-songwriter-multi-instrumentalist-producer-videographer-programmer who can also write the catchiest of pop tunes when he has the inclination. Rundgren turned his back on simply attempting to make hit records long ago and since the mid-'70s has focused most of his attention on those aspects of music that especially fascinate him. While fans of such early-'70s Rundgren hits as "We Gotta Get You a Woman," "I Saw the Light," and "Hello It's Me" continue to clamor for him to return to his early melodic-pop style, the singer has aggressively pursued a singular musical path that has taken him through a variety of styles but rarely returned him to the top of the charts. Interestingly—and part of what has made him an enigmatic rock figure—he hasn't seemed to have minded that in the least.

Rundgren's arrival on the scene came in the late 1960s via his superb Philadelphia-based rock band the Nazz, who ignored the fashionable San Francisco acid rock of the era to pursue the English rock sound of the Who, Yardbirds, and Rolling Stones. While the group had only one charting single— "Hello It's Me," which reached number 66 in 1969 and became a top five hit for Rundgren himself four years later—"Open My Eyes," the extremely Whoish opening track from its 1968 debut, *Nazz*, enjoyed considerable underground radio play at the time. Rundgren wrote and arranged nearly all of the material on the band's three albums, the third of which

saw release well after he'd left the group and scored a top 20 hit as a solo artist with "We've Gotta Get You a Woman."

The singer's new solo deal with Ampex Records came as the result of signing to the prestigious management firm of Albert Grossman. His in at the label and with Grossman allowed him to fully explore his interest in studio work; before long, he was producing and engineering many sessions for Grossman-related artists and the Bearsville label, including the American Dream, Ian and Sylvia's Great Speckled Bird, the Band, Jesse Winchester, the Paul Butterfield Blues Band, and early Sparks. Meanwhile, Rundgren's studio versatility allowed him to play most of the music on his own records, beginning with 1970's *Runt* through 1971's *The Ballad of Todd Rundgren* and 1972's gold two-LP tour de force album, *Something/Anything?*—the latter of which peaked at number 29 and remains his highest-charting album.

Rundgren's melodic gifts, evident from the start, owed much to the pop craft of Laura Nyro and the Brill Building sound of Goffin-King. Still, as the former lead guitarist of the Nazz, the singer was an able hard rocker and showed it on early tracks such as "Devil's Bite," "Parole," and "Black Maria." It was a dichotomy that would become more glaring as his career developed through the 1970s and the dazzling studio whiz needed to take his act on the road. Following 1973's *A Wizard/A True Star,* a remarkably seamless collection of pop, rock, and R&B that many feel to be his best work, Rundgren assembled a live band called Utopia with whom he would continue to regularly record into the 1990s.

Beginning with 1974's *Todd Rundgren's Utopia,* which bore a mixture of instrumental progressive rock midway between the arty sounds of Yes and the jazz fusion of John McLaughlin's Mahavishnu Orchestra, Rundgren began losing many of the loyal fans who came to him via his *Something/Anything?* hits "I Saw the Light" and "Hello It's Me." It was something that couldn't be helped, he maintained. "*Something/Anything?,* as much as I enjoyed the exercise, was unsatisfying for me in the end," he recalled in 1981. "Writing songs in that vein became so...automatic...that I didn't feel I was being creative. It started out being a single album, but by the time I was finished it was a double album. I was writing a song every day. In 15 minutes I'd come up with a song—it became too easy. It was all formula, essentially."

Rundgren began releasing albums alternately with Utopia and under his own name, the latter of which would typically feature him performing all the music via studio overdubs. Ironically, as the 1970s progressed, the Utopia albums became more hard-rock- and song-oriented, while his solo albums became more extended and musically diffuse. He began playing clever studio games that bore fascinating results, such as 1976's *Faithful*—on which he devoted one album side to near note-for-note replications of '60s classics by the Yardbirds, the Beach Boys, the Beatles, Bob Dylan, and Jimi Hendrix—and 1980's Utopia set *Face the Music,* a brilliant Beatles "parody" that perfectly captured the Mersey-beat-era style but then shunted it oddly sideways.

Meanwhile, Rundgren's future as a '70s pop superstar began to evaporate as all but one of his post-*Something/Anything?* solo albums failed to even enter the top 40. The exception, his excellent *Hermit of Mink Hollow,* marked a conspicuous return to his earlier pop style and featured his last hit, the top 30 single "Can We Still Be Friends." It became further apparent that only Rundgren's commercial pull, not his songwriting prowess, had dete-

riorated—that he wasn't kidding, he really did prefer not to write hits "by formula"—when England Dan and John Ford Coley scored a 1979 top 10 hit with his song "Love Is the Answer," otherwise found buried at the end of Utopia's middling 1977 set *Oops! Wrong Planet.*

By the mid-1980s Rundgren was immersing himself in music video and other projects, while neither Utopia's albums nor his own were succeeding in even breaking the top 100. He moved to Warner Bros. with 1985's *A Capella,* a solo set that featured only his multi-overdubbed vocals; its 1989 follow-up, *Nearly Human,* showcased yet another gimmick: it was recorded entirely live in the studio with a backing band of nearly 30 musicians—but, as was now the norm, it failed to catch fire. With his constant need to try something new—whether it be an a cappella album, studio replicas of other people's hits, or untouched live performances—Rundgren now often seemed to approach album making as more an intellectual exercise than a vehicle of artistic expression. "I have to have a context to work within," he explained in 1993. "Since I have a very short attention span, I need some kind of unifying theme; otherwise I'd be doing jazz or classical or electronic music all on the same album. Every record would be so eclectic and chaotic it would be impossible to retain an audience."

The singer once again claimed a technological first with 1993's *No World Order,* the first album

TOP ALBUMS

SOMETHING/ANYTHING? (Bearsville, '73, *29*)

A WIZARD/A TRUE STAR (Bearsville, '73)

TODD RUNDGREN'S UTOPIA (with Utopia, Bearsville, '74, *34*)

HERMIT OF MINK HOLLOW (Bearsville, '78, *36*)

ADVENTURES IN UTOPIA (with Utopia, Bearsville, '80, *32*)

TOP SONGS

WE GOTTA GET YOU A WOMAN (as Runt, Ampex, '70, *20*)

I SAW THE LIGHT (Bearsville, '72, *16*)

HELLO IT'S ME (Bearsville, '73, *5*)

CAN WE STILL BE FRIENDS (Bearsville, '78, *29*)

SET ME FREE (with Utopia, Bearsville, '80, *27*)

Additional Top 40 Songs: 1

ever recorded specifically for CD-interactive technology. With it, listeners were capable of playing various portions of his music in any sequence they liked. "Users would have to play the CD-I for 24 hours a day, seven days a week well into the next millenium to hear the same version of any song twice," Rundgren proudly announced at the time of its release. Habitually reluctant to repeat himself, Todd Rundgren is making certain in the 1990s that his fans won't allow him to do it either.

TOM RUSH

One of the most prominent figures to emerge from the burgeoning folk music scene of the early 1960s, Tom Rush (b. Feb. 8, 1941) was among the first in his genre to break out of blues and traditional folk modes and explore the works of other, more contemporary writers. While he himself gradually became an excellent composer—his song "No Regrets" being perhaps his best—his unerring taste in little-known songsmiths who'd soon become famous bordered on the phenomenal. His classic 1968 album *The Circle Game,* for example, provided many their first-ever hearing of songs by Joni Mitchell, James Taylor, and Jackson Browne; later the singer would cover works by Jesse Winchester, Bruce Cockburn, and even Gilbert O'Sullivan (who as Ray O'Sullivan had penned "Came to See Me Yesterday in the Merry Month Of" on Rush's 1970 album *Wrong End of the Rainbow*).

Rush, a Harvard student, got a comparatively early start in folk circles. In 1962, he released a live album on the small Ly Cornu label, *Tom Rush at the Unicorn,* after which he signed to Prestige, for whom he recorded *Got a Mind to Ramble* (1963) and *Blues/ Songs/Ballads* (1965). His material at the time was largely traditional and/or blues based, including such standards as "Rye Whiskey," "San Francisco Bay Blues," and "Rag Mama." While still a student, he signed to the blossoming Elektra label, which then concentrated largely on folk music. His three records for the imprint were distinctively for-

ward-looking; though the first two (1965's *Tom Rush* and 1966's *Take a Little Walk with Me*) included mostly traditional material such as "The Cuckoo" or "Sugar Babe," by the second, Rush was utilizing electric guitar (played by Al Kooper) and actually covering blues and rock and roll—by Willie Dixon, Chuck Berry, Bo Diddley, and even Buddy Holly. More interestingly, he included an atmospheric cover of "Joshua Gone Barbados" by Eric Von Schmidt, the Cambridge folk singer he has claimed as a major influence. It was a sign of what was to come: *Circle Game,* his final album for Elektra, signaled a move from traditional material to the newer folk-inspired pop of Mitchell, Taylor, and Browne. Whereas one of the highlights of its predecessor, *Take a Little Walk with Me,* was Rush's bluesy, "knife-style" guitar work on the traditional "Galveston Flood," *Circle Game,* in its way an early concept album, included orchestral backing, conducted by keyboardist Paul Harris. One of the true classics of the 1960s, the record peaked at number 68 and remains the singer's biggest hit.

Rush moved on to Columbia, where he continued covering the likes of Taylor and Browne but increasingly wrote his own material. His most frequent collaborator was Canadian guitarist Trevor Veitch; their best-known song, "Merrimack County," appeared on both *Wrong End of the Rainbow* (1970) and as the title track to its 1972 follow-up. Rush was by all means commercially successful—his Columbia albums all reached the bottom half of the chart—but after a 1986 hits collection, the singer lost major-label affiliation. One of the first '60s artists to recognize the potentially vast baby-boomer market for older artists, he then began a mail-order operation and record company called Night Light Recordings from his base in Hillsboro, New Hampshire. In 1982, he released *Live at Symphony Hall,* a superb concert recording of his best-known work; two years later, *Late Night Radio* similarly presented Rush live with guests including Steve Goodman, Mimi Farina, David Buskin, David Batteau, and Jake Holmes. It was a shrewd marketing move by a man to whom shrewdness—artistic or otherwise —had clearly never been a stranger.

TOP ALBUMS

TAKE A LITTLE WALK WITH ME (Elektra, '66)
THE CIRCLE GAME (Elektra, '68)
TOM RUSH (Columbia, '70)
WRONG END OF THE RAINBOW (Columbia, '70)

TOP SONGS

NO REGRETS (Elektra, '68)
MERRIMACK COUNTY (Columbia, '70)

LEON RUSSELL

An outstanding musician who's recorded with most of the major artists in rock and roll, Leon Russell (b. Apr. 2, 1941, Lawton, Oklahoma) was once nicknamed the "Master of Space and Time"—and on the basis of his resume alone, it wouldn't be wise to quibble. Russell worked with Jerry Lee Lewis in the 1950s; moved to L.A. and played on most of Phil Spector's classic sessions in the early '60s; performed on the Byrds' 1965 hit "Mr Tambourine Man"; co-wrote and arranged several top five hits for Gary Lewis and the Playboys; regularly appeared on the hit '60s TV show "Shindig!"; and later played individual sessions with Eric Clapton, Bob Dylan, the Rolling Stones, Delaney and Bonnie, and many more. He became internationally known both for organizing Joe Cocker's famous Mad Dogs and Englishmen tour of 1970 and for his memorable performance at George Harrison's 1971 Concert for Bangladesh at Madison Square Garden. And in the course of all this, he managed to make his own records, too.

Russell's first real album came in 1968, when he and songwriting partner Marc Benno recorded as the Asylum Choir for Smash Records. Though *Look Inside the Asylum Choir* sold poorly, it remains a remarkably good album; filled with upbeat songs and a fair share of sound effects, the musicianship is superb throughout—and Beatlesque tracks such as "Icicle Star Tree" will surprise anyone thinking Russell's roots lie solely in earthy, gospelish R&B. After arranging and performing on Delaney and Bonnie's 1969 Elektra album *The Original Delaney & Bonnie*, Russell was asked by British producer Denny Cordell to co-produce Joe Cocker's second album. The eventual result: the album went gold and entered the top 15, Cocker covered Russell's well-known tune "Delta Lady," the Mad Dogs and Englishmen tour got under way, and Russell and Cordell soon founded the Shelter Records label.

When Russell released his 1970 Shelter debut,

TOP ALBUMS

LEON RUSSELL & THE SHELTER
  PEOPLE (Shelter, '71, *17*)
CARNEY (Shelter, '72, *2*)
LEON LIVE (Shelter, '73, *9*)
STOP ALL THAT JAZZ
  (Shelter, '74, *34*)
WILL O' THE WISP (Shelter, '75, *30*)

Additional Top 40 Albums: 4

TOP SONGS

A SONG FOR YOU (Shelter, '70)
DELTA LADY (Shelter, '70)
TIGHT ROPE (Shelter, '72, *11*)
THIS MASQUERADE (Shelter, '72)
LADY BLUE (Shelter, '75, *14*)

Leon Russell, the depth of his connections became apparent: though contractual difficulties would not allow exact musician credits, the album was "dedicated to" a cast of musicians that included Beatles George Harrison and Ringo Starr, Rolling Stones Charlie Watts and Bill Wyman, Eric Clapton, Steve Winwood, and Delaney and Bonnie, among others. One of the better debut albums of the 1970s, the set included Russell's oft-covered "A Song for You," his own version of "Delta Lady," and "Hummingbird," which became a top 50 hit for B. B. King later that year. Though for some, Russell's Oklahoma drawl took some getting used to, the album was an early FM hit and reached number 60 without the benefit of a hit single.

Following the success of Joe Cocker's live *Mad Dogs & Englishmen* album, which reached number two at the end of 1970 and featured Russell prominently, the stage was set for 1971's *Leon Russell & the Shelter People*. One of Russell's best records, it featured four separate bands, entered the top 20—again, with no hit to speak of—and was his first gold album. As it made its way up the charts, so did a top five cover version of Russell and Bonnie Bramlett's "Superstar" by, of all people, the Carpenters; if anything, the ultra-straight duo's recognition of Russell's writing talents only added to his reputation as "Master of Space and Time." The success of the *Shelter People* set was enough for Russell and Cordell to buy back the master for a second Asylum Choir album that Mercury had chosen not to release; issued by Shelter in late 1971 as *Asylum Choir II,* the two-year-old album sounded much more in keeping with Russell's known style than did its predecessor and climbed to number 70 on the charts.

With 1972's *Carney*, which stayed at number two for four weeks, Russell reached the pinnacle of his commercial success. Its opening track, "Tight Rope," his first hit, reached number 11; also featured was "This Masquerade," which George Benson would later take to the top 10 in 1976. He followed it with a somewhat excessive three-LP set,

Leon Live—which despite its size entered the top 10 and went gold—then returned to his "country roots" with *Hank Wilson's Back,* an album covering country classics by the likes of Hank Williams, George Jones, and Bill Monroe.

Russell's next few albums continued to do well: *Stop All That Jazz* offered an early appearance by R&B hitmakers the Gap Band, and 1975's *Will O' the Wisp* went gold thanks to its inclusion of the top 15 hit "Lady Blue." He married Shelter-signed vocalist Mary McCreary in 1976; that same year, their joint *Wedding Album* reached number 34 on the charts, significantly higher than John Lennon and Yoko Ono managed with their own same-titled set seven years earlier. But by the end of the 1970s, things were slowing down for the singer. A second duet album, 1977's *Make Love to the Music,* hung on the charts for a scant five weeks, and *Americana,* Russell's first solo album since *Will O' the Wisp,* meagerly peaked at number 115. Though his 1979 collaboration with Willie Nelson, *One for the Road,* went gold, it did so largely because it had followed two of the biggest albums of Nelson's career. Russell's last charting effort was *The Live Album,* jointly recorded with bluegrass group New Grass Revival; it stayed on the charts for two weeks in 1981 and peaked at number 187.

An attempt by Virgin Records to rekindle Russell's recording career in the early 1990s was conspicuously unsuccessful. A very solid album that featured major songwriting input from co-producer Bruce Hornsby, *Anything Can Happen* disappointingly failed to find any kind of audience; the album never even entered the charts. And whether Russell remains in the mood for yet another comeback attempt is, of course, a question only the Master of Space and Time himself can answer.

DOUG SAHM

"**D**oug Sahm is the true rock hybrid," wrote critic John Swenson in his liner notes to Sahm's 1973 superb odds-and-ends compilation *Rough Edges,* "a psychedelic Texan with ice cold blues blood and an equal affinity for country-western music, the funky chicano sound from his home town and good ole rock 'n' roll." Swenson's colorful description hit it precisely on the nose: Doug Sahm (b. Nov. 6, 1941, San Antonio, Texas), like all truly great artists, has absorbed everything he's ever heard and created something distinctly original and timeless in its appeal. As founder of the Sir Douglas Quintet, who had a top 20 hit with 1965's "She's About a Mover," as a solo artist, and as one-fourth of '90s Tex-Mex supergroup the Texas Tornados, Sahm has produced one of the most distinguished and substantial bodies of work in pop music.

A musical prodigy who as five-year-old "Little Doug" won a radio singing contest, Sahm was playing triple-neck steel guitar while in elementary school in San Antonio. The town's diverse music scene gave him an early education in country music (at seven, he'd been photographed in the lap of the legendary Hank Williams), the Texas blues of T-Bone Walker, and the Mexican rock of Ricky Aguirre. The mixture would serve him well both in mid-'50s local bands such as the Knights and as a budding solo artist in 1960, when he scored local hits with "Why Why Why" and "Crazy, Crazy Feelin'." And, of course, it certainly played a role in the early 1960s, when he formed the nucleus of what would become the Sir Douglas Quintet. Given the "Sir Douglas" nickname by producer Huey Meaux, who sought to take advantage of the era's surge of British Invasion bands, Sahm recorded "She's About a Mover" for Meaux's Tribe Records label in early 1965 and had an international hit on his hands months later. By early 1966, a second hit, "The Rains Came," had followed. After an infamous drug bust in Corpus Christi that year, the original Quintet disbanded, and Sahm headed to San Francisco.

Beginning with 1968's *Honkey Blues,* Sahm's newly formed Quintet released a string of albums for various Mercury-affiliated labels that constitute most of the best work he's done. Very much the eclectic blend that writer Swenson describes above, the records boast a diversity of styles held together by Sahm's warm, raspy vocals, the distinctive organ playing of original Quintet member Augie Meyers (who rejoined Sahm in 1968), and the consistently strong material Sahm supplied regularly. He scored a 1969 top 30 hit with "Mendocino," memorably pumped up by Meyer's Farfisa organ—a sound that would later be blatantly imitated by Elvis Costello and the Attractions and fellow Texan Joe "King" Carrasco; from the album of the same name also came "At the Crossroads," later covered to great effect on the debut LP by England's Mott the Hoople.

Typically, Sahm blended rock, country (he'd cut Tom T. Hall's "the Homecoming"), early Tex-Mex

TOP ALBUMS

MENDOCINO (with the Sir Douglas Quintet, Smash, '69)
TOGETHER AFTER FIVE (with the Sir Douglas Quintet, Smash, '70)
ROUGH EDGES (Mercury, '73)
DOUG SAHM AND BAND (Atlantic, '73)
TEXAS ROCK FOR COUNTRY ROLLERS (with the Texas Tornados, Dot, '76)
HELL OF A SPELL (Takoma, '80)

TOP SONGS

SHE'S ABOUT A MOVER (with the Sir Douglas Quintet, Tribe, '65, 13)
MENDOCINO (with the Sir Douglas Quintet, Smash, '69, 27)
AT THE CROSSROADS (with the Sir Douglas Quintet, Smash, '69)
NUEVO LAREDO (with the Sir Douglas Quintet, Smash, '70)

(1971's *The Return of Doug Saldana* featured a cover of later Texas Tornado Freddy Fender's "Wasted Days and Wasted Nights"), and blues into a distinctive sound, then topped it off with originals with titles like "Lawd, I'm Just a Country Boy in This Great Big Freaky City" and "You Never Get Too Big and You Sure Don't Get Too Heavy, That You Don't Have to Stop and Pay Some Dues Sometime." His unique talents drew fans from high places, including producer Jerry Wexler, who signed Sahm to Atlantic Records in 1973, and Bob Dylan, who played harmonica and sang on his own previously unrecorded "Wallflower" for label debut *Doug Sahm and Band.* Sahm would later appear with Dylan on his memorable Rolling Thunder Revue tour of 1975–76.

Sahm moved to various labels throughout the 1970s, including Warner Bros. for 1974's *Groover's Paradise* (which featured the singer backed by the rhythm section of Creedence Clearwater Revival), Dot for 1976's *Texas Rock for Country Rollers,* and Takoma in 1980 for *Hell of a Spell.* By then, Augie Meyer's cheap-Farfisa sound had influenced an entire generation of punk and new wave bands; it was enough to give Sahm reason to reform his Quintet—which he did for 1981's *Border Wave,* also on Takoma. He spent most of the 1980s performing with the Quintet and recording for small labels, domestic or otherwise; two of his better sets are *Juke Box Music,* released on the Texan Antone's label in 1988, and *The Return of the Formerly Brothers,* a collaboration featuring Sahm, guitarist Amos Garrett, and pianist Gene Taylor.

Since 1990, Sahm has met significant success with the Texas Tornados, an all-star group also including Meyers, Fender, and accordionist Flaco Jimenez. A track from their debut album received a 1990 Grammy Award (in the category of Best Mexican/American Performance), and their 1991 follow-up set, *Zone of Our Own,* was similarly nominated. Fittingly, the group's hybrid style echoes the same eclecticism that has been a central part of Sahm's work since the days of "She's About a Mover." However varied it may be, Doug Sahm's music has never strayed so far from its San Antonio roots that it could lose its Texas heart—or soul.

"Black kids who are into rap, that's great," Sahm told writer Keith Gorman in 1993. "But they should know who T-Bone Walker is. And Guitar Slim—how funky can you get? Look what that guy did for Louisiana music. I've never heard people talk about those guys, and it bothers me. People should take their roots more seriously."

BUFFY SAINTE-MARIE

With her high-pitched, vibrato-filled voice and repertoire of meaningful political songs and touching romantic ballads, Native American singer-songwriter Buffy Sainte-Marie (b. Feb. 20, 1941, Piapot Reserve, Saskatchewan, Canada) cut a striking image in the early 1960s. A mixed-blood Cree Indian, she wrote and sang about controversial topics such as the Vietnam War ("Universal Soldier"), drug addiction ("Cod'ine"), and the plight of the American Indian ("My Country 'Tis of Thy People You're Dying") yet balanced all that with sensitive love songs like "Until It's Time for You to Go," later covered by Elvis Presley, Barbra Streisand, Bobby Darin, and Neil Diamond. She spent much of the later 1960s in an exploratory mode, recording a Nashville album at the invitation of Chet Atkins in 1968 (*I Wanna Be a Country Girl Again*) and an extremely forward-looking, quadraphonic album of electronic music (*Illuminations*) only a year later.

TOP ALBUMS

IT'S MY WAY (Vanguard, '64)
LITTLE WHEEL SPIN AND SPIN (Vanguard, '66)
I'M GONNA BE A COUNTRY GIRL AGAIN (Vanguard, '68)
SHE USED TO WANNA BE A BALLERINA (Vanguard, '71)
COINCIDENCE AND LIKELY STORIES (Ensign/Chrysalis, '92)

TOP SONGS

UNIVERSAL SOLDIER (Vanguard, '64)
UNTIL IT'S TIME FOR YOU TO GO (Vanguard, '65)
NOW THAT THE BUFFALO'S GONE (Vanguard, '68)
MISTER CAN'T YOU SEE (Vanguard, '72, 38)
THE BIG ONES GET AWAY (Ensign/Chrysalis, '92)

A graduate of the University of Massachusetts in Amherst, Sainte-Marie studied Oriental philosophy and education and later received a Ph.D. in fine arts. Having regularly performed at a campus coffee house while a student, she departed to New York upon graduation to try her hand in the city's burgeoning folk music scene and found success quickly. A series of press raves convinced Vanguard Records maven Maynard Solomon to offer the singer a deal, which she eventually accepted; between 1964 and 1973, she recorded 12 well-received albums for the label.

Perhaps because of her unique voice—which some felt to be an acquired taste—Sainte-Marie's better-known songs have typically been performed by other artists. Both Glen Campbell and Donovan, for instance, recorded "Universal Soldier," which originally appeared on her 1964 debut, It's My Way. In September 1965, both versions debuted the same week on the Hot 100, with Campbell's peaking at number 45 and beating Donovan's by a mere eight slots. Similarly, Quicksilver Messenger Service's version of "Cod'ine" became an early standard for the legendary San Franciscan rock group.

By the time of her first charting album, 1966's Little Wheel Spin and Spin, Sainte-Marie established a consistent pattern of performing for both the general public and Native American populations on assorted reservations. Her militant stance on the issue of Indian rights became increasingly pronounced in her repertoire, notably with such songs as "Now That the Buffalo's Gone," "My Country 'Tis of Thy People You're Dying," and "Bury My Heart at Wounded Knee." Eventually, the singer would speak of being "blacklisted" for her strong human rights stance. "On the 'Tonight Show,' " she has said, "I was told not to sing anything to do with the Indian people."

Upon departing Vanguard in 1973, she made two country-oriented albums for MCA, including 1974's Buffy, which caused a clamor with its revealing cover photo showing the singer's bared breast. "It stood for a woman's right to take her own shirt off," she later explained. "I was having trouble with my own reputation for being a 'serious artist.' " Sweet America, released on ABC in 1975, was the singer's final album for 15 years. In the interim she joined the cast of "Sesame Street" in a semi-regular role, gave birth to a son, Dakota, and scored the films Harold of Orange and Where the Spirit Lives. Unexpectedly, she won a 1982 Academy Award for co-writing "Up Where We Belong" from the Paramount film An Officer and a Gentleman.

In the 1990s, Sainte-Marie now composes much of her music on a Macintosh computer, and she actually used it to record most of her inspired 1992 comeback album, Coincidence and Likely Stories. Ironically, the disc was issued on Ensign Records, the same label for which Sinead O'Connor records; at the time of its release, several critics noted Sainte-Marie's onetime "acquired taste" of a voice in fact bears a marked resemblance to that of youthful alternative star O'Connor. A respected artist whose commitment to music and people has characteristically gone hand-in-hand, Buffy Sainte-Marie is now, happily, sounding better than ever.

LEO SAYER

Time has been kind to the memory of Leo Sayer (b. Gerard Sayer, May 21, 1948, Shoreham, England). It may simply be a case of absence making the heart grow fonder—he hasn't had a major hit since 1980, after all—but more likely, it's because there was never much to dislike in the first place. Sayer was a pop artist who made no grandiose claims about his own talent; he simply made unpretentious, catchy pop records that people liked and, not incidentally, often bought in great number. Which is easier said than done.

Discovered singing in the London streets in 1972 by former U.K. pop star Adam Faith and his eventual songwriting partner David Courtney, Sayer burst upon the scene somewhat indirectly. Roger Daltrey, the Who's lead vocalist, took the Sayer-Courtney collaboration "Giving It All Away" to the top of the British charts in 1973 and set the stage for Sayer's debut album, *Silverbird,* soon after. Despite a hokey performing gimmick Sayer used initially but then dropped—he wore full makeup and a clown costume onstage—he was an immediate success, and his single "The Show Must Go On" an instant U.K. smash.

In an era when Elton John reigned supreme, many noticed interesting parallels between John and Sayer. Both sang with distinctively high voices, both used regular songwriting partners (though Sayer wrote his own lyrics and Elton his own music), and both were highly charismatic live performers. Before long, America noticed, too. Sayer's second album, *Just a Boy,* reached the top 20 largely on the strength of the top 10 hit "Long Tall Glasses (I Can Dance)." And then Sayer lost his collaborator Courtney, who—in yet another Elton parallel—left to establish his own solo recording career (but didn't; Courtney's *First Day,* his 1975 solo set, flopped, and he'd eventually work with Sayer again). After a brief stint collaborating with onetime Supertramp bassist Frank Farrell for 1975's *Another Year,* Sayer flew to America to record *Endless Flight* with hotshot producer Richard Perry. The resulting album was the biggest

in Sayer's career—and a major change for him. He began covering other writers' material (in this case Andrew Gold, Danny O'Keefe, and Albert Hammond and Carole Bayer Sager) and writing with more than his habitual one collaborator. Wisely so, it turned out: both "You Make Me Feel Like Dancing" (co-written by Sayer and Vinnie Poncia) and "When I Need You" (by Hammond and Sager) hit Number One and remain Sayer's first and last times at the top.

The bad news: his next two albums, also Perry productions, bore only one hit, "Thunder in My Heart." And 1979's *Here,* which reunited Sayer with former partner Courtney, also proved a critical and commercial disappointment. Sayer's final chart appearance came in 1980 with the number two single "More Than I Can Say," originally a hit for Bobby Vee in 1961. His last two albums, *World Radio* and *Have You Ever Been in Love,* came and went quietly—and so, it seemed, did Sayer.

BOZ SCAGGS

Boz Scaggs (b. William Royce Scaggs, June 8, 1944, Ohio) remains one of pop music's most mysterious delights. A rocker since the early 1960s, he's been ahead of his time in many ways: at the forefront of the late-'60s San Francisco scene with the Steve Miller Band; as a solo act holding his own with the distinguished musicians of Muscle Shoals; credibly incorporating into his own music the black sounds of Motown and New Orleans's Allen Toussaint; redefining "blue-eyed soul" with his 1976 masterwork *Silk Degrees;* and finally, frustratingly, seemingly retiring from the music business altogether. If anyone deserves the tired appellation "eclectic," Scaggs is certainly the man.

Having met Miller while attending a Dallas prep school in the late 1950s, the 15-year-old Scaggs was invited to join Miller's band as vocalist; the relationship continued when both moved to the University of Wisconsin in Madison and played together in local band the Ardells. In 1963, Scaggs returned to Texas alone and formed an R&B band called the Wigs. A trip to Europe together the next year resulted in that group's eventual disbanding; while Scaggs' former band members went back to the States, the singer recorded a solo folk album in Stockholm for Polydor, released in 1965 and now extremely rare.

TOP ALBUMS

JUST A BOY (Warner Bros., '75, *16*)
ENDLESS FLIGHT (Warner Bros., '76, *10*)
THUNDER IN MY HEART (Warner Bros., '77, *37*)
LIVING IN A FANTASY (Warner Bros., '80, *36*)

TOP SONGS

LONG TALL GLASSES (I CAN DANCE)
   (Warner Bros., '75, *9*)
YOU MAKE ME FEEL LIKE DANCING
   (Warner Bros., '76, *1*)
WHEN I NEED YOU (Warner Bros., '77, *1*)
HOW MUCH LOVE (Warner Bros., '77, *17*)
MORE THAN I CAN SAY (Warner Bros., '80, *2*)
LIVING IN A FANTASY (Warner Bros., '81, *23*)

Additional Top 40 Songs: 2

Scaggs soon returned to the States and joined the Steve Miller Band, newly signed to Capitol, sticking around long enough to play on *Children of the Future* (1967) and *Sailor* (1968), now both regarded as classics. Scaggs' written contributions were minimal compared to Miller's; "Baby's Calling Me Home," his memorable track from *Future,* was later resurrected by the then soloist in the 1972 film *Fillmore: The Last Days.*

Scaggs came into his own artistically with 1969's *Boz Scaggs,* a superb album recorded at Muscle Shoals that neatly displayed his most notable influences, from country (a cover of Jimmie Rodgers' "Waiting for a Train") to blues (a version of Fenton Robinson's "Loan Me a Dime" featuring memorable playing by Duane Allman) to upbeat R&B ("I'm Easy," co-written by Scaggs and Barry Beckett). Two marvelous Scaggs originals, "I'll Be Long Gone" (later covered by Mother Earth) and "Finding Her," pointed toward the musical direction Scaggs would eventually explore most successfully; both were moody, soulful tracks, nearly mournful in tone but still delightful. They sounded, in fact, like the cover of Scaggs' next album looked.

Moments, released by Columbia in 1971, bore a photo of Scaggs staring reflectively at an ocean sunset. Three of its most memorable tracks were, like "Long Gone," moodily introspective: "Downright Women," "Near You," and the (surprisingly) instrumental "Can I Make It Last (Or Will It Just Be Over)" showed an overall maturity that would come to characterize the best work of Scaggs' career. His next few albums found him scampering from style to style, regularly covering Allen Toussaint, dropping his band in favor of studio musicians, and eventually hooking up with former Motown producer Johnny Bristol for 1974's *Slow Dancer.*

Grand success kicked in via 1976's *Silk Degrees,* with which Scaggs finally, irrefutably, created a perfect merger of rock, soul, and R&B, and which eventually went double platinum. It helped that he'd written some of his best songs ever, including top five hit "Lowdown" and "Lido Shuffle" (both co-written with keyboardist David Paich) and "We're All

TOP ALBUMS

BOZ SCAGGS (Atlantic, '69)
MOMENTS (Columbia, '71)
SILK DEGREES (Columbia, '76, 2)
DOWN TWO THEN LEFT
 (Columbia, '77, *11*)
MIDDLE MAN (Columbia, '80, 8)
HITS! (Columbia, '80, *24*)

TOP SONGS

LOWDOWN (Columbia '76, 3)
LIDO SHUFFLE (Columbia, '77, *11*)
LOOK WHAT YOU'VE DONE TO ME
 (Columbia, '80, *14*)
MISS SUN (Columbia, '80, *14*)

Additional Top 40 Songs: 4

Alone" (a top 10 hit for Rita Coolidge in 1977). Propelled by a studio band that would evolve into hit act Toto, *Silk Degrees* remains one of the best albums of the 1970s.

What could he do for a follow-up? That's essentially been the question ever since. Though his next two albums—1977's *Down Two Then Left* and 1980's *Middle Man*—went platinum, neither seemed more than a further refinement of *Silk Degrees'* admittedly winning formula. And Scaggs' increasing use of co-writers took its toll as well: of the 10 tracks on his 1980 *Hits!* compilation, only three were solely penned by Scaggs; the rest featured co-writers such as Paich, David Foster, and David Lasley. Furthermore, when Scaggs finally returned in 1988 with the disappointing *Other Roads,* he was writing even less: his name was buried amid a seeming committee of contributors including Jim Carroll, Marcus Miller, Bobby Caldwell, Dan and David Huff, Peter Wolf, and Patrick Leonard. Significantly, the album promptly took a nosedive off the charts.

Scaggs may seem gone since then, but he hasn't been forgotten. In 1991, he was part of Donald Fagen's New York Rock and Soul Revue with Michael McDonald, Phoebe Snow, and others; he sang "Drowning in the Sea of Love" on the resulting live album. And more than one review of *Grand Tour,* the 1993 album by New Orleans legend Aaron Neville, likened its overall texture, ironically, to *Silk Degrees.* Which very likely had Boz Scaggs—who has sung Allen Toussaint's songs and praises longer and more soulfully than most—grinning from ear to ear.

JOHN SEBASTIAN

There may be no greater mystery in rock and roll than, simply, what happened with John Sebastian? As leader of the legendary '60s pop group the Lovin' Spoonful, Sebastian (b. Mar. 17, 1944, New York) single-handedly composed some of the best rock and roll music of the decade—songs that met the challenge of the so-called British Invasion head-on and were nearly always better. On paper, the list is an eye-opener: Less than a year after the September 1965 release of top 10 hit "Do You Believe in Magic?," the Spoonful had four more chart toppers, including "You Didn't Have to Be So Nice," "Daydream," "Did You Ever Have to Make Up Your Mind?," and "Summer in the City," which held the Number One spot for three straight weeks in the summer of 1966. Before the New York–based quartet disbanded in 1968, they scored two more top 10 and three top 30 hits. And in 1970, when Sebastian released his superb debut solo album *John B. Sebastian,* it seemed likely the singer was only beginning what would be a long and extremely fruitful solo career. But John Sebastian had only one more hit record in his life—admittedly a Number One hit, 1976's "Welcome Back," from TV's "Welcome Back, Kotter"—before he faded from view for, incredibly, 17 years.

In fact, John Sebastian's promising solo career was riddled with misfortune from the very start. *John B. Sebastian* has the unlikely distinction of having been simultaneously pressed, distributed, and offered for sale by two different labels. Completing it shortly after departing from the Lovin' Spoonful in 1968 (the band's drummer, Joe Butler, kept the group name for a final Sebastianless Spoonful album, *Revelation: Revolution '69*), Sebastian presented the tapes to MGM Records and was told the label planned to release it under his former band's name. Sebastian refused to go along, and after a year's worth of legal wrangling, during which the singer signed a new deal with Reprise, the delayed album emerged with two different covers on both Reprise and MGM. "So, not only did I lose a lot of momentum," Sebastian told writer Bruce Pollock some years later, "but then people were going, 'Which is the real album?' "

Within six months, MGM further muddied the waters with *John Sebastian Live,* an unauthorized concert recording which spent three weeks on the charts before being pulled off the market. Reprise released its own live set six months later, but 1971's *cheapo-cheapo productions presents Real Live John Sebastian* contained a minimum of new Sebastian

TOP ALBUMS

JOHN B. SEBASTIAN (MGM and Reprise, '70, *20*)
CHEAPO-CHEAPO PRODUCTIONS PRESENTS REAL LIVE JOHN SEBASTIAN (Reprise, '71)
THE FOUR OF US (Reprise, '71)
WELCOME BACK (Reprise, '76)
TAR BEACH (Shanachie, '93)

TOP SONGS

SHE'S A LADY (Reprise, '70)
RED-EYE EXPRESS (Reprise, '70)
WELCOME BACK (Reprise, '76, *1*)

material, and even more career momentum was lost. When the singer's first post-debut album of new material, *The Four of Us,* followed five months later, its lack of a hit single was devastating: the album slid off the charts in nine weeks. And with Sebastian's 1974 "comeback," *The Tarzana Kid*—his best album since *John B. Sebastian*—came the final blow: it failed to chart at all. The unexpected 1976 success of "Welcome Back" was a financial boon to Sebastian, particularly due to the television residuals he received, but if he was looking for it to revive his ailing career, he was sorely disappointed—and soon without a label at all. He spent most of the time since in Woodstock, New York, playing harmonica and autoharp on recording sessions and performing occasional club dates.

In 1993, the small Shanachie label released *Tar Beach,* Sebastian's first album in 17 years. Received with open arms from those members of the press old enough to remember him, the record was surprisingly strong and clearly aimed at the now-graying generation of fans that once bought Lovin' Spoonful albums. Ample evidence that the singer's talents hadn't deserted him, it made his extended absence seem all the more wasteful. "The process of living and growing has nothing to do with the music industry," Sebastian told *Billboard*'s Jim Bessman. "Most of my new songs, it seems, have been rather well received by the general public. They've also been on the desk of every record company president for as long as I haven't had an album out."

NEIL SEDAKA

Like Carole King, Roy Orbison, Paul Anka, and to some extent Del Shannon, Neil Sedaka (b. Mar. 13, 1939, Brooklyn, New York) is one of the few performers to enjoy success with two distinct generations of the pop audience. From 1958 to 1963, the high-voiced singer-songwriter produced a string of 13 top 40 hits highlighted by his 1962 Number One, "Breaking Up Is Hard to Do." Then, his career revived in large part due to Elton John's intervention, Sedaka returned in 1974 and scored seven more top 40 hits, the biggest of which, "Bad Blood," held the Number One slot for a full three weeks.

Sedaka's colorful past extends as far back as the mid-1950s, when the Juilliard-educated pianist was selected as the best classical pianist in New York City by no less than Arthur Rubinstein. An interest in pop songwriting led him to form the earliest edition of later hitmakers the Tokens; under that name, he and three friends from Lincoln High School recorded a 1956 single on the Melba label. He then joined forces with yet another high school friend, Howard Greenfield, the lyricist with whom he would collaborate for nearly 20 years; together, the pair wrote late-'50s hits for Connie Francis ("Stupid Cupid," "Fallin'," "Frankie," and later, "Where the Boys Are") and songs covered by LaVern Baker, Dinah Washington, and Little Anthony and the Imperials. They soon became staff members at Don Kirshner and Al Nevins's illustrious Aldon Music, where they would work side by side with Carole King and Gerry Goffin, Barry Mann and Cynthia Weil, and others.

Sedaka's solo recording career began in 1958 at RCA, when he produced his own version of "The Diary" after Little Anthony's version bombed; he then watched his single soar to number 14 on the charts. His first top 10 hit, "Oh! Carol," came soon after; written for Aldon Music workmate King, it received an official response in 1960, when King recorded the "answer" song "Oh! Neil" on Alpine

TOP ALBUMS

SEDAKA'S BACK (Rocket, '74, 23)
THE HUNGRY YEARS (Rocket, '75, 16)
STEPPIN' OUT (Rocket, '76, 26)

TOP SONGS

OH! CAROL (RCA, '59, 9)
CALENDAR GIRL (RCA, '60, 4)
HAPPY BIRTHDAY, SWEET SIXTEEN (RCA, '61, 6)
BREAKING UP IS HARD TO DO (RCA, '62, 1)
NEXT DOOR TO AN ANGEL (RCA, '62, 5)
LAUGHTER IN THE RAIN (Rocket, '74, 1)
BAD BLOOD (Rocket, '75, 1)

Additional Top 40 Songs: 14

Records. Sedaka's run of chart hits between 1960 and '63 was consistent and impressive; his four top 10 hits ("Calendar Girl," "Happy Birthday, Sweet Sixteen," "Breaking Up Is Hard to Do," and "Next Door to an Angel") are among the best remembered of the era. But they distinctly were of an era—and it was an era that came to an abrupt end in 1963, when the Beatles began a British Invasion that stopped many American artists, including Sedaka, in their tracks.

Sidelined as a performer, Sedaka then continued his career as a songwriter. Though hits were not plentiful, he remained a presence on the top 40 via songs by the Fifth Dimension (1969's "Workin' on a Groovy Thing" and 1970's "Puppet Man"), Tom Jones (1971's "Puppet Man" remake), and Andy Williams (1970's "One Day of Your Life"). Oddly, while his American career had suffered at the hands of bands from Britain, England itself became more receptive to Sedaka's music in the early 1970s. An English recording deal then resulted in three albums: *Solitaire* (released in the U.S. in 1972 on Kirshner Records) and *The Tra-La Days Are Over,* both recorded with early 10cc, and *Laughter in the Rain.* All were well received, showing Sedaka to be a mature and accessible artist whose work was comparable to that of contemporary singer-songwriter Carole King. One major change was in evidence, though: Sedaka's longtime partner Howard Greenfield was nowhere to be found; lyricist Phil Cody had replaced him.

Upon hearing that Sedaka had no American label deal, longtime admirer Elton John immediately signed him to his fledgling Rocket Records label. The result was 1974's *Sedaka's Back,* a collection of tracks from the singer's three previous English albums that instantly rekindled Sedaka's American fame. Providing him his first Number One record since 1962 with "Laughter in the Rain," along with two additional top 40 hits ("The Immigrant" and "That's When the Music Takes Me"), the album also bore two tracks—"Love Will Keep Us Together" and "Solitaire"—that would become significant hits when later covered by the Captain and Tennille and the Carpenters. Sedaka's run at Rocket brought him two additional hit albums—the gold *The Hungry Years* (which contained "Bad Blood" and a top 10 remake of "Breakin' Up Is Hard to Do") and *Steppin' Out*—before he moved over to Elektra for 1977's *A Song* and 1980's *In the Pocket,* both softer, nearly middle-of-the-road efforts.

Perhaps appropriately, Sedaka's final hit record illustrated just how much time had passed since his first: "Should've Never Let You Go," which reached the top 20 during the summer of 1980, was jointly credited to the singer and his daughter, Dara Sedaka. Though he hasn't made a record since, Neil Sedaka's 22-year span of hits is surely record enough.

BOB SEGER

One of the cornerstones of the Detroit rock and roll sound, Bob Seger (b. Robert Clark Seger, May 6, 1945, Dearborn, Michigan) has in the course of his 30-year career proven to be one of America's most consistent songwriting talents. Like Bruce Springsteen, Seger has amassed an extremely loyal audience that has come to see him as representing the voice of everyman—as sharing the same beliefs, values, and working-class background, yet still rising above it all for the glory of rock and roll and the personal redemption it promises. In the blue-collar town long nicknamed the Motor City, Seger has struck a powerful alliance with rock fans who can relate all too well to songs like "Makin' Thunderbirds"; he is no elitist, he has no pretentions, and—perhaps most significantly—after the glories and temptations of superstardom, he continues to make Detroit his permanent home.

Raised in the university town of Ann Arbor, Seger started performing in early '60s Detroit-area bands such as the Decibels and the Town Criers. By 1965, he'd struck up a business relationship with manager Eddie "Punch" Andrews that continues even today; with Andrews at the helm, Seger scored a regional hit single with "East Side Story" that was soon picked up by the Cameo-Parkway label. Following a series of Cameo-Parkway singles such as "Persecution Smith" and "Heavy Music," both significant Michigan-area hits, Seger signed to Capitol Records, and by 1969, with his band the Bob Seger System, had a top 20 hit with "Ramblin' Gamblin' Man."

TOP ALBUMS

STRANGER IN TOWN (Capitol, '78, 4)
AGAINST THE WIND (Capitol, '80, 1)
NINE TONIGHT (Capitol, '81, 3)
THE DISTANCE (Capitol, '83, 5)
LIKE A ROCK (Capitol, '86, 3)

Additional Top 40 Albums: 3

TOP SONGS

NIGHT MOVES (Capitol, '77, 4)
STILL THE SAME (Capitol, '78, 4)
AGAINST THE WIND (Capitol, '80, 5)
SHAME ON THE MOON (Capitol, '82, 2)
SHAKEDOWN (MCA, '87, 1)

Additional Top 40 Songs: 14

Though Seger's workaholic nature made him a midwestern fixture throughout much of the late 1960s, all that roadwork did little to help the sales of his first few albums. While his first Capitol album, *Ramblin' Gamblin' Man,* enjoyed some success, reaching number 62 on the charts, its little-known follow-up, *Noah,* failed to chart at all; similarly, 1970's *Mongrel* peaked at number 171 and was off the charts in four weeks, and 1971's *Brand New Morning*—a completely solo recording, an adventurous concept at the time—failed to chart as well. Disheartened, Seger took some time off to attend college, but by 1972 he had resurfaced with Detroiters Teegarden and Van Winkle on *Smokin' O.P.'s,* issued by the independent Detroit label Palladium Records. Filled with covers of songs by Bo Diddley ("Bo Diddley"), Steve Stills ("Love the One You're With"), and Tim Hardin ("If I Were a Carpenter") and only two originals—his Cameo sides "Heavy Music" and "Someday"—the album attracted enough interest to be picked up by Reprise Records.

Seger's stint at Reprise was essentially a rerun of his Capitol days; *Smokin' O.P.'s* only reached number 180 on the charts, *Back in '72* did worse, peaking at number 188, and 1974's *Seven* didn't make the chart at all. Still, there was a difference. Seger was maturing as a writer, penning believable ballads about his wearying road life such as *Back in '72's* "Turn the Page" along with classic rock rave-ups like *Seven's* "Need Ya" and "Get Out of Denver." Other artists were listening and taking notice as well: Welsh rocker Dave Edmunds (and British punk group Eddie and the Hot Rods) later covered "Denver," and, unfortunately for Seger, Eric Clapton snared his excellent backing band, which included Dick Sims, Jamie Oldaker, and Marci Levy.

By now one of the most experienced performers on the Midwest circuit, Seger put together a new group, the Silver Bullet Band, and carried on. By 1975, he had re-signed to Capitol and issued an album that marked a significant turning point in his career. *Beautiful Loser*—which peaked at number 133 but has since gone platinum—was the album on which

Seger transformed himself from goodhearted Midwestern rocker to respected singer-songwriter of considerable depth. And by 1976, with the growing presence of saxophonist Tom "Alto Reed" Cartmell in the Silver Bullet Band, more than a few critics were starting to draw parallels between Seger and one of the hottest new artists of the decade: Bruce Springsteen and the E Street Band.

Just as Peter Frampton kickstarted his career into high gear that year with the double live *Frampton Comes Alive,* it took Seger's own double live set, *Live Bullet,* to finally take him over the top. While the album's chart peak of number 34 might seem unextraordinary, its duration on the album chart—a full 167 weeks—indicated how powerful a statement it became for the singer. Boasting the best songs of his long career, from "Heavy Music" and "Ramblin' Gamblin Man" to "Katmandu" and "Get Out of Denver," the album told the world what the Midwest had long known—that Bob Seger was one of the most exciting performers in rock and roll.

Seger has credited his viewing George Lucas's film *American Graffiti* as a personal turning point; the coming-of-age epic on the screen soon found parallels in the singer's newest songs, which often seemed a mixture of nostalgia ("Rock and Roll Never Forgets") and hometown provincialism ("Main Street"). Beginning with 1976's *Night Moves,* the title track of which became a top five smash, Seger began a lengthy hit streak that brought him enormous success. Between 1976 and 1981, the singer released eight top 20 singles, including "Still the Same," "Hollywood Nights," "We've Got Tonight," "Fire Lake, and "Against the Wind." Even more impressive was his streak of top-selling albums, including *Live Bullet* (quadruple platinum); *Night Moves* and *Stranger in Town* (both quintuple platinum); his first Number One album, *Against the Wind* (quadruple platinum); and 1981's *Nine Tonight* (triple platinum).

At that level of success, Seger began taking longer and longer to make albums; platinum seller *The Distance* emerged in 1983, *Like a Rock* in 1986, and—after nearly five-and-a-half years—*The Fire Inside* saw release in 1991. Still, for most of the 1980s, Seger was becoming something of an institutional figure in American pop: Tom Cruise captivated many with his underwear-only air-guitar performance of Seger's "Old Time Rock 'n' Roll" in 1983's *Risky Business,* while the singer's "Like a Rock" was later adapted for use—with his full blessing—in, appropriately, car commercials. Additionally, Seger closed out the decade with the first Number One single of his career, 1987's "Shakedown" from the soundtrack to *Beverly Hills Cop II.*

Though 1991's platinum *The Fire Inside* was one of Seger's most substantial albums ever, its failure to generate any charting single was a troubling sign. Five years away from the marketplace, particularly in the MTV-driven music industry of the 1990s, may have been too long for Seger, who will turn 50 in 1995. "The chance to play rock 'n' roll as an adult feels like a privilege to me," Seger said by way of acknowledgment in 1991. "I look at guys from Jagger and Springsteen to James Brown and Chuck Berry, and I figure they're damn nice company to be in." With a streak of consecutive platinum albums that extends back nearly 20 years, Bob Seger, it appears, will keep making music as long as Detroit keeps making cars.

DEL SHANNON

Very much ahead of his time, the late Del Shannon (b. Charles Westover, Dec. 30, 1934, Coopersville, Michigan) was one of the most fascinating pop figures of the early 1960s. His career launched by the huge hit "Runaway," which spent four weeks at Number One in 1961, Shannon instantly seemed a cut above such teen-idol contemporaries as Frankie Avalon, Bobby Vee, and Bobby Rydell, if only for the fact that he wrote much of his own material. There were other differences that also displayed the singer to be a pioneer of sorts: "Runaway" featured a futuristic electronic keyboard solo on the Musitron, a forerunner of the synthesizer; his 1963 cover of John Lennon and Paul McCartney's "From Me to You," which peaked at number 77, was the first American performance of a Beatles song; his 1964 album *Del Shannon Sings Hank Williams* marked him as one of the first rockers to show his affection for—and display his indebtedness to—country music; and finally, the persona he crafted with such hits as "Runaway," "Keep Searchin'," and "Stranger in Town"—that of the urban loner looking for personal salvation—was conspicuously echoed in the later work of Bruce Springsteen during his *Born to Run* period. Indeed, Shannon's influence could be seen in the eagerness with which many '70s stars wanted to work with him: Jeff Lynne of the

Move and Electric Light Orchestra produced several tracks for the singer in 1973 and most of his posthumous 1991 album *Rock On!*; likewise, longtime fan Tom Petty oversaw Shannon's 1981 album *Drop Down and Get Me*, which contained the singer's final top 40 single, his cover of Phil Phillips' 1959 hit "Sea of Love."

Shannon's entry into the music business came following a late-'50s army stint, when the performer was spotted at a Battle Creek, Michigan, nightspot called the Hi-Lo Club by Ann Arbor deejay-producer Ollie McLaughlin. At his recommendation, the singer signed with Detroit-based managers Harry Balk and Irving Micahnik, who sent him to New York to record some demos. When none initially proved fruitful, Shannon returned to the Hi-Lo Club, where he spent several months performing again before eventually co-writing "Runaway" with keyboardist Max Crook. Released by Big-Time Records in March 1961, the record was sitting at Number One a month later.

Shannon followed up his initial hit with a string of similar successes, including the top five "Hats Off to Larry," "So Long Baby," and "Hey! Little Girl." Interestingly—particularly in light of the British Invasion soon to come—the singer found himself becoming even more popular in England than in the States: while his 1962 single "Swiss Maid" failed to crack the American top 40, it shot to number two in Britain and was Shannon's biggest hit since "Runaway." Touring there in 1963, Shannon met the Beatles and thus was introduced to "From Me to You"; ironically, his version of the song outsold (and preceded) the group's original Vee-Jay version in America. To further the irony, British Invasion duo Peter and Gordon, after initially releasing three Lennon and McCartney–penned hits, cracked the top 10 with their version of a Shannon song: 1965's "I Go to Pieces." While other American performers felt the competitive heat from a seeming nonstop parade of new British bands, Shannon more than held his own with such hits as "Little Town Flirt," "Handy Man," the top 10 "Keep Searchin' (We'll Follow the Sun)," and 1965's "Stranger in Town."

Following a series of protracted legal battles with his management that preoccupied the singer during much of that time, Shannon moved to Los Angeles and signed with Liberty Records in 1966. There, unfortunately, his hits stopped. Part of the problem was the assembly-line hits formula used by producer Snuff Garrett, who had previously made successful

Del Shannon

records with Gary Lewis and the Playboys and Bobby Vee; while those artists prospered recording other writers' material, Shannon—already proven a superb writer—was forced to largely fill albums like 1966's *This Is My Bag* and 1967's *Total Commitment* with inappropriate cover material such as "Everybody Loves a Clown," "Summer in the City," "Sunny," and "Red Rubber Ball."

After recording an album with Rolling Stones producer Andrew Loog Oldham in 1967 called *Home and Away*, which Liberty opted not to release, and following it up with his best album in years, 1968's poor-selling *The Further Adventures of Charles Westover*, Shannon spent most of the 1970s going unrecorded and working with other artists. He produced longtime friend Bryan Hyland's 1970 Uni album, which bore a top five remake of "Gypsy Woman" and five songs he wrote or co-wrote; he also discovered the Dunhill group Smith, who had a top five hit with his arrangement of "Baby, It's You." While Shannon did release one album during the '70s—a superb 1973 oldies set, *Del Shannon Live in England*—his few recordings otherwise consisted of scattered singles for Dunhill, United Artists (in the U.K.), and Island.

Thanks to Petty, Shannon's recording career was briefly revived in the 1980s with 1981's *Drop Down and Get Me,* a welcome set filled with sparkling originals much like those of the Shannon of old. The album spent nearly four months on the chart and peaked at number 123; the singer toured nationally and garnered much press attention as a result. Afterward, however, he faded from the scene once again, resurfacing only briefly with a remake of "Runaway" that served as the theme for the 1987 TV series "Crime Story." While never exactly financially struggling—he'd done well in real estate, and such songs as "Runaway" had been profusely covered—the singer spent most of the decade performing on various oldies tours, which tended to undercut his edge as a "contemporary" artist.

When Roy Orbison died in 1988, there was much talk that Shannon might be drafted to fill his slot in the informal supergroup the Traveling Wilburys. It seemed likely, since the singer had previously worked with Petty and Lynne, Wilbury members both; but that never materialized. What did, unfortunately, was Shannon's death by a self-inflicted gunshot wound on February 8, 1990. A taste of what might have been surfaced in 1991 with *Rock On!,* Shannon's final album, produced by Jeff Lynne and featuring Tom Petty and the Heartbreakers. "Walk Away," the set's excellent opening track, was written by Shannon, Lynne, and Petty, and in any other circumstance it would have pointed the way

toward a bright and hopeful future of similar collaborations. Instead, it was a tragic memorial to a singer-songwriter who looked and looked but never found what he kept searching for.

JULES SHEAR

Considering the quality of his songs and the duration of his recording career, it's difficult to believe that Jules Shear has never had a charting record in his life. While the Pittsburgh-raised singer-songwriter has seen his work turn into hits for other artists—Cyndi Lauper took "All Through the Night" to the top five in 1984, and the Bangles had a top 40 hit in 1986 with "If She Knew What She Wants"—Shear's own output, certainly equally as accessible, has escaped the attention of nearly everyone who buys records. Which, of course, leaves out music critics—who have sung the man's praises for over 15 years, so far to little effect.

Shear's first band of note, formed after he departed Pittsburgh for Los Angeles in the mid-1970s, was the Funky Kings—whose 1976 Arista album included the original version of "Slow Dancing" (a.k.a. "Swayin' to the Music"), a top 10 gold record for Johnny Rivers the next year. Unfortunately for Shear, who'd contributed three songs to the album, "Dancing" was penned by Funky King Jack Tempchin. On the critical level, Shear came into his own as leader of Jules and the Polar Bears; the group's two Columbia albums—*Got No Breeding* (1978) and *Phonetics* (1979)—were a fine showcasing of his talents as songwriter, singer, and lyricist. Oddly, the band was marketed by Columbia as a "new wave" band; if anything, they sounded like a rocking Jackson Browne being backed by the Kinks. Still, they may have gotten lost in the radio shuffle as a result: CBS was then inundating consumers with a flood of bogus new wave groups (4 out of 5 Doctors, the Romeos, the Hitmen, the Laughing Dogs among them) that uniformly proved commercial nonentities. After two sales flops of their own, Shear and his group saw their third album, *Bad for Business,* rejected by Columbia; while material from it would eventually emerge on two EPs, the move ended up putting the Polar Bears on ice.

The real mystery in Jules Shear's discography remains his first solo album, *Watch Dog.* Produced by Todd Rundgren and released by EMI America in

TOP ALBUMS

Little Town Flirt (Big Top, '63, *12*)
The Further Adventures of Charles Westover
    (Liberty, '69)
Drop Down and Get Me (Elektra, '81)
Rock On! (Gone Gator/MCA, '91)

TOP SONGS

Runaway (Big Top, '61, *1*)
Hats Off to Larry (Big Top, '61, *5*)
So Long Baby (Big Top, '61, *28*)
Little Town Flirt (Big Top, '63, *12*)
Keep Searchin' (We'll Follow the Sun)
    (Amy, '64, *9*)
Stranger in Town (Amy, '65, *30*)

Additional Top 40 Songs: 3

1983, the record is Shear's masterwork, a collection of stylistically diverse, wonderfully hook-filled tunes that should have established him as a major recording star. Boasting Shear's original "All Through the Night," the moving album opener "Whispering Your Name," and the incredible Beach Boys pastiche "The Longest Drink," *Watch Dog* was easily one of that year's best albums; its commercial failure surely sent a troubling message to Jules Shear. Following the release of 1985's *The Eternal Return*—which contained future Bangles cover "If She Knew What She Wants" and proved another sales flop—Shear was again without a label.

Since then, Jules Shear's recording career has proceeded haphazardly: An excellent album of Shear demos saw release by Enigma Records as *Demo-Itis* (1986); an attempted new band, the Reckless Sleepers, produced a fair album (*Big Boss Sounds,* 1988) of collaborative songs, the one exceptional track, "If We Never Meet Again," being solely Shear's (and later covered by both Roger McGuinn and Tommy Conwell and the Young Rumblers); and solo follow-up *The Third Party* (1989) featured Shear singing his songs accompanied only by Marty Wilsson-Piper's acoustic guitar. The latter album's stripped-down format was indirectly responsible for the creation of MTV's enormously successful "Unplugged" series; Shear, in fact, hosted the series' first 13 shows. In 1991, the singer signed to Polydor, and with the next year's surprisingly strong *The Great Puzzle,* he seemed back on track in every way but one: commercially. It was one more in the seemingly endless series of Shear stiffs.

TOP ALBUMS

GOT NO BREEDING (with the Polar Bears, Columbia, '78)
PHONETICS (with the Polar Bears, Columbia, '79)
WATCH DOG (EMI America, '83)
THE ETERNAL RETURN (EMI America, '85)
DEMO-ITIS (Enigma, '87)
THE THIRD PARTY (IRS, '89)
THE GREAT PUZZLE (Polydor, '92)

TOP SONGS

ALL THROUGH THE NIGHT (EMI America, '83)
IF SHE KNEW WHAT SHE WANTS (EMI America, '85)
IF WE NEVER MEET AGAIN (IRS, '88)

By no means is Shear an unrecognized talent within the industry; he has collaborated with Marshall Crenshaw, Natalie Merchant, Aimee Mann, Maria McKee, Dion, Cyndi Lauper, and members of the Band, Cars, and Tom Petty's Heartbreakers. Singer Ian Matthews actually devoted an entire album to his songs; indeed, *Walk a Changing Line,* released by Windham Hill in 1988, may be the most gorgeous-sounding testimonial to one songwriter's talent ever. But as ridiculous as it may sound, after nearly 20 years, Jules Shear still remains one hit record away from the success he deeply deserves. And he's going to have to sing it.

MICHELLE SHOCKED

Any budding singer-songwriter who's spent the typical small fortune trying to get his or her music heard by virtually anyone in the industry must find the Michelle Shocked story astounding. English producer Pete Lawrence, visiting West Texas for the 1986 Kerrville Folk Festival, heard the young singer informally perform at the festival site, then politely asked if she could wander off and perform "a few songs" so that he might record them on his Sony Walkman. She did, he did, and Shocked's performance, the highly unorthodox 1986 album debut *The Texas Campfire Tapes,* was the result. As crickets chirped and a dying campfire crackled, Shocked recorded her audition, her demo, and her first album all at once.

Her entry into the music business wasn't the standard, but then again, neither was Shocked. By her own account—which some claim is heavily fictionalized—she was born in Dallas in 1962, the oldest of eight children and an army brat. In 1979, she ran away from her Mormon fundamentalist mother and stepfather to live with her father, "Dollar" Bill Johnston, whose vivid interest in music exposed her to the likes of Leadbelly, Doc Watson, Big Bill Broonzy, Norman Blake, Randy Newman, Guy Clark, and other highly respected American musicians. Soon she travelled, spending 1981–83 in Austin (where she began writing songs), then on to San Francisco, New York, and Amsterdam. After meeting producer Lawrence at the Kerrville Folk Festival, Shocked saw his campfire recording of her performances zoom to the top of the British independent charts, eventually netting her a U.S. deal with Mercury.

The resulting albums show Shocked to be a woman of many directions and ambitions—perhaps too many for her own good. With Dwight Yoakam's skilled producer Pete Anderson on hand, 1988's *Short Sharp Shocked* is a delightful showcasing of good songwriting mostly in the Texas tradition. But the package was noticeably slanted toward the alternative marketplace: the album's graphic cover photo depicted Shocked struggling with a policeman clutching her neck, and the album's final song was an uncredited punked-out version of *Campfire*'s "Fogtown" featuring hardcore Austin–San Francisco band MDC. The next album, 1989's *Captain Swing,* took still another tack: bluesy swing. It was a whole new direction for Shocked, and an outstanding showcase for Anderson, who not only produced but arranged the whole brass-heavy affair.

TOP ALBUMS

THE TEXAS CAMPFIRE TAPES (Mercury, '86)
SHORT SHARP SHOCKED (Mercury, '88)
CAPTAIN SWING (Mercury, '89)
ARKANSAS TRAVELLER (Mercury, '92)

TOP SONGS

5 A.M. IN AMSTERDAM (Mercury, '86)
ANCHORAGE (Mercury, '88)
IF LOVE WAS A TRAIN (Mercury, '88)

Though Shocked had redone *Campfire*'s "(Don't You Mess Around With) My Little Sister," stylistically there was little else that sounded familiar. 1992's follow-up, *Arkansas Traveller,* was even more diverse. Apparently meant to focus on black minstrelsy as roots music—and if it sounds vague, you're right—the album included bluegrass and old-timey string music and featured top players like the Red Clay Ramblers, Doc Watson, Norman Blake, Alison Krauss, Bela Fleck, Ireland's Hothouse Flowers, and Australian band the Messengers. With its cover credit "conceived, written and produced by Michelle Shocked," the album seemed a well-meaning, grandiose effort gone slightly awry.

In mid-1993, it looked as if Shocked's label was wondering if their artist was wandering too far astray. Print accounts claimed that Mercury had turned down a suggested budget for Shocked's next proposed stylistic romp: a gospel album. "Mercury decided the [gospel] album wasn't 'representative' of me," a disgruntled Shocked explained to the *Los Angeles Times,* adding that she next planned to assemble, believe it or not, a dance-funk-oriented band. Though one can't deny Shocked's talent, some say it's becoming increasingly difficult to figure out in which genre it lies.

JANE SIBERRY

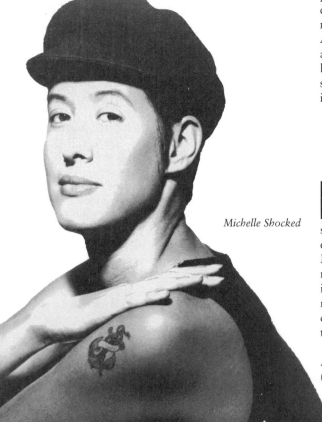

Michelle Shocked

In the course of a decade, Jane Siberry has, one by one, watched the qualifiers and comparisons slowly fade away. It's no longer an issue that she's Canadian and female; she's simply one very talented and creative singer-songwriter. And Joni Mitchell, Kate Bush, Laurie Anderson—the familiar names writers would typically invoke when describing Siberry's innovative approach—don't pop up as reference points so much anymore, either. To her credit, Siberry has neatly established herself as one of the most unique artists in the industry.

Which doesn't mean she can't have a good time. A Guelph University microbiology student, Siberry (b. circa 1956) was working in Toronto as a waitress

Jane Siberry

and, the story goes, used her tips to finance her independently released 1981 debut album, *Jane Siberry*. You can hear all about it on "The Waitress"—a semi-autobiographical number confiding, "I am a drag at parties/Cuz it upsets me/To see so many empties"—which begins her next album, 1984's *No Borders Here*. Because that record was her first to get widespread distribution both in Canada and the United States, the wryly humorous, fast-moving track was typically the first sampling of Siberry most people ever had. But finally getting most of the attention, and offering a better indication of where she was headed, was the lengthy, stunning "Mimi on the Beach," vividly allegorical in its lyric (involving a girl, a pink surfboard, and "the great leveller"), intri-

cately arranged, and featuring Siberry speaking as well as singing. What could have been a top-heavy, pretentious failure by anyone else was carried off charmingly by Siberry.

The next year's follow-up effort, *The Speckless Sky,* showed further growth, with increasingly sophisticated lyrics paired head-to-head with catchier melodies—"One More Colour" wasn't a hit, but it should have been—and fuller musical arrangements. Helping shape Siberry's artistic growth, and those arrangements, was a steady band featuring bassist John Switzer, guitarist Ken Myhr, and drummer Al Cross. *Speckless* went gold in her native Canada and was followed by a 50-city North American tour, the latter bringing her considerable (and valuable) exposure via an enthusiastic and supportive American press.

Siberry signed to Warner Bros. and released the dreamy, impressionistic *The Walking* in 1988. Her new label called it a "56-minute cinema-in-sound," and indeed it was heavily introspective, most tracks spanning 6 to 10 minutes in length apiece. She veered in the other direction with the next year's *Bound by Beauty,* which was more upbeat, easier to listen to than its predecessor, and from a career standpoint, much needed—particularly the hilarious "Everything Reminds Me of My Dog," an indirect reminder that this woman may be arty, but hey, she used to write songs about empty beer bottles.

In the summer of 1993, Siberry released *When I Was a Boy.* It was a departure: bassist Switzer, with whom Siberry had previously co-produced her albums, appeared on only one track, while Siberry herself received sole production credit for seven. New on the scene were Brian Eno—producer of both "Sail Across the Water" and (with Siberry co-producing) the album's memorable opening track, "Temple"—and fellow Canadian (and Eno associate) Michael Brook, who produced "Love Is Everything." Also included was "Calling All Angels," a duet with k. d. lang that Siberry had recorded for the soundtrack to Wim Wenders' film *Until the End of the World. When I Was a Boy* was at once Siberry's most intimate and forward-looking work; it prompted a very warm critical reception. Though no tour had been planned to promote the album, she still had much to do in late 1993: film director Wenders, very much a fan, asked her to contribute music to his planned sequel to *Wings of Desire.* Like her wonderful albums, Siberry continues to make friends and influence people.

TOP ALBUMS

No Borders Here (Open Air, '84)
The Speckless Sky (Open Air, '85)
The Walking (Reprise, '87)
Bound by Beauty (Reprise, '89)
When I Was a Boy (Reprise, '93)

TOP SONGS

Mimi on the Beach (Open Air, '84)
The Waitress (Open Air, '84)
One More Colour (Open Air, '85)

CARLY SIMON

A singer-songwriter very much of her time, Carly Simon (b. June 25, 1945, New York) grew popular in the 1970s singing sophisticated songs dealing largely with romance and self-actualization; many of her better-known songs seemed to draw inspiration equally from self-help books of the era and Woody Allen films. The third of four children from the Simon family—the same Simon of publisher Simon and Schuster fame—the singer had a plush, upper-class upbringing that provided her extraordinary exposure to the fine arts. "We were always encouraged to perform," the singer recalled in 1990. "We used to have a little theater in our barn, and my parents' friends would come and be a very patient audience for our plays and dances. Little did we know that the audience included some of the major contributors to the arts of the last century—Oscar Hammerstein, Richard Rodgers and Jessica Tandy, among others."

While a student at Sarah Lawrence College, Simon and her older sister Lucy formed a folk duo and signed to Kapp Records; they scored a minor hit with "Winkin', Blinkin' and Nod," which reached number 73 in May 1964. In 1966, Simon linked with Bob Dylan's manager Albert Grossman for an attempted Columbia solo LP that never emerged; instead, the singer eventually signed with Elektra and issued an eponymous debut in 1971.

Simon's initial top 10 hit "That's the Way I've Always Heard It Should Be," co-written with lyricist Jacob Brackman, exemplified the lyrical stance she'd utilize for most of the 1970s. "You say we'll soar like two birds through the clouds," she sang, "But soon you'll cage me on your shelf/I'll never learn to be just me first/By myself." Her combination of feminism and self-preoccupation perfectly suited the beginning of the "Me Decade"; while early bluesmen had soulfully wailed about demon whiskey and big boss men, Simon's unique brand of blues seemed addressed to lonely housewives sitting home alone in Connecticut while their husbands drew six-figure paychecks in midtown Manhattan. She was a natural, and quickly won the 1971 Best New Artist Grammy.

Simon had a consistent string of hits thereafter, including "Anticipation"—at this point remembered just as much for its ketchup-commercial affiliation as its chart position—and her first Number One single,

1972's "You're So Vain." The latter, which featured backing vocals by Rolling Stone Mick Jagger, was the center of much discussion regarding the identity of its subject; though Simon never said, many assumed the vanity in question was Warren Beatty's. The same year, Simon married James Taylor in what would become one of the most prominent show-biz marriages in the music industry. Chartwise, the union resulted in two top 40 singles for the pair: 1975's top five remake of Inez and Charlie Foxx's "Mockingbird," and 1978's "Devoted to You."

Interestingly, while Simon penned many of her hits alone, those written with longtime collaborator Brackman were often the ones making the most use of her post-feminist, liberated woman persona: "Attitude Dancing," "The Right Thing to Do," and "Haven't Got Time for the Pain," all top 30 hits between 1973 and '75, bore Brackman's credit and seemed aimed directly at the audience "That's the Way I Always Heard It Should Be" had cultivated. The downside of that strategy, unfortunately, is that two decades later, the songs seemed oddly dated and unlikely to be covered in the future.

Simon took several artistic stretches later in her career, including 1981's *Torch,* an excellent collection of pop standards (greatly enhanced by producer Mike Mainieri's tasteful arrangements); she returned to the format nearly a decade later (with full orchestration) with *My Romance.* Following her 1982 breakup with James Taylor, however, she has mostly been a stranger to the singles chart; her sole top 40 hit since was 1986's "Coming Around Again," written for the film *Heartburn.* Simon's work for films previously had included the number two single "Nobody Does It Better" from 1977's *The Spy Who Loved Me;* she'd later contribute songs to *Nothing in Common, Desperately Seeking Susan,* and *Postcards from the Edge.* Additionally, "Let the River Run," her contribution to *Working Girl,* earned her Grammy, Oscar, and Golden Globe awards in 1989.

Simon's most impressive artistic achievement came in 1992 with her complete scoring of Nora Ephron's film *This Is My Life.* Even more impressively, she spent much of 1993 working on a one-act opera commisioned jointly by the Metropolitan Opera and the Kennedy Center. While perhaps a far

Carly Simon

TOP ALBUMS

No Secrets (Elektra, '72, *1*)
Hotcakes (Elektra, '74, *3*)
Playing Possum (Elektra, '75, *10*)
Boys in the Trees (Elektra, '78, *10*)

Additional Top 40 Albums: 6

TOP SONGS

That's the Way I've Always Heard It Should Be
   (Elektra, '71, *10*)
You're So Vain (Elektra, '72, *1*)
Mockingbird (with James Taylor, Elektra '74, *5*)
Nobody Does It Better (Elektra, '77, *2*)
You Belong to Me (Elektra, '78, *6*)
Jesse (Elektra, '80, *11*)

Additional Top 40 Songs: 6

cry from her days of "Winkin', Blinkin' and Nod," it might have been what her parents had in mind for her back when Hammerstein and Rodgers were dropping by for showtime.

PAUL SIMON

Paul Simon

One of most distinguished singer-songwriters in American pop history, Paul Simon (b. Oct. 13, 1941, Newark, New Jersey) began his fourth decade of record making in the 1990s. One might suppose he'd therefore have an overflowing stock of songs in his repertoire, but it simply isn't so: a perfectionist of the highest caliber, and an admittedly slow songwriter, Simon has only recorded—both as a solo artist and with former partner Art Garfunkel—somewhere in the range of 125 original songs. In comparison, the singer's closest contemporary, Bob Dylan—whose recording career began only two years earlier, in 1962—passed the 300 mark years ago. Discounting live albums, compilations, and their contribution to the soundtrack of *The Graduate,* Simon and Garfunkel made only five albums between 1964 and 1971; likewise, Simon himself has recorded only seven albums of new material since his 1972 American solo debut, *Paul Simon.*

Luckily for Simon—and, of course, his fans—the singer's quality control operates at the highest level imaginable. He is one of the very few pop songwriters whose lyrics, stripped of their musical context, can generally stand alone as poetry. Still, because of the conspicuous literacy that informed even the earliest Simon and Garfunkel songs—"The Sounds of Silence," "Homeward Bound," and "I Am a Rock" —they have occasionally been criticized as overly melodramatic and pretentious; even Simon himself has occasionally grimaced while publicly performing some of his wordier early works. But before long, the singer learned the value of lyrical economy. "The easier it is for people to understand, the better it is," Simon told writer Paul Zollo in 1993, "as long as you're not sacrificing intelligence or insight or feeling in order to make it easier. But if you can capture something that you feel is real and express it in a way that a lot of people can understand, that's rare and there's something about that that makes a song have a certain kind of life."

Simon's well-documented life as a recording artist began in the late 1950s, when he and pal Art Gar-

funkel formed the Everly Brothers–influenced duo Tom and Jerry; the pair scored a minor 1957 hit with "Hey School Girl" and actually performed it on "American Bandstand," when Simon was only 16. After three follow-up singles flopped, Simon studied English literature at Queens College and began haunting New York recording studios, recording demos of his own songs and other artists'. He recorded several early singles under the name Jerry Landis and Tico and the Triumphs and began producing and arranging sessions for several little-known artists.

Eventually becoming attuned to the growing Greenwich Village folk scene of the early 1960s, Simon rejoined Garfunkel and the pair officially debuted at Gerde's Folk City in March 1964. Following an audition with Columbia Records, the duo inked a deal and recorded their debut album, *Wednesday Morning 3 A.M.* When it sold poorly, the pair temporarily split; moving to England, Simon recorded his first solo album, *The Paul Simon Songbook,* in a one-hour session in 1965. The album, which contained many songs later rerecorded by Simon and Garfunkel, was never released domestically. Meanwhile, in the States, Columbia producer Tom Wilson had taken an acoustic track from

Wednesday Morning 3 A.M. and dubbed in a rock background; the resulting single was "The Sounds of Silence," the historic Number One song that brought Simon back to America and established Simon and Garfunkel as major recording stars. Before disbanding in 1971, the duo released 13 top 30 singles and five albums, all but the first (which eventually went gold) enormously successful multi-platinum sellers.

Paul Simon's solo career in many ways has simply been a Garfunkel-less extension of his earlier work. The musical adventurism that fueled both 1986's *Graceland* and 1990's *The Rhythm of the Saints* was by no means a new development; Latin American instrumentation was, after all, an integral part of Simon and Garfunkel's "El Condor Pasa," from 1970's *Bridge over Troubled Water.* Simon showed the influence of reggae on his earliest solo hit "Mother and Child Reunion," and followed it with "Me and Julio Down by the Schoolyard," which featured skilled Brazilian percussionist Airto Moreira. Other stylistic forays for Simon have included a strong interest in gospel forms—evidenced on 1973's "Loves Me Like a Rock," featuring backing vocalists the Dixie Hummingbirds, and 1975's duet with Phoebe Snow, "Gone at Last," which also showcased the Jessy Dixon singers.

But it was indeed with the multiple-Grammy-winning *Graceland* that Simon reinvented himself as a true world musician; the project incorporated African musicians Youssou N'Dour and Ladysmith

Black Mambazo, as well as East L.A. Latino rockers Los Lobos and cajun/zydeco artist Rockin' Dopsie. Though some accused the singer of "cultural raiding"—and indeed, his working with South African musicians during the cultural boycott of the apartheid-ridden country caused a major political stir—Simon artfully merged his own writing style with the playing of the other musicians and created a fascinating, unique hybrid that "stole" from no one. (Several tracks, in fact, are credited as collaborations.) His 1990 follow-up, *The Rhythm of the Saints,* not quite as commercially successful, similarly incorporated South American percussionists and featured an astounding international cast, including Brazil's Milton Nascimento, Africa's Hugh Masekela, zydeco artist C. J. Chenier, American guitarist J. J. Cale, and the Brecker Brothers, among others.

Simon has had regular reunions with former partner Garfunkel, both in concert—they reunited for a national tour in 1981 (documented on 1982's *Reunion in Central Park*) and again in the 1990s for charity—and on record, via the 1975 hit "My Little Town" and James Taylor's 1978 remake, "What a Wonderful World." Interestingly, Simon appears able to have it both ways in the '90s: as a one-off "nostalgia" artist, playing his old hits with Garfunkel, and as a still vital, probing solo artist, singing new songs that are as sophisticated musically as they are lyrically. A figure of enormous international respect, Paul Simon quite amazingly remains a central pop figure 30 full years after he first sang "The Sound of Silence."

TOP ALBUMS

PAUL SIMON (Columbia, '72, 4)
THERE GOES RHYMIN' SIMON (Columbia, '73, 2)
STILL CRAZY AFTER ALL THESE YEARS
  (Columbia, '75, 1)
GRACELAND (Warner Bros., '86, 3)
THE RHYTHM OF THE SAINTS (Warner Bros., '90, 4)

Additional Top 40 Albums: 4

TOP SONGS

MOTHER AND CHILD REUNION (Columbia, '72, 4)
KODACHROME (Columbia, '73, 2)
LOVES ME LIKE A ROCK (Columbia, '73, 2)
50 WAYS TO LEAVE YOUR LOVER (Columbia, '76, 1)
SLIP SLIDIN' AWAY (Columbia, '77, 5)

Additional Top 40 Songs: 8

GRACE SLICK

One of the most recognizable faces and voices in rock and roll, Grace Slick (b. Grace Barnett Wing, Oct. 30, 1939, Evanston, Illinois) was a major factor in the success of San Francisco's legendary Jefferson Airplane during that band's Summer of Love heyday. She sang their only two hits, 1967's dual top 10 singles "Somebody to Love" and "White Rabbit," and stayed with the group through its evolution to the more commercial Jefferson Starship in 1974 and, finally, Starship in 1984. When she departed in 1988, Slick had been the only remaining Airplane member in the group for four years.

Though she was not a founder of the original Jefferson Airplane (she had joined in 1966, and first appeared on their second album, *Surrealistic Pillow*) and had left the Starship between 1978 and 1981, in her 19-year affiliation Slick saw her onetime pioneering and creative band gradually become transformed into a faceless and bland hitmaking entity playing precisely the sort of "corporate rock" the original Airplane would have naturally despised. The irony, unfortunately, was that corporate rock was a big seller during the Starship era—and that the Air-

Grace Slick

plane's two 1967 hits were dwarfed by the 14 top 40 Starship hits recorded between 1975 and 1989. Even worse, while Slick had at least written one of the two Airplane hits, she wrote none of the Starship's 14.

A former model who had been a member of San Francisco band the Great Society in 1965–66, Slick joined the Airplane to replace singer Signe Toly Anderson, who departed in 1966 on maternity leave and never returned. She brought with her two songs she had sung in her former band (which had includ-

ed her then-husband Jerry Slick and his brother Darby): "Somebody to Love" and "White Rabbit," the latter of which the singer herself had written. They were the first of many songs Slick would bring to the Airplane—a group already filled with capable writers such as Marty Balin, Paul Kantner, and Jorma Kaukonen.

As a songwriter, Slick alternately proved intelligent, witty, and cutting: her "rejoyce" from *After Bathing at Baxter's* (1967) borrowed themes from James Joyce's *Ulysses*; *Crown of Creation*'s "Greasy Heart" showed the former model rebelling against the facile '60s world of glamour, while the memorable "Lather" was an oddly moving tale of arrested development; and the ecologically conscious "Eskimo Blue Day" from *Volunteers* (1969), co-written with Kantner, featured the singer railing, "Consider how small you are/Compared to your scream/The human dream/Doesn't mean shit to a tree."

The Airplane's major success allowed them to create Grunt Records in 1971, which provided each of the band members numerous opportunities to record solo projects. During that period, while they readied the final two Jefferson Airplane albums—1971's *Bark* and 1972's *Long John Silver*—Slick also recorded 1971's *Sunfighter* with Kantner and 1973's *Baron Von Tollbooth & the Chrome Nun* with Kantner and future Starship member David Freiberg. Months before 1974's *Dragon Fly* emerged as the first work by the newly reconstituted Jefferson Starship, Slick also released her first solo album, *Manhole*. None of the albums were particularly inspired, however; despite quality backing musicians such as Jerry Garcia, David Crosby, the Pointer Sisters, Graham Nash, and others, the songs seemed weak and often poorly conceived. The meager chart showings of all three compared to regular Airplane albums—*Sunfighter* peaked at number 89, *Tollbooth* at number 120, *Manhole* at number 127—may have been the first indication to Slick and Kantner of the intrinsic value of the "Jefferson Airplane" brand name.

The vast commercial success of Jefferson Starship, and Slick's departure from the group in 1978, may explain why her second solo album, 1980's *Dreams*, remains her highest-charting effort. It surely can't be explained by the undistinguished songs—of which Slick wrote only half—or, for that matter, by the disappointing lack of subtlety in her formerly adventurous singing style. Still, that was a relative masterwork compared to 1981's near-heavy-metal outing *Welcome to the Wrecking Ball!,* which was completely dominated by the very ordinary songs of guitarist Scott Zito; Zito co-wrote four songs with Slick and the album's remaining six entirely on his own. Slick's next album, 1984's *Software,* was an ambitious synthesizer-driven collaboration with keyboardist Peter Wolf that failed to chart at all; it was no coincidence she was back in the Starship scant months after its release.

Slick's remaining work with Starship—*Nuclear Furniture* (1984), the top 10 *Knee Deep in the Hoopla* (1985), and *No Protection* (1987)—included five hit singles, two of which were Number One hits ("We Built This City" and "Sara"); additionally, the group scored a third Number One hit with "Nothing's Gonna Stop Us Now" from the film *Mannequin.* After she departed, she participated in a disappointing Jefferson Airplane reunion album, which peaked at number 85 and fell off the charts in less than two months.

Though Slick has made no new records since— and to some may now be best known for being the mother of onetime MTV veejay China Kantner—she likely will remain a major American pop cultural figure for years to come. As a performer who sang on the stages of Woodstock, Monterey, and Altamont during the 1960s; as a politically outspoken artist; and as a songwriter who actually told an entire nation to feed its head on top 40 radio, Grace Slick has inarguably touched an entire generation.

TOP ALBUMS

SUNFIGHTER (with Paul Kantner, Grunt, '71)
BARON VON TOLLBOOTH & THE CHROME NUN (with Paul Kantner and David Freiberg, Grunt, '73)
MANHOLE (Grunt, '74)
DREAMS (RCA, '80, 32)
WELCOME TO THE WRECKING BALL! (RCA, '81)
SOFTWARE (RCA, '84)

TOP SONGS

FATHER BRUCE (with the Great Society, Columbia, '68)
WHITE RABBIT (with Jefferson Airplane, RCA, '67, 8)
PLAY ON LOVE (with Jefferson Starship, Grunt, '75)

P. F. SLOAN

To be immortalized in song is one thing, but to be immortalized in a song bearing your name, written by a songwriter many feel to be among the best ever, is entirely another. The second track on Jimmy Webb's underappreciated 1970 album *Words and Music* bears the unmistakable title "P. F. Sloan," and on it, Webb sings, "I have been seekin' P. F. Sloan, but no one knows where he has gone/No one ever heard the song that boy sent winging." Still, however high the praise, Webb's album is long out of print, as are all of Sloan's, and the onetime ubiquitous songwriter has likely been forgotten.

But then there's the matter of the songs he wrote and how much they affected a generation of '60s music fans. P. F. Sloan (b. Philip Sloan, 1945) had a hand in some of the most memorable hits of the 1960s, was a founding father of the so-called folk-rock movement of that era, played and wrote surf music as part of the Fantastic Baggys, and helped father the enormously successful pop group the Grass Roots. Additionally, his song "Eve of Destruction," a Number One hit for former New Christy Minstrel Barry McGuire in 1965, was deemed so controversial at the time that many radio stations made disc jockeys follow it with the "positive" answer song "Dawn of Correction" by the rather dreary Spokesmen. In short, while he may have been a relatively anonymous figure to the general public, P. F. Sloan had a hand in some of the most influential music of the decade.

Sloan's music career began in the early 1960s in Los Angeles, where he and partner Steve Barri toiled as Screen Gems songwriters. Their demos were heard and liked by surf-rock duo Jan and Dean, who began singing the pair's songs (including "Summer Means Fun," "One-Piece Topless Bathing Suit," and "Horace, the Swingin' School-Bus Driver," among others) and including them as backup singers on their records. At producer Lou Adler's behest, Sloan and Barri were signed to Imperial Records and dubbed the Fantastic Baggys. Their sole album, issued in July 1964 as *Tell 'Em I'm Surfin',* failed to chart (though, oddly, it was reportedly a hit in South Africa), but no matter: the man who had been writing about one-piece topless bathing suits had heard the music of Bob Dylan and was moving on. As Sloan would later tell *Goldmine* magazine, "The questioning feeling of [Dylan's] 'Masters of War' is what opened my mind up to be able to think rationally and clearly about the problems that were haunting me." Before long, Sloan had written such socially conscious hits as "Eve of Destruction," "Let Me Be" (a top 30 hit for the Turtles in 1965, as was its Sloan-penned follow-up, "You Baby"), and "Take Me for What I'm Worth" (the title track of a 1965 album by Britain's formative folk-rock pop group the Searchers) and was busily writing material for the likes of Herman's Hermits. Furthering his '60s pop icon status: Sloan wrote the theme to the CBS television show "Secret Agent," a top three hit as "Secret Agent Man" by Johnny Rivers in 1966.

Sloan had recorded three albums of his own during the period—*Songs of Our Times* (1965), *Twelve More Times* (1966), and *Measure of Pleasure* (1968)—but none had found much of an audience. That wasn't the case, of course, with the Grass Roots. Though never actual members, producers Sloan and Barri ultimately formed the group by necessity, when a demo they'd recorded was sent to an L.A. radio station and became an instant hit. That song, "Where Were You When I Needed You," would be the first of 14 top 40 hits recorded by the Grass Roots between 1966 and 1972. Sloan, who parted ways with longtime partner Barri in 1968, was involved in the group's first three albums; with Barri, he co-wrote their early hits "Things I Should Have Said" and "Wake Up, Wake Up" and much other material.

Sloan's final solo album, *Raised on Records,* was released on the CBS-distributed MUMS label in 1972. By then, perhaps, he'd heard the song Jimmy Webb had written about him. "The last time I saw P. F. Sloan he was summer-burned and winter-blown," Webb had sung. "You know he turned the corner all alone, but he continued singin'." Sloan, whom many had considered to have been missing in action for

nearly five years, opened his long-awaited opus with a new version of his song "Let Me Be." To whom it was directed remains a mystery—and 20 years later, with no new album since, so does P. F. Sloan.

PATTI SMITH

A central figure in the earliest days of '70s punk rock, poet-turned-rocker Patti Smith (b. Dec. 30, 1946, Chicago) may be remembered not so much for her music as for the inspiration she provided to fledgling members of that growing scene. Preoccupied with art in all its forms, she was especially enraptured by rock and roll, and she claimed Jimi Hendrix, the Rolling Stones, Jim Morrison, and Bob Dylan as personal heroes. When Smith's 1975 album *Horses* arrived in the stores, the depth of its artistic intensity sounded a wake-up call for many—who saw Smith as an unschooled musician and singer who was nonetheless very capable of making a credible, sometimes profound personal statement via music. In many ways, Smith was America's first and best female punk-rock star.

Inspired in her early years by such cultural figures as Yeats, Modigliani, Greta Garbo, Lorca, and Arthur Rimbaud, Smith wrote poetry and found herself captivated by Bob Dylan's classic 1964 album *Another Side.* "I've always loved singing," she later said, "but I never knew how to approach singing out of my poems. Dylan released that in me." Moving to Manhattan's famous Chelsea Hotel in 1968, Smith became friends with playwright Sam Shepard; together they then collaborated on a book of plays (*Mad Dog Blues*) and performed in an off-Broadway production of their play *Cowboy Mouth.* Her name began appearing regularly in rock periodicals such as *Creem, Rolling Stone,* and *Crawdaddy*—though as a bylined journalist and record reviewer rather than performer. Her serious pursuit of poetry resulted in the publication of two collections, 1971's *Seventh Heaven* and 1973's *WITT.* When she began doing readings from the latter at St. Mark's Church in lower Manhattan, she decided to feature musical accompaniment, first in the form of music critic–guitarist Lenny Kaye, then in 1974 adding pianist Richard Sohl, drummer Jay Dee Daugherty, and guitarist-bassist Ivan Kral. The result was a rock band, the Patti Smith Group, that would eventually play at early local punk clubs such as CBGB's, record the

TOP ALBUMS

Songs of Our Times (Dunhill, '65)
Twelve More Times (Dunhill, '66)
Measure of Pleasure (Atco, '68)
Raised on Records (MUMS, '72)

TOP SONGS

Eve of Destruction (Dunhill, '65)
Take Me for What I'm Worth (Dunhill, '65)

Patti Smith

name; further, *Horses* was produced by John Cale of rock's legendary Velvet Underground. The album's opening lyrical passage—"Jesus died for somebody's sins, but not mine"—still ranks among the most vivid in all of rock and roll.

Despite one wrong career turn—the unfocused, lackluster follow-up to *Horses,* 1976's *Radio Ethiopia*—Smith had an extremely impressive reign during the tail end of the 1970s. A career-long critical favorite, she genuinely seemed excited by rock and roll as mythology, rather than as a business, and her enthusiasm was contagious. Unexpectedly, she continued to win fans from the legions of the era's self-professed "punk-rock haters"; largely helping matters was her 1978 top 20 single "Because the Night," written with Bruce Springsteen, who at the time was unheard from since 1975's *Born to Run.* The song pushed Smith's *Easter* into the top 20, and brought her increasing international acclaim.

In 1979, following the release of her most successful album yet—*Wave,* which peaked at number 18—Smith surprised the industry by retiring at the peak of her fame. Following her final show, in Florence, Italy, before an audience of 85,000, she took a lengthy, nine-year sabbatical. During that time, she married former MC5 guitarist Fred "Sonic" Smith (who had been the subject of *Wave*'s opener "Frederick") in Detroit, where they lived and had two children together. In the interim, her fame only grew; her song "Dancing Barefoot" from *Wave,* for example, saw several late-'80s and early-'90s covers by such prominent bands as U2.

Smith returned, again unexpectedly, in 1988 with *Dream of Life,* an album that purported to be Smith and her husband's "intensely personal statement of their happy communion," according to her label. Though not a massive success, the album reached number 65 on the charts and was convincing proof that Smith's talents had not evaporated in the decade of her absence. Unlike many artists who sprang up in her wake—who took advantage of the groundwork she had already laid, then grew lax in their own principles, artistically or otherwise—Patti Smith remains an artist of admirable integrity and substantial abilities.

early independent single "Piss Factory," and, in 1975, sign to Clive Davis's new label, Arista Records.

Horses, Smith's first album, was received with open arms both by critics—who called it one of the most inspired debut albums in rock history—and also by the public, who bought it in sufficient quantity to send it to the top 50 despite its lack of a commercial single. The album was unique: Smith's voice wasn't especially good, yet she sang so energetically and passionately it still dazzled; her song lyrics were poetic but not pretentious, filled with images that were surrealistic and emotionally wrenching at the same time. She borrowed from rock royalty by incorporating Van Morrison's mid-'60s hit (with Them) "Gloria" into her own song of the same

TOP ALBUMS

HORSES (Arista, '75)
RADIO ETHIOPIA (Arista, '76)
EASTER (Arista, '78, *20*)
WAVE (Arista, '79, *18*)
DREAM OF LIFE (Arista, '88)

TOP SONGS

BECAUSE THE NIGHT
 (Arista, '78, *13*)
DANCING BAREFOOT (Arista, '79)
PEOPLE HAVE THE POWER
 (Arista, '88)

PHOEBE SNOW

O wner of one of the most distinctive voices in the music industry, Phoebe Snow (b. Phoebe Laub, July 17, 1952, New York) has not had a similarly exceptional career. Coming from out of nowhere in the summer of 1974, her self-titled debut entranced a growing number of listeners and eventually became a top five album, spurred by its similarly top five single, "Poetry Man." Snow's smoky, mature voice proved captivating in the jazzy, understated setting the album provided; conspicuously helping shape that sound were two accompanying jazz giants, pianist Teddy Wilson and tenor saxophonist Zoot Sims. But a smooth career instantly proved difficult when Snow next found herself in the center of a lawsuit between Leon Russell's Shelter label, which had released her debut, and Columbia Records, who signed Snow and claimed the rights to produce her second album. Columbia eventually won and released Snow's next four records, but the legal maneuvering mired whatever career momentum Snow might have been able to take advantage of.

Raised in Teaneck, New Jersey, Snow had studied piano but finally settled on guitar as a teenager. She dropped out of college in 1969 and, after spending a few years performing at various Greenwich Village folk clubs, was signed to Shelter in 1973 via the intercession of Dino Airali, who produced her debut. While that album showcased an early style that seemed an interesting merging of blues, folk, and jazz, Snow seemed to gradually shift into rhythm and blues while at Columbia; her albums, impeccably produced by the likes of Phil Ramone, David Rubinson, and Barry Beckett, were filled with top-notch session players and often sounded slick compared to her sparsely arranged debut. Though all sold well—1976's *Second Childhood* went gold and reached the top 20—none provided her a second hit single. Snow's only return brush with the top 40 in fact came with "Gone at Last," a duet she'd recorded with Paul Simon for his 1975 album *Still Crazy After All These Years*.

Snow left Columbia after 1978's *Against the Grain* and came back three years later with *Rock Away,* an album she would later term "a three-chord rock 'n' roll record." By then, her writing had slowed; aside from her three originals, the disc included her interpretations of Rod Stewart's "Gasoline Alley," Bob Dylan's "I Believe in You," and Don Covay's "Mercy, Mercy, Mercy," among other covers. Next came nine years spent on what she called "the unsigned-act circuit," in which she recorded a duet with Dave Mason, occasionally performed with local New York band the Hudson River Rats, and provided vocals for television and radio commercials, a lucrative market for her.

Snow returned in semi-triumph in 1989 with *Something Real,* her sole album for Elektra, which bore four new original songs and was warmly received by critics. Two years later she popped up again as part of Donald Fagen's New York Rock and Soul Revue; on 1991's *Live at the Beacon,* she is heard singing Etta James's "At Last," the Temptations' "Shakey Ground," and (with Michael McDonald) Eddie Floyd's "Knock on Wood." The album's liner notes stated that she appeared courtesy of SBK Records, though as of late 1993, she had yet to release a follow-up to 1989's *Something Real.*

While in some ways Snow's recording career seems oddly unfulfilled, her track record—all of her albums have cracked the top half of the album chart—is still enviable.

TOP ALBUMS

PHOEBE SNOW (Shelter, '74, 4)
SECOND CHILDHOOD (Columbia, '76, 13)
IT LOOKS LIKE SNOW (Columbia, '76, 29)
NEVER LETTING GO (Columbia, '77)
AGAINST THE GRAIN (Columbia, '78)
ROCK AWAY (Mirage, '81)
SOMETHING REAL (Elektra, '89)

TOP SONGS

POETRY MAN (Shelter, '75, 5)
HARPO'S BLUES (Shelter, '74)

J. D. SOUTHER

O ne of the major movers and shakers of the '70s West Coast "laid-back" sound, J. D. Souther (b. John David Souther, circa 1946, Detroit, Michigan) has had his fair share of recording success but remains better known for writing songs that have been popularized by others. Among those who have covered his work are onetime paramour Linda Ronstadt, Bonnie Raitt, Don Henley and the Eagles, James Taylor, Roy Orbison, Jimmy

Buffett, and Crosby, Stills and Nash. On his own, Souther struck gold with both his top 10 1979 hit "You're Only Lonely" and the attempted '70s "supergroup," the Souther-Hillman-Furay Band. Very much a part of David Geffen's Asylum Records artist stable, Souther was a ubiquitous presence on many of that label's best-selling albums of the 1970s; even as late as 1989, his songs played a conspicuous part in the success of former Eagle Henley's multi-platinum *The End of the Innocence.*

Born in Detroit but raised in Amarillo, Texas, Souther met early musical success while still in high school with his band John David and the Senders, who scored a local hit in the mid-1960s. He moved to Los Angeles in 1968, worked with local group the Kitchen Cinq, and later played briefly in Natty Bumpo with Norman Greenbaum (of "The Eggplant That Ate Chicago" and "Spirit in the Sky" fame). His soon-to-blossom relationship with the Eagles began early on, when he and future Eagle Glenn Frey formed Longbranch Pennywhistle; their only album, released in 1970 on Amos Records, is now a rarity.

When Geffen founded Asylum in 1972, Longbranch Pennywhistle found a new home, albeit separately; Frey went off with Don Henley and formed the Eagles while Souther released his solo debut, *John David Souther.* Stylistically much in keeping with the country-tinged rock of the era, the record failed to chart, though its opening track, "The Fast One," later surfaced on Linda Ronstadt's gold 1973 album *Don't Cry Now.* The latter set, produced by Souther and including two additional songs by him ("I Can Almost See It" and the title track), was the first indication of how highly regarded his songwriting would become by his fellow Asylum artists. By

J. D. Souther

the next year, the Eagles would score a Number One hit with the Souther-Henley-Frey collaboration "Best of My Love"; as the decade wore on, that success was followed by two additional Number One Souther collaborations, 1976's "New Kid in Town" and 1979's "Heartache Tonight."

At David Geffen's suggestion, Souther teamed up with Chris Hillman (of the Byrds) and Richie Furay (of Buffalo Springfield and Poco) in 1974 to form the Souther-Hillman-Furay Band. Though their debut went gold and reached number 11, the group itself seemed vaguely artificial and was critically perceived as a deliberate attempt by Geffen to create his label's own Crosby, Stills and Nash–type supergroup. When 1975's follow-up, *Trouble in Paradise,* met near universal panning, the trio soon went their separate ways. Still, the experience helped heighten Souther's individual profile; his second solo album, 1976's *Black Rose,* secured a healthy number 85 chart position, and critics generally responded positively.

Souther's two brushes with the top of the charts came via 1979's *You're Only Lonely,* the title track of which reached number seven, and his 1981 duet

TOP ALBUMS

JOHN DAVID SOUTHER (Asylum, '72)
BLACK ROSE (Asylum, '76)
YOU'RE ONLY LONELY (Columbia, '79)
HOME BY DAWN (Warner Bros., '84)

TOP SONGS

HOW LONG (Asylum, '72)
SILVER BLUE (Asylum, '76)
YOU'RE ONLY LONELY (Columbia, '79, 7)
HER TOWN TOO (with James Taylor,
    Columbia, '81, *11*)

with James Taylor, "Her Town Too," a top 15 hit co-written by Souther, Taylor, and guitarist Waddy Wachtel. Any residual effect from the latter hit was negligible by the time of Souther's 1984 set *Home by Dawn;* the all-too-accurately-titled album failed to chart at all.

Since then, Souther has yet to make another record, focusing his attention mainly on songwriting (he penned the theme to ABC-TV's "Anything but Love") and—perhaps surprisingly—acting. Souther took on a recurring role in the late-'80s TV series "thirtysomething," and he has also appeared in the films *Always* (1989), *Postcards from the Edge* (1990), and *To Cross the Rubicon* (1991). With a publishing company that owns or shares the rights to over 50 songs, Souther continues to prosper from music in the 1990s; whether his future performances will be in the recording studio or on the screen—silver or otherwise—remains to be seen.

RICK SPRINGFIELD

The dilemma that has faced Rick Springfield (b. Richard Lewis Springthorpe, Aug. 23, 1949, Sydney, Australia) in America from the start was apparent in 1973, when his label, Columbia Records, took out ads for his album *Comic Book Heroes* that read, "Rick is more than a face." The handsome young singer, who in Australia had been in successful, respected rock outfits such as Rock House and Zoot (which also included future Little River Band member Beeb Birtles), was deemed just another cute teen idol by American tastemakers of the era. Why? Because Capitol Records had already signed the singer, rerecorded his Australian hit single "Speak to the Sky" and scored a top 15 hit with it in 1972, and then, thanks to a P.R. push, ensured that Springfield's face was swiftly plastered in such teen magazines as *Tiger Beat* and *16* alongside Partridge Family mainstay David Cassidy's.

"The songs are brilliant," Columbia wrote in its ad. "The performances are super. And Rick Springfield did it all. Nobody wrote the songs for him. Nobody told him how to sing. Rick is a new kind of teen idol. His talent is as beautiful as his face." In a year when top artists included Alice Cooper, Pink Floyd, Led Zeppelin, and the Allman Brothers, and the need for "artistic credibility" counted nearly above all else, Columbia killed Springfield with kindness.

The irony, unfortunately, is that the record was superb: well-written, Anglo-sounding pop that at the time was compared—by some astute, unprejudiced listeners—to the best work of David Bowie. It flopped, unfortunately, and was just one of several career disappointments the singer experienced in the 1970s. First, Columbia refused to release his 1974 follow-up, *Springfield;* then, following his 1976 release of *Wait for Night* on Chelsea Records, the label folded just as Springfield began touring to promote it. Springfield, who had been seriously studying acting, then signed a two-year contract with Universal; it brought him various television guest spots on such shows as "Six Million Dollar Man," "Wonder Woman," and "The Rockford Files." Before long, the singer had snagged a two-year role as Dr. Noah Drake on the long-running soap opera "General Hospital."

Thus, when RCA Records signed Rick Springfield in 1980, it almost needed to run its own version of Columbia's "not just another face" ad. The major difference this time, however, was the red-hot single "Jessie's Girl"—which gave his RCA debut, *Working Class Dog,* double platinum sales and won the singer a Grammy. Springfield's combination of syncopated rock and catchy pop hook was a radio favorite, and a sophisticated one; to a young audience, who had no idea of the singer's previous acting history, the Australian seemed nothing more than a talented—and very good-looking—pop craftsman.

Between 1981 and 1983, Springfield had an envi-

TOP ALBUMS

WORKING CLASS DOG (RCA, '81, 7)
SUCCESS HASN'T SPOILED ME YET (RCA, '82, 2)
LIVING IN OZ (RCA, '83, 12)
HARD TO HOLD (RCA, '84, 16)

Additional Top 40 Albums: 2

TOP SONGS

SPEAK TO THE SKY (Capitol, '72, 14)
JESSIE'S GIRL (RCA, '81, 1)
I'VE DONE EVERYTHING FOR YOU (RCA, '81, 8)
DON'T TALK TO STRANGERS (RCA, '82, 2)
AFFAIR OF THE HEART (RCA, '83, 9)
LOVE SOMEBODY (RCA, '84, 5)

Additional Top 40 Songs: 11

able run on the charts, scoring three platinum albums and nine top 40 singles, including top 10 hits "I've Done Everything for You" (penned by Sammy Hagar), "Don't Talk to Strangers," and "Affair of the Heart." The success continued with the soundtrack to Springfield's first movie, 1984's *Hard to Hold*—it went platinum and produced the top five single "Love Somebody"—but in some ways, his singing career never fully recovered. "It wasn't a real wise choice," he recalled four years later, noting that he regretted the time he'd spent making it. "I didn't need to have to do it. I didn't have to do a movie where I was playing a rock star. I think my acting chops are up enough that I could have tackled something with a little more meat. But the script was there, and my ego was saying, 'Yeah, yeah—movie, movie.' I was on a roll, but it just didn't happen."

Whether the movie role—and all that it entailed—actually knocked Springfield's career momentum askew is difficult to discern. But his 1985 album *Tao* was his first in five years to lack a top 10 single, and it went gold rather than platinum. The singer then took time off, both for the birth of his son and because, he said, "I just started looking into myself and had a crisis of faith—and a crisis of belief in myself. I lost perspective of myself and of what I really believe in, what I really want." Unfortunately, *Rock of Life,* Springfield's 1988 return to action, didn't help: it stalled at number 55 and was his first album that had failed to go gold since 1976's *Wait for Night.* Springfield hasn't made a record since.

BRUCE SPRINGSTEEN

The most important rock figure to emerge during the 1970s, Bruce Springsteen (b. Sept. 23, 1949, Freehold, New Jersey) borrowed from all the best sources in rock, folk, and rhythm and blues and created a style that has become uniquely his own—and itself widely imitated. A greatly admired and charismatic performer, Springsteen is renowned for his devotion to his fans, and has built a career pleasing them with three- and four-hour marathon shows that leave no doubt he has given his all. Since his 1973 debut album, *Greetings from Asbury Park, New Jersey*, his music has shifted from Dylanesque, wordy prose, to Phil Spector–influenced pop, to hard-driving rock and roll, to its current,

often deliberately threadbare lyrical style. The epitome of a musical perfectionist, Springsteen is well known for laboring intensely on each of his albums; the dual result has been infrequent releases and a wide supply of officially unreleased tracks often bootlegged and circulated among fans. Indeed, Bruce Springsteen's many fans are among the most fanatical in all of rock and roll.

Spending his early years in New Jersey–based bands such as the Castiles, Earth, Child, Steel Mill, and Dr. Zoom and the Sonic Boom—who collectively played a mixture of rock and roll, R&B, and hard rock—Springsteen was one of the last major talents to be signed to Columbia Records by distinguished producer-A&R man John Hammond. His first album, 1973's *Greetings from Asbury Park, New Jersey,* arrived in time for the singer to be pushed by his label and perceived by the press as one of the era's most prominent "new Dylan" types; it was an inaccurate tag that in some ways (in terms of galvanizing a generation) would later prove not totally off-base. Still, the verbal overload of Dylan's "Subterranean Homesick Blues" was indeed recalled by early Springsteen songs such as album opener "Blinded by the Light": "Madman drummers bummers and Indians in the summer with a teenage diplomat," he sang, "In the dumps with the mumps as the adolescent pumps his way into his hat."

But the decade's superstar-to-be created little stir with his first album: both it and its late-1973 followup, *The Wild, the Innocent and the E Street Shuffle,* would not even enter the charts until the summer of 1975. Regardless, the artistic transformation that had taken place between those two albums was apparent. While *Greetings* had almost seemed a stripped-down singer-songwriter demo, *E Street Shuffle* sounded very much the work of a fully cohesive band, playing rock arrangements midway between the work of Van Morrison and the Paul Butterfield Blues Band. And though Springsteen was only slightly less wordy, his lyrics seemed more focused, and filled with a noticeable romantic imagery that seemed slightly nostalgic and at times recalled *West Side Story.*

At the same time, Springsteen's reputation as a live performer was growing by leaps and bounds. Critic Jon Landau, who would later become the singer's producer and business associate, penned a review containing the infamous snippet, "I saw rock 'n' roll's future and its name is Bruce Springsteen." He was right, though, and by 1975, the New Jersey rocker was simultaneously on the cover of both *Time* and *Newsweek* and a top five star with his classic album *Born to Run*. While its Phil Spector–influenced title track climbed into the top 30, Springsteen and his superb backing group the E Street Band toured and began accumulating what would soon become a massive base of fanatical fans convinced the singer was the most electrifying live performer since Elvis Presley.

Legal problems with manager Mike Appel eventually resulted in an injunction that delayed Springsteen's next album until 1978. In the interim, his following swiftly grew—mostly due to extensive touring, growing agreement among journalists that the singer was an important figure, and cover versions of his songs by such artists as the Hollies (1975's "Sandy"), Manfred Mann's Earth Band ("Blinded by the Light," a Number One hit in 1977, and "Spirit in the Night"), Robert Gordon and the Pointer Sisters (both covered "Fire," with the Pointers' version a number two hit in 1979), and Patti Smith (who co-wrote 1978's top 20 hit "Because the Night").

When Springsteen returned with 1978's *Darkness on the Edge of Town,* there was a new depth to his music that might have reflected the preceding legal unpleasantness; many of the characters in such songs as "Racing in the Streets," "Something in the Night," and the title track seemed without hope or were regretful about some sort of profound loss. "Some folks are born into a good life," Springsteen sang in the latter song, "Other folks get it anyway, anyhow/I lost my money and I lost my wife/Them things don't seem to matter much to me now." It was a considerable step away from the joyfulness that populated earlier songs such as "Kitty's Back" or "Rosalita (Come Out Tonight)" from *E Street Shuffle* and in some ways a preview of many similarly downbeat songs to come from the singer.

Springsteen's first Number One album was 1980's ambitious two-LP *The River,* which spent four weeks at the top of the charts pushed by his bouncy top five single "Hungry Heart" and the top 20 hit "Fade Away." A sprawling set, the album clearly delineated the two separate sides of Springsteen's musical persona: the upbeat rocker whose "Hungry Heart" and "Sherry Darling" were concert crowd-pleasers, and the moody, soul-searching writer of the album's title track and the haunting "Wreck on the Highway." Discussing the album in a 1980 interview, Springsteen called *The River* a "romantic" album. "To me, 'romantic' is when you

Bruce Springsteen

see the realities, and when you understand the realities, but you also see the possibilities," Springsteen said. "And sometimes you write about things as they are, and sometimes you write about them as they should be, as they could be, maybe. And that's basically what I wanted to do, you know? And you can't say no to either thing. If you say no, you're cheating yourself out of feelings that are important and should be a part of you."

Springsteen's darkest album ever came via the home-recorded *Nebraska*, an acoustic set that was filled with songs about both urban and moral decay, including "Atlantic City," "Highway Patrolman," and the intense, mesmerizing "State Trooper." The album's title track, about a murderer facing the electric chair, was a clear indication the singer had weighty matters on his mind. "They declared me unfit to live, said into that great void my soul'd be hurled," the song's character says. "They wanted to know why I did what I did/Well sir I guess there's just a meanness in this world."

The singer's greatest commercial success came with 1984's *Born in the U.S.A.*, which contained an unprecedented series of seven top 10 singles, including "Dancing in the Dark," "Cover Me," "Born in the U.S.A.," "I'm on Fire," "Glory Days," "I'm Going Down," and "My Hometown." The album, which went platinum seven times over, in part marked a return to the uplifting rock style of "Hungry Heart," but also bore its share of darker material. Ironically, one of the darkest was the album's title track—which many at the time mistakenly took to be an expression of blind, my-country-right-or-wrong patriotism, when it was anything but. Springsteen, who wed actress Julianne Phillips in 1985, then followed the massively popular disc with a long-awaited live album, the 40-song *Bruce Springsteen & the E Street Band Live/1975–85*, which hit Number One and likewise went multi-platinum.

Tunnel of Love, perhaps the singer's most underrated album, followed in 1987 and marked a return

to the quiet, profound emotionalism to be found on the best songs from *Darkness* and *The River*. The album's title reflected its contents, and the songs themselves were an introspective lot dealing with human relationships and their frailties. When Springsteen divorced actress Phillips in 1989 and became romantically linked with his backing singer Patty Scialfa, many saw *Tunnel of Love* in retrospect as his most disarmingly autobiographical work to date.

Five years after the release of *Tunnel of Love*, Springsteen—by then a father of two children with Scialfa, and no longer with the E Street Band—returned with two albums at once, *Human Touch* and *Lucky Town*. The first was the more polished; the second, reportedly recorded quickly by Springsteen after he felt uneasy about the first, was the more informal. Both were superb, and both reflected the changes that Springsteen had undergone in five years' time: "Living Proof" was a moving song about being a first-time father, and "57 Channels (And Nothin' On)" touched on his move to the West Coast ("I bought a bourgeois house in the Hollywood Hills," he sang, "with a trunkload of hundred thousand dollar bills"). For the first time, however, critics began conspicuously picking at him, suggesting that the singer had "gone Hollywood" or had made a mistake by splitting with the E Street Band. The albums nonetheless entered the top five and went platinum, which was no mean feat for any artist following a five-year absence.

In the 20 years since his debut album, Springsteen's lyrical style has taken a noticeable turn toward the less-clever, more direct approach. It has worked very much in his favor. The seeming simplicity of such songs as "I Wish I Were Blind" gives them more of a timeless feel than the word-heavy likes of "Blinded by the Light" carry; one can imagine Springsteen singing the newer song in 20 years' time without it seeming the slightest bit dated. Like all the best artists in pop music, Bruce Springsteen continues moving forward, approaching his craft

---

TOP ALBUMS

BORN TO RUN (Columbia, '75, 3)
THE RIVER (Columbia, '80, 1)
BORN IN THE U.S.A. (Columbia, '84, 1)
BRUCE SPRINGSTEEN & THE E STREET
BAND LIVE/1975–85
 (Columbia, '86, 1)
TUNNEL OF LOVE (Columbia, '87, 1)
HUMAN TOUCH (Columbia, '92, 2)

Additional Top 40 Albums: 3

TOP SONGS

HUNGRY HEART (Columbia, '80, 5)
DANCING IN THE DARK
 (Columbia, '84, 2)
GLORY DAYS (Columbia, '85, 5)
BRILLIANT DISGUISE (Columbia, '87, 5)

Additional Top 40 Songs: 12

---

with an intelligence and desire for improvement that puts most of his contemporaries to shame. "You make your record like it's the last record you'll ever make," he said in 1980. "[When I] go out and play at night, I don't think, 'If I don't play good tonight, at least I played good last night.' It's like there are no tomorrows or yesterdays. There's only right now."

BILLY SQUIER

Billy Squier

A singer-songwriter whose initial ambition was, in his record company's words, to "combine hard rock rhythms with infectious melodies," Billy Squier became a major figure in the American hard-rock scene in the early 1980s doing precisely that—though how infectious those melodies were remains a point of critical argument. During his 1981–82 commercial peak, Squier (b. May 12, 1950, Needham, Massachusetts) vigorously objected to critics who persistently branded him a "Robert Plant clone" and his music too Led Zeppelin-derived; by 1993, however, when his future was looking much less assured, he candidly told one writer, "Those comparisons may have been valid 10

or 12 years ago—but I don't think there's any comparison now, to be honest."

Perhaps one reason critics were taking Squier to task was due to his prior status as a cult figure. In the early 1970s, he'd been a latter-day member of Boston's trendy glam–punk rock precursors the Sidewinders, whose sole RCA album, recorded before Squier came aboard, had been produced by future Patti Smith Group guitarist Lenny Kaye. By 1976, he was the focal point of Piper, a respected Boston rock and roll band that sounded more like the Rolling Stones and New York Dolls than Led Zeppelin. Though the recipients of much critical hoopla, Piper recorded two A&M albums that quickly sank, despite the group's affiliation with the red-hot Aucoin Management group, then handling Kiss at that band's commercial peak.

There was still considerable critical interest when Squier resurfaced in 1980 with his first solo album, *The Tale of the Tape* perhaps partly because of the participation of former E Street Band members David Sancious and Ernest "Boom" Carter, among others. *Tape* caused enough of a splash to secure a chart position (although it peaked low, at number 169) and helped set up Squier's all-time biggie, 1981's *Don't Say No*. That album, which soared to the top five, stayed on the charts for 111 weeks, and went triple platinum, was simply the right album—and the right sound—at the right time. What grabbed FM programmers across the country was Squier's loud and instantly addictive track "The Stroke," which, despite coming two years after Led Zeppelin had disbanded, could have been their brand-new single as far as radio was concerned. Squier became a hard-rock sensation, and when Capitol released his top five follow-up, *Emotions in Motion,* in July 1982, *Don't Say No* was still lodged comfortably on the album charts.

Unlike most other hard-rock singer-songwriters, Squier was also an excellent guitarist—which helped in his songwriting, providing more than one tune with a sense of dynamics that much hard rock of the time was lacking. It also provided him with top 40 hits—"The Stroke," "In the Dark," "Everybody Wants You," and "Rock Me Tonite"—which, considering the genre, was unusual. But those hits came in just a four-year streak, and by 1986's *Enough Is Enough,* Squier's career was sputtering down; since then, he hasn't managed an album that's even reached the top 50.

Ironically, Squier's 1993 album *Tell the Truth—*

TOP ALBUMS

DON'T SAY NO (Capitol, '81, 5)
EMOTIONS IN MOTION (Capitol, '82, 5)
SIGNS OF LIFE (Capitol, '84, 11)

TOP SONGS

THE STROKE (Capitol, '81, 17)
IN THE DARK (Capitol, '81, 35)
EVERYBODY WANTS YOU (Capitol, '82, 32)
ROCK ME TONITE (Capitol, '84, 15)

which seemed to arrive in the stores completely unannounced—was a significant departure from Squier's past work and unexpectedly delightful. Produced by Mike Chapman, the album was a pop-filled aural treat, at times reminiscent of both the Beatles and the (Chapman-produced) Knack. Though dismally received at retail and radio, had *Tell the Truth* been issued a decade earlier, it may well have changed the course of the singer's career. Its suggested title: *Different "Strokes" for Different Folks.*

CAT STEVENS

By far one of the most successful and popular singer-songwriters of the 1970s, Cat Stevens (b. Steven Georgiou, July 21, 1947, London) has had one of the most extraordinary careers in the music business: few of his contemporaries can claim, after all, to have chucked it all away—money, material possessions, gold records—and later be the subject of a radio boycott due to deeply held religious beliefs, as Stevens did and was. He may remain a personal enigma, but the now-retired singer's musical work has been understood and fully enjoyed by millions.

Even early on, Stevens's life was marked by peculiar twists and turns. The son of a Greek restaurant owner father and Swedish mother, he grew up fully immersed in Greek folk music styles and began playing folk music and writing his own music while at London's Hammersmith College. An opportune meeting with British producer Mike Hurst eventually led to a 1967 recording contract with London Records subsidiary Deram, with whom he scored several British hits including "I Love My Dog," "Matthew & Son," and "I'm Gonna Get Me a Gun." Each was a heavily produced pop record that would stand in marked contrast to the stripped-down simplicity of Stevens's later work. Additionally, two songs Stevens had penned were hits by other artists: "Here Comes My Baby," a top 20 American hit for the Tremeloes in 1967, and "The First Cut Is the Deepest," a U.K. hit for singer P. P. Arnold in 1967 and an international smash for Rod Stewart 10 years later. But a serious brush with tuberculosis sidelined Stevens for nearly two years, during which time he began radically reworking his music, aiming to strip away the glossy pop production, perhaps add into it a few classical elements, and ultimately make it simpler.

Stevens reemerged triumphantly in 1970 with *Mona Bone Jakon,* a folkish, mostly acoustic affair featuring only Stevens, his guitar and that of Alun Davies, and a simple bass-and-drums backing (with limited flute contributions from future Genesis and solo star Peter Gabriel). Though it proved a hit in England, the album charted in America only after Stevens's 1971 follow-up *Tea for the Tillerman* became a top 10 hit and established him as a major artist. Instrumental in doing that was his first hit, "Wild World," a top 20 charter in which Stevens's sentimentally advised a departing girlfriend that there was "a lot of bad out there" and to be careful. Fans found much more to like on *Tillerman,* including "Father and Son," a moving musical dialog that was uncluttered and warm and may be Stevens's all-time classic; it's the favorite of many fans today.

With America hooked, Stevens continued releasing increasingly ambitious packages that sold in even greater number. With *Teaser and the Firecat,* released in late 1971, Stevens hit the top 10 twice—first with "Peace Train," later covered with conspicuous irony by 10,000 Maniacs on their platinum 1987 set *In My Tribe,* then "Morning Has Broken," which at number six was his biggest hit to date. Stevens's first and only Number One album, *Catch Bull at Four,* followed; its strong sales were especially significant—and indicative of how wide the singer's appeal had become—since the album bore not a single hit. The onetime sparseness of Stevens's music had evolved into something much more complex as well; by 1973's *Foreigner,* which claimed as its centerpiece the 18-minute "Foreigner Suite," Stevens was joined by a large musical crew including Bernard Purdie, Phil Upchurch, Patti Austin, and influential keyboardist Jean Roussel, who'd joined him one album earlier. Hits were still coming regardless, including *Buddha and the Chocolate Box*'s top 10 track "Oh Very Young," and the 1974 single "Another Saturday Night."

Stevens, meanwhile, was coping with his fame in a revealing manner: he'd moved to Brazil to escape a backbreaking tax burden. A selfish move? Hardly, as he was donating much of his income to charities (such as UNESCO), finding himself drawn more and more to Eastern mysticism. Gradually his sales began to taper off, as did his hits. 1978's *Back to Earth* ended the gold-record streak that had begun with 1970's *Mona Bone Jakon*. More importantly, it also ended his recording career: In 1977, Stevens fully embraced Islam, changed his name to Yusuf Islam, and gave away all his material possessions. By 1983, he had founded the Islamia Primary School in Kilburn, London, and given up music altogether. "Art and music aren't the essence of life," he later told writer John Tracy. "They are ornamental, but people need this ornament when something substantial is missing in their lives." In 1989, when Stevens told the media that controversial writer Salmon Rushdie should be slain for his writing of *The Satanic Verses,* infuriated American radio stations called for an airplay boycott of all of Stevens's music—including, ironically, "Peace Train." One suspected, though, that that meant very little to former pop star Yusuf Islam.

Al Stewart

TOP ALBUMS

TEA FOR THE TILLERMAN (A&M, '71, 8)
TEASER AND THE FIRECAT (A&M, '71, 2)
CATCH BULL AT FOUR (A&M, '72, 1)
FOREIGNER (A&M, '73, 3)
BUDDHA AND THE CHOCOLATE BOX (A&M, '74, 2)
IZITSO (A&M, '77, 7)

Additional Top 40 Albums: 3

TOP SONGS

PEACE TRAIN (A&M, '71, 7)
MORNING HAS BROKEN (A&M, '72, 6)
OH VERY YOUNG (A&M, '74, 10)
ANOTHER SATURDAY NIGHT (A&M, '74, 6)

Additional Top 40 Songs: 7

AL STEWART

If it's a given that everybody in showbiz needs a gimmick, Al Stewart (b. Sept. 5, 1945, Glasgow, Scotland) seemed well supplied indeed. A one-time almost radically confessional folksinger, Stewart shifted gears mid-career, began singing "historical folk-rock," and instantly won an enthusiastic audience. And while his contemporaries were off singing drearily about Old John Barleycorn, there was Stewart singing songs about American president Warren G. Harding, pre–World War II Germany, and the prophesies of Nostradamus.

Stewart, who moved to London from the south England town of Bournemouth in 1965, entered the healthy British folk scene, sharing the stage with such well-known acts as the Incredible String Band, Fairport Convention, Pentangle, and Steeleye Span. Signing with British CBS, Stewart released one album (1967's *Bedsitter Images*) prior to his official American debut, 1969's *Love Chronicles*. Declared "folk album of the year" by influential U.K. rock paper *Melody Maker,* the latter disc boasted an impressive roster of musicians (including guitarists Jimmy Page and Richard Thompson), an overwhelming 18-minute title track devoted to every woman Stewart had apparently ever felt strongly about, and one of the earliest lyrical uses of the word "fucking" on record. Not that it mattered; few historical accounts of Stewart even note *Love Chronicles'* American release in the first place. Two more U.K.-only albums followed—*Zero She Flies* in 1970 and *Orange* in 1972—before Stewart hit the jackpot with *Past, Present and Future*, released in the U.S. on Janus Records.

"History is something I use for a backdrop, because 'A meets B' is just two-dimensional," explained Stewart to writer Stephen K. Peeples in 1976. "But if I say 'A meets B in 1934,' suddenly there's a whole context. The image becomes three dimensional." In short, that concisely explains how Stewart began retooling his career. After 1974's *Past, Present and Future* set the stage—FM radio in particular took to Stewart's track "Roads to Moscow"—the next year's follow-up, *Modern Times,* hit the top 30. Stewart's earlier folk sound was now thoroughly replaced by well-played rock provided by such top English players as Tim Renwick, Rick Wakeman, and B. J. Cole. The ultimate payoff came with 1976's *Year of the Cat,* Stewart's final album for Janus, which gave him his first top 10 single (the title track), a top five album, and a whole new pop audience. Thrilled, he then moved to the States.

Year of the Cat remains Stewart's all-time career high, though its follow-up, *Time Passages* on Arista, also reached the top 10. While Stewart's lyrical approach was sometimes wearing—who in 1978, after all, could get that excited about any song based on the French Revolution?—the superb production of Alan Parsons (himself a recording star) made each track a smooth, radio-ready gem. But soon after, when Parsons departed, Stewart's songs began getting a little too samey and his career started fading. Following a combination live/studio album (1981's *Indian Summer*), he disappeared for a while, finally emerging in 1984 with a slipshod album called *Russians and Americans,* which had been produced by Heart producer Mike Flicker and was reportedly passed on by Arista (it ended up on the independent Passport label). Four years later, *Last Days of the Century*—very much a rock album—came and went on Enigma Records without a peep. Stewart's last project was 1992's *Rhymes in Rooms,* a live "hits" album with Peter White, his guitarist partner since *Year of the Cat.* Though not much happened with it commercially, the set showed the singer was still in fine voice. However tempting it may be, it's simply too soon to say Al Stewart is, er, history.

JOHN STEWART

One of America's more respected and distinguished singer-songwriters, John Stewart (b. Sept. 5, 1939, San Diego, California) played a part in the success of two memorable '60s groups—the Kingston Trio and the Monkees, whose 1967 smash "Daydream Believer" he wrote—and had his own career rejuvenated by a landmark group of the 1970s, Fleetwood Mac.

Stewart's large repertoire is dominated by earthy tunes largely dwelling on American themes—not dissimilar to country music in its scope—and his voice at times sounds like Johnny Cash's might were it a half-octave higher.

Stewart's entry into the music business followed the demise of his rock and roll band the Furies, formed while he was a student at Pomona Catholic High School. Taken with the folk music of the Kingston Trio, he introduced himself to the band at a Pomona appearance and later sent them some of his material. Soon his "Molly Dee" opened their 1959 album *Here We Go Again!,* which stayed at Number One for eight weeks. "I got a check for $10,000, and I said, 'Hey, why am I going to college? This is the promised land!' " he later told writer William J. Bush. Via that connection, Stewart, John Montgomery, and Gil Robbins then signed with

TOP ALBUMS

PAST, PRESENT AND FUTURE (Janus, '74)
MODERN TIMES (Janus, '75, 30)
YEAR OF THE CAT (Janus, '76, 5)
TIME PASSAGES (Arista, '78. *10*)
24 CARROTS (Arista, '80, 37)

TOP SONGS

YEAR OF THE CAT (Janus, '77, 8)
TIME PASSAGES (Arista, '78, 7)
SONG ON THE RADIO (Arista, '79, 29)
MIDNIGHT ROCKS (Arista, '80, 24)

Roulette Records and released three albums as the Cumberland Three. When Kingston Trio founder Dave Guard departed to form the Whiskeyhill Singers in 1961, Stewart auditioned to replace him and did so, staying with them through June 17, 1967, when they gave their final performance at San Francisco's hungri i venue. "One More Town," which reached the lowly chart position of number 97, was the only Stewart-penned Trio single to crack the Hot 100.

Stewart then met up with his future wife, singer Buffy Ford; together they recorded *Signals Through the Glass,* released by Capitol in 1968 to scant commercial notice. Stewart thereafter decided to go it alone as a solo artist (though Ford would continue to sing with him), and the result was his classic *California Bloodlines,* regarded by many as his all-time best work. Recorded in Nashville precisely when Bob Dylan was working on his own country epic, *Nashville Skyline,* the 1969 album contained vital Stewart material such as "July, You're a Woman," "Never Goin' Back (To Nashville Anymore)," and the title track, and set the standard for many singer-songwriters to come. Not coincidentally, two of the genre's most famous practitioners, James Taylor and Carole King, showed up on Stewart's equally impressive *Willard*—released in August 1970, when Taylor's *Sweet Baby James* was topping the charts and King's *Tapestry* was still to come. Stewart, who had worked on the Bobby Kennedy election campaign, notably donated all the royalties from *Willard* track "Click Clack" to the Robert F. Kennedy Memorial Foundation.

Stewart recorded for several labels during the 1970s, including Warner Bros. and RCA, but was a

negligible chart presence until his second album for RSO Records, *Bombs Away Dream Babies.* The 1979 album was a surprise pop hit, largely due to the production participation of longtime fan Lindsey Buckingham, and it brought Stewart three hits; the top five single "Gold" conspicuously featured Stevie Nicks' backing vocals and Buckingham's crisp electric guitar, as did follow-up hit "Midnight Wind."

When RSO folded, Stewart formed his own label, Homecoming Records, and later began another creative/commercial venture called the Ship, created to promote talented artists who were slipping through the cracks in an industry increasingly dependent on big hits and massive budgets. It was a canny, artistically worthy business move by the man who once struck "Gold."

ROD STEWART

With his inimitable gravelly voice, one-of-the-lads demeanor, and longtime reputation as a master showman, Rod Stewart (b. Jan. 10, 1945, London) became one of the true superstars of the 1970s. A onetime soccer player, gravedigger, and street singer, Stewart began his career with U.K. singer Long John Baldry's group the Hoochie Coochie Men in 1964, moved on to later groups such as Steampacket and Shotgun Express, and established himself internationally in 1968 as lead vocalist of the Jeff Beck Group. Before leaving, he signed a solo deal with Mercury Records that would lead to 1971's international Number One smash "Maggie May"; at the same time, he and Beck Group bassist Ronnie Wood became key members of reconstituted '60s pop group the Small Faces. By the time the Faces disbanded in 1975, Stewart was an enormously successful solo act and has continued making top 10, platinum-selling albums well into the 1990s.

While Stewart's brilliance as an interpretive singer has often been the major focus of his acclaim—indeed, many think his readings of Cat Stevens's "The First Cut Is the Deepest" and Danny Whitten's "I Don't Want to Talk About It" are definitive—his songwriting skills are in many ways critically undervalued. While he has generally tended to use collaborators—most often band members or accompanying musicians such as Ronnie Wood or Martin Quittenton in the early days and Gary

TOP ALBUMS

CALIFORNIA BLOODLINES (Capitol, '69)
WILLARD (Capitol, '70)
WINGLESS ANGELS (RCA, '75)
BOMBS AWAY DREAM BABIES (RSO, '79, *10*)
DREAM BABIES GO HOLLYWOOD (RSO, '80)

TOP SONGS

JULY, YOU'RE A WOMAN (Capitol, '69)
GOLD (RSO, '79, *5*)
MIDNIGHT WIND (RSO, '79, *28*)
LOST HER IN THE SUN (RSO, '80, *34*)

Grainger, Jim Cregan, and Carmine Appice later on—several of his biggest hits, including "Tonight's the Night (Gonna Be Alright)," "Hot Legs," and "You're in My Heart (The Final Acclaim)" were entirely self-penned. In fact, during the earliest phase of his solo career—between 1969's *The Rod Stewart Album* and 1971's *Every Picture Tells a Story*—the singer drew as much critical attention for the folksy warmth of his songwriting style as for his singing prowess. Even later, while Stewart was scoring top 40 hits with the comparatively shallow lyrical fare of "Hot Legs," he was also producing sophisticated and intelligent work such as the top 30 "The Killing of Georgie (Part I and II)," a moving song about the death of one of his friends.

Stewart's first platinum single, 1978's "Da Ya Think I'm Sexy," co-written with drummer Carmen Appice, in a very real way marked a turning point in his career, particularly from a critical perspective. Accompanied by a driving dance beat, the song—about a young couple meeting at a club—was perceived by many as the singer's "sell out" to that era's disco trend; additionally, its very title led many to think Stewart himself was posing the question. "If I ever wrote a song which put a fly in the ointment or a spanner in the works—it's this one," Stewart pointed out in the liner notes to his 1989 career retrospective, *Storyteller/The Complete Anthology: 1964–1990*. "It was frightening, stirring up so much love and hate at the same time: Most of the public

Rod Stewart

loved it; all the critics hated it. I can understand both positions. Anyway, that was then. By the way, just to set the record straight. This song is not sung in the first person and your most humble vocalist is not singing about himself nor am I praising my minimal sex appeal. I am but a narrator telling a story about a couple."

During the same period, Stewart was dogged by press accounts of his glamorous personal life, which has included a string of notably beautiful blonde girlfriends and wives (including Britt Ekland, Alana Hamilton, and current spouse Rachel Hunter), and his tax-driven 1975 move to glitzy Los Angeles—which made him a prime target of celebrity-cruising paparazzi for much of the decade. Nonetheless, as musical trends came and went, whether disco or punk and new wave rock, Stewart's noteworthy consistency throughout the 1980s won him back much of the critical admiration he'd lost during the "Sexy" period. Alternative heroes such as the Replacements spoke warmly of the singer's early '70s work with the Faces, and in the 1990s, hugely popular bands such as the Black Crowes reached the top of the charts playing music obviously deeply influenced by Stewart. Additionally, the fact that the singer's 1989 top five hit "Downtown Train" was penned by a

TOP ALBUMS

EVERY PICTURE TELLS A STORY (Mercury, '71, *1*)
NEVER A DULL MOMENT (Mercury, '72, *2*)
A NIGHT ON THE TOWN (Warner Bros., '76, *2*)
FOOT LOOSE & FANCY FREE (Warner Bros., '77, *2*)
BLONDES HAVE MORE FUN (Warner Bros., '78, *1*)

Additional Top 40 Albums: 14

TOP SONGS

MAGGIE MAY (Mercury, '71, *1*)
TONIGHT'S THE NIGHT (GONNA BE ALRIGHT) (Warner Bros., '76, *1*)
YOU'RE IN MY HEART (THE FINAL ACCLAIM) (Warner Bros., '77, *4*)
DA YA THINK I'M SEXY (Warner Bros., '78, *1*)
DOWNTOWN TRAIN (Warner Bros., '89, *3*)

Additional Top 40 Songs: 27

critical favorite like Tom Waits suggested Stewart's taste was as contemporary as ever; at 45, he was still no dinosaur.

Stewart became (and remains) an enormously popular concert attraction, and he was one of many older artists to resolidify his career via one of MTV's many "Unplugged" sessions. His resulting 1993 set *Rod Stewart Unplugged...and Seated* shot to number two and went double platinum; further, it provided him dual hits via his remakes of Van Morrison's "Have I Told You Lately" and Tim Hardin's "Reason to Believe," the latter of which he'd originally covered on 1971's *Every Picture Tells a Story*. By late 1993, Stewart had yet another large hit on his hands with "All for Love," taken from that year's film *The Three Musketeers* and featuring the triple-talent lineup of Stewart, Bryan Adams, and Sting. In all, three decades into a hit-filled career, Rod Stewart remains very much in the picture—and that picture, as the song goes, tells one very fascinating story.

STEPHEN STILLS

Stephen Stills

As a key member of both Buffalo Springfield and Crosby, Stills, Nash and Young, Stephen Stills (b. Jan. 3, 1945, Dallas, Texas) has been responsible for writing and performing some of the best-loved pop music of the 1960s and '70s. His early song "For What It's Worth," a top 10 hit in 1967 for the Buffalo Springfield, was a hook-filled, early political statement that would catch the ear of the decade's growing baby boomer audience; additionally, his appearance at the 1969 Woodstock Festival with partners Crosby, Nash, and Young was one of the celebrated gathering's true highlights. Throughout the 1970s, whether with CSN&Y, his group Manassas, the short-lived Stills-Young Band, or on his own, Stills was viewed as a member of rock's royal elite. Though his star significantly faded through the 1980s and into the '90s, due mostly to his erratic solo career, few critics dispute the relevance or quality of his early work with both the Buffalo Springfield and CSN&Y.

Raised in Florida, Stills spent a significant part of his earlier years in San Jose, Costa Rica, where his family moved in 1961. He later briefly audited some classes at the University of Florida in Gainesville and relocated to New Orleans, but by 1964 he had moved to Greenwich Village in search of a music career. He found work there with the Au Go-Go Singers, who also included a young Ohio-born singer named Richie Furay in their ranks; both Stills and Furay were present on *They Call Us Au Go-Go Singers,* issued by Roulette Records in 1964. During a gig in Ontario, the group performed with a Canadian band known as the Squires, led by a singer-guitarist named Neil Young, and within two years, Stills, Furay, and Young joined forces in Los Angeles to form the Buffalo Springfield.

Stills's earlier attempt to start a group with Van Dyke Parks resulted in a top 40 hit with his song "Sit Down, I Think I Love You," issued by the Parks-produced Mojo Men in early 1967. But by the time that song had entered the charts, the Buffalo Springfield—who had been signed by Atco in 1966—had released their first album and were riding high on the success of Stills's "For What It's Worth." Though the group was troubled by constant instability—largely due to Young, who departed and returned several times during the band's two years together—and had only that one hit, their three albums (1967's *Buffalo Springfield* and *Buffalo Springfield Again* and 1968's *Last Time Around*) easily rank among the best American rock of the 1960s. Stills's finest songs with the band included "Bluebird," "Rock and Roll Woman," "Everydays," and "Go and Say Goodbye," the latter track serving as a precursor to what would soon become known as country rock.

When the group finally split in 1968, Stills put in an appearance on one side of *Super Session*—the top 15, gold-selling "jam" album also featuring Al Kooper and Mike Bloomfield—and then joined ex-Byrd David Crosby and former Hollies singer Graham Nash in Crosby, Stills and Nash.

Stills's best work within the Crosby, Stills, Nash and Young context remains the group's brilliant pre-Young 1969 debut, *Crosby, Stills & Nash*, containing the top 25 hit "Suite: Judy Blue Eyes," which Stills wrote for Judy Collins, as well as his "You Don't Have to Cry," "Helplessly Hoping," "Wooden Ships" (co-written with Crosby and the Jefferson Airplane's Paul Kantner), and "49 Bye-Byes." Most of the songs' lyrics dwelt on love relationships that were over or going sour; it was a lyrical area in which Stills excelled, though his later work often looked elsewhere for inspiration.

With the addition of Neil Young, CNS&Y released two other albums—1970's *Déjà Vu* and 1971's *4 Way Street*—before temporarily disbanding. Stills's presence was not as deeply felt on either album; *Déjà Vu*'s opener, Stills's "Carry On," borrowed liberally from his Buffalo Springfield song "Questions," his "4+20" lasted less than two minutes, and the surging album closer "Everybody I Love You" was co-written with Young. In fact, it seemed Stills had saved much of his own work for his 1970 solo debut album, *Stephen Stills*, an excellent set that easily stands as his finest. Featuring guest appearances by both Jimi Hendrix and Eric Clapton and Stills's top 15 single "Love the One You're With," the album was one of the era's few solo sets that truly served its purpose: the singer stretched out and explored areas that might not have been appropriate in the context of his group, including gospelish rock ("Church [Part of Someone]"), straight blues-inspired material ("Black Queen" and "Go Back Home"), big-band rock ("Cherokee"), and orchestrated pop much in the style of early Tim Hardin ("To a Flame").

Stills's solo album quickly found its audience,

peaked at number three, and went gold. Its follow-up, *Stephen Stills 2,* issued only seven months later, likewise hit the top 10 and was certified gold. Unlike its predecessor, however, it seemed less inspired and more businesslike, which did not bode well for the singer. When not writing about such subjects as faded romance, Stills wrote lyrics that often seemed labored, preachy, or both, as in this snippet from his "Sugar Babe": "How do turtles talk to one another?/They just look, there's no reason to cower/Just like people, they're drawn to each other/They don't live in no ivory tower."

With CSN&Y no longer functioning, Stills rebounded tastefully by forming a new group, Manassas, that included former Byrd and Flying Burrito Brother Chris Hillman. His addition was a stroke of brilliance, as the two cuts bearing both his and Stills's co-writing credit—"It Doesn't Matter" and "Both of Us (Bound to Lose)"—are a cut above nearly everything else Stills recorded for the remainder of the decade. After 1973's *Down the Road*, however, the group disbanded when Hillman and other group members opted to join the ill-fated Souther-Hillman-Furay Band.

For the first time in his career, Stills shifted to a label other than Atlantic/Atco with *Stills*, issued by Columbia in 1975. It was one of many works to come that would receive negative reviews from critics who collectively felt Stills was ailing as a songwriter. No hits emerged from any of the singer's three Columbia albums, including *Illegal Stills*

TOP ALBUMS

STEPHEN STILLS (Atlantic, '70, 3)
STEPHEN STILLS 2 (Atlantic, '71, 8)
MANASSAS (with Manassas, '72, 4)
STILLS (Columbia, '75, 19)

Additional Top 40 Albums: 4

TOP SONGS

LOVE THE ONE YOU'RE WITH (Atlantic, '70, *14*)
SIT YOURSELF DOWN (Atlantic, '71, *37*)
CHANGE PARTNERS (Atlantic, '71)
MARIANNE (Atlantic, '71)
IT DOESN'T MATTER (with Manassas, Atlantic, '72)
BOTH OF US (Bound to Lose) (with Manassas, Atlantic, '72)

(1976) and *Thoroughfare Gap* (1978), with the latter peaking at number 83, Stills's worst chart showing ever. Meanwhile, there was a lesson to be learned in the other successes Stills was enjoying in group contexts—first with the Stills-Young Band, whose 1976 album entered the top 30 and went gold, then with the reunited Crosby, Stills and Nash, whose 1977 album *CSN* stayed at number two for a month and went platinum. That lesson, unfortunately for Stills, seemed to be that his future might best be spent playing with his former band members.

With the exception of his 1984 solo album *Right by You,* again on Atlantic and peaking at number 75, Stills was heard throughout the 1980s only with Crosby, Stills and Nash (on 1982's *Daylight Again* and 1983's *Allies*) and once with the reunited CSN&Y (1988's *American Dream*). The poor chart showing of CSN's 1990 album *Live It Up,* which only reached number 57, was a discouraging sign that even the onetime baby-boomer appeal the trio had enjoyed was beginning to fade—and indeed, before long, Stills found himself reduced to releasing a new solo album on a small, independent Florida-based label.

If it seemed the record-buying market had passed Crosby, Stills and Nash by, the gold-certified success of late 1991's *CSN*—a four-CD boxed-set retrospective of the group's work together and apart—indicated the degree of fandom the trio still maintained 22 years after their formation. For Stephen Stills, one suspects, his fourth consecutive decade of gold-level success was much-anticipated and welcome indeed. In late 1993, the onetime radio regular was wrapping up a deal that would make him co-owner of a Daytona Beach, Florida, classic-rock radio station.

STING
• • • • • • • • •

As the focal point of the enormously popular British rock trio the Police, Sting (b. Gordon Sumner, Oct. 2, 1951, Newcastle-upon-Tyne, England) became one of the most famous faces of the 1980s. Aside from writing a memorable string of hit singles and albums between 1979 and 1983, highlighted by the Number One song "Every Breath You Take" from 1983's hugely successful *Synchronicity,* the onetime schoolteacher turned pop star regularly appeared in such films as *Quadrophenia* (1979), *Brimstone and Treacle* (1982), *Dune*

(1984), and *The Bride* and *Plenty* (both 1985). It surprised few when, as the band's sole singer-songwriter, he finally opted to record his own solo album, 1985's platinum-selling *Dream of the Blue Turtles;* it surprised even fewer when, after a one-off appearance at a 1986 Amnesty International Conspiracy of Hope concert in Atlanta, the Police unofficially disbanded, and the former Gordon Sumner began what has since turned into an equally successful solo career.

Nicknamed Sting due to a black and yellow shirt he favored in the early 1970s, the blonde singer was part of a Newcastle, England, fusion-jazz quartet called Last Exit prior to joining with drummer Stewart Copeland to form the Police in early 1977. Following the release of a debut single featuring early guitarist Henri Padovani—whom Sting and Copeland replaced with renowned session guitarist Andy Summers—the Police began a lengthy relationship with A&M Records via the 1978 single "Roxanne," a colorful, reggae-tinged song about a prostitute written by Sting. Within a year, the song had cracked the top 40 and begun a streak of nine top 40 hits for the Police between 1979 and 1984, six of which made the top 10, including "De Do Do Do, De Da Da Da," "Don't Stand So Close to Me," "Every Little Thing She Does Is Magic," "Every Breath You Take" (Number One for eight weeks), "King of Pain," and "Wrapped Around Your Finger."

The band did not play by pop's traditional business rules of the time: they toured the U.S. before they'd released an album, and they signed a deal for a minimal advance that then guaranteed them high royalties. As a result, they acquired a very loyal early audience and became extremely wealthy: all six of their albums were certified gold, five going platinum or multi-platinum. *Synchronicity,* the trio's 1983 bestseller, was Number One for 17 weeks and certified quadruple-platinum; it would have been the year's top album had it not been for Michael Jackson's phenomenal *Thriller.*

Sting's progression as a songwriter was a fascinating step-by-step evolution from writing lightweight, wry songs about prostitutes and the seeming baby-babble of "De Do Do Do, De Da Da Da" to addressing weightier political topics influenced by philosopher Arthur Koestler (on *Ghost in the Machine*) and German psychologist Carl Jung (*Synchronicity*). In 1983, the singer explained how his world view was playing an expanding role in the

Sting

Sting's incorporation of such players indicated how the former fusioneer had come to feel hemmed in by the Police's guitar-bass-drums trio format; while most of the band's later albums were marvelously textured, the *Blue Turtles* lineup was able to provide an even more varied musical context for Sting's increasingly sophisticated compositions. Furthermore, *Bring on the Night*, a 1986 double live album documenting the singer's *Blue Turtles* tour, which went unreleased in the U.S., ably demonstrated that the group was more than capable of playing Police songs such as "Bring on the Night," "Driven to Tears" and "Tea in the Sahara" as well as, if not better than, the original trio.

The new band, plus guests Eric Clapton, jazz arranger Gil Evans, and even Police guitarist Summers accompanied Sting for his double platinum 1987 album *Nothing Like the Sun*. With three top 20 hits, including the number seven single "We'll Be Together," the record was actually his first since the Police's breakup, and it showed the singer had made the transition to solo artist seamlessly. A successful world tour followed, and his status as an international superstar was further cemented by the 1988 release of *Nana Como el Sol*, a Spanish and Portuguese version of *Nothing Like the Sun*. He returned in 1991 with *The Soul Cages*, a dark album written after the death of his father and largely reflecting the emotional ramifications of his loss throughout. Unusually—but to be expected, considering its overall downbeat theme—the album contained only one hit, the top five "All This Time."

Then in 1993, Sting rebounded with *Ten Summoner's Tales*, an album that even in its punning

songs he was writing. "I'm pretty angry at the world," he said. "And I think it's my duty to be angry. Because a lot of people are asleep, you know? They don't know what's going on. They don't know the place is being wrecked by fools. Fools we call politicians. I am angry, and I am sour about the political state of the world. I think it sucks. But that doesn't mean to say that I'm crying in my beer." Sting's political involvement showed itself through his alignment with such causes as Amnesty International, for whom he appeared in concert in 1986 and 1988, as well as his celebrated solo appearance in 1985 at Live Aid.

The latter performance coincided with the release of his long-expected platinum solo album *The Dream of the Blue Turtles*—which held the number two slot for six weeks, included the top 10 singles "If You Love Somebody Set Them Free" and "Fortress Around Your Heart," and boasted a topline backing band that included jazz stars Branford Marsalis, Kenny Kirkland, and Omar Hakim.

TOP ALBUMS

THE DREAM OF THE BLUE TURTLES (A&M, '85, 2)
. . . NOTHING LIKE THE SUN (A&M, '87, 9)
THE SOUL CAGES (A&M, '91, 2)
TEN SUMMONER'S TALES (A&M, '93, 2)

TOP SONGS

IF YOU LOVE SOMEBODY SET THEM FREE
  (A&M, '85, 3)
FORTRESS AROUND YOUR HEART (A&M, '85, 8)
WE'LL BE TOGETHER (A&M, '87, 7)
ALL THIS TIME (A&M, '91, 5)

Additional Top 40 Songs: 6

title (summoner = Sumner) offered an upbeat contrast to the dour *The Soul Cages*. "Being on the rebound from that very dark record," the singer explained upon its release, "this time I wanted to make one for the fun of it, the craft of it—to engage the band musically. There's a clash of styles and motifs that's quite deliberate." The album launched a series of popular singles—including "If I Ever Lose My Faith in You," "Fields of Gold," and "Nothing 'Bout Me"—and by the end of 1993 was double platinum and still selling strongly. Additionally, the singer was perched in the top 10 with the single "All for Love" as one-third of an unusual vocal trio also featuring hitmakers Bryan Adams and Rod Stewart. His marketplace clout was further confirmed that fall with the release of *Message in a Box,* a four-CD boxed set purporting to include every recording the Police had ever made—but, added some picky critics, still missing one or two obscure tracks. One of the few genuine superstars to emerge from the punk and new wave scene of the late 1970s, Sting remains one of pop's most vital and probing singer-songwriters.

JAMES TAYLOR

Credited as the central figure of the so-called singer-songwriter "renaissance" of the early 1970s, James Taylor (b. Mar. 12, 1948, Boston) has made a fascinating transition in the near quarter-century of his career. Beginning as an extraordinarily sensitive, inner-directed singer-songwriter, Taylor took his past, built upon it, and later transformed himself into a capable pop interpreter of such well-known hits as "Handy Man," "How Sweet It Is (To Be Loved by You)," and "Up on the Roof"—all the while retaining the uniquely melancholic edge that gave his earlier work its fascinating appeal. Initially autobiographical to a fault—earliest criticisms contended the singer's songs were far too solipsistic for their own good—Taylor's original material has matured during his career as well. It may have lost some of its intensity and drive in the process, but its appealing warmth—which arguably was the major attraction for the fans who first made him famous—remains and has grown even stronger during the past decade.

Born in Boston, the second of five musical children, Taylor moved to Chapel Hill, North Carolina, in 1951, when his father was appointed dean of the

medical school at the University of North Carolina. Inspired by his brother Alex, Taylor began playing guitar as a youth; by the summer of 1963, he met guitarist and longtime friend Danny "Kootch" Kortchmar on Martha's Vineyard, and the pair won a local hootenanny contest. At the age of 16, he joined Alex's rock band the Fabulous Corsairs for a year. Troubled by depression, Taylor committed himself to a mental institution during his senior year at Milton Academy, a private school outside Boston. Following his discharge, he moved to New York City in 1965, where by the next year he'd formed the Flying Machine with friend Kortchmar. Though the group failed to get a record deal, their demo tape was later issued in 1971 as *James Taylor and the Original Flying Machine*. The group disbanded in the spring of 1967, at which time Taylor, then a heroin addict, moved to London's Notting Hill Gate district.

While in England, the singer recorded several demo tapes and auditioned for various record companies. He eventually drew the interest of Peter Asher, formerly of hitmaking duo Peter and Gordon, who liked Taylor enough to make him the first outside signing to the Beatles' legendary Apple label. In late 1968, the company issued *James Taylor,* a superb debut that in many ways remains the singer's all-time peak. Lushly orchestrated in spots, with innovative musical "links" between tracks, the album contains many of Taylor's most darkly autobiographical songs, including "Something's Wrong," "Knockin' 'Round the Zoo" (about his earlier days in the mental hospital), "Sunshine Sunshine," and his well-known "Carolina in My Mind." Disappointingly, the album made no impact whatsoever at the time of its release; only later, after Taylor's success with "Fire and Rain," would the album show up on the charts, where it ultimately peaked at number 62.

Taylor returned to America in late 1968 and again entered a mental institution, this time to treat his ongoing heroin addiction. During the course of his near half-year stay, friend Asher—who had produced Taylor's debut—negotiated a new recording deal for him at Warner Bros. In March of 1970, *Sweet Baby James* resulted—and in the course of its 102 weeks on the charts, that triple-platinum album would establish Taylor as one of America's premier singer-songwriters. Key to its success was his eventual signature tune "Fire and Rain," a disturbing autobiographical number with veiled references to his hospital commitment and the suicide of a close

friend. Not exactly the stuff of hit records, but the record profoundly connected with the pop audience and became a top five hit.

Between the release of *Sweet Baby James* and its 1971 follow-up, *Mud Slide Slim and the Blue Horizon,* Taylormania ensued. Both Taylor's Apple debut and his Flying Machine demos entered the top 100; albums by three of his siblings—Livingston, Alex, and Kate—were released; Taylor himself starred with Beach Boy Dennis Wilson in the film *Two Lane Blacktop;* and the singer was the subject of a cover story in *Time* magazine. *Mud Slide* became his highest-charting album and spawned his first Number One hit with his version of Carole King's "You've Got a Friend." King, who played piano and sang on the album, was actually in Taylor's 1971 touring band immediately prior to the release of her historic bestseller *Tapestry.*

Taylor became major rock royalty in short order. His songwriting became even more inner-directed, which sometimes resulted in peculiarly self-conscious lyrics—as on "Nobody But You" from his 1972 album *One Man Dog,* in which he sang, "Everybody knows that I'm just a joe/That likes to hang around/Talking about my problems/Bringing other people down." But a flip side to that was emerging as well: Taylor married singer Carly Simon in late 1972, and together they soon charted with a duet cover of Inez and Charlie Foxx's 1963 hit "Mockingbird." That top five single—actually made for Simon's *Hotcakes* album—signaled a new "cover artist" phase in Taylor's career. More than half of the singer's remaining seven top 40 singles were well-known oldies, including "How Sweet It Is" (1975), "Handy Man" (1977), "(What a) Wonderful World" (1978), and "Up on the Roof" (1979).

At the same time, Taylor's albums were settling into an agreeable consistency that clearly pleased his fans; all but two of those following *One Man Dog* were certified gold or platinum. Much of the singer's original material remained autobiographical, but never as harrowingly so as on his earliest albums. The only exception came on the revealingly titled *Dad Loves His Work,* recorded the year before Taylor and Simon divorced. On the song "Her Town Too"—his last top 20 hit, written and sung with J. D. Souther—Taylor sang, "Well people got used to seeing them both together/But now he's gone and life goes on/Nothing lasts forever, oh no/She gets the house and garden/He gets the boys in the band."

Since then, Taylor has indeed spent much of his life with the boys in the band. He married Kathryn Walker in 1985 and otherwise spent most of the 1980s and '90s recording and performing onstage. His albums continue to sell strongly; as recently as 1993, his double-CD *(Live)* made the top 20. Unlike many other artists of his era, Taylor has maintained both a solid career and a reputation that has only been enhanced over time: many of Nashville's new wave of country performers in fact claim the singer as a major songwriting inspiration. A distinguished artist whose eventful life has been uniquely documented in his own work, James Taylor deserves every bit of the respect he is accorded.

TOP ALBUMS

SWEET BABY JAMES (Warner Bros., '70, 3)
MUD SLIDE SLIM AND THE BLUE HORIZON
   (Warner Bros., '71, 2)
ONE MAN DOG (Warner Bros., '72, 4)
GORILLA (Warner Bros., '75, 6)
JT (Columbia, '77, 4)

Additional Top 40 Albums: 10

TOP SONGS

FIRE AND RAIN (Warner Bros., '70, 3)
YOU'VE GOT A FRIEND (Warner Bros., '71, 1)
MOCKINGBIRD (with Carly Simon, Elektra, '74, 5)
HOW SWEET IT IS (TO BE LOVED BY YOU)
   (Warner Bros., '75, 5)
HANDY MAN (Columbia, '77, 4)

Additional Top 40 Songs: 9

LIVINGSTON TAYLOR

Though he's spent most of his nearly 25-year career in the shadow of his famous older brother James, Livingston Taylor (b. Nov. 21, 1950, Boston) has distinctly been his own man since releasing his first album in 1970. In the blur of years, the singer-songwriter's beginnings are often inaccurately remembered: Though it's true many Taylor siblings had their careers kick-started by brother James's massive success—including James's older brother Alex and sister Kate—Livingston's Capricorn debut emerged only four months after James's triple platinum classic *Sweet Baby James* was released. It would in fact be months before "Fire and Rain" became a hit, and even longer before that song pushed *Sweet Baby James* into the top 10.

Taken on its own, *Livingston Taylor* stands as an immaculately realized debut album, as deeply personal in its own way as *Sweet Baby James,* but a much more comforting listen. Like his brother, Livingston had voluntarily committed himself to a psychiatric hospital as a teen; several tracks on that first album reflected the experience, some surprisingly profoundly. Among the best were "Doctor Man," "Packet of Good Times," "Can't Get Back Home," and the marvelous, autobiographical "Carolina Day," in which Taylor painted a memorable picture of his early family life in North Carolina, actually mentioning his siblings—including the only one not to make a record, Hugh—in the lyric. Being James Taylor's sibling was one thing, but unlike gruff-voiced Alex or sister Kate, Livingston actually sounded like him most of the time; the major distinction, never more evident than it was here, was Livingston's tendency to slur and mumble some lyrics to the edge of incomprehensibility. Though it was difficult to discern whether "Hush a Bye" actually did contain the line "But you were lost to Ritalin," the song was equally moving in spite— maybe even because—of it.

Taylor never surpassed that album either artistically or commercially; it peaked at number

82 and was the highest-charting set of his career. As he progressed, he noticeably improved his enunciation and, perhaps predictably, began sounding more like his brother than ever. Similarly, he'd take to including cover versions of familiar songs on his albums—"On Broadway" on 1971's *Liv,* and later "Somewhere over the Rainbow" and "Dancing in the Street," among others. He had two encounters with the top 40: his charming adult-contemporary hit "I Will Be in Love with You" reached number 30 in 1979; "First Time Love," written by Pat Alger and Peter Kaminsky, peaked at number 38 the next year.

Taylor went on to do two unexpected things in the 1980s. He hosted the syndicated television show "This Week's Music" in 1984, and—for the first time on record—sang a duet with his brother James on "City Lights," from 1988's *Life Is Good.* Unfortunately, anyone who heard it probably assumed Taylor had merely double-tracked his own voice. Like other American singer-songwriters (Robbie Dupree, Peter Gallway, and Andrew Gold among them), Taylor eventually found himself more in demand in Japan than in his own country. In 1991, he released his excellent *Our Time to Dance* there; two years later, it saw American release on the small, revitalized Vanguard label. Continuing to devote most of his time to the concert stage, Taylor now plays an average of 100 to 150 live dates per year.

TOP ALBUMS

LIVINGSTON TAYLOR (Atco, '70)
LIV (Capricorn, '71)
OVER THE RAINBOW (Capricorn, '73)

TOP SONGS

IN MY REPLY (Atco, '70)
SIT ON BACK (Atco, '70)
CAROLINA DAY (Atco, '70)
I WILL BE IN LOVE WITH YOU (Epic, '78, *30*)
FIRST TIME LOVE (Epic, '80, *38*)

RICHARD THOMPSON
· · · · · · · · · · · · · · · · · ·

If only for his role as a founder of England's legendary folk-rock band Fairport Convention, Richard Thompson (b. Apr. 3, 1949, London) would be deemed a major figure in British contemporary music. But the enormously talented guitarist and songwriter was only beginning his career when he departed Fairport in 1971 following five years with the pioneering group. As a solo artist, freed from the constraints of his former band's determined shift to pure traditional folk music, Thompson took all he'd learned from Fairport—which was considerable—and further developed an inimitable, near-timeless style that has placed him among the highest ranks of singer-songwriters. In his liner notes to *Watching the Dark,* Hannibal Records' outstanding 1993 Thompson anthology, esteemed critic Greil

Livingston Taylor

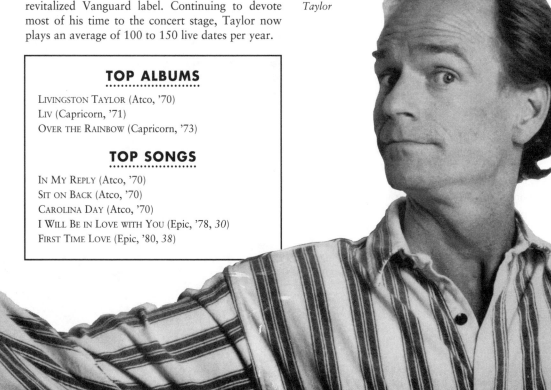

Marcus precisely touched on what has made the guitarist's work so special: "Trace Thompson's songs and performances over time," Marcus wrote, "and there is little or no sense of development, maturity, refinement. As with Van Morrison or Neil Young, perhaps Thompson's only true pop likenesses, a listener can believe it was all there from day one . . ."

If an artist can be said to be the sum of his influences, Thompson's wildly divergent taste—which encompasses Celtic folk, Scottish reels, jigs, American rock and roll and blues, and even classical and jazz forms—may explain why his best songs sound both instantly familiar and oddly unlike anything else out there. Throw in his bleak, dark sense of humor and his mid-'70s conversion to Sufism, and he seems an even stranger character. From the wacky humor of "Nobody's Wedding," which appeared on his 1972 solo debut, *Henry the Human Fly,* to the ominous "Did She Jump or Was She Pushed," from his landmark 1982 album *Shoot Out the Lights,* Richard Thompson has amassed one of the most curious song catalogs in pop—as well as one of the most consistently satisfying.

Following *Henry,* Thompson spent over a decade recording in tandem with his then wife Linda, a Glaswegian backup singer whom he met while recording *Rock On,* a 1972 one-off oldies project by Fairport offshoot the Bunch. A perfect coupling, Linda's honey-sweet voice provided a valuable counterbalance to many of Thompson's deliberately dour songs, while the gruff-voiced guitarist was given a broader musical range to write music within. They recorded six full albums together during the course of their 1972–82 marriage, of which three—*I Want to See the Bright Lights Tonight* (1974), *Pour Down Like Silver* (1976), and *Shoot Out the Lights* (1982)—rank among Thompson's very best. The latter album, a huge critical favorite, was named one of 1982's best by the *New York Times, Time* magazine, and the *Village Voice*'s massive yearly rock critics' poll.

The pair's divorce during the same year was the focus of much media attention at the time, largely because many of Thompson's songs seemed so blatantly autobiographical; indeed, many were unsettled that the guitarist—who would soon leave his his wife for another woman—had her sing "Did She Jump or Was She Pushed" on their final album together. Six years later, Thompson suggested that the critics were overreacting. "Every line from every

Richard Thompson

song for years after [the divorce], it was 'You know, he's writing about her and she's writing about him.' People take it very personally when you're writing the song and singing it at the same time. They say, 'It's him, poor fellow, he really has got the blues. He is going to put his head on the railroad track.' People won't accept that you're writing from another persona, they want the song to be your life."

Beginning with 1983's solo *Hand of Kindness,* Thompson's albums have generally made respectable showings on the album chart, though none as yet has surpassed 1985's *Across a Crowded Room,* which peaked at number 102. His superb guitar playing—heard on literally scores of classic pop albums since his days in Fairport—began showing up in the company of an increasingly wide range of artists, including Beausoleil, avant-rocker David Thomas of Pere Ubu, Loudon Wainwright III (for whom he also produced 1985's *I'm Alright*), Crowded House, and T-Bone Burnett. Additionally, his songs have been covered by Elvis Costello, the Pointer Sisters, and Jo-El Sonnier, among others. He has also served as one-fourth of a part time "alternative supergroup"—also featuring Fred Frith, John French, and Henry Kaiser—that to date has released two albums.

Thompson's nonstop creativity has yet to slow after 25 years, and there's little indication it's likely to. "It'd be nice to be like the old blues guys," he said in 1988, "like B.B. King, to still be playing at 60-plus. That'd be very good. I mean, hell, Shakespeare was just hitting his stride at 40."

TOP ALBUMS

HENRY THE HUMAN FLY (Reprise, '74)
I WANT TO SEE THE BRIGHT LIGHTS TONIGHT
  (with Linda Thompson, Island, '74)
POUR DOWN LIKE SILVER (with Linda Thompson,
  Island, '76)
SHOOT OUT THE LIGHTS (with Linda Thompson,
  Hannibal, '82)
HAND OF KINDNESS (Hannibal, '83)
ACROSS A CROWDED ROOM (Polydor, '85)
RUMOR AND SIGH (Capitol, '91)

TOP SONGS

WALKING ON A WIRE (with Linda Thompson,
  Hannibal, '82)
WHEN THE SPELL IS BROKEN (Polydor, '85)

PETE TOWNSHEND

One of rock and roll's most venerated spokesmen and performers, Pete Townshend (b. Peter Dennis Blandford Townshend, May 19, 1945, London) electrified the baby-boomer generation of the 1960s as the leader of the Who—a band that stood alongside the Beatles, Rolling Stones, and Kinks as the best and most influential of the groups to emerge from the '60s British Invasion. As the band's main songwriter and colorful lead guitarist, Townshend gained renown for his "windmill"-style strum, his expert early use of electronic feedback, and, of course, his many wonderful songs, 16 of which became top 40 hits between 1967 and 1982. But if there is one thing for which the former Who leader will forever be linked, it is his band's famous "rock opera" *Tommy*—a 1969 album that was rerecorded by the London Symphony Orchestra in 1972, became a film by noted director Ken Russell in 1975, and was adapted to a full stage musical in 1992. In 1993, *Tommy* opened on Broadway to record-breaking box office sales and garnered five Tony Awards, including one for best original score. In many ways—and not necessarily to his liking—*Tommy* has proved to be the focus of Pete Townshend's musical career.

Beginning in the early 1960s as the Detours, then the High Numbers, and finally the Who, Townshend, singer Roger Daltrey, bassist John Entwistle, and drummer Keith Moon met only minimal American success with their initial single, "I Can't Explain," but by 1967 had a top 10 hit with "I Can See for Miles." Though they had begun as an R&B cover band, Townshend's original material was in ready supply and became increasingly sophisticated with each album. His early interest in so-called "rock opera" was first evidenced by the nine-minute extended track "A Quick One While He's Away" from the group's 1967 album *Happy Jack;* by the next year's *The Who Sell Out,* Townshend concluded the album with a fascinating story-song called "Rael," which contained musical themes that would soon be expanded in 1969's *Tommy.*

Tommy's massive success—it entered the top five and stayed on the charts for 126 weeks—made the Who internationally famous. Journalists were pleased to see that its creator, Townshend, was at least as fascinating as the album he'd created; after his band's memorable appearances at both the Mon-

Pete Townshend

terey and Woodstock festivals, the guitarist soon found himself unofficially appointed by the same press as spokesman for an entire generation. The effect, whether intended or otherwise, was Townshend's perceived need to express himself through increasingly grand musical statements. An attempted follow-up music/film project called *Lifehouse* failed to gel, but the guitarist used many of its songs for both 1971's *Who's Next* and his first official solo album, 1972's *Who Came First*. (An admirer of guru Meher Baba, Townshend had privately released two albums—1970's *Happy Birthday* and 1971's *I Am*—to fellow Baba followers.) By 1973, Townshend had readied the Who's *Quadrophenia*, a second two-LP

"rock opera" that was extremely well received; it became the group's highest-charting album and was similarly made into a film in 1979.

Following *Quadrophenia*, most Who albums to come were discussed by critics and fans purely in terms of their relation to that album or *Tommy*. In essence, despite his attempts to make quality pop records—among them, 1975's *The Who by Numbers* and 1978's *Who Are You*—Townshend was continually working in the shadow of his previous, more ambitious projects. Additionally, the success of the 1979 retrospective documentary film *The Kids Are Alright*—which followed the tragic 1978 death of Who drummer Keith Moon—only helped make the Who seem an increasingly over-and-done-with proposition. Having received good reviews for both *Who Came First* and 1976's *Rough Mix*—an informal duo album he'd recorded with longtime friend Ronnie Lane of the Small Faces—Townshend began pondering further outside Who activity.

With 1980's *Empty Glass*, Pete Townshend effectively proved he no longer needed the Who. His best work since *Quadrophenia*—and for that matter, his best solo work—the album was a top five hit and went gold, helped by its top 10 single "Let My Love Open the Door." Though his next effort, 1981's *Face Dances*, would again be with the Who—and do even better saleswise, going platinum—it was generally panned by critics, who felt Townshend was remaining with the band merely for the sake of maintaining its high-profile brand name. The guitarist returned the next year with still another solo album, *All the Best Cowboys Have Chinese Eyes*, and attempted to explain why he was following two distinct career paths. "There are limitations in writing for the band we all call the Who," he said, "based on the preconceptions that we all share about what the function of that band is. It should stick to what it always has done, because what it always has done has been so important. Form follows function." Nonetheless, by 1982, the group released its final album, *It's Hard*, and disbanded.

Without a band, Townshend began looking backward and forward at the same time. He released two fascinating double albums consisting of home recordings and early demos, *Scoop* (1983) and *Another Scoop* (1987), and accepted a position as an editor for the distinguished U.K. publishing house Faber and Faber. In 1985 he released his first book, *Horse's Neck,* a collection of fiction he'd written during the previous five years; well received, the book confirmed the songwriter had clearly been frustrated by the limitations that the song form alone presented. It came as no surprise the same year, therefore, that his first record in three years would have some literary aspirations, and indeed, from its title alone, 1985's *White City—A Novel* seemed an ambitious affair. Written about a working-class housing development located near the guitarist's birthplace, the album was also accompanied by a long-form video, still more proof that Townshend was attempting to be more than a simple tunesmith. "I called it a novel," he later explained, "because I was trying to deal with the same scale of storytelling."

Townshend's next venture was a turning point in his career. Impressed by a stage production of the musical *Les Miserables,* but vexed at its old-fashioned score, the singer decided to take on writing his own musical—but one that would be driven by a rock and roll soundtrack. The result was 1989's colorful *The Iron Man,* a work based on a children's story penned by British poet Laureate Ted Hughes. No longer hemmed in by the constraints of writing songs that would be sung only by himself or the Who's Roger Daltrey, Townshend stretched considerably with guest vocalists John Lee Hooker and Nina Simone. Though the album met only middling success—it peaked at number 58—Townshend later ascribed its comparative failure to the frenzy of activity surrounding that year's Who reunion tour, which he claimed drew attention away from the project.

Deeply involved with the stage production of *Tommy,* which was launched in La Jolla, California, in 1992, Townshend got a further taste of inspired musical theater. In 1993, following that show's extremely enthusiastic Broadway reception, the singer released the texturally dense *Psychoderelict;* including a full narrative, character dialog, and several songs, the album was described by an enthusiastic Townshend as "a novel form." His record company, getting even more to the point, declared, "Not a rock opera, it is something akin to a radio-play catapulted into the virtual reality of the '90s." Interestingly, however, when the album failed to generate much excitement at radio (it fell off the

TOP ALBUMS

EMPTY GLASS (Atco, '80, 5)
ALL THE BEST COWBOYS HAVE CHINESE EYES
    (Atco, '82, 26)
SCOOP (Atco, '83, *35*)
WHITE CITY—A NOVEL (Atco, '85, 26)
THE IRON MAN: THE MUSICAL BY PETE TOWNSHEND
    (Atlantic, '89)
PSYCHODERELICT (Atlantic, '93)

TOP SONGS

PURE AND EASY (Track, '72)
LET MY LOVE OPEN THE DOOR (Atco, '80, 9)
ROUGH BOYS (Atco, '80)
FACE THE FACE (Atco, '85, 26)

album chart in two weeks) and some consumers complained about the dialog between songs, the label quickly reissued the album in a special "music-only" package—an indication, perhaps, that Townshend's bottom-line appeal may remain as a songwriter, not a writer of radio plays.

If so, however, he isn't taking the hint. "I'd love to be able to tell myself that all I have to do for the rest of my life is write and perform songs," he told the Associated Press in late 1993. "But in music you deal in generalizations—the chase, the seduction, the melodrama of relationships—and never with the subtleties. As an adult, as I grow, one of the things that excites me is the specificity of theater, the subtlety that's possible there."

DWIGHT TWILLEY

There is a fine line between exploring a past musical genre while bringing something new to it and simply replicating a style. In the 1960s, Sha Na Na made a career of replaying '50s-style rock; in the 1970s, the Stray Cats likewise took '50s rockabilly songs and either directly covered them or borrowed their style for their own so-called "originals." But one of the very few artists to make something new of something old—in his case, the rocking sound of Elvis Presley combined with the melodicism of the '60s British pop of the Beatles and Searchers—was '70s singer-songwriter Dwight Twilley (b. June 6, 1951, Tulsa, Oklahoma). While music critics of the late 1970s were quibbling over such terminology as "punk" and "new wave," most agreed the rising sound of "power pop" drew direct inspiration from the mid-'70s work of Twilley.

A superb melodicist, Twilley and his early partner, drummer-singer Phil Seymour, had been musical misfits in their hometown of Tulsa since the late 1960s. Both were fascinated by the hook-filled sound of '60s pop, at a time when progressive rock and the "gospel rock" sound of fellow Tulsa resident Leon Russell were beginning to dominate the charts. Recording numerous pop songs in Twilley's informal home studio during the course of several years, the pair eventually (and ironically) ended up on Russell's own label, Shelter Records, after trekking out to Los Angeles in 1974 in search of a record deal. Then called Oister, the duo changed their name to the Dwight Twilley Band and instantly scored a hit with their first single, "I'm on Fire"—which reached number 16 on the Hot 100 in the summer of 1975, despite the absence of any accompanying album.

But Twilley's career was dogged by bad luck. Distribution problems between Shelter and its distributor, ABC Records, meant that Twilley's first album would not emerge until a year after "I'm on Fire" had hit; while Sincerely reached a respectable number 138 on the charts, it lost whatever momentum the single might have generated. Still, reviews could not be more effusive in their praise of Twilley and his catchy pop sound; Sincerely was voted debut album of the year by Rolling Stone magazine. A second album, licensed from Shelter and issued on Arista, did even better, peaking at number 70 even without a charting single. Given the considerable visual appeal of both Twilley and Seymour, it seems likely they might've exploded had MTV been around to bring their faces to middle America's living rooms. But it wasn't, and after working together 10 years, the pair split up.

Twilley continued on in a solo career that seemed slightly erratic; his debut album, Twilley, was similarly licensed by Shelter to Arista—and like Eric Carmen, another former rocker at the latter label, his sound began to soften somewhat, noticeably so on the sweeping ballad opener, "Out of My Hands." While ex-partner Seymour had signed a deal with Boardwalk Records and managed a 1981 hit with "Precious to Me," Twilley himself remained hitless—for a while. A new deal with EMI America Records resulted in two albums, Scuba Divers (1982) and Jungle (1984), the second of which finally brought the singer his much-needed hit "Girls," which peaked at exactly the same chart position (number 16) "I'm on Fire" had reached nine years earlier.

But if a strong career requires consistency and momentum, Dwight Twilley seemed to have neither. After two years of silence, his comparatively weak Wild Dogs was quietly released

TOP ALBUMS

SINCERELY (Shelter, '76)
TWILLEY DON'T MIND (Arista, '77)
TWILLEY (Arista, '79)
SCUBA DIVERS (EMI America, '82)
JUNGLE (EMI America, '84, 39)

TOP SONGS

I'M ON FIRE (Shelter, '75, 16)
GIRLS (EMI America, '84, 16)

on the CBS Associated label in 1986 and failed to chart at all. Since then, Twilley has been without a label. And while one of his songs ("Why You Wanna Break My Heart") did end up on 1992's platinum *Wayne's World* soundtrack, it was sung by actress-turned-singer Tia Carrere rather than Twilley himself. One upbeat note remains, however: in late 1993, DCC Compact Classics issued *The Great Lost Twilley Album,* a welcome collection of unreleased tracks from 1974 to 1980 that delighted Dwight Twilley's small—but still very loyal—pop audience.

Why Dwight Twilley's career did not take off in the same manner as that of another Shelter Records alumnus—Tom Petty, who in fact played guitar on some Twilley Band songs—ultimately remains a mystery. Some attribute it to inconsistent live performances, others to label problems, and still others to poor career advice. But—almost uniformly—very few attribute it to his songwriting. One suspects, though, that that may not offer him very much comfort.

MIDGE URE

Midge Ure

However global the international music market may appear, regional hits still exist. In the case of Midge Ure (b. James Ure, Oct. 10, 1953, Glasgow, Scotland), whose music has been heard throughout the world, his "region" is most definitely Great Britain. At one point in the late 1980s, it was estimated that Ure—who had prolifically recorded with the groups Ultravox and Visage, as well as on his own—had had more British hit records during the decade than any other individual.

How many? Twenty-nine. And in America? How does *one* sound?

To be fair, Ure did have a slight hit in the States in 1989 with "Dear God"—if peaking at number 95 is your idea of a minor smash. And six years earlier, as a member of Ultravox, he also watched his group's single "Reap the Wild Wind" ascend mightily to number 71. Still, most Americans are familiar only with "Do They Know It's Christmas?," the massive international hit he co-wrote in 1984 with Bob Geldof to benefit Ethiopian famine victims. Recorded by Band Aid—a British all-star

group including Phil Collins, Paul McCartney, David Bowie, U2, George Michael, Boy George, Duran Duran, and Sting—the record remains the all-time best-selling single in the U.K., and it reached number 13 in the States.

One reason Ure has enjoyed such popularity in Britain lies in the simple fact that he's had a hand in nearly every sort of band his trend-conscious country has had to offer in the past two decades. When teen idols the Bay City Rollers were at their peak between 1974 and 1976, Ure was a member of Slik, a similarly poppy combo that had a Number One U.K. hit with "Forever and Ever." When original Sex Pistol Glen Matlock

TOP ALBUMS
THE GIFT (Chrysalis, '85)
ANSWERS TO NOTHING (Chrysalis, '89)
PURE (RCA, '91)

TOP SONGS
THE GIFT (Chrysalis, '85)
DEAR GOD (Chrysalis, '89)

departed that infamous punk group in 1977, he started up a new punk band called the Rich Kids and recruited Midge Ure as guitarist. When the so-called New Romantic sound arose in the early 1980s, to be popularized by the likes of Spandau Ballet and Duran Duran, Ure was already in its forefront as a member of Visage, scoring top 10 hits with such singles as 1980's "Fade to Grey." He became even more prominent the same year when he replaced departing singer John Foxx in Ultravox.

With Ure at the helm, Ultravox produced four albums that reached the charts between 1980 and 1984; their most popular, *Quartet,* peaked at number 61 in 1983. Early proponents of rock video, the band appeared often on MTV. Further, both Ure and bandmate Chris Cross themselves produced rock videos, not only for their own band, but for Bananarama, Phil Lynott, and Fun Boy Three, among other artists. In 1982, Ure had released a solo single (a cover of Tom Rush's "No Regrets") that reached the U.K. top 10; in 1985, he went all the way and made a solo album, *The Gift,* the title track of which became his first British Number One single. Meanwhile, Ure's star was rising as a major figure in such international events as Band-Aid and Live Aid; he actually accompanied the first Live Aid shipment to Ethiopia. Additionally, he was music director of the U.K.'s renowned Prince's Trust Concerts and put together an all-star band for the internationally broadcast Nelson Mandela Freedom Fest at Wembley Stadium.

In 1988, Ure officially left Ultravox to concentrate on his solo career. The resulting album, *Answers to Nothing,* sounded considerably different than the slick electro-pop Ultravox was known for; it reached a respectable number 88 on the album charts. Worth noting was its inclusion of special guest Kate Bush on the duet "Sisters and Brothers," with members of UB40 supplying backup vocals. Ure continued his journey away from the synthetic sound on 1991's *Pure,* a solid collection of songs mostly centered around the distinctly unhip lyrical theme of love. More than ever, he announced at the time, he wanted to concentrate on the distinguished craft of songwriting. "I'm a melody-oriented person," he said. "I like melody and I like structure, as old-fashioned as that may be." Some cynics have noted, however, that his newfound enthusiasm for songwriting might stem from his getting a look at the size of the songwriting royalty check the Band Aid charity single generated.

SUZANNE VEGA

Like another onetime folksinger who now can't be so easily classified—hint: he was born Robert Zimmerman—Suzanne Vega (b. Aug. 12, 1959, New York) has followed her muse to very strange places indeed. Raised in Spanish Harlem by a mother who was a musician and a Puerto Rican stepfather who wrote novels, Vega began writing poetry at an early age and songs when she was 14. Within two years, guitar in hand, she was playing at New York clubs like Folk City and the Speakeasy, drawing raves from the likes of the *New York Times,* and attracting major label interest. A&M Records signed her and, for her first two albums, astutely paired her with co-producer Lenny Kaye. Why "astutely"? Because Kaye was a well-respected former rock/folk critic, a performer himself, and perhaps most importantly, an integral figure in the Patti Smith Group—whose leader was one of the most pivotal female vocalist-poets of the punk-rock era. Thus Vega's eponymous solo album, released in April 1985, caught the ears of folk fans who'd heard the buzz about this fresh-faced and captivating New York folkie, and punky post-moderns who knew they wouldn't exactly be getting the next Odetta. "I wanted to take the folk tradition and make it contemporary," Vega told the *Los Angeles Times* in 1987, "toughen it up and harden the language, learn how to use words differently."

From the start, Vega's career zoomed, thanks to songs like "Marlene on the Wall," which—like much of her best work—was rich with imagery, tinged both with hopefulness and regret, and endearingly (considering her folk "roots") minimalist. Though the success of her first record was by no means

TOP ALBUMS

SUZANNE VEGA (A&M, '85)
SOLITUDE STANDING (A&M, '87, *11*)
DAYS OF OPEN HAND (A&M, '90)
99.9 F (A&M, '92)

TOP SONGS

MARLENE ON THE WALL (A&M, '85)
LUKA (A&M, '87, *3*)
TOM'S DINER (featured with D.N.A., A&M, '90, *5*)

Suzanne Vega

minor—it spent 27 weeks on the Top Pop Albums chart—album number two, *Solitude Standing,* really remains her landmark. What propelled the album to gold status was the number three hit "Luka," Vega's supremely memorable, haunting tale of an abused tenement child, which was promoted by an equally stark music video often played by MTV. The album, very much in the public consciousness at the time, garnered three Grammy nominations.

Having earlier contributed a song ("Left of Center") to the platinum-selling *Pretty in Pink* soundtrack album and lyrics to two tracks on avant-composer Philip Glass's *Songs from Liquid Days* set—she had heavy friends—Vega now seemed primed to be a bigger pop sensation than ever. Or so it appeared. Though her 1990 follow-up album, *Days of Open Hand,* was warmly received by critics—most of whom felt Vega was swiftly moving from her folkish roots to a new pop-rock hybrid—it lacked a hit single, and thus sold accordingly.

What happened next was, in one sense, a singer-songwriter's dream: she had a hit record that she had nothing to do with. Her a cappella performance of "Tom's Diner" was, without her permission, lifted from her *Solitude Standing* album, given a hip-hop backing by U.K. group D.N.A., and transformed into a hit dance record. Vega heard it, loved it, and asked for its legitimate release, thrilled that her music was being heard by a whole new audience. "If I thought it was bad," she disarmingly told the press at the time, "I would have sued them."

What began as a fluke soon became a mini-phenomenon: in 1991, A&M released *Tom's Album,* a hilarious compilation of 13 different "versions" of "Tom's Diner"—by such artists as reggae singers Michigan and Smiley and informal R.E.M. spin-off group Bingo Hand Job— that included the Vega/D.N.A. "original." If there is a lesson to be learned from this, it may be that despite the context, it's the song that matters. That Vega was writing better ones than ever was noted in nearly every rapturous review of 1992's *99.9 F*— which, with its startling use of electronic and industrial noises, was called "Suzanne Vega meets Nine Inch Nails" by a few smarmy critics, albeit affectionately.

Very few singer-songwriters—perhaps really only Joni Mitchell—have managed to so conspicuously grow in musical and lyrical presentation simultaneously, and at so rapid a rate. For that matter, even fewer have inspired another performer's stage name, as Reprise Records singer Luka Bloom will happily attest. No one knows what Vega will do next—and what more could any artist ask for?

BILLY VERA

A man who learned the ins and outs of the music business as a songwriter and performer during the 1960s, Billy Vera (b. William McCord, Jr., May 28, 1944, Riverside, California) must have seen his unexpected mid-'80s success as par for the extremely wacky course. There could be no more flukish a hit than "At This Moment," which held the Number One slot on the singles chart for two weeks in 1987—five full years after its initial release. How did it happen? Following two 1985–86 airings on the NBC situation comedy "Family Ties"—placed there by the show's producer, who liked the tune—the song generated over 9,000 phone calls to NBC (reportedly the most in the network's history) and a flood of radio requests across the country. Any station lucky enough to locate the track—before Rhino Records quickly reissued it—would have found it on *Billy & the Beaters,* issued on the obscure Alfa label in 1981 and then quickly deleted.

Born in southern California but raised in New York, Vera began writing songs as a teenager; among his first charting tunes were Ricky Nelson's 1965 single "Mean Old World" and Barbara Lewis's top 30 hit "Make Me Belong to You," the latter of which got Vera his own deal with Atlantic Records. Paired with R&B singer Judy Clay at the suggestion of Atlantic's Jerry Wexler, the singer then recorded the duet "Storybook Children" (penned with regular collaborator Chip Taylor), which peaked at number 54 in January 1968. A few months later, Vera and Clay scored their sole top 40 hit with "Country Girl–City Man" then parted ways when Stax Records, to whom Clay was officially signed, ended its distribution deal with Atlantic. Vera managed his

own top 50 solo hit a few months later—"With Pen in Hand," written by Bobby Goldsboro—but then slowly faded from view. Aside from his mid-'70s album *Out of the Darkness,* released on Midsong International, little was heard from the singer during the '70s.

Vera's career picked up notably in 1979: Dolly Parton scored a Number One country hit with his song "I Really Got the Feeling", he took a staff position at WB Music Corp. in Los Angeles, and he formed Billy and the Beaters, who amassed a strong local following via weekly gigs at the famous Troubadour club. Signed to the Japanese Alfa label, the group released two albums, the first of which bore hit-to-be "At This Moment," the second of which was issued immediately prior to Alfa's folding its American operation.

In 1986, Rhino Records issued *By Request (The Best of Billy & the Beaters)* and saw those five-year-old recordings become the best-selling release in the company's history; they then issued a compilation of Vera's Atlantic material. By 1988, Vera himself had moved over to Capitol Records. His resulting album, *Retro Nuevo,* proved a sales disappointment—it didn't even chart—and Vera became a free agent once more, again par for the wacky course. Since then, the singer has acted in films (he'd had a small role in 1984's *Buckaroo Banzai*) and television, hosted a much-praised weekly R&B radio show in L.A., and done exemplary work compiling and annotating early R&B and rock and roll reissues for several major labels. A fervent record collector, Vera has a passion for music befitting a man who has made a lifelong living in its pursuit. Hits are great, he's learned, but you just can't count on them.

TOP ALBUMS

BILLY & THE BEATERS (Alfa, '81)
BY REQUEST (THE BEST OF BILLY VERA & THE BEATERS) (Rhino, '86, *15*)
RETRO NUEVO (Capitol, '88)

TOP SONGS

COUNTRY GIRL–CITY MAN (with Judy Clay, Atlantic, '68, *36*)
I CAN TAKE CARE OF MYSELF (Alfa, '81, *39*)
AT THIS MOMENT (Rhino, '86, *1*)

LOUDON WAINWRIGHT III

Few singer-songwriters can match the wit and biting irony that have spiced the songs of Loudon Wainwright III (b. Sept. 5, 1946, Chapel Hill, North Carolina) since his 1970 debut launched him as one of an unending series of so-called "new Dylans." It was an inappropriate tag—one that Wainwright himself made fun of years later with his hilarious "Talking New Bob Dylan"—but its implication that he was a masterful and intelligent songwriter was precisely on the mark. Over the course of 14 albums, Wainwright has crafted a repertoire of songs that are alternately funny, bitter, and at their best, profoundly moving.

The son of the late, well-known *Life* magazine columnist and editor Loudon S. Wainwright, Jr., the singer led a comfortable early life and attended an Episcopalian boarding school. He studied acting at Carnegie Mellon University for 18 months, then dropped out in 1967; hitchhiking cross-country to San Francisco, young Wainwright became an actual local during that city's famous Summer of Love. A return hitchhike eventually brought him to Cambridge, where he began writing songs in 1968. By 1969, after a well-received stint at the Village Gaslight, he signed to Atlantic Records.

Wainwright's 1970 debut drew considerable notice, for both its stark presentation—he sang accompanied only by his own guitar—and the intensely confessional nature of many of its songs. A heavy user of irony, Wainwright excelled at combining humor, self-deprecation, and pathos all into one lyric. A memorable example, taken from his 1971 set *Album II,* was "Motel Blues," in which the singer described "romance" on the road: "Chronologically, I know you're young/But when you kissed me in the club, you bit my tongue/I'll write a song for you and put it on my next LP/Come up to my motel room, sleep with me."

Wainwright's 1972 switch to Columbia Records brought him an unexpected top 20 hit with "Dead Skunk," a song he claimed to have written in 15 minutes (which wasn't hard to believe) that became the Number One single in Little Rock, Arkansas, for six weeks. Its success was ample proof that Wainwright's humorous approach could bear commercial fruit. Unfortunately, the singer's "humorous" songs weren't necessarily his best, or most rewarding.

Through 1974's *Attempted Mustache* and parts of 1975's *Unrequited,* Wainwright's material was often dominated by similarly comic turns, and while his sense of humor was unassailable, the songs wore out their welcome faster than they might have otherwise. Still, Wainwright's commercial peak came during that mid-'70s era; his only charting albums were *Album III* (which peaked at number 102), *Unrequited*

Loudon Wainwright III

(number 156), and *T Shirt* (number 188), his first recording for Arista.

Wainwright's recordings since then have appeared on a variety of labels; ironically, considering the singer's nationality, those released in the 1980s came about through separate deals with English labels, who then licensed the records to America's Rounder. In 1985, Wainwright himself moved to London, where he recorded *I'm Alright* (1985), *More Love Songs* (1986), and *Therapy* (1988), the first two of which were nominated for Grammys. He moved back to the States in 1988, due to his father's terminal illness and what he described as "the pull" of his children—whose respective mothers were singers Kate McGarrigle and Suzzy Roche.

When not performing, Wainwright has regularly acted in television, films, and theatre. In 1975, he played Captain Calvin Spaulding on the television show "M*A*S*H"; additionally, he appeared in the 1985 film *The Slugger's Wife* and 1989's *Jackknife* and had a stage role in *Pump Boys and Dinettes*. If these other activities have hampered his songwriting, so far there's been no evidence: as a songwriter, Wainwright is getting better with age. His 1992 album *History* may be his finest work ever; devoted to the many relationships in his extended family— father, son, daughter, ex-wife, mother, sister—the work was at once caustic, hilarious, and extremely touching. Once in danger of becoming a parody of himself, Wainwright still retains his edge—and the blade isn't duller, it's larger. He is settling into middle age with the gracelessness for which his fans have undoubtedly hoped.

TOP ALBUMS

LOUDON WAINWRIGHT III (Atlantic, '70)
ALBUM II (Atlantic, '71)
ALBUM III (Columbia, '72)
ATTEMPTED MUSTACHE (Columbia, '74)
UNREQUITED (Columbia, '75)
T SHIRT (Arista, '76)
THERAPY (Silvertone, '88)
HISTORY (Charisma, '92)

TOP SONGS

DEAD SKUNK (Columbia, '73, *16*)
RUFUS IS A TIT MAN (Columbia, '75)

JOHN WAITE

In the course of his career, John Waite (b. July 4, 1955, England) has been luckier than most performers: he's had time to get it right. From the peaks-and-valleys run of his first band, the Babys, through his own solo career, and back as part of Bad English, Waite has seen how the business works and obviously knows how to use it to his advantage.

As lead vocalist with Chrysalis Records act the Babys, Waite watched his group send three singles into the top 40 during its five-year run. Unfortunately, none of the three—"Isn't It Time," "Every Time I Think of You," and "Back on My Feet Again"—had been penned by him, though he and other band members collaborated on most Babys material. Other singer-songwriters might have resented the fact that the hits were coming from outside sources; Waite, who'd already established a reputation for having significant business savvy, simply carried on.

When the Babys disbanded in 1981, Waite launched his own solo career with 1982's *Ignition* and continued in the same pattern. Though the majority of the tunes were written by Waite and musicians he worked with, outside writers like Holly Knight, Paul Sabu, and Chas Sandford were called in as needed. The payoff came in 1984, when he moved to EMI America with his *No Brakes* album: "Missing You," a collaboration between Waite, Mark Leonard, and Sandford, became his biggest record ever, topping the Hot 100 chart and firmly establishing him as a solo artist. (Further evidence that Waite was experiencing a career high came when Chrysalis slapped a new cover on 1982's *Ignition* and shipped it out to take advantage of the success of "Missing You.")

With the exception of a remake of Marvin Gaye's "Ain't That Peculiar," Waite's 1985 follow-up, *Mask of Smiles,* was also filled with collaborations. Though opening track "Every Step of the Way" reached number 25 on the Hot 100, the lack of other strong singles had an obvious chilling effect on album sales. And despite "These Times Are Hard for Lovers"—a dynamic collaboration with hit songwriter Desmond Child—matters worsened with Waite's 1987 follow-up, *Rover's Return.*

The solution? Bad English, Waite's 1989 "supergroup," reuniting him with former Babys Jonathan

TOP ALBUMS

IGNITION (Chrysalis, '82)
NO BRAKES (EMI America, '84, *10*)
MASK OF SMILES (EMI America, '85, *36*)
ROVER'S RETURN (EMI America, '87)

TOP SONGS

MISSING YOU (EMI America, '84, *1*)
TEARS (EMI America, '84, *37*)
EVERY STEP OF THE WAY
  (EMI America, '85, *25*)

Cain and Ricky Phillips and including guitarist Neal Schon of Journey. Their debut album swiftly went platinum, and, in traditional Babys fashion, the biggest single, "When I See You Smile," was penned by an outsider—in this case, Diane Warren. It shot straight to Number One. Though John Waite has had his share of critical detractors over the years, no one will argue that he doesn't know his way around a hit record—regardless of who wrote it.

John Waite

TOM WAITS
· · · · · · · · · · · · · · · · · · ·

Few performers have grown so vividly before our eyes as has Tom Waits (b. Dec. 7, 1949, Pomona, California). Beginning his career in the early 1970s as a slightly off-center, traditional singer-songwriter, Waits developed into a beatnik-styled hipster whose combination of mumbles and growls were accompanied by slick jazz-combo backing. Then, perhaps sensing a dead end ahead, he shifted gears and became a daring sonic experimen-

talist whose image-laden lyrics suggested a combination of European theatre, Martin Scorsese, and skid row. And Waits's artistic evolution took place on more than one front: a series of small acting roles beginning with Sylvester Stallone's 1978 film *Paradise Alley* blossomed into a full-fledged acting career for the singer, who by 1987 was starring alongside Jack Nicholson and Meryl Streep in Hector Babenco's *Ironweed*.

Waits's earliest recordings, made under the direction of his manager Herb Cohen in late 1971 but never released, unexpectedly surfaced in the early

1990s when Cohen released them on his reactivated Bizarre label. They revealed a colorful young songwriter preoccupied with life's seamier side—as in "I'm Your Late Night Evening Prostitute"—and characters generally down on their luck ("Looks Like I'm Up Shit Creek Again"). Those themes would recur with regularity throughout most of Waits's songs, though their musical context would shift tremendously. His earliest album, 1973's *Closing Time,* arrived on David Geffen's singer-songwriter–heavy Asylum label and suggested another typical addition to its roster—albeit a slightly more colorful one. Opening track "Ol' 55" was quickly covered by both Ian Matthews and the Eagles; "Martha" was likewise redone by Cohen's own DiscReet Records artist Tim Buckley.

By album two, *The Heart of Saturday Night,* Waits was beginning his Kerouac-inspired hipster phase, memorably documented by 1975's double-LP *Nighthawks at the Diner:* accompanied by an extremely able jazz trio, Waits let his colorful words fly a mile a minute, more often speaking than singing, rambling about the ghost of Gene Krupa, Chubb's Pool and Snooker, and Big Joe and Phantom 309. To hear it once was captivating; with repeated listenings, though, the shtick grew thin. By his next album, Waits managed to consolidate every stylistically scattered direction he'd pursued into one very cohesive, triumphant package. *Small Change,* which reached number 89 on the charts, Waits's career high, was the singer's best album by far, and with "Tom Traubert's Blues" and "The Piano Has Been Drinking (Not Me)," he showed that despite his jive-talkin' persona, he was still capable of writing songs that tugged at the heart.

Waits's next few albums continued in the same direction, and while there were some surprises—Bette Midler duetting on *Foreign Affairs'* "I Never Talk to Strangers," his cover of *West Side Story's* "Somewhere" on *Blue Valentine* —beat-inspired songs like 1977's "Jack and Neal" were becoming too predictable a part of Waits's repertoire. After recording 1980's *Heartattack and Vine*—which contained "Jersey Girl," later covered by well-known

---

TOP ALBUMS

CLOSING TIME (Asylum, '73)
NIGHTHAWKS AT THE DINER (Asylum, '75)
SMALL CHANGE (Asylum, '76)
BLUE VALENTINE (Asylum, '80)
SWORDFISHTROMBONES (Island, '83)
RAIN DOGS (Island, '85)
BONE MACHINE (Island, '92)

TOP SONGS

OL' 55 (Asylum, '73)
MARTHA (Asylum, '73)
TOM TRAUBERT'S BLUES (Asylum, '86)

Jerseyite Bruce Springsteen—he stepped back to act in Francis Ford Coppola's strangely surrealistic film *One from the Heart.* The exceptional soundtrack, written by Waits himself, featured the singer duetting with unexpected partner Crystal Gayle and was a genuine pleasure.

Waits's giant leap came with 1983's self-produced *Swordfishtrombones,* a musically adventurous album on which Waits said he "tried to listen to the noise in my head and invent some junkyard orchestral deviation." His voice deeper than ever, he sang to the accompaniment of tuba, trombone, marimba, banjo, and harmonium to stunning effect. The series of albums that have followed since—*Rain Dogs, Frank's Wild Years, Big Time,* and *Bone Machine*— were again all produced by Waits and the subjects of near-universal critical acclaim. Waits has explored theater (*Frank's Wild Years* contained songs from the 1986 theatrical production of the same name he co-wrote with his wife, Irish playwright Kathleen Brennan) and continues to work in film, both as an actor and a soundtrack composer (most recently for Jim Jarmusch's 1992 film *Night on Earth*). An uncompromising figure still viewed by the industry as a growing talent, Tom Waits now mostly does what he wants—and commands tremendous respect from critics, film directors, and his fellow musicians at the same time.

JERRY JEFF WALKER

A much-admired Texas troubadour who has become a musical institution unto himself, Jerry Jeff Walker (b. Ronald Clyde Crosby, Mar. 16, 1942, Oneonta, New York) is best known for penning the pop perennial "Mr. Bojangles," a top 10 hit by the Nitty Gritty Dirt Band in 1971, also covered by an extremely wide range of artists. Walker's breadth of experience is similarly impressive: he began as a folksinger, worked in a duo with guitarist David Bromberg, was a member of the late-'60s psychedelic band Circus Maximus, became a solo artist

Jerry Jeff Walker

Bojangles" was the singer's only Hot 100 entry). The song (and the album itself) became one of the earliest entries in the burgeoning "progressive country" movement that would soon boom with such Texas artists as Clark, Michael Murphey, and, of course, Willie Nelson. Walker's next effort, *Viva Terlingua!*, was a major step forward in establishing both his sound and career; the album, which went gold, introduced Walker's highly skilled Lost Gonzo Band and featured a blend of originals and songs by Ray Wiley Hubbard, Murphey, and Clark. The latter's contribution, "Desperadoes Waiting for a Train," became yet another signature tune for Walker and further shaped his growing "Texas outlaw" mystique.

Walker's reputation as a good-time troubadour continued to blossom, particularly through his wayward, sometimes boozy live performances, which were ably documented on three sides of the 1977 double-LP *A Man Must Carry On*, his highest-charting album ever. Walker's own songwriting had started to slow down somewhat by the mid-'70s, however; as early as 1975, the singer had penned only two of the 10 songs on *Ridin' High*. Still, one of them, album closer "Pissin' in the Wind," became a major part of his repertoire; a humorously autobiographical track, the song ends with Walker singing, "The answer my friend is just/Pissin' in the wind/The answer is pissin' in the sink."

Walker continued steadily through the 1970s, though he still remained a cult artist by decade's end. His Lost Gonzo Band, which had released its own MCA album in 1975, departed in 1977 and was replaced by the Bandito Band; that group backed up the singer on 1978's *Contrary to Ordinary* and *Jerry Jeff* and the next year's *Too Old to Change*. The latter two albums, recorded for Elektra, were further evidence that Walker was becoming more of a singer than songwriter; though they contained well-chosen covers of songs by Paul Siebel, Rodney Crowell, and

in 1968 with "Mr. Bojangles," then in three years moved to Austin, Texas, where he continues to live even now. Since the early 1970s, his music has drifted somewhere between folk, country, and rock—and it's that middle "somewhere" region that has come to define him as a wholly unique entity as well as one of the central figures in Austin's enormously influential music scene.

In many ways, Walker's career as it is known today began with his signing to MCA Records (then Decca) in 1972. His eponymous label debut, recorded both in Austin and New York, was a solid showcasing of the musical direction he'd pursue thereafter: featured amid a wealth of original material such as "Hill Country Rain" and "Hairy Ass Hillbillies" were two songs by Austin songwriter Guy Clark, one of which—"L.A. Freeway"—would become a standard for Walker (and aside from "Mr.

TOP ALBUMS

VIVA TERLINGUA! (MCA, '73)
RIDIN' HIGH (MCA, '75)
A MAN MUST CARRY ON (MCA, '77)
GYPSY SONGMAN (Tried & True/Rykodisc, '87)

TOP SONGS

MR. BOJANGLES (Atco, '68)

Willis Alan Ramsey, there was only one Walker original ("Her Good Lovin' Grace") to be found on either. Returning to MCA once more, Walker made his final major label album with 1982's *Cowjazz*.

In 1986, Walker and his longtime wife Susan formed their own label, Tried & True music, on which the singer released his lauded *Gypsy Songman* career retrospective. The pair then made a deal with Massachusetts indie label Rykodisc, which has since released all of Walker's work through 1992's *Hill Country Rain*. While not a major player in the industry, Walker today deserves kudos for the efficiency of his business organization and fan club—among the best in the business—and for his sheer ability to keep his audiences wildly entertained for nearly a quarter of a century. It's just one more aspect of his fabled Texas mystique.

JOE WALSH

The former leader of the James Gang and a latter-day member of the Eagles, Joe Walsh (b. Nov, 20, 1947, Wichita, Kansas) is as well known for his sarcastic wit as his considerable abilities as a guitarist. His 1978 top 20 hit "Life's Been Good," which came after three years at the top with the Eagles, deliciously summarized the lifestyle change he'd undergone: "My Maserati does 185/I lost my license, now I don't drive/I have a limo, ride in the back/I lock the doors in case I'm attacked/I make hit records, my fans they can't wait/They write me letters, tell me I'm great." Next seen astride a tank that had just demolished a house—his cover for 1981's *There Goes the Neighborhood*—Joe Walsh, it was understood, was one funny guy.

While there was little comparable humor to be found on the records of Walsh's 1969–71 band the James Gang, the four records on which he played boasted guitar playing that was even more impressive. Among those impressed was the Who's Pete Townshend, who spoke highly of Walsh's fretboard talent and asked the James Gang to open the Who's 1971 European tour. After recording four albums with the group—three of which made the top 30 on the basis of Walsh's "Walk Away" and "Funk #49" (co-written with the band)—Kent State alumnus Walsh departed to form a new group called (briefly) Barnstorm with drummer Joe Vitale and bassist Kenny Passarelli. 1973's *The Smoker You Drink, the*

Player You Get—its title growing evidence of Walsh's wackiness—became the first top 10 album of Walsh's career, thanks to its memorable radio hit "Rocky Mountain Way," which has since become Walsh's signature tune.

By late 1974's *So What*, Walsh was getting significant studio help from various members of the Eagles—with whom he shared management—and had co-written "Falling Down" with Don Henley. Though it came as some surprise when, with two recent top 20 albums to his credit, he accepted an invitation to replace Bernie Leadon in the Eagles, in retrospect it seems a wise move. He gave the Eagles a much-needed harder rock edge, as heard on *Hotel California*'s top 20 hit "Life in the Fast Lane," co-written by Walsh, Henley, and Glenn Frey; the Eagles, meanwhile, gave him enhanced visibility and, one suspects, significant cash incentive. It may not be coincidental that the sole platinum album of Walsh's career was *But Seriously Folks…*: It arrived in stores in 1978, when the Eagles were at their commercial zenith, and contained a hit in "Life's Been Good" that drew its inspiration directly from his newfound super-celebrity.

Walsh stayed with the Eagles through their 1982 breakup, moving on to release a series of albums that typically bore humorous titles (*There Goes the Neighborhood, You Bought It—You Name It, Got Any Gum?*) but fewer obvious hits. After the top 30 "A Life of Illusion," the guitarist had only one more charting single—1983's "Space Age Whiz Kids," which peaked at number 52—before his sales began

TOP ALBUMS

THE SMOKER YOU DRINK, THE PLAYER YOU GET (Dunhill, '73, 6)
SO WHAT (Dunhill, '75, 11)
YOU CAN'T ARGUE WITH A SICK MIND (ABC, '76, 20)
BUT SERIOUSLY, FOLKS… (Asylum, '78, 8)
THERE GOES THE NEIGHBORHOOD (Asylum, '81, 20)
YOU BOUGHT IT—YOU NAME IT (Warner, '83)

TOP SONGS

ROCKY MOUNTAIN WAY (Dunhill, '73, 23)
LIFE'S BEEN GOOD (Asylum, '78, 12)
ALL NIGHT LONG (Full Moon, '80, 19)
A LIFE OF ILLUSION (Asylum, '81, 34)

to noticeably taper off. By 1992, his album *Songs for a Dying Planet* failed to enter the charts at all—and life in the fast lane, sad to say, had become an increasingly distant memory for Joe Walsh.

JIMMY WEBB

O ne of the most fascinating figures in all of pop music, and by far one of the most acclaimed, Jimmy Webb (b. Aug. 5, 1946, Elk City, Oklahoma) was blessed—or cursed—with staggering success so early in his career that the nearly three decades that have followed in some ways seem peculiarly anticlimactic. Webb, who moved with his family from Oklahoma to southern California in 1964, started out in a recording studio transcribing other people's music for $50 a week; by the end of the 1960s, he was a Grammy-winning multimillionaire whose songs were ubiquitous on the radio and—in the case of "Up, Up and Away," a 1967 top 10 hit by the Fifth Dimension—even as television commercials.

Webb's rapid ascension came via his marvelous ear for melodic hooks, sophisticated chord changes, and lyrics that typically cut straight to the heart. Beginning as a contract composer for Jobete Music, for whom he penned "Honey Come Back" in 1965 (a top 20 hit by Glen Campbell five years later), Webb at times seemed almost divinely inspired. His song "By the Time I Get to Phoenix" instantly caught the ear of hitmaker Johnny Rivers, who covered the song on his 1967 album *Changes* and paired Webb with the Fifth Dimension, a group he'd signed to his Soul City label. After taking a ride in a hot air balloon, Webb penned their hit "Up, Up and Away," which TWA would later use regularly on their TV commercials (and inspire Webb to create his own commercial music production company). The Fifth Dimension continued recording Webb's music—they scored two top 40 hits with "Paper Cup" and "Carpet Man"—but by 1968, the writer was branching out. Glen Campbell had scored a hit with Webb's "Phoenix" and kept coming back for more: by 1970, he'd put four

Webb songs in the top 30, including "Wichita Lineman" (a number three hit), "Galveston" (which peaked at number four), "Where's the Playground Susie," and "Honey Come Back."

Webb's unique collaborations with British actor-singer Richard Harris resulted in two well-received 1968 albums, *A Tramp Shining* and *The Yard Went on Forever*. The former had included the massive hit "MacArthur Park," unusual not only for its seven-minutes-plus length, but for its colorful orchestration and infamously surrealistic lyrics (ten years later, disco diva Donna Summer's remake of the song was a Number One hit for three weeks). By 1969, Webb couldn't have been more deeply enmeshed in the industry. He'd won two Grammys (for "Up, Up and Away," 1967's Best Song, and "MacArthur Park," 1968's Best Arrangement), he'd produced a gorgeous album for Thelma Houston (*Sunshower*) and another for his sister Susan Webb, and hits were coming from all directions—even from the Brooklyn Bridge, when the group of the same name, led by Johnny Maestro, took Webb's "Worst That Could Happen" to number three and scored a gold record.

Toward the end of that that year, during a period he later called "a kind of insanity," Webb took a breather. He traveled, practiced extensively, and finally decided to establish himself as a solo performer. Though Epic had released an earlier album of demos against his wishes in 1968 (*Jim Webb Sings Jim Webb*), his official debut—*Words and Music* on Reprise—was released in 1970. It met mixed reaction. Some critics contended Webb was not an especially good singer; others, such as *Rolling Stone*'s Jon Landau, held that his lyrics, "which were excellent in the pop song context, are now often overdone, pretentious and empty." Landau also pointedly dismissed as the album's "low point" its extended song, "Music for an Unmade Movie." Perhaps ironically, the song contained a revealing segment called "Dorothy Chandler Blues" in which Webb railed heavily against all critics, including his own: "How many songs of love have you written in your life sir?" he sang. "How many have you destroyed?/Who is the man who doesn't pay to see the play sir?/And angry with his

TOP ALBUMS

WORDS AND MUSIC (Reprise, '70)
AND SO ON (Reprise, '71)
LETTERS (Warner Bros., '72)
LAND'S END (Asylum, '74)
EL MIRAGE (Atlantic, '77)
SUSPENDING DISBELIEF (Elektra, '93)

TOP SONGS

P. F. SLOAN (Reprise, '70)
SANDY COVE (Elektra, '93)

Jimmy Webb

wife, takes out his knife and puts the show away."

Webb released a series of albums thereafter, each garnering mixed critical response and selling next to nothing. While his songs were still being performed by other artists—the Supremes, Judy Collins, Joe Cocker, Lowell George, Art Garfunkel (who devoted most of his 1978 *Watermark* to Webb songs, highlighted by the moving "Crying in My Sleep")—his own recording career floundered. He moved from label to label—Reprise, Asylum, Atlantic, Columbia—and became involved in film scoring, providing the music for such films as *Doc, The Naked Ape, Voices,* and *The Last Unicorn,* as well as the television shows "Tales from the Crypt," "Amazing Stories," and "Faerie Tale Theater." By

1983, Webb had relocated to New York in hopes of writing musicals.

In 1993, prodded by longtime friend and fan Linda Ronstadt, Webb released his most polished album ever, *Suspending Disbelief.* Many of the songs were quite dark—especially the introspective "Sandy Cove" (sample lyrics: "But I've got cracks in all my mortar/I've got holes in all my bricks")—but Webb's voice, noticeably improved after 10 years, sang them with a convincing, often moving compassion. With an agenda that included plans for collaborating on two musicals (*Love Me, Love My Dog* with Peter Stone and *Dandelion Wine* with its original author, Ray Bradbury), Webb ended 1993 busily and with great expectations. As he looks forward, so should we.

BOB WEIR

A founding member of the Grateful Dead and an active, ambitious solo artist, Bob Weir (b. Robert Hall, Oct. 16, 1947, San Francisco) has written and sung many of the Dead's best-liked tunes, though he generally has remained very much in the shadow of the band's other, better-known singer-guitarist, Jerry Garcia. Usually preferring to collaborate with a lyricist, Weir has written several songs with the Dead's stalwart wordsmith Robert Hunter but has most often worked with his prep-school friend and band's road manager, John Barlow. Beginning with *Ace,* his 1972 "solo" album —which was essentially a Dead album he fronted— Weir has recorded with his own bands such as Kingfish and Bobby & the Midnites, steadily with the Dead, and entirely on his own.

A onetime member of Mother McCree's Uptown Jug Champions along with Garcia, Weir was there from the beginning—as the group changed its name to the Warlocks in 1965 and to the Grateful Dead soon after. Though early Dead compositions were often credited to the entire band—either under that name or the pseudonymous McGannahan Skjellyfetti—Weir's serious move into songwriting began in the early 1970s, with such Dead songs as "Sugar Magnolia" (from 1970's *American Beauty*) and "Jack Straw" (from 1972's *Europe '72*). Both songs were co-written with Hunter; along with "Greatest Story Ever Told" and "Playing in the Band" (both of which also share co-writing credit with Dead drummer Mickey Hart), those Weir-Hunter compositions have remained staples in the Dead's live set now for over 20 years. The latter two tracks surfaced on *Ace,* Weir's highly regarded solo debut, which also showcased the first collaborations between Weir and Barlow. "I have a tendency not to want to write the sort of things Weir wanted in his songs at that time," lyricist Hunter later explained to writer David Gans in his book *Playing in the Band* (St. Martin's Press, 1985). "He wasn't looking for the telling phrase, the really apt combination of words to fire off a thought or emotional process; he was more interested in water colors, the texture of the words." Weir's ensuing partnership with Barlow—highlighted on *Ace* via "Looks Like Rain" and "Cassidy"—apparently satisfied all parties; it has continued ever since.

Full-time membership in the Grateful Dead has never been a hindrance for band members looking to explore other creative avenues. Just as Garcia pursued side projects such as the New Riders of the Purple Sage and Old and in the Way during the 1970s, Weir, too, played a major role in both Kingfish—for whose 1976 self-titled debut album he and Barlow wrote half the material—and Bobby and the Midnites, who released two albums in 1981 (*Bobby & the Midnites*) and 1984 (*Where the Beat Meets the Street*). Where Weir had joined a preexisting group with Kingfish (other key members included bassist Dave Torbert and guitarist Matthew Kelly), which continued without him following his 1977 departure, Bobby and the Midnites was another story. A bizarre "supergroup" pairing the singer with jazz pros Billy Cobham and Alphonso Johnson and former Steppenwolf guitarist Bobby Cochran, the band was a mildly successful unit put together purely for recording and touring purposes. Though their records were somewhat disappointing, such tracks as "Festival," "Carry Me," and "Josephine" were solely penned by Weir and showed him to be a fully capable lyricist on his own.

Between both side projects, Weir released another solo album, 1978's *Heaven Help the Fool.* Consisting mostly of Weir-Barlow tunes, the album was produced by Fleetwood Mac producer Keith Olsen and featured a top-notch cast of L.A. studio musicians; band biographer Blair Jackson rightly termed the result "an album which sounds like Bob Weir singing in front of tracks recorded for a Boz Scaggs album." Like virtually all of Weir's side projects, the album met only middling success: his two solo albums charted in the upper 60s, and the Bobby and

---

TOP ALBUMS

ACE (Warner Bros., '72)
KINGFISH (with Kingfish, Round, '76)
HEAVEN HELP THE FOOL (Arista, '77)
BOBBY & THE MIDNITES (with Bobby and the Midnites, Arista, '81)
WHERE THE BEAT MEETS THE STREET (with Bobby and the Midnites, Columbia, '84)

TOP SONGS

GREATEST STORY EVER TOLD (Warner Bros., '72)
PLAYING IN THE BAND (Warner Bros., '72)
ONE MORE SATURDAY NIGHT (Warner Bros., '72)
CASSIDY (Warner Bros., '72)

the Midnites records peaked at numbers 158 and 166 respectively; only the 1976 Kingfish set entered the top 50.

From a musical standpoint, Weir's music seems equally drawn from rock, R&B, and countryish sources. "There are certain places in 'Sugar Magnolia' where a certain chord would fit in naturally," former Dead keyboardist Brent Mydland revealingly told journalist Gans, "but Bob put in different ones. I asked him once why he'd put some weird chord where another one would go right in, and he said, 'That's my signature lick. That makes it my sound. Anybody could have stuck those other chords in there.' "

In 1991, Weir and his sister Wendy produced a children's book and accompanying cassette called *Panther Dream: A Story of the African Rainforest*. Weir, both with the Dead and on his own, has been a vocal supporter of preserving the world's rainforests; he testified before both Congress and the United Nations about the issue. All proceeds from the book were directed to fund rainforest reforestation and educational projects in Africa. "Children are open," Weir said at the time. "Maybe their innocent vision can bring the adult world greater respect for our planet." Weir's own vision, on display now for nearly three decades, remains a major factor in the driving force that will likely take the Grateful Dead into the next century.

TONY JOE WHITE

At the time in the late 1960s when rock and roll was beginning its evolution into a top-heavy series of genre hyphenates—be it the jazz-rock of Blood, Sweat and Tears, the acid-rock of the Jefferson Airplane, or the country-rock of Poco—Tony Joe White (b. July 23, 1943, Goodwill, Louisiana) carved out his own specific niche: swamp rock. Looking not unlike an early Elvis Presley (who would later cover one of his songs) and literally raised on a Louisiana cotton farm, White burst into pop consciousness in the summer of 1969 with his spookily mesmerizing growl of a top 10 hit, "Polk Salad Annie." Though that song remains his sole recording to reach the top 40 (his only other charting record, "Roosevelt and Ira Lee [Night of the Mossacin]," peaked at number 44 the same year), White's other accomplishments as a writer are even

more impressive: for one, his "Rainy Night in Georgia," a top five gold record for Brook Benton in 1970, has been covered by more than 100 artists.

White has said his earliest inspirations included bluesmen Lightnin' Hopkins and John Lee Hooker, the latter to whom he was, at times, obviously stylistically indebted. Part of a large musical family, White once credited his "daddy" for "coming up with the soulful licks on 'My Kind of Woman' " from his self-titled 1971 Warner Bros. album. His early years as a performer were spent fronting such bands as Tony and the Mojos and Tony and the Twilights, a club band that played the Louisiana and Texas circuit. Eventually, a 1967 audition in the office of Nashville music publisher Bob Beckham—just White and his guitar—led to a deal with Monument Records. Paired with producer Billy Swan, White recorded three superb albums for the label, each featuring his inimitably gruff voice singing and sometimes speaking (as with the intro to "Polk Salad Annie") and a uniquely fluid guitar style he himself described as "whomper stomper."

Oddly, perhaps, White first drew notice outside the States—in Paris, in fact, where his early single "Soul Francisco" fascinated a French-speaking populace taken with his distinctly American sound. "I would watch these people talk and dance around when I was playing over there," White recalled to journalist Robert K. Oermann. "They were just dancing their hearts out. I knew they couldn't understand what I was singing. I used to see guys and women dressed up like some of the characters in my songs, even in rural France and places way out in the woods. There's a lot of swampy people out there."

But it would be "Annie" that would bring White attention in the States. He initially toured here as a pop act, but his records and songs were being heard—and covered—by an amazingly diverse group of fellow artists: Benton, Elvis Presley ("I Got a Think About You Baby"), Dusty Springfield ("Willie and Laura Mae Jones"), Ray Charles ("3/4 Time"), Jerry Reed ("I Get Off on It"), Jacky Ward ("That's the Way a Cowboy Rocks and Rolls"), and even Wilson Pickett ("Hold On to Your Hiney"). After his Monument deal, he recorded three albums for Warners variously produced by Jerry Wexler and Tom Dowd, Peter Asher, and White himself (as co-producer). Though hits weren't forthcoming, White acquitted himself fairly well critically at that juncture, though some of that wore off as he rapidly moved to other labels (1977's *Eyes*, on 20th Century; 1980's *Real Thing*, on Casablanca; and 1983's *Dangerous*, on Columbia, his last major label) and began collaborating with other writers.

In 1986, Tony Joe White began marketing his music via his own independent label, Swamp Fox Records. Though he might seem to have been lying low, in some ways his profile was never higher: Tina Turner (with whom he shares a management company) recorded four of his songs for her gold 1989 album *Foreign Affairs*, resulting in the international hit "Steamy Windows," which hit the top 40 in America. Additionally, his two recent albums *Closer to the Truth* (1991) and *Path of a Decent Groove* (1993), released on the European Remark label, charted throughout Europe, Australia, and New Zealand—the former selling over 100,000 copies in France alone. And back in the States—where he'd been heard in commercials for McDonald's McRib sandwich and singing "You're Gonna Look Good in Blues" for Levi's 501 jeans—a superb 1993 Warner Bros. compilation of his 1969–73 material served as a welcome reminder of his one-of-a-kind talent.

BRIAN WILSON

Along with the Beatles and Bob Dylan, Brian Wilson (b. June 20, 1942, Hawthorne, California) stands as the most influential artist to emerge in pop music during the 1960s. As leader of the Beach Boys, Wilson produced, wrote, arranged, and sang on many of the decade's most memorable hits—most of which built the foundation for rock's

so-called "California Sound"—and advanced the overall state of pop music as much as if not more than any other performer in the genre. As chief architect of 1966's enormously far-reaching album *Pet Sounds,* Wilson directly contributed to the creation of the Beatles' 1967 masterwork *Sgt. Pepper's Lonely Hearts Club Band* by inspiring Paul McCartney, who fell in love with the album and played it repeatedly upon its release. "It may be going overboard to say it's the classic of this century," McCartney said years later to writer David Leaf, "but to me, it certainly is a total, classic record that is unbeatable in many ways." Following an incredibly productive streak of recording that resulted in 10 top 10 Beach Boys albums between 1963 and 1966, Wilson ran into difficulty completing his legendary "lost" album, *Smile,* and gradually lessened his involvement with the band, though still occasionally contributing moments of inspired brilliance in later years. After a period of semi-retirement from music making, Wilson returned in 1988 with a stirring solo album and has since been attempting to follow up that comeback. The subject of TV movies and a vast wealth of books (including his own) dealing both with him and the still-functioning Beach Boys, Wilson has lived a life of both triumph and tragedy.

Consisting of Wilson, his two brothers Carl and Dennis, his cousin Mike Love, and friend Al Jardine, the Beach Boys issued their first record, "Surfin'," in 1961. The Hawthorne, California–based quintet, and especially Wilson himself, was captivated by the vocal harmonies practiced by such groups as the Four Freshman; their early success came from blending their own sophisticated vocal style with the rock rhythms of the day and in the process creating something new. After being signed to Capitol Records in 1962, the group soon had their first top five single with "Surfin' U.S.A.," which indeed took the music of Chuck Berry (specifically his hit "Sweet Little Sixteen") and added topical lyrics about the then-local surfing craze. With such other hits as "Surfin' Safari" and "Surfer Girl," the group was instrumental in creating the early '60s surf music genre further popularized by friends Jan and Dean, the Rip Chords, and a host of others.

Typically, Wilson would provide the music while others such as Mike Love, producer Gary Usher, disc jockey Roger Christian, or later Tony Asher and Van Dyke Parks, would contribute the lyrics—which, early on at least, dealt with such subjects of teen interest as surfing, drag racing, and high school.

Often, however, Wilson provided both music and lyrics, and many of those songs are among the group's best work, including the Number One singles "I Get Around" and "Help Me, Rhonda," as well as "California Girls," "Surfer Girl," "When I Grow Up (To Be a Man)," "She Knows Me Too Well" and "Let Him Run Wild."

Wilson's most stunning creative stretch with the Beach Boys extended from 1964's *All Summer Long* through 1965's *The Beach Boys Today!* and *Summer Days (And Summer Nights!!)* to 1966's *Pet Sounds.* All were top five albums except, ironically, for *Pet Sounds,* which peaked at number 10 and was viewed as a failure in some quarters—largely because many of the lyrics (mostly supplied by Tony Asher) reflected more adult-oriented topics than surfing and drag racing.

Wilson, who had quit touring with the band in 1964 to devote more time to studio recording, was a remarkably advanced producer and arranger, and his songs, becoming increasingly complex, reflected that sophistication. His first post–*Pet Sounds* single, 1966's Number One hit "Good Vibrations," was not only one of the group's most successful records but one of the most intricately constructed sound montages in pop.

Expectations were high for *Smile,* an album that Wilson declared would be "a teenage symphony to God," but for many reasons—most of them well-documented in innumerable Beach Boys histories—the album went unfinished and never saw official release. (Lengthy excerpts from it were finally released in 1993—27 years later—on Capitol's superb five-CD boxed set, *Good Vibrations: Thirty Years of the Beach Boys.*) Dribs and drabs of songs intended for the album later emerged as a single (1967's "Heroes and Villains") and on later albums such as *Smiley Smile* (1967), *20/20* (1969), and *Surf's Up* (1971); but otherwise, the complexity of "Good Vibrations" and "Heroes and Villains" was soon replaced by a less ambitious, more laid-back feel on the albums to come.

A tumultuous and eventful personal life took its toll on Brian Wilson in the late 1960s and early '70s, and his contributions to each Beach Boys album began to diminish; yet his few songs on *Sunflower* and *Surf's Up* were typically gorgeous. The group had temporarily wound down by 1973, but even then their timeless appeal was demonstrated by the huge success of compilations such as 1974's *Endless Summer* (a Number One set that stayed on the charts

for 155 weeks) and 1975's top 10 *Spirit of America.* By 1976, Wilson had rejoined the Beach Boys for the tepid *15 Big Ones,* which featured the singer in surprisingly poor shape physically and vocally; still, the album went gold and included his moving rendition of the 1965 Righteous Brothers hit "Just Once in My Life." Though its successor, the much-underrated *Love You,* was a surprising return to form and featured Wilson's best songs in years—including "The Night Was So Young" and "I'll Bet He's Nice"—it was a sales stiff and failed to even crack the top 50. A series of uninspired Beach Boys albums then followed, most of which barely featured Wilson at all.

Involved in intense and sometimes controversial therapy with psychiatrist Eugene Landy, Wilson essentially produced no major works until his unexpected 1988 "comeback" album, *Brian Wilson.* A thrilling set that often recalled his illustrious work of the past, it received enthusiastic reviews and suggested the singer was back on the productive track. Still, the continued association of Landy—who was listed as executive producer and took co-writing credit on five of the album's songs—rubbed many critics and fans the wrong way. A series of further misfortunes followed, including the refusal of Warner Brothers to release Wilson's intended 1991 follow-up, *Sweet Insanity;* bootleg tapes of the album have since surfaced that make the label's decision seem puzzling, as it seems as good as if not better than its predecessor.

Wilson was the center of several legal battles in the early 1990s, including a lawsuit filed by former

---

TOP ALBUMS

BRIAN WILSON (Sire, '88)

TOP SONGS

The Beach Boys:
SURFIN' U.S.A. (Capitol, '63, 3)
SURFER GIRL (Capitol, '63, 7)
BE TRUE TO YOUR SCHOOL (Capitol, '63, 6)
FUN, FUN, FUN (Capitol, '64, 5)
I GET AROUND (Capitol, '64, 1)
HELP ME, RHONDA (Capitol, '65, 1)
CALIFORNIA GIRLS (Capitol, '65, 3)
WOULDN'T IT BE NICE (Capitol, '66, 8)
GOOD VIBRATIONS (Capitol, '66, 1)

Additional Top 40 Songs: 25

partner Mike Love involving writing credits, another suit against Irving Music regarding the publishing deal struck by his father, and a custody fight that resulted in a court order finally separating Wilson and Landy. Such struggles have tended to cloud the perception of Wilson as a viable artist in the 1990s —yet, on the evidence of the unreleased *Sweet Insanity,* the artist is still very much a major talent to be reckoned with. Were Brian Wilson to have faded from sight after *Pet Sounds,* he would still be regarded as one of pop music's greatest talents; luckily he didn't—and his legacy continues to be enjoyed more than 30 years after the first, historic Beach Boys single.

JESSE WINCHESTER

Singer-songwriter Jesse Winchester's first album arrived in this country on the now-defunct Ampex label in 1970—courtesy of Canada, however indirectly. Shreveport, Louisiana, native Winchester (b. May 17, 1944), whose father was in the military, was literally a draft dodger. After leaving Memphis to study in Munich, Germany, in 1967, the singer faced his draft notice back home and opted instead to move to Canada. That sense of the poet-in-exile only heightened the artfulness of Winchester's wonderful, distinctly American debut. Produced by another Canadian with an instinctive grasp of musical Americana—Robbie Robertson of the Band—the album seemed an astonishingly mature statement. Most notable were two tracks, "Biloxi" and "Yankee Lady," beautiful, longing ballads that painted unforgettable pictures of times, places, and relationships long gone. Those who heard the album—and there weren't many who did, thanks to Ampex's less-than-powerhouse promotional abilities—instantly loved it. Furthermore, artists who knew a good song when they heard one—like Joan Baez, Tom Rush, Ian Matthews, Tim Hardin, and more—instantly rushed to cover both tracks, which can now fairly be termed standards.

Winchester returned in 1972 with the markedly more upbeat *Third Down, 100 to Go,* self-produced except for three tracks overseen by Todd Rundgren (who had engineered his debut). There was humor in many of the songs that hadn't quite been evident earlier, but the peculiar sense of detachment and classicism that so dominated his earlier album wasn't much in evidence. That didn't prevent Winchester

from making his first impression on the charts, although a peak position of number 193 wasn't much to write home about, regardless of your country of origin. (That Ampex had folded and the singer was now on the more powerful Warner Bros.-distributed Bearsville label may have helped him chart, too.)

By 1973, Winchester was a full-fledged Canadian citizen; his next album, *Learn to Love It,* appropriately bore two songs he wrote in French Canadian and two by band member Russell Smith that would later become chart hits by Smith's next group, the Amazing Rhythm Aces: "Third Rate Romance" and "The End Is Not in Sight." Winchester's own fortunes would improve two albums later with 1977's *Nothing But a Breeze,* his most commercially successful set. It included his first charting single in the title track and a thematically appropriate cover of "Bowling Green," a 1967 hit for the Everly Brothers (who'd been courteous enough to cover Winchester's "Brand New Tennessee Waltz" on their 1972 album *Stories We Could Tell*). President Carter's declaration of amnesty for draft dodgers then allowed Winchester his first legal entry to the United States in 10 years; he entered, toured to much acclaim, and then hightailed it back to his adopted country of Canada. Four years later, he'd achieve his first brush with the top 40 with "Say What," produced by Memphis R&B legend Willie Mitchell; it would also be his last.

Had Winchester never released another album after that galvanizing debut, he'd be nearing legendary status. But he did, and his string of workmanlike albums may, unfortunately, have taken away some of his allure. Like other singer-songwriters whose moment in the pop world seems to have come and gone, Winchester continues to record—most recently for the Sugar Hill label—and doesn't spend much time looking backward.

TOP ALBUMS

JESSE WINCHESTER (Ampex, '70)
THIRD DOWN, 110 TO GO (Bearsville, '72)
NOTHING BUT A BREEZE (Bearsville, '77)
A TOUCH ON THE RAINY SIDE (Bearsville, '78)

TOP SONGS

BILOXI (Ampex, '70)
YANKEE LADY (Ampex, '70)
THE BRAND NEW TENNESSE WALTZ (Ampex, '70)

STEVE WINWOOD

From his teenage days as lead singer and focal point of England's Spencer Davis Group, multi-instrumentalist Steve Winwood (b. May 12, 1948, Birmingham, England) seemed an extraordinary figure. Most captivating was his astounding, R&B-charged voice, which most often resembled that of Ray Charles—no mean feat in itself, but even more impressive considering boy-wonder Winwood was barely 15 when he'd joined the band. Scoring his first U.K. Number One with the Davis Group's "Keep on Running" in 1965, the youthful singer had an early, filling taste of the "high life" he'd name an album after a full 21 years later.

Following two top 10 hits that brought him even more renown—1967's "Gimme Some Lovin' " and "I'm a Man," both penned by Winwood with band collaborators—the singer reacted by dropping out of the pop world to form Traffic. The latter, much-loved group featured Winwood with drummer friend Jim Capaldi, guitarist Dave Mason, and reed player Chris Wood; together they wrote and played some of the finest pop music of the decade. Merging rock, pop, psychedelia, and R&B into a uniquely eclectic, high-spirited musical whole, Winwood and company were a near-perfect combination that ultimately proved too good to last. Divided into two musical camps at the start, Winwood, Capaldi, and sometimes Wood typically collaborated on classic tracks such as "Paper Sun," "Coloured Rain," and "Heaven Is in Your Mind," while guitarist Mason generally preferred to work on his own. Following the U.K. top five success of Mason's poppy "Hole in My Shoe," Mason quit and rejoined the band numerous times; by the time the group's debut album, *Mr. Fantasy*, reached American shores, the group was depicted as a trio, and only two Mason-penned songs were included. Mason remained long enough to contribute some exceptional tracks to the band's second album, 1968's *Traffic*, before starting his own successful solo career; as far as America was concerned, however, Winwood was the band's dominant force from Day One.

With an occasional side trip—such as Winwood's breaking up the band in 1969 while he co-led the ill-fated supergroup Blind Faith with Eric Clapton, only to reform it again in 1970—Traffic recorded a string of extremely well-received albums between 1967's *Mr. Fantasy* and 1974's *When the Eagle Flies*, eight

Steve Winwood

of which made the top 40. Mainly using drummer Capaldi as lyricist, Winwood found his songwriting style marked by two distinct phases while in Traffic: Prior to and including 1969's *Last Exit,* the singer wrote tightly knit, shortish tracks that drew from standard pop, rock, and R&B (mostly Stax-inspired) forms. Following the group's reformation with 1970's *John Barleycorn Must Die,* however, Traffic became more of a "jamming" band, working on a loose, repetitive groove over which Winwood's voice generally soared, alternately powerfully or dreamily. Tracks such as 1971's 11-minutes-plus "Low Spark of High-Heeled Boys" became the general norm, and while album sales remained strong, the group never had a top 40 American hit in its duration.

When Winwood finally disbanded the group in late 1974, he worked as a session musician with several artists before finally reemerging with 1977's *Steve Winwood,* a debut solo album that, perhaps unexpectedly, sounded very much like Traffic had prior to their split. Still collaborating on songs with Capaldi—who had begun a successful solo career of his own as far back as 1972—Winwood had also continued his writing relationship with former Bonzo Dog Band member Vivian Stanshall, who'd penned the lyrics to "Dream Gerrard" on Traffic's 1974 finale, *When the Eagle Flies.* Very much a solo album, *Steve Winwood* essentially featured the singer playing an assortment of instruments—mostly keyboards and guitars—over a hired rhythm section.

TOP ALBUMS

STEVE WINWOOD (Island, '77, 22)
ARC OF A DIVER (Island, '81, 3)
BACK IN THE HIGH LIFE (Island, '86, 3)
ROLL WITH IT (Virgin, '88, 1)
REFUGEES OF THE HEART (Virgin, '90, 27)

Additional Top 40 Albums: 2

TOP SONGS

WHILE YOU SEE A CHANCE (Island, '81, 7)
HIGHER LOVE (Island, '86, 1)
THE FINER THINGS (Island, '86, 8)
ROLL WITH IT (Virgin, '88, 1)
DON'T YOU KNOW WHAT THE NIGHT CAN DO?
   (Virgin, '88, 6)

Additional Top 40 Songs: 5

It's arguable that Winwood's "real" post-Traffic solo career in fact began with 1981's *Arc of a Diver.* First, it marked the beginning of his very productive songwriting relationship with lyricist Will Jennings; although both Stanshall and George Fleming contributed lyrics, Jennings' predominated. He thereafter provided nearly all of Winwood's lyrics. Secondly, Winwood had returned to the simple pop songcraft that made early Traffic so appealing, most notably with *Diver's* opening track, "While You See a Chance," which in 1981 became his first top 10 American single since his days with the Spencer Davis Group. As a result, the album went top five, and Winwood established himself as a major solo star.

During much of the 1980s, Winwood consolidated that burst of success with a number of similarly successful albums, most of which fruitfully provided regular top 20 hits. A major career surge ensued in 1986 via his top five *Back in the High Life;* the album was nominated for six Grammys, won three, and included Winwood's first-ever Number One single, "Higher Love." The high esteem in which Winwood was held became evident when it was announced that he'd been signed by Virgin Records —then launching in America—for an extremely lucrative sum. Their faith in the singer paid off: his 1988 Virgin debut, *Roll with It,* went double platinum and became his first Number One album.

Winwood's music became more R&B-based in the late 1980s, and indeed there was some controversy that his "Roll with It" shared too many similarities with Jr. Walker and the All Stars' 1966 hit "(I'm a) Road Runner." Regardless, the singer, who now lives in America, is generally perceived as one of the most creative voices to emerge from the U.K. in the 1960s. Still in his mid-40s, he has escaped the "dinosaur" tag often bestowed by younger critics and listeners on his '60s contemporaries and at the same time is generally accorded the respect usually reserved for performers 10 or 20 years his elder.

GARY WRIGHT

There's a good chance nobody was more surprised than Gary Wright (b. Apr. 26, 1943) to discover that the producers of the early '90s hit movie *Wayne's World* not only wanted to use his 1976 smash "Dream Weaver"—they wanted to use it as, er, comic relief. For when Mike Myers, playing

Gary Wright

nitwit Wayne, looked at Tia Carrere and knew at once he was in love forever, the music he heard in his head—and we heard in the theatre—was Wright's omnipresent '70s theme. The money must've been great, sure...but the association with one of cinema's main meatheads might have stung.

In retrospect, Gary Wright (who himself had been a child actor), like similar '70s radio stars the Bee Gees and Peter Frampton, may be one of those unfortunate few performers forever tied to a specific time, place, and clothing style. But, again like the Bee Gees and Frampton, Wright's distinguished track record and pedigree aren't so easily dismissed. Prior to his solo career, Wright's best-known band was Spooky Tooth, which formed in 1967 when Island Records head Chris Blackwell paired the New Jersey native with Art, a four-piece British band already on his label. Much respected during their three years together, Spooky Tooth uniquely featured two keyboard-playing singers: the high-voiced Wright (who often sang falsetto) and menacingly deep-voiced Mike Harrison. Each played off the other as if they were the psychedelic Righteous Brothers, singing high and low while frenetic lead guitarist Luther Grosvenor howled away scarily. The original group

recorded three albums before Wright departed to go solo.

Wright's first two solo albums, 1970's *Extraction* and 1971's *Footprint,* contained all-original material (including two collaborations with guitarist Hugh McCracken) and seemed compositionally the equal of Spooky Tooth; additionally, each featured superstar sessioneers such as George Harrison (under the pseudonym George O'Hara), King Curtis, Klaus Voorman, and Jim Keltner. No matter: each sold poorly, and before long, after attempting to launch a new group called Wonderwheel, Wright reunited with Spooky Tooth. "That came out of frustrations on just about everyone's part from not having much success with our individual efforts," Wright later recalled. "I really didn't like the albums we did." Those albums numbered three, and—regardless of his sentiments—the first two contained some of Wright's most dynamic material to date, including "Cotton Growing Man" (from 1973's *You Broke My Heart, So I Busted Your Jaw,* later covered by singer Tim Rose) and "Ocean of Power" (from 1973's *Witness*).

Only after Wright kissed off Spooky Tooth forever, in 1974, did things gel. The first fruit of his new solo deal with Warner Brothers was 1975's platinum-selling *Dream Weaver,* which gave Wright his first two top 10 singles (both the title track and "Love Is Alive" reached number two) and, of course, a music credit in a hit movie two decades later. Though Wright took great pains to note on its cover that *Dream Weaver* was different—"an album of keyboard music," he proudly called it, for which he didn't even need a band—in terms of material, it wasn't much different than what he'd been doing in Spooky Tooth. Moot point though it was, one could easily imagine Tooth's Mike Harrison singing new material like "Blind Feeling" and maybe even making it better. *Dream Weaver* contained more than hits, too: Wright had begun practicing yoga, and would credit Paramahansa Yogananda on many albums to follow. That this became his first to feature lyrics about such things as "astral planes"—and that later album jackets would feature Wright bedecked in a robe, arms outstretched and wearing a mystic amulet—may help explain his later appeal to the *Wayne's World* crew.

In 1981, "Really Wanna Know You," from his final Warners album, *The Right Place,* became Gary Wright's last hit single, peaking at number 16. Like several songs on that set, it had been co-written, in this instance with Ali Thompson. When Wright returned seven years later with the quite respectable *Who I Am,* half of those songs were collaborations as well. A dry spell? Considering the strength of new originals like the title track and "Rose," not likely. And though the album didn't click at retail, one suspects the next might. If there is a next one. If the Wayne and Garth soundtrack royalties, painful as they must be, ever stop kicking in.

TOP ALBUMS

EXTRACTION (A&M, '70)
FOOTPRINT (A&M, '71)
THE DREAM WEAVER (Warner Bros., '75, 7)
THE LIGHT OF SMILES (Warner Bros., '77, 23)
TOUCH AND GONE (Warner Bros., '77)
THE RIGHT PLACE (Warner Bros., '81)

TOP SONGS

DREAM WEAVER (Warner Bros., '76, 2)
LOVE IS ALIVE (Warner Bros., '76, 2)
REALLY WANNA KNOW YOU (Warner Bros., '81, *16*)

ROBERT WYATT

Though likely to go down in pop history as an intriguing but minor cult figure, Robert Wyatt (b. Robert Ellidge, Jan. 28, 1945, Bristol, England) is in fact one of the most distinguished singers, songwriters, and politically committed performers to emerge from Great Britain. As drummer and lead vocalist in the '60s psychedelic rock group Soft Machine, Wyatt began as a wryly humorous, incomparably sweet-voiced singer; evolved into an idiosyncratic band leader with his own '70s group Matching Mole; and finally forsook performing his own material to record the little-heard songs of international artists who had faced severe political repression. A one-of-a-kind performer whose material, however difficult, captivates listeners with the honesty of its expression, Wyatt is a maverick figure of heroic proportions.

A member of Canterbury pop group the Wilde Flowers between 1963 and 1965, Wyatt formed Soft Machine in 1967 with former schoolmate Mike Ratledge, Australian guitarist Daevid Allen, and bassist-singer Kevin Ayers. That version of the group lasted long enough to record one unsuccessful single; following an early American tour with the Jimi Hendrix Experience, the group (minus guitarist Allen) recorded their first album, *Soft Machine,* in New York in 1968. The album, which peaked at number 160 in early 1969, remains Wyatt's major brush with American chart success. The group disbanded temporarily, then reformed with bassist Hugh Hopper and released 1969's brilliant *Volume Two,* for which Wyatt penned the lyrics and arranged much of the music. Perhaps the finest standing example of truly psychedelic music to emerge from Britain in the 1960s, the album caught the group midway between its evolution from a deliberately experimental, joyfully excessive rock band to a less interesting, refined fusion jazz unit. Wyatt hung around long enough to record his side-long extravaganza "Moon in June" on 1970's *Third,* but after the next year's *Fourth*—on which he was no longer permitted to sing with the now totally instrumental group—he departed to form his own group, Matching Mole.

With Matching Mole, Wyatt was able to utilize his skillful jazz-inflected drumming and vocals in both a pop and wordless scat-style context. He wrote both beautiful, sentimental ballads ("O Caroline") and spacey instrumental pieces ("Instant Pussy")—

and, as he did in Soft Machine, typically injected humorously self-conscious lyrics into songs such as "Signed Curtain." "This is the second verse," sang Wyatt. "And this is the chorus/Or perhaps it's a bridge/Or just another part of the song that I'm singing." Though the group's first album was released only in the U.K., its second, *Little Red Record*—produced by King Crimson's Robert Fripp and featuring Brian Eno—was released domestically on Columbia in 1972, albeit to minimal sales.

Plans for a third Matching Mole album fell through when, horrifyingly, Wyatt broke his back in 1973 in a four-story fall that left him a paraplegic. What might have reasonably ended any artist's career only temporarily derailed his, however; following a lengthy period of hospitalization, Wyatt returned with his stunning 1974 solo album, *Rock Bottom,* which that year won the top French music award, Prix Charles Cros, and remains one of the most moodily magnificent records of the 1970s. "In a way it was the easiest record I've ever had to make," Wyatt recalled in 1986. "It was the first record where I didn't have to spend half the time trying to carry the drum kit around all over the place. Before, I'd been trying to get about drumming and the kit, and writing and arranging and organizing gigs, and singing and writing songs. So cutting it down to those last two—just concentrating on the bits I could handle and leaving more to other people—was quite liberating."

Wyatt followed the critically hailed album with a cover version of the Monkees' "I'm a Believer" and had the first U.K. hit single of his career. But after releasing one more album, 1975's *Ruth Is Stranger than Richard,* the singer took an extended hiatus from recording. "There seemed to be this consensus in the rock world that it was a new and semi-legitimate art form, and it was sort of a natural vehicle for new and rebellious ideas," said Wyatt. "And it became quite clear to me that we were, as rock musicians, members of the establishment. You were getting to funny stages where people who deliberately maimed themselves onstage were selling themselves as brave and courageous—whereas you had someone like Victor Jara in Chile, who because he sang for democracy in Chile, was tortured to death. If we're going to talk about brave rebels in the music business, let's talk about Victor Jara, not people who mutilate themselves on groovy videos."

Wyatt then issued a series of cover versions of songs that he felt had both personal and political

meaning for him. Their sources ranged from Cuban folk songs ("Caimanera") to Jara ("Yolanda" and "Te Recuerdo Amanda") to the Golden Gate Jubilee Quartet ("Stalin Wasn't Stallin' ") to Billie Holiday ("Strange Fruit") to Chic ("At Last I Am Free"); most were compiled and issued by Gramavision Records in 1986 as *Nothing Can Stop Us.* Additionally, Wyatt scored a top 40 U.K. hit in 1983 with "Shipbuilding," a commentary on the Falklands War penned for him by Elvis Costello and Clive Langer. His unique voice has also been heard on albums by a wide variety of other artists, including Pink Floyd drummer Nick Mason, jazz artists Carla Bley and Mike Mantler, Roxy Music guitarist Phil Manzanera, Hatfield and the North, and Everything but the Girl's Ben Watt.

Wyatt's own records have come less and less frequently. 1986's *Old Rottenhat* was a mesmerizing but sparse effort, with lyrics considerably less humorous than those of his days in Soft Machine and Matching Mole—as on the opening track "Alliance": "I know what you're frightened of more than anything/Is knowing you need workers more than they need you/'A herd of independent minds,' Chomsky got it right/Jogging into battle wearing old school ties." Five years later he returned with *Dondestan,* another dreamily atmospheric work that this time incorporated several lyrics by his wife, artist Alfreda Benge. His last release was *A Short Break,* a brief EP of low-key instrumentals recorded in 1992 and issued on the small Voiceprint label. Still one of the most fascinating figures on the pop scene, Robert Wyatt continues to follow his conscience and muse simultaneously; where both will take him should be rewarding and perhaps even more interesting.

TOP ALBUMS

LITTLE RED RECORD (with Matching Mole, Columbia, '72)
ROCK BOTTOM (Virgin, '74)
NOTHING CAN STOP US (Gramavision, '86)
OLD ROTTENHAT (Gramavision, '86)
DONDESTAN (Gramavision, '91)

TOP SONGS

SEA SONG (Virgin, '74)
I'M A BELIEVER (Virgin, '74)

JESSE COLIN YOUNG

Jesse Colin Young

Jesse Colin Young (b. Perry Miller, Nov. 22, 1941, Long Island) dropped out of Ohio State University at 18 to pursue a career in music—inspired, he'd later claim, by blues guitar great T-Bone Walker. After briefly pursuing an *On the Road* lifestyle while hitchhiking through the South, Young ended up in New York in 1962, intermittently performing while working for the Rockefeller Foundation. Upon meeting producer Bobby Scott while performing at Gerdes' Folk City in Greenwich Village, Young recorded his 1964 debut album, *Soul of a City Boy,* in all of four hours at New York's A&R studios. The starkly recorded album, featuring just guitar and vocals, was a good, albeit typical, East-Coast-folkie affair: half traditional tunes ("Drifter's Blues," "Rye Whiskey") and a mix of similar-sounding originals, with "Four in the Morning" (written by Holy Modal Rounder Robin Ramaily)—a memorable, eerie tune that showcased Young's distinctive high-pitched voice—the clear high point. Scott also produced Young's second album, *Young Blood,* issued in 1965 by Mercury, which featured the singer backed with a band including future Lovin' Spoonful John Sebastian and dobro player Peter Childs.

But the action in the mid-1960s clearly came via the pop groups, and eventually, after Young met folk singer Jerry Corbitt in Boston, the Youngbloods were born. Comprising Young, Corbitt, keyboardist-guitarist Lowell "Banana" Levinger, and drummer Joe Bauer, the group played a captivating blend of folk, rock, and blues. The group's commercial zenith was unquestionably their version of Dino Valenti's "Get Together," for many one of the true anthems of the 1960s, which hit the Hot 100 both in 1967 and 1969, when its use in a popular public service announcement sent it soaring to the number five slot. After recording two albums and moving to Marin County in 1967, the group lost Corbitt midway through the making of *Elephant Mountain.* It remains their best work by far and contains what some think are Young's best tunes: "Darkness, Darkness," "Sunlight," and "Ride the Wind." As a trio, the group moved to Warner Bros. in 1970 and were one of the first artists to be awarded their own label, Raccoon Records. Four unsuccessful albums later, they parted.

Young's ensuing solo career began with a focus the latter-day Youngbloods albums had lacked. A string of substantial 1974–76 works (*Song for Juli, Light Shine, Songbird*) highlighted by meaty songs and a superb backing band, helped make Young a significant touring attraction—as did his opening slot on Crosby, Stills, Nash and Young's pioneering 1974 stadium tour. Three of Young's albums of that era consecutively reached the top 40—*Light Shine, Songbird,* and *On the Road*—but eventually he faded, moving to Elektra Records in the late 1970s for his last two major-label recordings. Young spent three years work-

---

TOP ALBUMS

THE SOUL OF A CITY BOY (Capitol, '64)
SONG FOR JULI (Warner Bros., '73)
LIGHT SHINE (Warner Bros., '74, 37)
SONGBIRD (Warner Bros., '75, 26)
ON THE ROAD (Warner Bros., '76, 34)

TOP SONGS

JOSIANE (Warner Bros., '75)
SUGAR BABE (Warner Bros., '75)

---

ing on 1982's *The Perfect Stranger,* an album of collaborations with writers like Wendy Waldman, Tom Snow, Danny O'Keefe, and Michael McDonald— but all to no avail, as it quickly stiffed. Young, frustrated, later blamed its failure on its being released "just as [Elektra's] president left."

Like countless other artists of his era in the same situation, Young stopped recording, spent time on the road, and eventually resurfaced on the adult-oriented "boomer" label, Cypress Records. Issued in 1987, *The Highway Is for Heroes* was major perhaps only to rock historians, who noted that former Youngblood Jerry Corbitt had been involved in the mixing of two tracks. Since then, Young has rerecorded several earlier solo tracks for his own privately distributed *Classics Volume 1* and reportedly plans a new album called *Turning Point.* Though by no means one of the most colorful pop stars of the mid-'60s, Young continues to remain on course while his onetime contemporaries have long since faded out of the picture entirely.

NEIL YOUNG

The number of artists whose careers began in the 1960s and whose work has continued to command critical respect through the '90s can be counted on the fingers of one hand. Somewhere on that hand is Neil Young (b. Nov. 12, 1945, Toronto). A brilliant songwriter; a quirky, high-pitched singer; and a guitarist whose piercing style has influenced an entire generation of young alternative-rock fans, Young has spent his career exploring nearly every genre of popular music. Beginning with the countrified pop-rock of '60s legends Buffalo Springfield, he has played rock (*Neil Young,* 1968), hard rock (*Re-ac-tor,* 1981), singer-songwriter-style pop (*After the Gold Rush,* 1970), synth-rock (*Trans,* 1983), '50s-style rock and rockabilly (*Everybody's Rockin',* 1983), country music (*Old Ways,* 1985), rhythm and blues (*This Note's for You,* 1988), protest rock (*Freedom,* 1989), feedback-heavy art rock (*Arc,* 1991), and, of course, the mandatory MTV *Unplugged* set (1993). Through it all, though, he has always sounded like Neil Young—which may be the major reason he remains such a vital artist.

Young began as a folk singer in Toronto, where he first met future bandmates Stephen Stills and Richie Furay in the early 1960s and played in the

Mynah Birds with future R&B star Rick James, Steppenwolf's Goldy McJohn, and bassist Bruce Palmer. In 1966, Young drove with Palmer to Los Angeles, where he soon met up with Stills and Furay; together with drummer Dewey Martin, the five musicians formed Buffalo Springfield and were soon signed to Atco Records. The group recorded three classic albums between 1966 and 1968 and then disbanded; each member then pursued a career either in a solo or new group context, with Young, Stills, and Furay achieving the most notable success.

Though Young's 1969 solo debut, *Neil Young,* failed to chart, in some ways it remains one of his best—and most overlooked—efforts. A stylistic extension of his better work with Buffalo Springfield (particularly his collaborations with producer-arranger Jack Nitzsche), the album featured Young working within a gorgeously melodic pop framework; including some of his best early material, such as "The Loner" (covered the next year by Three Dog Night), "I've Been Waiting for You," and "What Did You Do to My Life," the album also featured two atmospheric instrumentals and the extended, surrealistic folk-dirge "The Last Trip to Tulsa."

Needing a band, Young soon found one in Crazy Horse, who as the Rockets had already recorded a 1968 album for White Whale Records. Backed by guitarist Danny Whitten, bassist Billy Talbot, and drummer Ralph Molina, Young then recorded *Everybody Knows This Is Nowhere,* an album that has since assumed classic status in his canon. Crazy Horse was a near-perfect match for Young; by no means seasoned studio pros, they played hard and emotionally, providing drama and adrenalized surges to Young's sometimes bare-boned songs. Featuring "Cinnamon Girl," "Cowgirl in the Sand," and "Down by the River"—a song that would be covered by Buddy Miles, Roy Buchanan, and every high school band formed in the next 10 years— *Everybody Knows This Is Nowhere* was the first of seven albums Young would record with Crazy Horse.

In the meantime, Young had rejoined his former bandmate Stephen Stills as part of Crosby, Stills, Nash and Young. Always seeming more an appendage than part of the original core trio, Young played with the group at Woodstock and contributed to both 1970's multi-platinum *Déjà Vu* and the next year's live *4 Way Street.* That group's immense popularity helped set up the success of his third album, 1970's *After the Gold Rush,* which

Neil Young

went top 10, stayed on the charts 66 weeks, and was certified double platinum. His success was further consolidated by its follow-up, *Harvest*—his all-time bestseller, thanks largely to its Number One gold single "Heart of Gold" and top 40 hit "Old Man."

The Neil Young heard on *Harvest* was a far cry from the rocker of *Everybody Knows This Is Nowhere;* a soft, countryish singer-songwriter album (with appearances by both James Taylor and Linda Ronstadt), the disc might have established Young as a soft-rock superstar had he so desired. But he didn't. On his 1976 compilation *Decade,* Young revealingly wrote of the track "Heart of Gold": "This song put me in the middle of the road. Travelling there soon became a bore so I headed for the ditch. A rougher ride but I saw more interesting people there."

The "ditch," as Young described it, comprised a series of seeming slapdash, erratic albums that were the antithesis of the smooth, polished sound of *Harvest.* Among them were the confusing soundtrack to Young's rarely seen film *Journey Through the Past* (1972); a rough-sounding live set by Young and his new band the Stray Gators called *Time Fades Away* (1973); the sluggish, but semi-return-to-form *On the Beach* (1974); and Young's all-time depressing landmark, *Tonight's the Night* (1975), a harrowing, emotional tribute to Crazy Horse guitarist Danny Whitten and CSN&Y roadie Bruce Berry, both victims of drug overdoses.

Since then Young has enjoyed two major career surges. The first was in 1979, when his *Rust Never Sleeps* album found him again paired triumphantly with Crazy Horse; the title track, which mentioned punk-rock star Johnny Rotten by name, both opened and closed Young's most captivating album in over a decade. It was followed by *Live Rust* (1979) and a film documentary of the same name, marking a period of artistic renewal for Young, who, unlike his former bandmates in Crosby, Stills and Nash, still seemed a vibrant, probing artist. The second peak came 10 years later with *Freedom,* not incidentally his first gold album since *Live Rust.* Young—more

politically outspoken than he'd been since penning "Ohio" for CSN&Y in 1970—took on the subjects of homelessness and crime (belittling President George Bush's "thousand points of light" phrase in the powerful "Rockin' in the Free World") yet balanced that harshness with acoustic tracks such as "Hangin' on a Limb," which featured guest vocalist Linda Ronstadt. Young then rejoined Crazy Horse for 1990's much-praised *Ragged Glory* and the live *WELD,* which featured the bizarre, 35-minute instrumental bonus CD *Arc,* a so-called "sonic pastiche" digitally edited by Young and featuring waves of feedback and grungy electronic howls.

If there was a low point in Neil Young's career, it came in the mid-1980s. After delivering a series of stylistically quirky albums (from 1983's *Trans* through 1987's *Life*) to Geffen Records, with whom he'd signed in 1983, the label actually sued him for producing "non-typical" work. It was extremely ironic, since Young's work had habitually flitted from style to style for a decade prior to his Geffen signing.

The one constant in Young's body of work, however, is Crazy Horse, whose playing on *Everybody Knows This Is Nowhere,* 1975's *Zuma, Rust Never Sleeps,* and *Ragged Glory* made the albums the most acclaimed in Young's catalog. Why hasn't he simply made the group his permanent band? "I saw where Crazy Horse worked the best," Young said in 1990, "and I saw where what I tried to do got in the way of what Crazy Horse did. And my answer to that was to not use Crazy Horse to do things Crazy Horse shouldn't do —and to be more careful, and more respectful of what I have with Crazy Horse than to ever try to make it something it isn't."

Twenty years after *Harvest,* Young returned to "complete the circle" with the warmly accessible *Harvest Moon,* which stylistically echoed its predecessor in large part due to its inclusion of the Stray Gators, who'd played on the original. It was his first top 20 album in 13 years. Young's follow-up was his 1993 *Unplugged* session, which included material spanning his career from Buffalo Springfield through

TOP ALBUMS

AFTER THE GOLD RUSH
  (Reprise, '70, *8*)
HARVEST (Reprise, '72, *1*)
ON THE BEACH (Reprise, '74, *16*)
COMES A TIME (Reprise, '78, *7*)
RUST NEVER SLEEPS (Reprise, '79, *8*)
LIVE RUST (Reprise, '79, *15*)
HARVEST MOON (Reprise, '92, *16*)

Additional Top 40 Albums: 11

TOP SONGS

ONLY LOVE CAN BREAK YOUR HEART
  (Reprise, '70, *33*)
HEART OF GOLD (Reprise, '72, *1*)
OLD MAN (Reprise, '72, *31*)

his early solo days and underrated *Trans* period on through *Harvest Moon.* It peaked at number 23—significantly higher than he'd managed with the Buffalo Springfield a quarter-century earlier—and was only the latest chapter in an ongoing story that is one of rock and roll's most fascinating and original.

WARREN ZEVON

A fiercely intelligent Los Angeles–based songwriter, Warren Zevon (b. Jan. 24, 1947, Chicago) is renowned for his sardonic, often bitter lyrics, which provided a welcome contrast to the laid-back rock typically emerging from the West Coast during the 1970s. Like the best fiction writers, Zevon has a knack for personalizing absurd characters and situations that in less skillful hands would seem two-dimensional and transparent. Consider, for example, the opening lines to his 1982 song "The Hula Hula Boys": "I saw her leave the luau/With the one who parked the cars/And the fat one from the swimming pool/They were swaying arm in arm."

Still, though Zevon's fame as a songwriter may stem from the bizarre characters he has created—whether it be Roland the Headless Thompson Gunner or the Werewolves of London—his real artfulness has been displayed in the emotional territories he has chosen to explore. While other writers such as Tom Waits or even Rickie Lee Jones have touched on the themes Zevon pursues, they have generally used romantic, beat-inspired characters with '50s-era nicknames; Zevon's best songs, on the other hand, portray contemporary life at its most realistic—and, typically, its worst. Much of his work has focused on the hollowness of Los Angeles; his songs have used familar sites such as the Tropicana and Hollywood Hawaiian hotels, Mulholland Drive, the Le Dome restaurant, and the San Fernando Valley. He has written about drug addicts, crazed soldiers, mass murderers, Lear Jet S.W.A.T. teams, and gorillas at the L.A. Zoo. Yet even in the most absurd situations, his songs' protagonists sometimes aim only to find their way out of the chaotic muck surrounding them and simply get home, where life is semi-peaceful and the only moral treachery to be dealt with is one's own. That Zevon's best work can convey both pain and humor simultaneously is what often makes it most special.

Born in Chicago and raised in California and Ari-

zona by a Russian immigrant father and midwestern mother, Zevon has claimed an early encounter with composer-conductor Igor Stravinsky to be "a formative experience in my life." His earliest recordings include duo work with female vocalist Tule Livingston as Lyme and Cybelle; his first album, *Wanted Dead or Alive,* was released by Imperial Records in 1969 and credited solely to "Zevon." "She Quit Me," a song from that album, had been featured in the *Midnight Cowboy* soundtrack; sung by Leslie Miller, it was retitled "He Quit Me Man." Following an early '70s stint writing jingles and working as bandleader for the Everly Brothers, Zevon moved to Spain in 1975; he was convinced to return to the States by friend Jackson Browne, who had arranged a deal for him with Asylum Records.

Zevon's first album for Asylum, produced by Browne and released in mid-1976, was well received by critics, most of whom were captivated by Zevon's literate, often hilarious lyrics. Though the record peaked at number 189 and spent just two weeks on the chart, its influence was quickly felt: Linda Ronstadt recorded Zevon's "Hasten Down the Wind" and made it the title track of her 1976 platinum album; she'd later record three additional tracks from the album, including "Carmelita," "Mohammed's Radio," and "Poor Poor Pitiful Me," the latter of which became a top 40 hit in 1978. Zevon's next album, *Excitable Boy,* also produced by Browne, featured the singer's top 30 hit "Werewolves of London" and became his only gold album.

Following a rough patch of personal problems

TOP ALBUMS

WARREN ZEVON (Asylum, '76)
EXCITABLE BOY (Asylum, '78, 8)
BAD LUCK STREAK IN DANCING SCHOOL
  (Asylum, '80, 20)
THE ENVOY (Asylum, '82)
SENTIMENTAL HYGIENE (Virgin, '87)
LEARNING TO FLINCH (Giant, '93)

TOP SONGS

HASTEN DOWN THE WIND (Asylum, '76)
POOR POOR PITIFUL ME (Asylum, '76)
WEREWOLVES OF LONDON (Asylum, '78, 21)
THE INDIFFERENCE OF HEAVEN (Giant, '93)

that included a divorce and alcoholism—the singer checked into rehab for a month in 1978—Zevon resumed his career in 1980 with the strong *Bad Luck Streak in Dancing School,* which included "Jeannie Needs a Shooter," co-written with Bruce Springsteen. After two more albums for Asylum, Zevon stopped recording for five years; his 1987 comeback, *Sentimental Hygiene,* featured a very strong cast of supporting musicians and friends, including Bob Dylan, Neil Young, Don Henley, R.E.M., and even the Red Hot Chili Peppers' Flea. It met only mild chart success and peaked at number 63.

Since then, Zevon's career has stalled somewhat; his only charting album has been the one-off *Hindu Love Gods* project, featuring Zevon and members of R.E.M. covering songs by Robert Johnson, Prince, and Willie Dixon, among others. His most recent album, 1993's *Learning to Flinch,* was a low-budget live affair recorded direct-to-DAT and issued on Giant Records. An excellent set featuring some brilliant new material—particularly "The Indifference of Heaven"—it displayed a Warren Zevon still very much in top form...and still very much worth hearing.

Warren Zevon

INDEX

INDEX

ABOUT THE AUTHOR

Photo: Janet DiMartino

Dave DiMartino is the former editor-in-chief of *Creem* magazine, was the Los Angeles bureau chief of *Billboard* magazine between 1986 and 1991, and has worked as a senior writer at *Entertainment Weekly.* His writing has appeared in *Musician, Rolling Stone, Mojo, Spin,* the *Village Voice,* and other publications. He is currently serving as the West Coast editor of *Musician* magazine.